CRIMINAL COURTS

STRUCTURE, PROCESS, *and* ISSUES

GARY A. RABE
Minot State University

DEAN J. CHAMPION
Texas A & M International University

Upper Saddle River, New Jersey 07458

Library of Congress Cataloging-in-Publication Data

Rabe, Gary A.
    Criminal courts : structure, process, and issues / by Gary A. Rabe and Dean J. Champion.
        p.   cm.
    Includes bibliographical references and index.
    ISBN 0-13-780388-5
    1. Criminal justice, Administration of—United States.   2. Criminal courts—United
States.   I. Champion, Dean J.   II. Title.
KF8700.Z9 R33 2002
345.73'01—dc21

                                                                            2001034048

Publisher: Jeff Johnston
Executive Acquisitions Editor: Kim Davies
Assistant Editor: Sarah Holle
Managing Editor: Mary Carnis
Production Management: Stratford Publishing Services
Production Editor: Judy Ashkenaz, Stratford Publishing Services
Interior Design: Stratford Publishing Services
Production Liaison: Adele M. Kupchik
Director of Manufacturing and Production: Bruce Johnson
Manufacturing Buyer: Cathleen Petersen
Cover Design Coordinator: Miguel Ortiz
Formatting: Stratford Publishing Services
Marketing Manager: Ramona Sherman
Marketing Assistant: Barbara Rosenberg
Printer/Binder: Phoenix Color Printers
Copy Editor: Joy Matkowski
Proofreader: Marsha Kunin
Cover Design: Scott Garrison
Cover Illustration: Alan E. Cober, SIS/Images.Com
Cover Printer: Phoenix Color Printers

Pearson Education LTD.
Pearson Education Australia PTY, Limited
Pearson Education Singapore, Pte. Ltd
Pearson Education North Asia Ltd
Pearson Education Canada, Ltd.
Pearson Educación de Mexico, S.A. de C.V.
Pearson Education—Japan
Pearson Education Malaysia, Pte. Ltd

10 9 8 7 6 5 4 3

ISBN 0-13-780388-5

CONTENTS

Chapter 12
Courts, Media, and the Litigation Explosion   377

PREFACE

Criminal Courts: Structure, Process, and Issues is about processing criminal offenders from the point when they are arrested and charged with crimes. This book provides a comprehensive examination of the trial process by which their guilt or innocence is ascertained by a judge or a jury.

The book begins with an examination of law and its social and political origins. Law is as ancient as time itself. Despite the different eras into which scholars have divided world history, the pervasiveness and continuity of law are apparent. Laws have always existed in one form or another, largely intended to fulfill the same general purposes regardless of the culture. The major functions of law are social control, dispute resolution, and social change. Over time, technology has changed and social ideas have evolved that have contributed to how people orient themselves to others. Whether through verbal traditions passed from one generation to another in simple societies or in lengthy compendia in more complex social systems, the primary objectives of law have remained constant over time.

Laws can be differentiated according to whether they pertain to civil or criminal matters. Statements about what the law says and how people should comport themselves in the company of others have to do with substantive law. In less complex social systems, substantive law tended to be espoused by the courts in the form of common law. Common law is traditional, dependent on the particular needs and desires of groups of people living together. As social systems have become increasingly complex, more elaborate legal schemes and more formal mechanisms have been devised to maintain the social order and regulate human conduct. How the law should be applied is the province of procedural law. In the United States, one of the world's most complex legal systems has been contrived. Today, there are all types of laws pertaining to different aspects of our society. These laws are either civil or criminal, and a whole body of law focuses on administrative law.

It is a legal reality that applications of the law from the beginning of time have favored particular interests over others. Some people believe that our laws have been created to preserve the status quo for those who possess political and economic power. Thus, there are inherent disparities wherever applications of the law are implemented. Historically, those suffering most from legal disparities have been women, children, and minorities. In recent decades, sociolegal movements have prompted substantial social changes in response to disparate treatment of minorities and women in the courts. From these movements, different types of sociological jurisprudence, legal realism, critical legal studies, and feminist legal theories have emerged.

Understanding the laws of the United States begins with a critical examination and description of the dual court system in this country. The principal components of the dual court system are federal and state court apparatuses. Chapter 2 describes federal and state court organization and various functions of these different types of courts. There are diverse court systems, and there is little continuity across states concerning what these different courts should be called. We do not have a universal nomenclature that can be applied to all state and local courts at various levels. However, there is considerable continuity within the federal court system. Federal and state court jurisdictions are distinguished, and the processes and functions of different types of courts are described and discussed.

The court work group consists of the same types of actors in both federal and state jurisdictions. The government has created a prosecutorial system that enforces the laws passed by the different legislatures. Whenever one or more of these laws are violated, prosecutors at the state or federal level act against alleged offenders to bring them to justice. Thus, Chapters 3 and 4 examine prosecutors and defense counsels in some detail, identifying their principal functions and duties. The U.S. Constitution and Bill of Rights have vested all citizens with particular rights to ensure that they will be treated equally under the law. All those who are charged with a criminal offense are entitled to counsel if they are obligated to appear in court to answer criminal charges. Under particular circumstances, anyone may enjoy the right to a jury trial by one's peers. The roles and functions of both prosecutors and defense counsels are examined and discussed.

The most important actor in the court system is the judge. Judges, as discussed in Chapter 5, oversee all court proceedings and make important decisions. There are several types of systems used for judicial selection, and these systems are described. Although legal backgrounds are strongly recommended for those functioning as judges, it is not necessarily true that all judges have legal training or experience. Thus, different methods for selecting judges are explained, together with the weaknesses and strengths of these methods. Merit selection of judges seems to be favored in many jurisdictions, although often the best judges do not gravitate into these important posts. A segment of the judiciary clearly lacks the qualifications and commitment to make good decisions. Some judges are corrupt and commit deliberate acts that call their integrity into question. Judicial misconduct of various kinds is described, and some of the remedies available to the public for recalling bad judges are examined.

At the heart of the legal system is the jury process, the topic of Chapter 6. Juries are made up of individuals from the general population. Methods of jury selection vary greatly among jurisdictions. In fact, juries account for only about ten percent of all criminal cases that are pursued. Nevertheless, the jury process and how jurors are selected to judge the conduct of others are quite important. Both prosecutors and defense counsel conduct voir dires or oral questioning of prospective juries from a list of veniremen or a venire. Sometimes experts are used as consultants, because some people believe that jury selection can enhance the chances of a conviction or an acquittal. Various methods for discharging prospective jurors are examined, including challenges for cause and peremptory challenges. Various standards among the states and the federal system are described to show the different criteria applied for determining the appropriate jury size and the process of jury decision making. The decision-making process of juries is examined in some detail, and the important topics of jury nullification and juror misconduct are explored.

Chapter 7 deals with pretrial procedures. Not all those charged with crimes are ultimately processed by the criminal justice system. Some are diverted to civil courts or into civil dispute-resolution programs, where their cases can be concluded in noncriminal ways. Victims and offenders are often brought together in alternative dispute-resolution actions, in which victim compensation and restorative justice are sought as remedies for wrongdoing. For those who are eventually prosecuted criminally for violating the law, the arrest and booking process are described. The issue of bail is discussed. In some states, various laws are being scrutinized for the purpose of decriminalizing criminal acts through legislative changes, and this process is examined.

Perhaps the most frequently used resolution strategy for criminal offenders is plea bargaining, discussed in Chapter 8. Plea bargaining is a preconviction agreement between prosecutors, defense counsels, and their clients in which guilty pleas are entered to criminal charges in exchange for some type of leniency. Plea bargaining results in a criminal conviction, but the penalties imposed are often less harsh than the penalties imposed through trial convictions. Different types of plea bargaining, as well as the pros and cons of plea bargaining, are discussed. Furthermore, some jurisdictions have abolished plea bargaining, and their reasons for doing so are examined.

The actual trial process is illustrated in Chapter 9. Those charged with crimes may undergo either bench trials, in which a judge decides the case, or jury trials. The criminal trial process is described in some detail by way of fictional scenarios that parallel some actual legal cases of the recent past. In any criminal trial, due process requires considering any defendant innocent of a crime until proved guilty beyond a reasonable doubt. This standard is difficult to achieve in many cases. Prosecutors who pursue criminal cases against particular suspects believe that they can convince juries of the defendant's guilt. However, the defendant is represented by counsel who attempts to show that the defendant is innocent. Various witnesses are brought forth and testify, either for or against particular defendants. Some of these witnesses are eyewitnesses; others are expert witnesses who testify about the quality and significance of collected evidence. Juries deliberate and decide defendants' guilt or innocence.

Chapter 10 deals with sentencing and appeals. If the decision is a guilty verdict, then the offender undergoes a sentencing hearing. Sentencing hearings are conducted by trial judges and are, to some extent, replays of the court case originally presented. However, sentencing hearings permit victims or relatives of victims to make victim impact statements in either verbal or written form. Others testify on behalf of defendants. Judges are the final arbiters and impose different sentences, depending on the seriousness of the crime, the offender's prior record, and other factors. The several types of sentencing systems used by U.S. courts today are discussed in some detail, together with their implications for the early release of sentenced offenders. In the event that convicted offenders are dissatisfied with the verdict, they are entitled to appeal their cases to higher courts. The appellate process is discussed. Featured are death penalty cases, which are always automatically appealed. The appeals process is especially lengthy, and even those who are sentenced to death in states with capital punishment laws may not be executed for ten or more years.

A parallel system of justice exists for juvenile offenders. Chapter 11 examines the juvenile justice system in detail, with particular emphasis on how the juvenile court system is structured and operated. A different language applies to juvenile processing, and various comparisons are made between the juvenile and criminal justice systems. Several landmark juvenile cases are cited in which the U.S. Supreme Court has granted certain constitutional rights. Over time, juvenile courts have taken on the characteristics of criminal courts. Some people believe that in several years the juvenile court may be abolished in favor of a unified court for both juveniles and adults.

Chapter 12 examines the influence of the media on the court process. As society has become increasingly complex in a technological sense, more information is delivered to more people through different media, such as television and the Internet. At the same time that people have been increasingly exposed to what goes on in the courtroom, there has been a major litigation explosion, with increasing numbers of lawsuits filed. A very litigious society has evolved. One reason for the increase in litigation is the publicity derived from courtroom coverage by the media and the sensationalization of particular cases. Media in the courtroom are explored in this chapter, and the pros and cons of media coverage are examined in terms of how public opinion is shaped.

Ancillaries and desirable features of this book include numerous questions at chapter ends for review. Key terms are boldfaced throughout the text and listed at chapter ends, and the back of the book contains a comprehensive glossary of these and other terms. Suggested readings accompany each chapter so that those interested in learning more about particular subjects can locate further reading for their edification and education. An up-to-date bibliography of both research publications and legal cases is also provided at the back of the book. A particularly interesting feature is the liberal use throughout each chapter of interesting vignettes adapted from local newspapers that feature stories and events that complement the text itself. These boxes often show criminal justice in action, and real people and events are described. They are intended to heighten student interest in learning more about the court system.

An instructor's manual is available to professors and others. This manual contains true–false, multiple-choice, and short-answer essay test questions. The instructor's manual is available on diskette and CD-ROM for ease of use. It also lists Internet sites to enable those wishing to learn more about particular subjects to establish various Internet links and download useful information.

The two authors of this book acknowledge that the final result is the work of many persons. We wish to thank Kim Davies, our Prentice Hall Career and Technology editor, for her confidence in our ability to produce a useful text about the court system. We are also indebted to the following reviewers who made helpful suggestions and criticisms at critical points: H. Todd Locklear of Florida Metropolitan University. Dr. Roger E. Hartley of Roanoke College, Lynn Jones of the University of Scranton, Dr. Paul Katsampes of Metropolitan State College of Denver, and Dr. Tod Burke of Radford University. Finally, we wish to thank the production staff at Ohlinger Publishing in Columbus, Ohio. They have done a remarkable job of fashioning this project to enhance student interest and use.

Gary A. Rabe
Minot State University

Dean J. Champion
Texas A & M International University

LAW: THE LEGAL BATTLEFIELD

KRIS ANN HADDAD. It happened on I-95 in West Palm Beach, Florida. A mother was traveling at speeds up to 95 mph when, suddenly, she dangled her 2½-year-old son, Stephen, from the car window and dropped him onto the highway amid heavy traffic. Just as soon as she threw her infant from the car, she stopped by the roadside and ran to him. Motorists who witnessed the scene also stopped and came to Stephen's aid. According to authorities who interviewed Haddad later, she wanted to save her son from "this world."

Haddad had been in trouble with the law before. She had been accused of child abuse in the case of her daughter. She taped the baby's mouth shut in order to keep it from crying. Police detective Pat Galligan said, "The woman's got some serious problems. Back then she had some serious problems, and I'm not surprised that this happened." Haddad was held in jail on $60,000 bond and charged with attempted murder and child abuse. Her son, Stephen, was in serious condition and suffered numerous broken bones. What penalties should be imposed for someone who does this to a child? Was the earlier incident of child abuse against Haddad a warning of more serious problems? What could state authorities have done to prevent the most recent child abuse incident? If you were the judge, how would you judge Haddad if she is proven guilty of attempted murder and child abuse? What do you think? (*Source:* Adapted from the Associated Press, "Mother Admitted to Child Abuse Before." *Minot* (N.D.) *Daily News,* February 21, 1998:A2.)

MEGAN K. HOGG, 25, EX-MOTHER OF THREE. It happened in Daly City, California, in March 1998. A woman, Megan K. Hogg, 25, went into one of her daughters' bedrooms and bound the child's hands behind her back with duct tape. Then, Hogg took more duct tape and taped the daughter's nose and mouth so that she couldn't breathe. After five minutes, the child was dead. Then, Hogg walked into another daughter's bedroom and repeated the act. She did this three times. When finished, Hogg had suffocated to death her three daughters: Antoinette, 7; Angelique, 3; and Alexandra, 2. Then she attempted to kill herself with a prescription medicine overdose, but police found her in time to save her life. Investigating police are skeptical as to whether Megan Hogg really intended to kill herself. It was more of a suicide gesture, according to one police investigator. Several notes were found, indicating what she had planned to do and how she planned to do it. Police did not release the contents of the notes they had found. Lieutenant Steve Lowe, the principal police investigator, said, "In 29 years, I've seen a lot of evil . . . but nothing like this." Lowe also said, "It takes about five minutes to suffocate someone. Multiply that by three." Hogg was taken into custody and booked for investigation of homicide. She was transferred to a psychiatric facility to undergo a full psychiatric examination. If Hogg is subsequently convicted, should she be executed? What should be the proper punishment for someone who deliberately suffocates her own children in an especially heinous manner? What do you think? (*Source:* Adapted from the Associated Press, "Sisters Suffocated; Mom Accused." *Minot* (N.D.) *Daily News,* March 25, 1998:A2.)

ETHARINE PETTIGREW, 41, SLASHER. It happened in a Milwaukee supermarket. Vickie Lemons, a 27-year-old woman with a cartload of groceries, headed for the checkout lane, but she picked the wrong one. She entered the "10 items or fewer" lane with numerous items and paid a terrible price for this mistake. She was even encouraged to enter that lane by a checker, who motioned for her to bring her cart to him. Suddenly, apparently from nowhere, came Etharine Pettigrew, 41, brandishing a knife. She swung the knife at the victim, who happened to be in the wrong line. The knife cut off a substantial part of Lemons's nose and caused deep facial wounds. Emergency surgery was needed to keep Lemons from bleeding to death. Etharine Pettigrew was charged with second-degree reckless endangerment of safety, which carries a maximum sentence of a $10,000 fine and two years in prison. Meanwhile, Vickie Lemons has no nose. What should the penalty be for someone who causes another such injuries? Is a two-year prison term and a $10,000 fine sufficient punishment for such a heinous assault over such a petty incident? Is there anything grocery stores can do to protect their customers from assaults by other customers? What punishment would you impose on Pettigrew if she is convicted of that offense? What do you think? (*Source:* Adapted from the Associated Press, "Woman Charged for Slashing Woman." *Minot* (N.D.) *Daily News,* April 12, 1998:A2.)

Introduction

Attempted murder, murder, and aggravated assault: These scenarios are real examples of three very different types of crimes. For each crime alleged, there are elements that must be proved beyond a reasonable doubt in a subsequent trial. The different states and the federal government define crimes in particular ways, with much variation about the nature and seriousness of different types of offenses.

There are also many definitions of criminal law. These definitions are important to learn, but understanding the different functions of law and the consistency and inconsistency of its application is also important. This chapter describes types of law and examines various perspectives about the purposes and functions of law. The final section describes some of the more important contributions of sociolegal scholars who have investigated the interplay between law and society.

What Is Law?

Law is the body of rules of specific conduct, prescribed by existing, legitimate authority, in a particular jurisdiction, and at a particular point in time (Champion, 1997:72). Other definitions of law exist. For example, Quinney (1974) says that law is an expression of the needs of the ruling class. Depending on one's particular view of the legal system, law might be perceived as either liberating or oppressive, preserving the status quo or providing the means and opportunity to challenge the existing social order. Law has been used both to perpetuate and eliminate slavery, to dominate and liberate women, and to convict and acquit the innocent. Law is related closely to all of these different definitions.

The Dred Scott Case and the Law

The role of law was apparent in the nineteenth-century Dred Scott case when the slavery issue was raised. This case was more about citizenship than about slavery. Dred Scott was the slave of an army officer, who took Scott from Missouri to Wisconsin and eventually to Illinois. When Scott returned to Missouri, he claimed that he was no longer a slave because slavery was not recognized in either Wisconsin or Illinois. Therefore, an important constitutional question arose: Were citizenship and freedom vested in former slaves as the result of their relocating in states where slavery was prohibited? The U.S. Supreme Court heard and decided the case in 1857. Recognizing the rights of individual states, the Supreme Court held that citizenship was not a federal issue. Rather, the issue of slavery was to be determined by the individual states. Thus, according to this decision, Dred Scott was still considered a slave, because the U.S. Supreme Court chose not to interfere in states' rights. This decision encouraged antislavery activists to make federal citizenship take priority over state citizenship (Friedman, 1985). Subsequently, the efforts of these activists resulted in the ratification of the Fourteenth Amendment, which Amendment became the instrument that ensured the citizenship and freedom of former slaves wherever in the nation they might choose to reside (Johnson, 1988:201).

Women and the Law

The status and roles of women in society have been continually restructured through the law. The law plays a powerful but not exclusive role in shaping and maintaining women's subordination. The law has operated directly and explicitly to prevent women from attaining independence in the public sphere, thereby reinforcing their dependence upon men. Simultaneously, the law's continued absence from the private sphere, where women were relegated, not only has deprived women of formal legal remedies but also has devalued and discredited them as a class.

The Law and Reproduction

The law has also been used to control women's reproduction (*Webster v. Reproductive Services,* 1989), access to professional credentials (*Bradwell v. Illinois,* 1873), and role in the work force (*Muller v. Oregon,* 1908). The law has been used to redress these inequalities through affirmative action, which provides, in part, for fair and equitable hiring and promotion practices.

Determining precisely what the law should be has proved to be elusive. Adamson Hoebel (1954:18) has said that seeking a precise definition of law is like the quest for the Holy Grail. Prosecutors, defense attorneys, judges, defendants, businesspeople, consumers, the wealthy, and the poor all have different perspectives about what the law is and how it should be applied. Despite these diverse views of the law, there are several fundamental assumptions about the functions of law.

The Functions of Law

Various legal scholars have studied the functions of law in different social systems and at different points in time. Their many observations about the functions of law can be classified according to (1) social control, (2) dispute resolution, and (3) social change.

Social Control

Social control is society's efforts to regulate the behavior of its members. The most visible form of social control is application of the law (e.g., being arrested, prosecuted, and sentenced). For most citizens, this method of control is often the subject matter of the evening news and happens only to other people who we believe deserve to be controlled by the state. We seldom realize that we are subject to these same social controls in our daily lives.

Legal scholars distinguish between informal and formal social controls. Informal social controls are an integral feature of the socialization process. From early childhood, we are constantly taught the norms of behavior that our parents and the social world expect of us. These norms are a product of cultural expectations regarding dress, language, and behavior and our biological capacity to comprehend and adapt to these expectations. These informal social controls are effective because we are rewarded or punished by people who are important to us, our significant others.

For example, if we do things that offend our parents, close friends, or significant others, the sanctions administered by these people that we have grown to love and respect are very powerful, and we often refrain from engaging in these offensive behaviors. If our grandparents learn that we have been engaging in underage drinking, they issue stern words to us, and their glances have great influence on our personal conduct. The usual impact of this informal social pressure is that we refrain from those behaviors that tend to elicit harsh words, warnings, or glares. Gossip is another form of informal social control. Gossip flourishes in offices around the water cooler and during smoking breaks from our workplaces, as well as at weekly bridge games, in conversations with our friends over the telephone, and through computer e-mail. The effects of gossip are fairly consistent. Our behaviors are influenced significantly by the verbal and nonverbal cues we receive from others, either directly or indirectly. Through these different informal sanctions, we conform with what we believe are social expectations of us.

Dispute Resolution

A second function of law is **dispute resolution**. People frequently engage in disputes with others. Spouses might disagree about the division of labor in their household. Employees may disagree with their employers about their work effectiveness and quality. Sometimes total strangers disagree about how to drive on the interstate highways or how we or our children should behave in shopping centers. Historically, people involved in disputes have relied on informal methods for dispute resolution. In Colonial times, families or individuals relied on their village elders to settle disputes. Not so long ago, disputes about many issues were considered private matters settled in nonlegal ways. In more recent decades, informal nonlegal resolutions of disputes have changed considerably. Increasingly, **disputants** rely on the legal system to resolve issues that once were settled privately. A major change in our social dynamics is largely responsible for this shift. Informal methods for dispute resolution used to be more effective in small, closely knit, homogeneous societies. Often, the members of these communities were closely related through family ties or economically. Therefore, disputes disrupted the stability of the community and had to be resolved quickly. It was not deemed necessary to use legal means for resolving disputes because these disputes rarely rose to such formal levels.

One additional benefit of nonlegal methods to resolve disputes is that the agreements reached are usually satisfactory to both parties. In traditional courtroom litigation, legal dispute resolution resulted in winners and losers. One side was dissatisfied with whatever decision was rendered, but tradition called for accepting that decision without further argument. However, as social systems became increasingly complex and heterogeneous, informal dispute resolution methods were less effective. There was no clear interdependence among the disputants, and no one had the authority to informally resolve the dispute. This social evolution generated more formal methods for dispute resolution, which gradually replaced less formal methods. Although formal, legal methods may settle the disputes to the satisfaction of the legal system, this result does not necessarily mean that the dispute will never recur. It has been claimed, for instance, that a legal resolution of a conflict does not necessarily lead to a reduction of the tension or antagonism between the aggrieved parties (Vago, 1997:17–18). Richard Abel (1990) argues that disputes are never fully resolved; rather, they are temporarily quelled but eventually are resurrected into new conflicts and disputes.

Social Change

Social change is another important function of law. Social change is the process in which ideas and practices are modified, either actively or passively, through natural forces or deliberate social actions. Law is the principal avenue through which social ills and biases are resolved. History is replete with examples of law used to effect social changes of various kinds. State legislatures continually implement new laws to change the existing social order. Legislative actions are diverse and change our lives in various ways. For instance, new laws legislatures pass may require us to wear seat belts, pay increased taxes, raise or lower the speed limit, or observe new national holidays. Judges also create social change through their own interpretations of the law and how it should be applied. Because of greater attention given to police methods by the media, most Americans are aware of their Miranda rights during custodial interrogations. Most citizens are aware of their right to counsel if they cannot afford an attorney (*Gideon v. Wainright,* 1963). The judiciary has been most influential in social change through issuing their decisions in legal cases. Thus, precedents judges establish have formed the bases of changes in various social policies. These changes are the functional equivalent of lawmaking. Legislators regard this activity as **judicial activism** and are opposed to it; they believe that legislatures, not the judiciary, should have the exclusive authority to make law. Beyond this, law is also a method by which to initiate broader societal changes.

The Evolution of Disputes

Disputes occur frequently among citizens. We may have disputes with our spouses and bosses; however, we rarely rely on the legal system to resolve these types of disputes. There is a system for seeking legal remedies only when several important factors converge. Some investigators have conceptualized the dispute process as consisting of various stages.

Naming, Blaming, and Claiming

To develop a conceptual framework of the evolution of disputes before they reach the courts for formalized resolution, Felstiner, Abel, and Sarat (1980) identified three stages: naming, blaming, and claiming. Their view of disputes starts with classifying injuries as either perceived or unperceived. For instance, sometimes we are victimized or injured but are unaware of being victimized or suffering any injuries. If we do not understand that we have been victimized, then we do not consider the viability of a dispute. Have you ever wondered why all of the gasoline prices in your neighborhood are the same? Perhaps this reflects a free and open market in which competition has driven down gas prices as low as they can go, or maybe all of the gas station owners have secretly conspired to set fuel prices at fixed levels so that they can all benefit from higher prices. The point is that you never know when this situation actually occurs and whether you are being victimized. Each time you refuel your vehicle, you may be benefiting from the free market system, or you may be the unwitting victim of the crime of price fixing. In the latter case, even though you are a victim, no dispute arises. However, when you are able to identify yourself as a victim through **naming**, this is the first stage in formulating a legitimate dispute.

The second stage in the dispute process is **blaming**. In this stage, you translate your victimization into a formal grievance. For this event to occur, you must blame someone else for your victimization. Smokers move from naming to blaming when they allege that the tobacco companies have failed to inform them about the hazards of smoking.

The final stage in the formulation of disputes is **claiming**, which occurs whenever victims believe that they have been injured, have identified a particular victimizer, and formally express a grievance against the person or organization responsible for their victimization. In most cases, victims seek monetary remedies. These claims ultimately evolve into disputes when the claim is initially rejected by another person or an organization. Not surprisingly, most disputes do not result in formal lawsuits. Most injuries are never perceived; if they are perceived, it is difficult to identify a particular victimizer. Therefore, the courts are faced with and address only the small fraction of disputes that evolve into formal complaints and a search for legal remedies.

A similar typology of disputes has been developed by Nader and Todd (1978) and Nader (1979). Like Felstiner, Abel, and Sarat (1980), Nader and Todd describe three stages in the dispute process: (1) the grievance or preconflict stage, (2) the conflict stage, and (3) the dispute stage. The **grievance** or **preconflict stage** requires that individuals or groups must perceive that they have been involved in an unfair or unjust situation. If the grievance is not resolved at this stage, then it progresses to a conflict stage, and the victims confront the party they believe is the cause of their victimization. The dispute fully evolves when it reaches the **dispute stage** and the dispute is made public.

Types of Law

Substantive Law

Typologies of law are both important and necessary. Law varies according to who prosecutes, the nature and types of existing penalties, and its particular historical origins. A broadly applicable typology that includes all types of law is difficult to develop. A distinction is commonly made between **substantive law** and **procedural law**. Substantive law is the **law in books**. Substantive law is what the law says. Basically, it is the compilation of local, state, and federal laws created by legislatures. A law exists that defines when someone is under the influence of alcohol when operating a motor vehicle. States have different intoxication standards. Most states have either 0.10 or 0.08 blood alcohol content (BAC) as the intoxication standard. Thus, if a motorist has a BAC of 0.10 or higher in a state where the intoxication standard is 0.10, then the motorist is legally intoxicated. If the motorist has a BAC level of 0.09 or lower, then the motorist is not legally intoxicated. Under other laws, those who take money from others by force commit robbery. If they use a weapon to take money from others by force, they commit armed robbery. Laws exist that define these and other criminal acts. Many additional laws combine to form the substance of substantive law.

Procedural Law

Procedural law, or the **process of law**, pertains to how the law is applied. Procedural law is also called the **law in action**. It specifies how police officers must obtain and execute a search warrant. It also details how jurors should be selected, how witnesses should be sworn when testifying in court, and how evidence should be admitted in the courtroom.

Procedural law also includes how those convicted of one or more crimes should be sentenced. For example, in North Dakota, judges are required to consider the following factors to determine the desirability of sentencing an offender to imprisonment:

1. The defendant's criminal conduct neither caused nor threatened serious harm to another person or his property.
2. The defendant did not plan or expect that his criminal conduct would cause or threaten serious harm to another person or his property.
3. The defendant acted under strong provocation.
4. There were substantial grounds which, though insufficient to establish a legal defense, tend to excuse or justify the defendant's conduct.
5. The victim of the defendant's conduct was induced to facilitate its commission.
6. The defendant has or will make restitution or reparation to the victim of his conduct for the damage or injury that was sustained.
7. The defendant has no history of prior delinquency or criminal activity, or has led a law-abiding life for a substantial period of time before the commission of the present offense.
8. The defendant's conduct was a result of circumstances unlikely to recur.
9. The character, history, and attitudes of the defendant indicate that he is unlikely to commit another crime.
10. The defendant is particularly likely to respond affirmatively to probationary treatment.
11. The imprisonment of the defendant would entail undue hardship to himself or his dependents.
12. The defendant is elderly or in poor health.
13. The defendant did not abuse a public position of responsibility or trust.
14. The defendant cooperated with law enforcement authorities by bringing other offenders to justice, or otherwise cooperated. (North Dakota Century Code, 12.1-32-04)

Common Law

Another type of law is **common law**. Common law is whatever is prevalent, traditional, or customary in a given jurisdiction. It is the law of precedent. There are no specific statutes that govern particular situations. Judges decide cases by common law on the basis of whatever is customary or traditional, not what is written down or codified.

Common law originated in England. Common law is judicially created law, as compared with law made by legislatures. English judges would travel to different cities and towns and decide cases on their circuits. Their decisions and the sentences they imposed were a combination of existing precedent and local custom. Because customs vary, common law varies among jurisdictions. For example, a judge in one jurisdiction may find that local residents are very tolerant of political dissent. If a defendant is arrested and charged with political dissent in this jurisdiction, it may be customary for the judge to impose a lenient sentence. The judge would probably not impose a harsh sentence because the citizenry would oppose it. However, in another jurisdiction where political

TWO EXAMPLES OF COMMON LAW

The Case of Ghen, the Whale Hunter

It happened in Massachusetts Bay. A whale hunter, Ghen, shot a whale with a bomb lance off the coast, and the whale swam away and died about twenty-five miles from where it had been shot. Rich, a wandering beachcomber, came upon the dead whale lying on the beach. He stripped the blubber from the beached whale and converted the fat to oil, which he later sold at a nearby market. Subsequently, he bragged about his luck to others, and eventually word reached Ghen about where his whale had gone. Ghen tracked down Rich and accused him of converting the whale remains for profit, thus denying Ghen any revenue from the whale he had shot. Rich refused to turn over the money he had received from the whale remains, arguing that he had found the whale, did not know it was someone else's property, and did a lot of work to convert the remains to oil. Ghen sued Rich, seeking to recover damages.

An interesting case was presented to the presiding judge. In the Cape Cod area, there were *no laws* governing whale rights. However, it was customary for those finding whales to alert the whale hunters where the whale had washed ashore so that the whale hunters could obtain the blubber and make valuable oil from the remains. The bomb lances used by different whalers were thus marked distinctively, so that anyone familiar with whaling knew whose lance it was and, thus, who owned the whale. In Massachusetts, the custom was that the original whale hunter who shot a whale possessed it through a type of ownership, regardless of where the whale eventually swam or washed ashore. When Rich found the beached whale, he either knew or should have known the proper procedure to follow regarding turning the whale remains over to the rightful owner. In this case, Rich ignored custom and precedent and converted the whale remains for his own benefit. Thus, the judge ruled against Rich and in favor of Ghen, who was subsequently reimbursed for his loss by Rich.

The Case of Bradbury's Dead Sister

Bradbury lived in a large two-story building with his sister, Harriet, in a Maine community. During a particularly severe winter, his sister became ill and died in the apartment. Bradbury had little money and could not afford to pay for a funeral for his sister. Therefore, he concluded, he could dispose of his sister in the large apartment house furnace in the basement. He dragged her body to the basement, where he cremated it in the furnace. Neighbors detected a foul odor and called police, who investigated. They determined what Bradbury had done and arrested him. At the time, there was no law or written statute prohibiting anyone from disposing of a dead body in a home furnace. However, the court

(continued)

The Case of Bradbury's Dead Sister *(continued)*

determined that Bradbury had violated the common law, which spoke against indecent burials of bodies. The fact that Bradbury had indecently disposed of his sister's body and had not given her a Christian burial was sufficient to find him in violation of the prevailing common law.

In both the *Ghen* and *Bradbury* cases, no statutes existed during those times to prohibit the specific conduct described. In both cases, judges decided these matters strictly on the basis of prevailing precedent established by common agreement through common law. Today in the United States, many states continue to have common laws, although statutory law has replaced much of it. At the federal level, there is no common law anymore, replaced entirely by statutory law.

Sources: Ghen v. Rich, 8 F. 159 (1881) and State v. Bradbury, 136 Me. 347 (1939).

dissension is unpopular, a judge might impose a harsh sentence upon a political dissident and have substantial community approval.

Although American society has become formalized and the laws at all jurisdictional levels are largely codified, common law has not ceased to exist. In the United States, more than a few jurisdictions have common law and utilize it. Also, they might supplement their common law with codified statutory law. For example, many urban areas do not condone prostitution, although some prostitution exists and is accepted informally. In a certain area of town, prostitution goes on. If prostitutes are arrested, they are fined a nominal amount and are soon back on the street and engaging in more prostitution. In many rural areas of the United States, prostitution might be treated quite differently. If police arrested a prostitute, the prosecutor would be expected by the community to pursue the case against the prostitute as a serious crime. Therefore, certain crimes vary in their seriousness according to jurisdictional variations and prevailing customs and definitions of criminal conduct.

Civil Law

Civil law originated in ancient Roman law. Contrasted with common law, civil law stresses codification. Early civil law existed as compilations of rules and laws that were made under Emperor Justinian. Rather than rely on local custom to resolve disputes, common-law judges referred to written law when deciding cases. Civil law in America is used to resolve disputes between private parties. Unlike criminal law, a private party rather than the prosecutor originates a case against another person or an organization. The penalties sought are typically monetary. If one party is found to be at fault, damages are assessed. These damages are largely financial. Another feature of civil law is the standard of proof. In a civil case, the plaintiff must prove that the defendant was negligent by a **preponderance of the evi-**

COMMON LAW AND THE ABUSIVE WITCH

The Case of Kerri Lynn Patavino

Witches come in all shapes and sizes. They may even be mothers. In Bridgeport, Connecticut, Kerri Lynn Patavino, a twenty-eight-year-old mother of three, claimed to be a witch. She professed to be a follower of Wicca, an ancient, nature-based religion practiced by witches. On October 11, 1996, Patavino was convicted of five counts of second-degree burglary, six counts of risk of injury to a minor, third-degree burglary, and sixth-degree larceny. The total years she could have received as punishment was 115. She received a six-year prison sentence, to be followed by five years' probation. What did Patavino do?

Kerri Patavino was a school bus driver. She drove a bus of fourteen- and fifteen-year-olds on their way to school. One of these children, a fourteen-year-old boy, became Patavino's target for love letters and other attention. At one point, she induced the boy to her home, where she allegedly cast a spell on him, made him drink her blood, and made him have sex with her. The love letters she sent to the boy were written in her own blood. On other occasions, she gave the boy drugs. She stole from the boy various items, including videotapes, rings, and skateboards. According to the boy, the sexual relationship with Patavino continued from March through June of 1995.

Many of Patavino's friends, also professed witches and Wicca practitioners, raised the $2,750 needed to keep her free on bond while she appealed her sentence. "I think this whole thing is a mockery of the witch trials," said a friend, Patti Clark of Derby. "It doesn't matter whether you're a witch, a Christian, a Jewish person—you should be afraid today." Other friends of Patavino condemned the judge's sentence as reminiscent of the witch trials of Colonial days. The prosecutor said that the case had nothing to do with Patavino's religion and that it was entirely based on the idea that it is wrong for an adult to use a child for sexual purposes.

Did Patavino receive the appropriate punishment for her deeds? Was this indeed a "witch" trial reminiscent of the Colonial period or a clear case of child sexual abuse? How would common law apply to this situation? What do you think?

Source: Adapted from Associated Press, "Self-Proclaimed Witch Gets 6 Years." *Minot* (N.D.) *Daily News,* October 12, 1996:A2; "Witch Sentenced to Six Years in Jail for Sex with 14-Year-Old Boy." *Minot* (N.D.) *Daily News,* October 13, 1996:A2.

dence, which means more than fifty percent. Most Americans were made aware of this difference in the case of O. J. Simpson. Although O. J. Simpson was acquitted of murder charges in a criminal case in California in 1995, subsequently he was found at fault in the wrongful deaths of his former wife, Nicole Brown Simpson, and her friend Ron Goldman in the civil case that followed. The media attributed the different outcomes of the two trials to the different standards of proof required for criminal and civil cases. In O. J. Simpson's criminal case, the more difficult standard of **beyond a reasonable doubt** caused jurors to question the evidence against him and find him not guilty of the crimes. However, in the civil case that followed, another jury believed the plaintiffs who asserted that Simpson was responsible for the two deaths. In the latter case, Simpson's culpability was demonstrated according to the civil standard of the preponderance of evidence or weight of the evidence, not the criminal standard of beyond a reasonable doubt.

Criminal Law

For many citizens, the evening news on television is their primary source of information about how the criminal justice system operates. Television dramas such as *Law & Order, Matlock,* and *N.Y.P.D. Blue* feature stories about the legal system and do much to shape our views about criminal law. We might see a story about an offender sentenced in California to life in prison because he stole a pizza, or a story about a serial sex offender released by a parole board who subsequently commits a new sex crime. For most people, the efficacy of the justice system is measured by the sound application of criminal laws or the poor application of these laws.

Criminal law is differentiated from civil law according to the following criteria:

	Criminal Law	*Civil Law*
Who the victim is	State	Individual
Who prosecutes	State	Individual
Possible punishments	Fine, probation, or imprisonment	Monetary awards

In both civil and criminal law, the victim is a person or class of persons, such as an aggregate of smokers, inmates in a jail, or those who use marijuana. In criminal law, however, the offense is regarded as so disruptive to the social order that society as a whole is the nebulous victim. Under criminal law, society is considered harmed by someone's illegal actions; in civil law, someone is the victim and brings suit against the victimizer. Punishments under criminal law are more severe than the punishments prescribed under civil law. People convicted of crimes may be fined or incarcerated. The most severe form of criminal punishment is the death penalty. In civil cases, however, victimizers who are found liable are not imprisoned or put to death. In most instances, they are obligated to compensate victims for their losses and suffering. These penalties are monetary judgments or awards for damages.

Again, the O. J. Simpson case demonstrates this difference. If Simpson had been convicted in that criminal case, he would have been sentenced to prison. In the subsequent civil case against him, Simpson was found liable and ordered by the court to pay $25 million in punitive damages, which were intended to punish him for his conduct, and he was further ordered to pay $8.5 million in compensatory damages, which were intended to compensate the families of his victims for their pain and suffering.

MAN RAPES A COMATOSE WOMAN

The Case of John Horace

In August 1995, a twenty-nine-year-old woman was lying comatose in a Rochester, New York, nursing home. She had been comatose for ten years. Doctors described her condition, stemming from an accident and severe brain injury, as a "chronic vegetative state." On March 18, 1996, she gave birth to a two-month premature but healthy baby boy. Doctors were flabbergasted. This was the first time in modern history that a woman in such a vegetative state had actually given birth to a baby. No immediate explanation for the birth or her pregnancy was offered.

A subsequent investigation revealed that a nurse's aide, fifty-two-year-old John Horace, had worked at the nursing home in Rochester during the period when the woman's pregnancy could have occurred. Sample DNA from the baby's umbilical cord was preserved for later comparison with various suspects. John Horace was one of these suspects. He had been fired from the facility in early 1996. Eyewitness testimony given to police revealed that Horace had been seen in the woman's room during August 1995 and that he had been "acting suspiciously."

Horace was brought in for questioning by police. Also, a search warrant was obtained to acquire some of Horace's personal effects to make a DNA comparison possible with that of the newborn baby. New York State Supreme Court Judge Charles J. Siragusa ordered Horace to provide police with a blood sample. In the meantime, police obtained a saliva specimen from a stamp on a letter Horace had mailed. The DNA match between Horace's saliva specimen and the baby's DNA showed a 99.55 percent chance that he had impregnated the woman. The baby's paternity had all but been established, according to New York Deputy District Attorney General Russell Buscaglia. Prosecutors deliberated on what specific charges they would file.

What laws have been violated here? Should Horace be charged with rape? What parental rights does Horace have? Should New York give the baby to the natural father, John Horace? Is DNA conclusive to establish Horace's guilt on a rape charge? What are the rights of the comatose woman?

Source: Associated Press, "Suspect in Rape of Woman in Coma Ordered to Provide Blood Sample." *Minot* (ND) *Daily News*, April 2, 1996:A2.

Administrative Law

Administrative law is the body of laws, rules, orders, and regulations created by administrative agencies. Although other forms of law may not directly affect us in our daily lives, administrative law is pervasive and affects all of us in various ways. There are more than fifty federal regulatory agencies that promulgate and enforce a diverse array of regulations.

Other administrative agencies exist at the state and local levels. The result is an over-whelming amount of bureaucratic control. When we travel on an airline, for example, we are subject to the administrative rules developed by the Federal Aviation Administration. The food and drugs we consume are approved and regulated by the Food and Drug Administration. When we telephone others, this communication is regulated by the Federal Communications Commission. If we purchase a house, our actions are influenced by interest rates, which are indirectly related to the actions of the Federal Reserve.

An interesting example of the high degree of governmental regulation and control is given by Vago (1997). Vago notes that a couple may be awakened by the buzz of an electronic clock or perhaps by a clock radio. This signals the beginning of a highly regulated existence for them. The clock or radio that wakes them is run by electricity provided by a utility company, regulated by the Federal Energy Regulatory Commission and by state utility agencies. They listen to the weather report generated by the National Weather Service, part of the Commerce Department. When they go to the bathroom, they use products, such as mouthwash and toothpaste, made by companies regulated by the Food and Drug Administration (FDA). The husband might lose his temper trying to open a bottle of aspirin that has a childproof cap required by the Consumer Product Safety Commission (CPSC). In the kitchen the wife reaches for a box of cereal containing food processed by a firm subject to the regulations of the U.S. Department of Agriculture (USDA) and required to label its products under regulations of the Federal Trade Commission (FTC). When they get into their car to go to work, they are reminded by a buzzer to fasten the seat belts, compliments of the National Highway Traffic Safety Administration. They paid slightly more for the car than they wanted to because it contains a catalytic converter and other devices stipulated by the Environmental Protection Agency (EPA) (Vago, 1997:128–129).

Sociolegal Perspectives and the Law

Just as there are various types of law, there are also many perspectives about the interaction between society and law. The analysis of the interaction of law and society has its early American roots in the writings of Oliver Wendell Holmes Jr., Louis Brandeis, and Roscoe Pound, who were among the first to criticize classical jurisprudence. Classical jurisprudence was concerned with strict interpretation and application of the law. This formal and mechanical method of jurisprudence did not permit the courts to effect changes in social policy. Holmes, Brandeis, and Pound believed that law should be active, dynamic, and useful for changing the social order. The perspective on law proposed by these authorities is **sociological jurisprudence**.

Sociological Jurisprudence

Sociological jurisprudence indicates that a part of law should concern itself with making social or public policy. Today, this legal agenda is called judicial activism. Oliver Wendell Holmes believed that law should be responsive to and incorporate changing social conditions, although the legislature should remain the primary method of social change. Holmes said that "for the rational study of the law the black letter man may be seen as the man of the present, but the man of the future is the man of statistics and the master of economics" (Holmes, 1897:457). This statement suggests that law and/or judges should acknowledge and utilize social science to further develop and answer legally relevant questions.

The first person to use social science in litigation was Louis Brandeis. Brandeis embraced sociological jurisprudence and utilized social science to win cases. He often incorporated social science results into briefs to the court to bolster his arguments. One noteworthy case was *Muller v. Oregon* (1907), a dispute about the working hours of women. Two years earlier, the case of *Lochner v. New York* (1905) had been decided by the U.S. Supreme Court, which declared a statute unconstitutional that limited working hours to sixty per week. Aware of this case and holding, Brandeis believed that he had to show that it was harmful for women to work more than sixty hours per week. To substantiate his claim, Brandeis wrote a brief that included statements arguing that women were deleteriously affected by long hours of work. Brandeis used labor statistics and statements from international conferences about labor legislation as his scientific sources. Dr. Theodore Wely had written that women bear the following generation, whose health is essentially influenced by that of the mothers, and the state has a vital interest in securing for itself future generations capable of living and maintaining it (Wely, 1904).

Breckenridge supported this sentiment by suggesting that the assumption of control over the conditions under which industrial women are employed was one of the most significant features of legislative policy. In many advanced industrial countries at that time, the state not only prescribed minimum standards of decency, safety, and healthfulness but also specified minimum limits for wage earners. The state also took cognizance of several ways for distinguishing sex differences and sex relationships. Furthermore, the state sometimes took cognizance of the peculiarly close relationship between the health of its women citizens and the physical vigor of future generations. It had been declared a matter of public concern that no group of its women workers should be allowed to unfit themselves by excessive hours of work, by standing, or other physical strain for the burden of motherhood that each of them should be able to assume. He added that the object of such control is the protection of the physical well-being of the community by setting a limit to the exploitation of the improvident, unworkmanlike, unorganized women who are the mothers, actual or prospective, of the coming generation (Breckenridge, 1906).

The U.S. Supreme Court was persuaded by this argument and held that the adverse effects of women's long working hours were detrimental to the public interest. There is no doubt that the justices of the U.S. Supreme Court were influenced by the social science evidence provided by Brandeis in his brief. The court reasoned in *Muller* that a woman's physical structure and the performance of maternal functions place her at a disadvantage in the struggle for subsistence, especially when the burdens of motherhood are upon her. Even when they are not, by abundant testimony of the medical fraternity, continuance for a long time on her feet at work, repeating this from day to day, tends to injurious effects on the body, and as healthy mothers are essential to vigorous offspring, the physical well-being of women becomes an object of public care in order to preserve the strength and vigor of the citizenry (*Muller v. Oregon*, 1907).

Roscoe Pound elaborated on the purpose and goal of sociological jurisprudence in several of his essays. He recognized that law was not and could not be autonomous or

---

On the Possible Legalization of Marijuana

Proposed Decriminalization in California

Yes, it's on the ballot. In the November 1996 elections, a California citizen-initiated proposal was put before residents for a vote: Should marijuana for medical purposes be legalized?[1] This is not the first time that states have considered decriminalizing the use of previously controlled or illegal substances. In recent years, Washington and Oregon have called for similar voting, although voters rejected these suggestions to legalize the use of marijuana. As of 1996, twenty-four states permitted citizen-initiated proposals to be placed on ballots independent of legislative action. California was also considering Proposition 209, a proposal that would terminate affirmative action and affirmative action programs in California. Other states, such as Louisiana, have considered eliminating riverboat gambling and imposing taxes on previously tax-exempt churches.

As a public policy issue, do you think marijuana should be legalized? How much crime would be eliminated through the legalization of marijuana? Should the same decriminalization be applied to heroin and cocaine?

Source: Adapted from Associated Press, "On the Ballot: Legalize Marijuana?" *Minot* (N.D.) *Daily News*, October 28, 1996:A2.

[1]Subsequently, in 1998, California legalized the use of marijuana for medicinal purposes. However, a federal judge issued an injunction against the California law because the use of marijuana for *any* purpose violated the federal law governing controlled substances. At this writing, the marijuana issue in California is unresolved.

---

uninfluenced by social conditions. He wrote that the important part of our system is not the trial judge who dispenses justice to litigants but rather the judge of the appellate court who uses the litigation as a means of developing the law (Pound, 1912:489). Pound developed five strategies by which sociolegal jurists could distinguish themselves from more traditional jurists.

1. They are looking more to the working of the law than to its abstract content.
2. They regard law as a social institution which may be improved by intelligent human effort, and hold it their duty to discover the best means of furthering and directing such effort.
3. They lay stress upon the social purposes which law subserves rather than upon sanction.
4. They urge that legal precepts are to be regarded more as guides to results which are socially just ills less as flexible molds.
5. Their philosophical views are very diverse. (Pound, 1912:489–490)

These legal scholars and practitioners represented a dramatic change in thinking about the law. They believed that classical jurisprudence and jurists should be the only ones to strictly apply existing law. These jurists believed that law and society were inextricably linked. One influenced the other, and one was necessary for the other. Judges cognizant of or trained in sociological jurisprudence realized that one of the major functions of law was social change. Lawyers and jurists should apply law with the idea of fostering social change.

Legal Realism

Sociological jurisprudence provided the foundation for **legal realism**. This perspective is described in the work of Karl Llewellyn (1931). Llewellyn had a broader agenda than his predecessors. He argued that law was dynamic and often inconsistent. Interestingly, West Publishing Company's development of the *National Reporter* system is believed to have contributed to this perspective by disclosing that similar cases or existing legal precedents were actually applied or interpreted differently, depending on the jurisdiction. For an example, an appellate judge in California applied a particular legal precedent differently than another appellate court judge in Texas applied the same legal precedent.

Karl Llewellyn also believed that the existing understanding of law was inadequate. He believed that law and society were constantly evolving. Realists also believed that law should be the means to a social end rather than an end in itself. Realists were distrustful of legal rules and the perspectives of rule formation. Rather, they were interested in determining the effects of law (Llewellyn, 1931).

Critical Legal Studies

Critical legal studies is one of the most dynamic and controversial perspectives on law. This movement began with a group of junior faculty members and law students at Yale in the late 1960s. In 1977, the group organized itself into the Conference of Critical Legal Studies, which presently has more than four hundred members and holds annual conferences that attract a thousand or more participants (Vago, 1997:57).

The critical legal studies movement involves a thorough examination of the entire legal system. The theoretical underpinnings of critical legal studies is most often attributed to Roberto Unger. The movement had its origins in legal realism. Similarly, critical legal studies takes issue with formal rational law and contends that we must recognize that the law is subjective rather than objective (Unger, 1986).

Critical legal scholars believe that law is not value-free. Essentially, they believe that the law serves to preserve existing power relations in society. Duncan Kennedy (1982) has provided us with a fundamental examination of legal education from the critical legal studies perspective. He argues that law schools train students for hierarchy. In the classroom, students learn their social position during lectures. Law school teachers rely heavily on the Socratic method, whereby teachers ask students about different points of the law. The students, regardless of their responses, are always incorrect. The teacher relies on either lower or higher levels of abstraction to fit particular situations. Law schools justify this method because many law professors believe that it makes students

Changing the Law: Lawsuits against Drug Dealers?

Drug Users Suing Their Connections?

California is one of a few states with legislation that permits consumers of illegal drugs to sue their suppliers. The son of actor Carroll O'Connor committed suicide after becoming addicted to drugs and despondent over marital problems. O'Connor's son, Hugh O'Connor, was supplied cocaine by Harry Perzigian, who was subsequently convicted of selling cocaine and sentenced to a year in jail.

Governor Pete Wilson of California signed into law the new bill, which became effective January 1, 1997. Although Carroll O'Connor cannot recover damages in any wrongful death action against Perzigian, other victims or relatives of victims suffering from drug abuse will be able to sue their suppliers and anyone else who provides them with illegal drugs. The California state law allows suspected drug dealers to be sued for any deaths, injuries, or damage they cause. The same strict liability standards are applied to drug suppliers that are also applied to legitimate businesses. "We're going to financially bankrupt these leeches," said Governor Wilson of the new law.

If any dealers are believed to have caused damage or injury by selling drugs, then they can be sued by the victim's family, employers, hospitals, insurers, and others who suffer from drug users' reckless actions. Suspected drug dealers do not have to be convicted of any crime first. Even drug users can sue their drug suppliers under the new law. A person who believes that he or she was injured while still in the womb can also sue.

Do you think that laws permitting drug addicts to recover damages from their suppliers are effective deterrents to the illegal distribution of drugs in the United States? How much liability should users of illegal drugs assume in such situations? Do you see any potential problems with such laws?

Source: Adapted from Associated Press, "Law Allows Lawsuits against Drug Dealers." *Minot* (N.D.) *Daily News,* September 26, 1996:A3.

think like lawyers. However, Duncan Kennedy says that this experience is humiliating for the students and only further reinforces the hierarchy of law.

To remedy certain problems associated with acquiring a legal education, Kennedy advocates a radical restructuring of law school curricula and how law is taught. In Kennedy's version of an ideal legal education, there would be few legal skills classes (e.g., learning legal rules and the categorization of cases), and the major focus in law school would be mastering social and political theory and an analysis of the existing social system (e.g., housing, welfare, and criminal justice).

On the Legality of Assisted Suicide

The Case of Dr. Jack Kevorkian

His name is Jack Kevorkian. He is a physician. He assists people who wish to end their lives. He enables them to commit suicide. Is he a monster? Is he a savior? According to police, prosecutors, and his victims, he is both.

Kevorkian is a long-time advocate for euthanasia, the practice of ending one's life when one has a terminal illness and is suffering intense pain. If there is no hope for survival or a prolonged useful life, many patients in this condition want to end their pain and suffering in the most painless way possible. Kevorkian has supplied numerous persons with "suicide kits," enabling them to use their own automobiles as personal death chambers through death by carbon monoxide poisoning.

Kevorkian has been in several courtrooms to defend himself against various types of murder charges. Testifying in his behalf have been many family members of those who have terminated their lives with his assistance. Living wills recorded on videotape from the deceased themselves have absolved Kevorkian from beyond the grave. Yet, prosecutors and state legislators continue to bring Kevorkian into court, attempting to secure a murder conviction.

One dilemma is that Kevorkian took an oath when he became a physician. The oath required him to prolong a person's life, not terminate it. Yet, Kevorkian insists that in all cases where he has assisted the terminally ill, he has merely provided the means by which they can die with dignity, instead of screaming to death in a lonely hospital bed from the unbearable pain of cancer and other diseases.

Kevorkian almost always delivers the bodies of victims to hospitals where they can be properly examined. He insists that although he is referred to in the media as Dr. Death, he does not deserve such an appellation. Rather, he sees his role as alleviating the suffering and pain of terminally ill patients. Other doctors reject his philosophy and claim that doctors should do everything they can to prolong life.

What do you think? Do you believe that people should be allowed to choose whether they live or die, if they are suffering a terminal condition and are in great pain? What should the decision be about Dr. Jack Kevorkian? Is he guilty of multiple murders under the guise of assisted suicide? Is this a moral issue? What values are evident in this debate over medically assisted suicide? How should it be resolved?

Source: Adapted from Associated Press, "Kevorkian Assists Suicide No. 33." *Minot* (N.D.) *Daily News,* July 11, 1996:A2.

Feminist Legal Theory

Another perspective on the law has its origins in feminism. The diverse experiences of women in respect to the law have evolved into various perspectives on the relationship between law and gender. The feminists' perspective of the law, or **feminist legal studies**, ranges from the radical to the pragmatic. Some feminists have examined how the law protects male interests. Some have argued that the law treats women as objects of men (Abrams, 1995). Other feminists have examined the impact of women on the legal system as law students and attorneys (Menkel-Meadow, 1986) and as judges (Friedman, 1984). The rationale for this view is that women reason differently than men; therefore, as lawyers and judges, women use a different type of logic to apply the law. Women may be less adversarial and confrontational than men, which is quite possibly a positive result. The confrontational, adversarial process has a winner and a loser. Frances Olsen (1982) says that women express dissatisfaction with the win-lose nature of litigation because the real needs of the litigants are never addressed or accommodated. Female lawyers might advocate a process involving less litigation, more mediation, and fewer winner-take-all results (Menkel-Meadow, 1986).

Summary

Law has a variety of functions. It is often used as a method of social control or to regulate our behavior. When people violate the law, the law is used to punish them for their past behavior and to control their future behavior. Another function of the law is dispute resolution. The law provides for rules of evidence and procedure that are employed to hear and process disputes. Another function of the law is social change. In the United States, law is often used as an agent of social change. State legislatures are constantly passing laws to change the existing social order. Legislative action or law has changed how we as a society perceive and react to various criminal offenses.

Four types of law were identified in this chapter. Common law originated in England and was made by judges who traveled in circuits and dispensed justice according to the customs common to the region. Civil law is codified, or written and documented. It originated in ancient Roman law. Unlike common law, judges refer to the written law when deciding cases. Criminal law is differentiated from other types of law in that society as a whole is a victim when a criminal law is violated. Punishments under criminal law are more severe than those under civil law. Administrative law is the body of law, rules, orders, and regulations created by administrative agencies. Administrative law affects our lives almost daily.

Another important aspect of law is how it interacts with society. This chapter presented four perspectives that explore this interaction: sociological jurisprudence, legal realism, critical legal studies, and feminist legal theory. Each of these offers different perspectives on the interaction between law and society.

KEY TERMS

Administrative law
Beyond a reasonable
  doubt
Blaming
Civil law
Claiming
Common law
Criminal law
Critical legal studies
Disputant

Dispute resolution
Dispute stage
Feminist legal studies
Grievance
Judicial activism
Law
Law in action
Law in books
Legal realism
Naming

Preconflict stage
Preponderance of the
  evidence
Procedural law
Process of law
Social change
Social control
Sociological jurisprudence
Substantive law

QUESTIONS FOR REVIEW

1. What is law? What are two different types of law? Differentiate between them.
2. What was the significance of the Dred Scott case?
3. Name and describe four functions of law.
4. What is the significance of the view containing naming, blaming, and claiming?
5. Compare and contrast substantive law with procedural law. What do these different types of law govern? Explain.
6. What is common law? How do judges decide cases on the basis of common law?
7. What is meant by administrative law? Why is it important for social change?
8. What is sociological jurisprudence? How is sociological jurisprudence related to social change?
9. What is meant by legal realism? How does critical legal studies compare with legal realism? Explain.
10. How has feminism affected the development of law in the United States?

SUGGESTED READINGS

Beckett, Katherine. (1997). *Making Crime Pay: Law and Order in Contemporary American Politics.* New York: Oxford University Press.

Friedman, Lawrence. (1985). *History of American Law,* 2nd ed. New York: Simon and Schuster.

Henry, Stuart and Dragan Milovanovic (eds.). *Constitutive Criminology at Work: Applications to Crime and Justice.* Albany: State University of New York Press.

Johnson, Herbert. (1988). *History of Criminal Justice.* Cincinnati, OH: Anderson.

McDonald, William F. (ed.). (1997). *Crime and Law Enforcement in the Global Village.* Cincinnati, OH: Anderson.

Pestritto, Ronald J. (2000). *Founding the Criminal Law: Punishment and Critical Thought in the Origins of America.* DeKalb: Northern Illinois Press.

Thurbin, Daye. (1998). *Crime and Punishment: A Critical Survey of the Origins and Evolution of the Common Law.* Surrey, UK: Idle Press.

Vago, Steven. (1997). *Law and Society,* 5th ed. Upper Saddle River, NJ: Prentice Hall.

THE STRUCTURE OF AMERICAN COURTS

JOHNNY DEVIANT works long days at the factory and after work has a few beers with the boys to unwind. At first, his wife was extremely upset with his shenanigans. But as time passed, Johnny's wife didn't seem to care. In fact, Johnny felt that she was adjusting to the traditional housewife role, and he felt that he was happily married. Unbeknownst to Johnny, the source of his wife's joy was Johnny's staying at the bar after work. This is because, in his absence, she had started an affair with the mailman. As time passed, Johnny grew suspicious. His wife seemed happier than ever. Johnny began to take sick days from work and watch his house from down the block. He began to notice a pattern. The mailman came to the house every day. But often Johnny found no new letters or bills. In a fit of rage, Johnny picked up the most recent copy of *Soldiers of Misfortune* to look for an ad for a hitman. After perusing the advertisements and interviewing several interested parties, Johnny soon found the right man for the job. Together, they quickly began to plan the best way to eliminate Johnny's problem. However, Johnny did not realize that the hitman was an undercover police officer. Finally, Johnny was arrested and charged with conspiring to kill his wife. He was assigned an attorney, and his trial date was set in the Supreme Court and was to be televised. Criminal justice students from a nearby state could not understand how the Supreme Court could hold a trial. How could this event be explained?

Introduction

For many people from foreign countries, the American court system is one of the most confusing in the world. Many countries have a centralized court system that is uniform and easy to understand. Even students of the American court system often find it difficult to understand the structure and operations of U.S. courts. There are fifty-one different court structures in the United States. Each state, as well as the federal government, has its own structure and process for resolving disputes and prosecuting criminals. Moreover, acquiring an awareness of only the state and federal court systems ignores other court systems, such as military tribunals, juvenile and family courts, probate courts, tribal courts, chancery courts, and housing and land courts.

This chapter examines the structure of the American court system. It is beyond the scope of this book to list and describe all the subtle differences of every type of court structure. Rather, this chapter classifies these court structures according to jurisdictions. It does not focus strictly on court names, however, because the meaning associated with a particular court name varies among counties and states. The opening scenario is an example of such confusion. Correctly, it may be assumed that the supreme court is an appellate court of last resort at the state and federal levels. Most trial courts are called circuit courts or district courts. In New York, however, felony trials are within the purview of the Supreme Court. New York supreme courts are the functional equivalent of criminal courts in other states and simply use the term *supreme court* for this type of court. This conceptual Tower of Babel needs to be understood in order to compare and contrast the different courts and their functions.

Classifying America's Courts

One way of classifying American courts is by **jurisdiction**. Jurisdiction is the legal authority or power of a court to hear specific kinds of cases. Jurisdiction varies most often according to where the offense occurred, the seriousness of the offense, and whether the case is being heard for the first time or on appeal. There are three types of jurisdiction: subject matter jurisdiction, geographic jurisdiction, and hierarchical jurisdiction.

Subject Matter Jurisdiction

Subject matter jurisdiction refers to the type of case the court has authority to hear. Usually misdemeanors and preliminary hearings are processed or conducted by courts of **limited jurisdiction**. For example, if a person burglarizes a house and steals $499 worth of goods, the case typically will be heard by a court of limited jurisdiction (e.g., municipal court, city court, county court). However, if the same person burglarizes the same house and steals $500 or more worth of goods, this case will likely be heard in a court of **general jurisdiction** (e.g., district court, circuit court, superior court). Thus, the actual dollar value of property stolen determines whether the jurisdiction is limited or general. The greater the dollar value of property stolen, the more likely the case will be heard in a court of general jurisdiction. Courts of limited jurisdiction most often decide petty offenses involving minor monetary sums.

In many areas of the country, courts of limited jurisdiction are responsible for processing the initial stages of felony cases. These courts usually issue warrants, conduct initial appearances, establish bail, and advise felony defendants of their rights and the charges they are facing, as well as a date for a preliminary hearing to determine whether probable cause exists.

Geographic Jurisdiction

Geographic jurisdiction is determined by the political boundaries where the crime was committed. It is the clearest type of jurisdiction to understand. A defendant's case will be heard by a court within the political boundary where the offense occurred. If a crime is committed in a county outside the city limits, a county court will preside if there is a later trial. However, if the crime occurs in the city, then a city criminal court will preside. In Knoxville, Tennessee, for instance, there are courts of general jurisdiction known as **general sessions courts**. Anyone who commits a crime within the city limits of Knoxville will be tried in one of these courts. However, if the crime is committed in Knox County, where Knoxville is located, but beyond the city boundaries, then a different court will hear the case. In this instance, the case will be heard in **circuit courts**. Tennessee is one of a few states that has retained the circuit court concept. In the early 1800s, circuit court judges would ride the circuit—that is, ride on horseback or in buggies—to remote, sparsely populated areas of Tennessee to conduct trials for those charged with crimes. These circuit judges would hold court, probably once a month, to hear both civil and criminal cases. In recent times, circuit courts in urban areas of Tennessee hear criminal and civil matters that occur outside city limits but within county boundaries. Furthermore, Tennessee cities also have **criminal courts** that hear more serious criminal cases that are beyond the jurisdiction of general sessions courts. Thus, Tennessee has a more complex and overlapping court system than most other states.

There are other types of geographic jurisdiction besides the political boundaries of cities and counties. For instance, almost every military base, fort, or installation and Native American reservation is located within a particular state or territory. If someone commits a crime in Sequoia National Park in California, geography itself would seem to indicate that California would have jurisdiction. Because Sequoia National Park is a federally protected area, however, the federal court has jurisdiction. Many offenses occurring in federally protected areas are heard by U.S. magistrates. Also, if a crime is committed on the premises of Minot Air Force Base in North Dakota, it is not relevant that the crime took place within the geographic boundaries of North Dakota. Minot Air Force Base is a federal military installation, and military police and courts will arrest, prosecute, and try criminal defendants. North Dakota state courts do not have jurisdiction in these cases, even though the land on which Minot Air Force Base rests is centered within the geographical boundaries of North Dakota. Politically, the jurisdiction of North Dakota courts ends at the Minot Air Force Base gates.

Geographic jurisdiction may also be influenced by the perpetrator and victim (e.g., federal agent or federal property). For instance, in the case of *Morrissette v. United States* (1952), Morrissette, a civilian, was hunting deer one afternoon on a U.S. Army artillery range in Michigan. Although there were signs stating "Danger—Keep Out—Bombing Range," the area was known as good deer country, and Morrissette hunted there anyway. In the course of his hunting, he came across a number of spent copper bomb casings that appeared to be discarded. After a frustrating day of hunting, Morrissette decided to offset some of his trip expenses by gathering some of these casings and selling them for their copper value. He was arrested and charged with stealing U.S. government property. He was tried in federal district court, convicted, sentenced to imprisonment for two months, and fined $200. The U.S. Supreme Court reversed Morrissette's conviction, holding that Morrissette had no intention of committing a crime. Furthermore, he did not know that what he was doing was unlawful, and through his good character and openness in the taking of the casings, he demonstrated that his action was not deliberately criminal. It is significant here that Morrissette's case was not heard in a military tribunal. Morrissette was a civilian and not subject to military law and sanctions. If the perpetrator had been a soldier in the U.S. Army, however, the soldier would have been tried by a military court for the criminal trespass offense.

Hierarchical Jurisdiction

Hierarchical jurisdiction is basically the difference between appellate and trial courts. Trial courts are often referred to as courts of fact, whereas appellate courts are referred to as courts of law. **Trial courts** are courts of fact because they are the forum where a judge or jury listens to the facts presented in the case and determines whether the defendant is guilty or not guilty. Trial courts are also responsible for sentencing the defendant. In contrast, **appellate courts** do not hear testimony or impose sentences. Appellate courts determine if the law was applied correctly. For example, a trial court judge during the course of a trial may make many decisions regarding the admissibility of evidence and testimony. For each of these decisions, the judge relies on an understanding of constitutional and procedural law. When a case is appealed, appellate court judges review whether the trial court judge followed constitutional law in those decisions.

Federal Court Structure

The court system in the United States can be divided into two separate entities. One court system is at the federal level and consists of the U.S. Supreme Court, the U.S. Circuit Courts of Appeal, U.S. District Courts, and the U.S. Magistrate. The other court system is established through the authority of the states and consists of state and local courts. These court structures at the state and federal levels are referred to as a **dual court system**. The federal court system has the authority to hear cases identified by the U.S. Constitution. Article III, Section 2 of the U.S. Constitution identifies disputes that may be heard by federal courts, including cases in which the U.S. government or one of its officers is being sued. The Constitution also grants authority to the federal courts to hear "Controversies between two or more states; between Citizens of the same State claiming land under grants from other states." For example, one state might sue another state for exporting hazardous waste. The case is heard at the federal level because the impartiality of the state courts in either state jurisdiction might be questioned.

The Constitution also extends federal courts the authority to hear cases involving counsels, ambassadors, and other public ministers. The federal courts are authorized to hear cases involving laws enacted by Congress, treaties and laws related to maritime jurisdiction, and commerce on the high seas. Because of this authority, the federal courts often decide disputes involving interstate commerce. Congress has determined that some of these cases may also be heard by state courts, giving state and federal courts **concurrent jurisdiction**. An example is a citizen from one state who sues a citizen from another state. The case may be heard in the state courts or in a federal district court. However, the case is heard at the federal level only if the amount of the dispute exceeds $50,000. Again, the amount of money involved in a dispute often determines which court will hear the case. The federal court structure consists of four basic levels: the U.S. Magistrate Courts, U.S. District Courts, U.S. Circuit Courts of Appeal, and the U.S. Supreme Court.

U.S. Magistrate Courts

The lowest court of limited jurisdiction at the federal level is the U.S. Magistrate. In 1968, Congress created the judicial office of federal magistrate. The magistrate's office was created to alleviate the workload of the U.S. district court judges. In 1990, the position title was changed to magistrate judge. The **U.S. magistrates** are appointed by the district judge and assigned as either full-time or part-time magistrates, depending on the caseload of the district court. Full-time magistrates are appointed to an eight-year term, whereas the terms of part-time magistrates are four years.

The duties of the magistrate judge are similar to the duties of judges who serve in courts of limited jurisdiction at the state level. Magistrate judges hear disputes involving civil consent matters, misdemeanor trials, and the preliminary stages of felony cases, including preliminary hearings, pretrial motions, and conferences. In 1994, there were 494 magistrate judge positions. Of these, 406 were full-time magistrates, 85 were part-time magistrates, and 3 were assigned duties of clerk of court and magistrate (Maguire and Pastore, 2000).

U.S. District Courts

At the federal level, **U.S. District Courts** are courts of general jurisdiction. Most civil and criminal cases are tried and disposed of in the U.S. District Courts. Approximately eighty-five percent of all federal court cases are civil, and fifteen percent are criminal. There are ninety-four district courts in the United States. Each state has at least one federal district court, and these courts can also be found in the U.S. territories of Guam, Puerto Rico, the U.S. Virgin Islands, and the Northern Mariana Islands. Thirty-one states and the U.S. territories have only one district court with the jurisdiction to hear federal cases. The remaining states have two or more federal district courts.

Federal judgeships are lifetime appointments. There is no mandatory retirement age, and federal district court judges may serve as long as they desire. In the language of the Constitution, they "hold their office during good behavior, and shall at stated Times, receive for their services a compensation, which shall not be diminished during their Continuance in Office." This provision for an independent judiciary allows judges to make decisions without the threat of being removed from office or having their salaries reduced.

U.S. Circuit Courts of Appeal

The U.S. Circuit Courts of Appeal are often referred to as **circuit courts**. At the federal level, they are basically intermediate appellate courts, serving as buffers between the U.S. District Courts and the U.S. Supreme Court. Congress created the U.S. Circuit Courts of Appeal in 1891 to relieve the caseload of the U.S. Supreme Court.

There are thirteen courts of appeal. Twelve of these appellate courts have jurisdiction over specific geographic areas. At a minimum, a circuit court hears appeals from three states (e.g., the 2nd and 5th Circuits). The 9th Circuit, located in San Francisco, includes the largest geographical area, nine states and two U.S. territories (Alaska, Arizona, California, Hawaii, Idaho, Montana, Nevada, Oregon, Washington, Guam, and the Northern Mariana Islands). The 12th Circuit has jurisdiction over cases in the District of Columbia. The 13th Circuit is the U.S. Court of Appeals for the Federal Circuit, which was created in 1982 by consolidating the U.S. Court of Claims and the U.S. Court of Customs and Patent Appeals. This court hears cases from the specialized federal courts (e.g., the U.S. Court of Federal Claims, the U.S. Court of Veteran Appeals, and the U.S. Court of International Trade). On occasion, the court hears cases appealing decisions from the secretaries of the Departments of Commerce and Agriculture.

In 1998, there were 179 appellate court judges. The number of authorized judgeships varies by circuit court. The 9th Circuit has the most appellate judges with twenty-eight, and the 1st circuit has the least with six judges. The numbers of judges in each circuit court is determined by the sheer case volume, which varies greatly among the thirteen circuits. More judges are needed to hear more cases in some areas, whereas a lower caseload might require fewer judges (Maguire and Pastore, 2000).

Typically, circuit courts hear cases with three-judge panels. In certain circuits, the volume of cases may be such that several three-judge panels may be convened simultaneously. These three-judge panels hear appeals from decisions in U.S. District Courts. On rare occasions, a case may be heard *en banc*, and the entire aggregate of judges in the circuit hears and decides the case appeal. Usually, appeals heard *en banc* involve important constitutional issues, and input from the larger number of judges is deemed important.

Like district court judges, appellate judges are appointed for life by the president and confirmed by the Senate. One of these judges is designated as the chief judge. Usually, the chief judge has the most seniority and is under sixty-five years of age. Chief judges perform additional duties apart from hearing cases, and their maximum term in this role is seven years.

The U.S. Supreme Court

The court of last resort at the federal level is the **U.S. Supreme Court**. It is the only court specifically mentioned in Article III, Section 1 of the Constitution. The Constitution states that "the judicial power of the United States, shall be vested in one supreme court, and in such inferior courts as the Congress may from time to time ordain and establish." Like the other federal courts, U.S. Supreme Court justices hold their positions for life. They are nominated and appointed by the president, with Senate confirmation. The Supreme Court has eight associate justices and one chief justice. The chief justice has the additional responsibility of conducting conferences, supervising the federal judiciary, and assigning the task of writing case opinions to a member of the judicial majority. Each of the associate justices is assigned to one of the appellate circuits for emergencies, such as death penalty appeals. In 1998, the annual salary of U.S. Supreme Court justices was $164,100 (Maguire and Pastore, 2000).

The U.S. Supreme Court is in session from the first Monday of October until the following June. The year of the annual session is the year when the session is commenced. When the U.S. Supreme Court convenes in October 2003, all cases decided during that term are considered as cases decided during the 2003 term, even though a particular case might not be heard until May or June of 2004.

Annually, the court decides approximately five thousand case appeals. Most appeals are disposed of when the U.S. Supreme Court decides not to hear the case because of the subject matter or because it is not significant enough to merit court review. The decision to hear a case is made when the justices meet to review all cases. For all of the justices to hear a particular appeal, the case must pass a screening known as the **Rule of Four**. At least four of the nine justices must agree that the case has constitutional merit or national importance and that it should be heard by the entire court. If a case receives four or more votes from the justices, it is placed on the docket and scheduled to be heard.

Most cases reach the court through a petition known as a **writ of *certiorari***. This is an order issued by the Supreme Court to the lower court to send the record for review. When the court decides to hear a case, it is scheduled for written and oral arguments by the opposing lawyers. The written arguments are filed with the court and made available to the public. In some cases, other interested parties may file briefs for the court to hear, on behalf of other parties. These types of filings are called ***amicus curiae*** briefs. *Amicus curiae* means "a friend of the court" and refers to a broad class of briefs that may be filed by one party on behalf of one or more other parties. For instance, an *amicus curiae* brief was filed on behalf of Gary Gilmore, a convicted murderer in Utah, by Amnesty International, an organization opposed to capital punishment. The brief was on behalf of Gilmore, who was scheduled to be executed. The brief sought relief in the form of a stay of Gilmore's execution, until the U.S. Supreme Court had time to hear and consider new arguments for why the death penalty should not be imposed in Gilmore's case. Although the brief was successful, in that it gave Gilmore several additional weeks, Gilmore did not wish to pursue further appeals. He declared that he wanted to die and that the state should be allowed to execute him, despite the objections of Gilmore's family and Amnesty International. Gilmore was subsequently executed by a Utah firing squad.

Appearances by attorneys before the U.S. Supreme Court are highly regimented by prevailing protocol. The attorneys for the opposing sides are permitted thirty minutes each to present oral arguments. Green, yellow, and red lights, similar to those that regulate automobile traffic, flash for the different litigants. A green light means oral argument may proceed, a yellow light flashes when the thirty-minute oral argument time limit is approaching, and a red light means that the oral argument terminates. During this time, justices are allowed to ask questions of the attorneys presenting the oral arguments. After oral arguments, the justices schedule a meeting, which is called a case conference. In this meeting, the justices take an initial position.

Traditionally, if the chief justice is in the majority, this justice assigns the writing of the majority opinion to one of the other majority justices. The senior justice for the minority or dissenting opinion assigns the writing of this opinion to one of the dissenting justices. The writing of the opinion may be quite complicated, especially when the justices on both sides have conflicting opinions about the case. For instance, not all of the majority justices may believe the case should be decided in a given way for the same reasons. Thus, each majority justice may write an independent opinion explaining why the justice voted a certain way. Accordingly, dissenting justices do not have to agree about why they dissent, and several dissenting justices may write independent opinions explaining why they dissented. These opinions make for interesting reading for Supreme Court historians and others because often the personal views of justices are made evident in their opinions.

When the topic of the opinion is controversial, such as a case involving abortion or the death penalty, each justice expresses different views about the issue. For example, in *Furman v. Georgia* (1972), all justices wrote separate opinions. In most cases, the opinion goes through several drafts before it is approved by the majority or dissenting justices and before it is subsequently made available to the public. Unlike cases heard at the appellate level, the U.S. Supreme Court hears all cases *en banc*. All nine justices hear each case.

There are exceptions. Sometimes, a death or resignation from the U.S. Supreme Court leaves the court with seven or eight members temporarily, until a new justice or justices can be appointed. While the court does not have nine justices, it may still convene and hear and decide appeals. A majority of justices is still required, although a majority is more difficult to achieve. Eight justices may divide equally on a given issue, with a 4–4 vote. Such a vote results in no decision rendered about that particular appeal. Five or more justices are required to support any appeal. When a 4–4 vote occurs, the case is simply discarded and not scheduled for rehearing. The litigants may bring the case before the U.S. Supreme Court again, provided that they raise a different and meaningful issue as the basis for challenging a lower court decision. And the Rule of Four exists for all new case filings, regardless of whether a particular case has been previously heard. Four or more justices must agree to hear the case before it will be docketed.

State Court Structure

Studying the American courts would be relatively easy if we did not have to consider state court organization. But, as we have seen, states such as Tennessee provide numerous court structures and jurisdictions that create some complexity, and each state is different from the others in state court organization and function. Thus, we must add to the federal system the different court systems found in all fifty states.

The organization and functions of the fifty different state court structures are diverse and complex. For example, Massachusetts has its Supreme Judicial Court, Appeals Court, Superior Court, District Court, Probate/Family Court, Juvenile Court, Housing Court, Municipal Court, and Land Court. In contrast, South Dakota has only a two-tiered system, with a Circuit Court and a Supreme Court. State courts often have overlapping and

THE POWER OF THE U.S. SUPREME COURT

The 1996–1997 Term

The U.S. Supreme Court decides many important cases annually. Most of these cases involve constitutional issues. Compared with Congress, the country's law-making body, the U.S. Supreme Court interprets the law and how the law should be applied. However, the U.S. Supreme Court outdid itself during the 1996–1997 term. At issue were many important matters. A citizen, Paula Jones, had accused President Bill Clinton of sexual misconduct while he was governor of Arkansas. President Clinton's lawyers claimed that the president should be immune from lawsuits while he was still in office, in that such lawsuits might impair his effectiveness and performance of his presidential duties. The Brady Bill was being tested, whereby local law enforcement agencies were being required to conduct background investigations on all firearms applicants. Gun lobbyists and others claimed that this was too much government intrusion and imposed undue hardship on gun dealers and law enforcement personnel. The Internet was being censored for transmitting obscene materials. The American Civil Liberties Union claimed that censoring the Internet in this regard amounted to a violation of the right to free speech under the First Amendment. What did the Supreme Court decide?

First, President Clinton could be sued by Paula Jones while he was president. He was not above the law and could not insulate himself from such lawsuits, if substantial grounds existed for their origination. Second, gun dealers and law enforcement personnel are not required to perform extensive background checks on handgun applicants. Third, the Internet cannot prevent obscene materials from being transmitted to those wishing to receive the materials.

In other decisions, the U.S. Supreme Court upheld the laws of two states that prohibited physician-assisted suicides of terminally ill patients. The court ruled that police officers in all jurisdictions have the right to require all passengers to exit vehicles that have been stopped for routine traffic violations. The court also ruled that sexual predators can be locked up for periods beyond their original maximum sentences if they are deemed to pose a danger to others. Last but not least, the court ruled that the Religious Freedom Restoration Act of 1993 was unconstitutional.

Do you think these powers are within the scope of authority originally vested in the U.S. Supreme Court? Should the U.S. Supreme Court be subject to the scrutiny of other bodies, such as the executive branch or Congress? What do you think?

Source: Adapted from Associated Press, "Judicial Power: Supreme Court's 1996–1997 Term Proved a Showcase of Ultimate Legal Influence." *Minot* (N.D.) *Daily News,* June 29, 1997:A4.

conflicting jurisdictions. The state courts are also very busy with variable caseloads. Millions of cases are filed and disposed of each year. In 1992, more than 93 million disputes were heard by state courts. By 1994, this number had declined to 86.5 million (Kauder and LaFountain, 1996). Most of these cases (more than 50 million) were traffic offenses. Juvenile cases increased most, eighteen percent, between 1992 and 1994.

Many jurisdictions do not require that judicial officers have a law degree. In fact, thirty-six states do not require that judges in a court of limited jurisdiction must be educated in the law. One reason is that many judges are elected rather than appointed or selected through some other form of merit selection. In short, these judges need to convince the electorate that they have the ability to serve rather than be legal practitioners with professional credentials. The lack of education and knowledge of the judicial process among many state court judges has caused a number of problems. Most of these courts are not courts of record, and so it is difficult to monitor their activities formally. Because many elected judges do not know the limits of their authority or are unfamiliar with the processes of the judicial system, many states have established a legal training requirement for newly elected judges. Most of these judges are required to attend a legal training seminar sponsored by the state judicial conference or a committee or a program sponsored by the Administrative Office of the U.S. Courts.

Despite provisions for the legal training of new judges in most jurisdictions, research about courts of limited jurisdiction has revealed that more than a few inequities exist. Some of these problems, such as judicial incompetence, have been highlighted in U.S. Supreme Court cases. For example, the U.S. Supreme Court was confronted with the matter of judicial competence in the case of *North v. Russell* (1976). Judge Russell worked in the coal mines of Kentucky after he dropped out of high school. Later he was elected as a judge and presided over the case of Lonnie North, who had been accused of drunk driving. Judge Russell denied North's request for a jury trial, did not inform North of his right to counsel, and denied North's right to appeal the subsequent decision. Judge Russell listened only to the arresting officer's version of the incident and did not permit North to testify on his own behalf and provide his version of events. Judge Russell sentenced Lonnie North to thirty days in jail, although the statute provided a maximum sentence of a fine and no jail time. In this case, North's conviction was set aside by the U.S. Supreme Court, and Judge Russell was criticized for his incompetence.

Generally, state courts have a four-tiered structure. These tiers are courts of limited jurisdiction, courts of general jurisdiction, intermediate courts of appeal, and courts of last resort.

Courts of Limited Jurisdiction

Courts of limited jurisdiction have the greatest variability among the states. These courts hear minor offenses such as violations of traffic laws, minor civil cases, and infractions. They also perform other administrative duties. Courts of limited jurisdiction are about eighty percent of the total number of state courts. They are the courts with the highest caseloads in the nation (National Institute of Law Enforcement and Criminal Justice; 1979). On average, they dispose of more than fifty percent of all cases brought before the

TECHNOLOGY AND ACCESS TO THE FEDERAL JUDICIARY

Technological advances have affected all of us in some way. The federal judiciary is not immune to this trend. Since the 1990s, the federal courts have made available to the public a number of resources to access information about the cases before the courts and the decisions reached by the courts. The services offered allow the public to obtain information about the actions of the courts without ever setting foot inside a courthouse. Some of the services offered by the court are:

The U.S. Supreme Court Electronic Bulletin Board System

The U.S. Supreme Court Electronic Bulletin Board System (EBBS) service provides on-line access to the court docket, opinions, argument calendar, rules, and bar information forms. Additional information includes general and tour information and special notices.

U.S. Supreme Court Clerk's Automated Response Systems

The U.S. Supreme Court Clerk's Automated Response System (CARS) provides callers with information about the status of cases by instructing callers to respond to telephone prompts.

Appellate Bulletin Board System

The Appellate Bulletin Board System (ABBS) is a source of information about judicial opinions that is offered to the public by federal circuit courts of appeal. These courts provide public access to court decisions, argument calendars, case dockets, reports, notices, and press releases. Information can be downloaded and viewed on-line by computer users. Currently, there is a fee of sixty cents per minute for this service.

Public Access to Court Electronic Records

The Public Access to Court Electronic Records (PACER) allows users to dial into the bankruptcy court computer to access information about cases and decisions. Again there is a charge of sixty cents per minute. Users must first register with the PACER service center before they can use this service. Many district and circuit courts have established toll-free numbers, and users do not incur the additional costs of long-distance telephone calls.

(continued)

Technology and Access to the Federal Judiciary
(continued)

Party/Case Index

In 1977, the courts started a new service to allow users to conduct searches of the bankruptcy court by party name or social security number. Searches can also be conducted to locate civil or criminal cases or cases being appealed. The search will retrieve the case filing date and filing location.

Electronic Filing and Attorney Docketing Service

The Electronic Filing and Attorney Docketing Service (EFADS) is being tested in selected district courts. This service allows attorneys to submit pleadings and other docket entries through the Internet. The case file and official docket can be viewed on-line or downloaded electronically.

state courts. Iowa, South Dakota, Idaho, and Illinois are the only states without courts of limited jurisdiction, and the District of Columbia also has no such court.

State courts of limited jurisdiction have many different names. Most of these courts are called municipal courts, county courts, city courts, or justice of the peace courts. Other courts are specialized courts of limited jurisdiction. Some of these courts might be called juvenile court, family court, probate court, or court of workers compensation. Caseload estimates indicate that between 1984 and 1994 traffic cases in municipal courts decreased by fifteen percent. However, these courts continued to be busy with heavy caseloads because the decrease in traffic cases was replaced by a fifty-nine percent increase in juvenile cases heard by these same courts during the same period (National Center for State Courts, 1995).

Courts of General Jurisdiction

Courts of general jurisdiction have jurisdiction over all major civil and criminal cases. These courts differ from courts of limited jurisdiction because they are **courts of record** and **general trial courts**. They are courts of record because a record is made of all the proceedings. Various methods are used to make records of these proceedings. Court reporters use tape recorders and other devices to record whatever is said. With a few exceptions, courts of general jurisdiction are called circuit courts, district courts, superior courts, courts of common pleas, and supreme courts. A list of names of these courts for the different states is provided in Table 2.1.

TABLE 2.1 Courts of General Jurisdiction for Each State

Circuit Court

Alabama, Arkansas, Florida, Hawaii, Illinois, Indiana,[a] Kentucky, Maryland, Michigan, Mississippi, Missouri, Oregon, South Carolina, South Dakota, Tennessee, Virginia, West Virginia, Wisconsin

Superior Court

Alaska, Arizona, California, Connecticut, Delaware, District of Colombia, Georgia, Maine, Massachusetts, New Hampshire, New Jersey, North Carolina, Rhode Island, Vermont,[b] Washington

District Court

Colorado, Idaho, Iowa, Kansas, Louisiana, Minnesota, Montana, Nebraska, Nevada, New Mexico, North Dakota, Oklahoma, Texas, Utah, Wyoming

Court of Common Pleas

Ohio, Pennsylvania

Supreme Court

New York[c]

---

[a]Indiana has both circuit courts and superior courts.
[b]Vermont has superior courts and district courts.
[c]New York also has county courts.

In 1994, state courts processed and sentenced more than 870,000 adults for felony offenses. This figure does not include civil filings (Bureau of Justice Statistics, 1997). Contrary to what is reported and portrayed by the media, criminal jury trials are relatively rare events. More than ninety percent of all criminal convictions are secured through plea bargaining, by which guilty pleas are entered in exchange for some form of leniency from prosecutors and judges. Thus, criminal trials are conducted only for about ten percent of all criminal cases.

In recent years, the criminal courts have been processing cases more rapidly than in past years. In 1988, for instance, state courts processed 667,366 cases, and the average case-processing time from arrest to conviction was about seven months. In 1994, the courts processed 872,217 cases, and the average time between arrest and conviction was six and a half months (Maguire and Pastore, 2000). Many factors account for this decrease in processing time. One reason is that courts, faced with increasing caseloads, have incorporated more efficient caseload management processes to reduce court delays. Courts may also deliberately limit the number of delays and continuances that were allowed in past years. The workload of a court is strongly associated with where the court is located. Typically, urban courts have more cases to process than rural courts. For example, Los Angeles, the busiest court system in the nation, processed 50,197 felony cases in 1994 (Maguire and Pastore, 2000). This figure is higher than all of the felony cases processed in the entire federal system during that same year.

The demand for court services fluctuates greatly in different areas of the country. In 1994, for example, Lawrenceville, Georgia, processed only 2,732 cases. However, between 1992 and 1994, the number of cases processed declined in Los Angeles. In contrast, Lawrenceville had a forty-seven percent increase in the number of cases processed (Kauder and LaFountain, 1996).

Judges in the courts of general jurisdiction usually have practiced law either as prosecutors or in a law firm before becoming judges. However, in Delaware, Maine, and Massachusetts, judges at this level are not required to have a law degree. The only requirement is that they are learned in the law (Rottman, Flango, and Lockley, 1995). Surprisingly, Maine requires that judges who preside over courts of limited jurisdiction have law degrees, whereas their counterparts in the trial courts have no such requirement. Most states require some combination of a law degree, membership in the state bar for five to ten years, and local and/or state residency. Some states have age limitations for judges at this level. Usually, the minimum age is twenty-five to thirty years, and the maximum age is seventy to seventy-five. The median salary for judges in trial courts is $90,154. Judges in New Jersey's general courts were the highest paid in the nation, with a salary of $115,000. The lowest paid trial judges were in Montana, with a salary of $67,513 (Maguire and Pastore, 2000).

Intermediate Courts of Appeal

Eleven states and the District of Columbia do not have intermediate courts of appeal. Most states have developed an intermediate court of appeal (see Table 2.2) to review and screen the caseload of the state supreme court. These intermediate courts of appeal became necessary shortly after 1900. A few states such as Alabama, Tennessee, and Texas have separate appellate courts for civil and criminal cases. North Dakota has a statutory provision providing for an appellate court at this level, although these judges must be called to action by the state supreme court. Such an event rarely occurs in North Dakota. Most cases are heard with a panel of three judges. Unlike courts of last resort, they do not have discretionary appellate review. Thus, they are required to hear all cases that are properly filed.

Most of the judges at this level are appointed by the governor after being selected by a nominating commission. Appellate court judges make slightly more than their colleagues in the general trial courts. The median salary was $98,727. Appellate court judges in New Jersey were paid the most at $124,200, and appellate court judges in New Mexico were paid the least, making $79,413 (Maguire and Pastore, 2000).

Courts of Last Resort

The highest court structures at the state level are called **courts of last resort**. Usually these are also called supreme courts. In states with an intermediate court of appeals, these courts have discretionary appellate review; that is, they decide which cases they will hear. By refusing to hear a case, they are allowing the decision of the lower court to stand.

TABLE 2.2 Intermediate Courts of Appeal

Appeals Court Massachusetts	**Appellate Division of Superior Court** New Jersey
Appellate Court Connecticut, Illinois	**Appellate Division of Superior Court** New York Hawaii
Appellate Terms of Supreme Court New York	**Superior Court** Pennsylvania
Commonwealth Court Pennsylvania	
Courts of Appeal California, Louisiana, Texas	
Court of Civil Appeal Alabama	
Court of Appeals Alaska, Arizona, Arkansas, Colorado, Georgia, Idaho, Indiana, Iowa, Kansas, Kentucky, Michigan, Minnesota, Missouri, Nebraska, New Mexico, North Carolina, North Dakota, Ohio, Oklahoma, Oregon, South Carolina, Tennessee, Utah, Virginia, Washington, Wisconsin	
Court of Criminal Appeal Alabama, Tennessee	
Court of Special Appeals Maryland	
District Court of Appeals Florida	

In states with no intermediate court of appeal, the state supreme court has no discretionary authority. Oklahoma and Texas are unique in this regard because they have two courts of last resort. One is designated to hear civil cases, and the other hears only criminal cases. Judges who preside in state supreme courts are usually selected by a nominating commission and appointed by the governor. In order to remain in their positions, they must receive a majority vote in a retention election. The median salary for the states' highest court is $100,645. The highest paid supreme court justices reside in Florida and make $133,600. The lowest paid supreme court justices are in Montana, where they receive annual salaries of $68,874 (Maguire and Pastore, 2000).

Summary

The American court system is the most confusing in the world. Each state has its own court structure, and in many cases courts that perform the same functions are referred to by different names. Therefore, to understand American court structure, we must understand how each court functions and compare these courts in the different states. The best way to understand the American court structure is to classify these courts according to their particular jurisdiction. Courts of limited jurisdiction are granted the legal authority to hear misdemeanor cases or the preliminary stages of felony cases. Courts of general jurisdiction are basically felony trial courts. They are also referred to as courts of fact. However, appellate courts are called courts of law because they do not determine the facts of the case. Rather, they are charged with determining whether the law has been applied correctly. Geography also defines the limits of a court's authority. A court's legal authority is limited by political boundaries. For example, a state court in Arizona does not have the legal authority to hear a criminal case from Nevada. Many municipalities have their own court systems, and their jurisdiction is limited to cases that occur within the city limits.

The scenario of court systems at both the state and federal levels is often referred to as the dual court system. The basic trial courts in the federal system are the U.S. District Courts. The federal system has thirteen appellate jurisdictions or circuit courts of appeal. The U.S. Supreme Court is the court of last resort, the highest court in the land. Its nine justices hear an average of five thousand cases per year and write opinions in about two hundred of them. Unlike trial courts, which have no control over what cases are presented to them, most state courts of last resort and the U.S. Supreme Court decide which case appeals they will or will not hear.

KEY TERMS

Amicus curiae	General jurisdiction	Trial courts
Appellate courts	General sessions courts	U.S. Circuit Courts of
Circuit courts	General trial courts	Appeal
Concurrent jurisdiction	Geographic jurisdiction	U.S. District Courts
Courts of last resort	Hierarchical jurisdiction	U.S. magistrates
Courts of record	Jurisdiction	U.S. Supreme Court
Criminal courts	Limited jurisdiction	Writ of *certiorari*
Dual court system	Rule of Four	
En banc	Subject matter jurisdiction	

QUESTIONS FOR REVIEW

1. Differentiate between courts of limited and general jurisdiction.
2. What is meant by geographic jurisdiction? What is the power of courts with geographic jurisdiction?
3. Describe the U.S. Magistrate and the duties of this particular type of court.
4. What is the basic trial court for the federal system?
5. When a defendant in a U.S. District Court case is found guilty of a crime, where is the appeal directed? What are the jurisdictional limits of this appellate court?
6. What is the court of last resort? Why is it called the court of last resort?
7. What are courts of limited jurisdiction? What are some of the functions of courts of limited jurisdiction?
8. Describe intermediate courts of appeal. Are these courts the same in all states? Why or why not?
9. What is meant by *en banc*?
10. What is the function of an *amicus curiae*?

SUGGESTED READINGS

Felkenes, George T. (1993). "Extraterritorial Criminal Jurisdiction: Its Impact on Criminal Justice." *Journal of Criminal Justice* **21**:583–594.

Flango, Victor E. and David B. Rottman. (1992). "Research Note: Measuring Trial Court Consolidation." *Justice System Journal* **16**:65–74.

Henderson, Thomas A. (1994). *The Significance of Judicial Structure: The Effect of Unification on Trial Court Operations*. Washington, DC: Institute of Economic and Policy Studies, National Institute of Justice.

Hughes, John C. (1995). *The Federal Courts, Politics and the Rule of Law*. New York: HarperCollins.

Kadish, Sanford H., et al. (1994). "Supreme Court Review." *Journal of Criminal Law and Criminology* **84**:679–1175.

Meador, Daniel John. (1991). *American Courts*. St. Paul, MN: West.

Rottmann, David, Carol Flango, and R. Shedine Lockley. (1995). *State Court Organization 1993*. Washington, DC: U.S. Bureau of Justice Statistics.

Rottman, David B. and William E. Hewitt. (1996). *Trial Court Structure and Performance: A Contemporary Reappraisal*. Williamsburg, VA: National Center for State Courts.

THE PROSECUTION

SAMANTHIA CARROLL, 32, a singer, model, and girlfriend of investment banker John Holder Jr., had photographs to prove Holder had physically abused her. The photos clearly showed dark bruises on Carroll's legs, arms, and back, a bloody mouth, and shoeprints on her belly and breast. Holder was arrested for aggravated assault. When the jury saw the photos, the case was quickly concluded with Holder's conviction. He lost his lucrative job at J.P. Morgan in New York City. He was socially disgraced and shunned. He was expected to serve at least a year in jail following his conviction.

The most damning evidence against him were the photographs, taken in December of 1994 by Carroll. These photographs, together with Carroll's riveting testimony in court, were enough to convince the jury that Holder was indeed the culprit and ought to pay for his crime. But wait! The Polaroid photos taken of Carroll's injuries were from a batch of film that had been stored in a photo supply warehouse until late February 1995! Weren't these photos supposed to have been taken three months earlier, in December 1994?

We've heard of DNA. We've heard of fingerprints. We've even heard of voiceprints and footprints. These are all incriminating pieces of evidence to fill in the blanks at crime scenes. But what about the funny numbers on the backs of Polaroid photos? Someone decided to check them out. To everyone's amazement, except John Holder's, the photographs were fake. They couldn't possibly have been taken in December 1994 because the film itself wasn't even sold to the public until late February 1995!

The judge threw out the case against Holder. Will J.P. Morgan give him his job back, now that everything has been put back together again? As it turned out, Holder had given Carroll $20,000 to help her get herself on her feet and produce a music video. But Carroll wanted more money. Speculation is that she wasn't content with the $20,000 and wanted more. The threat of aggravated assault against John Holder Jr. was a good way of extorting more money from him. He was punished, wrongfully, and almost went to jail. Samanthia Carroll still has John's money and her freedom—for now.

What should the prosecutor in this case do, if anything, to help Holder regain his job and self-respect? Do you think that the prosecutor knew about the fake photos and used them anyway? (*Source:* Adapted from Associated Press, "Photo Code Reverses Beating Conviction." *Minot* (N.D.) *Daily News,* July 4, 1996:A5.)

RAY BOEGER, 77, was an otherwise successful advertising executive and businessman in Santa Ana, California. Living in a nice house and driving a Cadillac, Boeger seemed to have it all. In fact, Boeger was deeply in debt from costly medical bills and bad business deals. His wife's kidney problems only made his bad financial situation worse. Trying to bury his troubles with booze, Boeger went to a local bar one morning and began drinking beer. He downed at least four pints of English ale. Then he got a bright idea. According to Boeger, "The beer and bad feelings triggered something in me." Boeger donned a Halloween costume, picked up an unloaded gun, and went to the nearest branch of the World Savings and Loan. Boeger entered the bank and handed a teller an $800 check. Then he advised her that he had a gun and demanded money. She accommodated by handing Boeger $1,100 in cash, together with an exploding dye packet. When Boeger left the bank, the dye packet exploded, spraying him with red dye. Depressed, Boeger stopped by another bar and had more to drink. He was apprehended a few hours later by police, when quick-thinking observers recalled his car license plate number. His wife reportedly was "disappointed" in him. "I guarantee you I won't do it again, because I'm not going to drink anymore," said Boeger when questioned by police. But armed robbery is not to be taken lightly, even if the perpetrator was drunk.

As a prosecutor, how would you proceed against Boeger? Would you charge him with armed robbery and pursue the prosecution in court? Would you recommend diversion for Boeger? (*Source:* Adapted from the Associated Press, "Blaming Crime on Booze, Bills." *Minot* (N.D.) *Daily News,* September 22, 1997:A5.)

Introduction

This chapter examines the roles of one of the most important players in American courtrooms: the prosecutor. The American system of justice is adversarial in nature. The key adversaries are prosecutors, who pursue criminal charges against defendants, and defense counsel, who represent these defendants and defend them against the criminal charges alleged.

The first section of this chapter briefly explores the adversarial system of justice in the United States. At both the state and federal levels, prosecutors represent the interests of government. Prosecutors are described, as well as their functions. Prosecutors have wide-ranging discretion. From time to time, some prosecutors are accused of abusing this discretion by engaging in unethical conduct. Thus, an integral part of the description of prosecutors is the ethical framework within which the criminal justice process is couched.

The Adversary System

When a crime is committed, law enforcement officers frequently arrest a suspect who is believed to have committed the crime. Criminal suspects become defendants charged with one or more crimes. Although all criminal defendants in the United States are entitled to the presumption of innocence before their guilt is established in court beyond a reasonable doubt, they are also entitled to counter the charges against them. Therefore, defendants are represented by defense counsel, whose job it is to defend their clients against these criminal charges (Beckman, 1986). Presumably, defense counsel who represent clients in court are more or less effective according to their training, expertise, and practical trial experience (Klein, 1986; Uphoff, 1992). The system of alleging criminal charges against defendants and defending them against such charges is known as the **adversary system**.

The adversarial nature of the criminal court is evident in the different roles of the **prosecutor** and **defense attorney**. The prosecutor's aim is to prove that the defendant committed a crime, beyond a reasonable doubt. The defense attorney contests any criminal allegations made against the defendant and seeks to dissuade the court or a jury from thinking that the defendant is guilty of a criminal offense.

In 1996, for instance, O. J. Simpson, a football player and actor, was charged with the 1994 double murder of his ex-wife, Nicole Brown Simpson, and her friend, Ronald Goldman, in Los Angeles. Because of the high-profile nature of the defendant, a prosecution team was established that sought to show why he was a murderer. An equally capable defense team was hired by Simpson, including such notable attorneys as F. Lee Bailey, Johnnie Cochran, and Robert Shapiro. This so-called dream team sought to show why the government's case against Simpson was flawed in various respects. Thus, for several months in 1995–1996, the public saw the adversarial system very much at work in a Los Angeles court. In Simpson's case, the defense team was able to show sufficient weaknesses in the state's case that Simpson was acquitted of these murders. The defense team won, as a professional football team might win the Super Bowl (Green, 1988).

The idea of comparing criminal court to a game being played out from beginning to end is not new. The gamelike nature of the courtroom is reinforced by using court-relevant terminology such as **sides** and prosecutorial or **defense strategy**. Prosecutors are on one side and use a particular strategy that they believe will enable them to win the game. For prosecutors, a win is a conviction against the accused. For the defense side, a win is the defendant's acquittal. Prosecutors and defense counsel are often labeled as players by writers who seek to characterize courtroom procedures (Uphoff, 1992). The more skillful player using the better strategy will win the game by defeating the other player (Feeley, 1983; Lipetz, 1983).

The adversarial system of justice in the United States is rooted in a tradition of English jurisprudence dating back several centuries (Green, 1988; Schulhofer, 1986). In U.S. courts, the key players—prosecutors, defense attorneys, and judges—are bound to observe standardized **Rules of Criminal Procedure**, as well as a well-defined **ethical code**. Thus, there are specific rules governing the order in which a case is presented against a defendant and the response from defense counsel. Besides following a predetermined pattern or protocol for presenting a case against and for a defendant, other rules govern the nature and types of evidence and witnesses who may be called for either side. Each side attempts to manipulate the evidence presented in ways that enhance its own arguments. **Witnesses** are examined and cross-examined by the different sides in an effort to bolster the conflicting arguments. Ideally, the side with the most persuasive and compelling argument, either against or for the accused, wins. Juries decide the facts in the case before them, and their deliberations most often favor either guilt or acquittal. On rare occasions, juries may not be able to reach agreement as to which side, the prosecution or the defense, has the more persuasive argument. In these instances, juries are deadlocked or hung, and mistrials are declared. Subsequently, the adversarial process begins anew with another trial. In each trial proceeding, it is expected that both sides will adhere to an accepted ethical code and conduct themselves accordingly.

Throughout the criminal trial, evidence is presented by both sides for its persuasive effect. Prosecutors usually present **inculpatory evidence**, which is testimony and other forms of evidence that tends to show the guilt of the defendant. For instance, the defendant's fingerprints might have been found on the murder weapon, or eyewitnesses may have seen the defendant pull the trigger of the gun that killed the defendant. This evidence would be considered inculpatory, because it shows the guilt of the accused. In contrast, defense counsel introduces **exculpatory evidence**, which is testimony and other forms of evidence that show the innocence of the defendant. For example, one or more persons may testify that the defendant was with them at the time the murder was committed. Theater ticket stubs in the defendant's possession may indicate that the defendant was watching a movie when the crime occurred. In this way, alibis and other relevant information may show that the defendant could not have committed the crime when it occurred.

The Prosecution

Besides the judge who makes important rulings in criminal cases and oversees trial proceedings, the prosecutor has perhaps the most powerful position in the criminal justice system (Lithner, 1967; Holten and Jones, 1982). Prosecutors are either elected or appointed officials who pursue criminal cases against those charged with crimes. Prosecutors are held to the same standards of ethical conduct as defense counsel (Morgan, 1983; Green, 1988; Pollock-Byrne, 1989). Depending on the jurisdiction, prosecutors are known by different names. In Tennessee, for example, prosecutors are known as **district attorneys**. Their assistants are called *assistant district attorneys*. In North Dakota, prosecutors are called **state's attorneys** or **assistant state's attorneys**.

In the federal system, each U.S. district court has a **U.S. Attorney's Office**. The **U.S. attorney** in each federal district is appointed by the president of the United States with the advice and consent of Congress. The **attorney general** of the United States, also a presidential appointee, appoints one or more **assistant U.S. attorneys (AUSAs)** to serve in each of these district offices. The number of AUSAs varies from district to district, depending on the civil and criminal caseload.

The Roles of Prosecutors

The primary roles of all prosecutors in criminal courts are to represent the government's interests and pursue criminal charges against those alleged to have committed crimes. For state's attorneys or district attorneys, their roles are similar throughout the different U.S. jurisdictions (Ray, 1984).

1. To screen cases for prosecution (Chilton, 1993)
2. To determine the best strategy for prosecuting cases (Brannigan, Levy, and Wilkins, 1985)
3. To make case assignments to assistant district attorneys
4. To interview prospective witnesses against the accused (Belsky, 1984; McBarnet, 1983)
5. To work closely with law enforcement officers to determine the nature of inculpatory evidence against the accused (Lithner, 1967)

In the federal system, the U.S. attorney's offices in the various federal districts are charged with the following broad roles:

1. Prosecute all offenses against the United States
2. Prosecute or defend, for the government, all civil actions, suits, or proceedings in which the United States is concerned
3. Appear on behalf of the defendants in civil actions and suits or proceedings pending in the district against collectors or other officers of the revenue or customs for things they have done or for the recovery of any money exacted by or paid to them
4. Institute and prosecute proceedings for the collection of fines, penalties, and forfeitures incurred for violation of any revenue law
5. Report as the attorney general directs

SCREENING CASES. **Screening cases** means to assign priority to different cases on the basis of which ones are most deserving of prosecution. The screening function of prosecutors is very important as it relates to obtaining guilty pleas from criminal defendants. Most convictions are obtained through plea negotiations between prosecutors and defense counsel, in which some form of leniency from the prosecution is extended in exchange for a defendant's guilty plea (Albrecht and Backes, 1989). Prosecutors have broad discretionary powers concerning which cases to pursue and what types of offers to extend to those charged with crimes as inducements for guilty pleas (Chilton, 1993; Pollock-Byrne, 1989).

Prosecutors have the power to determine the types of cases that will be prosecuted more vigorously than others. Drunk-driving cases may receive high priority in certain jurisdictions where strong interest groups, such as Mothers against Drunk Driving (MADD), may wish to decrease alcohol-related driving accidents and deaths in their communities. Prosecutors can assist them in their prevention and deterrence efforts by pursuing drunk-driving cases and seeking maximum penalties (Moskowitz, 1992).

Organized crime may have high priority for prosecutions in certain jurisdictions (Edel-hertyz and Overcast, 1990).

Prosecutors seek convictions, and prosecutorial effectiveness is often gauged by the number of convictions they obtain. The greater the number of convictions, the more effective the prosecutors. Therefore, it is in the prosecutor's interest to select for prosecution the cases that are the easiest to prosecute. If clear and convincing evidence exists against an accused, prosecutors are in a stronger position to succeed in obtaining a conviction. More than a few cases have little incriminating evidence and are based purely on circumstantial evidence (Holten and Lamar, 1991). Prosecutors must decide whether cases are worth pursuing if the conviction of the accused is less of a certainty compared with a case with considerable inculpatory evidence (Belsky, 1984).

DETERMINING COURT STRATEGY. Prosecutors must devise their theory of how and why the crime was committed. They must attempt to link the defendant to the crime in such a way that the jury will be convinced beyond a reasonable doubt of the accused's guilt. There are many potential explanations for a defendant's conduct relative to the crime. The prosecutor need not select the true explanation, only a plausible one. The theory of the crime and its commission is often suggested by the nature and quality of the evidence against the defendant. For example, if one spouse was violently killed and the surviving spouse stands to collect on a $1 million life insurance policy, then this fact provides a motive for why the surviving spouse might have committed murder. If the surviving spouse has had an affair, then the motive for the murder may be love and not money. Different spins easily can be given to any criminal scenario.

When O. J. Simpson was charged with the murders of his ex-wife and her friend in Los Angeles in 1994, for instance, prosecutors spun a theory of uncontrollable jealousy and rage that presumably gripped Simpson to the point that he killed his ex-wife in the heat of passion. However, Simpson's defense counsel offered alternative explanations for the deaths. They suggested to the jury that the deaths might have been caused by Colombian drug lords seeking revenge against Simpson's ex-wife's friend, who lived with her for a time. That they happened upon Simpson's ex-wife instead of her friend was an unfortunate circumstance that led to his ex-wife's death. Further, the defense counsel argued, certain incriminating evidence found at Simpson's home shortly after the murders might have been planted by the investigating detectives themselves. Thus, when the defense raised other possibilities for Simpson's ex-wife's killers, the prosecution sought to dissuade jurors from thinking about these alternative explanations by overwhelming the jury with forensic evidence of different types. These maneuvers by both sides in Simpson's trial were strategies calculated to persuade jurors to think one way or another about how the crime was committed and who might have committed it.

ASSIGNING CASES. Prosecutors in most jurisdictions have assistant prosecutors who handle some of the case workload (Holten and Lamar, 1991). In fact, most large-city district attorney's offices are bureaucratized to the extent that there are specialty areas for different types of legal cases. A general civil–criminal distinction exists; some of the assistant district attorneys may be assigned civil cases, and other assistants are assigned criminal ones. Further subdivisions may be made, depending on case volume. Criminal cases may be divided into sex crimes, property crimes, and other logical categories. Certain prosecutors acquire considerable expertise in selected legal areas, and this expertise enables them to prosecute such cases more effectively than other prosecutors who lack this expertise (Cirincione, 1996; Weinreb, 1993). For instance, prosecutors with substantial experience with forensic evidence, such as DNA testing, may be more skillful at eliciting compelling testimony from expert witnesses and also may do a better job of cross-examining defense experts on the same subject matter. Other prosecutors may have considerable experience and facility with child eyewitnesses. Each case poses certain types of problems for prosecutors, and it is prudent for prosecutors to make strategic case assignments on the basis of which assistant district attorneys can do the best job of prosecuting under the circumstances.

INTERVIEWING WITNESSES. Prosecutors and their assistants must interview people who have knowledge about the crime. Often, witnesses for both the prosecution and defense are **deposed**. A deposition is a sworn written record of oral testimony. Those who are deposed are **deponents.** The purpose of a deposition is to have a written record of the testimony and an indication of its relevance to the case (Gorman, 1983; Lithner, 1967). When witnesses testify in court later, their depositions can be used to refresh their recollections (Kleinig, 1986). Sometimes depositions can be used to impeach witnesses if they lie or say things that are inconsistent with their earlier depositions (Nagel, 1986b).

Information witnesses provide to prosecutors can be interpreted in various ways. Witness interviews can help prosecutors formulate their strategy for prosecuting a case. The state may use expert witnesses to verify whether a defendant is sane or insane, competent or incompetent (Cirincione, 1996). If certain defendants are sufficiently incompetent to stand trial, then prosecutors can use this information to seek their commitment indefinitely in a mental hospital (West, 1986).

Prosecutors can determine in which order they will present their witnesses against the accused later in court. Thus, they can use witnesses to build their case against defendants. In complex, serious criminal cases, there will probably be numerous witnesses called by both sides. It is important, therefore, that some effort should be made to organize the witnesses into an orderly presentation that will create the most convincing case against the accused. Observations of actual criminal trials reveal such orderly presentations of witnesses for both sides.

WORKING CLOSELY WITH LAW ENFORCEMENT OFFICERS. It is important for prosecutors to develop a working rapport with law enforcement officers. Law enforcement officers have direct crime scene experience and can testify about their conversations with the defendant. If a confession has been obtained or if the defendant has provided police officers with incriminating information, this information can be developed in court to the defendant's disadvantage.

Law enforcement officers are subject to cross-examination by defense counsel. Experienced defense attorneys can seriously impair the state's case against a defendant by evoking inept-sounding responses from officers. Prosecutors and their assistants can assist officers in learning how to give testimony that will minimize any weaknesses in the state's case.

Police officers also testify about the evidence they collected at the crime scene that incriminates the defendant. Their testimony is quite important in this respect, and it is vital that prosecutors have the trust of these officers when they are questioned under direct examination in court. In federal district courts, AUSAs work closely with Federal Bureau of Investigation (FBI) agents and other federal authorities in presenting evidence against those charged with federal crimes. The FBI agents learn to permit AUSAs the latitude of presenting the case against the defendant in a particular way. They also learn to give testimony in certain ways that will heighten the inculpatory or incriminating effect of it. In a criminal case in the U.S. District Court in Knoxville, Tennessee, an FBI agent advised the AUSA that he would not get on the stand and lie. The AUSA advised him that he (the prosecutor) did not want the agent to lie; rather, the prosecutor wanted the FBI agent to "tell the story *our way.*" This comment implies that there was more than one way to relate the testimony and that the prosecutor wanted the FBI agent to put a spin on the story that would place the defendant in the most incriminating light. It would be up to the defense counsel, therefore, to attempt to get the FBI agent to admit that the jury might make less sinister interpretations of his testimony.

Prosecutorial Misconduct

Whether prosecutors are elected or appointed, there are many pressures on them from different sources. First, there is the immediate pressure to win cases and obtain convictions against defendants. Second, there is pressure to make a weak case look like a strong case, which means that the evidence may have to be manipulated or collected in ways that are inconsistent with proper police procedure (Jonakait, 1987).

Just as there are varying degrees of attorney competence, there are also varying degrees of prosecutorial misconduct. Not all forms of misconduct have the same weight or importance. Some misconduct may be trivial, although the cumulative effect of minor or trivial misconduct may arouse juror suspicions to the degree that a guilty verdict is subsequently rendered. Prosecutors may encourage experts to exaggerate their claims or evidence to enhance their case against a defendant, overwhelm grand juries with purely inculpatory evidence and deliberately exclude any exculpatory evidence, bluff defendants and threaten or intimidate them, suppress certain types of exculpatory evidence from the defense, exclude prospective jurors who have views favorable to defendants, offer inadmissible evidence in court, and engage in malicious prosecutions.

ENCOURAGING DECEIT FROM EXPERTS AND OTHER TYPES OF WITNESSES. When prosecutors construct their case presentations, they arrange the testimony of various expert witnesses and others who have relevant evidence to present. Often, expert witnesses may be able to provide too much information in court, and prosecutors must work with them to ensure that only selected pieces of information are disclosed about the case. Thus, experts have their testimony shaped and tailored by prosecutors so that it fits more closely with the scenario of the crime and its commission as envisioned by the state (*Georgetown Law Journal,* 1987; Wolf, 1986). In a federal case involving two co-conspirators on charges of interstate transportation of stolen property, one of the co-conspirators pleaded guilty and accepted a lenient sentence in exchange for his testimony against the other co-conspirator. The other co-conspirator went to trial after entering a plea of not guilty to the stolen property charges. While the guilty conspirator was being coached by AUSAs, he said at one point, "I'm not going to go into court and lie." The lead AUSA said to him, "No, no, no. We don't want you to lie either. But we *do* want you to tell the story [about the other co-conspirator] *our way*" (emphasis mine).

Therefore, much of the prosecutorial melodrama in court is carefully orchestrated in advance. If certain witnesses are considered weak and have little direct inculpatory information against the accused, they may be brought to the witness stand to testify early in the trial, so that the jury has forgotten about their weaknesses toward the end of the trial.

Seemingly innocent expert witness statements can appear very incriminating. The prosecutor may ask, "Was the blood found on the defendant's shirt consistent with the blood of the victim?" If the expert witness says, "Yes, I can say definitely that there was such a consistency," the jury is transfixed by such riveting testimony. However, the defense breaks this bubble on cross-examination by asking the expert witness, "Can you say positively that the blood on the defendant's shirt is the victim's blood?" And the expert witness lowers his head and says, "No, I can't say positively that the blood found is that of the victim's. I can only say that it is consistent with the victim's blood." The defense probes further. "In what respect is the blood found consistent with the victim's blood?" The expert witness says, "It is type O positive." And the defense asks, "And is it not so that the defendant also has type O blood?" And the expert says, "Yes, that is true." And the defense asks, "And is it not possible that the blood on the defendant's shirt is the defendant's own blood from a cut on the defendant's arm?" And the expert witness says, "Yes, that is true."

Although DNA matching is increasingly important to show precisely whose blood is found at crime scenes, the fact remains that contamination of blood can make blood typing and identification somewhat unreliable. This does not prevent prosecutors from using this evidence, regardless of its potential unreliability, to the disadvantage of the defendant. Only a skillful defense counsel can undo the damage done by a prosecutor who twists the facts to fit the state's case against the defendant (Green, 1988).

OVERWHELMING GRAND JURIES. When grand juries are convened, prosecutors are interested in obtaining indictments against defendants. Grand juries consider evidence presented by the prosecutor and determine whether there is sufficient probable cause to believe that a crime was committed and that the defendant probably committed it. Grand juries do not determine the guilt or innocence of the accused. They merely determine whether probable cause exists and whether a case should go forward to trial for a legal resolution.

Prosecutors are in a unique position relative to grand juries. Prosecutors direct which evidence and testimony will be presented to the grand jury. A prosecutor who has considerable evidence and numerous witnesses may decide to present only the most damaging evidence and the most incriminating testimony (Robinson et al., 1993). Some

ON DNA GENETIC FINGERPRINTING AND GRAND JURY INDICTMENTS

The Case of the "John Doe" Rapist

Since 1996, at least sixteen women have been attacked and raped by an unknown assailant. The most recent attack occurred on September 15, 1998. Nicknamed the "East Side Rapist of Manhattan," the unidentified rapist left semen samples behind in at least four of the rape sites. These semen samples have been tested for DNA matches and have proved to be from the same man. Four days before the statute of limitations expired on the original rape incident, a New York grand jury handed down an indictment against an unknown "John Doe" rapist on the basis of the rapist's DNA profile. This is a first for New York.

"Although this is New York state's first grand jury indictment of a 'John Doe' identified by DNA, I am certain it will not be the last," said District Attorney Robert Morgenthau. His office is reviewing hundreds of open rape cases that DNA technology might help to solve. At least two other states, Wisconsin and Utah, use DNA profiling for obtaining arrest warrants. However, New York is the first state to use such DNA profiling for issuing grand jury indictments. A "John Doe" indictment is legal if it contains a sufficient description of the suspect, said H. Richard Uviller, a Columbia University Law School professor. DNA certainly fits this bill, according to Uviller, and he labeled such evidence the "genetic fingerprint."

Although the rapist is still at large at the time of this writing, it is probably only a matter of time before the suspect is eventually apprehended and his identity revealed through DNA fingerprinting.

If a suspect is subsequently apprehended and matches the DNA taken from the rape scenes, should this evidence alone be sufficient to convict the person of one or more of the rapes? How should courts interpret this evidence? What do you think?

Source: Adapted from the Associated Press, "A First: Grand Jury Indicts on Basis of DNA." *Minot* (N.D.) *Daily News,* March 16, 2000:A2.

witnesses interviewed by the prosecutor may actually provide an alibi for the defendant, showing that the defendant may not have been where the crime was committed at time it occurred. Prosecutors exercise their discretion here and determine to present only the evidence and witnesses that show the defendant's guilt (Holderman, 1980).

Because grand juries see only one side of the case against an accused, they are inclined to think only the worst about the defendant (Johnston, 1974). Indictments are issued, therefore, when grand juries are convinced that there is sufficient probable cause to

CANDY BAR THIEF GETS 16 YEARS

Kenneth Payne, III, Candy Bar Thief

It happened in Tyler, Texas. In March 2000, Kenneth Payne III stole a Snickers candy bar from a convenience store and was quickly apprehended by police. It was determined from court records that this was not Payne's first brush with the law. He had a prior conviction for stealing a bag of Oreo cookies from another convenience store. But Payne's sweet tooth did not go over well in court.

Assistant District Attorney Jodi Brown tried Payne as a habitual offender, thus bumping the misdemeanor shoplifting charge to felony theft and making Payne eligible for a sentence of up to twenty years in prison. A jury heard the case and recommended a sixteen-year sentence for Payne, largely based on the habitual offender charge. Payne's attorney, Linda Altier, was outraged by the sixteen-year sentence for the theft of a dollar chocolate bar. She indicated that she would appeal.

Are habitual offender laws targeting the right people for extended incarceration? Should shoplifters, although chronic and habitual, be subject to lengthy prison terms such as life without parole or even sixteen years? What standards should govern whether defendants are prosecuted as habitual offenders? Should we be more specific about the types of crimes qualifying for such charges, or should we simply have a general rule applicable to everyone? What do you think?

Source: Adapted from the Associated Press, "Candy Bar Thief Gets 16 Years." *Minot* (N.D.) *Daily News,* April 5, 2000:A2.

believe that the defendant committed the crime. They are not permitted the luxury of a presentation by the defense counsel to rebut whatever was presented by the prosecutor.

Several attempts have been made by different court systems to monitor prosecutorial conduct before grand juries. For instance, in federal grand jury proceedings, tape recordings have been made and reviewed later by federal district court judges. Misconduct before the grand jury has been referred to as pre-indictment impropriety, and it is often detected only by chance (Holderman, 1980). However, recordings of grand jury proceedings can help to uncover prosecutorial misconduct. Some of these federal judges have recommended that a full disclosure of grand jury proceedings be made available later to defense counsel and others. Presumably, these recommendations are intended to cause prosecutors to engage in more ethical conduct. It is doubtful that such recordings of grand jury proceedings and subsequent disclosures have curbed prosecutorial abuses of discretion in grand jury proceedings, however (*Georgetown Law Journal,* 1987; Gershman, 1985, 1995).

PROSECUTORIAL BLUFFING WITH CRIMINAL DEFENDANTS: THREATS OR INTIMIDATION? When criminal defendants are not represented by counsel or are represented by weak defense lawyers, and/or when the cases against criminal defendants are weak, prosecutors may engage in **prosecutorial bluffing** (Jonakait, 1987). Prosecutorial bluffing means to threaten defendants with a lengthy list of charges, each of which carries serious penalties of fines and lengthy incarceration. The intent of prosecutorial bluffing is to cause a defendant to enter a guilty plea to one of the more minor charges in exchange for prosecutorial leniency (Sheriff, 1981). For instance, if the defendant pleads guilty to one felony charge, the prosecutor will drop the other twenty felony charges. Or maybe the prosecutor will accept the defendant's guilty plea to a misdemeanor, in exchange for a sentence of probation and dropping more serious felony charges.

This overcharging tactic is successful in many cases, even where more competent defense counsel are involved. In one case, a twenty-one-year-old restaurant waiter ran over and killed two drunk men who were wrestling in the middle of a poorly lit street late at night. The waiter had completed his 11:00 P.M. shift at the restaurant, had a few beers, and drove home at 1:00 A.M. He obeyed all traffic laws and was not legally intoxicated. Nevertheless, when he turned a corner near his apartment on a secondary road near a major highway, he suddenly saw two men wrestling on the road in front of him. Although he was only traveling about twenty miles per hour, he could not stop his vehicle in time to avoid running over them. The prosecutor charged the waiter with vehicular homicide. Vehicular homicide includes the elements of intent to commit homicide with an automobile. Because it was never the waiter's intent to drink some beer and then drive his car until he could run over two drunk men fighting in the middle of the road, it was doubtful that the vehicular homicide charge could be sustained. Subsequently, the prosecutor said that if the waiter would plead guilty to involuntary manslaughter, he would drop the vehicular homicide charge. The defense counsel rejected the offer and insisted on a trial for his client. Later, the prosecutor offered to drop the vehicular homicide charge if the waiter pleaded guilty to reckless driving. Again, the waiter's defense attorney rejected the offer. A few months later, the prosecutor advised that the case against the waiter had been dropped. There was no criminal conduct on the part of the waiter. The prosecutor attempted to bluff, but the defense counsel called his bluff and insisted on a trial to clear the waiter's name.

Prosecutorial bluffing is not limited to criminal defendants. Prosecutors may also threaten or intimidate prospective witnesses (Koenig and Godinez, 1982). In 1998, for example, independent counsel and special prosecutor Kenneth Starr was investigating alleged illegal campaign contributions by the Democratic party and President Bill Clinton. Starr cast a wide net in an effort to implicate Bill Clinton in any type of wrongdoing. At one point, one of Clinton's former White House interns, Monica Lewinsky, 24, had disclosed to a friend that she and Clinton had been sexually intimate. However, in a sworn affidavit in another matter, Lewinsky said that she had never had any sexual encounters with Clinton. Starr engaged in various tactics designed to threaten and intimidate Lewinsky into giving testimony that would implicate Clinton. The intimidation included surrounding her with FBI agents and prosecutors at a hotel and interrogating her for two days about her presidential encounters and statements made to her friend. Various informed sources said in newscasts that Starr had engaged in misconduct when interrogating Lewinsky and that this misconduct was grounds to have him removed as a special independent counsel in the case. Starr countered these allegations of misconduct by saying that he was merely seeking the truth in matters involving Bill Clinton.

SUPPRESSING EVIDENCE FROM THE DEFENSE. Prosecutors are able to view all evidence collected from the police and material witnesses in criminal cases. Although some of this evidence may tend to show the guilt of the defendant, other evidence may show the defendant's innocence. A prosecutor who has such exculpatory evidence is obligated to disclose this evidence to the defense for its use (Carr, 1995). Much of the time, however, exculpatory evidence seems to be deliberately suppressed by prosecutors, even in capital cases (Death Penalty Information Center, 1992; Gershman, 1995; U.S. Congress Committee on the Judiciary, 1993).

During the trial of O. J. Simpson on double-murder charges in Los Angeles in 1995, for instance, a Los Angeles police detective, Mark Fuhrman, gave substantial incriminating testimony about evidence he had found that linked Simpson to the crime. In other testimony Fuhrman gave about his feelings toward blacks, he denied being prejudiced. Furthermore, he denied under oath that he had made any derogatory racial slurs or statements for more than a decade. Later, defense attorneys produced a witness who had tape-recorded interviews with Fuhrman. These tape recordings clearly revealed that Fuhrman had made numerous racially derogatory statements against blacks, sharply contradicting what he had previously said on the witness stand under oath. Subsequently, Fuhrman entered a guilty plea to perjury charges. However, the damage had already been done to his earlier testimony incriminating Simpson, and defense counsel implied that the prosecutors knew about Fuhrman's racism in advance of his testimony about it. Further, defense counsel alleged, prosecutors caused Fuhrman to let them tell the story their way, and they deliberately withheld from the jury any reference to Fuhrman's racism, although the prosecutors knew about it. This is an example of suppressing evidence.

EXCLUDING PROSPECTIVE JURORS WHO ARE FAVORABLE TO DEFENDANTS. When prospective jurors are being questioned about their qualifications, beliefs, and prejudices, both prosecution and defense have an opportunity to challenge them. Particularly in high-profile trials involving well-known people, a concerted attempt is made by both sides to configure the best jury most favorable to either side. Although jury voting cannot be predicted by either side in advance, prosecutors and their associates attempt to select jurors who will favor the prosecution in their views.

In a capital murder case, for instance, prospective jurors with strong feelings against the death penalty may be excluded because these prospective jurors believe that their own feelings might not permit them to impose the death penalty if they find the defendant is guilty of the capital crime. When prosecutors dismiss these jurors, they narrow the pool of prospective jurors who might be favorably disposed toward the defendant. Frequently, prosecutors dismiss prospective jurors who exhibit other views that are associated with anti–death penalty sentiments. Defense counsel can engage in similar behavior by excluding those who favor capital punishment. Always, the number of jurors who can be dismissed by either the prosecution or the defense because of the juror's sentiments is limited. Despite these limitations, prosecutors can skillfully maneuver and create a jury composition that they believe is unfavorable to a defendant. Because of the diffuse grounds used to dismiss particular prospective jurors, it is not easy to determine when prosecutors are engaging in this type of misconduct (Pettegrew, 1986).

OFFERING INADMISSIBLE EVIDENCE IN COURT. A prosecutorial tactic sometimes used in a weak criminal case is to backdoor hearsay evidence. **Backdooring hearsay evidence** means to mention or comment about evidence against the accused that is not admissible evidence. Perhaps the defendant, charged with trafficking in heroin, has been arrested five times in the past for heroin and cocaine possession. However, these arrests have resulted in case dismissals. There was insufficient evidence to move forward with criminal prosecutions in each of these five arrest situations. In many jurisdictions, prosecutors may introduce evidence only about one's prior criminal convictions. It is not permissible for prosecutors to mention any arrests that never resulted in convictions. But the prosecutor might ask a witness, "Were you with the defendant when he was arrested for cocaine and heroin possession on five different occasions during the last three years?" Before the witness can speak, an objection is made by the defense and the judge sustains the objection, admonishing the jury to disregard the prosecutor's question. But the damage has already been done. The question has been raised and heard by the jurors. They now know that the defendant has been arrested in the past for heroin and cocaine possession. More important, the jurors have no way of knowing that these arrests never resulted in prosecutions or convictions on the drug charges (Celebrezze, 1987). Inadmissible evidence has been admitted through the back door, although the judge has declared that the jury should ignore it. Jurors cannot ignore whatever they have heard (Gershman, 1995).

It is difficult for the court to determine whether the utterances of prosecutors are deliberate or willful, intentional or unintentional (*Georgetown Law Journal,* 1987). Prosecutors may claim that they had no intention of violating court rules by mentioning inadmissible evidence, although they may have done so deliberately. Most courts interpret such utterances as harmless error (Gershman, 1995; U.S. Congress Committee on the Judiciary, 1993).

MALICIOUS PROSECUTIONS. The pressure on prosecutors to obtain convictions may induce them to file charges against certain defendants who are innocent of any crime (Green, 1988; Jonakait, 1987). When prosecutors bring charges against the accused with the full knowledge that the accused is innocent of the crimes alleged, this is a **malicious prosecution**.

CONFESSION TO A PRIEST OR TO THE PROSECUTOR?

The Case of the Questionable Confession

It happened in Portland, Oregon. Conan Wayne Hale was charged with the shooting deaths of three teenagers. Hale, twenty years old, became a suspect in the shooting deaths of three teens in a forest near Springfield, Oregon, 110 miles south of Portland. Hale was being held in a county jail awaiting trial on unrelated charges of burglary and theft.

When Hale asked for a priest from the local Roman Catholic Church, a priest was sent to the jail to hear his confession. Unknown to Hale and the Catholic priest was the fact that the entire conversation was being tape-recorded by jail authorities. During the confession to the priest, Hale confessed to the three teen killings, furnishing details about the crime only known to the killer and the police.

The prosecutor, Dopug Harcleroad, has suggested that the state may use the tape in court as incriminating evidence against Hale. However, Hale's attorney, Terri Wood, said she would fight against the admissibility of the taped confession. Wood told reporters, "I don't want anyone confusing a criminal confession with the religious term of art called confession."

According to Oregon law, jail conversations other than those between an attorney and a client may be recorded by jail officials, without the consent of anyone involved. However, another Oregon law says that conversations between clergy and their followers are confidential. Prosecutor Harcleroad said, "We determined it [the tape] was legal and we are investigating the deaths of three children in this community." According to various law experts in Oregon and elsewhere, the issue of the tape's admissibility is already resolved by former U.S. Supreme Court proclamations about consensual tape-recorded conversations. "They will never be able to use the actual confession in a trial unless they prove [Hale] waived confidentiality," said law professor David Schuman. What is even worse for the prosecution is that a sheriff's investigator and an assistant prosecutor have heard the tape, which could jeopardize the entire case. If the taping is found to have been improper, then the prosecutors will have to prove that no information from the tape was used in their investigation. An exception is that inevitable discovery may be used to show that inculpatory or incriminating material or evidence would eventually be revealed independent of any confession and crime details yielded in Hale's confession to a priest.

Should the government have its hands tied in a murder investigation because of technical details when a murderer confesses his crime to others? Under what circumstances should tape recordings be used to secure evidence against criminal suspects? Was the government acting properly in Hale's case?

Source: Adapted from Associated Press, "Can Police Use Taped Confession?" *Minot* (N.D.) *Daily News,* May 11, 1996:A8.

Misconduct Risks and Sanctions

When prosecutors commit **prosecutorial misconduct**, particularly in the courtroom, there is always the chance that the misconduct will be detected and sanctioned in some way. Prejudicial commentary by the prosecutor will cause defense counsel to object. Judges will sustain these objections, but the harm has already been done (Gershman, 1985). The jury has heard the prejudicial commentary, and despite an admonition from the judge to disregard such prejudicial commentary, the jury cannot forget about it entirely. For instance, a prosecutor may be barred from mentioning a defendant's sexual preferences in a murder trial occurring in a small religious community. However, the prosecutor may allude to a homosexual defendant's gay rights activism, even though this commentary has nothing to do with the case before the court. Defense counsel will object strenuously, and the judge will sustain this objection. But the jury cannot erase from their memories the prosecutor's statement about the defendant's gay rights activities. Jurors may assume that the defendant is gay, and this assumption may be sufficient to prejudice some of them. Because some of the jurors may dislike gays, they may punish the defendant by voting for his guilt, despite the fact that the defendant's guilt has not been established beyond a reasonable doubt. The prosecutor is successful, therefore, in prejudicing jurors against the defendant by alluding to one or more extralegal factors.

AN ABSENCE OF ETHICAL NORMS. Prosecutors can get away with their courtroom misconduct largely because of an absence of ethical norms as standards against which to gauge their conduct (Gershman, 1985). In case after case in which prosecutorial misconduct is alleged, the U.S. Supreme Court has failed to articulate clear and consistent ethical norms to guide prosecutors (Gershman, 1985, 1986; Wolf, 1986).

Interestingly, juries are more inclined to consider inadmissible evidence favorable to defendants than inadmissible evidence unfavorable to defendants (Gershman, 1986). Despite this factor of defense favoritism, prosecutors might be tempted to sway the jury by introducing highly prejudicial inadmissible evidence. By doing so, they risk jeopardizing any resulting conviction. However, the likelihood of having the conviction overturned in these instances is extremely remote. The most significant reason for the continued presence of prosecutorial misconduct is the **harmless error doctrine** (Gershman, 1986). Under this doctrine, an appellate court can affirm a conviction despite the presence of serious prosecutorial misconduct during the trial. Thus, the desirability of the doctrine is undermined when the prosecutor is able to commit misconduct without fear of sanction.

Also, the standards currently used in ruling on motions for retrial based on false testimony fail to strike an acceptable balance between the right of the accused to a fair and impartial trial and the demand for efficient administration of the criminal justice system in court (Cardinale and Feldman, 1978; Wright and Lewis, 1978). Ideally, motions for retrial based on false testimony presented by prosecution witnesses should be governed by a standard drawn from newly discovered evidence and prosecutorial misconduct. The proper test for a new trial based on newly discovered evidence of false testimony is

THE KLEPTOMANIAC ASSISTANT U.S. ATTORNEY

The Case of AUSA Dennis Fisher

It happened in Fargo, North Dakota. Dennis Fisher, a fifty-two-year-old assistant U.S. attorney (AUSA), was apprehended by police for a second time following his theft of a small fishing tool from a sporting goods store in Grand Forks. Earlier, Fisher had stolen two pairs of shorts from a department store by concealing them in a grocery bag. He was arrested for that crime as well, although police diverted the incident because of Fisher's position with the U.S. Attorney's Office. However, Fisher had been advised to seek counseling. At the time of his second arrest, Fisher was being treated for depression and had been seeing a counselor. In May 1997, Fisher resigned his position as AUSA, citing personal reasons for his resignation.

Although these crimes are admittedly minor ones, should federal prosecutors be granted any special privileges regarding *any* criminal conduct? When Fisher was arrested the first time, what do you think the U.S. Attorney's Office should have done? Should any formal action have been taken? What do you think?

Source: Adapted from the Associated Press, "U.S. Attorney Resigns after Second Arrest." *Minot* (N.D.) *Daily News*, May 24, 1997:B5.

whether there is a significant chance that a jury with a knowledge of the false testimony would avoid convicting the defendant (Wolf, 1986).

Summary

Prosecutors, who represent governmental interests, are key players in the adversarial system in U.S. criminal courts. The adversarial system has been characterized as a game with very serious outcomes for criminal defendants. Each side devises one or more strategies whereby criminal cases are approached and explained. The objective of each side is to devise a winning strategy. Prosecutors want to convict defendants. Prosecutors present their cases, usually before juries, where the issue of one's guilt is decided.

Prosecutors are expected to abide by codes of ethics, or rules that regulate professional conduct. The American Bar Association has promulgated an ethical code that most attorneys respect. Prosecutors are expected to have sound bases for charging specific defendants with crimes. Frivolous prosecutions are unwarranted and unjustified. They screen and prioritize cases for prosecution, interview prospective witnesses, and work closely with law enforcement to determine the competency of evidence.

Whenever the prosecution acts in unprofessional ways or in manners inconsistent with their codes of conduct and professional responsibilities, misconduct may occur. Prosecutorial misconduct may involve encouraging deceit from expert witnesses and overwhelming grand juries with misleading evidence against the accused. Some evidence favorable to defendants may be deliberately suppressed, and prosecutorial bluffing sometimes occurs. Some prosecutions may be malicious and motivated by reasons other than legal merit. Various types of sanctions can be imposed on prosecutors who engage in misconduct.

KEY TERMS

Adversary system
Assistant state's attorneys
Assistant U.S. attorneys
   (AUSAs)
Attorney general
Backdooring hearsay
   evidence
Defense attorney
Defense strategy
Deponent

Depose
District attorneys
Ethical code
Exculpatory evidence
Harmless error doctrine
Inculpatory evidence
Malicious prosecution
Prosecutor
Prosecutorial bluffing

Prosecutorial misconduct
Rules of Criminal
   Procedure
Screening cases
Sides
State's attorneys
U.S. attorney
U.S. Attorney's Office
Witnesses

QUESTIONS FOR REVIEW

1. What is meant by the adversary system? Which actors make up the adversary system? What rules govern the adversary system in courts?
2. At the federal and state levels, who are the prosecutors?
3. What are the functions of prosecutors?
4. Under what circumstances might prosecutors engage in misconduct? What are four types of prosecutorial misconduct?
5. How do prosecutors overwhelm grand juries?
6. How do prosecutors perform screening functions in criminal cases?
7. What is meant by prosecutorial bluffing? What are some examples of prosecutorial bluffing?
8. How can prosecutors bias a case in favor of the prosecution? Give some examples.
9. What is meant by backdooring hearsay evidence?
10. What is a malicious prosecution? What are some sanctions the court might use to reprimand district attorneys who engage in malicious prosecutions of suspects?
11. What is meant by the harmless error doctrine?

SUGGESTED READINGS

Baker, Mark. (1999). *Prosecutors in Their Own Words.* New York: Simon and Schuster.

DeFrances, Carol J. and Greg W. Steadman. (1998). *Prosecutors in State Courts.* Washington, DC: U.S. Bureau of Justice Statistics.

Finkelman, Byrgen (ed.). (1995). *Perpetrators, Victims, and the Courts.* New York: Garland.

Glaser, Edward L. and Bruce Sacerdote (2000). *The Determinants of Punishment: Deterrence, Incapacitation, and Vengeance.* Cambridge, MA: National Bureau of Economic Research.

THE DEFENSE

WASHINGTON IS ONE of the few states that reimburses acquitted defendants and their attorneys when self-defense is used to justify crimes. The intent of the Washington law was to give victims of crime a break. The law was established in 1977 and authorizes reimbursement of legal costs for those found not guilty on grounds of self-defense.

In the case of Timothy Myers, he became involved in a bar fight. He defended himself, and in the process his attacker was killed. Myers was charged with murder, but the jury acquitted him. His defense was self-defense; that is, he acted to protect himself. Washington mailed him and his attorney a check for $71,600 to cover attorney's fees and lost wages for Myers.

Defense attorneys like Washington's law for reasons unrelated to the reimbursement factor when their clients are acquitted. They believe that it discourages prosecutors from filing charges in weak cases. Between 1977 and 1997, Washington has had to pay out more than $6 million to murder and assault defendants who have acted in self-defense. The law was intended to address violent crimes, but it doesn't specify precise charges. The largest check issued by the state for such a defense was to Clyde Fondren in 1989. Fondren received $128,000 when he was found to have acted in self-defense when he fatally shot a man who followed him home after an argument in a Trout Lake, Washington, bar.

Prosecutors disagree that the law deters them from filing charges against criminal suspects, regardless of the soundness of the case. One prosecutor, Tom McBride, says, "I don't think it has any effect on filing decisions. I filed a lot of cases where I've had to think about self-defense, and I never think about reimbursement. You think about the decision to file up front, and then you take your lumps." (*Source:* Adapted from the Associated Press, "Washington's Self-Defense Law: One of a Kind." *Minot* (N.D.) *Daily News,* July 13, 1997:A4.)

RONALD L. SHANABARGER, 30, confessed to police that he sought revenge against his wife by purposely fathering their child and then killing the boy. Shanabarger told police that his father passed away in October 1996. At the time, he and his wife were on a cruise vacation. The wife, Amy Shanabarger, refused to cut short their cruise vacation so that Ronald could attend his father's funeral. At that time, Ronald Shanabarger planned the crime to kill his own child to exact punishment against his wife. On June 22, 1999, just hours after the funeral of his 7-month-old son, Tyler, Shanabarger confessed to his wife that he had smothered their son in his crib three nights earlier and told her why he did it. Police arrested Shanabarger after his wife notified police, and he was ordered held without bail.

Earlier, a coroner had ruled the baby's death to be the result of sudden infant death syndrome (SIDS), and no charges were filed in the case. Following being charged, Shanabarger was asked by the judge whether he had enough money to hire his own attorney, and Shanabarger said, "I'll have to ask my wife." The judge suggested that help was unlikely to come from his wife and assigned a public defender to defend him. In Indiana, child murderers are eligible for the death penalty because of the special circumstances of their cases. Also, those charged with capital murder are not eligible for bail. (*Source:* Adapted from the Associated Press, "No Bail for Dad Who Allegedly Killed Own Baby for Revenge." *Minot* (N.D.) *Daily News,* June 29, 1999:A3.)

FOLLOWING THE MASS MURDERS of twelve students at Columbine High School in Colorado in April 1999 by students Eric Harris and Dylan Klebold, Michael Ian Campbell, an aspiring 18-year-old actor from Cape Coral, Florida, sent a message to the Colorado high school threatening to "finish the job." Eventually, the message was traced back to Campbell, and he was arrested by FBI agents and Florida authorities. He was charged with transmitting a threat to another person in interstate commerce, punishable by up to five years in prison and a fine of $250,000. He was scheduled for trial in federal court on February 28, 2000.

His attorney, Miami lawyer Ellis Rubin, said that he planned to use an "Internet intoxication defense" to defend his client and explain his actions, which he regarded as an innocent prank. Rubin said, "To intoxicate is to elevate yourself into a state of euphoria, even into madness. You've logged on and gone into this imaginary world, this playland, this make-believe arena. That's why I call it Internet intoxication. The more they go into the Internet, the more bizarre their role-playing becomes." The U.S. Attorney's Office in Florida was not available for comment about the Internet intoxication defense planned for Campbell. However, some legal experts say that there is little difference between the authors of anonymous Internet threats and people who make obscene telephone calls. Diane Cabell, a fellow at the Berkman Center for Internet and Society at Harvard Law School, says that "they know what they're doing. It's just a cheaper way to stalk others." Lawyer Rubin used a similar defense previously in the case of Ronny Zamora, 15, who was convicted of murdering an elderly neighbor in Miami Beach. In Zamora's case, however, Rubin argued that Zamora was under the influence of "television intoxication." (*Source:* Adapted from the Associated Press, "Lawyer Plans 'Internet Intoxication' Defense in Columbine Threat Case." *Minot* (N.D.) *Daily News,* January 13, 2000:A3.)

IN DECEMBER 1995, when he was 15, Marlon Comes and two other youths, Adrian Alex, 17, and Wayne Greywater, 16, were at a wild party getting drunk. After drinking heavily, the trio decided to rob a convenience store for some extra cash. Linking up with another youth to drive them, they drove around Devils Lake, North Dakota, until they came to a convenience store that looked convenient. While the fourth boy waited in the car, Alex, Greywater, and Comes entered the store where the night clerk, 31-year-old Donald Jerome, was on duty. Jerome was ordered by Comes to get on his knees. Comes carried a sawed-off 12-gauge shotgun. He put the shotgun to the back of Jerome's head and pulled the trigger, splattering the surrounding area with Jerome's blood. Some of this blood got on Comes's clothing, which was later matched by police with blood from the crime scene. Also, when Comes got back into the car following the murder, he told the driver that he had "killed the clerk." The trio was apprehended later. From jail while awaiting trial, Comes wrote letters to many of his acquaintances nicknaming himself as "Mr. One Slug," referring to the single shotgun shell that killed Jerome. When police interrogated the trio, Alex and Greywater confessed to police and admitted that Comes was the shooter. Comes himself admitted the crime as well. Public defenders Scott Thompson and Todd Burianek were assigned to defend the trio on murder charges. The evidence against the three was overwhelming. The lawyers advised Comes and his associates to plead guilty to escape a harsher punishment if the case ever went to trial. Subsequently, a judge accepted Comes's guilty plea and sentenced him to life in prison with the possibility of parole within 25 years. Now Comes wants the North Dakota Supreme Court to reopen his case, alleging that his attorneys were incompetent and that he should have been permitted to go to trial, which was his right. Lonnie Olson, the Ramsey County, North Dakota, state's attorney, said that the evidence against Comes was overwhelming. Olson said, "I know this may sound sarcastic, but I don't think O. J. Simpson's legal defense team could have gotten Marlon Comes out of this case. I can't even fathom a jury finding Mr. Comes not guilty in this matter. I can't foresee of any possible way that there would have been a different result, had we gone to trial." (*Source:* Adapted from the Associated Press. "Teen-Ager Says Attorneys Gave Bad Advice." *Minot* (N.D.) Daily News, June 27, 2000:A1, A7.)

IT HAPPENED IN HOUSTON, TEXAS, in 1984. Calvin Herold Burdine, 30, was on trial for murder. Burdine was subsequently convicted in the slaying of W. T. Wise, 50, a former housemate, who was stabbed to death in 1983. Burdine had told police that he had argued with Wise and moved out of their trailer because Wise wanted him to work as a prostitute. Evidence showed that Burdine and an accomplice, Douglas McCreight, were involved in the burglary during which Wise was stabbed to death. McCreight was convicted of a lesser crime and sentenced to eight years in prison. He was subsequently paroled. Burdine was sentenced to death and placed on death row. In 1999, an appeal by Burdine alleged that his attorney had actually slept throughout the lengthy murder trial and that this attorney incompetence led to Burdine's capital sentence. A federal district court heard Burdine's appeal and threw out Burdine's murder conviction. Texas prosecutors were given 120 days to give Burdine a new trial or set him free. The 120 days expired, and no action had been taken by the prosecutor's office. The judge ordered Burdine freed from prison. Texas prosecutors objected, but the judge declared,

"The state must adhere to the same rules as defendants. A similar procedural error by defense counsel in a capital case could result in a defendant's execution." Burdine himself had the following to say, following his release from prison: "The state of Texas don't have to worry about Calvin Burdine. We've got 80 acres in Oklahoma and I can get out there and fish and relax—out of sight and out of mind. I don't want them to think I'm going to roar down those streets and in those bars. I'm not like that anymore." Although U.S. District Court Judge David Hittner threw out Burdine's conviction because Burdine's lawyer slept through long stretches of his 1984 trial, he did not bar prosecutors from seeking to retry Burdine on the same murder charges at a later date. (*Source:* Adapted from the Associated Press, "Judge Orders Death Row Inmate Released." *Minot* (N.D.) *Daily News,* March 2, 2000:A4.)

Introduction

This chapter is about **defense counsel** or defense attorneys. These are persons who represent and defend criminals and are an integral part of the **courtroom work group**. The courtroom work group consists of the judge, prosecutor, defense counsel, court reporter, bailiff, and others who ensure that cases will be processed efficiently and effectively. The first section of this chapter describes the legal ethics and professional responsibilities of defense attorneys. All attorneys are expected to adhere to a code of ethics promulgated by the American Bar Association and other professional legal organizations.

All criminal defendants are entitled to counsel, either privately acquired or court appointed. The conditions under which criminal defendants, including indigents, are entitled to counsel and to have jury trials are listed and examined, and the functions of defense counsel are described. The issue of attorney competence is highlighted. Similar to prosecutors, defense misconduct may occur, because defense counsel must adhere to the same code of ethics that governs prosecutorial conduct. A description of defense practices, including misconduct, is provided.

Defense counsel must work closely with prosecutors in most major criminal cases. The interaction or interplay between prosecutors and defense counsels is examined. A key element in this process is discovery, whereby each side discloses certain evidentiary information obtained that may have relevance for the case outcome. The discovery process is described. The chapter concludes with an examination of some of the strategies defense counsels use to counter allegations of criminal conduct against their clients. These are criminal defenses, and their use is dependent upon the circumstances of the offense and the offender.

On Legal Ethics and Professional Responsibility

Lawyers have been the butt of more than a few jokes. For instance, there's the one about a lawyer who was fishing with his lawyer friends in the Atlantic Ocean. Suddenly a big wave washed over the boat, spilling one of the lawyers into the shark-infested waters. A twenty-foot great white shark came along and grabbed the flailing lawyer between its teeth. But instead of heading to the depths of the ocean with the lawyer, the shark swam alongside the boat and placed the lawyer back on the deck. The shark started to swim off, but the lawyer called out, "Hey, why didn't you eat me?" The shark turned around, smiled, and said, "Professional courtesy."

There are several reasons for such jokes. First, some lawyers have engaged in disreputable or dishonest activities. When they have been caught, they often make headlines in their local newspapers. There are hundreds of disbarment proceedings against lawyers every year, with different forms of misconduct alleged. The U.S. Supreme Court has rejected most of their appeals for reconsideration. Also, some lawyers have bad reputations for taking advantage of their clients and exploiting them. The public seems to have a general mistrust of lawyers as well, as shown in public opinion polls regarding the honesty of lawyers and other professionals. In 1997, for instance, lawyers were ranked nineteenth in honesty behind funeral directors, newspaper reporters, dentists, police officers, and real estate agents (Maguire and Pastore, 1999:108). Between 1976 and 1997, the public's low or very low rating of the honesty and ethical standards of lawyers rose from 26 percent to 40 percent (Maguire and Pastore, 1999:108). In 1997, a national poll showed that 15 percent of those surveyed rated the ethical standards and honesty of lawyers as very high or high, whereas 41 percent rated them as low or very low.

In an effort to improve the image of lawyers throughout the United States, legal professional associations and organizations have evolved codes of ethics or standards by which lawyers should conduct themselves. For instance, the American Bar Association (ABA) first published its **Canons of Professional Ethics** in 1908 (Morgan, 1983:3). Intended as a means of self-regulation, the Canons of Ethics are part of the **ABA Model Code of Professional Responsibility**. Attorneys in all U.S. jurisdictions ideally are expected to adhere to this code on a voluntary basis. Whenever violations of this code occur or are alleged, disciplinary rules are invoked to sanction those who are believed to have engaged in unethical conduct. There are nine Canons of Ethics.

1. A lawyer should assist in maintaining the integrity and competence of the legal profession.
2. A lawyer should assist the legal profession in fulfilling its duty to make legal counsel available.
3. A lawyer should assist in preventing the unauthorized practice of law.
4. A lawyer should preserve the confidences and secrets of a client.
5. A lawyer should exercise independent professional judgment on behalf of a client.
6. A lawyer should represent a client competently.
7. A lawyer should represent a client zealously within the bounds of law.
8. A lawyer should assist in improving the legal system.
9. A lawyer should avoid even the appearance of professional impropriety. (Morgan, 1983:3.)

All states have **state bar associations**. These associations are powerful enough to require that all those who practice law in these states must be approved in advance by these bars. Thus, attorneys who attend law school and graduate with a law degree must first pass one or more state bar examinations to qualify as practicing lawyers in those states.

Defense counsel are practicing lawyers who must pass state bar examinations to demonstrate their familiarity with local and state laws. Besides passing tests and taking other types of examinations, all lawyers are expected to adhere to codes of ethics and to conduct themselves in a way that will not compromise their integrity. It is expected that the ABA Canons of Ethics and the ABA Model Code of Professional Responsibility are applicable to virtually all practicing attorneys in the United States. Although not all attorneys in the United States belong to the ABA, the ethical and professional responsibility provisions promulgated by the ABA are generally and implicitly applicable to them anyway.

The Right to Counsel

The Sixth Amendment to the U.S. Constitution says that all defendants shall have the right to a speedy trial by an impartial jury, the right to be informed of the nature of the charges against them, the right to confront their accusers in court, and the right to have assistance of counsel for their defense. Although the Sixth Amendment does not declare that counsel must be competent, we have the *Strickland* guidelines by which to gauge attorney effectiveness and competence (Echikson, 1986a; Nagel, 1986).

The right to counsel as guaranteed under the Sixth Amendment has not always been clearly defined by the states (Bowman, 1986; Klein and Spangenberg, 1993). It was assumed for many decades, for instance, that the right to counsel meant that people charged with crimes were free to hire their own attorneys to represent them. However, **indigent defendants**—those without the money or means to hire their own counsel—were often tried and convicted without benefit of any defense counsel (Puritz et al., 1995). States had their own legislative provisions for providing attorneys in criminal cases. Until the 1960s, indigent defendants in Florida courts were not entitled to a court-appointed attorney unless they were charged with a capital crime, such as murder. Indigents who were charged with noncapital offenses were unable to compel courts to furnish them with an attorney. Without an attorney to defend them, therefore, many indigents were convicted, whether or not they were guilty of the crime(s) alleged (Miller et al., 1995).

In 1942, the U.S. Supreme Court condoned these state practices. In the case of *Betts v. Brady* (316 U.S. 455 [1942]), Betts, a robbery suspect, claimed that he was indigent and demanded a court-appointed attorney to defend him on the robbery charge. The court said that Betts could be appointed counsel only in rape or murder cases, and his request for an attorney was denied. In felony cases in which life or death was not an issue, the U.S. Supreme Court ruled that the states were not required to furnish counsel to indigent defendants in every case. It should be noted, however, that many states *did* provide counsel for indigent defendants during this period because it was required by the state legislatures (Weinreb, 1993).

THE U.S. SUPREME COURT CHANGES ITS MIND. In 1963, the U.S. Supreme Court reviewed and decided the case of *Gideon v. Wainwright.* Clarence Gideon broke into a Florida poolroom with the intent to commit larceny, a felony in Florida. Gideon was indigent and asked for a lawyer to represent him. He was advised by the judge that counsel could be appointed to indigents only if they were charged with a capital crime. Because he was denied an attorney, Gideon represented himself. Subsequently, he was convicted and appealed. The U.S. Supreme Court overturned Gideon's conviction, holding that all indigent defendants are entitled to court-appointed counsel in any serious case. The Florida courts interpreted *serious case* to mean any felony. Thus, the *Gideon* case established that court-appointed counsel would be provided to any indigent defendant who was charged with a felony.

Nine years later, the case of *Argersinger v. Hamlin* (407 U.S. 25 [1972]) was decided by the U.S. Supreme Court. This case also arose in Florida. Argersinger was an indigent charged with carrying a concealed weapon, a misdemeanor in Florida that was punishable by a fine and six months' imprisonment. Argersinger claimed to be indigent and demanded that the court appoint counsel to represent him. Argersinger's request was denied because, according to *Gideon*, only felony charges entitled indigent defendants to court-appointed counsel. Argersinger was convicted of the misdemeanor and sentenced to ninety days in jail. He appealed, and the U.S. Supreme Court overturned his misdemeanor conviction. Essentially, the U.S. Supreme Court said that anyone facing possible imprisonment is entitled to court-appointed counsel if they are indigent and cannot afford to hire private counsel.

SELF-REPRESENTATION. Under certain circumstances, defendants may wish to represent themselves in court rather than use the services of a defense attorney. All criminal defendants may elect to defend themselves and reject court-appointed counsel. When defendants engage in **self-representation**, they are said to be proceeding ***pro se***, which means "on his or her own behalf." Defendants who defend themselves do not have to be trained lawyers, nor do they have to be skilled in criminal law or trial techniques. However, in most instances when defendants have elected to represent themselves in court, judges have appointed lawyers to assist or advise them anyway, although the roles of these counsel are somewhat passive.

One of the most sensational cases of self-representation is the case of Colin Ferguson, a Jamaican immigrant living in New York in 1993. Ferguson, who was unemployed and divorced, had recently been rejected for public assistance by New York officials. One afternoon, armed with a semiautomatic pistol, he boarded a Long Island commuter train. After the train was in motion, he rose from his seat and methodically began shooting passengers at point-blank range. He paused only long enough during the shooting to change clips in his pistol. Eventually, while he was changing clips and reloading, some of the passengers rushed him and wrestled him to the floor of the car. They disarmed him and, at the next train stop, turned him over to waiting police. Ferguson had killed six people and seriously wounded nineteen others. Numerous eyewitnesses saw Ferguson shoot them or others. Ferguson left behind a note that explained his actions to those finding his body; clearly, he did not expect to be taken alive.

At his trial, Ferguson was appointed counsel. Two prominent criminal defense attorneys, William Kunstler and Ron Kuby, were assigned to represent him. Kunstler believed that, given the overwhelming direct and conclusive evidence against Ferguson, Ferguson's best and only chance to escape punishment was to claim temporary insanity. Kunstler also

About Self-Representation and Assistance of Counsel

Hamilton v. Alabama, 368 U.S. 52 (1961). Hamilton, an indigent, was indicted for murder by a grand jury. At his arraignment following the indictment, he was not represented by counsel, and he was subsequently convicted of murder. He appealed, contending that he had been disadvantaged by not having counsel present during the arraignment. The U.S. Supreme Court overturned his conviction, saying that arraignments are critical stages requiring the presence of a court-appointed attorney in indigent cases. In Alabama at the time, defendants were required to show that they were in need of counsel. Hamilton had not requested counsel at the time, but counsel had not been offered either.

Gideon v. Wainwright, 372 U.S. 335 (1963). Gideon broke into a poolroom, allegedly with the intent to commit larceny. This act was regarded as a felony in Florida. Gideon was indigent and asked for a lawyer to represent him. He was advised by the judge that counsel could be appointed only if the offense involved the death penalty. Therefore, Gideon represented himself and was convicted. He appealed. The U.S. Supreme Court overturned his conviction, saying that all indigent defendants are entitled to court-appointed counsel in felony cases. (See *Argersinger v. Wainwright* [1972] for a narrowing of this provision to minor crimes or misdemeanor cases.)

Illinois v. Allen, 397 U.S. 337 (1970). Allen was charged with robbery. He waived his right to counsel and elected to represent himself. During the jury selection and trial, he was abusive and argued constantly with the trial judge until eventually he was ordered removed from the courtroom. The trial was held anyway, and he was convicted. Later, Allen appealed to the U.S. Supreme Court; he argued that his Sixth Amendment right had been violated because he had not been present at his own trial when convicted. The U.S. Supreme Court upheld his conviction, saying that repeated warnings to Allen from the judge had had no effect on his conduct, which was so disruptive as to prevent the jurors from properly considering the evidence. Thus, there was nothing unconstitutional about the judge's removing Allen from the courtroom.

Argersinger v. Hamlin, 407 U.S. 25 (1972). Argersinger was an indigent charged with carrying a concealed weapon. In Florida, this crime is a misdemeanor punishable by imprisonment of up to six months and a $1,000 fine. Argersinger was not allowed to have court-appointed counsel, as required for a *felony,* because his crime was not a felony.

Baldasar v. Illinois, 446 U.S. 222 (1980). Baldasar was convicted in a theft of property not exceeding $150 in value. Although this offense was a misdemeanor, it was Baldasar's second offense; therefore, it became a felony. He was sentenced to one to three years in prison. He appealed, claiming that he had not been represented by counsel at the time of his first conviction. Therefore, the enhanced penalty from the second conviction was not constitutional. The U.S. Supreme Court agreed with Baldasar and overturned his conviction, holding that no indigent criminal defendant shall be sentenced to a term of imprisonment unless the state has afforded him the right to assistance of counsel. Baldasar had requested but been denied counsel in the trial for his original misdemeanor, which became a crucial step in enhancing the penalty resulting from his second conviction.

Faretta v. California, 422 U.S. 806 (1975). Faretta, who was charged with grand theft, desired to represent himself. The judge ruled that he had no constitutional right to represent himself in the case and appointed a public defender to defend him. Faretta was convicted. He appealed, arguing that he had a right to represent himself. The U.S. Supreme Court overturned his conviction, holding that Faretta, indeed, had a right knowingly and intelligently to waive his right to counsel and represent himself in the criminal proceeding. Thus, he had been denied his constitutional right to act as his own counsel.

Godinez v. Moran, 509 U.S. 389 (1993). Moran was charged with several murders, although he had entered a plea of not guilty by reason of insanity. Several doctors reported test results that indicated Moran was competent to stand trial. Following these psychiatric reports, Moran advised the Nevada court that he wished to dismiss his attorneys and plead guilty to the multiple murders. The court determined that Moran made these guilty pleas knowingly, intelligently, and voluntarily. Further, Moran waived his right to assistance of counsel and other rights associated with guilty pleas. Subsequently, after he was convicted and sentenced to death, he filed a habeas corpus petition alleging that even though he had earlier requested to represent himself, he was incompetent to do so. The U.S. Supreme Court upheld the conviction and death sentence, holding that the competency standard for pleading guilty or waiving the right to counsel is the same as the competency standard for standing trial. Moran had been found competent in both instances and had knowingly and intelligently waived the rights he was now alleging had been violated.

briefly entertained the "black rage" defense, which suggested that Ferguson had gunned down white persons he felt were oppressive and against him. Early in the trial proceedings, Ferguson dismissed Kunstler and Kuby and requested that the judge permit him to defend himself. He advised the judge that he considered himself to be a "formidable opponent." The judge appointed a psychiatrist to examine Ferguson, and the psychiatrist pronounced Ferguson sane. Therefore, the judge permitted Ferguson to represent himself.

The trial itself was a sham because Ferguson was attempting to refute irrefutable evidence against him. At one point, Ferguson told the jury, "There are ninety-three counts against me. Ninety-three counts. That is because the year was 1993. If it had been 1925, there would have been twenty-five counts." He cross-examined several people he had wounded on the commuter train. All this action was futile, although Ferguson acquired considerable sophistication and experience during the trial. Toward the end of the proceedings, Ferguson attempted to call President Bill Clinton as a witness, based on the fact that Clinton had given a pair of cufflinks to one of the train survivors who had visited the White House. Ferguson contemplated calling another witness who purportedly was on the train when Ferguson began to shoot the other passengers. The potential witness claimed to have seen an Asian man place a computer chip in the back of Ferguson's neck, then take out a black box and move some dials, thereby activating Ferguson to shoot passengers. That witness did not testify. Subsequently, at the sentencing hearing, Ferguson's victims testified against him. When Ferguson rose to rebut them and tell the court why he should not receive the full measure of the law against him, the entire courtroom cleared, as spectators simply walked out in an expression of their contempt for Ferguson. Ferguson was convicted and sentenced to life imprisonment for the train murders. Ron Kuby said that, in retrospect, he believes Ferguson should never have been permitted to defend himself, because he was clearly mentally ill.

ATTORNEY–CLIENT PRIVILEGE AND CONFIDENTIALITY. Other rules have evolved as well to cover the relation between attorneys and their clients (Canon 4). **Attorney–client confidentiality and privilege** is intended to protect clients from having their attorneys disclose incriminating details of their lives to others, such as prosecutors. If a defense attorney hears a confession from a client, the attorney is vested with considerable legal protection. Prosecutors cannot compel defense counsels to provide them with incriminating information about their clients (Suny, 1987). The attorney–client privilege is as inviolate as the relation between parishioners and their priests.

ATTORNEY COMPETENCE AND EFFECTIVE ASSISTANCE OF COUNSEL. Probably all attorneys think that they are competent. However, a troubling number of allegations arise from convicted offenders who believe that their defense counsel was incompetent and ineffective (R. Klein, 1986). There is considerable variation among lawyers regarding **attorney competence**, both defense counsel and prosecutors, concerning their quality and effectiveness. Attorneys of all types vary considerably according to their expertise, years on the job, personal and professional experience, and enthusiasm for defending or prosecuting. However, attorneys are tacitly expected to zealously perform their defense tasks in a competent manner (Canons 5, 6, and 7).

Ideally at least, attorneys are expected to do their best, whether they are prosecuting or defending someone on a criminal charge. Counsel competence is difficult to assess objectively. It is more frequently the case that the effectiveness and competence of counsel are assessed subjectively (Hutton, 1987; Uphoff, 1992). It is precisely because of the diffuseness of the concepts of effectiveness and competence that convicted offenders often call into question the performance of their attorneys. These questions pertain to the ineffective assistance of counsel.

The leading case concerning attorney competence is *Strickland v. Washington* (466 U.S. 668 [1984]). Whether ineffective assistance of counsel was rendered in this case was measured according to the following standards: Was the counsel's conduct such that it so undermined the functioning of the adversarial process that a trial cannot be relied upon to render a just result? Did the counsel's behavior fall below the objective standard of reasonableness? There must be a reasonable probability that, but for counsel's unprofessional errors, the result of the proceedings would be different.

Thus, *Strickland* established the standards of (1) whether counsel's behavior undermined the adversarial process to the degree that the trial outcome is unreliable and (2) whether counsel's conduct was unreasonable to the degree that the jury verdict would have been different otherwise. This does not mean that all attorney conduct must be flawless and that every stone, large or small, has been overturned in all cases. Most attorneys make one or more mistakes and exercise bad judgment occasionally when defending a client. But many of these mistakes or instances of bad judgment are inconsequential and would not ordinarily affect the trial outcome. There is no obligation on the part of any attorney to raise every nonfrivolous issue in a criminal case (*Jones v. Barnes,* 463 U.S. 745 [1983]; *Murray v. Carrier,* 477 U.S. 478 [1986]).

INEFFECTIVE ASSISTANCE OF COUNSEL. The U.S. Supreme Court has decided instances of **ineffective assistance of counsel** on occasion. For instance, in the case of *Lozada v. Deeds* (498 U.S. 430 [1991]), José Lozada was convicted of four crimes relating to narcotics. He was earlier convicted in Nevada on four counts of possession and sale of controlled substances. Following the trial proceedings, Lozada's attorney failed to notify him of his right to appeal, of the procedures and time limitations of an appeal, and of his right to court-appointed counsel. Further, Lozada alleged that his attorney failed to file a notice of appeal or to ensure that Lozada received court-appointed counsel on appeal. Finally, it was alleged that the attorney misled Lozada's sister, and hence Lozada, when he told her that the case had been forwarded to the public defender's office, which it had not. Lower appellate courts dismissed Lozada's subsequent **habeas corpus petition** that he had ineffective assistance of counsel as the result of these alleged events. The U.S. Supreme Court found otherwise, however, and reversed his convictions, holding that Lozada had made a substantial showing that he was denied the right to effective assistance of counsel.

Defendants should have a reasonable expectation, therefore, that the counsel representing them is competent and effective. But this expectation should not be that the defense counsel is necessarily the best defense available. The standard of reasonableness is very important because of the varying degrees of counsel competence and effectiveness that are within the reasonable parameters articulated in *Strickland.* Furthermore, defendants may assume with some confidence that defense counsel will adhere to the ethical codes and manner of professional responsibility articulated by their state bar associations and other professional organizations established to regulate attorney quality and performance.

The Right to a Trial by Jury

One of the most significant cases challenging the court's authority to grant or deny a defendant the right to a **jury trial** was *Duncan v. Louisiana.* Duncan was convicted in a bench trial of simple battery in a Louisiana court. The crime was a misdemeanor, punishable by a maximum prison term of two years and a fine of $300. However, Duncan was sentenced to only sixty days and fined $150. He appealed, contending that he was denied his constitutional right to a jury trial under the Sixth Amendment. The U.S. Supreme Court agreed with Duncan, saying that any crime carrying a maximum punishment of two years is a serious crime, despite the fact that a jail sentence of only sixty days was imposed. Thus, for serious crimes, under the Sixth Amendment, Duncan was entitled to a jury trial as a matter of right.

Eventually, the standard was established whereby criminal defendants are entitled to a jury trial as a matter of right. The standard was set in the case of *Baldwin v. New York*. Baldwin was arrested and prosecuted for jostling or **pickpocketing**, a class A misdemeanor punishable by a maximum term of imprisonment of one year in New York. Baldwin asked for a jury trial, but he was denied one. At the time, New York law defined jostling as a petty offense, which did not require a jury trial. Baldwin was subsequently convicted and sentenced to ninety days in jail. He appealed. The U.S. Supreme Court heard Baldwin's appeal and declared that **petty offenses** carrying a one-year incarcerative term are *serious* in that jury trials must be provided if requested by defendants. Specifically, the wording of *Baldwin* gives substantial significance to the *months* of imprisonment that define a serious crime. The U.S. Supreme Court said that a potential sentence in excess of six months of imprisonment is sufficiently severe by itself to take an offense out of the category of petty as respects one's right to jury trial (at 1886, 1891). Therefore, the U.S. Supreme Court overturned Baldwin's conviction on these grounds. At present, jury trials must be granted to any defendant whose possible punishment involves incarceration beyond six months.

NO JURY TRIALS FOR DEFENDANTS CHARGED WITH PETTY OFFENSES. The U.S. Supreme Court has made clear its position about jury trials and when defendants are entitled to them. According to *Baldwin*, jury trials are available as a matter of right only to defendants charged with serious crimes, when their loss of liberty is beyond six months. Jury trials are not available as a matter of right in other nonserious cases. For instance, in *United States v. Nachtigal* (507 U.S. 1 [1993]), Nachtigal was convicted of drunk driving while operating a motor vehicle in a national park. When he appeared before the U.S. Magistrate, Nachtigal asked for a jury trial but was denied one. His offense carried a maximum incarceration of six months in jail, and thus it did not qualify for a jury trial. Nachtigal appealed his conviction on the Sixth Amendment grounds that he was denied a jury trial, but the U.S. Supreme Court upheld his conviction, saying that jury trials may not be granted in petty offense cases.

Another drunk-driving case was *Blanton v. City of North Las Vegas*. Blanton was convicted in Nevada for operating a motor vehicle while under the influence of alcohol. Blanton demanded a jury trial but was denied one because the charge was considered a petty offense. Blanton was convicted in Nevada, where the maximum prison term for drunk driving is six months. However, the court also required Blanton to pay a fine and perform forty-eight hours of community service. Blanton's driver's license was also revoked for ninety days, and the court required Blanton to attend a victim-impact panel and a course on alcohol abuse. Blanton appealed to the U.S. Supreme Court, arguing that the cumulative effect of all these sanctions and conditions elevated his case to the level of a serious one, thus entitling him to a jury trial. However, the U.S. Supreme Court was not persuaded by Blanton's argument and rejected his appeal. Thus, the other conditions of one's sentence, including attending courses and panels and performing community service, are not considered as relevant factors in determining a crime's seriousness.

One exception to *Baldwin* is as follows: Sometimes judges conduct bench trials without juries when a defendant is charged with a serious crime, but these judges advise the defendant in advance that if the defendant is found guilty, the incarcerative punishment will be six months or less. Judges must keep this promise. Thus, if a defendant is found guilty by the judge following court proceedings in a bench trial, then the judge cannot impose an incarcerative sentence longer than six months. If a judge violates this promise to a defendant and sentences him or her to a term of imprisonment beyond six months, then the convicted offender has solid grounds to have a higher court review the judge's action and overturn the conviction. Judicial promises must be kept.

The Defense

Defense counsel are attorneys who represent those charged with crimes. Defense attorneys adhere to the ABA code of professional responsibility and are obligated to do all that is ethically possible to defend their clients. All criminal defendants are entitled to an attorney as a matter of right. Many defense counsel are retained privately by defendants able to afford them. Other defense counsel are appointed by the courts in their jurisdictions to represent clients without money to hire their own attorneys. Thus, both indigents and others are entitled to counsel. Defense counsel who are hired by the state or are appointed to represent indigent defendants are called public defenders.

FORMS OF LEGAL AID FOR INDIGENTS. By 1992, about eighty percent of all criminal defendants charged with felonies were represented by court-appointed counsel (Smith and DeFrances, 1996:1). Court-appointed legal representation for indigent criminal defendants plays a critical role in the criminal justice system. About $357,000 was spent on court-appointed counsel for indigents in 1979, $1,336,000 in 1990, and $2.6 million in 1999 (Maguire and Pastore, 2000; Smith and DeFrances, 1996:3). Table 4.1 shows various types of public defender systems in the United States from a National Prosecutors Survey conducted in 1992.

Not every state has the same type of public legal aid for indigent defendants (Smith and DeFrances, 1996:1). Each state is at liberty to establish its own particular form of legal aid services, and different states have evolved different public defense systems. The most common public defender system, used in twenty-eight percent of all U.S. counties, is called simply the **public defender system**. This system is state- and county-funded and serves the needs of numerous persons unable to afford legal aid. The public defender system began in 1914 in Los Angeles (Klein and Spangenberg, 1993). Public defenders are hired by the state and county to represent indigent clients who are in need of defense. They draw salaries and are expected to mount the best defense possible,

TABLE 4.1 Indigent Defense Delivery Systems Used by Local Jurisdictions

Type of System	Percentage of Prosecutors' Offices Indicating the Type of Counsel Provided by Their Jurisdiction
Total	100%
Public defender program only	28%
Assigned counsel system only	23%
Assigned counsel and public defender	23%
Contract attorney system only	8%
Public defender and contract	8%
Assigned counsel, public defender, and contract system	6%
Assigned counsel and contract system	3%
Other	1%

Source: Steven K. Smith and Carol J. DeFrances, *Indigent Defense* (Washington, DC: U.S. Department of Justice, 1996), 2.

under the limited resources of their agencies. Quite often, their funds for legal defense are limited, and they do not enjoy investigative luxuries and other expenditures that might be available to the privately acquired counsel of more affluent defendants.

Two other types of systems are the **assigned counsel system** and the **contract system**. The assigned counsel system, the sole system in twenty-three percent of all local jurisdictions, is used in cities and towns where there are not many attorneys. Small towns and sparsely populated counties may not have many practicing lawyers. Local bar associations function as liaisons between association members and the courts to provide legal services for indigent clients on a voluntary basis. Ordinarily, the local bar association submits a list of attorneys' names to judges, who select defense counsel to represent indigent defendants on a case-by-case basis. In most jurisdictions where assigned counsel systems are operative, assigned counsel are paid a fixed rate per day for compensation. Compensation may range from $50 to $125 per day for these attorneys, a small sum compared with what an attorney might charge a private client. Actually, these per diem rates are closer to the hourly rates charged by attorneys who are affiliated with small law firms. Experienced attorneys in large law firms may bill their clients $500 per hour or more. About twenty-three percent of all local jurisdictions use a combination of the assigned counsel and public defender systems.

Because the compensation for indigent client legal services is inadequate, those who furnish their legal services to indigent clients under such a system are not particularly enthusiastic about defending their clients. Many of these attorneys merely want to go through the motions of negotiating the best deals for their clients with prosecutors. They often encourage their clients, though innocent, to plead guilty to a lesser criminal charge in exchange for a short jail term or probation. They may persuade their clients to waive their right to a jury trial and opt for a quick plea bargain. The saying "You get what you pay for" is often applicable to attorneys who work as either public defenders or assigned counsel for indigents. The lack of incentives (e.g., monetary remuneration for legal services) causes them to lack the motivation and zeal they should have, in view of the Canons of Ethics and professional responsibility codes they should abide by through the ABA and other state professional legal affiliates.

The contract system involves competitive bidding among different law firms in various jurisdictions for providing legal services to indigent clients. A law firm may submit a bid to represent indigent clients on the basis of a fixed amount of money per hour or per day. The state or county accepts the most attractive bid to hold down defense costs. About eight percent of all U.S. counties use only the contract system (Smith and DeFrances, 1996:2). Another eight percent of all local jurisdictions use a combination of the contract and public defender systems, and ten percent use other combinations of the three systems.

One drawback is that the low bidders under the contract system may not be the most competent counsel. A law firm may assign its newest and least experienced lawyers to defend indigent clients charged with serious crimes. When the least trained attorneys are expected to defend indigent clients in serious and complex cases, they may not be qualified to perform an adequate defense job. In fact, their defense of indigent clients may be downright incompetent, to the extent that ineffective assistance of counsel charges may be alleged by convicted indigents.

Despite the flaws of these and other defense systems for indigents and others, the fact remains that all criminal defendants are entitled to counsel. The U.S. Supreme Court has never made explicit the exact nature of attorney competence, other than what has previously been articulated in *Strickland v. Washington* (1984). In the *Strickland* case, the U.S. Supreme Court declared that an attorney's performance should not be such that the adversarial process is undermined or that but for the attorney's conduct, the trial verdict may have been different. The *reasonableness* of attorney conduct was stressed by the court, although it failed to give precise definition to reasonableness. Therefore, the U.S. Supreme Court has left this determination up to individual state supreme courts and lower courts whenever allegations of attorney incompetence are lodged by convicted offenders.

ARE PUBLIC DEFENDERS AS EFFECTIVE AS PRIVATELY RETAINED COUNSEL? Under the assigned counsel, public defender, and contract systems, states and the federal government set fixed hourly rates for remunerating attorneys who defend indigent clients. These hourly rates, which may range from $25 to $50, are well below the rates charged by private counsel who are hired by more affluent criminals. Many public defenders who work in a public defender's office are fresh out of law school and interested in acquiring courtroom experience. They are willing to work for low pay in exchange for this experience. Other public defenders and court-appointed counsel who work on an assigned-counsel basis may be apathetic or hostile toward their clients and the general job of defending criminals. In many of these cases, public defenders attempt to rush their clients into plea agreements and conclude these low-paying cases quickly, without adequately testing the strength of the case (Hanson et al., 1992). This rapid case processing is particularly prevalent in those jurisdictions with contract systems. A primary consideration in contracting is economizing on resources and expediting case processing for maximum efficiency. Such rapid resolution of criminal cases may deprive some defendants of an adequate defense and seriously jeopardize their chances of obtaining equity (Worden, 1991).

At the federal level, the Federal Defender Services program provides legal counsel for those who cannot afford attorneys (U.S. General Accounting Office, 1995). The cost of operating this program tripled during the 1990–1995 period, and projections are that costs will go much higher in future years. In some jurisdictions, budget cutbacks have directly influenced the numbers of court-appointed counsel available for indigent defendants, as well as the amount of time allocated to each of these cases (Worden, 1993; U.S. General Accounting Office, 1995). In Fulton County, Georgia, for instance, the indigent defense system is at best fragmented and disjointed (Spangenberg, 1990). Communication, coordination, and cooperation are lacking among the various agencies providing indigent defense services. The number of staff is insufficient in every category to handle the current caseload, and early representation in the public defender's office is lacking. There is virtually no training for public defenders and little supervision. Salaries are low, as is morale. Greater use of technology has enabled many jurisdictions to cut their operating costs while maintaining fairly high-quality attorney representation for indigents, however (Spangenberg et al., 1999).

The general question therefore arises, Are court-appointed counsel as effective as their privately retained counterparts? Some early research suggests that defense services for indigents in certain jurisdictions such as Hamilton County, Ohio, have been substandard, especially in homicide cases (Steelman and Conti, 1987). More extensive continuing education requirements have been recommended for many of these defense attorneys to improve their criminal law skills. More recent research suggests that inadequate compensation of attorneys for indigents in capital cases produces increasing numbers of appeals from convicted offenders who allege ineffective assistance of counsel (McCoy and Lichtenberg, 1999). Despite these criticisms, public defender programs have been defended as being on par with private counsel who defend indigent clients. In short, public defenders have been found to be equally effective at defending indigent clients as private counsel, thus contradicting long-standing portrayals of indigent defenders as incompetent, ill equipped, and poorly trained (Hanson et al., 1992).

In sum, there is perhaps an element of truth to both views of public defender and assigned-counsel systems. Particularly in larger urban jurisdictions, the public defender's office is often staffed with new attorneys with little or no criminal trial experience. This fact operates to their disadvantage vis-à-vis prosecutors and configuring plea agreements beneficial to criminal defendants. But in assigned-counsel and contract systems, there are also many seasoned attorneys with considerable criminal law experience. At present, there is great diversity in the quality of court-appointed legal representation for indigent criminal defendants. At least eighty percent of all criminal defendants continue to have court-appointed counsel, and it is likely that this figure will not change substantially in future years (Smith and DeFrances, 1996).

Functions of the Defense

The functions of defense counsel are to represent their clients faithfully, attack the prosecution's case vigorously, counsel with the defendant as to the best course of action in the case, negotiate with prosecutors for a case resolution most favorable to their client, vigorously cross-examine prosecution witnesses to attack and undermine their credibility in front of jurors, and use all legal means to defeat the government's case.

REPRESENTING CLIENTS FAITHFULLY. It is expected that defense counsel will represent their clients faithfully. They will take an active interest in the case rather than a detached, passive interest. They will strive to collect relevant exculpatory evidence, interview crucial witnesses, and engage in proper trial preparations. They will consider the defendants' needs and give them every consideration. They will assume that their clients are innocent, despite incriminating evidence to the contrary.

ATTACKING THE PROSECUTION'S CASE VIGOROUSLY. Defense counsel are expected to attack the government's case in a vigorous manner. They should take steps to point out all aspects of the prosecutor's case that are weak or that raise reasonable doubt about the defendant's guilt. They should be aggressive and promote their clients' interests to the best of their ability.

COUNSELING WITH DEFENDANTS CONCERNING THE BEST COURSE OF ACTION IN A CASE. Sometimes defense counsel will be assigned cases with overwhelming direct and conclusive evidence about the defendant's guilt. In these types of cases, a vigorous defense should be implemented, designed to provide a plausible explanation for why the crime was committed. One part of the counseling process involves determining the client's view of the case and a disclosure of crime details. This shared information and subsequent defendant disclosures are confidential through attorney-client confidentiality and privilege. Whatever the defendant tells his or her attorney will remain private and confidential. If the defendant admits guilt to the attorney, the defense counsel must continue to represent the client with enthusiasm. Defense counsel are in crucial positions to understand the consequences of a trial. In some cases, it may be more prudent to work out deals for clients with prosecutors instead of proceeding with a trial. These bargains often involve some measure of leniency for their clients. The prosecutor may be amenable to reducing more serious charges to less serious ones in exchange for a defendant's guilty plea. If a counsel's client were to reject the bargain offered by the prosecutor and proceed with a trial, a conviction would almost guarantee an increase in the harshness or severity of the penalty imposed by the judge. Therefore, good defense counsel should explain all viable options to their clients and work out what is best for them through close collaboration. Good advice to a client might be to plead guilty to a lesser charge and accept a less severe punishment rather than take a chance in court, where a conviction and more severe sentence are imminent.

NEGOTIATING WITH PROSECUTORS FOR A CASE RESOLUTION MOST FAVORABLE TO CLIENTS. Prosecutors determine which charges should be filed against defendants. Defense counsel are expected to negotiate with prosecutors in an effort to reach a compromise favorable to their clients. Sometimes, defense counsel may request diversion for their clients; that is, their cases are temporarily removed from the criminal justice system. Under diversion, clients are expected to be law abiding, pay monthly maintenance fees, and perhaps pay restitution to victims or engage in community service. The result of a successful diversion might be that the prosecutor would drop all criminal charges against the defendant or downgrade the charges eventually filed from felonies to misdemeanors. Defense attorneys are key players in facilitating such negotiations between prosecutors and defendants.

VIGOROUSLY CROSS-EXAMINING PROSECUTION WITNESSES AND UNDERMINING THEIR CREDIBILITY. Good defense attorneys engage in vigorous cross-examinations of prosecution witnesses in an effort to undermine their credibility. Often, eyewitness testimony is damaging to defendants, and defense counsel can sometimes cause eyewitnesses to express doubt about what they observed. If defense counsel can encourage prosecution witnesses to admit to uncertainty about what was seen, this strategy undermines the prosecution's case considerably.

USING ALL LEGAL MEANS TO DEFEAT THE GOVERNMENT'S CASE. Within the limits of propriety and the code of ethics that bind together defense counsel throughout the United States, defense attorneys are encouraged to use any and all legal means at their disposal to defeat the government's case against their client. Some of the means may be considered unsavory, although they may be entirely legal. For instance, if a man is suspected of killing his wife and if there are older children or relatives who did not get along with the deceased, it is proper for the defense counsel to suggest to the jury that others might have been motivated to kill the defendant's wife. Certain relatives might be named as possible suspects, even though the defense attorney may not believe that they were involved in the woman's death. Rather, the intent of such a strategy is to plant a seed of doubt in the minds of jurors. Someone else may have committed the crime. Others besides the defendant may have had strong motives to kill. If sufficient doubt can be raised by deflecting possible guilt to others, then the jury may acquit the defendant.

One fact that operates to the disadvantage of defense counsel everywhere is that other types of attorneys do not hold criminal defense lawyers in particularly high regard. Defending criminals is viewed by more than a few citizens as an unsavory profession. Defending criminals means having to interact with them. For many attorneys, interacting with criminals is undesirable. Therefore, criminal defense counsel often engage in thankless tasks. They may even be viewed with disdain by their own criminal clients. If they win their cases, they are accused of getting guilty defendants off and escaping punishment. If they lose, their clients may appeal and allege that their defense was incompetent or ineffective. Even criminal court judges regard defense counsel with a certain amount of contempt. Thus, for many criminal defense attorneys, considerable stress is generated.

Defense Misconduct

Much of the misconduct that occurs in court is the result of prosecutorial actions or abuses of judicial discretion. However, some misconduct is committed by the defense

LAWYERS ARE A DIME A DOZEN?

The Case of Too Many Lawyers

It is happening all over the United States. There is a lawyer glut! Just too many lawyers! What can be done about it?

Is there an overabundance of lawyers in the United States? There were twice as many lawyers per capita in 1997 as in 1947. Many lawyers have been pushed out of their law firms, often because of layoffs or because they did not reach partner status. Nowadays, graduating lawyers have to be creative in finding sufficient legal work to make ends meet. Many lawyers have had to seek additional employment and work at least two different jobs for a decent paycheck each month.

Some lawyers have turned to other professions for additional income. For instance, Sondra Sellars has twenty-eight years of experience as a lawyer, but her true love is acting. Since 1994, Sellars has worked as a temporary lawyer for various firms, while she spends the major portion of her time seeking acting work.

Several enterprising businesses have capitalized on the overabundance of legal experts. One company, the Wallace Law Registry, was started in 1987. During the 1987–1997 interval, the company has placed thousands of lawyers in temporary assignments in numerous businesses throughout the United States. The company pays its lawyers from $30 to $100 per hour, depending upon their experience. President Shelley Wallace, based in Hartford, Connecticut, says that her lawyers average forty to fifty hours of work per week, and some earn as much as $100,000 per year. This compares very favorably with the typical eighty-hour week many lawyers must work in traditional law firms.

The temp lawyering business is booming, catching on throughout the United States. In 1991, for instance, professional temping was a $335 million business. In 1997, it was a $2 billion business. There is no question that temporary lawyering is growing. It is increasingly popular because contract attorneys are much cheaper than staff attorneys, they can work through a crunch, they leave when the overload is done, and they free a firm's own attorneys for more important work. "When you get a large project, with maybe twenty people doing document review over the course of two months, those cost savings are pretty significant," says Jim Michaliwicz, manager of the DuPont Company in Wilmington, Delaware.

Source: Adapted from Associated Press, "Temporary Lawyers: Temps Becoming Multimillion-Dollar Industry." *Minot* (N.D.) *Daily News*, August 11, 1997:B3.

counsel. Prosecutors are barred from mentioning or admitting into evidence certain types of incriminating information; defense counsel are likewise admonished to avoid saying anything that might prejudice the jury in favor of their client. Certain scientific advances, for instance, may not be sufficiently reliable for introduction as evidence in courtrooms (Moenssens et al., 1993).

DNA: A NEW SIGNATURE OF A CRIME?

The Case of Marv Albert, NBC Sportscaster

Marv Albert, a forty-two-year-old NBC sportscaster, was by all accounts a very popular celebrity, adding colorful remarks and witticisms to his sportscasts. However, accusations of sodomy and sexual assault were lodged against Albert by an unnamed woman in Arlington, Virginia. The woman alleged that Albert threw her onto a bed in an Arlington motel room, bit her back repeatedly, and forced her to perform oral sex. Albert was arrested by Arlington police and charged. In his initial appearance, he pleaded not guilty to all charges and was released on his own recognizance pending a subsequent trial.

In the interim, police investigators collected semen and saliva specimens from the woman alleging the sexual assault. They also obtained blood, hair, and saliva samples from Albert. A DNA analysis and testing were completed several months later. According to the Virginia State Crime Laboratory, there was only a 1 in 2.6 billion chance that some of the samples taken from the woman could have come from someone other than Albert. The lab found consistencies between a blood sample provided by Albert and sperm samples recovered from the woman's skin and underwear and DNA from bite wounds on her back.

Meanwhile, Marv Albert's attorney, Roy Black, said, "Marv Albert reasserts his innocence and will establish his innocence in court when he finally gets an opportunity." A professor at New York's John Jay College of Criminal Justice, Lawrence Kobilinsky, said, "I think that Mr. Albert is in very serious trouble. I think that the defense is going to be very hard-pressed to explain how his saliva and semen were found on her person."

How important do you think DNA is in establishing one's guilt or innocence? Although Marv Albert's DNA seems to match that found on the alleged victim, does this by itself prove sexual assault and sodomy? Trial was commenced for Albert in September 1997. In the middle of the trial, however, Albert pleaded guilty to a lesser included offense and was sentenced to probation.

Source: Adapted from the Associated Press, "DNA Tests Link Albert to Accuser." *Minot* (N.D.) *Daily News*, August 12, 1997:A1, A6; Associated Press, "Albert Pleads Guilty in Middle of Trial." *Minot* (N.D.) *Daily News*, October 15, 1997:A4.

For instance, it is widely accepted that testimony about **polygraph tests** (**lie detectors**) is inadmissible. Lie detector results are unreliable and cannot be interpreted with the same degree of precision as fingerprint evidence or other tangible direct evidence. But suppose the defendant submitted to a lie detector test administered by the local police department. Further assume that the defendant passed the lie detector test. The test results would be interpreted to mean that the defendant was telling the truth and that this fact might be considered exculpatory evidence. However, the prosecutor

WHO SAYS LAWYERS DON'T GET INTO TROUBLE WITH THE LAW?

The Conviction of George Parker, Former Attorney-at-Law

It happened in Honolulu, Hawaii. A large drug ring was operating there, with drug kingpin Frank Moon at the helm. A federal strike force made up of DEA and FBI agents moved to catch Moon and end his lucrative drug trade.

During Moon's successful drug operations, he paid off many people, including an attorney, George Parker, who enjoyed a fairly good reputation within the Hawaiian legal community. But there was a dark side to Parker. He accepted large amounts of money from Moon in exchange for legal favors. In at least one instance, he accepted $20,000 in cash from another drug dealer, William Batkin, to persuade Moon not to cooperate with federal authorities once Moon had been indicted and charged with several serious drug offenses. Ultimately, Parker was convicted of money laundering, witness tampering, and conspiracy.

During Parker's sentencing in federal court, Federal District Judge David Ezra sentenced Parker, age thirty-six, to thirteen years in prison for his convictions. The day following his conviction, Parker reappeared in court and pretended to have a weapon. In fact, it was his cellular telephone wrapped in a jacket, but police did not know this. Parker threatened to shoot the weapon, possibly wounding or killing innocent citizens who happened to be in the federal court building. Despite Parker's threats, police were able to subdue him with nonlethal foam and wooden bullets.

Parker's actions were cited by Judge Ezra as additional evidence of Parker's lack of good judgment in the Moon case. The exceptionally harsh sentence was imposed because Parker was an attorney who knew or should have known that witness tampering and conspiracy were criminal offenses. Ezra characterized Parker as seeking to enhance his own reputation by making large amounts of money via becoming Moon's lawyer and knowingly accepting illegal cash payments for bribery from other Moon conspirators. Interestingly, Moon was convicted and sentenced to twelve years. An attorney for Parker, William Harrison, argued that Parker's sentence should not have been greater than Moon's because Moon had been involved in a multi-million-dollar drug operation and distributed enormous quantities of narcotics. However, U.S. Attorney Steven Alm said that the sentence was just, in that Moon had helped authorities in their apprehension of other co-conspirators.

Do you think that Parker's sentence was proportionately fair relative to the sentence received by Moon? Which man committed the greater crime? Should one's position as an attorney be used to increase one's sentence because of established attorney ethics? What do you think?

Source: Adapted from Ken Kobayashi, "Lawyer in Standoff Sentenced to 13 Years." *Honolulu Advertiser*, August 5, 1997:B1, B4.

decided to move forward with the prosecution anyway, feeling that the polygraph test results were unreliable. What if the defense counsel asked a police officer who was testifying for the state, "My client took a lie detector test about this crime and passed, didn't he?" The prosecutor would object, and the judge would sustain the objection. Just as prosecutors would be guilty of committing harmless errors by backdooring inadmissible evidence, defense counsel would be equally guilty of backdooring another type of inadmissible evidence, the lie detector test results. The judge can order the jury to disregard the defense counsel's question, but can the jury ever forget the question by the defense? No. This is one example of defense misconduct.

Another type of defense misconduct occurs whenever the defense attorney knows that the defendant is guilty. The defendant has confessed a crime to the defense counsel, and it is expected that this confession will remain confidential. The privilege of confidentiality exists between the attorney and the client, and it is unethical for an attorney to violate this privilege. Although the defense counsel is obligated to defend the client despite the confession, the defense counsel is prohibited from advising the client to take the stand and lie about the crime. Advising one's client, or advising one's client's witnesses to lie, is the **subornation of perjury**. Suborning perjury means to encourage someone to lie under oath. If a defense attorney were to suborn perjury, this would constitute defense misconduct. Further, it would be a crime (Subin, Mirsky, and Weinstein, 1993).

Interactions between Prosecutors and Defense Attorneys

Most of us are quite familiar with courtroom drama. We see programs on television such as *Law and Order, Murder One*, and *Perry Mason* reruns. These shows focus on the courtroom as the major contact point between prosecutors and defense counsel. But these programs give us only one dimension of a much larger picture of interaction between the defense and the prosecution. Both prosecutors and defense attorneys are integral parts of the courtroom work group. Actually, their interactions with one another and other members of the courtroom work group are more frequent outside than inside the courtroom. For instance, defense attorneys who maintain good relations with various court officers can benefit by being assigned more cases. Defense attorneys, especially recent law graduates, need to earn a living. Being assigned more cases enables these attorneys to earn more money to support themselves and establish their law practices. Defense attorneys with poor attitudes may lose out on case assignments that are given to more compliant defense counsel.

Defense attorneys consult frequently with prosecutors concerning defendants. Prosecutors work closely with the police and detectives who gather incriminating evidence of crimes, interviews with suspects, and conversations with various experts and eyewitnesses. Some of this information is made available to defense attorneys so that they may advise their clients concerning which course of action is best.

Although the interactions between defense counsel and prosecutors are often characterized as adversarial and antagonistic, the fact is that most of these people have amicable relations with one another both on and off the job. Most prosecutors are known by defense counsel on a first-name basis. Their relationships are almost always friendly, even though in the courtroom their respective demeanors might suggest otherwise.

Another consequence of close interactions between prosecutors and defense attorneys is that they both learn about each other's interests and objectives. They are able to assess each other's skills and strategies. Thus, some prosecutors know that they can expect a serious challenge from some defense attorneys who have been successful in garnering acquittals for their clients. This mutual understanding between prosecutors and defense counsel facilitates the process of deciding whether defendants will enter guilty pleas to certain charges in exchange for leniency.

Also, it is important for both prosecutors and defense counsels to maintain good relations because they are both interested in ensuring that justice is served. The wheels of justice turn more smoothly to the extent that relations between prosecutors and defense counsel are cordial and cooperative. However, some prosecutors resent having to share case information with defense attorneys. Some defense attorneys are openly antagonistic toward prosecutors. Information exchanges from both sides are slowed and hampered by formality. Under a cooperative scenario, for example, prosecutors willingly share case information with defense attorneys because it is important for these attorneys to know what they are facing in regard to inculpatory evidence against their clients. Under less cooperative conditions, defense counsel are obligated to write detailed letters to request case information to which they are entitled. Prosecutors might drag their feet and delay turning over case materials in a timely manner. Ultimately, however, both sides exchange information in the process known as discovery.

The Discovery Process

Discovery is the procedure or mechanism whereby the prosecution shares information with the defense attorney and the defendant. Specific types of information are made available to the defendant and defense counsel before trial, including results of any tests conducted, psychiatric reports, and transcripts or tape-recorded statements made by the defendant. Also shared between prosecution and defense is the list of witnesses both sides plan to call to testify at the trial.

If the defendant confessed to the crime, and if the confession was videotaped and transcribed, then the defense is entitled to see a copy of the videotape and have a transcription of it for use in the subsequent trial. Accordingly, if the defense has certain types of information, it is also discoverable by the prosecution. Thus, discovery involves an exchange between the prosecution and defense of relevant information in the case. Both sides must allow the other to see certain types of information they plan to introduce as evidence at the subsequent trial.

The premise on which discovery is based is that all defendants are entitled to a fair and impartial trial. If the government with its immense resources restricted access to various test results and tangible evidence, even oral testimony and reports of experts, this restriction would jeopardize a defendant's right to a fair trial. Fundamental fairness is that the defense shall not be deprived of a fair trial. This means that the disclosure of certain types of evidence by the prosecution is mandatory.

In several jurisdictions, defense counsel must make a motion for discovery, itemizing the testimony and other evidence it wants. If the defense does not ask for specific items in the possession of the government, the government is not obligated to volunteer them to the defense. This fact is underscored in the case of *Kimmelman v. Morrison* (477 U.S. 365, 1986). In this case, Neil Morrison was convicted of rape in a bench trial in New Jersey. During the trial, a police officer testified about some evidence, a bedsheet found at the crime scene, which had been seized without a proper search warrant. The defense attorney objected and moved to suppress statements about the bedsheet. The judge, however, ruled that it was too late to register such an objection and that the proper time would have been during discovery, when the items seized and to be used as evidence against Morrison were disclosed to him. Following his conviction, Morrison filed a habeas corpus petition, alleging ineffective assistance of counsel relating to the bedsheet issue and the motion to suppress it. Because of the defense attorney's incompetence in not raising a motion at an earlier and more proper time, Morrison argued, he was deprived of the effective assistance of counsel, and this problem led to his conviction. An appellate court reversed his conviction on these grounds, and the state appealed to the U.S. Supreme Court. The U.S. Supreme Court heard the case and affirmed the lower appellate court, concluding that Morrison's counsel was ineffective because of his failure to conduct any pretrial discovery and determine what the state had planned to present as incriminating evidence. Further, the counsel clearly failed to make a timely motion to suppress such evidence. On these grounds, Morrison's conviction must be reversed.

It is beyond the scope of this book to list all types of discoverable information. Furthermore, there is considerable interstate variation concerning what is or is not discoverable material or statements. Confession statements are always discoverable in all jurisdictions. However, the statements of material witnesses may or may not be immediately discoverable. Usually, when lists of witnesses are exchanged by prosecution and defense, each side seeks to interview the witnesses to be called. This is to avoid a trial by ambush, in which a witness gives testimony unknown to the other side, and the testimony given influences the trial outcome. Neither side wishes to be surprised by the other.

A leading case about discovery is *Brady v. Maryland* (373 U.S. 83 [1963]). Brady was convicted of murder and sentenced to death. He appealed on the grounds that he was denied access to various statements made by a confederate, Boblit. Actually, Brady took the stand in his own defense and admitted to participating in the crime, but Brady declared that Boblit was the one who actually killed the victim. Various statements had been made to police and prosecution by Boblit. The prosecutor denied the defense access to these statements, alleging confidentiality. Following Brady's conviction, some of this evidence came to light and proved favorable and exculpatory to Brady. He sought an appeal, claiming that he was denied due process by having these important statements withheld during his trial. The U.S. Supreme Court agreed with Brady and overturned his murder conviction, saying that suppression by prosecution of evidence favorable to an accused upon request violates due process if evidence is material either to guilt or to punishment, irrespective of the good faith or bad faith of prosecution. Subsequently, both prosecutors and defense attorneys have referred to discoverable materials and evidence as **Brady materials**. When the prosecutor or defense counsel withholds certain discoverable information, this is called a **Brady violation**.

LEFT HOLDING THE BAG

Pleading Guilty to Possession of Bread Crumbs

What will some people do to avoid going to jail and losing their jobs? In Belleville, Illinois, a man pleaded guilty to possession of drugs. The plea bargain cut with prosecutors enabled him to be released from an eighteen-day jail stay. He entered the guilty plea after being assured that he would receive only probation. Further, he did not want to lose his job. He had stayed in the jail since his arrest because he did not have $2,500 for the bond required to be released on his own recognizance before the trial.

It all started on February 14, 2000, when James McClain, age thirty-three, was stopped by police for a traffic violation. While writing up the ticket for the traffic offense, an overzealous officer spied a plastic bag in McClain's coat pocket. The officer grabbed the bag and noted that there were some brown particles in the bottom of the bag. McClain was arrested and charged with possessing a controlled substance.

In the meantime, McClain was appointed a public defender, Herb Lantz, to represent him in the case. Lantz advised McClain to plead guilty to simple possession and then he could be freed from jail with probation. McClain entered the plea. At the sentencing hearing, Chief Judge Stephen Kernan was advised by the prosecutor that after analysis and testing, the substances in the bag seized from McClain turned out to be bread crumbs from McClain's cousin's lunch. The judge threw out the guilty plea and scolded both the prosecutor and Lantz for allowing McClain to plead guilty. McClain said that he had been wearing a coat borrowed from his cousin and that the bag contained remnants of a sandwich. McClain said he pleaded guilty because he was worried about losing his job at Granite City Steel Company and he wanted a speedy resolution of his case.

McClain said that if anyone is to blame in the incident, then the St. Clair County and Fairmont City police should be. McClain said, "If they are going to charge me with having a controlled substance, they should have checked it. It's not Mr. Lantz's fault." The charges were dismissed, and McClain was able to keep his job after all.

What does this case say about the criminal justice system and the pressure for arrests and convictions? Are the police to blame for failing to test the substance seized from McClain? Should McClain receive any type of compensation for his jail stay of eighteen days? How often do you think people plead guilty to criminal charges when they are innocent, simply because they want to "get it over with quick"? What do you think?

Source: Adapted from the Associated Press, " 'Drugs' Turn Out to Be Bread Crumbs." *Minot* (N.D.) *Daily News,* May 12, 2000:A2.

Actually, an earlier case involving a similar issue was *Jencks v. United States* (353 U.S. 651, 1957), in which prosecutors withheld from the defense prior inconsistent statements by a key government witness against Jencks. In *Jencks,* the U.S. Supreme Court ruled that the government must disclose such inconsistent statements to the defense prior to a criminal trial. In Brady's case, the U.S. Supreme Court overturned his conviction and held that according to the ruling in the Jencks case, such information is discoverable and should be turned over to the defense by government attorneys. In a way similar to the case of *Brady v. Maryland* (1963), *Jencks* has led to discoverable evidence being called **Jencks materials**.

In another similar case, *Campbell v. United States* (365 U.S. 85, 1961), Campbell was charged with bank robbery and tried in federal court. During the testimony of a government witness, it became known that a previous statement had been made by that witness. The defense sought to obtain that statement under discovery, but the court denied them access to the statement. The government also denied the existence of the statement, when, in fact, it did exist. Campbell was convicted and appealed, arguing that under an earlier case, *Jencks v. United States* (1957), this statement was discoverable. The U.S. Supreme Court agreed and reversed Campbell's conviction. The U.S. Supreme Court held that under these circumstances Campbell's right to a fair and impartial trial was violated by the misconduct of the prosecutor.

Discovery of key prosecutorial information has been upheld by the U.S. Supreme Court in several subsequent cases. For example, in the case of *Gardner v. Florida* (430 U.S. 349, 1977), Gardner was charged with and convicted of first-degree murder. Following the conviction, a sentencing hearing was held. The jury advised the judge in the sentencing phase that their recommendation was life imprisonment. However, the judge cited extensive aggravating factors and imposed the death penalty. Importantly, portions of the presentence investigation (PSI) report relied upon by the judge for his knowledge of aggravating and mitigating factors were not given to the defense under discovery. Several mitigating factors were not included in the version of the report submitted to the judge at the time of sentencing. The U.S. Supreme Court heard Gardner's appeal and overturned his conviction, acknowledging that the government had not complied with the discovery law in that it failed to give Gardner a complete PSI report. The report contained information to support a life sentence rather than the death penalty. The U.S. Supreme Court declared that the failure of the Florida Supreme Court to consider or even read the confidential portion of the PSI report violated Gardner's right to due process under the Fourteenth Amendment.

Finally, in the case of *Kyles v. Whitley* (514 U.S. 419, 1995), Kyles was convicted by a Louisiana jury for first-degree murder and sentenced to death. During the trial, the prosecution failed to disclose to Kyles favorable and exculpatory evidence under discovery. For instance, eyewitness testimony and statements favorable to Kyles were withheld; also, statements made to police by an informant, Beanie, were withheld, and a computer print-out of all car license numbers at or near the murder scene, but which did not include Kyles's car license number, was in the possession of the prosecution and not made available to Kyles or his attorney when they demanded discovery. Appeals by Kyles to higher state courts resulted in affirmation of his original conviction and sentence. Thus, he sought relief by an appeal to the U.S. Supreme Court. The U.S. Supreme Court overturned Kyles's conviction, holding that the prosecution had violated his Brady rights to have relevant exculpatory information made available to him by the prosecution. The significance of this case is that it is now the constitutional duty of prosecutors to disclose to defense counsel any favorable evidence to defendants in criminal prosecutions.

Defense Attorneys and Their Defenses for Criminal Conduct

WHO BEARS THE BURDEN OF PROOF IN CRIMINAL PROSECUTIONS? In any criminal prosecution, it is the responsibility of the state to prove beyond a reasonable doubt that the defendant committed the crime(s) charged. This means that prosecutors must prove beyond a reasonable doubt that a crime was committed and that the defendant committed the crime. Thus, the prosecutor bears the **burden of proof** in asserting a criminal charge. This burden is providing the jury with **evidence** of the crime.

The burden of proof standard, also known as the **evidentiary** standard, in all criminal cases does *not* mean that prosecutors must produce witnesses or victims who can furnish **conclusive evidence** of a defendant's guilt. Conclusive evidence might suffice if several persons watched a defendant commit the crime in plain view. Such evidence is so compelling and strong that it cannot be disputed or contradicted. For instance, a man might shoot his wife, killing her. Then he turns the gun on himself, intending to commit suicide. But somehow he survives the bullet wound and is subsequently tried for his wife's murder. He might have left a highly incriminating suicide note indicating his reasons for killing his wife. The suicide note is a type of **derivative evidence**, or written evidence. The weapon he used has his fingerprints on it, his hands have powder residue from firing the weapon, and he is found holding the weapon after his neighbors report the sound of gunshots to police. In this instance, the facts are generally not disputed. District attorneys sometimes prosecute cases with this sort of conclusive evidence.

Also, the burden of proof standard does *not* mean that prosecutors must produce any **direct evidence** of the crime. As in the case of conclusive evidence, direct evidence is incriminating information such as fingerprints or eyewitness testimony. Rather, prosecutors may be able to convince a jury that a defendant is guilty of the crime based on **circumstantial evidence** alone. In one New York murder case, for example, a physician, Robert Bierenbaum, was suspected of killing his wife, Gail Katz Bierenbaum, in the summer of 1985. Prosecutors believed that he loaded her body aboard a rented airplane, flew over the ocean, and dumped her body into the water. No trace of his wife was ever found. Furthermore, police investigators never found any traces of Bierenbaum's wife's blood in Bierenbaum's automobile trunk or inside the airplane. If such evidence would have been found, this would have been **demonstrative evidence** or derivative evidence, because it is tangible and does not relate to eyewitness testimony. Neighbors reported that they often heard Bierenbaum arguing with his wife. On the day his wife disappeared, Bierenbaum was seen taking off from the airport and flying in the direction of the ocean in a rented airplane, although the police did not know Bierenbaum had rented the airplane until a year had elapsed. The case was dormant for fifteen years because police did not have sufficient evidence to charge Bierenbaum with a crime. Subsequently, a check of airport records showed that Bierenbaum had altered his flight log to show that his flight occurred on a different day and time. Also, on the day his wife disappeared, she had spoken with a friend that morning and said that she was leaving Bierenbaum and moving in with a new boyfriend. When the person called her back forty minutes later, Bierenbaum answered the telephone and told the caller that his wife had just left and he did not know when she was returning. All of these circumstances and **corroboration** did not prove that Bierenbaum killed his wife. But prosecutors eventually decided to indict Bierenbaum for his wife's murder in December 1999. He was tried and convicted of murder in New York on October 24, 2000. Although the case against Bierenbaum was entirely circumstantial, the jury drew inferences from all of this information and found him guilty of second-degree murder (Rogers, Cotliar, and Erwin, 2000:91).

In another murder case, this time in Atlanta, Georgia, a man was accused of killing his wife and setting his own home on fire to cover up any incriminating evidence. He managed to crawl out of a second-story window of his home while it went up in flames. He told passers-by that his wife was inside and had been overcome with smoke. He said that the fire seemed to come from the kitchen in a downstairs area and that he and his wife were sleeping. He claimed that his wife was too overcome with smoke to assist in her own flight to safety and that he was too weak to carry her to a window. Thus, he was able to save only himself. Again, like the New York murder, this man had taken out a large life insurance policy on his wife a few months earlier, and he had named himself as the primary beneficiary. It was also found that he was deeply in debt and that his business was failing. Prosecutors surmised that he killed his wife in an effort to save his company from bankruptcy by using the insurance money from her death. The case was purely circumstantial, but the jury was convinced that the man did, indeed, murder his wife, and he was convicted of her murder.

Usually, prosecutors must convince a jury that the accused had the means, motive, and opportunity to commit the crime(s) alleged. Because many criminals perform their criminal acts in secret and do not brag about what they have done because they do not want to get caught and convicted, the prosecutor's burden is a somewhat difficult one. Judges eventually instruct jurors about how they should regard the evidence presented during the trial and how to weigh that evidence.

The defense is under no obligation to prove anything to the jury. It is not their place to prove their client's innocence. Rather, they may simply offer alternative explanations for how the crime may have occurred. When television and movie personality O. J. Simpson was accused of murdering his ex-wife, Nicole Brown Simpson, and her friend Ron Goldman in 1994, his attorneys suggested alternative scenarios that may have accounted for the murders. Because Nicole Brown Simpson had been known to use cocaine and other drugs, Simpson's defense team suggested that she was the victim of drug dealers. Furthermore, they offered a reward leading to the arrest and conviction of these drug dealers they believed had executed Simpson's ex-wife. They also suggested that other people who knew her had motives to murder her. All of their alternative scenarios about how the two victims were murdered were intended to dissuade jurors from considering O. J. Simpson as the guilty party. He was subsequently acquitted of these crimes. One factor that contributed to his acquittal was that one of the investigating detectives committed perjury during his trial, and the detective's perjury was detected and brought to the attention of jurors. Another factor was that some of the inculpatory evidence against Simpson, blood evidence, had allegedly been planted in Simpson's home by investigating detectives. All of this information was weighed by the jury. The fact that the case was largely circumstantial did not help prosecutors either.

Defense counsel often recommend that their clients should not testify. The fact that defendants do not often testify in their own criminal trials is greatly misunderstood by the public, even many defendants. One of the first things innocent defendants want to do is get up on the witness stand and proclaim their innocence to the jurors. But prosecutors have many clever ways of distracting and upsetting innocent defendants and twisting their own words to prosecutorial advantage. The defendant's demeanor and self-control are important factors that jurors can observe. On more than one occasion, prosecutors have disturbed defendants so much on the witness stand that they lose their tempers and act guilty, even though they are innocent. It is a fundamental right of defendants, therefore, to remain silent while the prosecution attempts to prove their guilt. This is due process, and all defendants are entitled to it. Some jurors might believe that if the defendant does not take the stand and testify, then this is some sort of guilt by omission; that is, if defendants do not declare their innocence on the witness stand, an inference may be drawn that they have something to hide. This is absolutely untrue. Although all defendants have the right against self-incrimination, they also have the right to due process, which means in part that if they do not testify, this is *not* a form of incrimination. Ordinarily, judges read jury instructions to jurors and highlight this fact so that jurors must not and cannot consider a defendant's refusal to testify as evidence of their guilt. In fact, *no* inferences may be drawn by jurors about the defendant's guilt or innocence when the defendant does not testify.

However, defense attorneys are seldom content to allow the prosecutors' allegations to go unchallenged. A vigorous defense is expected from any competent defense attorney. But most frequently these defenses are designed to explain away the case prosecutors have crafted against the accused. As we have seen, defense attorneys may provide jurors with alternative explanations for why the crime occurred and who might have committed the crime. But when there is direct evidence that a defendant committed the crime, the defense must act aggressively here as well. Under these circumstances, when criminal conduct is alleged, the defense attempts to counter the criminal charges with one or more **defenses to criminal conduct**. Defenses to criminal conduct are also known as **affirmative defenses**. These defenses include automatism, intoxication, coercion or duress, necessity, alibi, entrapment, defense of property, ignorance or mistake, and self-defense.

Automatism and/or Insanity

The defense of **automatism** says that defendants were incapable of formulating criminal intent because they blacked out or were acting unconsciously. For example, the defendant may sleepwalk and commit the crime of breaking or entering by entering the home of another when he thinks he is entering his own home. The *mens rea* or guilty mind is eliminated as a criminal element.

Insanity is occasionally raised in criminal cases. **Insanity** is defined different ways among U.S. jurisdictions. Usually, it means acting under an irresistible impulse, an inability to conform one's conduct to the requirements of the law, a mental disease or defect, and not knowing the difference between right and wrong. If the defendant was not sane when the crime was committed, then the *mens rea* component of a crime can be overcome. Therefore, a crime is not committed.

When John Hinckley shot and wounded President Ronald Reagan and James Brady in 1981, for example, he was charged with attempted murder. His defense counsel raised the **insanity defense**, claiming that Hinckley was not sane at the time he attempted to kill President Reagan. The act itself was never denied. Hinckley was acquitted, largely because of the great burden on the prosecution to prove Hinckley was sane when he committed these crimes. The public and various state legislatures were incensed over Hinckley's acquittal and sought to reform existing insanity provisions in courts. Currently, most states and the federal government have adopted the guilty but mentally ill plea, in which it is no longer the burden of the prosecution to show that one is sane.

Intoxication

Intoxication is often raised in criminal cases to show that the defendant was not fully capable when the crime was committed. However, intoxication rarely excuses criminal conduct. Intoxication may be used to show that certain elements of the crime may not be present. For instance, in premeditated murder cases, the intoxication of the defendant may help the defense show that the defendant was not capable of premeditating the crime. States differ in the weight given to intoxication as a way of negating criminal intent.

In Tennessee, for instance, Wayne Adkins was charged with and convicted of first-degree murder in the death of Junior Adams (*State v. Adkins,* 1983). Witnesses testifying about what they saw said that Adkins had consumed a case of beer shortly before the shooting and was drunk when he killed Adams. The jury recommended the death penalty nevertheless. The Tennessee State Supreme Court set aside the death penalty, however, and ruled that Adkins was not capable of premeditating the murder as the result of intoxication. This holding is not necessarily indicative of how other state supreme courts might rule on similar issues.

Coercion or Duress

When people act under **coercion** or **duress**, they feel compelled to act in certain ways to avoid harm from others. In youth gang activities, for instance, the gang may pressure younger members of the gang to commit crimes. The older gang members may threaten younger gang members with bodily harm. "We will beat you up, maybe even kill you, if you don't steal these things from the store," the gang might say to younger gang members. Thus, when the younger gang members commit theft and are caught, they may claim duress. They allege that the gang made them do it or else.

In another case involving duress, two female inmates held in a California minimum-security prison were charged with escape when they walked away from the prison. They fled the prison when they were threatened by other inmates, lesbians, with physical harm if they did not submit to sexual advances. Later, when the women were free of the prison and the circumstances that might have caused them physical harm, they surrendered themselves to local law enforcement authorities. They claimed duress resulting from the threats of lesbian inmates. They were convicted of escape in a lower California court, but an appellate court set their conviction aside, accepting their defense of duress as valid (*California v. Lovercamp,* 1974). This does not mean that prisoners are always entitled to flee from their prison confines if they feel threatened by other prisoners. Each case must be resolved on an individual basis. However, in this California case, duress was successfully used. Thus, if a defendant is made to perform conduct that is criminal, duress or coercion may be an affirmative defense to remove it from criminal conduct.

Necessity

In 1996, a man was arrested in Minot, North Dakota, for breaking and entering a car dealership. However, his case was dismissed during trial when he cited necessity as the reason for his actions. In his case, he was driving a car toward Minot from Bismarck when a storm struck. The powerful snow and winds caused a whiteout, and he could not see the road in front of him. During this blizzard, his car slid off the road, and he was stranded. He knew that he must seek shelter or die. He walked in the blizzard for about a mile, finally coming to a large automobile dealership on the outskirts of Minot. He broke a window to gain entry into the facility and climbed into an automobile on the showroom floor to keep warm. Employees found him asleep in one of the showroom cars a day later, when the storm subsided. They called police, and he was arrested. His defense of **necessity** was accepted as valid by the court. He was merely trying to save his life.

Alibi

Defendants who claim an alibi intend to show that they were somewhere else when the crime was committed. Thus, if a crime is committed in St. Louis, Missouri, at 10:00 P.M. on a Monday night, and the defendant can show that he or she was in New York City at 10:00 P.M. on that same Monday evening, the witnesses who testify to that fact provide the defendant with an alibi. Depending upon the veracity or truthfulness of these other witnesses, an **alibi** defense is a strong defense to criminal conduct.

Entrapment

Entrapment occurs whenever a defendant is lured into criminal conduct by another. Usually, the conduct is something that is extraordinary for the defendant, and not conduct that is normally a routine or practice. Law enforcement officers often seek to induce people to commit a crime so that they can make an arrest. Female officers pose as prostitutes in an effort to arrest those seeking to buy sexual favors. Many prospective customers of prostitutes are thus snared in police stings. However, sometimes the police go out of their way to encourage others to violate the law. They may knock on motel doors until they find someone willing to invite the officer-prostitute in for sex. This aggressive policing often leads to charges of entrapment, in which customer-defendants are lured into committing acts they do not ordinarily contemplate.

A high-profile example of entrapment was the case of John DeLorean, an automobile manufacturer. DeLorean was becoming financially destitute after his attempt to market a particular type of automobile was unsuccessful. Desperately in need of operating capital, DeLorean was susceptible to undercover police suggestions that he purchase a large quantity of cocaine for resale. The profits from the resale of cocaine, according to undercover police officers, would be sufficient to bail out DeLorean and save his failing automobile company. DeLorean succumbed to their suggestions and arranged for the purchase of a large quantity of cocaine. DeLorean was videotaped purchasing cocaine from these undercover officers and charged with possessing cocaine for resale. However, his attorney raised the defense of entrapment. The jury agreed with DeLorean and acquitted him of the criminal charges. They believed that he had been illegally entrapped by police in the cocaine sale. If one is entrapped, then one is not guilty of criminal conduct.

Defense of Property

Defense of property can sometimes be cited as an excuse for criminal conduct. If someone attempts to steal one's car, for example, a defendant is entitled to use reasonable force to deter criminals from committing this crime. Although deadly force is never an acceptable defense of property, it is plausible that a defendant might engage in aggravated assault to discourage criminals from stealing her or his valuables. Thus, more than a few defendants have been acquitted of criminal charges when they have been able to demonstrate that they were merely defending their property when they attacked their attackers.

Ignorance or Mistake

The old adage that ignorance is no excuse is applicable here to a degree. The fact that someone does not know what the law is regarding a certain type of conduct should reduce the seriousness of whatever they do. People who visit foreign countries, for instance, may not know what the laws of the foreign country are. They may unwittingly violate a criminal law by engaging in conduct that might be acceptable in their own country.

In certain cultures, for example, it is customary to remove the clitoris of all female children. This ritual is condoned and socially and religiously approved. However, it is against the law in the United States for such a procedure to be performed. In California and other states, some people have been prosecuted for performing these rituals. Thus, the courts have had to weigh the religious and cultural significance of these illegal rituals and their legality in other countries.

Mistake or ignorance may be acceptable under other conditions. For example, Morrissette was a hunter who routinely hunted on an army artillery range. It seems that this particular artillery range, although enclosed by a perimeter wire fence, was considered a good deer-hunting area by local hunters. Furthermore, a section of the army post wire fence had been cut away so that private citizens could drive their trucks through to more easily hunt deer. One afternoon, Morrissette drove his truck into the military artillery range and hunted deer. After a long, unsuccessful afternoon of deer hunting, Morrissette was about to leave when he spied a pile of copper artillery shell casings. Weeds had grown up around the pile of copper shell casings, and it appeared to Morrissette that these casings, some of which were rusting away, had been abandoned. Morrissette loaded the shell casings into his truck and sold them subsequently at a local flea market for their metal value. With the money, he went to a bar and treated his friends to several rounds of drinks. Nearby enlisted men from the military post overheard Morrissette brag about the copper shell casings he had found, and he was reported to police, who arrested him for theft of military property. He was convicted, but he appealed, arguing that he did not know that he was stealing government property when he took the copper shell casings. In this instance, the appellate court believed Morrissette and overturned his conviction. However, this is a relatively rare instance of a court accepting ignorance or mistake as an excuse for otherwise criminal conduct.

Self-Defense

If someone commits a crime and raises the affirmative defense of **self-defense**, it must be shown that the conduct was justified because the defendant believed his or her life was in jeopardy. Self-defense is often raised in homicide cases. If the facts are unclear, a murder charge may be filed against the defendant. Later in court, the defendant raises self-defense as the explanation for the conduct. The trial provides the factual forum, where witnesses and others testify about what happened. If the defendant persuades the jury that the only course of action available was to kill the aggressor and eliminate the threat, then the jury will acquit the defendant of the murder charge. Self-defense is always a good defense to this type of criminal conduct if there is sufficient factual information to back up that particular defense.

Summary

Defense attorneys are important components of the courtroom work group. They must work closely with prosecutors and judges in an effort to ensure that their clients are adequately represented. The American Bar Association and other professional organizations have promulgated various standards of ethical responsibility. One of these standards is the ABA Model Code of Professional Responsibility. Nine canons of ethics relate to how attorneys should conduct themselves and relate to their clients and others. Attorneys must observe the privilege of confidentiality between themselves and their clients.

Defense counsel are expected to defend their clients aggressively and in a competent manner. All criminal defendants are entitled to counsel, although there is no constitutional provision that entitles defendants to the most expensive defense. Defense counsel are expected to provide their best advice to clients, negotiate with prosecutors, and use all legal means at their disposal to challenge the credibility of the prosecutor's case.

Many criminal clients are indigent and require court-appointed counsel. Several systems have evolved over the years for assigning counsel to indigents: the public defender system, the assigned counsel system, and the contract system. Several criticisms have been directed at those who defend indigents. These criticisms suggest that indigent clients do not receive effective assistance of counsel from public defenders. However, research shows that in many instances the quality of representation from court-appointed counsel is comparable with that of private attorneys who are hired to represent affluent criminal clients. Under some conditions, criminal defendants may choose to represent themselves. Self-representation is a right and is considered a *pro se* action, although most attorneys and judges do not recommend it.

Defense counsel must work closely with prosecutors and interact on a daily basis with other members of the courtroom work group. When representing criminal clients, defense attorneys are entitled access to information and evidence obtained by the prosecutor's office. This is a process known as discovery.

Among the strategies used by defense counsel to absolve their clients of criminal intent and nullify prosecution arguments that suggest their clients have committed crimes, defense counsel may argue that their clients are insane and did not know what they were doing. They may argue that their clients were intoxicated, were acting under coercion or duress, or were acting out of necessity. Some defense attorneys have used alibi, entrapment, defense of property, self-defense, and ignorance or mistake to show that their clients did not commit crimes intentionally. These are known as affirmative defenses and are used to negate either the *mens rea* or *actus reus* as components of criminal conduct. The *actus reus* is the overt criminal act.

KEY TERMS

ABA Model Code
    of Professional
    Responsibility
Affirmative defenses
Alibi
Assigned counsel
    system
Attorney–client
    confidentiality and
    privilege
Attorney competence
Automatism
Brady materials
Brady violation
Burden of proof
Canons of Professional
    Ethics
Circumstantial evidence
Coercion

Conclusive evidence
Contract system
Corroboration
Courtroom work
    group
Defense counsel
Defense of property
Defenses to criminal
    conduct
Demonstrative evidence
Derivative evidence
Direct evidence
Discovery
Duress
Entrapment
Evidence
Evidentiary
Habeas corpus petition
Indigent defendants

Ineffective assistance of
    counsel
Insanity
Insanity defense
Intoxication
Jencks materials
Jury trial
Lie detectors
Mistake
Necessity
Petty offenses
Pickpocketing
Polygraph tests
Pro se
Public defender system
Self-defense
Self-representation
State bar associations
Subornation of perjury

QUESTIONS FOR REVIEW

1. What are five defenses to criminal conduct? Explain in each case how each might be used.

2. What are the general rules governing discovery? What is discovery, and what are its purposes?

3. Under what circumstances are criminal defendants entitled to an attorney? Under what circumstances are defendants entitled to a jury trial? What are some leading legal cases having to do with the right to counsel and to jury trials?

4. What is meant by ineffective assistance of counsel? What are some leading cases in which ineffectiveness of counsel is defined?

5. What are some major canons of ethics that are part of the ABA Model Code of Professional Responsibility? Why are they important?

6. What is meant by the courtroom work group, and who are its key components? Why is it important for defense attorneys to work closely with the courtroom work group?

7. Name several forms of legal aid for indigent defendants.

8. Are court-appointed counsel as effective as privately retained counsel at representing criminal defendants? Why or why not? Explain.

9. Compare the assigned counsel system with the contract system. What are the benefits of each?

10. What is meant by defense misconduct? What are some different forms of defense misconduct?

11. What is meant by subornation of perjury?

12. What is meant by a Brady violation?

13. Who bears the burden of proof in criminal prosecutions? Under due process, what can be assumed about the guilt or innocence of the accused?

14. Can defendants be convicted of crimes solely on the basis of circumstantial evidence? Why or why not? Explain. Give an example.

SUGGESTED READINGS

Beck, James C. and Robert Shumsky. (1997). "A Comparison of Retained and Appointed Counsel in Cases of Capital Murder." *Law and Human Behavior* 21:525–538.

Becker, Ronald F. (2000). *Criminal Investigation.* Gaithersburg, MD: Aspen.

Hanson, Roger A. et al. (1992). *Indigent Defenders Get the Job Done and Done Well.* Williamsburg, VA: National Center for State Courts.

Wessler, Stephen. (2000). *Addressing Hate Crimes: Six Initiatives That Are Enhancing the Efforts of Criminal Justice Practitioners.* Washington, DC: U.S. Bureau of Justice Assistance.

JUDGES

IT HAPPENED IN URBANA, ILLINOIS. On Tuesday, April 8, 1997, a man threw a fire-bomb at a judge during a medical malpractice trial. An explosion caused a fire that sent many attendees scampering for the exits. At least four people were injured by the explosion. A juror, Abra Bonnell, said that a man simply walked into the courtroom during the trial. He had a bottle filled with an amber liquid. He lit a rag sticking out of the top of the bottle, threw it at the bench, and ran from the courtroom. "It was pretty obvious that he was aiming the [bomb] at the judge," said Bonnell. "We all smelled gas, and everyone just left the jury box screaming." Although she didn't see a burst of fire, she did smell the smoke as she left the burning courtroom. No information was readily available about the bomber or his motives. Who ever said that being a judge was a soft job? (*Source:* Adapted from the Associated Press, "Man Throws Bomb at Judge." *Minot* (N.D.) *Daily News,* April 9, 1997:A5.)

IT HAPPENED IN BISMARCK, NORTH DAKOTA. A 21-year-old man, David V. Anderson, was arrested after allegedly engaging in various sex acts with a 12-year-old girl. Anderson was a first offender, but he was labeled a sexual predator after extensive psychological and psychiatric examinations and tests. Anderson's lawyer cut a deal with the state's prosecutor, and they agreed that if Anderson would plead guilty to having sex with a 12-year-old girl, the prosecutor would recommend an 8½-year sentence, with 4½ years suspended. When Judge James Vukelic saw the plea agreement, he rejected it outright. He sentenced Anderson to 8 years in prison, to be followed by 10 years of probation. During the probationary period, Anderson would be monitored closely, and his activities would be greatly restricted. The judge said, "I think the sentence recommended here doesn't go far enough." Consulting a thick presentence investigation report submitted by a probation officer, Judge Vukelic said, "I don't find anything in here in your favor. Another thing that jumped out at me [in the reports] is how easy it is for you to find victims. We naively assume here in North Dakota that kids are safe." Anderson further admitted to raping young boys. He had previously been prosecuted in juvenile court on these charges, and his admissions were admitted into his present court record. Judge Vukelic said that Anderson had resisted treatment for sex offenders and had little or no control over his sexual impulses. He also said that Anderson seemed to derive great pleasure from his ability to control his victims. The judge worried that the sex offender treatment wouldn't be successful in Anderson's case, but he ordered Anderson to undergo it anyway at the Bismarck State Penitentiary where Anderson would be confined. (*Source:* Adapted from Associated Press, "Judge Doubles Prosecution's Request." *Minot* (N.D.) *Daily News,* September 6, 1996:A3.)

IT HAPPENED IN FORT LUPTON, COLORADO. After seven teenagers were arrested for disturbing the peace with their loud music, Municipal Judge Paul Sacco decided to impose an innovative punishment. All convicted teens were ordered to meet once a month, on a weekend night, and listen to music, with a policeman as a DJ. This doesn't sound like much of a punishment. However, the music selections and the circumstances under which they are played may make a good case for cruel and unusual punishment. The music is largely lounge music, including hits from Wayne Newton, some Navajo flute music, and John Denver songs. One of the judge's own compositions, "I'm Sleeping with My Car," was featured, as was the theme song from the television show *Barney.* The terms of listening to this court-ordered music once a week include no laughter, no dancing, no bouncing, and no talking. The policeman who performs the DJ work, Joe Morales, says, "There's something annoying for everyone, and it works." Morales recalled one youth he had trouble with three or four times for disturbing the peace: "He came here once and he hasn't been back." (*Source:* Adapted from the Associated Press, "Judge Punishes Noise Offenders with Music." *Minot* (N.D.) *Daily News,* March 6, 1999:A2.)

IN 1995, A CONGRESSIONAL STUDY was planned to investigate the effectiveness of the federal judiciary in how they perform their jobs. A self-administered questionnaire was to be mailed to all federal court judges, seeking detailed information about the amount of time these judges actually devote to official tasks. Chief Justice William H. Rehnquist most vigorously opposed this study. "There can be no doubt that answers to some form of such questions could aid Congress in making decisions about judicial salaries, permitted outside income from teaching, creating new judgeships, and filling existing vacancies. There can also be no doubt that the subject matter of the questions and the detail required for answering them could amount to an unwarranted and ill-considered effort to micromanage the work of the federal judiciary." Rehnquist hoped that the committee's inquiries were designed to obtain information that was the legitimate prerogative of Congress without infringing on judicial independence. Congressional leaders defended their study by saying that their purpose was simply to initiate dialogue between Congress and members of the judiciary. (*Source:* Associated Press, "Rehnquist: Congress Threatens Justice." *Minot* (N.D.) *Daily News,* January 1, 1996:A1.)

IT HAPPENED IN YOUNGSTOWN, OHIO. Cheryl Richard, 24, was found guilty of drug use in a local municipal court. Because Richard was nine months' pregnant with her fourth child, Municipal Court Judge Patrick V. Kerrigan gave her the choice of either three months in jail, a $750 fine, and two years' probation or a sterilization operation. In the latter scenario, Richard would still be placed on probation for two years and required to have counseling. Cheryl Richard elected to have the sterilization operation. The judge said, "I'm not punishing her for her lifestyle, but I'm recognizing she can't seem to break out of crime and drug dependency unless some drastic measures are taken." Richard waived her right to an attorney and pleaded guilty in early February 1995 to two counts of possession of crack cocaine pipes and one count each of disorderly conduct and possession of marijuana. Richard told Judge Kerrigan that she used cocaine regularly. (*Source:* Adapted from Associated Press, "Woman Chooses Sterilization over Jail." *Minot* (N.D.) *Daily News,* February 12, 1995:A2.)

IN MEMPHIS, TENNESSEE, Judge Joe Brown dispenses justice daily to a variety of low-level law-breakers. Judge Brown has his own television program, *Judge Joe Brown,* which is syndicated throughout the United States. Brown's career in television began when he was interviewed by Ted Koppel on ABC's *Nightline.* A representative from the *Judge Judy* show happened to be watching and sent a producer to observe him in his courtroom. Peter Brennan, a producer, says that Brown has a dynamic anger, rising from his bench like a gale force of wind. Impressed with Brown's courtroom demeanor, Brennan and others offered Brown a chance to star in his own television show. Twice a month, Judge Brown flies to Los Angeles, where he tapes ten different court cases a day. He earns about $10,000 for each week of shows. What is interesting about Judge Brown is his approach to justice. He dispenses what is known as alternative sentencing, which is growing in popularity as a nontraditional, nonincarcerative alternative to costly imprisonment. In one case, Judge Brown was listening to a woman who was facing minor drug charges. The woman had 11 children and was pregnant again. Judge Brown: "What's wrong with you, fool? Why didn't you use birth control?" Instead of sending the woman to jail, Judge Brown referred her to classes to learn parenting skills and earn a GED. She also had to write a 150-page essay on birth control and give him installments every time she came to court for a monthly status review. "I don't care about grammar," Brown said. "But you will give me a report."

Through the Freedom of Information Act, Judge Brown and the show's producers gain access to small claims court cases and find plaintiffs and defendants who agree to be tried by Brown. In exchange, the producers pay all of the expenses incurred by both parties, and participants also receive a $150 appearance fee. Thus, the program works out well for everyone concerned. Not everyone takes the show up on the offer, however. Some people don't want their cases aired on national television.

Judge Brown says that he had a tough time growing up in Los Angeles. His parents were both schoolteachers and taught him never to do something just because someone else was doing it. Brown also had to reckon with unfair teachers in school. He said that one teacher flunked him on an examination and told him that the exam was too good for him to have written; therefore, the teacher said, Brown must have cheated. Brown said, "If you were black, they assumed you were stupid." But Brown changed the minds of teachers by the end of his sophomore year, when he made the dean's list. Brown was elected to the bench in 1990 in Memphis. He was re-elected in 1998, when his television show began. Brown has been through a divorce and had to raise two sons, and he admits, "My interpersonal relationships have not been the best." But today, Brown says that he can moralize to his heart's content on television. He has always wanted to make a difference, and that is his motivation in life. He's not interested in the money or the notoriety. He believes his role as judge is to teach personal responsibility to adults and, more important, to children. The main thing, as far as Judge Brown is concerned, is that people must promote their neighborhood and make it economically viable and safe. (*Source:* Adapted from Ponchitta Pierce, "Jail Isn't Always the Best Option." *Parade Magazine,* April 4, 1999:22.)

Introduction

There are many kinds of judges with diverse **judicial powers**. The public has general conceptions about judges and what they are supposed to do, but many of these conceptions are actually misconceptions. This chapter examines judges and their qualifications. Not all judges have the same degree of legal expertise, nor are all judges lawyers. They differ greatly in their personalities and idiosyncrasies, and they have many prejudices and limitations. How all these people become judges in the different jurisdictions is described in this chapter.

In recent years, the judiciary has come under close scrutiny by various interests and agencies, and some evidence of judicial misconduct has surfaced. Different forms of judicial misconduct and abuses of discretionary powers are presented in this chapter.

Judges and Their Qualifications

In any courtroom, the key figure is the **judge**, who makes decisions that affect the lives of defendants. All judges have certain rules to follow that are an integral feature of **judicial process**. Sometimes judges make decisions that are reversed by higher courts. A judge may allow the introduction of incriminating evidence against a defendant, or the judge may decide to exclude such evidence. The judge decides what is or is not relevant testimony. Overall, the judge controls the conduct of all trials.

It is a common misconception among citizens that all judges are lawyers and have legal expertise. However, in numerous jurisdictions throughout the United States, many judges have no legal training. For instance, among the 2,000 judges who served in the various townships and villages in New York State in 1980, 1,600 were not lawyers. Only 400 of these passed the New York State bar exam (Zimmerman, 1981:265–268). Similar distributions of nonlawyer judges can be found in most other states (Provine, 1986). One implication is that, in many jurisdictions, judicial selection is more a matter of politics than of judicial expertise. The political nature of judicial selection has its roots in seventeenth-century England (Volcansek, 1990). Table 5.1 shows qualification requirements for judges in state appellate and trial courts of general jurisdiction.

In 1998, the minimum age for appellate and trial court judgeships ranged from eighteen to thirty (Maguire and Pastore, 2000:66–67). The minimum age requirements shown in Table 5.1 are somewhat deceptive because it might appear that an eighteen-year-old can qualify as an appellate or trial court judge. States with these minimum age provisions eliminate this possibility by requiring that their prospective judges have been

TABLE 5.1 Selected Qualification Requirements of Judges of Appellate and Trial Courts of General Jurisdiction, by Type of Court and Jurisdiction, as of January 1, 1998

Jurisdiction	U.S. Citizenship		Years of Minimum Residence				Minimum Age		Member of State Bar (years)		Other	
			In State		In District							
	Appellate	Trial	Appellate	Trial	Appellate	Trial	Appellate	Trial	Appellate	Trial	Appellate	Trial
Alabama	(a)	(a)	5[b]	5[b]		1	25	25				
Alaska	Y	Y	5[b]	5[b]					Y[c]	Y[c]		
Arizona			10[d]	5	(e,f)	1	30	30	10[d]	5	(g,h)	(g,h)
Arkansas	Y	Y	2	2			30	28	(i,j)	(i,j)	(g)	(g)
California									10[j]	10[j]		
Colorado			(f)			(f)			5	5	(h)	(h)
Connecticut							18	18	10	10		
Delaware			(b)	(b)					(i)	(i)		
Florida			(f)	(f)	Y[k]	Y[k]			10	5	(h)	(h)
Georgia	(a)	(a)	Y[k]	3[b]				30	7	7		
Hawaii	Y	Y	Y[b,k]	Y[b,k]					10	10		
Idaho	Y	Y	2	1		(f)	30	30	10	10		
Illinois	Y	Y	Y[k]	Y[k]	Y[k]	Y[k]			Y[k]	Y[k]		
Indiana	Y	Y			Y[k]	Y[k]			10[j]	Y[k]		
Iowa									Y[k]			
Kansas						Y[k]	30	30	Y[k,j]	Y[j,k]		
Kentucky	Y	Y	2	2	2	2			8	8		
Louisiana			2	2	2	2			5	5		
Maine					(l)				(i)	(i)		
Maryland			5[b,f]	5[b,f]	(l)	(l)	30	30	Y[k]	Y[k]	(g)	(g)
Michigan			(f)	(f)	(f)	(f)			Y[k]	Y[k]	(g)	(g)
Minnesota									Y[i,k]	Y[i,k]		
Mississippi			5[b]	5[b]			30	26	5	5	(h)	(h)
Missouri	(a)	(a)	(f)	(f)	Y[k]		30	30	Y[k]	Y[k]		
Montana	Y	Y	2	2		1		30	5	5		

(continued)

101

TABLE 5.1 (continued)

Jurisdiction	U.S. Citizenship Appellate	U.S. Citizenship Trial	In State Appellate	In State Trial	In District Appellate	In District Trial	Minimum Age Appellate	Minimum Age Trial	Member of State Bar (years) Appellate	Member of State Bar (years) Trial	Other Appellate	Other Trial
Nebraska	Y	Y	3		Y[f,k]	Y[k]	30	30	5[j]	5[j]		
Nevada			2[f]	2[f]			25	25	Y[k]			
New Hampshire											(m)	(m)
New Jersey				(n)		(n)			10	10		
New Mexico			3	3		Y[k]	35	35	10[i,j]	6[i,j]		
New York			Y[k]	Y[k]			18	18	10	10		
North Carolina						Y[k]			Y[k]	Y[k]		
North Dakota	Y		Y[k]	Y[k]		Y[k]			Y[i,k]	Y[i,k]		
Ohio			(f)	Y[k]	(f)	Y[k]	30		6[j]	6[j]	(h)	(h)
Oklahoma			(f)		(f)	(f)			5[j]	4[j]		
Oregon	Y	Y	3	3		1			Y[k]	Y[k]		
Pennsylvania	Y	Y	1[b]	1[b]		Y[k]			Y[k]	Y[k]		
Rhode Island							21					
South Carolina	Y	Y	5[b]	5[b]			26	26	5	5		
South Dakota	Y	Y	Y[k]	Y[k]	Y[f,k]	Y[f,k]			Y[k]	Y[k]		
Tennessee			5[b]	5		1	35[o]	30	Y[i,k]	Y[i,k]		
Texas	Y	Y	(b)	(b)	(e)	2	35		Y[j,k]	Y[j,k]		
Utah	Y	Y	5[p]	3		Y[k]	30[q]	25	Y[k]	Y[k]		
Vermont			5	5					Y[j,k]	Y[j,k]		
Virginia			Y[k]	Y[k]	Y[k]	Y[k]			5	5		
Washington			1	1	1				Y[k,r]	Y[k]		
West Virginia			5	Y[k]		1	30	30	10[j]	Y[j,k]		
Wisconsin			(s)	(s)	(s)	(s)			5	5		
Wyoming	Y	Y	3	2			30	28	9[i,j]	(i)		

102

District of Columbia	Y	Y		(t)	(t)	5[j]	5[j]	(u)
Northern Mariana Islands	Y				30	5[j]	(i)	
Puerto Rico	Y	Y	5		25	10	Y[j,k]	

"Appellate" refers to judges of courts of last resort and intermediate appellate courts. "Trial" refers to judges of courts of general trial jurisdiction. In some instances, information on the length of time for residency and legal experience requirements was not supplied. There are no qualification requirements for judges in Massachusetts. In the table, "Y" indicates that the requirement applies.

[a]Citizen of the United States. Alabama—5 years, Georgia—3 years, Missouri—15 years for appellate court, 10 years for trial courts.

[b]Citizen of the state.

[c]Length of time as member of state bar not specified but must have been engaged in active practice of law for a specific number of years: 8 years for appellate court, 5 years for trial court.

[d]For court of appeals, 5 years.

[e]For court of appeals judges only.

[f]Qualified elector. For Arizona court of appeals, must be elector of county of residence. For Michigan Supreme Court, elector in state; court of appeals, elector of appellate circuit. For Missouri supreme and appellate courts, elector for 9 years; for circuit courts, elector for 3 years. For Oklahoma Supreme Court and Court of Criminal Appeals, elector for 1 year; court of appeals and district courts, elector for 6 months. For Oregon court of appeals, qualified elector in county.

[g]Specific personal characteristics. Arizona, Arkansas—good moral character. Maine—sobriety of manners. Maryland—integrity, wisdom, and sound legal knowledge.

[h]Nominee must be under certain age to be eligible. Arizona—under 70 years. Colorado—under 72 years, except when name is submitted for vacancy. Florida—under 70 years, except upon temporary assignment or to complete a term. Michigan, Ohio—under 70 years.

[i]Learned in law.

[j]Years as a practicing lawyer and/or service on bench of court of record in state may satisfy requirement. Arkansas—appellate: 8 years; trial: 6 years. Indiana—10 years admitted to practice or must have served as a circuit, superior, or criminal court judge in the state for at least 5 years. Kansas—appellate: 10 years; trial: 5 years. Texas—appellate: 10 years; trial: 4 years. Vermont—5 of 10 years preceding appointment. West Virginia—appellate: 10 years; trial: 5 years. Puerto Rico—appellate: 10 years; trial: 5 years.

[k]Length of time not specified.

[l]6 months.

[m]Record of birth is required.

[n]There are 260 restricted superior court judgeships that require residence within the county at time of appointment and reappointment. There are 144 unrestricted judgeships for which assignment of county is made by the chief justice.

[o]30 years for judges of court of appeals and court of criminal appeals.

[p]Supreme court is 5 years; court of appeals is 3 years.

[q]Supreme court is 30 years; court of appeals is 25 years.

[r]For court of appeals, admitted to practice for 5 years.

[s]10 days.

[t]90 days.

[u]Superior court judges must also have 5 years of legal government practice or serve as law school faculty.

Source: Maguire and Pastore, 2000:66–67.

members of the state bar association for five or ten years or longer, which disqualifies these young prospective judges.

About half of the states in 1998 did not require U.S. citizenship for appellate or trial judge posts. The years of residence within the state to qualify for a judicial post varied from one to ten years, and several states had no provisions for minimum residence times for either appellate or trial court judges (Maguire and Pastore, 2000:66). Some states specified personal characteristics as qualifications, including good moral character, sobriety of manners, integrity, wisdom, and sound legal knowledge.

THE POLITICIZATION OF JUDICIAL SELECTION. The politicization of the judicial selection process cannot be overstated. When politics is the dominating factor in judicial appointments, a candidate's qualifications for a judgeship are practically irrelevant. Whether a partisan election or a gubernatorial or presidential appointment leads to a judgeship, the result is often a judicial appointment that reflects party politics rather than professional qualities for deciding cases fairly. Political judicial appointees are not incapable of being fair in judging cases; rather, they are expected to adhere to a fixed political agenda associated with the party that places them in power (Pinello, 1995).

Political influence works to the detriment of women in judicial appointments. Gender bias has been found in systems in which judges are appointed by politicians and women are routinely excluded from judicial consideration (Missouri Task Force on Gender and Justice, 1993).

Several critics argue that political appointments of judges place too much power in the hands of the appointer, such as the governor or president (Swain, 1985). Politically appointed judges have considerably lower levels of accountability, and weak sanctioning mechanisms are in place for their discipline or removal. Those who oppose election of judges say that voter apathy and lack of interest, political influence, and a general lack of information about candidates and their qualifications make this process meaningless. During the first term of the Reagan administration (1980–1984), approximately ninety-seven percent of all federal judicial appointments were Republicans, a higher partisanship level than the previous five presidential administrations. Fewer than one percent of these judicial appointments were black; only nine percent were women (Goldman, 1985).

Earlier, President Jimmy Carter had created nominating commissions for federal circuit courts and district courts. Under the Carter administration, judicial appointees were more likely to have professional experience, to be older and have more years at the bar, to have acquired a legal education, and to receive higher American Bar Association ratings than subsequent Reagan appointees (Fowler, 1984). Subsequently, President Reagan discontinued the nominating commission method of judicial appointments.

Nominating commissions have identified the following criteria for their judicial selections: age, communication skills, health, industry, integrity, judicial temperament, justice (e.g., impartiality, fairness, objectivity), professional skills, and social consciousness (American Judicature Society, 1983). However, no precise guidelines have been established to indicate how these qualities should be measured or assessed. There is historical precedent for these ambiguities in the judicial selection process. In early England, for example, much secrecy was involved in the process by which judges were selected (Pickles, 1987). Judicial selection criteria were purposely diffuse and ambiguous, so that only con-

HERE COMES THE JUDGE

The Case of Judge Justin Weaver

Justin Weaver is the Honorable Justice Justin Weaver, of Randolph, New York. Weaver became judge as the result of a town election to fill of a judicial vacancy. He did no campaigning. He did not even tell most people that he was running for the judgeship. In fact, he was a write-in candidate. Justin Weaver, a twenty-one-year-old college dropout with no legal training, wrote in his own name on the ballot during the election in Randolph and won the election in a 1–0 vote! Justin was floored. However, he is determined to be the best judge he can be, even taking a crash course on his new job, a six-day state training course for new judges. However, he may have to get himself a lawyer. The town has offered to pay him only $30 a week, compared with the former judge's salary of $166 a week. Some people in the community say that Weaver should resign, but he's not about to. After all, he voted.

Source: Adapted from Barbara Runnette, "Unlearned Hand." *People,* February 24, 1996:41.

servative types of people could hold judicial posts. These judges were often manipulated by politically influential constituencies (Pickles, 1987). Further, men have dominated the legal profession in England and the United States in past years (Sachs and Wilson, 1978).

In some jurisdictions, guidelines assist judges in learning about courtroom protocol and the diverse functions of courtroom personnel. For instance, the National Center for State Courts in Williamsburg, Virginia, has produced a resource manual that is designed to enhance the performance of trial judges (Hewitt, 1995). The manual includes a discussion of terminology interpretation, judicial training issues, and general court interpreter services.

Reform movements in judicial selection are not new (American Judicature Society, 1971; Hoff, 1969). Aggressive court reforms have been undertaken for many decades, as different waves of state and federal judges have manifested characteristics that suggest inexperience and ineffectiveness (Flango and Ducat, 1979; Powell, 1980; Uppal, 1974). Many formal recruitment and judicial selection systems have been proposed, but relatively few have come up with any conclusive data indicating the kinds of qualitative differences that might result from alternative selection systems (Canon, 1972; Klein and Wilztum, 1973). Interviews with judges themselves suggest mixed reactions to any type of selection system, whether it is through appointment or election (Sheldon, 1971).

State Judicial Selection Methods

Judges are either appointed or elected (Dubois, 1990). Alfini (1981:253) has identified five methods of judicial selection as basic variations on appointments or elections: partisan election, nonpartisan election, gubernatorial appointment, selection through the merit plan, and legislative appointments.

PARTISAN ELECTIONS. **Partisan elections** of judges are the same as elections for other public offices. Democrats, Republicans, and other parties advance their own slate of candidates for various offices, including judicial vacancies. The public votes for their choice by secret ballot. The winners become judges for a fixed term, such as four years. In 1999, the following eight states used partisan elections for selecting the highest appellate judges: Alabama, Arkansas, Illinois, Louisiana, North Carolina, Pennsylvania, Texas, and West Virginia (Maguire and Pastore, 2000:69–70).

NONPARTISAN ELECTIONS. In **nonpartisan elections**, candidates are simply listed to fill judicial vacancies, regardless of their political affiliation. In 1999, thirteen states used nonpartisan elections to fill the highest appellate court posts: Georgia, Idaho, Kentucky, Michigan, Minnesota, Mississippi, Montana, Nevada, North Dakota, Ohio, Oregon, Washington, and Wisconsin (Maguire and Pastore, 2000:69–70).

PROBLEMS WITH PARTISAN AND NONPARTISAN ELECTIONS OF JUDGES. There are several problems with electing judges by popular vote. One criticism is whether either partisan or nonpartisan elections actually reflect the people's choices (Beechen, 1974). Usually, some amount of private financing is behind each judicial candidate. The slate of candidates is generated by political parties and special interest groups, regardless of whether elections are partisan or nonpartisan (Beechen, 1974; Hall, 1984). People whose names are placed on the ballot may not be those most likely to represent the interests of the general public.

Despite the partisan nature of judicial voting, there are indications of an attentive public that makes informed selections of judges in their voting booths (Sheldon and Lovrich, 1983). Interestingly, investigations of voter knowledge of the judicial selection process show that although voters may not fully understand the nature of voting reforms, they are informed about the opinions and views of the respective judicial candidates (Lovrich and Sheldon, 1984).

In some sections of the country, there is significant partisanship in public voting. For instance, in the South, the Democratic party has been successful most of the time in the promotion of partisan judicial candidates. Many incumbents in southern criminal courts have been reelected repeatedly, reflecting the public's interest in maintaining the status quo for both major and minor judgeships (Volcansek, 1983). Other areas of the country exhibit strong differences from the South, such as the moralistic and individualistic political culture of the West. Less money is spent on campaign financing for judicial elections in the West than in the South. Despite the differential impact of money spent, the overriding variable influencing the outcome of judicial elections in almost every jurisdiction was party affiliation (Volcansek, 1983).

Perhaps the most significant criticism of using elections for filling judicial vacancies is that the most popular judges may not be the most qualified judges. There are no objective criteria used to evaluate judicial qualifications. Most jurisdictions do not require judges to pass tests or engage in any qualifying competition for these important posts.

Those elected to judicial positions who lack judging experience are often sent to schools that offer crash courses on how to act like judges. These schools attempt to familiarize judges with the rules of criminal procedure and evidence associated with their jurisdictions, but it is doubtful that any such short course can instill the competence and experience to make the best decisions in important criminal cases. For better or worse, however, partisan or nonpartisan elections are prevalent in most states, and it is unlikely that these states will change their methods of judicial selection in the near future. Other methods for judicial selection, judicial appointments by executives, are equally flawed.

Appointments of Judges by Governors

In 1999, governors made the highest appellate **judicial appointments** in four states: California, Maine, New Hampshire, and New Jersey (Maguire and Pastore, 2000:69–70). Governors may or may not make use of state and local bar association recommendations for judgeships, and gubernatorial appointments are not necessarily made on the basis of which candidates are best qualified to serve. Rather, these judgeships are political appointments. Thus, major contributors to a governor's election campaign make recommendations to the governor for particular judgeships, and quite often these recommendations result in particular judges being appointed (Iowa Equality in the Courts Task Force, 1993).

In many other jurisdictions, people campaign for judgeships much as candidates run for political offices. In fact, politics accounts for the large numbers of nonlawyers in posts such as municipal judges, justices of the peace, and county court judges. There has been considerable debate about whether judges should be appointed or elected, although no judicial selection method has been found superior to others (Dubois, 1990; Feeley, 1983). Some researchers have observed that gubernatorial judicial appointments in certain jurisdictions result in racial or gender bias in judicial decision making (Louisiana Task Force on Women in the Courts, 1992).

A study was conducted in 1980–1981 of state supreme court judicial selection according to gubernatorial appointments versus merit plans. The 135 questionnaires returned by political science professors, judges, and court administrators enabled researchers to describe and compare judges selected by different methods (Glick and Emmert, 1987). Most judges selected by governors rather than the merit system tended to be born out of state, although these judges were from similar regions (e.g., Southern governors tended to appoint Southern judges, Northern governors tended to appoint Northern judges). The merit system resulted in judges who graduated from more prestigious law schools (e.g., Harvard, Yale, Columbia) than those who were appointed by governors. Protestant judges were more abundant in Southern courts, and Catholic and Jewish judges were more prevalent in Northern and Eastern courts (Glick and Emmert, 1987). One interesting outcome of this study was that merit selection tended to result in fewer appointments of women and minorities as judges. Thus, gubernatorial appointments are more likely to yield women and minority judges (Berkson and Vandenberg, 1980). Tables 5.2, 5.3, and 5.4 show the method of selection, length of term, and retention conditions of the highest state appellate court justices, intermediate appellate court judges, and judges in courts of general jurisdiction.

TABLE 5.2 Method of Selection and Length of Initial and Retention Terms of the Highest Appellate Court Justices by State, as of July 1999

State	Initial Selection		Retention	
	Method[a]	Term	Method	Term (in Years)
Alabama	Partisan election	6 years	Partisan election	6
Alaska	Nominating commission	Until next general election but not less than 3 years	Retention election	10
Arizona	Nominating commission	Until next general election but not less than 2 years	Retention selection	6
Arkansas	Partisan election	8 years	Partisan election	8
California	Appointed by governor	Until next general election	Retention election	12
Colorado	Nominating commission	Until next general election but not less than 2 years	Retention election	10
Connecticut[b]	Judicial selection commission	8 years	Commission reviews, governor renominates, legislature confirms	8
Delaware	Nominating commission	12 years	Reappointment by governor	12
District of Columbia[c]	Nominating commission	15 years	Reappointment by judicial tenure commission or president	15
Florida	Nominating commission	Until next general election but not less than 1 year	Retention election	6
Georgia	Nonpartisan election	6 years	Nonpartisan election	6
Hawaii	Nominating commission	10 years	Reappointment by commission	10
Idaho	Nonpartisan election	6 years	Nonpartisan election	6
Illinois	Partisan election	10 years	Retention election	10
Indiana	Nominating commission	Until next general election but not less than 2 years	Retention election	10
Iowa	Nominating commission	Until next general election but not less than 1 year	Retention election	8
Kansas	Nominating commission	Until next general election but not less than 1 year	Retention election	6

State	Initial selection	Term	Retention	
Kentucky	Nonpartisan election	8 years	Nonpartisan election	8
Louisiana	Partisan election[d]	10 years	Partisan election[d]	10
Maine	Appointed by governor	7 years	Reappointment by governor	7
Maryland[e]	Nominating commission	Until next general election but not less than 1 year	Retention election	10
Massachusetts	Nominating commission	To age 70	X	X
Michigan	Nonpartisan election	8 years	Nonpartisan election	8
Minnesota	Nonpartisan election	6 years	Nonpartisan election	6
Mississippi	Nonpartisan election	8 years	Nonpartisan election	8
Missouri	Nominating commission	Until next general election but not less than 1 year	Retention election	12
Montana	Nonpartisan election	8 years	Nonpartisan election, but if unopposed, retention election	8
Nebraska	Nominating commission	Until next general election but not less than 3 years	Retention election	6
Nevada	Nonpartisan election	6 years	Nonpartisan election	6
New Hampshire	Appointed by governor[f]	To age 70	X	X
New Jersey	Appointed by governor	7 years	Reappointment by governor	To age 70
New Mexico	Nominating commission	Until next general election	Partisan election for first time; after that, winner runs in retention election	8
New York[e]	Nominating commission	14 years	Reappointment by governor	14
North Carolina	Partisan election	8 years	Partisan election	8
North Dakota	Nonpartisan election	10 years	Nonpartisan election	10
Ohio[g]	Nonpartisan election	6 years	Nonpartisan election	6
Oklahoma[h]	Nominating commission	Until next general election but not less than 1 year	Retention election	6
Oregon	Nonpartisan election	6 years	Nonpartisan election	6
Pennsylvania	Partisan election	10 years	Retention election	10
Rhode Island	Nominating commission[i]	Life tenure	X	X
South Carolina	Nominating commission[i]	10	Reelected by legislature	10
South Dakota	Nominating commission	Until next general election but not less than 3 years	Retention election	8

(continued)

TABLE 5.2 (*continued*)

State	Initial Selection		Retention	
	Method[a]	Term	Method	Term (in Years)
Tennessee	Nominating commission	Until the biennial general election but not less than 30 days	Retention election	8
Texas[h]	Partisan election	6 years	Partisan election	6
Utah	Nominating commission	Until next general election but not less than 3 years	Retention election	10
Vermont	Nominating commission	6 years	Retained by vote in general assembly	6
Virginia	Elected by legislature	12 years	Reelected by legislature	12
Washington	Nonpartisan election	6 years	Nonpartisan election	6
West Virginia	Partisan election	12 years	Partisan election	12
Wisconsin	Nonpartisan election	10 years	Nonpartisan election	10
Wyoming	Nominating commission	Until next general election but not less than 1 year	Retention election	8

Note: These data were compiled through a survey of state statutes; they were then verified by personnel of the American Judicature Society.

"Initial selection" is defined as the constitutional or statutory method by which judges are selected for a full term of office. "Retention" refers to the method used to select judges for subsequent terms of office. "Partisan election" refers to elections in which the judicial candidates' names appear on the ballot with their respective party labels; "nonpartisan election" refers to the situation when no party labels are attached to judicial candidates' names on the ballot. "Retention election" refers to an election in which a judge runs unopposed on the ballot and the electorate votes solely on the question of the judge's continuation in office. In the retention election, the judge must win a majority of the vote in order to serve a full term, except in Illinois, which requires 60%, and New Mexico, which requires 57%. "Nominating commission" is a merit selection procedure that refers to the nonpartisan body, composed of lawyers and nonlawyers, which actively recruits, screens, and nominates prospective judicial candidates to the executive for appointment. The nominating commission method of selection was established by executive order in Delaware, Maryland, and Massachusetts and by constitutional or statutory authority in all other jurisdictions.

[a]In states that use nominating commissions, the governor generally makes the appointment.

[b]The judicial selection commission submits a list of prospective judges to the governor, who nominates one to fill a vacancy. The legislature then votes to approve or disapprove that nomination.

[c]Initial appointment is made by the president of the United States and confirmed by the Senate. If the president does not wish to reappoint the judge, the District of Columbia Nomination Commission compiles a new list of candidates.

[d]Although party affiliation of judicial candidates appears on ballots, judicial primaries are open. This gives judicial elections a nonpartisan character.

[e]The highest state court is named the Court of Appeals.

[f]Subject to approval of an elected five-member executive council.

[g]Ohio's primary elections are partisan, but in general elections, party affiliations are not listed on the ballot.

[h]Oklahoma and Texas have two courts of final jurisdiction: the supreme court, which has final civil jurisdiction, and the court of criminal appeals, which as final criminal jurisdiction. The selection process is the same for both.

[i]The Judicial Merit Selection Commission was established on July 1, 1997. The commission screens and then recommends a list of three judicial candidates to the legislature. The legislature votes only on the list submitted by the commission. If all candidates on the list are rejected, the process begins again with the commission.

Source: Maguire and Pastore, 2000:69–70.

TABLE 5.3 Method of Selection and Length of Initial and Retention Terms of the Intermediate Appellate Court Judges in 39 States, as of July 1999

State	Initial Selection		Retention	
	Method[a]	Term	Method	Term (in Years)
Alabama[b]	Partisan election	6 years	Partisan election	6
Alaska	Nominating commission	Until next general election but not less than 3 years	Retention election	8
Arizona	Nominating commission	Until next general election but not less than 2 years	Retention selection	6
Arkansas	Partisan election	8 years	Partisan election	8
California	Appointed by governor	Until next general election	Retention election	12
Colorado	Nominating commission	Until next general election but not less than 2 years	Retention election	8
Connecticut	Nominating commission	8 years	Commission reviews, governor renominates, legislature confirms	8
Florida	Nominating commission	Until next general election but not less than 1 year	Retention election	6
Georgia	Nonpartisan election	6 years	Nonpartisan election	6
Hawaii	Nominating commission	10 years	Reappointment by commission	10
Idaho	Nonpartisan election	6 years	Nonpartisan election	6
Illinois	Partisan election	10 years	Retention election	10
Indiana	Nominating commission	Until next general election but not less than 2 years	Retention election	10
Iowa	Nominating commission	Until next general election but not less than 1 year	Retention election	6
Kansas	Nominating commission	Until next general election but not less than 1 year	Retention election	4
Kentucky	Nonpartisan election	8 years	Nonpartisan election	8
Louisiana	Partisan election[c]	10 years	Partisan election[c]	10
Maryland	Nominating commission	Until next general election but not less than 1 year	Retention election	10

(continued)

TABLE 5.3 (*continued*)

| State | Initial Selection | | Retention | |
	Method[a]	Term	Method	Term (in Years)
Massachusetts	Nominating commission	To age 70	X	X
Michigan	Nonpartisan election	6 years	Nonpartisan election	6
Minnesota	Nonpartisan election	6 years	Nonpartisan election	6
Mississippi	Nonpartisan election	8 years	Nonpartisan election	8
Missouri	Nominating commission	Until next general election but not less than 1 year	Retention election	12
Nebraska	Nominating commission	Until next general election but not less than 3 years	Retention election	6
New Jersey	Appointed by governor	7 years	Reappointment by governor	To age 70
New Mexico	Nominating commission	Until next general election	Partisan election for first time; after that, winner runs in retention election	8
New York	Nominating commission	5 years	Reappointment by governor	5
North Carolina	Partisan election	8 years	Partisan election	8
Ohio[d]	Nonpartisan election	6 years	Nonpartisan election	6
Oklahoma	Nominating commission	Until next general election but not less than 1 year	Retention election	6
Oregon	Nonpartisan election	6 years	Nonpartisan election	6
Pennsylvania[e]	Partisan election	10 years	Retention election	10
South Carolina	Nominating commission[f]	6 years	Reelected by legislature	6
Tennessee[b]	Nominating commission	Until the biennial general election but not less than 30 days	Retention election	8
Texas	Partisan election	6 years	Partisan election	6
Utah	Nominating commission	Until next general election but not less than 3 years	Retention election	6

State			
Virginia	Elected by legislature	8 years	Reelected by legislature	8
Washington	Nonpartisan election	6 years	Nonpartisan election	6
Wisconsin	Nonpartisan election	6 years	Nonpartisan election	6

Note: See Note, Table 5.2. Sates not listed do not have intermediate appellate courts.

[a] In states that use nominating commissions, the governor makes the appointment.

[b] Alabama and Tennessee have two intermediate appellate courts: the court of civil appeals, which has civil jurisdiction, and the court of criminal appeals, which has criminal jurisdiction. The selection process is the same for both.

[c] Although party affiliation of judicial candidates appears on ballots, judicial primaries are open. This gives judicial elections a nonpartisan character.

[d] Ohio's primary elections are partisan, but in general elections, party affiliations are not listed on the ballot.

[e] Pennsylvania has two intermediate appellate courts: the superior court and the commonwealth court. The selection process is the same for both.

[f] The Judicial Merit Selection Commission was established on July 1, 1997. The commission screens and then recommends a list of three judicial candidates to the legislature. The legislature votes only on the list submitted by the commission. If all candidates on the list are rejected, the process begins again with the commission.

Source: Maguire and Pastore, 2000:71.

TABLE 5.4 Method of Selection and Length of Initial and Retention Terms of General Jurisdiction Court Judges by State and Name of Court, as of July 1999

State/Name of Court(s)	Initial Selection		Retention	
	Method[a]	Term	Method	Term (in Years)
Alabama				
Circuit court	Partisan election	6 years	Partisan election	6
Alaska				
Superior court	Nominating commission	Until next general election but not less than 3 years	Retention election	6
Arizona				
Superior court[b]	Nominating commission	Until next general election but not less than 2 years	Retention selection	4
Arkansas				
Circuit court	Partisan election	4 years	Partisan election	4
California				
Superior court	Nonpartisan election or gubernatorial appointment[c]	6 years	Nonpartisan election[d]	6
Colorado				
District court	Nominating commission	Until next general election but not less than 2 years	Retention election	6
Connecticut				
Superior court	Nominating commission	8 years	Commission reviews, governor renominates, legislature confirms	8
Delaware				
Superior court	Nominating commission	12 years	Reappointment by governor	12

	Initial selection	Term	Retention/reappointment	
District of Columbia Superior Court[e]	Nominating commission	15 years	Reappointment by judicial tenure commission or president	15
Florida Circuit court	Nonpartisan election	6 years	Nonpartisan election	6
Georgia Superior court	Nonpartisan election	4 years	Nonpartisan election	4
Hawaii Circuit court	Nominating commission	10 years	Reappointment by commission	10
Idaho District court	Nonpartisan election	4 years	Nonpartisan election	4
Illinois Circuit court	Partisan election[f]	6 years	Retention election	6
Indiana Circuit court	Partisan election[g]	6 years	Partisan election[g]	6
Superior court	Partisan election[h]	6 years[i]	Partisan election[j]	6
Iowa District court	Nominating commission	Until next general election but not less than 1 year	Retention election	6
Kansas District court	Nominating commission[k]	Until next general election	Retention election[l]	4
Kentucky Circuit court	Nonpartisan election	8 years	Nonpartisan election	8
Louisiana District court	Partisan election[m]	6 years	Partisan election[m]	6
Maine Superior court	Appointed by governor	7 years	Reappointment by governor	7

(continued)

TABLE 5.4 *(continued)*

State/Name of Court(s)	Initial Selection		Retention	
	Method[a]	Term	Method	Term (in Years)
Maryland				
Circuit court	Nominating commission	Until next general election but not less than 1 year	Nonpartisan election	15
Massachusetts				
Trial Court of the Commonwealth	Nominating commission	To age 70	X	X
Michigan				
Circuit court	Nonpartisan election	6 years	Nonpartisan election	6
Minnesota				
District court	Nonpartisan election	6 years	Nonpartisan election	6
Mississippi				
Circuit court	Nonpartisan election	4 years	Nonpartisan election	4
Chancery court	Nonpartisan election	4 years	Nonpartisan election	4
Missouri				
Circuit court	Partisan election[n]	6 years[o]	Partisan election[p]	6
Montana				
District court	Nonpartisan election	6 years	Nonpartisan election, but if unopposed, retention election	6
Nebraska				
District court	Nominating commission	Until next general election but not less than 3 years	Retention election	6
Nevada				
District court	Nonpartisan election	6 years	Nonpartisan election	6
New Hampshire				
Superior court	Appointed by governor[q]	To age 70	X	X

				To age 70
New Jersey				
Superior court	Appointed by governor	7 years	Partisan election the first time; after that, winner runs in retention election	6
New Mexico				
District court	Nominating commission	Until next general election	Reappointment by governor	
New York				
Supreme court	Partisan election	14 years	Partisan election	14
North Carolina[r]				
Superior court	Partisan election	8 years	Partisan election	8
North Dakota				
District court	Nonpartisan election	6 years	Nonpartisan election	6
Ohio[s]				
Common Pleas court	Nonpartisan election	6 years	Nonpartisan election	6
Oklahoma				
District court	Nonpartisan election	4 years	Nonpartisan election	4
Oregon				
Circuit court	Nonpartisan election	6 years	Nonpartisan election	6
Pennsylvania				
Common Pleas court	Partisan election	10 years	Retention election	10
Rhode Island				
Superior court	Nominating commission	Life tenure	X	X
South Carolina				
Circuit court	Nominating commission[t]	6 years	Reelected by legislature	6
South Dakota				
Circuit court	Nonpartisan election	8 years	Nonpartisan election	8
Tennessee				
Circuit court	Partisan election	8 years	Partisan election	8
Texas				
District court	Partisan election	4 years	Partisan election	4

(continued)

117

TABLE 5.4 (continued)

State/Name of Court(s)	Initial Selection		Retention	
	Method[a]	Term	Method	Term (in Years)
Utah				
District court	Nominating commission	Until next general election but not less than 3 years	Retention election	6
Vermont				
Superior court	Nominating commission	6 years	Automatic retention unless legislature votes against it	6
Virginia				
Circuit court	Elected by legislature	8 years	Reelected by legislature	8
Washington				
Superior court	Nonpartisan election	4 years	Nonpartisan election	4
West Virginia				
Circuit court	Partisan election	8 years	Partisan election	8
Wisconsin				
Circuit court	Nonpartisan election	6 years	Nonpartisan election	6
Wyoming				
District court	Nominating commission	Until next general election but not less than 1 year	Retention election	6

Note: See Note Table 5.2. Courts of general jurisdiction are defined as having unlimited civil and criminal jurisdiction (Larry C. Berkson, "Judicial Selection in the United States: A Special Report," *Juricature* 64 [October 1980], p. 178).

[a] In states that use nominating commissions, the governor makes the appointment.

[b] Counties with populations under 250,000 select and retain superior court judges in nonpartisan elections for 4-year terms.

[c] Local electors can choose either nonpartisan elections or gubernatorial appointment.

[d] Judge must be elected to a full term on a nonpartisan ballot at the next general election. If the election is not contested, the incumbent's name does not appear on the ballot.

e Initial appointment is made by the president of the United States and confirmed by the Senate. If the president does not wish to reappoint the judge, the District of Columbia Nomination Commission compiles a new list of candidates.

f Circuit court associate judges are appointed by the circuit judges in each circuit for 4-year terms, as provided by supreme court rule.

g In Vanderburgh County, initial selection and retention are by nonpartisan election.

h A nominating commission is used for the superior court judges of Lake and St. Joseph Counties. In Vanderburgh County the election is nonpartisan.

i In Lake and St. Joseph Counties each appointed judge serves until the next general election but not less than 2 years.

j Nonpartisan elections are used in Allen and Vanderburgh Counties. Retention elections are used in Lake and St. Joseph Counties.

k Seventeen of 31 districts use a nominating commission for district judge selection; the remaining 14 select district judges in partisan elections.

l Fourteen of 31 districts use partisan elections.

m Although party affiliation of judicial candidates appears on ballots, judicial primaries are open. This gives judicial elections a nonpartisan character.

n Nominating commissions are used for selecting circuit court judges in Jackson, Clay, and Platte Counties and the City and County of St. Louis.

o An associate circuit court judge's term is 4 years; also in counties that use nominating commissions, the appointed judge serves until the next general election but not less than 1 year.

p Retention elections are used in Jackson, Clay, and Platte Counties and the City and County of St. Louis.

q Subject to approval by an elected five-member executive council.

r In addition, a small number of special judges of superior court are appointed by the governor for terms of varying length.

s Ohio's primary elections are partisan, but in general elections, party affiliations are not listed on the ballot.

t The Judicial Merit Selection Commission was established on July 1, 1997. The commission screens and then recommends a list of three judicial candidates to the legislature. The legislature votes on the list submitted by the commission. If all candidates on the list are rejected, the process begins again with the commission.

Table 5.2 shows that as of July 1999, eight states used partisan elections for selecting judges and thirteen states used nonpartisan elections. Twenty-four states used nominating commissions, and governors appointed judges in four states. Only one state, Virginia, used a legislative election (Maguire and Pastore, 2000:69–70). Judicial terms for state supreme court justices range from six to fifteen years, with a median of ten years, although in three states (Massachusetts, New Hampshire, and Rhode Island) these selections are for life or until age seventy. Most of these states have retention elections following the initial judicial terms.

Table 5.3 shows the method of selection, length of term, and retention process for judges in state intermediate appellate courts. For the most part, the selection methods for intermediate judiciary are the same as those for state supreme court justices. However, the terms are somewhat shorter, ranging from six to twelve years, with a median of eight years. Most of these states also have retention elections following the initial judicial terms (Maguire and Pastore, 2000:71).

Table 5.4 shows the method of selection and the length of initial and retention terms for state general jurisdiction judges. More than thirty of these states used partisan or nonpartisan elections for these judges in 1999. The terms of these general jurisdiction judges ranged from four to fifteen years, with a median of six years (Maguire and Pastore, 2000:72–73).

PROBLEMS WITH POLITICALLY APPOINTED JUDGES. Some of the problems raised by politically appointed judges are the same as those in jurisdictions where partisan and nonpartisan elections fill judicial vacancies. Are the most qualified people selected for the judgeship? An investigation of elected and appointed judges for the California Superior Court from 1959 to 1977 compared their demographic characteristics, educational backgrounds, and prejudicial career experiences (Dubois, 1990). Of the 739 judges investigated, 662 had been appointed. Most had earlier careers as attorneys or some other previous legal experience. When their decisions were examined for technical accuracy and legal justification, however, no significant differences between elected or appointed judges were found (DuBois, 1990). No conclusions could be drawn about which selection method was better on the basis of the quality of their judicial decision making.

Another issue is whether political appointments contribute to corruption among the judiciary (Blankenship, Spargar, and Janikowski, 1994; Scheb, 1988). Because of their powerful positions, judges may influence trial outcomes, dismiss cases, or find innocent defendants guilty. They can also regulate the harshness of penalties imposed whenever a jury verdict of guilty is rendered. All states have judicial sanctioning boards. They are usually operated through state bar associations and have provisions for officially questioning judicial behavior. Studies comparing the qualities of judges elected versus those appointed tend to show little difference in placing high-quality judges on the bench (Blankenship, Spargar, and Janikowski, 1994). Judicial accountability versus judicial independence models do not seem to differ significantly as a means for improving the quality of judges generally.

Some jurisdictions, such as Pennsylvania, have attempted to hold the governor primarily accountable for political judicial appointments of incompetent or corrupt judges

(*Villanova Law Review,* 1982). Particularly with respect to gubernatorial appointments of appellate judges, insufficient monitoring methods have historically resulted in occasional selections of poor judges. Suggested alternative judicial selection methods include a gubernatorial appointment system whereby the records of prospective judicial appointees can be carefully scrutinized by the press and state bar associations. Further, all gubernatorial candidates would have to be approved by the state legislature through some type of confirmation process (*Villanova Law Review,* 1982). Perhaps the best method of judicial selection is on the basis of merit.

Merit Selection of Judges

Prior to 1933, no state had any type of **merit selection** plan for filling vacant judgeships (Uppal, 1974). By far the most popular method of selecting judges was partisan or nonpartisan elections. Other systems used included gubernatorial or legislative appointments. One reason for the slow adoption of merit systems for judicial appointments is the strong sentiment in predominantly rural communities for the elective process (Uppal, 1974). By the early 1990s, fifteen states (Alaska, Arizona, Colorado, Connecticut, Delaware, Hawaii, Iowa, Kansas, Maryland, Massachusetts, Nebraska, New Mexico, Utah, Vermont, and Wyoming) and the District of Columbia had developed merit systems for filling judicial vacancies (Holten and Lamar, 1991). By 1999, twenty-four states had nominating commissions to select judges to fill the highest appellate vacancies (Maguire and Pastore, 2000:69–70).

THE MISSOURI PLAN. A popular method of judicial selection that has been adopted by several states is the **Missouri plan**. The Missouri plan, introduced in 1940, uses a merit system for appointments to judgeships (President's Commission on Law Enforcement, 1967:66–67). The essential features of the Missouri Plan follow:

1. A nominating committee of lawyers and nonlawyers appointed by the governor and chaired by a judge
2. A listing of qualified candidates nominated by the committee for each judicial vacancy
3. Judicial vacancies filled by the governor from the list of candidates nominated by the committee
4. Retention elections for appointed judges

The Missouri plan is a version of the 1914 **Kales plan** (Kales, 1914). The Kales plan has survived in various forms in several states over the years, and its influence on the Missouri plan is evident. The Kales plan requires a nonpartisan committee of lawyers, judges, and nonjudicial personnel to draft a list of the most qualified judicial candidates on the basis of their records and expertise. This list is then submitted to the governor to make judicial appointments. Judicial vacancies occur because of death, retirement, or removal because of incompetence. Any choice a governor makes from the approved list would, by definition, be a good choice. Ideally, politics is removed from such gubernatorial appointments.

Some critics question whether *any* merit plan, including the Kales and Missouri versions, can eliminate politics from judicial selection (Blankenship, Sparger, and Janikowski, 1994; Champagne, 1988). Other analysts find the merit plan useful for promoting greater accountability and fairness among judges (Scheb, 1988).

One way of making the merit selection plan more palatable to the public is to ensure that the qualification procedures for judicial applicants are rigorous (Dubois, 1990). A thorough screening procedure should provide a standard against which to compare different judicial candidates so that the public knows that all judicial nominees have been tested for competency and ability (Dubois, 1990; Scheb, 1988).

One troubling aspect of merit selection occurs in those states where governors have the power to appoint **interim judges** to fill unexpected vacancies. When judges die, become infirm, or are otherwise unable to perform their duties in midterm, governors make temporary judicial appointments without consulting any merit selection committee. Interim judges generally have an easier time as **incumbents** when it comes time to appoint a new judge for a subsequent term (Baum, 1983). The politicization of the interim judicial appointment process is furthered by gubernatorial appointments of nominating committee members who convene later to review the credentials of applications for new judicial vacancies (Haynes, 1977).

Some researchers have suggested that governors should remove themselves entirely from the judicial selection process, even from the process of appointing interim judges to fill temporary vacancies (Vandenberg, 1983). In New Mexico, for instance, a judicial nominating commission is in place to screen and fill temporary judicial vacancies. The nominating commission submits its recommendations to the governor, and the governor appoints people from the list to vacant judgeships. Thus, the governor does not directly screen candidates or select judges independent of a nominating commission. Other states that have nominating commissions are Delaware, Georgia, Maryland, Massachusetts, Minnesota, New York, North Carolina, Pennsylvania, Rhode Island, and West Virginia.

Under President Jimmy Carter, Executive Order 11972 established the U.S. Circuit Judge Nominating Commission. This commission radically altered the method of selecting federal judges. Carter wanted to devise a system whereby judges would be appointed on the basis of their professional merit and potential for high-quality service on the bench. Further, he wanted to develop a mechanism that would enable him to place more women and minorities in judgeships. One criticism of this method of judicial selection is that Carter may have undermined the merit system in favor of affirmative action considerations. During his presidency, Carter selected eighty-six percent of the judges from his own Democratic party. He dramatically increased the presence of women (25 percent of his appointments) and minorities (29 percent) on the federal bench (Berkson and Carbon, 1980). Subsequently, other U.S. presidents have made partisan judicial appointments (Goldman, 1983, 1987; Gottschall, 1983, 1986; Rowland, Songer, and Carp, 1988).

Legislative Appointments of Judges

In 1999, only Virginia raised judges to the highest appellate bench through legislative elections. In this process, nominating committees advance a list of judicial candidates for legislative approval. Legislative voting results in the appointment of judges to benches in various state jurisdictions. Although legislative appointments of judges affect only a small portion of the judiciary, the impact of legislatively selected judges has been studied by several researchers. Daniel Pinello (1995) has characterized their subsequent performance as judges as acquiescent and inactive. Governor-appointed judges tend to choose the interests of individuals over state interests more often than legislatively appointed judges.

Legislative appointments are extremely political and reflect the political leanings of legislators who have been voted into office by the citizens of the state. Thus, a legislature controlled by Democrats might be disposed to appoint Democratic judges, and Republican-dominated legislatures would be expected to appoint Republican judges. Relatively little depends on the qualifications of those considered for judgeships in these jurisdictions. There is a great propensity on the part of state legislators to appoint former legislators to judicial vacancies. Also, any person in the state who has formerly held a political office stands a much greater chance of receiving a judicial appointment from the legislature than someone without political experience. Does the legislature appoint the most qualified people to vacant judgeships? Not if these appointments are based on former political ties to the legislature or other political offices within the state. Virtually the same thing can be said of gubernatorial appointees, who most often have held one or more state political offices.

ARE MERIT SYSTEMS FOR JUDICIAL SELECTION BETTER THAN ELECTION METHODS? The debate over which judge selection plan is best assumes that it makes some kind of measurable difference which plan is used—that one plan results in better judges. However, research has tended to show that there are few discernible differences among the various plans in terms of the quality of judges (*Northern Kentucky Law Review*, 1982). Partisan elections may not produce better judges than other means of selection, but neither, apparently, do they produce worse ones (Swain, 1985). According to one view, the legal profession tends to ignore research findings and blindly and steadfastly adheres to the Missouri merit selection method. One proposed but unlikely modification would be to democratize the Missouri plan by rectifying some of its major weaknesses (*Northern Kentucky Law Review*, 1982).

For many decades, the public has assumed that judicial selection systems that emphasize merit rather than political interests create greater judicial accountability and independence. Elections are perceived as popularity contests, often rigged to accommodate one vested interest group or another. Gubernatorial selection methods result in the appointment of political hacks who cater to the interests of the governor and the governor's friends. Merit selection, it is argued, results in the most qualified judges. However, several researchers have raised questions about whether any of these methods is better than the rest. Blankenship, Sparger, and Janikowski (1994) suggest that the election–merit selection dichotomy is more myth than fact. They contend that appointive methods for selecting judges are no more effective than the elective process in placing qualified judges on the bench. They add that neither elections nor appointments of judicial candidates succeed in fulfilling the long-range philosophical expectations of judicial accountability and independence. Other researchers who investigated the attitudes and opinions of judges in various jurisdictions have reported similar results (Canon, 1972; Flango and Ducat, 1979).

Federal Judicial Selection Methods

THE NATURE OF U.S. SUPREME COURT APPOINTMENTS. The president of the United States exerts direct influence on U.S. Supreme Court appointments and judicial appointments to lower federal courts. The president recommends people for district, circuit, and supreme court judgeships, with the advice and consent of Congress (Solomon, 1984). Supreme Court appointments have not necessarily required previous judicial experience, however. From 1930 to 1967, twenty-three U.S. Supreme Court justices were appointed. Only seven of them had previous experience as a federal judge, and only one had served at least five years on the federal bench. Further, only four of these twenty-three appointees had experience as state judges. Only Justice Cardozo, appointed in 1932, had more than eight years on a state bench; he served eighteen years in state courts.

U.S. Supreme Court justiceships are appointments by the president of the United States, subject to Congressional approval. They are lifetime appointments with an annual salary of $175,400 (1999). Because these positions are presidential appointments, they often reflect a president's vested interests. Therefore, judges with judicial philosophies consistent with those of the president are appointed instead of more qualified judges who hold contrary philosophies (Goldman, 1985; Solomon, 1984). When former President George Bush, a Republican, nominated Clarence Thomas, also a Republican, to fill a U.S. Supreme Court vacancy, the nomination was hotly debated by the U.S. Senate Judiciary Committee after examining Thomas's views on various issues. Those most critical of Thomas were Senate Democrats. Political philosophy was influential in Judge Thomas's eventual acceptance as a Supreme Court justice.

During the 1990s, two U.S. Supreme Court justices were appointed by President Bill Clinton, a Democrat. Ruth Bader Ginsburg was the first Democrat to serve on the U.S. Supreme Court in twenty-six years, as well as the second woman appointed.

Presidential appointments to the U.S. Supreme Court are also characterized according to whether the appointees are conservative, liberal, or moderate. Republican appointees have tended to be very conservative or conservative, and justices appointed under Democratic administrations have tended to be moderate or liberal. These philosophical orientations have been crucial in determining various social policies during the last fifty years. For instance, Chief Justice Earl Warren was appointed to the high court in 1953 by President Dwight Eisenhower. When Warren became chief justice, the court became known as the "Warren court." Under Warren's guidance, the U.S. Supreme Court made a number of rulings that regulated police tactics in custodial interrogation and search and seizure. Critics felt the U.S. Supreme Court was anti-police during Warren's tenure as chief justice, because they thought many of its rulings tied the hands of law enforcement officers who were investigating crimes. The most notable rulings included *Mapp v. Ohio* (1961), which required police officers to have search warrants before conducting searches of a suspect's premises, and *Miranda v. Arizona* (1966), which required police officers to advise suspects of their right to an attorney prior to being interrogated.

Later U.S. Supreme Court rulings created various exceptions to warrantless searches and "untied" the hands of police. Under Warren E. Burger, appointed chief justice by President Richard M. Nixon in 1969, the "Burger court" established the "totality of circumstances" and "good faith" exceptions to the exclusionary rule, which permitted law enforcement officers considerable latitude to conduct warrantless searches of a suspect's premises, person, and automobile. During the 1990s, the newly configured U.S. Supreme Court presided over by Chief Justice William H. Rehnquist, the "Rehnquist court," issued more conservative rulings regarding search and seizure. These rulings resemble those of the Warren court forty years earlier.

Thus, the influence of presidential appointments on the composition of the U.S. Supreme Court cannot be ignored. These appointments, which are highly political, are intended to increase the likelihood of particular social agendas the president favors. During any presidential election year, a key factor for voters is what types of Supreme Court justices will be appointed and what will be the nature of their decision making in future years. The long-term social policy implications of these lifetime appointments are quite clear.

CIRCUIT COURT JUDGESHIPS. Judges who serve in Circuit Courts of Appeal are appointed by the president of the United States, and their nomination must be approved by Congress. The salary of U.S. circuit judges was $145,000 in 1999. The Senate Judiciary Committee hears arguments for and against these presidential appointees and either approves or rejects them. One example of a rejection is the case of Miami U.S. District Court Judge Kenneth L. Ryskamp, who had been appointed a federal district judge by President Ronald Reagan in 1986. At that time, the Senate Judiciary Committee recommended his nomination, and his appointment was eventually confirmed. However, during his next five years on the federal bench, Judge Ryskamp made numerous disparaging remarks about racial and ethnic minorities. When the Senate Judiciary Committee conducted a subsequent hearing of Ryskamp's qualifications for a Circuit Court of Appeals judgeship in April 1991, committee members called to Ryskamp's attention remarks that he had made once to four black plaintiffs who filed suit after being mauled by police dogs. Ryskamp told them, "It might not be inappropriate to carry around a few scars to remind you of your wrongdoing," even though two of the four were never even charged with any crime. He also complained from the federal bench that people were thin-skinned if they took offense at calling a black area "colored town."

Judge Ryskamp also belonged to a Miami country club that excluded blacks and Jews. While in Washington, Ryskamp failed to follow recommendations from Washington politicians or adhere to advice from his aides. When President George Bush nominated Ryskamp to the Circuit Court of Appeals encompassing Florida, Georgia, and Alabama, his elevation would have created a conservative majority in that court. Although President Bush had seventy-six previous confirmation victories and the Senate Judiciary Committee had not rejected any Republican president's nomination since 1988, they did reject Ryskamp. Even Ryskamp contributed to his own demise. He confided to an aide to Senator Paul Simon that "Miami is like a foreign country where the store clerks speak Spanish and stock only ethnic food. Cubans always show up two hours late to weddings" (Cohn, 1991:31). Other Reagan judicial appointees have been labeled as ideological extremists (Tomasi and Velona, 1987).

Table 5.5 shows the characteristics of appellate judicial appointees by presidential administration for the years 1963–1998. Presidential appointments in most cases involve nominees who are members of the president's political party. Table 5.5 shows, for instance, that 95 percent of Democratic President Lyndon Johnson's circuit court judicial appointments were Democrats, 93 percent of Republican President Richard Nixon's appointments were Republicans, 92 percent of Republican President Gerald Ford's appointments were Republicans, 82 percent of Democratic President Jimmy Carter's appointments were Democrats, 96 percent of Republican President Ronald Reagan's appointments were Republicans, 90 percent of Republican President George Bush's appointments were Republicans, and 85 percent of Democratic President Bill Clinton's appointments were Democrats. The American Bar Association regarded Johnson's and Clinton's circuit court judge appointments as exceptionally well qualified, whereas Ford and Reagan had the lowest ratings for their circuit judgeship appointments, with less than 60 percent regarded as exceptionally well qualified.

Table 5.5 also shows an interesting pattern of circuit judicial appointments over time according to gender of appointees. Presidents Johnson, Nixon, and Ford made almost exclusively male appointments to circuit judgeships during their administrations. President Carter was the first to appoint women to nearly 20 percent of these posts. President Reagan's appointments returned the pattern to the Johnson-Nixon-Ford years, with more than 95 percent male circuit judgeship appointments. But Presidents Bush and Clinton again began appointing more women to these positions. President Clinton, in fact, nominated women in about a third of all appointments, a percentage unprecedented during all previous presidential administrations.

President Carter appointed the greatest percentage of blacks (16.1 percent) to circuit court posts, followed by President Clinton (10.4 percent), and President Clinton appointed the largest percentage of Hispanic judges to these positions (10.4 percent).

U.S. DISTRICT COURT JUDGES. There were more than 650 federal district judges in 1999 (Title 28, U.S.C. Sec. 133, 2001). Federal district judges are also appointed by the president of the United States and serve life terms. Their annual salaries in 1999 were $136,700. Federal district judges who serve ten or more years with *good behavior* are entitled to retire at their option at any time thereafter and receive their annual salary for life. Although judicial appointments are ideally made without regard to race, color, sex, religion, or national origin, these appointments are primarily political and reflect the interests and views of the president. The advice and consent of Congress is required for all such appointments.

President Jimmy Carter made various appointments that were considered liberal. Of his fifty-six appointments to federal circuit courts of appeal (Gottschall, 1983), twenty-two were either female or a member of a racial minority. These judges were tracked over time to see whether there was corresponding liberal decision making on appeals from convicted minority offenders in 301 criminal and prisoner's rights cases, 169 sex discrimination cases, and 295 racial discrimination cases. Minority appointees by Carter cast 79 percent of their votes to favor the rights of accused minorities and women, as did only 53 percent of the white male judges he had appointed. Race and gender discrimination cases disclosed more liberal rulings from these judges than prisoner's rights cases.

TABLE 5.5 Characteristics of Presidential Appointees to U.S. Courts of Appeals Judgeships by Presidential Administration, 1963–1998[a]

	President Johnson's Appointees 1963–1968[b] (N=40)	President Nixon's Appointees 1969–1974 (N=45)	President Ford's Appointees 1974–1976 (N=12)	President Carter's Appointees 1977–1980 (N=56)	President Reagan's Appointees 1981–1988 (N=78)	President Bush's Appointees 1989–1992 (N=37)	President Clinton's Appointees 1993–1998 (N=48)
Sex							
Male	97.5%	100%	100%	80.4%	94.9%	81.1%	63.7%
Female	2.5	0	0	19.6	5.1	18.9	33.3
Race, ethnicity							
White	95.0	97.8	100	78.6	97.4	89.2	77.1
Black	5.0	0	0	16.1	1.3	5.4	10.4
Hispanic	0	0	0	3.6	1.3	5.4	10.4
Asian	0	2.2	0	1.8	0	0	2.1
Education, undergraduate							
Public-supported	32.5	40.0	50.0	30.4	24.4	29.7	45.8
Private (not Ivy League)	40.0	35.6	41.7	51.8	51.3	59.5	33.3
Ivy League	17.5	20.0	8.3	17.9	24.4	10.8	20.8
None indicated	10.0	4.4	0	0	0	0	0
Education, law school							
Public-supported	40.0	37.8	50.0	39.3	41.0	29.7	39.6
Private (not Ivy League)	32.5	26.7	25.0	19.6	35.9	40.5	25.0
Ivy League	27.5	35.6	25.0	41.1	23.1	29.7	35.4
Occupation at nomination or appointment							
Politics or government	10.0	4.4	8.3	5.4	6.4	10.8	4.2
Judiciary	57.5	53.3	75.0	46.4	55.1	59.5	56.3
Law firm, large	5.0	4.4	8.3	10.7	14.1	16.2	18.8
Law firm, moderate	17.5	22.2	8.3	16.1	9.0	10.8	12.5
Law firm, small	7.5	6.7	0	5.4	1.3	0	0
Professor of law	2.5	2.2	0	14.3	12.8	2.7	8.3
Other	0	6.7	0	1.8	1.3	0	0

(continued)

TABLE 5.5 (continued)

	President Johnson's Appointees 1963–1968[b] (N=40)	President Nixon's Appointees 1969–1974 (N=45)	President Ford's Appointees 1974–1976 (N=12)	President Carter's Appointees 1977–1980 (N=56)	President Reagan's Appointees 1981–1988 (N=78)	President Bush's Appointees 1989–1992 (N=37)	President Clinton's Appointees 1993–1998 (N=48)
Occupational experience							
Judicial	65.0	57.8	75.0	53.6	60.3	62.2	62.5
Prosecutorial	47.5	46.7	25.0	32.1	28.2	29.7	35.4
Other	20.0	17.8	25.0	39.3	34.6	32.4	27.1
Religion							
Protestant	60.0	75.6	58.3	60.7	NA	NA	NA
Catholic	25.0	15.6	33.3	23.2	NA	NA	NA
Jewish	15.0	8.9	8.3	16.1	NA	NA	NA
Political party							
Democrat	95.0	6.7	8.3	82.1	0	5.4	85.4
Republican	5.0	93.3	91.7	7.1	96.2	89.2	6.3
Independent or none	0	0	0	10.7	2.6	5.4	8.3
Other	0	0	0	0	1.3	0	0
American Bar Association Rating							
Exceptionally well/well qualified	75.0	73.3	58.3	75.0	59.0	64.9	77.1
Qualified	20.0	26.7	33.3	25.0	41.0	35.1	22.9
Not qualified	2.5	0	8.3	0	0	0	0

Note: These data were compiled from a variety of sources. Primarily used were questionnaires completed by judicial nominees for the U.S. State Judiciary Committee, transcripts of the confirmation hearing conducted by the committee, and personal interviews. In addition, an investigation was made of various biographical directories including *The American Bench* (Sacramento: R. B. Forster), *Who's Who in American Politics* (New York: Bowker), *Martindale-Hubbell Law Directory* (Summit, NJ: Martindale-Hubbell, Inc.), national and regional editions of *Who's Who*, *The Judicial Staff Directory* (1994 edition), and local newspaper articles.

Law firms are categorized according to the number of partners/associates: 25 or more associates for a large firm, 5 to 24 associate for a moderate firm, and 4 or less for a small firm. Percent subtotals for occupational experience sum to more than 100 because some appointees have had both judicial and prosecutorial experience.

The American Bar Association's (ABA) ratings are assigned to candidates after investigation and evaluation by the ABA's Standing Committee on Federal Judiciary, which considers prospective federal judicial nominees only upon referral by the U.S. attorney general or at the request of the U.S. Senate. The ABA's committee evaluation is directed primarily to professional qualifications—competence, integrity, and judicial temperament. Factors including intellectual capacity, judgment, writing and analytical ability, industry, knowledge of the law, and professional experience are assessed. Prior to the Bush administration, the ABA's Standing Committee on Federal Judiciary utilized four ratings: exceptionally well qualified, well qualified, qualified, and not qualified. Starting with the Bush administration, the ABA Standing Committee on Federal Judiciary dropped its "exceptionally well qualified" rating so that "well qualified" became the highest rating. Nominees who previously would have been rated "exceptionally well qualified" and nominees who would have been rated "well qualified" now receive the same rating. The "exceptionally well qualified" and "well qualified" categories are combined for all administrations' appointees, and therefore figures prior to President Bush's administration may differ from previous editions of *Sourcebook*. Some data have been revised by the source and may differ from previous editions of *Sourcebook*.

[a]Percents may not add to 100 because of rounding.

[b]No ABA rating was requested for one Johnson appointee.

Source: Magure and Pastore, 2000:58.

The pattern of partisanship indicated by presidential appointments to circuit court judgeships is also evident in presidential appointees to federal district courts through 1998. More than 90 percent of all federal district court judges have been of the same political party as their appointing president (Table 5.6). The ratings of federal district court judges by the American Bar Association were fairly consistent across the different presidencies—from 46 to 58 percent were exceptionally well qualified—regardless of the president's party (Maguire and Pastore, 2000:58–59).

Regarding the gender and race or ethnicity of U.S. district court judge appointments, President Bill Clinton appointed the largest percentage of women (28.2 percent), followed by President Bush (19.8 percent) and President Carter (14.4 percent). President Clinton had a higher percentage of black appointees (19 percent) than President Carter (14 percent); all other U.S. presidents have appointed fewer than 7 percent black judges to these district court judgeships. Both President Carter (6.9 percent) and President Clinton (5.2 percent) appointed the most Hispanic federal district court judges.

U.S. MAGISTRATES. U.S. magistrates have jurisdiction over petty federal crimes. They may conduct the preliminary stages of felony cases and set bail for criminal defendants, and they decide numerous civil cases (Table 5.7). They are appointed by U.S. district court judges and serve terms of either eight years or four years, depending on whether they are full-time or part-time magistrates (Smith, 1987, 1992). The salary of U.S. magistrates in 1999 was $125,764.

Besides having jurisdiction over cases involving federal misdemeanors and petty offenses, these magistrates also issue search warrants, arrest warrants, and summonses; hold detention hearings; review bail for arrestees; issue seizure warrants; and conduct preliminary examinations. These magistrates have civil duties as well as criminal ones, although their criminal responsibilities outweigh their civil responsibilities 2 to 1. They hold pretrial conferences, rule on motions, conduct evidentiary hearings, appoint special masterships, and hear some prisoner litigation involving habeas corpus petitions and civil rights submissions.

By far the bulk of a U.S. magistrate's duties consist of preliminary proceedings, such as issuing search warrants, arrest warrants, and summonses; conducting initial appearances; and setting bail. Much of their civil work relates to conducting pretrial conferences, ruling on motions, and screening prisoner litigation (Maguire and Pastore, 2000:63).

WHAT DO JUDGES THINK ABOUT DIFFERENT JUDICIAL SELECTION METHODS?
When judges themselves are surveyed, they seem to favor merit plans over elections (Scheb, 1988). In 1987, for instance, a national survey of 562 state appellate judges solicited their attitudes toward alternative judicial selection methods. When asked to compare the Missouri plan of merit selection with political appointment and partisan election, the judges responded overwhelmingly that the merit plan was the more professional selection method. By this, the judges meant that the Missouri merit plan tended to professionalize the courts. Judges selected under the merit system were far less likely to become involved in political causes or debates than those judges who were either gubernatorial appointees or elected (Scheb, 1988).

In some jurisdictions, such as Texas, judges believed that performance evaluations are made unfairly because the judicial selection methods used in their state have not been

TABLE 5.6 Characteristics of Presidential Appointees to U.S. District Court Judgeships by Presidential Administration, 1963–1998[a]

	President Johnson's Appointees 1963–1968 (N=122)	President Nixon's Appointees 1969–1974 (N=179)	President Ford's Appointees 1974–1976 (N=52)	President Carter's Appointees 1977–1980 (N=202)	President Reagan's Appointees 1981–1988 (N=290)	President Bush's Appointees 1989–1992 (N=148)	President Clinton's Appointees 1993–1998 (N=248)
Sex							
Male	98.4%	99.4%	98.1%	85.6%	91.7%	80.4%	71.8%
Female	1.6	0.6	1.9	14.4	8.3	19.6	28.2
Race, ethnicity							
White	93.4	95.5	88.5	78.7	92.4	89.2	73.8
Black	4.1	3.4	5.8	13.9	2.1	6.8	19.0
Hispanic	2.5	1.1	1.9	6.9	4.8	4.0	5.2
Asian	0	0	3.9	0.5	0.7	0	1.6
Native American	NA	NA	NA	0	0	0	0.4
Education, undergraduate							
Public-supported	38.5	41.3	48.1	56.4	36.6	44.6	43.6
Private (not Ivy League)	31.1	38.5	34.6	33.7	49.7	41.2	42.3
Ivy League	16.4	19.6	17.3	9.9	13.8	14.2	14.1
None indicated	13.9	0.6	0	0	0	0	0
Education, law school							
Public-supported	40.2	41.9	44.2	50.5	42.4	52.7	41.1
Private (not Ivy League)	36.9	36.9	38.5	32.7	45.9	33.1	39.5
Ivy League	21.3	21.2	17.3	16.8	11.7	14.2	19.4
Occupation at nomination or appointment							
Politics or government	21.3	10.6	21.2	5.0	13.4	10.8	10.9
Judiciary	31.1	28.5	34.6	44.6	36.9	41.9	46.8
Law firm, large	2.4	11.2	9.6	13.9	17.9	25.7	15.7
Law firm, moderate	18.9	27.9	25.0	19.8	19.0	14.9	15.3
Law firm, small	23.0	19.0	9.6	13.4	10.0	4.7	8.5
Professor of law	3.3	2.8	0	3.0	2.1	0.7	1.6
Other	0	0	0	0.5	0.7	1.4	1.2

(continued)

131

TABLE 5.6 *(continued)*

	President Johnson's Appointees 1963–1968 (N=122)	President Nixon's Appointees 1969–1974 (N=179)	President Ford's Appointees 1974–1976 (N=52)	President Carter's Appointees 1977–1980 (N=202)	President Reagan's Appointees 1981–1988 (N=290)	President Bush's Appointees 1989–1992 (N=148)	President Clinton's Appointees 1993–1998 (N=248)
Occupational experience							
Judicial	34.4	35.2	42.3	54.0	46.2	46.6	51.2
Prosecutorial	45.9	41.9	50.0	38.1	44.1	39.2	40.7
Other	33.6	36.3	30.8	30.7	28.6	31.8	29.8
Religion							
Protestant	58.2	73.2	73.1	60.4	NA	NA	NA
Catholic	31.1	18.4	17.3	27.7	NA	NA	NA
Jewish	10.7	8.4	9.6	11.9	NA	NA	NA
Political party							
Democrat	94.3	7.3	21.2	90.6	4.8	5.4	89.1
Republican	5.7	92.7	78.8	4.5	91.7	88.5	4.8
Independent or none	0	0	0	5.0	3.4	6.1	5.7
Other	NA	NA	NA	0	0	0	0.4
American Bar Association rating							
Exceptionally well/well qualified	48.4	45.3	46.1	51.0	53.5	57.4	58.1
Qualified	49.2	54.8	53.8	47.5	46.6	42.6	40.7
Not qualified	2.5	0	0	1.5	0	0	1.2

Note: Percentage subtotals for occupational experience may sum to more than 100 because some appointees have had both judicial and prosecutorial experience. Some data have been revised by the source and may differ from previous editions of *Sourcebook.*

[a] Percentages may not add to 100 because of rounding.

Source: Maguire and Pastore, 2000:59.

TABLE 5.7 Duties Performed by Magistrates in U.S. District Courts

Activity	1988	1994	1995	1996	1997	1998
Total	471,085	517,397	512,741	554,041	579,450	612,440
Trial jurisdiction cases	89,996	87,519	72,868	74,806	85,257	96,832
Misdemeanors	13,418	12,138	9,875	10,356	10,177	10,633
Petty offenses	76,578	75,381	62,993	64,450	75,080	86,199
Preliminary proceedings	143,352	196,990	206,612	224,647	240,338	262,600
Search warrants	14,246	26,250	25,966	27,811	29,563	30,371
Arrest warrants/summonses	16,408	20,513	21,202	21,119	23,116	26,252
Initial appearances	47,956	50,645	52,654	55,206	60,419	68,982
Detention hearings	11,935	21,711	24,060	26,800	28,996	32,948
Bail reviews	6,665	7,394	8,558	9,456	9,628	9,874
Preliminary examinations	6,805	8,406	8,969	10,303	13,049	14,436
Grand jury returns	4,259	5,208	5,411	6,057	6,172	6,125
Arraignments	29,569	35,061	37,198	40,715	41,559	45,524
Attorney appointment hearings	NA	6,116	6,488	8,219	8,055	8,998
Seizure warrants	NA	2,529	1,782	1,798	2,254	2,359
Fee applications	NA	8,655	9,389	11,048	11,278	10,585
Other[a]	5,509	4,502	4,935	6,115	6,249	6,146
Additional duties	231,834	225,053	224,294	244,640	243,774	242,669
Criminal	38,884	47,780	48,366	55,594	55,421	53,396
Motions	28,709	28,240	26,282	28,444	27,329	24,071
Evidentiary hearings	1,355	2,154	2,031	1,990	1,788	1,998
Pretrial conferences	3,462	4,555	5,090	5,837	5,737	5,763
Calendar calls	1,679	2,183	1,955	2,577	2,869	3,636
Motion hearings/arguments	NA	3,752	5,124	8,113	8,955	8,234
Other[b]	3,679	6,896	7,884	8,633	8,743	9,694
Civil	167,486	146,814	144,949	155,830	158,929	161,889
Pretrial conferences	48,359	54,703	56,286	62,130	64,548	63,220
Motions	103,608	65,639	63,203	66,203	66,535	69,517
Evidentiary hearings	1,784	774	523	602	660	740
Social Security	7,258	5,623	5,384	4,603	4,553	5,261
Special masterships	1,213	825	682	1,080	963	886

(continued)

TABLE 5.7 (continued)

Activity	1988	1994	1995	1996	1997	1998
Civil (*continued*)						
Calendar calls	2,184	1,792	1,658	2,576	2,867	3,017
Motion hearings/arguments	NA	13,535	14,458	15,577	15,851	16,178
Other	3,080	3,923	2,755	3,032	2,952	3,070
Prison litigation	25,464	30,459	30,979	33,216	29,424	27,384

Note: The Federal Magistrates Act (28 U.S.C. 636[b]) provides the authority under which magistrates assist courts in the performance of "additional duties." This authority was both broadened and clarified by Public Law 94–577, Oct. 21, 1976, and by new procedural rules governing most habeas corpus proceedings in the district courts, effective Feb. 1, 1977. The changes make clear the ability of the parties of a civil case to consent to have the case referred to a magistrate for trial as a special matter; the changes also empower magistrates to conduct evidentiary hearings in prisoner petition cases. Additionally, the role of magistrates in providing pretrial assistance to district judges in both dispositive and nondispositive matters has been clarified. A magistrate's authority to conduct arraignments following indictment in a criminal case is provided under Rule 10 of the Federal Rules of Criminal Procedure in 86 districts. Data for 1988 and 1994 are reported for the 12-month period ending September 30. Beginning in 1995, data are reported for the federal fiscal year, which is the 12-month period ending June 30.

[a]Beginning in 1994, category includes contempt proceedings and other hearings.

[b]Beginning in 1994, category includes hearings for mental competency.

Source: Maguire and Pastore, 1996:67.

changed since 1891 (Greenhill and Odam, 1971). They felt that creating new jurisdictional divisions among Texas's existing courts could do much to improve case-processing efficiency and that specific organizational reforms could enhance judges' performance. One such reform would be to empower presiding judges in different jurisdictions to move other judges to courts on an as-needed basis and to control court dockets. They thought restricting the monetary jurisdiction of various criminal and civil courts to $5,000 would also improve court efficiency (Greenhill and Odam, 1971).

Judicial Training

Theories of management and organization have sometimes been applied in the judicial selection and training process (Gazell, 1975). For instance, **bureaucracy** and its derivative bureaucratic theory emphasize **centralization** of authority in decision making, thus creating a degree of standardization in judicial selection (Council of State Governments, 1978). However, strict adherence to bureaucratic principles may not always result in selection of the most qualified judges in local jurisdictions. A departure from bureaucratic theory would be to decentralize the judicial selection process and place greater decision-making power in the hands of local commissions for judicial appointments, with some authority given to state supreme courts to oversee the selection process. The legislative electoral process is one way of rationalizing and objectifying the selection process. Local bar elements could recommend those most qualified for judgeships, and the legislature would make the best judicial selections with state supreme court approval (Berkson and Hays, 1977).

In the late 1970s, a survey by the American Judicature Society disclosed no uniformity or pattern of organization in different lower courts of state jurisdictions (Knab, 1977). The qualifications for state judges were diverse and inconsistent from one jurisdiction to the next, and there were different standards for selecting judges, determining their qualifications, compensating them, and providing for their retirement or removal.

The U.S. Advisory Commission on Intergovernmental Relations (1971) suggested setting uniform rules to govern the conduct of judges, as well as standard procedures for judicial retirement, removal, and discipline. The commission also recommended mandatory retirement ages and a term limit to eliminate the possibility of certain judges serving for long periods. To upgrade and improve the quality of judicial selection, the American Judicature Society (1973) called for codes of judicial ethics, together with explicit judicial compensation and qualification criteria.

Other recommendations for standardizing the qualifications, training, and selection of judges are for public financing of judicial elections so that judges are not dependent on private contributions. A standard amount of money could be available to all judicial candidates for their election campaigns, and no private contributions of any kind would be allowed. Further, filing fees should not be required of anyone seeking a judgeship (Beechen, 1974). In some county elections, more affluent judges have spent considerably more of their own money on judicial campaigning than less affluent candidates have. The relative difference in campaign money spent by the different candidates can create the appearance of improper influence (Nicholson and Weiss, 1986). Further, candidates of modest means are disadvantaged and may be deterred from seeking public office.

Whether a judicial candidate is an incumbent or seeking a judgeship for the first time makes a substantial difference in the amount of financial support generated for the campaign. In the 1984 Cook County Circuit Court elections, for instance, judicial incumbents raised substantially more money for their campaigns from lawyer contributions than did fresh candidates. Even sitting judges who were sure losers were able to generate substantially more funding than winning candidates (Nicholson and Weiss, 1986).

Subsequent studies of partisan judicial elections that revealed private contributions and frivolous candidate expenditures have raised questions about judicial ethics and fairness (Keil et al., 1994). Further, the bars of various states have disclosed that they have little influence on the nature of voting for one judicial candidate or another in terms of their comparative qualifications (Keil et al., 1994).

Evidence suggests that voters are more attentive to judges' policy preferences and ideological inclinations than researchers have predicted. Based on a random sample of 1,012 ballots cast in the November 1988 Marion County, Oregon, judicial race, which occurred simultaneously with the Bush-Dukakis presidential campaign, voters were very much aware of the political philosophies and personal ideologies of those competing for judicial vacancies (Lovrich and Sheldon, 1994). In nearby Washington state, a survey of voters in a 1986 judicial election indicated that voter knowledge about judicial candidates and their views was critical to their participation in voting (Lovrich, Pierce, and Sheldon, 1989). In other states such as California, however, voters in judicial elections did not appear to be as informed or educated about the issues involved in judicial selections (Grodin, 1987).

Judicial Misconduct and Abuses of Discretion

Judicial conduct is monitored by different individuals and organizations in different jurisdictions. For instance, in New York, judicial conduct is monitored by the Commission on Judicial Conduct (League of Women Voters of New York State, 1979). The commission receives or initiates complaints with respect to the conduct, qualifications, fitness to perform, or performance of official duties of any judge in New York state. After investigation and a hearing, the commission may admonish, censure, remove, or retire a judge. Decisions by the commission may be appealed to the court of appeals.

Forms of Judicial Misconduct

There are several forms of judicial misconduct, but most relate to the performance of one's job as judge. A judge is a powerful entity who dominates the courtroom. Judges make rulings that have immense influence over trial outcomes.

JUDGES CAN INFLUENCE TRIAL OUTCOMES BY EXHIBITING PREJUDICE IN EVIDENTIARY RULINGS. One of the most frequent types of judicial misconduct is to prejudice the court proceedings in such a way that the trial outcome is favorable to one side or the other. Such behavior on a judge's part is difficult to detect, however. Simply ruling unfavorably against one side can be explained by numerous frivolous motions filed by that side. Further, most judges can rationalize their conduct if pressed to do so.

JUDGES CAN DELIBERATELY AGGRAVATE OR MITIGATE AN OFFENDER'S SENTENCE FOLLOWING CONVICTION. When offenders are convicted, judges can deliberately increase or decrease the severity of the sentence imposed. Again, it is difficult for court watchers to detect whether judicial intervention is the result of objective decision making or personal vindictiveness.

JUDGES CAN ACCEPT BRIBES FROM VARIOUS PARTIES IN COURT ACTIONS. Judges may also accept bribes from politicians or others when their rulings are influential. Especially in bench trials, when judges themselves decide the outcomes of cases, it is easy for judges to decide in favor of someone if a financial bribe has been received. Again, this form of misconduct is difficult to detect, but it is not completely undetectable. Bribery and judicial corruption were targeted in Operation Greylord in the late 1970s.

CORRUPT JUDGES AND OPERATION GREYLORD. In 1978, one of the largest and most successful investigations of judicial misconduct was launched. **Operation Greylord** was an FBI undercover sting operation that targeted the judges of Cook County, Illinois (Bensinger, 1988). The history of judicial corruption in and around Chicago was notorious and known throughout the United States. Politically corrupt judges would accept bribes for favorable bench decisions. Organized crime was able to flourish because of judicial participation in illicit activities.

The FBI task force fabricated a variety of court cases to be heard in Cook County courts. Conversations were tape-recorded between judges and undercover FBI agents posing as attorneys and defendants. Electronic surveillance and telephonic wiretaps were installed in different judges' offices in an effort to acquire incriminating information. The results of Operation Greylord were shocking. More than sixty judges and judicial adjuncts were prosecuted and convicted of various forms of judicial misconduct and corruption, including accepting bribes and prejudicing judgments in favor of certain undercover clients.

The immediate public reaction to Operation Greylord was a general loss of confidence in the Illinois judiciary, despite the fact that only Cook County was targeted. In later years, public confidence in the judiciary was restored through a series of judicial selection reforms. The Illinois Bar Association and judicial organizations adopted new ethical standards and modes of professional conduct. Merit selection of judges throughout Illinois became the rule rather than the exception. The administration of justice in Cook County was drastically overhauled and revised. Although judicial corruption and misconduct have not been entirely eliminated, Operation Greylord did much to reduce its existence (Illinois Supreme Court, 1993).

Criticisms of Judges

SOME JUDGES ARE INCOMPETENT AND INEXPERIENCED. Judicial incompetence is often associated with inexperience as a judge. When inexperienced judges rule on motions from the prosecution or defense, these judges may not fully understand the rules of evidence and whether the motion should be granted or denied. Often, inexperienced judges

Man Bites Dog? How about "Judge Bites Nose"?

Judge Joseph Troisi

It happened in St. Marys, West Virginia. Bill Witten, twenty-nine, was appearing before Judge Joseph Troisi, forty-seven, in the Pleasants County Circuit Court on grand larceny and burglary charges. The bail had been set at $40,000 for Witten, and he objected loudly. Witten became so vulgar and vocal that Judge Troisi lost his temper, stormed down from the judge's bench, and bit Witten on his nose. The two were separated by court officers, and Witten was led out of the courtroom.

In the aftermath, Judge Troisi was charged with assault and battery and resigned his judgeship. He pleaded no contest to a battery charge. Troisi faced one year in jail and a $500 fine. At the time of his plea, Judge Troisi faced federal civil rights charges carrying up to ten years in prison. Ray Witten, Bill Witten's father, said, "It once again proves that no matter who you are, you're not above the law."

Other observers claimed that Judge Troisi had had trouble on the bench in past years. Specifically, he could not control his temper. He was first elected to the bench in 1992 and had temper problems ever since.

Should judges be elected or appointed? Should these appointments be on the basis of one's skills as a judge or on political favoritism? How should Judge Troisi be punished for what he did? What do you think?

Source: Adapted from the Associated Press, "Judge Bites Defendant in the Nose." *Minot* (N.D.) *Daily News,* October 24, 1997:A2.

make these decisions on the basis of their emotional sentiment during the trial. Whenever judges make mistakes of judgment in ruling on motions, these are errors. They vary in their importance. Many errors are harmless, meaning that the outcome of the trial would not have been affected if the judge had ruled differently. Other types of errors are **harmful errors** or **reversible errors**.

Harmful or reversible errors may lead higher appellate courts to overturn judicial decisions. However, (1) not all errors are detected in a trial, (2) not all *guilty* verdicts are appealed, and (3) not all appeals are heard on their merits by higher courts. The U.S. Supreme Court hears only about four percent of the appeals it schedules annually.

For instance, in a murder case, a judge admitted into evidence photographs of the mutilated corpse of the victim, and the photographs had absolutely no bearing on the guilt or innocence of the accused. There were eyewitnesses to the murder, and the defendant's guilt had been proven beyond a reasonable doubt without the photographs. But the photographs obviously inflamed the jury and influenced their decision to impose the death penalty. The murder conviction was appealed, but the verdict was affirmed by a

ARE JUDGES ABOVE THE LAW?

The Case of Illinois Supreme Court Justice James Heiple

James Heiple was the chief justice of the Illinois Supreme Court until May 1997. He had served in that capacity for seven years of a ten-year term, but bad publicity and a call for his removal as a judge prompted him to resign. Nevertheless, various agencies and prosecutors are going after him for assorted violations of the law and for conduct unbecoming a judge.

One characteristic of Heiple, according to his critics, is his arrogance. He is also considered by some to be abrasive. In his personal life, Heiple snubbed his son's wedding and gloated over an opponent's loss. Professionally, it has been alleged that Heiple abused his judicial powers by waving his judicial card to avoid speeding tickets on several occasions. In one instance, officers stopped Heiple on suspicion of drunk driving, but Heiple drove off. Later, they tested Heiple and found that he was within the legal blood alcohol concentration limit and not intoxicated.

Beyond these traffic incidents, Heiple is alleged to have used his judicial office to obtain loans from banks. Further, Heiple appointed a personal friend to the Illinois Courts Commission when he learned that he was about to be sanctioned by that body. One of Heiple's former clerks, Bonita Welch, claims that Heiple cut her salary after she campaigned for one of Heiple's rivals in 1990.

Those who know Heiple intimately give a different impression of him. Rich Craig, a Chicago lawyer who clerked for Heiple in the 1980s, says that he can be gruff but is not the ogre portrayed in the media. But he still rubs people the wrong way, Craig admits. However, his defense attorney, former governor James Thompson, says, "If judges can be impeached for being arrogant or difficult, we'll have a lot of empty benches."

What standards should be imposed for regulating judicial conduct? Should judges have special privileges to escape police arrests for alleged traffic offenses? Do you believe that arrogant judges should be impeached? What do you think?

Source: Adapted from Debbie Howlett, "Impeachment Sought for 'Arrogant' Judge." *USA Today,* May 6, 1997:3A.

higher court. In that case, the court said there was so much evidence against the accused that the admission of these inflammatory materials into evidence resulted in harmless error. Under other circumstances, however, the admission of inflammatory photographs might be the final element necessary to persuade a jury to render a guilty verdict in an otherwise weak case against the defendant. Again, the trial judge controls the courtroom and influences the general course of the trial, as well as the defendant's chances for conviction or acquittal.

It is assumed by all appellate courts that the original judgment or verdict rendered by a lower trial court was the correct one. Therefore, a defendant must present clear and convincing evidence supporting a reversal of a verdict by the trial judge or jury. It is insufficient simply to prove that errors were committed. Even harmful errors are insufficient to overturn a judge's decision under certain conditions.

SOME JUDGES CONTRIBUTE TO COURT DELAYS AND CLOGGED COURT CALENDARS. Serious court delays are commonplace in most jurisdictions. A study of case processing in New York City, for instance, revealed that a significant obstacle contributing to court delays is inadequate judicial training (Correctional Association of New York, 1993). Technology facilitates case processing in many modern court systems, but some New York City judiciary have been slow to acquire new technology. Further, courses offered for judges on case management have relatively low enrollments. Realistic timetables are not adhered to, and more than a few judges inadvertently impede a defendant's right to a speedy trial because of their inefficient case management practices (Correctional Association of New York, 1993).

Other factors besides judicial inexperience contribute to case-processing delays. In some cases, there are attorney appearance conflicts, witness unavailability, attorney unpreparedness, vacations, and illness-precipitated court absences (Jacobs, Chayet, and Meara, 1986). Court delays in various jurisdictions are also due to a lack of resources and judicial support staff and equipment (Citizens Crime Commission of Connecticut, 1984). Increasing judges' knowledge through mandatory education programs is one means of facilitating case processing (National Center for State Courts, 1976).

MANY JUDGES IMPOSE DISPARATE SENTENCES. Judicial discretion in sentencing is often criticized by researchers who say that judges make decisions primarily on extralegal factors rather than legal ones (Pollack and Smith, 1983; Zumwalt, 1973). Legal factors include prior record, seriousness of the current offense, age, and acceptance of responsibility. Extralegal factors refer to race or ethnicity, gender, socioeconomic status, and attitude (Schulhofer, 1979). Sentencing disparities attributable to race, gender, socioeconomic status, and other extralegal factors have plagued judges for years (Coppom, 1979; Evans and Gilbert, 1975; Gazell, 1972). Commissions and state legislatures have attempted to create greater sentencing consistency and bind judges to nonarbitrary standards (McFatter, 1986; U.S. House Committee on the Judiciary, 1984). Sentencing guidelines have been created in most jurisdictions to make the punishments for various offenses more uniform (Hennessey, 1976; Wilkins et al., 1976). Some observers question whether structured sentencing guidelines will eliminate disparities in judicial decision making, however (McDonald, 1983). Experiments with various types of sentencing reforms have shown some success in improving judicial fairness (Federal Judicial Center, 1981; Miller, Roberts, and Carter, 1981; Stern, 1980).

IT TAKES ONLY ONE BAD JUDGE

U.S. District Judge James Ware

They sit in judgment of federal law violators. They are a proud and arrogant lot who dominate their courtrooms like kings in early England. They get away with much in the federal courtrooms that would typically result in mistrials in state courts. Who are they? Federal district judges. They are appointed for life by the president of the United States, with the consent of Congress. They may take early retirement at full salary after serving only ten years on the federal bench. Salaries in 1998 were approaching the $200,000 mark for federal district court judges.

The public therefore expects from U.S. district court judges a high standard of integrity and job performance. When we see one or more of these judges act in inappropriate ways, it causes us serious problems. We know that these judges must be squeaky clean and have nearly perfect personal histories. When these facts are challenged, so is our faith in the judicial system.

Judge James Ware, fifty-one, was a U.S. district court judge in San Jose, California, in November 1997, when he was nominated by President Bill Clinton for an appointment to the Ninth Circuit Court of Appeals. In fact, many political insiders considered Judge Ware to be another potential black Supreme Court justice in future years.

On more than one occasion, Judge Ware reminded vast audiences of his early childhood in Birmingham, Alabama. He recited how he was there when his brother, thirteen-year-old Virgil Ware, was shot to death by an angry white mob who opposed Martin Luther King Jr. and integration. Judge Ware told his audiences, "When I went through the death of my brother, I came very close to becoming someone who could hate with a passion. What happened to me was a defining experience, a turning point in my life." Comments from Judge Ware from the 1960s? No. These comments were made and reported in the *San Jose Mercury News* on August 26, 1994. The main problem with the article was that it was not true. Ware did indeed have a brother named Virgil Ware, but not the one killed in Birmingham.

The real brother of Virgil Ware was hot under the collar. "I couldn't believe a judge would do something like that, being a man of the law. I think it was wrong. He was trying to better himself off somebody else's grief." Judge Ware was appointed to the federal bench by President George Bush in 1990, after Ware had served as a state court judge in California from 1988 to 1990. Bill Clinton nominated Ware to the Circuit Court on June 27, 1997.

Following the revelation that Ware was unrelated to the dead Virgil Ware from Birmingham, the judge withdrew his name from consideration for the

(continued)

It Takes Only One Bad Judge *(continued)*

Circuit Court judgeship. Then he backpedaled. He claimed that he did have a brother. Further, he said his father had a vague relation with a woman who bore him a son named "Virge." "I did live in Birmingham at the time of the event. But I did use my tenuous connection with the Wares and my own feeling of loss as a basis for making a speech about Virgil Ware's death." Virgil Ware's brother was unimpressed.

Should Judge Ware be forced to resign as a U.S. district court judge? How important is this lie about his brother's death in Birmingham in the 1960s? Did he use this lie to get sympathy from President Bush and the position of district court judge? Should this lie disqualify him as a district court judge? What do you think?

Source: Adapted from the Associated Press, "Judge Acknowledges Lie, Withdraws Nomination." *Minot* (N.D.) *Daily News*, November 7, 1997:A3.

Removing Judges from Office

Whenever corrupt or incompetent judges are identified, there are relatively few mechanisms available to remove them from office. In New York, judicial conduct is monitored by the Commission on Judicial Conduct (League of Women Voters of New York State, 1979). The commission receives or initiates complaints with respect to the conduct, qualifications, fitness to perform, or performance of official duties of any judge in New York. After investigation and a hearing, the commission may admonish, censure, remove, or retire a judge. However, decisions made by the commission are directly appealable to the New York Court of Appeals.

Independent commissions to oversee judicial misconduct are not new. Proposals have been made or adopted in North Carolina, Kentucky, Alaska, Colorado, Idaho, Iowa, Oklahoma, Nebraska, Utah, and Vermont (American Judicature Society, 1971; North Carolina Courts Commission, 1971; Uppal, 1974).

The first state to implement a commission to deal with judicial misconduct was California. In 1960, California created a **judicial conduct commission** that was charged with investigating complaints against judges. The attorneys, judges, and politically prestigious other people who are commission members function as a part of the California Supreme Court. They meet in secret, and their findings are confidential. They investigate misconduct reports against California state trial judges and make recommendations to the California Supreme Court. Their array of sanctions includes recommendations for private censure, removal from the bench, and retirement. The California Supreme Court has the final authority concerning recommendations made by the judicial conduct commission (Brooks, 1985; Miller, 1991). Table 5.8 shows states that had judicial conduct organizations for the years 1996–1997.

ANOTHER BAD JUDGE?

The Case of Judge Randall Hoffman, Jamestown, North Dakota

Judicial codes of conduct exist in every state. These codes are intended to provide guidance about how judges should conduct themselves, both inside and outside the courtroom. These codes also prescribe sanctions and methods for imposing them whenever allegations of judicial misconduct are determined to be true.

In Jamestown, North Dakota, Judge Randall Hoffman was elected in 1994 to serve a term as judge in the North Dakota Southeast Judicial District. However, in March 1997, things went sour for Judge Hoffman. Divorced, he was bitter and hostile toward his ex-wife. On more than one occasion, it is alleged, Hoffman engaged in abusive conduct around her, either through threatening telephone calls or scenes in public places. A restraining order was issued, barring Hoffman from any further contact with his ex-wife, by telephone or otherwise. However, this did not deter him from further antagonistic conduct.

According to police reports filed by his ex-wife and a mutual friend, Hoffman entered the home of the friend one morning in August 1997 by going through a garage door and knocking on the screen door. Although he did not actually enter the house, he stood in the garage and shouted obscenities at his friend and ex-wife through the screen door. Police were called to remove Hoffman. Before the police arrived, however, his ex-wife walked into the garage to confront Hoffman, where, she said, he kicked her. Hoffman later claimed that his ex-wife tripped while coming into the garage and that the bruises on her legs were from the accidental fall.

On another occasion, Hoffman relayed to police officers misleading information about his ex-wife in order to solicit their assistance in recovering her automobile, which he claimed he owned. While trying to get his ex-wife's vehicle, he made obscene gestures and used vulgarities.

Hoffman is also accused of being abusive to the judge who issued the restraining order. He called out in the courtroom, "Judge Smith's petition and order are bullshit! They are a fiasco!" Later, Hoffman admitted making the remarks in court, but he denied that these remarks constituted judicial misconduct or violated any judicial conduct rules.

In April 1998, the Judicial Conduct Commission was served with a complaint against Judge Hoffman, alleging all of those actions and, further, that Hoffman had demeaned his office and undermined public confidence in the judiciary. He was accused of stalking and engaging in abusive conduct toward his ex-wife. If the charges against Hoffman are sustained, he could face the penalties of removal from office, retirement, suspension, restrictions on his judicial duties, and/or censure. In the meantime, he has consented to an

(continued)

ANOTHER BAD JUDGE? *(continued)*

agreement reached by the attorney general's office whereby he will refrain from contacting his ex-wife in any way and not break any state laws. Under this agreement, he does not have to admit guilt to any of the charges and will retain his judgeship.

What do you think of the Judicial Conduct Commission in North Dakota? Does a judge cross the line as a judge when his personal behavior becomes a matter of public record, such as stalking and assault? How would you punish Judge Hoffman if the charges were substantiated? What do you think?

Source: Adapted from the Associated Press, "Jamestown Judge Accused of Violating Judicial Code of Conduct." *Minot* (N.D.) *Daily News*, April 10, 1998:B4.

Unfortunately, the United States has a poor record for sanctioning the behaviors of bad judges. Compared with other nations such as France, Italy, and Great Britain, judicial conduct organizations in the United States institute relatively few cases of judicial sanctioning (Volcansek, DeFranciscis, and Lafron, 1996). One reason for this lack of commitment to sanction bad judges is that American judges enjoy near-absolute judicial independence. They face relatively little accountability. However, bad judges can be removed either through impeachment or recall elections. Table 5.9 shows judicial misconduct complaints and dispositions handled by judicial conduct organizations for 1996–1997.

During that period, 10,588 misconduct complaints were received by state judicial conduct organizations. About seventy-six percent (9,856) of these complaints were dismissed outright, and most of the remaining cases were informally disposed of with reprimands, short-term suspensions, and fines. Only 111 cases resulted in judges vacating their offices (Maguire and Pastore, 2000:450–451). Thus, the system is weighted heavily in favor of judges, even bad ones. The likelihood that a complaint against any given judge will be sustained is less than five percent. It is even more alarming that there are few provisions for issuing severe sanctions against the worst judges. Although the existence of judicial conduct organizations is commendable, these organizations have relatively little power in administering judicial sanctions.

Impeachment

Impeachment means to allege wrongdoing against a judge or other public official before a legislative or judicial body vested with the authority to remove that judge or public official from office. For impeachment to be successful, the allegations must be well founded and upheld by compelling evidence against the accused. In many jurisdictions,

TABLE 5.8 Staff and Budget of Judicial Conduct Organizations by State, 1996–1997

State	Total Employed	Administrative or Executive Director	Attorneys	Investigators	Administrative Assistants, Secretaries	Other Staff	Budget Amount[a]	Judges Subject to Jurisdiction
Alabama[b]	3	1	0	0	1	1	$175,411	645
Alaska	2	1	0	0	1	0	225,400[c]	62
Arizona	4	1	0	1	1	1	312,000	444
Arkansas	4	1	0	1	1	1	289,176	400[d]
California	25	1	14	0	8	2	3,010,000	1,580
Colorado	2	1	0	0	1	0	108,000	284
Connecticut	2	1	0	(e)	1	0	191,263[f]	271
Delaware[g]	X	X	X	X	X	X	X	112
District of Columbia	3	1	1	0	1	0	120,004[h]	89
Florida	4	1	2	0	1	NA	458,888	789
Georgia	3	1	0	1	1	0	166,000	1,800[d]
Hawaii	8	0	0	0	1	7[i]	70,882	117
Idaho	2	1	0	0	1	0	109,300	120
Illinois	5	1	0	2	2	0	548,300	914
Kansas	5	1	1	2	1	0	38,032[j]	500[k]
Kentucky	5	1	1	2	1	0	93,986	404
Maine	2	1	0	0	1	0	40,000	68[k]
Michigan	7	1	3	0	3	0	920,600	1,077[k]
Minnesota	2	1	0	0	1	0	258,000	359
Mississippi	5	1	1	1	2	0	321,478	700
Missouri	3	1	0	0	2	0	190,581	650
Nebraska	3	1	0	0	2	0	15,000[f]	137
Nevada	2	1	0	0	1	0	318,081	149
New Hampshire	3	1	0	0	2	0	15,000[l]	240
New Jersey	3	1	0	1	1	0	175,000	825
New Mexico	NA	NA	NA	NA	NA	NA	180,832	NA
New York	21	1	7	4	7	2	1,736,500	3,500
North Carolina	2	1	0	0	1	0	105,270	317
North Dakota[m]	4	0	2	0	2	0	248,000	125

(continued)

145

TABLE 5.8 *(continued)*

State	Total Employed	Administrative or Executive Director	Attorneys	Investigators	Administrative Assistants, Secretaries	Other Staff	Budget Amount[a]	Judges Subject to Jurisdiction
Ohio	13	1	4	1	5	2	1,215,278	1,125
Oklahoma	2	1	0	0	1	0	250,000[n]	600[d]
Oregon	1	1	0	0	0	0	50,996[c]	500[d]
Pennsylvania	9	2	2	2	2	1	838,000	1,000[d]
Rhode Island	1	0	0	0	0	1	84,473	134[d]
South Carolina	2	1	0	0	1	0	500,633[f]	775
South Dakota[e]	X	X	X	X	X	X	29,539	57
Tennessee	5	1	1	0	1	2	100,000	590
Texas	16	1	8	0	5	2	690,793	3,500[d]
Utah	3	1	0	2	0	0	211,000	233
Virginia	3	1	1	0	1	0	392,083	819
Washington	6	1	0	2	2	1	618,120	406[d]
West Virginia[o]	7	2	0	5	0	0	(l)	342
Wisconsin	2	1	0	0	1	0	199,300	850
Wyoming	1	0	0	0	1	0	75,283	130[d]

Note: The Center for Judicial Conduct Organizations conducts annual surveys of judicial conduct organizations. These organizations are typically state agencies created by statute or constitutional amendment with the mandate to receive, investigate, and dispose of complaints regarding judicial misconduct. Figures presented include both full- and part-time staff. Information was not available for Indiana, Iowa, Louisiana, Maryland, Massachusetts, and Vermont.

Judicial conduct organizations use different reporting periods. Many of the figures are for calendar year 1997. Other reporting periods are: 9/26 to 8/97 for Texas; 8/97 to 8/98 for Tennessee; 9/96 to 9/97 for New Jersey; 1/96 to 12/96 for Maine, Minnesota, Ohio; 7/97 to 6/98 for Georgia, Illinois, Pennsylvania, South Carolina, South Dakota, Utah, New Mexico; 7/96 to 6/97 for Connecticut, Hawaii, Kentucky, Missouri, Nevada, Washington, Florida; 10/96 to 9/97 for Alabama, District of Columbia.

[a]Cross-jurisdiction comparisons of budgets should be done with caution. Some judicial conduct organizations have their offices in private buildings and must pay rent, while other organizations are located in state buildings and incur no rental expense. The budgets of some judicial conduct organizations include all salaries of their personnel, while other organizations receive personnel support from state agencies.

[b]Alabama has a two-tier judicial disciplinary system; figures are for the Judicial Inquiry Commission, the first tier.

[c]The commission may request additional funds for litigation, investigations, or hearings.

[d]Approximate.

[e]Personnel are hired as needed.

[f]Does not include litigation costs. In most cases, these costs are borne by the state attorney general's office.

146

[g]The Court on the Judiciary does not have a budget or staff. The supreme court designates a clerk and may designate one or more deputy clerks, who have powers prescribed by the court. At the time of the survey, a staff attorney with the supreme court was designated as the clerk.

[h]The budget of the Commission on Judicial Disabilities and Tenure also covers the costs for its evaluation of active judges who seek reappointment and the reviews of retired judges who wish to continue their judicial service as senior judges.

[i]The seven members of the Commission on Judicial Conduct perform many staff functions.

[j]Includes litigation costs only and does not accurately reflect the dollars spent operating the Commission on Judicial Qualifications each year. Staff salaries, office space, telephone, copying, and faxing are absorbed in the appellate clerk's budget. If these items were included, the budget would exceed $150,000.

[k]In addition, the commission has jurisdiction over certain other court personnel, such as retired judges and pro tem judges.

[l]The budget is part of the supreme court budget.

[m]Staff and budget are shared by the Judicial Conduct Commission and the Disciplinary Board of the Supreme Court.

[n]Does not include litigation costs.

[o]West Virginia has a two-tier judicial disciplinary system; figures are for the Judicial Investigation Commission, the first tier.

Source: Maguire and Pastore, 2000:74.

TABLE 5.9 Judicial Misconduct Complaints and Dispositions Handled by Judicial Conduct Organizations by Type of Disposition and State, 1996–1997

	Complaints							Disposition of Complaints	
	Pending at beginning of reporting period	Received during reporting period	Pending at end of reporting period	Dismissed without formal or informal action	Informal action taken	Judge vacated office[a]	Case dismissed after formal hearing	Judge privately censured, admonished, or reprimanded	Judge publicly censured, admonished, or reprimanded
Alabama[c]	8	264	27	239	9	0	0	(d)	1
Alaska	12	49	19	39	1	0	0	1	0
Arizona	60	254	48	227	30	2	0	30	0
Arkansas	115	250	157	196	1	2	0	(d)	7
California	107	1,183	108	1,114	43	2	4	10	5
Colorado	2	114	0	109	0	3	0	4	0
Connecticut	17	102	15	0	0	0	NA	0	1
Delaware	8	32	3	33	(d)	0	3	(d)	1
District of Columbia	4	14	1	16	1	0	0	0	0
Florida	4	513	2	424	13	4	0	(d)	2
Georgia	16	74	9	62	7	1	0	7	0
Hawaii	2	51	12	41	1	0	0	0	0
Idaho	26	202	12	55	3	0	0	2	(d)
Illinois	161	41[f]	217	283	97	0	0	0	0
Kansas	9	347	11	311	10	0	0	1	4
Kentucky	18	200	13	190	10	1	0	1	2
Louisiana	138	—	81	210	122	27	1	2	2
Maine	7	38	5	40	4	0	0	0	0
Michigan	203	630	231	563[f]	25[f]	3	0	10	2
Minnesota	14	111	13	106	12	0	0	0	2
Mississippi	41	335	46	297	16	0	1	1	5
Missouri	35	202	28	189	16	0	0	16	0
Nebraska	10	64	14	6	0	0	0	(d)	0
Nevada	32	110	19	100	1	2	0	(d)	1
New Hampshire	17	80	25	61	6	0	0	5	0
New Jersey	55	267	35	271	3	3	0	12	1

State									
New Mexico	NA	NA	NA	118	15	14	1	0	0
New York	172	1,403	152	1,317	49	28	2	(d)	14
North Carolina	17	202	25	179	0	1	0	5	1
North Dakota	12	36	11	36	0	0	0	1	0
Ohio[h]	11	463	20	365	(d)	0	0	(d)	2
Oregon	10	118	3	119	6	0	0	(d)	0
Pennsylvania[i]	167	532	128	541	24	0	0	0	2
Rhode Island	4	19	3	18	1	0	0	2	0
South Carolina	24	206	60	91	10	1	0	6	4
South Dakota	1	13	1	13	0	0	0	0	0
Tennessee	198	224	215	193	0	4	0	7	(d)
Texas	386	789	348	758	(d)	3	0	32	7
Utah	49	95	66	76	6	1	0	1	2
Washington	60	251	83	205	(d)	6	0	(d)	3
West Virginia	43	244	28	243	4	2	2	(d)	4
Wisconsin	7	344	10	343	4	1	0	(d)	1
Wyoming	6	28	6	27	0	0	0	0	(d)

Note: The Center for Judicial Conduct Organizations conducts annual surveys of judicial conduct organizations. These organizations are typically state agencies created by statute or constitutional amendment with the mandate to receive, investigate, and dispose of complaints regarding judicial misconduct. The judicial conduct organizations handle complaints such as judicial prejudice or bias, slow processing of orders, procedural or administrative irregularity, courtroom demeanor, and conflict of interest. (The Center for Judicial Conduct Organizations, *Judicial Conduct Reporter* 3 (Fall 1981), p.2.) A confidentiality provision prohibits revealing disposition of complaints in Virginia. Information was not available for Iowa, Massachusetts, Montana, Oklahoma, and Vermont. Cross-jurisdiction comparisons should be done cautiously due to differences among the states in reporting periods, definitions of complaints, authorized sanctions, and recording practices. For the states of Alabama, Alaska, Arizona, California, Connecticut, Idaho, Illinois, Kansas, Kentucky, Michigan, Mississippi, Missouri, Nevada, North Carolina, Rhode Island, South Carolina, Tennessee, Utah, Washington, and West Virginia, any discrepancies in totals are due to multiple or consolidated complaints and/or dispositions.

Judicial conduct organizations use different reporting periods. Many of the statistics in this table are for calendar year 1997. Other reporting periods are: 9/26 to 8/97 for Texas; 8/97 to 8/98 for Tennessee; 9/96 to 9/97 for New Jersey; 1/96 to 12/96 for Maine, Minnesota, Ohio; 7/97 to 6/98 for Georgia, Illinois, New Mexico, Pennsylvania, South Carolina, South Dakota, Utah; 7/96 to 6/97 for Connecticut, Florida, Hawaii, Kentucky, Missouri, Nevada, Washington; 10/96 to 9/97 for Alabama, District of Columbia.

[a]Includes judges who vacated office while investigation was pending or after formal charges were filed.

[b]This category encompasses a number of statues including misconduct cases that were pending before the supreme court, judges who were suspended as an interim sanction, orders for education, retirement, and disability.

[c]Alabama has a two-tier judicial disciplinary system. The Judicial Inquiry Commission receives and investigates complaints. The Court of the Judiciary hears complaints filled by the commission and issues a judgment.

[d]Sanction not available in the jurisdiction.

[e]The Delaware Constitution empowers the Court on the Judiciary to "censure, remove or retire" any judicial officer. The constitution does not specifically provide that the court may suspend, fine, or assess fees or costs; however, case law has made it clear that the power to suspend a judicial officer is inherent in the express powers granted to the court by the constitution. Whether the court has the inherent authority to impose other lesser sanctions, such as a fine, fees, or costs or interim suspension, is not clearly settled.

[f]Approximate.

[g]The supreme court has not decided if it has the authority to impose a fee.

[h]Figures are from the Disciplinary Counsel for the Supreme Court, which handles over 90% of the complaints against Ohio judges. The balance are handled by state or local certified grievance committees.

[i]Pennsylvania has a two-tier judicial disciplinary system. These numbers are for the Judicial Conduct Board, which files charges with the Court of Judicial Discipline.

Source: Maguire and Pastore, 2000:450.

149

the state supreme court is the sanctioning body that hears impeachment allegations against judges and has the power to act to either remove the judge or dismiss the allegations (American Bar Association, 1975).

For instance, suppose a judge continually fails to safeguard the rights of indigents in criminal cases. A judge might require a defendant to plead without representation by court-appointed counsel. A judge may tell a jury that he believes a defendant is guilty (Becker, 1985). A judge might set a particularly high and arbitrary bail amount for someone who is not dangerous or likely to flee the jurisdiction. The judge may coerce defendants out of their appeal rights. These forms of disrespect for the law occur from time to time in U.S. courts (Feldman, 1973). However, few mechanisms have existed to remove these judges from office (Braithwaite, 1971).

In more recent years, procedures have been suggested to systematize the judicial sanctioning process. Certain rules have been promulgated by the Federal Judicial Center to govern how complaints are filed, the review of complaints by chief judges, the review of the chief judge's disposition of the complaint, an investigation and recommendation by a special committee, rules dealing with **confidentiality**, public availability of decisions rendered, disqualification, and withdrawal of complaints and petitions for review (Browning, Seitz, and Clark, 1986).

Recall Elections

Another mechanism is the **recall election.** A petition is circulated by interested citizens or by city council in response to complaints against a judicial official. A special election is held, with alternative candidates presented to fill the judicial post. A popular vote results in the bad judge's removal from office, as well as support for a new judge to replace the bad one. Recall elections depend heavily on citizen involvement and concern (Tauro, 1968).

One other option is for a bad judge to simply resign. For instance, in Lakewood, Washington, a suburb of Seattle, Lakewood Municipal Judge Ralph H. Baldwin admitted to drinking beer with a defense lawyer and the prosecutor while the jury deliberated the fate of a defendant facing drunk-driving charges. Even after the case was over and the jury had rendered a verdict of guilty, the judge invited the jury members into his chambers and served them alcoholic beverages. Some jurors were clearly offended by the judge's actions, and his conduct was immediately reported to the Lakewood City Council. When the city council confronted Baldwin with the allegations, he admitted them, stating, "I want you to know that none of my words or actions on that evening arose from malice but rather from a misguided sense of congeniality and extremely poor judgment. To each of you, I extend my sincere apologies." Baldwin had served for only three months as municipal judge, at an annual salary of $65,000, when the incident occurred (Associated Press, 1998:A2). Baldwin was not available for comment about his resignation when reporters attempted to contact him.

Summary

In any court proceeding, the key official is the judge. At the local, state, and federal levels, judges are either elected or appointed. Among state courts, partisan and nonpartisan elections account for about two thirds of all judicial positions. State governors and the U.S. president make other judicial appointments. The president selects U.S. district court judges, appellate judges, and U.S. Supreme Court justices, subject to congressional approval. An increasingly popular judicial selection method is appointment on the basis of merit. One of these merit plans is known as the Missouri plan.

The backgrounds of judges are varied. Many performing the judicial role have limited legal experience or expertise, and a large portion lack law degrees. To ensure better judicial performance among those less skilled in the law, many judges are required to undergo judicial training. This training familiarizes judges with procedural and evidentiary law, and it socializes them concerning different motions that may be made by prosecutors or defense counsel, as well as how to rule on such motions.

In virtually every U.S. jurisdiction, the judiciary is flawed in some ways, and judges vary in their judicial effectiveness and how their courts are managed. Some judges deliberately engage in misconduct, such as influencing trial outcomes because of bribery or aggravating or mitigating the sentences they impose. Some judges are simply incompetent, and their poor decisions cause appellate courts to reverse their verdicts or sentences. Other judges sentence particular offenders according to extralegal criteria, such as race, ethnicity, socioeconomic status, or gender. These sentencing disparities reflect bias or prejudice.

When appeals are filed by either side following a judgment, appellate courts assume that the original trial judge's decision was the correct one, regardless of whether it was. This presumption is quite difficult to overcome because appellants must prove by a preponderance of the evidence that the ruling was wrong. Errors cited by appellants may be harmless, harmful, or reversible. Harmless or harmful errors may be insufficient to change the original trial outcome. Reversible errors often result in convictions being set aside or simply overturned. Under these circumstances, prosecutors must decide whether to retry the case and expend scarce resources for a new trial.

It is difficult to recall judges and remove them from office. Some states have judicial conduct commissions, where people, usually convicted offenders, can lodge complaints about their treatment in court and how judicial misconduct or abuse of office caused their convictions. Most complaints are rejected. Hard evidence must be presented for a judge to be sanctioned, and removing a judge from office requires even harder evidence. In some jurisdictions, judges may be removed from their positions through recall elections. Another strategy for removing judges from office is impeachment. Under the rules of impeachment, evidence must be presented to a legislative body of a judge's wrongful conduct. Again, a high standard of proof is required to sustain particular charges of misconduct against judges and to justify sanctioning actions.

KEY TERMS

Bureaucracy	Judge	Merit selection
Centralization	Judicial appointments	Missouri plan
Confidentiality	Judicial conduct	Nonpartisan elections
Harmful errors	commission	Operation Greylord
Impeachment	Judicial powers	Partisan elections
Incumbents	Judicial process	Recall election
Interim judges	Kales plan	Reversible errors

QUESTIONS FOR REVIEW

1. Are there any national qualifications for judges in state courts? What kinds of qualifications would you propose?

2. Distinguish between partisan and nonpartisan elections of judges. Is one type of election better than the other? Why or why not?

3. In some states, judges are appointed by governors. What are some criticisms of gubernatorial appointees?

4. How are U.S. Supreme Court justices appointed? Who must approve these appointments?

5. Describe how Federal Circuit Court judges, U.S. District Court judges, and U.S. magistrates are appointed.

6. What is a popular merit method for selecting judges? Why is it favored in various states?

7. Is the merit plan for judicial selection superior to legislative or gubernatorial appointment methods? Why or why not?

8. Differentiate between the Kales plan and the Missouri plan.

9. What sort of training do judges typically receive before becoming judges?

10. Identify four types of judicial misconduct.

11. How can we sanction judges who engage in misconduct?

12. What are two mechanisms for removing bad judges from the bench? Describe each process briefly.

SUGGESTED READINGS

American Bar Association. (1999). *Perceptions of the U.S. Justice System.* Chicago: American Bar Association.

Calhoun, Frederick S. (1998). *Hunters and Howlers: Threats of Violence against Federal Judicial Officials in the United States, 1789–1993.* Washington, DC: U.S. Marshals Service.

Gottfredson, Don M. (1999). *Effects of Judges' Sentencing Decisions on Criminal Careers.* Washington, DC: U.S. National Institute of Justice.

Murphy, Timothy R., Paul L. Hannaford, and Genevra Kay Loveland. (1998). *Managing Notorious Trials.* Williamsburg, VA: National Center for State Courts.

Ostrom, Brian J. and Roger A. Hanson. (1999). *Efficiency, Timeliness, and Quality: A New Perspective from Nine State Criminal Trial Courts.* Williamsburg, VA: National Center for State Courts.

Ostrom, Brian J. and Neal B. Kauder. (1995). *Examining the Work of State Courts, 1993: A National Perspective from the Court Statistics Project.* Williamsburg, VA: National Center for State Courts.

Pizzi, William T. (1999). *Trials without Truth: Why Our System of Criminal Trials Has Become an Expensive Failure and What We Need to Do to Rebuild It.* New York: New York University Press.

Stith, Kate and Jose A. Cabranes. (1998). *Fear of Judging: Sentencing Guidelines in the Federal Courts.* Chicago: University of Chicago Press.

Wrightsman, Lawrence S. (1999). *Judicial Decision Making: Is Psychology Relevant?* New York: Kluwer Academic/Plenum.

JURIES

IT WAS FINALLY TIME, time to kill. Time to end the years of abuse and torment. While her common-law husband lay passed out drunk in the pickup, Jane Stafford shot and killed him. When arrested by police, Jane admitted killing her husband while he was unarmed and unconscious. She was charged with first-degree murder. However, during the trial the jury would hear the alarming details of her husband's abuse for more than five years. The jury learned that many in the community, even law enforcement, feared Jane's husband. He weighed over 250 pounds and had abused and assaulted two previous wives and their children. Jane was also sexually abused by her husband, even forced to have sex with a dog. How would the jury decide the case? She had admitted killing him when he was passed out drunk and no immediate threat to her. To the surprise of almost everyone, the jury returned a verdict of not guilty. Did the jury return the correct verdict? This murder was obviously not self-defense. How could the jury justify the verdict? If you were a juror in this case, how would you vote? (*Source:* J. Steed. "Will Battered Wife Face a New Murder Trial?" *Toronto Globe and Mail.* February 4, 1983:A1.)

A NEW MEANING was given to being high in March 1998. Matthew Smith, 28, was a juror in a criminal trial involving three defendants who were charged with selling illegal drugs. On the evening prior to jury deliberations, Smith met with the three defendants, who had been released on bail, and smoked marijuana with them. The following day, the defendants were convicted of the drug charges. However, immediately following the conviction, the offenders' lawyers filed juror misconduct allegations with the court on appeal, alleging what Smith had done. According to the convicted offenders, Smith spoke to one defendant and then to another after retrieving a dollar bill that one of the defendants had dropped in the court parking lot. After closing arguments on the last trial day, Smith joined the three defendants in one of their rooms, where they consumed a large quantity of marijuana. The trial had lasted 3½ weeks in federal court. Although the three defendants were convicted, five others named as co-conspirators were acquitted. Smith was immediately indicted by a federal prosecutor on the basis of testimony from the convicted offenders. Subsequently, in December 1997, he pleaded guilty to contempt of court for smoking marijuana during the trial with the criminal defendants. He was sentenced on March 27, 1998, to six months of home confinement and two years of probation. How would you guard against such juror misconduct in such a trial? Should jurors be tested for drugs during trial proceedings? Do you think Smith was sufficiently punished for his misconduct in smoking pot with three federal criminal defendants? What do you think? (*Source:* Adapted from the Associated Press, "Juror Confined for Getting High." *Minot* (N.D.) *Daily News,* March 31, 1998:A2.)

Introduction

Many people assume that the right to a jury trial has always been an important part of most societies. However, history suggests that using juries to judge disputes is relatively rare. In ancient times, disputes or conflicts were resolved through direct interpersonal violence. The disputants engaged in some form of physical confrontation (e.g., duel or battle), and the winner of the confrontation was also the winner of the dispute. If this were the case today, prizefighter Mike Tyson might never have been convicted of rape and incarcerated in an Indiana prison.

The role of the jury has often been challenged and revised. In the last few decades, the integrity of the jury system has been questioned as defendants who seem guilty are freed when the jury announces a verdict of not guilty. Often, juries award multimillion dollar damages to plaintiffs on the basis of allegations against defendants that seem questionable. Many legal scholars argue that juries should be replaced with panels of experts who would be more likely to see the merits of a case, understand the law, and avoid being swayed by emotion (Adler, 1994).

The History of Juries

The jury system in America has not had a direct, linear evolution. The ancient Greeks were the first to rely on certain people in their community to pass judgment on a variety of cases. At one point, the entire population of Athens was required to hear appeals from the magistrates, a process that became difficult to administer. Subsequently, jury members were drawn from a cross-section of the community to work with the magistrate and render decisions in criminal cases. This new jury was called a dicastery.

The ancient Romans also relied on an early form of the jury. In 190 B.C., for instance, magistrates could assemble a jury for certain criminal acts, including forgery, counterfeiting, and embezzlement. A jury of thirty-five to seventy-five people decided the guilt of the accused. There were no provisions for appeals of verdicts.

In earlier times, common-law juries had the dual function of investigating crimes and conducting trials of the accused. After the Norman invasion in England, these two responsibilities were divided into separate functioning units. The grand jury was created to investigate and report crimes, and the petit jury determined a defendant's guilt or innocence. Today, these different jury systems continue to perform the same functions.

The Development of the Grand Jury

The earliest forms of the **grand jury** can be traced back to Germanic tribal law and Anglo-Saxon dooms. The earliest versions of the grand jury had its origins in the Assize of Clarendon in 1166. An assize is essentially an order by the king that is binding throughout the kingdom. On this occasion, King Henry II ordered that twelve of every hundred family heads be placed under oath to report offenses or known criminals to the authorities. The most commonly reported offenses were robberies, murders, and theft. This practice resembled our contemporary neighborhood watch programs.

In American colonial times, judges traveled in circuits and visited certain cities or towns only every few months. Members of a grand jury were responsible for gathering information about known criminal activity and presenting their information to the authorities whenever the circuit judge was in town. Most often, when judges heard the cases presented to them by the grand jury, they ordered the defendant banished from the community. In essence, all trials during these early years were bench trials. The judge decided the guilt or innocence of defendants and determined the nature of the punishment. The petit jury or trial jury as we know it did not descend directly from the grand jury. Rather, it gradually replaced trials by ordeal.

The Development of the Petit Jury

Medieval England used trials by ordeal to determine a defendant's guilt or innocence. The prevailing practice was to have the process blessed by a priest in the belief that a proceeding endorsed by the church and ultimately by God would be just. The trial participants believed that God would intervene to protect an innocent defendant from harm. For example, the trial by hot water required defendants to remove a rock placed at the bottom of a pot of boiling water. Their hands were then wrapped in bandages. When, after a specified time, the bandages were removed, defendants with burned hands were believed to be guilty because God had not intervened to protect the accused from harm. This practice went unchallenged for centuries.

As of the Fourth Lateran Council in 1215, the church withdrew its support of the trial by ordeal and no longer supplied priests to bless the trial. The trial by ordeal was gradually replaced by the **petit jury** or trial jury. Initially, those accused of crimes were reluctant to accept a jury trial because being found guilty meant they would lose their property and their descendants would lose their inheritance, a penalty not applied to those who opted for the bench trial.

Another significant event occurred in 1215. King John of England was forced to sign the Magna Carta, a document that provided the foundations for due process and the right to a jury trial by one's peers. The section of the Magna Carta that established this concept reads, "No Freeman shall be taken, or imprisoned or be disseized of his Freehold, or Liberties, or Free Customs, or be outlawed, or exiled, or otherwise destroyed; nor will we not pass upon him nor condemn him, but by lawful judgement of his peers, of by (a) the Law of the land. (2) We will sell to no man, (b) we will not deny or defer to any man either Justice or Right" (McCart, 1964:5).

Originally, these rights extended to only nobility, and most people were still denied justice and the due process of law. The rights of a jury trial and due process were addressed in the Statute of Westminister of 1275. The relevant portions of this statute mandated that "no City, Borough, nor town nor any maybe amerced [fined or punished arbitrarily] without reasonable cause, and according to the Quality of his Trespass, that is to say, every Freeman saving his Freehold, a Merchant saving his Merchandise, a Villain saving his Gaynage [his rights in agricultural land, his tools and the product thereof] and that by his or their Peers" (McCart, 1964:6).

During this period, there were no lawyers to act as advocates. To address this deficiency, Parliament authorized forty men to practice law throughout England. This number was believed adequate to fulfill the needs of the entire country. The trial jury during this period differed in one significant respect from the jury system in America today. The medieval jury was expected to have some knowledge of the case to assist them in determining the guilt or innocence of the accused. Today, our notions of an impartial jury exclude those who have knowledge of the case. Historically, jurors were considered qualified if they were familiar with the facts of the case; now jurors are considered qualified if they have little or no knowledge of the facts of the case.

The Jury Selection Process

Venire

In medieval England, jurors were selected by the king from the wealthy landowners. Throughout history, those who were allowed to serve on juries were few in number. The selection of the **venire** or the **venireman list** of those qualified to serve as jurors has changed dramatically over time. For example, during most of American history, women were excluded from jury service. Some of the most prominent legal scholars of the eighteenth century argued that women should not be allowed to serve on juries because their defect of sex made it impossible for them to engage in the intelligent decision making required for jury service (Hans and Vidmar, 1986). In 1919, Utah became the first state to allow women to serve as jurors. The national sentiment against women as prospective jurors changed dramatically after the passage of the Nineteenth Amendment, which gave women the right to vote, and after that most states allowed women to serve on juries. However, in many jurisdictions, women were not automatically included in the venire. As recently as 1966, three states did not permit women to serve on juries. In many other jurisdictions, women who wanted to serve on juries had to go to the courthouse and ask to be included in the list of potential jurors. This process was known as **affirmative registration**. In 1966, the U.S. Supreme Court upheld the practice of excluding women from the jury pool when it reasoned, "The legislature has a right to exclude women so they may contribute their services as mothers, wives, homemakers, and also to protect them . . . from the filth, obscenity, and noxious atmosphere . . . of the courtroom" (*Hoyt v. Florida,* 1961:57). Not until 1975, in the case of *Taylor v. Louisiana,* did the U.S. Supreme Court rule that the affirmative registration process was unconstitutional.

Currently, most jurisdictions use voter registration lists to obtain prospective jurors for the jury pool. Once names have been drawn from the list, the court sends prospective jurors a notice summoning them for jury service and asking them to complete a short questionnaire to determine if they are qualified. Questions are asked that might automatically exclude them from jury service. The standard questions include but are not limited to the following:

1. Are you a U.S. citizen?
2. Are you at least 18 years old?
3. Do you have any mental or physical disability?
4. Have you ever been convicted of a felony?

The wrong answer to any of these questions may be grounds to exclude a person from the jury pool. Those who pass the initial screening are sent a letter advising them to appear for jury service at the courthouse on a particular date and time.

Some have argued that relying solely on voter registration lists systematically excludes segments of the population, perhaps sixty percent (Levin, 1988). Who does this process exclude? The poor, the undereducated, minorities, and women are less likely to register to vote. Most defendants in the criminal court share characteristics with those who are excluded from jury service. Ultimately, voter registration lists are ineffective for obtaining a cross-section of the community. Levin (1988) suggests drawing on voter registration lists, tax rolls, public utility records, driver's license records, and the telephone directory to increase the representativeness of those who are called to jury service.

Voir Dire

Jurors are expected to be unbiased and impartial when they hear the facts of a case. The process of determining a person's appropriateness or worthiness to serve as a juror is called ***voir dire***. *Voir dire,* meaning "to speak the truth," is the opportunity to learn about the existing prejudices of prospective jurors (Hans and Vidmar, 1986). It is the crucial process by which attorneys attempt to uncover prospective juror biases that might prevent them from providing defendants with a fair and impartial trial. Although *voir dire* has frequently been called jury selection, this term is inappropriate because *voir dire* does not so much select those who sit on a jury as it eliminates those who are unsuitable (Fay, 1979).

Hans and Vidmar (1986) describe the *voir dire* process as follows: the trial judge and/or attorneys may ask questions of prospective jurors to determine their qualifications for jury service, their knowledge of the defendant and the case, and their attitudes toward issues or individuals in the case that bias their views of the trial evidence. For example, questions may be wide ranging or more specifically related to the case, depending on what the trial judge allows.

A Case of Jury-Tampering

A Case of Bribery and a Hung Jury

It happened in Fort Lauderdale, Florida. An important federal case was being prosecuted in U.S. District Court. Thomas Schwab, forty-three, was on trial for money-laundering $770,000 in drug profits. A jury had been selected, and the case against Schwab was being presented. Then, something unexpected happened.

Two men, Ray Hernandez and Ricardo Canword, approached Schwab during a break in the trial. They advised him that they "owned a juror" and could get a "mistrial" or even an acquittal for the "right price." Schwab wanted to know what they meant. If Schwab paid them $175,000, they said, they would have their juror vote in favor of Schwab's acquittal. Schwab said that the men referred to "their" juror as their "ace in the hole."

Next, something else unexpected occurred. Schwab contacted his attorney to share this information. They both approached federal prosecutors and advised them what Schwab had been told by Hernandez and Canword. U.S. Attorney Thomas E. Scott was impressed with Schwab's candor, and the U.S. Attorney's Office decided to spring a trap.

Schwab went back to Hernandez and Canword, asking them how they could prove to him that the juror would do as they said. Hernandez and Canword told Schwab that while he was at the defense table, he should drink a glass of water and then place the empty glass upside down on the table. Then, they said, Juror No. 11 would take off her green jacket and fold it neatly over her chair. Later in court, Schwab did as they said, and Angela Chiles, twenty-seven, Juror No. 11, promptly took off her green jacket, folded it, and placed it over her chair. Hidden cameras recorded all of these events.

The very next day before court commenced, Angela Chiles, together with Hernandez and Canword, was arrested by FBI agents, on charges of conspiracy, obstruction of justice, and bribery. The judge declared a mistrial in Schwab's money-laundering trial. The judge said in disgust, "I've never seen anything like it in twenty-seven years on the bench. What you have here is a man who by day is defending himself against these very serious charges at trial, and by night he's wearing a wire and working with his prosecutors."

How easy is it to influence jurors with money or other incentives to vote certain ways? What punishment should be imposed on Angela Chiles if she is convicted of these charges? How can the court system guard against jury tampering? What do you think?

Source: Adapted from the Associated Press, "Hidden Cameras Capture Jury-Tampering." *Minot* (N.D.) *Daily News,* August 28, 1998:A3.

Despite the purpose of the *voir dire* process to remove prospective jurors with biases, many have argued that the process actually achieves the opposite result. Both prosecutors and defense attorneys attempt to select jurors who might be sympathetic to their position. If one side is successful in soliciting crucial information during *voir dire,* they can use this information to remove unsympathetic jurors and increase jury bias either against or in favor of the defendant. Typically, prosecutors seek prospective jurors who are middle-aged, white, and middle class in the belief that they are more likely to support the prosecution. However, defense counsel seek to remove prospective jurors with extreme views (Brady, 1983; Simon, 1980).

The Elimination of Jurors

Challenges for Cause

During the *voir dire* process, the trial judge and attorneys attempt to uncover any biases that might hinder prospective jurors from serving in an impartial manner. There are two methods used to eliminate biased jurors or those considered undesirable by either side for whatever reason, the **challenge for cause** (or strike for cause) and the peremptory challenge. Prospective jurors may be challenged for cause and removed from the jury if they do not meet state mandatory requirements (e.g., underage or not a U.S. citizen), for a specific bias (e.g., related by blood or marriage to the accused), or for a nonspecific bias (e.g., expressing prejudice toward the defendant) (Bermant and Shapard, 1981). Either the judge or the attorney may ask these questions. However, to have a juror removed by challenge for cause, the attorney must provide the judge with a compelling reason. The judge is the final arbiter of whether the juror stays or goes.

For instance, a prominent black defense attorney from Nashville, Avon Williams, was noted for his ability to dismiss prospective white jurors for cause whenever he represented black defendants. He would ask these prospective jurors if they were prejudiced against blacks. Most would answer no. Then Williams would ask them where they lived and if they belonged to any country clubs. Many of these white jurors lived in all-white neighborhoods, and some belonged to country clubs. He would then ask if these country clubs barred or admitted blacks. When these white prospective jurors became agitated and said that their country clubs and neighborhoods did not include blacks, Williams would ask the judge to strike them for cause. The judge usually granted Williams' request, based on the nature of his *voir dire* questioning.

Peremptory Challenges

The second method for removing prospective jurors is by **peremptory challenge**. Unlike challenges for cause, peremptory challenges do not require any explanations from attorneys for either side. Both prosecutors and defense counsel are given a limited number of these peremptory challenges, which varies according to the seriousness of the case. In the most serious cases or those with a lot of pretrial publicity, attorneys are given more

---

THE CHIEF OF POLICE AS A JUROR?

Portland Chief of Police Charles Moose

It happened in Portland, Oregon. Juror No. 27 looked very familiar to a lot of court personnel. In turn, he knew just about everyone at the courthouse. Portland Police Chief Charles Moose turned in his blue uniform for civilian clothes and reported for jury duty. His first call involved a drug case, but he was bounced in a hurry.

According to the chief, "The defense lawyer asked me to leave before they even got started. I just stood up and told the judge that there's a problem. I hope he didn't take it personally." Defense lawyer Philip Lebenbaum was not amused by the prospect of having the chief of police on his client's jury.

Ordinarily, law enforcement officers may be ejected from jury service through challenges for cause because they have a vested interest in criminal cases. However, court administrator Doug Bray said that the chief *could* sit on a jury if there were no objections from the prosecution or defense counsels. "He is qualified to sit, and he might very well be called for a civil case," said Bray.

Do you think that law enforcement officers should be permitted to sit as jurors in criminal cases? What possible sources of conflict might disqualify police officers from such jury service?

Source: Adapted from the Associated Press, "Officer Bounced from Jury Duty." *Minot* (N.D.) *Daily News,* February 25, 1999:A2.

---

challenges. For instance, in most misdemeanor and less serious felony cases, each side is given six peremptory challenges. For more serious cases such as murder trials, each side is given a dozen or more peremptory challenges. In some jurisdictions, as many as twenty peremptory challenges may be given to each side for their use in striking prospective jurors they do not like, for whatever reason.

How do prosecutors and defense counsel know which prospective jurors to remove? During the *voir dire* process, attorneys usually ask members of the jury pool about their occupations, their attitudes toward law enforcement, and their general perceptions about the offense. For example, a defense attorney in a drunk-driving case may ask prospective jurors if it is a crime to drink and drive. If members of the jury pool say that drinking and driving is a crime, some defense counsel use this opportunity to educate the jury pool that drinking and driving is not a crime and that it rises to the level of a criminal offense only when someone becomes legally intoxicated and drives a vehicle. Attorneys for both sides also use the information gathered from the *voir dire,* together with juror demographics (e.g., age, gender, race), to develop a profile of how prospective jurors with similar characteristics feel about certain issues that might arise during the trial.

Social scientists have discovered that demographic characteristics are often quite important and influence a person's perceptions and attitudes. For example, Winston and

Winston (1980) found that jurors who were opposed to the death penalty were usually under forty-five years old, had at least a high school education, were employed, and did not watch news on television. Those favoring the death penalty tended to be men age sixty and older who had less than a high school education, were unemployed or retired, and watched news on television. If either the prosecution or the defense wishes to strike particular prospective jurors, they may simply excuse them by using a peremptory challenge.

Several serious allegations have been made about prosecutors who systematically remove minorities from juries when the criminal defendants are also minorities, even in high-profile cases. For example, Suggs and Sales (1981) describe prosecutors who use most of their peremptory challenges to remove blacks from the jury panel when a black defendant is on trial for a serious offense. Defense attorneys have also been accused of using peremptory challenges to remove types of people they believe would be unsympathetic to their position. For example, in the trial of the Harrisburg Seven, the defense used its twenty-eight challenges to remove those who were wealthy and exhibited conservative views (O'Rouke, 1972).

For many decades, the use of peremptory challenges was inviolate. In 1986, however, the U.S. Supreme Court decided to review the issue of using peremptory challenges to systematically remove black jurors in the case of *Batson v. Kentucky*. Batson, a black defendant, had been charged with burglary. During the jury selection process, the prosecutor used all of his peremptory challenges to exclude the few black prospective jurors from the jury pool. Batson was ultimately convicted of second-degree burglary by an all-white jury. The use of peremptory challenges in the *Batson* case was most transparent, and Batson appealed, arguing that he did not receive a fair trial because of how the jurors were selected and that his equal protection rights under the Fourteenth Amendment had been violated. The U.S. Supreme Court agreed with Batson and ruled that a prima facie case of discrimination exists whenever a prosecutor uses his peremptory challenges in a racially discriminatory manner. The court also extended this provision to intentional discrimination on the basis of gender. In 1991, the court applied the equal protection argument to defense counsel (*Georgia v. McCollum*) and in civil cases such as *Edmonson v. Leesville Concrete Co.* (1991).

Jury Consultants and Scientific Jury Selection

F. Lee Bailey and Melvin Belli have been credited as being the first defense attorneys to hire experts to assist them in the jury selection process. However, not until the Berrigan brothers' trial did **scientific jury selection** become an important trial tactic. Daniel and Philip Berrigan were Catholic priests who had been charged with conspiracy to kidnap Secretary of State Henry Kissinger, raid draft boards, and bomb tunnels in Washington, D.C. (Hans and Vidmar, 1986). Jay Schulman, a social scientist who sympathized with the defendants, decided to use his skill in social research methods to assist the defendants. To determine how several demographic characteristics (e.g., age, political philosophy, gender) influenced prospective jurors' perceptions of the issues surrounding the case and their attitudes toward the defendants, he and his colleagues conducted telephone interviews of 840 randomly selected registered voters and then personal interviews of 262 people. During the face-to-face interviews, the respondents were asked questions in the following areas:

(A) Media contact—Respondents were asked their choice of newspapers, magazines, radio, and television stations and their amount of contact with each.

(B) Knowledge of the defendants and their case—The names of the defendants were embedded with the names of other people in the news and respondents were asked if they had heard of the person and what they had heard about them.

(C) Greatest American of the past 10 or 15 years (to seek respondents' values).

(D) Trust in government—Three questions were asked relating to the government's decisions and attempts to do what is right.

   (1) "How much time do you think you can trust the Government in Washington to do what is right?"

   (2) "Do you feel that the people who are running the Government are smart people who usually know what they are doing?"

   (3) "Would you say that the Government is pretty much run for a few big interests looking out for themselves, or is it run for the benefit of the people?"

(E) Ages and activities of respondents' children.

(F) Religious attitudes and commitment.

(G) Spare-time activities.

(H) Organizational memberships.

(I) Attitudes that were potentially related to the trial. The interviewers sought the extent of agreement with eight statements concerning issues, such as right to private property, support for the government, police use of force, and the like.

(J) Scale of acceptable antiwar activities. (Wanamaker, 1978:348)

Using the results of this survey, the Harrisburg Seven researchers were able to determine that conservatives who had higher levels of education and who received their news from metropolitan news sources held opinions that were unfavorable to the defendants. Surprisingly, the researchers found that religious affiliation was an important factor that defense counsel should consider. Members of Protestant denominations, such as Methodists, Presbyterians, and Episcopalians, were more likely than others to condemn defendants for their actions. The research revealed that from the defendant's perspective, the most favorable type of juror was a female Democrat who expressed no religious preference and who was employed as a white-collar professional or possibly in a skilled blue-collar job (Wanamaker, 1978:349). It is impossible to determine if the information collected was useful in selecting a sympathetic jury for these defendants, but the jury in the actual case voted 10–2 to acquit the defendants. Had the jury voted to convict them, then the scientific jury selection process engaged in by Schulman and his colleagues might never have received much attention. But because the outcome of the trial favored the defendants, the legal community took special notice, and scientific jury selection subsequently became an important component of the jury selection process.

CAN JURY CONSULTANTS SELECT PREDICTABLE JURIES?

The Case of Jo-Ellen Dimitrius

At the outset of the 1991 rape trial of William Kennedy Smith in Florida, a jury was selected. Each side, the prosecution and defense, had a limited number of peremptory challenges to strike any prospective juror without having to provide a reason or rationale. In the 1994 and 1995 trials of Lyle and Erik Menendez, who admitted killing their parents, both sides again eliminated prospective jurors through peremptory challenges. In the O. J. Simpson murder trial, both sides again used their peremptory challenges to eliminate certain prospective jurors.

Jury selection is serious business. Many experts believe that certain juror characteristics are logically linked with particular verdicts, given the nature of the crime and type of criminal defendant. If the right kinds of jurors are included, these experts say, then the trial outcome becomes more predictable. Indeed, whenever a defendant is acquitted, jury consultants for the defense boast that their assistance had been critical to the outcome. Can jury consultants accurately predict how prospective jurors will vote after they have heard the evidence against a particular defendant?

Some consultanta believe that *race* is a crucial feature of jury composition, particularly when the defendant is a racial minority. A black defendant fares better if the jury is black or predominantly black, and white defendants do best if juries are white or predominantly white, or so the experts would have us believe. Is it that simple?

Jo-Ellen Dimitrius is a highly paid jury consultant who has assisted many criminal defendants and their attorneys in selecting the "right" juries. Dimitrius commands $150 to $300 an hour for her consultation services, and she is a member of the American Society of Trial Consultants.

The goal of jury consultants is to aid both defense and prosecuting attorneys in selecting jurors who have attitudes favorable or unfavorable to defendants. Often, they use focus groups from a cross-section of the community that are questioned as **shadow juries**, or replicas of actual juries who hear real cases. These groups give their opinions about how they would regard certain evidence or view particular defendants.

In the O. J. Simpson murder trial, a seventy-eight-page questionnaire was distributed to all prospective jurors. Its purpose was to screen prospective jurors who had obvious biases that would render them incapable of serving objectively or who had infirmities or hardships that would interfere with their jury duties. On the basis of the questionnaire, presiding Judge Lance Ito eliminated numerous prospective jurors. The remaining prospective jurors were then asked

(continued)

CAN JURY CONSULTANTS SELECT PREDICTABLE JURIES? *(continued)*

additional questions by both defense and prosecuting attorneys. Depending on their answers, each side used peremptory challenges to eliminate certain prospective jurors, until a suitable jury was selected. When Simpson was acquitted, charges were leveled against Dimitrius and the defense team that the jury was stacked in some way—that only jurors favorable to Simpson were included. However, these allegations lacked merit.

We do not know whether jury consultants can accurately predict how particular jurors will behave when voting for guilt or acquittal. Jury consultants point to their victories in court as evidence of their prowess in selecting those jurors most favorably disposed toward defendants, but these same consultants fail to mention the numerous juries they helped to select that convicted defendants. It may be possible to describe a particular profile or constellation of jury characteristics that would yield favorable outcomes for a particular type of defendant. For example, a handsome male defendant might fare better with a largely female jury than with a largely male one, whereas a largely male jury might be more inclined to acquit an attractive female defendant than would a largely female jury. No one knows for sure, but jury consultants *think* they know.

One important function of jury consultants is to help determine a witness's credibility. In the O. J. Simpson case, for example, a focus group said that they did not believe a particular witness, the maid of a Simpson neighbor. A tape of her proposed testimony was played for the focus group, who were not convinced that she was telling the truth. Thus, Simpson's defense decided not to call her as a witness, because her testimony might do more harm than good.

Should peremptory challenges be eliminated to level the playing field of jury selection? Do you think that the "right" kinds of jurors can be picked for particular defendants? What juror characteristics do you think are most important?

Source: Adapted from Bernard Gavzer, "Are Trial Consultants Good for Justice?" *Parade Magazine,* January 5, 1997:20.

The process of scientific jury selection has evolved into an entirely new professional enterprise. In recent high-profile criminal cases (e.g., O. J. Simpson, William Kennedy Smith, and Rodney King), jury consultants have assisted both prosecutors and defense counsel in their selection of jury members. For example, in the O. J. Simpson criminal trial, the defense team hired Jo-Ellen Dimitrius from Trial Logistics, and the prosecution hired Don Vinsom from DecisionQuest to aid in jury selection. Dimitrius and Vinsom conducted extensive surveys and relayed this information to their clients during trial strategy sessions. Interestingly, Dimitrius assisted during the entire trial, but Vinson was dismissed by the prosecution after two court appearances (Lafferty, 1994).

Jury consultation has become big business, with over 350 members in the American Society of Trial Consultants. Despite this rapid growth, there is much skepticism about the quality of scientific jury selection. Litigation Sciences boasts a ninety-five percent success rate, although this success rate may not be attributable to scientific techniques. Most of the jury consultants were hired in high-profile cases or political trials. In these trials, the defense attorneys are often in the best position to prepare their cases such that acquittal of their clients is more a matter of good lawyering than a matter of the advice received from professional jury consultants. Some have equated scientific jury selection with jury tampering (Parker, 1980) and suggest that the integrity of the jury is undermined or compromised (Etzioni, 1974).

Jury Size

People who are unfamiliar with the court process and are charged with a felony may be surprised to see only six people sitting as jurors to decide their guilt or innocence. Doesn't the Constitution guarantee them the right to a twelve-member jury? What effect do smaller jury sizes have on jury deliberations? Are smaller juries more likely than larger juries to convict defendants? These are just some of the questions defendants have raised about smaller jury sizes. These same questions have been asked and researched by legal scholars.

For instance, what is the special significance associated with the number 12? Why is this number given such importance in our common law legal history? Are twelve jurors better able to understand the evidence and reach a decision? One reason the number 12 is so deeply ingrained in our perception of the trial process has nothing to do with any scientific or legalistic reasoning. Rather, it has everything to do with historical tradition. Throughout most of the last several centuries, juries were comprised of twelve members.

Several legal scholars have studied the origins of the twelve-member jury. Despite their intensive investigative efforts, there is still no definitive conclusion as to the origin of the number 12. Some scholars have traced the twelve-member jury to ancient Greek mythology; others have found its antecedents in biblical writings (Moore, 1988). The most direct lineage of the twelve-member jury in America is traced to the Constitution of Clarendon, the Assize of Clarendon, and the Magna Carta.

The Constitution of Clarendon was signed by King Henry II of England in 1164. It provided that the sheriff was to administer an oath to twelve men of the neighborhood that they would declare the truth and render verdicts in cases brought to them. The Assize of Clarendon was a court Henry II created to give litigants a legal option to resolve a dispute rather than resolve it in the traditional manner, which was often a duel to the death. If a disputant chose the court rather than the duel, the court would issue a writ to the king to have four knights from the region select twelve jurors. The litigants were allowed to challenge the knights' decisions. This process continued until twelve acceptable jurors were selected. Finally, the Magna Carta, signed by King John, established the constitutional importance of the jury. The right to a twelve-member jury remained

CAN THE PERFECT JURY BE HANDPICKED?

Jury Selection in North Dakota

How are jurors chosen for criminal trials? How do lawyers choose prospective jurors, and what criteria do they use for rejecting jurors? Answers to these and other questions have been provided by a jury selection psychologist, Jim Rasicot of Minneapolis.

Rasicot worked as a defense jury consultant for the Mike Tyson trial in Indiana. He assisted in the jury selection for the trial on which the movie *Paradise Lost* was based and also was in the movie as an extra.

Rasicot has said there are several steps in choosing the right jurors. First, get rid of those jurors who pose the most danger to the defense. Second, gain rapport with potential jurors and, having done that, drop the seeds of the case into their minds. This is accomplished while questioning potential jurors about their past experiences in an attempt to gain access to their biases that they do not like to discuss. Rasicot said that these things are important because they can cause problems for the defense later on during the trial.

Another essential step in preparing to challenge jurors is developing the right type of questionnaire and keeping questions short and concise. He said, "Get the information you need [about the potential juror] and get out." Questionnaires for jury trials can be sixty pages or longer. It might take someone weeks to go through all the answers. Another important factor in choosing a juror or having one removed for cause is attitude. A lawyer has to consider how the juror's past experiences can affect attitude. He urged lawyers to confirm an attitude the juror might already have, such as "If someone breaks a window, they should have to pay for it, right?"

An important tactic is to get a potential juror to change an attitude. For instance, a juror might suppose that the defendant must have done something wrong if he was charged with a crime. "You have to try to change that attitude and create a new one," Raiscot said. He added, "Jurors don't want to talk to you, and so your job is to get them to talk. Let them know that there are no right or wrong answers during the jury selection, and to put them at ease."

Rasicot suggests talking to jurors about their occupations and being sure to ask them about any past occupations. One time, he said, a potential juror told the lawyer that he was in the sheet metal business and managed the company. During questioning, he later said he knew about trial proceedings because he had been a chief of police—and possibly pro-prosecution—before going to work for the sheet metal company. The juror was dismissed from further consideration after that. "It's important to find out about things like that," Rasicot said. "Remember, people might change occupations several times."

Another tip included not insulting any juror. He gave an example of a lawyer who was questioning a female juror who said that she was a housewife. The lawyer said, "Oh, you don't work, then." The woman replied curtly, "I work very hard." She did not serve on that jury. Rasicot also said that you need to let the jury know where you are going with the case. Start off with easy questions about things they like to talk about, such as occupations and education. Then ease into more controversial subjects that might show juror bias.

Can the perfect jury be selected? Do you think jury consultants are effective at selecting the best juries for their clients? Should lawyers be allowed to question prospective jurors at length concerning their qualifications for jury service? Should police officers or former law enforcement officers automatically be excluded as jurors? What do you think?

Source: Adapted from Ken Crites, "Psychologist Discusses Jury Selection Process." *Minot* (N.D.) *Daily News,* June 16, 2000:B1.

essentially the same for almost eight hundred years. This tradition was changed by the U.S. Supreme Court in *Williams v. Florida* (1972).

At the time Johnny Williams was charged with robbery, Florida permitted six-member juries to hear all noncapital criminal cases. Williams argued that his case should be heard by a twelve-member jury. His motion was denied, and he was tried and convicted by a six-person jury. He was ultimately sentenced to life in prison. He appealed his conviction on the grounds that the Sixth Amendment guaranteed him a right to a twelve-member jury. The court held that the Sixth Amendment does not require a twelve-person jury. The U.S. Supreme Court majority reasoned that the twelve-member jury is a historical accident and unnecessary for the proper functioning of a jury. Justice White said that the essential feature of the jury obviously lies in the interposition between the accused and the accuser of the commonsense judgment of a group of laymen and in the community participation and shared responsibility that result for the group's determination of guilt or innocence. The performance of this role is not a function of the particular number of people who make up the jury (*Williams v. Florida,* 1972 at 100).

With authority from the U.S. Supreme Court, many states began to challenge other aspects of the Sixth Amendment. For instance, the use of nonunanimous verdicts was upheld by the U.S. Supreme Court in *Apodaca v. Oregon* (1972) and *Johnson v. Louisiana* (1972). In the Apodaca case, the U.S. Supreme Court upheld the Oregon statute, which allowed a 10–2 vote for either conviction or acquittal. In Louisiana, the law allowed jury verdicts with a 9–3 vote. The U.S. Supreme Court also accepted this practice as not violating the Sixth and Fourteenth Amendments. One year later, in *Colgrove v. Battin* (1973), the court ruled that six-member juries were acceptable in civil cases. In the majority opinion, the court cited social science evidence that they believed indicated that there was no substantial difference between twelve-member and six-member juries. The *Colgrove* court cited four studies as providing "convincing empirical evidence of the correctness of the *Williams* conclusion that there is no discernable difference between the results reached by the two different-sized juries" (*Colgrove v. Battin,* 1973:47). With the *Colgrove* decision, the court seemed to give states the license to decrease their jury sizes. Georgia attempted this, with a statute allowing convictions based on deliberations by five-member juries. This practice was challenged in *Ballew v. Georgia* (1978). Ballew was a theater manager in Atlanta who was charged with violating a Georgia ordinance that prohibited the distribution of obscene material by showing a pornographic and sexually explicit movie starring Marilyn Chambers, *Behind the Green Door.* Ballew appealed his conviction by a five-member jury and contended that it violated his Sixth and Fourteenth Amendment rights. Ballew's conviction was set aside after the U.S. Supreme Court declared that five-member juries are too small to constitute a representative cross-section of the community. Thus, the minimum jury size was established as six.

In all previous U.S. Supreme Court decisions, the justices were reluctant to specify a minimum jury size. But with the *Williams* decision, the court was faced with a potentially serious dilemma. Again relying on social science, the U.S. Supreme Court argued that their conclusion rested on the assumption there was no difference between twelve- and six-member juries. The court believed that the deliberative ability, representativeness, verdict reliability, likelihood of conviction, and the minority ability to resist majority pressure were not hindered by decreasing jury size. However, the court's reading of the literature was seriously flawed. Most of the studies they relied on had several empirical flaws or limitations. Additionally, the U.S. Supreme Court misinterpreted some of the results of the studies they cited that had credibility and were empirically sound. The court cited a study conducted by Asch (1966) that examined the minority's ability to resist group pressure. Asch found that when the minority position has an ally, it is better able to resist pressure from the majority position. In the context of jury deliberations, this means that in a jury vote of 10–2, the minority jury voters are better able to withstand group pressure than minority jury voters when the jury vote is 5–1. However, the court erred in its interpretation and understanding of the social research and concluded that there was no functional difference between the two juries. In any case, a decision based on a 5–1 jury vote is unconstitutional, inasmuch as all six-member jury voting must be unanimous.

Jury Sequestration

Historically, **jury sequestration** has been used to isolate jurors from the potential biasing influence of the press and community sentiment. Preventing outside information from reaching jurors allows jurors to be influenced only by the information and evidence presented to them at trial, the instructions of judges, and their fellow jurors. Although jury sequestration has many critics, it may have some positive affects. Apart from the obvious benefit of not having jurors influenced by outside forces, sequestration, on many occasions, has fostered a group bonding process among the jurors. Following trials, jurors have often referred to themselves as becoming a family who plan to see each other after the trial (Yarrow, 1992), and the emotional connection developed as a result of sequestration may have a positive effect on deliberations. Researchers have

THE CHRISTMAS GIFT?

The Case of Terry Nichols

It had been a typical December in Denver. The Rocky Mountains were covered with snow, holiday decorations could be seen everywhere, and a holiday spirit was in the air. The stores were bustling with last-minute Christmas shoppers. However, this was not the case for everyone. A certain group of people were not allowed to go shopping or enjoy the other holiday festivities. In fact, every move they made was monitored by law enforcement officials. All of what they read and the visitors who came to see them had to be approved by those guarding them. Who were these people? Were they incarcerated offenders? No. They were the jurors in the Terry Nichols Oklahoma City bombing conspiracy case. These twelve jurors had been sequestered during their deliberations. With one shopping day before Christmas, after six days of deliberations, the jury convicted Nichols. Did the impending Christmas holiday influence the verdict? Some have described the verdict as a "Christmas compromise."

How does sequestration influence a jury? Do you believe that sequestration influenced the deliberative process of this jury? What are the pros and cons of jury sequestration?

Source: Adapted from Ian Fisher, "Justice Is Blind, but She Does Wear a Watch." *New York Times* (December 28, 1997).

learned that group communication is enhanced when individuals have formed an interpersonal connection (Cook, 1978). Therefore, jurors who have developed relationships with one another are more willing to listen to each other and discuss their differences. When this occurs, sequestration has enhanced the deliberative process. These positive effects of jury sequestration, however, are far outnumbered by criticisms of sequestration.

During sequestration, if the jury develops intergroup rivalries and animosity toward each other, the deliberative process suffers. People are more likely to gravitate toward people like themselves. This tendency highlights the differences between group members, and they begin to resent one other. Alliances are formed between certain jurors, and they form coalitions that become fairly powerful during jury deliberations. Sequestration also puts pressure on jurors who disagree with the majority. The jurors in the minority position see themselves as prolonging the sequestration. If they would only capitulate and agree with the majority, then all could go home and get back to their lives.

Jury sequestration is also expensive. In the O. J. Simpson criminal trial, the jury was sequestered for 266 days at a cost to the taxpayers of almost $1 million. Cost was one of the primary reasons the New York court system eliminated its practice of mandatory sequestration, and the savings was almost $4 million each year. Sequestration may also be why people try to get out of jury service. For many jurors, being confined to a hotel and treated like a prisoner in a potentially hostile environment may be a good reason to refuse to answer their calls for jury service.

Jury Decision Making and Voting

Considerable research has examined jury decision-making and voting behavior. For instance, women approach jury duty differently, perceive things differently, and often vote differently than men (Fischer, 1991, 1997). Not only do gender differences influence decision making but also jurors' type of occupation, ethnicity, and socioeconomic status exert a profound influence on how they perceive things and process large amounts of evidence and other important information. The differences in juror decision making and final jury verdicts are highlighted the most in civil cases when damages are sought. For example, in the case of *Sterling v. Bechenheimer's Inc.* (1985), a jury awarded Debra Sterling $25,000 in compensatory damages and $1,501,000 in punitive damages after she had been handcuffed and thrown to the ground by a security guard who believed she had stolen a soda worth $1.49. Compare the jury actions in this case with the jury actions in the case of Patricia James. In *James v. K-Mart* (1987), a jury awarded $2 to James and $502 to each of her teenage daughters after a security guard had twisted the daughters' arms behind their backs and strip-searched them in the belief that the daughters had been shoplifting. Why are there such different jury decisions and monetary awards?

Several important trial and victim factors influence jury voting behavior. Factors associated with guilty verdicts are physical evidence, a defendant's prior criminal record, and victim attractiveness (Reskin and Visher, 1986). Male jurors seem more likely to vote not guilty when the victim puts up some resistance against the offender. Guilty verdicts are more likely when jurors have had prior jury service (Dillehay and Nietzel, 1985). Not-guilty verdicts have been associated with employed offenders, attractive offenders, and some degree of victim facilitation (e.g., victims allow a stranger to take them home from a bar). Jurors who have a tendency to blame the victim are also more likely to vote not guilty (Deitz, Littman, and Bentley, 1984; Muehlenhard and Cook, 1988).

Another factor is whether jurors are verdict-driven or evidence-driven. Research indicates that once juries reach the jury room, they commence the decision-making process by following one of two patterns or methods (Hastie, Penrod, and Pennington, 1993). The first pattern is called an **evidence-driven jury**. In evidence-driven cases, juries come together and begin discussing how to proceed. Most jurors or at least a vocal few decide that they should review the evidence as a group before they can contemplate a verdict. With this method, all the evidence is discussed, not simply the evidence individual jurors believe is relevant. However, a **verdict-driven jury** believes that discussing the evidence before a vote is unnecessary. Why debate the evidence if all jurors might vote the same way without a review of the evidence? Using this method, the jury votes first to see how many jurors favor guilt or acquittal. When evidence is discussed, it is used to support one position or the other. Verdict-driven deliberations often take less time than evidence-driven deliberations because little or no time is taken to review the evidence before the jury votes.

Some research shows that the jury deliberation process may not have much impact on the final verdict. In Kalven and Ziesel's (1966) classic study of the jury system, they compared the initial jury vote to the final verdict. In the vast majority of cases, the first vote was the same as the final verdict. For example, on a twelve-person jury, if seven of the jurors initially voted not guilty, the subsequent verdict tended to be not guilty. However, if the majority of jurors voted guilty, the final verdict would almost always be guilty. Only on rare occasions does the minority succeed in convincing the majority to change their vote. Kalven and Ziesel have said that the real decision is often made before the deliberation begins. The deliberation process can be likened to what the developer does for an exposed film: a picture is developed, but the outcome is predetermined (1966:488–489).

Jury Verdicts

The media always seem willing to report how the justice system has failed in one respect or another to convict guilty defendants. Most often, we perceive that an obviously guilty person is found not guilty, or the jury delivers an excessive damage award to a plaintiff in a civil case. Armed with this anecdotal evidence, critics have called for reforming the jury system. When we advocate changing the jury system, we have to make two assumptions. First, we have to assume that the jury made a mistake. Second, we have to assume that there is a better alternative. In most cases, advocates for jury reform believe that juries composed of laypeople from the community are often unable to understand the complex information presented at a trial. Stephen Adler has argued in favor of the complexity exception, by which a judge who thinks the jury will not understand a particular civil case can decide it without a jury (Adler, 1995:143). He argues that jury reform should include a return to the **blue-ribbon jury**. During the 1960s and 1970s, blue-ribbon juries were formed from the best educated or socially placed members of society because it was believed a jury should be made up of such persons. Most people who serve on juries today would not have been placed on these blue-ribbon juries in past years. In fact, the reverse is now often practiced in many jurisdictions. New York's judicial rules allow automatic exemption for lawyers, doctors, clergy, dentists, optometrists, psychologists, podiatrists, registered and practical nurses, embalmers, police officers, correctional officers, firefighters, sole business owners, and many other professional groups.

If we agree with the idea that juries cannot understand the information presented to them and therefore are unable to arrive at a competent verdict, who do we want to replace them? Most critics would shift the responsibility for determining guilt or innocence to the judges themselves. Are juries unable to understand the material presented to them? In an effort to answer this question, Kalven and Ziesel (1966) investigated how juries arrived at verdicts and how these jury verdicts differed from judicial decisions about the same cases. Kalven and Ziesel gathered data from 3,576 trials. To compare the differences between judges and juries, the researchers asked judges how they would have ruled in each case. The research showed that the verdicts of judges and juries were essentially the same in 78 percent of the cases. Conversely, judges and juries disagreed on the outcome in 22 percent of the cases. The data indicate the largest disagreement came where judges said they would have convicted defendants that the juries acquitted. In essence, judges were more likely to convict than juries, and juries seem to be more lenient.

ARE JURIES PRO-POLICE?

The Death of Amadou Diallo

A tragic event occurred in New York City in 1999. An unarmed black man, Amadou Diallo, was killed by forty-one shots from four police officers in a small alcove of a dark building. In February 2000, the four officers went on trial for his murder. The trial was held in Albany, a middle-class, ninety percent white community with a strong Irish Catholic heritage. An Albany defense attorney, Terence Kindlon, said, "If there's a better place to defend a police officer, I haven't heard of it." Another observer, *New York Post* columnist Bob McManus, agreed. He said, "Irish Catholic conservative Albany has a civil service view of the world. They like their cops."

The murder trial of the four police officers charged in Diallo's death was moved to Albany from the Bronx in New York City because, according to authorities, it has a reputation for being hostile to police. It is two-thirds black or Hispanic, and the police have become outsiders. Does it really make a difference where the trial is held?

In January 2000, a jury in Albany was convinced that a well-respected detective forged a confession in the murder of an 82-year-old former minister and that police were overzealous in arresting a man who helped an alleged cop shooter to escape. In fact, in that particular case, camouflage-clad police officers were caught on videotape roughing up some store clerks while searching for the alleged shooter. The videotape led to internal disciplinary action against the police officers that once would have been unthinkable.

Some criminal justice experts around the country believe that the location of trials has become less important in recent years. More jurors are able to make sounder and fairer judgments, according to these observers. One observer, Boston College law professor Robert M. Bloom, said, "Confidence in police around the country is weakening because of such things as the Rodney King beating in Los Angeles and the Abner Louima case in New York City, where a black defendant was sodomized with a broomstick in a police station bathroom."

Amid allegations of pro-police bias, there have been numerous incidents around the United States to undermine public confidence in police officers. For example, police officers on highways throughout America have been routinely pulling over black drivers in what is known as racial profiling. *Albany Times Union* columnist Fred LeBrun said, "Even in a place like Albany, conservative with an almost Midwestern feel, there is the general feeling that you just can't take a police officer's word anymore."

Echoing these comments and opinions is a law professor from Fordham University, James Cohen, who says, "The feeling is people in power—the white people—tend to treat people without power differently." But there is some concern among those prosecuting the case against the four officers in Albany. In 1999 in Albany, a black basketball player at the College of Saint Rose claimed he was beaten by two off-duty police officers in a police garage following a bar fight. The officers were acquitted.

Are juries in one part of the state likely to be more pro-police than juries in other parts of a state? What about your own state? Is it likely that juries in different parts of the state would arrive at different verdicts if police officers were accused of crimes? How can juries be selected in ways that minimize their possible bias and unfair attitudes toward either the prosecutor or the defense? What do you think?

Source: Adapted from the Associated Press, "Albany Is a Pro-Police Setting for Murder Trial of N.Y. City Cops." *Minot* (N.D.) *Daily News,* February 8, 2000:A3.

Those critical of the jury system might argue that juries are not more lenient; rather, the differences in judge and jury case outcomes can be attributed to jury incompetence. They would infer that juries disagreed with judges and acquitted defendants that judges would have convicted largely because the jurors did not understand the law and the evidence presented to them at trial. To address this criticism, Kalven and Ziesel had the judges rate the evidence as difficult or easy to comprehend. If jury incompetence was the reason for the differences, we would expect a higher rate of disagreement in cases the judges rated as difficult to understand. However, the results indicate that judges and juries disagreed equally in both complex and simple cases.

Jury Nullification

Jury nullification is the refusal of juries to apply the law when they believe that following the letter of the law would be a miscarriage of justice (Hans and Vidmar, 1986). In a criminal trial, the jury is the finder of fact and has the absolute authority to acquit the defendant regardless of the evidence (Brody, 1995). The jury is also our protection from the oppressive powers of the state. The constitutional protection against double jeopardy makes the jury's acquittal irreversible, and the prosecution has no right to appeal the jury verdict. The only exception is jury tampering or some other irregularity that has caused the jury to disregard the evidence against the accused. In a system designed with checks and balances to control state power, the jury system provides ordinary citizens with more power than our highest elected and appointed government officials.

Although we have observed jury nullification in some recent spectacular cases (e.g., Marion Barry, Lorena Bobbit, and John Delorean), it is not unique to our times. Juries have nullified the law or, more accurately, the actions of the state for as long as juries have

THE STRESS OF JURY DUTY

The Stressful Jury in New York

Jury duty is more of a tedious chore than an exciting experience. However, jurors can get stress and burnout, especially when serving on juries that last for weeks or months.

Juries are made up of local citizens who pay taxes, vote, or drive cars. Public records are canvassed and jury pools are determined. Letters are sent to prospective jurors to appear at a courthouse on a particular date. When prospective jurors known as the venire or venireman list are questioned by the prosecution and defense, the experience can be both humiliating and stressful. Once particular people are selected for jury duty and impaneled, their stress intensifies. If the case they must decide is a murder charge, there may be the additional stress of determining whether to impose the death penalty.

Interviewed jurors say that their experience of being thrust into a gut-wrenching trial exacts a psychological toll that persists long after the verdict. Following the trial of a man who raped and murdered a young woman in her own home, a forty-one-year-old female juror said, "I'm paranoid. I can't shake it. I went to the Smoky Mountains and twice ran into a fellow who looked like him. I flipped out. I got hysterical, shook and just ran. I dreamed he broke into my apartment on several occasions. I have this same dream over and over. I'd wake up in a cold sweat."

One former juror expressed shock over the fact that he was shown a videotape of police digging up a murder victim's head from a garden. For many weeks after the trial, the juror would look out the kitchen window at his own garden and, in his mind's eye, see the buried head. Another juror said that she always remembered the picture of the murder victim with the slashed throat and a large footprint on her chest. She dreamed about it long after the verdict.

Judge Dennis M. Sweeney of Howard County, Maryland, said, "We do a very cruel thing to jurors, psychologically, during trials. We tell them that they cannot talk to anybody during the trial about the case . . . that's not a natural thing for people." Jurors also feel angered and frustrated by the legal system over the community reaction to their decisions, if they are not popular decisions. In the O. J. Simpson criminal trial in 1995, for instance, jurors were criticized widely in the media for ignoring certain "factual information" that showed Simpson's guilt. However, the jurors in the Simpson trial said that they were not convinced beyond a reasonable doubt. They voted their consciences, based on the facts as they saw them.

Mental health professionals say that jurors ought to go through a period of *debriefing,* when they can unload their emotions in a confidential forum, to decrease the stresses of jury life. Not only are jurors exposed to stomach-churning crime details—things that they have never encountered before—but also they are not allowed to discuss the experience before they can deliberate. This process is unhealthy, say mental health professionals.

What provisions should there be to counsel those who have served on juries? Are there limits to the types of evidence jurors should be shown? Should juries be psychologically screened before assuming the role of jurors? What do you think?

Source: Adapted from Associated Press, "Stress of Jury Duty Gets Attention from Courts." *Minot* (N.D.) *Daily News,* April 12, 1994:A3.

functioned in American and English courts. Jury nullification was common in England during the Bloody Code of the eighteenth and nineteenth centuries. The Bloody Code prescribed more than two hundred offenses that were punishable by death, including such minor offenses as stealing bread and pickpocketing. Because of the severity of the punishment relative to the offense, juries were reluctant to find defendants guilty of these offenses. The authority of the jury to engage in the practice of nullification was not challenged in England until 1670 in the Bushell case and later in America in the John Peter Zenger case.

In 1670, William Penn and William Mead were being tried at the Old Bailey, the Central Criminal Court of England. Penn, subsequently founder of the colony of Pennsylvania and a leading proponent of correctional reform, was a Quaker like Mead, and the authorities saw both of them as radicals and extremists. Consequently, they were banned from preaching in the streets. However, their only forum was the streets because the authorities had barred them from their churches. On one occasion while they were preaching in the streets, they were arrested and charged with unlawful assembly. Their fate ultimately rested in the hands of the jurors selected to hear the case. The witnesses included those who testified that Penn and Mead had preached on Gracechurch Street.

At the conclusion of the testimony, the jury was instructed to retire to the jury room and reach a verdict. When they returned with a verdict of not guilty, they were instructed to return to the jury room and deliberate until they reached a correct verdict. When they returned a second time, they found Penn guilty of speaking on Gracechurch Street but refused to convict him on unlawful assembly charges. The court reacted to this verdict by threatening Edward Bushell, who was identified as the leader of the jury revolt. They were sent back to deliberate once again, and when they returned, they announced that they had again found Penn guilty of speaking on Gracechurch Street, but they persisted and did not find him guilty of unlawful assembly. Additionally, they declared Mead innocent of any wrongdoing. The court was in turmoil. The court announced that Bushell and the rest of the jury would not be dismissed until they reached a verdict acceptable to the court. The judge ordered them locked up without "meat, drink, fire, and tobacco" until they reached an acceptable verdict. Facing this demand, the jury retired to deliberate and returned with an acquittal for Penn. The were ordered to go

What Happens When Juries Can't Agree on a Verdict?

The Matter of Hung Juries

In Indianapolis, Indiana, on August 27, 1996, four policemen were accused of inciting a drunken brawl after attending a minor-league baseball game that was supposed to be their reward for outstanding police work. The officers were Paul Tutsie, age thirty-four; Edward P. Brickley Jr., twenty-eight; Gregory C. Gehring, thirty-three; and Jason D. Hansman, twenty-seven. Since the brawl, the officers have either been fired or suspended without pay. In September 1997, a jury trial was conducted to hear the charges against the officers.

Following the presentation of the case during the next four weeks, the jurors deliberated. After ten hours of heated deliberation, the jury sent a message to the judge, Ruth Reichard, Marion Superior Court, indicating that they were hopelessly deadlocked; there was a **hung jury**. The judge thanked the jurors for the four-week trial and dismissed them. The prosecutor said that he would retry these officers in a second trial.

There is no limit to the number of times a trial may be conducted against defendants when earlier juries were deadlocked. Ordinarily, judges declare a mistrial, which is essentially interpreted to mean that no trial ever occurred, and retrying the defendants does not constitute double jeopardy. In some cases, defendants have been convicted after the fourth or fifth retrial. Some prosecutors have retried defendants six or more times before deciding to quit.

Should there be a limit on the number of times a prosecutor can seek to retry a case when juries are hung and cannot agree? What do you think?

Source: Adapted from the Associated Press, "Hung Jury in Police Brawl Case." *Minot* (N.D.) *Daily News,* October 26, 1997:A2.

back and deliberate again, but this time they refused. The judge was outraged. Bushell and the rest of the jurors were fined forty marks each and sent to jail until they could pay the fine. The jurors filed a habeas corpus appeal requesting their release from prison. The appellate court ordered their release and declared that the jury had the right to render a verdict according to their belief about the fairness of the law and did not have to act consistently with what the court deemed appropriate.

Jury and Juror Misconduct

Juror misconduct falls into two categories. The first is engaging in delinquency or lying to avoid jury service. The second is engaging in improper or prohibited behavior while serving as a juror. The first type of behavior is perceived as misconduct largely by those

Juror Accepts Bribes from Defendant

Juror Miguel Moya

It happened in Miami. Defendants Augusto "Willie" Falcon and Salvador Magluta were on trial for drug smuggling and large-scale drug dealing. Overwhelming and persuasive evidence of their guilt was presented at trial, but the trial took a peculiar turn when the jury deliberated and came back with an acquittal. Later, jurors said that they had deliberated for three days when they sent a note to the judge that they were "hopelessly deadlocked." The judge ordered them to continue deliberating and "reach a verdict." That's when they decided to throw in the towel and acquit the alleged drug smugglers.

Following the trial, one of the jurors, Miguel Moya, suddenly became wealthy. He bought a $200,000 home in the Florida Keys, jewelry, furniture, vacations, season tickets to the Florida Marlins games, and a sports car. Moya explained that he had recently come into some money from his cousin, Ramon "Ray" Perez, a convicted drug smuggler and former Miami policeman. Perez said that he had given Moya approximately $485,000 as a gift. At about the same time, Moya's parents retired, bought a new home in the Florida Keys, and took a Hawaiian vacation.

Prosecutors were more than a little suspicious about Moya's newfound wealth, and they investigated. They discovered that Moya had received nearly $500,000 from Falcon and Magluta following the trial in exchange for his persuasiveness with other jurors in arriving at an acquittal. Prosecutors charged Moya with money laundering, witness tampering, conspiracy, bribery, obstruction of justice, and filing a false tax return. Moya was convicted in July 1999 of the different crimes alleged. He faced 138 years in prison, plus substantial fines. His father, José, pleaded guilty to witness tampering and was sentenced in October 1999. Falcon and Magluta, reportedly the top drug traffickers in the United States during the 1980s, were charged with smuggling seventy-five tons of cocaine into the United States and making $2 billion. Their 1996 acquittal was a sound defeat for federal prosecutors, although both men were imprisoned later on lesser unrelated charges.

What safeguards should exist to protect juror integrity and insulate jurors from potential bribes from criminal defendants? What policies would you put in place to ensure that jury tampering can be prevented? What do you think?

Source: Adapted from the Associated Press, "Jury: Juror Guilty of Accepting Bribes." *Minot* (N.D.) *Daily News,* July 25, 2000:A2.

who believe that jury service is a civic duty and that all U.S. citizens are obligated to serve on juries when called to do so. Juror misconduct prior to trials most often involves jurors who lie to avoid jury service. Another problem is jurors who lie and fail to disclose important information during *voir dire* so that they can remain on the jury. Those who are called to jury service often want to avoid it because of certain hardships jury service would pose. Although jurors are compensated for their service, serving on a jury is still regarded by many persons as a financial hardship.

The financial hardship for jurors today is quite different from the financial burden on jurors in the 1700s. Jurors were usually compensated one to two dollars per day. However, many jurors had to travel long distances on foot or horseback to the courthouse. Because they could not return home each day, they had to pay for food and lodging. Often, these expenses were considerably more than the amount of their compensation received from the court for their jury service. Today, jurors continue to have the hardship of traveling to the courthouse, although in most instances they are able to return to their homes each evening. In past centuries, judges routinely refused to feed jurors while they were deliberating in order to starve out a verdict, another hazard that contemporary jurors do not endure. The reasons for avoiding jury service have changed over time, although some persons still consider serving on a jury to be a hardship and that jury service is an activity to be avoided.

Another form of juror misconduct is lying to avoid jury duty. In the early 1900s in Cleveland, for example, residents from the wealthiest neighborhoods claimed illnesses more often than those from poorer neighborhoods. Still others fabricated stories about how they were related to defendants in criminal cases simply to be dismissed as jurors. It was later revealed that they had no particular relationship with the accused and that their lies were ruses to avoid jury service (Stalmaster, 1931:74).

Engaging in inappropriate or prohibited behavior while serving as a juror is the most serious form of juror misconduct. Although juror misconduct has always plagued the jury system, it is more of a problem today than in the past. Over time, the definition of misconduct has not changed substantially, though what is different today is that jurors of the past had fewer opportunities to engage in inappropriate behavior. For instance, in past decades, a felony trial might have only one or two witnesses, and the trial lasted only a few hours. During this time, jurors were closely watched by the bailiff, who prevented any misconduct from occurring. Today, trials are much longer, and jurors have more unsupervised time and more opportunities to be exposed to external influences and bribes from a defendant's friends, visit the crime scene, discuss the evidence and the case prior to final deliberations, drink alcohol, and read, listen to, and watch prohibited media.

What are the implications of juror misconduct? For jurors themselves, they are most often held in contempt and ordered to pay a fine or serve a short jail term. In rare instances, they are charged with criminal behavior by the prosecutor. Interestingly, jurors most often charged with misconduct by the prosecutor were members of juries whose result was an acquittal or a mistrial. A common form of juror misconduct is drinking alcohol during the trial or deliberations. Judges have been reluctant to declare a mistrial when they learn that jurors have been drinking. However, most judges consider drinking during deliberations more serious than drinking during the trial (Conrad, 1998). In short, it appears that judges believe that jurors must have a clearer head for deliberating the evidence than for hearing the evidence.

Jurors who engage in misconduct are rarely punished, primarily because jurors are short-term actors in the criminal justice process. Jurors who engage in misconduct are punished after the trial, and so their fellow jurors are unaware of any punishment. Simi-

LAPD IN TROUBLE AGAIN

A Case of Jury Bias?

Three Los Angeles Police Department officers were convicted of conspiracy and other crimes on Wednesday, November 15, 2000, following a lengthy trial. The police officers were part of a department scandal involving an antigang unit at the police department's Rampart station. It began when former police officer Rafael Perez was caught stealing cocaine from an evidence locker and agreed to become an informant and government witness. Perez told the investigators that other officers framed people, planted evidence, committed perjury, and even shot innocent victims. More than a hundred convictions of innocent suspects have been thrown out as the result of the scandal.

When the officers were convicted on November 15, an alternate juror came forward and disclosed to authorities that the jury foreman had decided the defendants were guilty before any testimony had been presented. Another juror agreed and supported the alternate juror's assertions. Furthermore, the alternate juror said that other jurors often discussed the case outside court before deliberations began, in direct violation of the judge's instructions. Alternate juror Wendy Christiansen, thirty, who did not participate in deliberations, told the judge that on the day the jurors were selected, she had lunch with another alternate and the jury foreman, Victor Flores. Flores commented that he believed the defendants were guilty. Christiansen said also that throughout the trial, other jurors openly said they thought the prosecution's witnesses were lying when they claimed they did not remember things. They did not like the defense attorneys.

When Flores was interviewed by KNBC-TV in Los Angeles, he denied the assertion that he had made up his mind about the defendants before the trial and that he absolutely stood by the guilty verdicts. Flores said, "No, I did not say that, that wouldn't be something I'd even utter, because the law says they're innocent until proven guilty." In support of Flores, another voting juror, Ingrid Utke, said that Flores had acted appropriately and had not uttered what had been alleged by Christiansen. Utke said, "We pointedly made sure that we never talked about the case. If someone veered toward that, we'd say, 'Anyone see a movie lately?' so we wouldn't talk about it. Also, every time we came back from being out here [in the courtroom], there were lots of comments being made about the defense attorneys. They didn't like the defense attorneys. The person they did like was Joel Isaacson," Utke said.

Defense attorneys for the convicted police officers were quick to say that this new evidence warranted a new trial. The district attorney's office refused to comment on the case. Sergeant Brian Liddy, Sgt. Edward Ortiz, and Officer Michael Buchanan were convicted of conspiracy and other crimes involving gang members four years earlier. Barry Levin, one of the officer's attorneys, said, larly, new jurors are entering the system every day, and they typically have no knowledge of prior punishment of deviant jurors. Therefore, when judges do punish jurors, it has little or no potential deterrent value.

When jurors engage in misconduct there is always the possibility that the judge will declare a mistrial. In fact, some defendants prefer mistrials, which minimize the likelihood of a successive prosecution. One way to decrease the adverse effects of juror misconduct is the use of alternate jurors. Judges can replace offending jurors and continue with the trial.

Summary

The role of the jury in the common-law legal system has changed over time. Initially, juries resembled neighborhood watch programs that reported criminal behavior to the authorities. Over time, juries were granted more power and autonomy, and they have become an essential component of the American court process. Most attorneys would agree that one of the most important stages in the criminal court process is the selection of the jury. It is during the jury selection process that lawyers decide who will hear the case. Both sides in the adversarial process attempt to select jurors who might be sympathetic with their position. Additionally, jurors who lawyers believe will not be sympathetic are removed. Two methods for removing potential jurors from the jury pool are challenges for cause and peremptory challenges.

After the case is given to the jury for deliberations, they usually engage in one of two methods of reaching a decision about the guilt or innocence of the defendant. The first method is the evidence-driven jury; all evidence is examined and discussed before a jury vote is taken. The second form of decision making is the verdict-driven jury. In this scenario, the jury first conducts a vote. If all jurors agree on the verdict, their deliberations are concluded. If not, the evidence is examined and discussed. Jury nullification is the process of returning a verdict contrary to the evidence presented in the case; in most cases, a jury finds a defendant not guilty although the evidence strongly suggests the defendant's guilt.

KEY TERMS

Affirmative registration	Juror misconduct	Shadow juries
Blue-ribbon jury	Jury nullification	Venire
Challenge for cause	Jury sequestration	Venireman list
Evidence-driven jury	Peremptory challenge	Verdict-driven jury
Grand jury	Petit jury	*Voir dire*
Hung jury	Scientific jury selection	

QUESTIONS FOR REVIEW

1. Describe the history and development of the grand jury.
2. How has jury size changed over time?
3. What is jury nullification? Should juries have this power?
4. Describe the difference between evidence-driven juries and verdict-driven juries.
5. Should defendants be allowed to hire scientific jury consultants? If so, does this give them an unfair advantage?
6. What is *voir dire*?
7. What is the relevant case law that has shaped our current constitutional requirement on jury size?
8. What are some of the types of hardships cited by contemporary prospective jurors to avoid jury duty?
9. What are several different forms of juror misconduct?

SUGGESTED READINGS

Abramson, Jeffrey. (1994). *We, the Jury: The Jury System and the Ideal of Democracy.* New York: Basic Books.

Adler, Stephen. (1995). *The Jury: Disorder in the Court.* New York: Doubleday.

Bornstein, Brian H. and Robert J. Nemeth. (1999). "Jurors' Perception of Violence: A Framework for Inquiry." *Aggression and Violent Behavior* 4:77–92.

Cockburn, J. S. and Thomas A. Green (eds.). (1988). *Twelve Good Men and True: The Criminal Trial Jury in England, 1200–1800.* Princeton, NJ: Princeton University Press.

Hans, Valerie and Neil Vidmar. (1986). *Judging the Jury.* New York: Plenum.

Harrington, Matthew P. et al. (1999). "The American Jury." *Wisconsin Law Review* 43:377–606.

Kalven, Harry Jr. and Hans Zeisel. (1970). *The American Jury.* Chicago: University of Chicago Press.

Kennedy, Randall. (1997). *Race, Crime, and the Law.* New York: Pantheon.

Wishmen, Seymour. (1986). *Anatomy of a Jury.* New York: Penguin Books.

PRETRIAL PROCEDURES

Initial Appearance, Bail Decision Making, and Alternative Dispute Resolution

JIM BROOKMAN broke into the home of an elderly woman at 2 A.M. The woman was asleep. While in her home, the man stole diamond necklaces and bracelets and some rare coins. On his way out, Brookman took a small television set and a gold watch. However, as he climbed out of the window, Brookman knocked over a lamp. The noise awakened the old woman. As Brookman drove out of town, a county deputy sheriff pulled him over for speeding and driving an automobile with no license plates. When the deputy shined his flashlight into the car, he saw the television and a bag with some of the jewelry and coins exposed. Immediately, he suspected something was wrong and ordered the man from the car at gunpoint. He handcuffed Brookman, radioed the dispatcher with this information, and found out that a woman had just reported a burglary in her home. Later at the station, the woman identified the television, coins, and jewelry as hers. Charges were filed against Brookman. He was booked, photographed, fingerprinted, and held without bail. A court-appointed lawyer eventually discussed Brookman's case with the prosecutor. The defense counsel pointed out that Brookman was a first offender who had recently divorced. He had lost his home and job. The night of the burglary, he had been drinking heavily and was depressed. Brookman, the defense counsel argued, should be treated, not incarcerated. The prosecutor was agreeable and advised that if Brookman underwent counseling for one year, made victim restitution, and performed four hundred hours of community service, then perhaps the charges might be downgraded or dropped. The prosecutor said that he would discuss the matter with the woman and that an arbiter would be appointed to oversee the agreement. Later, Brookman met the woman, Mrs. Saunders, face to face in an alternative dispute resolution meeting. The woman was upset but said that she would agree to having Brookman perform community service and make restitution for the damage to her property. Brookman performed the community service, attended the required counseling sessions, and, after fourteen months, the prosecutor dropped all charges against him.

FRED JOHNSON left a bar late at night after having several drinks. On his way down the road, he sideswiped a parked car, damaging the passenger door and fenders. A few miles later, Johnson was pulled over for weaving. Police gave him a breathalyzer test and determined that his blood-alcohol level was 0.11, just slightly over the legal limit of 0.10 for intoxication. Johnson was charged with driving while intoxicated. He also admitted to scraping another car before he was stopped by police. Subsequent investigation disclosed that he had, indeed, sideswiped another car and that the damage to the other vehicle was $2,200. Later, a prosecutor met with his defense counsel and discussed various plea options. Because of Johnson's clean record (i.e., he had never been charged with any crime; he had lived in the community all of his life; he had never been convicted of any alcohol-related offense), the prosecutor suggested that Johnson might be able to participate in a diversion program. Johnson could make restitution to the person whose car was damaged, pay a monthly fee, and report to the probation department that he was remaining sober and not getting into trouble. After one year, the prosecutor said, if Johnson had completed the diversion program successfully and fully compensated the victim for the automobile damage, then perhaps the charges would be dropped. The prosecutor reasoned that Johnson's blood alcohol content was above the legal limit for intoxication but borderline, thus qualifying Johnson for diversion. Fred Johnson and his attorney agreed to the terms of the diversion program, and over the next year, Johnson complied with all program requirements and made restitution to the victim. His DWI charge was dropped, and his record remained clean.

Introduction

This chapter is about what happens to offenders before they are prosecuted for crimes. When people commit crimes and are subsequently arrested, they are booked. They make an initial appearance before a magistrate who determines whether they are entitled to bail. Persons who cannot afford counsel will have an attorney appointed to represent them. Bail is ordinarily granted to those who have established community ties and are unlikely to flee the jurisdiction, as well as those unlikely to pose a danger to themselves or to others. The bail process will be described.

Prosecutors screen many cases and determine that certain cases should be diverted from the criminal justice system temporarily. If one or more victims suffer injuries, property damage, or loss, their participation in diversion or alternative dispute resolution programs is solicited. Prosecutors and defense counsel meet with offenders and their victims and attempt to resolve things to the satisfaction of all concerned. One advantage to the state is avoiding a lengthy and costly trial, and the offender avoids a criminal conviction. Victims are compensated for their losses or injuries and have the satisfaction of participating in the punishment of the offenders.

Arrest and Booking

Arrest

An **arrest** means taking offenders into custody. Usually, arrests of criminal suspects are made by police officers. Arrested persons are referred to as **arrestees**. Arrests of suspects may be made directly by police officers who observe law violations. If a **felony** is alleged, officers must have at least reasonable suspicion to stop and detain for investigating a suspect. If subsequent developments provide the officers with **probable cause** to believe that the suspects they have detained probably committed the alleged offense, the officers can arrest the suspect(s) and take them to jail for further processing and identification. If a **misdemeanor** is committed and not directly observed by the officer, the officer may stop suspects and make inquiries. But without **reasonable suspicion** to inquire further, officers are not empowered to arrest possible misdemeanants if they lack probable cause.

In a felony case, for instance, officers in a cruiser sitting on the shoulder of Highway 55 may receive a report that a Mary's Convenience Store was just robbed by two men wielding shotguns. The men were described as two black males, one wearing a red cap and the other wearing a green cap. The men were last seen driving east on Highway 55 in a black 1966 Chevrolet van. Just then a black 1966 Chevrolet van goes by, driven by a black man in a red cap. The officers give chase and eventually stop the van. The officers cautiously approach and order the suspects to exit from the van. When the suspects are out of the van, the officers observe that the passenger is also black and is wearing a green cap. The officers shine their flashlights into the van's interior and see some moneybags marked "Mary's Convenience Store." These similarities are overwhelming, and thus the officers arrest the two men on suspicion of robbing Mary's Convenience Store. Although these officers did not see the actual robbery, the descriptions of the fleeing suspects, their vehicle, and the moneybags in the van have provided the officers with probable cause to make the arrests.

Booking

Once suspects have been arrested, they are usually booked. **Booking** is an administrative procedure to obtain personal background information about arrestees for law enforcement officers. Booking compiles a file for each defendant, including name, address, telephone number, age, place of work, relatives, and other personal data. The extensiveness of the booking procedure varies among jurisdictions. Most jurisdictions photograph and fingerprint criminal suspects. Sometimes, arrestees are merely detained for several hours and released. They are usually required to face charges in court later. For example, those arrested for drunk driving may be held temporarily in a local jail overnight. When they are sober in the morning, they are released but must appear before a judge to face charges later.

Initial Appearance

The **initial appearance** of a defendant before a magistrate is a formal proceeding during which a magistrate or other judicial official advises the defendant of the charges. An initial appearance follows the booking process. The magistrate determines from a reading of the charges whether they are petty offenses. Petty or minor offenses vary in interpretation among states. Indicators of petty offenses are usually small fines (less than $500) and short sentences (six months or less) associated with the criminal offense. More serious offenses involve larger fines and longer sentences, usually one year or longer in duration.

Crime seriousness has been critical in determining whether defendants have a right to a jury trial. For instance, the case of *Duncan v. Louisiana* (1968) involved a nineteen-year-old man who was convicted and sentenced to serve sixty days in jail and pay a $150 fine for simple battery. Duncan requested a jury trial but was denied one. Louisiana claimed that Duncan's crime was a petty offense and thus did not entitle him to a jury trial. The U.S. Supreme Court disagreed. The high court observed that Louisiana's law pertaining to battery, although a misdemeanor or petty offense, carried a two-year maximum sentence and a $300 fine. The U.S. Supreme Court observed that most states define petty offenses as punishable for terms of less than one year, and in some jurisdictions the maximum sentence is no more than six months and a $50 fine. Without defining precisely the meaning of a petty offense, the U.S. Supreme Court said, "We need not . . . settle in this case the exact location of the line between petty offenses and serious crimes. It is sufficient for our purposes to hold that a crime punishable by two years in prison is . . . a serious crime and not a petty offense." Duncan's conviction was overturned.

The Sixth Amendment says that all defendants in criminal prosecutions are entitled to a speedy and public trial, by an impartial jury of the state. But this amendment is interpreted differently, depending on the jurisdiction where the petty offenses are committed. Some jurisdictions discourage jury trials to resolve petty offense charges. In a New Jersey case, a defendant was indicted by a federal grand jury on federal misdemeanor charges, and the prosecutor for the government strongly expressed the opinion that the man ought to waive his jury trial rights. The man refused, and so the prosecutor brought new felony charges against the man in retaliation. In this case, the court dismissed all charges against the man as the fair remedy, and the prosecutor was criticized for his misconduct (*United States v. Lippi,* 1977).

When any crime is alleged, it is important for defendants to be advised of the specific charges against them. They should also be advised of their rights under the circumstances. When people are arrested by police, their initial appearance before a magistrate, therefore, is a formal proceeding in which defendants are advised of the charges against them. At that time, the magistrate advises the defendants of their rights, and bail is considered. This is also the occasion for magistrates to determine the date for a **preliminary examination** or a **preliminary hearing** to establish whether probable cause exists to move forward toward a trial. Between the time of a defendant's initial appearance and the preliminary hearing or examination, defendants can hire defense counsel to represent them. If a defendant is indigent, then an attorney is appointed by the court to represent him or her.

The Right to Bail

Bail has its roots in New England in the 1690s (McManus, 1993). Early English common law applicable during that period encompassed many of the guarantees later included in the Bill of Rights, including rights against unreasonable searches and seizures, double jeopardy, and compulsory self-incrimination; grand jury indictment; trial by jury; and the right to bail (McManus, 1993). Bail is not unique to the United States. Other countries, such as Australia, have done much to establish bail provisions for criminal defendants and the conditions under which bail is granted (*Michigan Yearbook of International Legal Studies,* 1983; Queensland, 1993).

RELEASE ON ONE'S OWN RECOGNIZANCE. Following an arrest, a decision is made about whether the defendant will be brought to trial. If a trial is imminent because of case seriousness, most defendants can obtain their temporary release from jail. Many arrestees may not have to post bail, in that they are eligible for **release on their own recognizance (ROR)** (Harmsworth, 1996). If they have strong community ties and are unlikely to flee from the jurisdiction, they may be freed on their own recognizance (ROR) by the magistrate or judicial officer (National Center for State Courts, 1990).

BAIL BONDS. When the character of the defendant is unknown or the offenses alleged are quite serious (e.g., aggravated assault, rape, armed robbery), the magistrate often sets bail or specifies a **bail bond**. Bail is a surety to procure the release of those under arrest, to assure that they will appear to face charges in court at a later date. A bail bond is a written guarantee, often accompanied by money or other securities, that the person charged with an offense will remain in the court's jurisdiction to face trial at a time in the future (Hawaii Office of the Auditor, 1992).

Motorists may be required to post a **cash bail bond** for minor traffic violations such as speeding or reckless driving. These cash bonds guarantee the motorist's appearance in court later to face charges of violating traffic laws. If the motorist fails to appear, the cash bond is forfeited. The bond set is often the exact amount of the fine for violating the traffic law.

When arrestees do not have the money to post their bail, they may use **bail bond companies**. These companies are usually located near jails. For a fee, they provide the service of posting bail for arrestees. **Bail bondsmen** or **bondspersons** appear at the jail and post bond for defendants. Defendants are usually required to pay the bonding company a fee for this service, which is ten percent of the bail bond set by the magistrate. For instance, if the bond set by the magistrate for a particular offense is $25,000, the bonding company may post this bond for the defendant if the defendant is considered a good risk, and if the defendant or an associate of the defendant pays the bonding company a nonrefundable fee of $2,500. If a defendant is unable to pay the fee and no one else will pay it, the defendant must remain in jail until trial is held.

A Murder Is a Murder Is a Murder . . .

The Case of Cameron Lee Smith

It happened in Norman, Oklahoma. One Friday evening, a neighbor saw a man walk naked from a rooming house to a trash bin and throw in a large, bloody object. The naked man returned to his rooming house up the street. The neighbor investigated and found a bloody head inside a knapsack. He reported this to the police.

An investigation led to the arrest of Cameron Lee Smith, thirty-three. The decapitated head was that of Roydon Dale Major, forty-four, whose body was found in another room near Smith's. The trash bin where Major's head was dumped was near a shopping district next to the University of Oklahoma. According to the neighbor who found the head, "The bag was bloody so I zipped it carefully and opened it up and saw the head."

No apparent motive had been given for the beheading. Smith's landlord, Thekla Mendros, said that she had ordered him to leave the rooming house by the weekend because he had been acting erratically and tearing down walls. Smith was being held on first-degree murder charges.

Should bail be granted in Smith's case? Can circumstantial evidence be used to deny a person bail? What do you think?

Source: Adapted from Associated Press, "Police Arrest Man in Beheading." *Minot* (N.D.) *Daily News,* May 26, 1996:A2.

Bail Bondsmen and Bonding Companies

Bail bondsmen either own or work for bonding companies. Bonding companies are authorized to post bail for various criminal suspects up to a fixed amount. Bonding companies usually have property investments and other capital that they use as a type of insurance with a city or county government. For example, a bonding company may be authorized by a city to post bonds of up to $5 million for various arrestees charged with crimes. The bonding company may have stocks, securities, property, and other assets that it has assigned to the city or county as collateral. Thus, the city or county is protected from the potential loss of revenue if the bonding company guarantees the bond amount for the release of a defendant. If the defendant fails to appear later in court, the bonding company forfeits the bond it has posted unless it can produce the defendant.

If the bonding company is authorized to write bonds of up to $5 million, once this ceiling has been reached, the bonding company can no longer write bonds for defendants. Bonding companies are released from their obligations to cities or counties once defendants have been convicted or acquitted of crimes or the bail bonds are canceled. Bonding companies profit from the ten percent nonrefundable fees they collect from those who want to be released from jail before their trials are held. In most jurisdictions, several bonding companies can provide bail for various arrestees.

Competing Goals of Bail

EXCESSIVE BAIL. Under the Eighth Amendment, citizens are advised that **excessive bail** shall not be required, nor excessive fines imposed. Some citizens believe that, regardless of the offense alleged, bail will be set and defendants will be permitted to remain free until the date of trial. This is not true. Depending on the circumstances of a particular criminal offense and the evidence obtained, some defendants may have a very high bail, and others may not be granted bail at all. They are required to remain in jail until trial.

The Eighth Amendment provision against excessive bail means that bail shall not be excessive in those cases in which it is proper to grant bail (*United States v. Giangrosso,* 1985). The right to bail is not absolute under the Eighth Amendment (*United States v. Bilanzich,* 1985; *United States v. Provenzano,* 1985). In some cases, suspects are detained for trial without bail (*United States v. Acevedo-Ramos,* 1984); in others, defendants are subject to detention even if they are unable to pay high bail ranging from $25,000 to $1 million (*United States v. Szott,* 1985; *United States v. Jessup,* 1985). If a murder suspect is caught in the act or is a habitual offender, bail will probably be denied because such defendants will probably attempt to flee the jurisdiction to avoid prosecution. Are certain suspects dangerous to others? States vary in permitting judges the discretion to make this decision. In thirty-one states and the District of Columbia, this is a judicial consideration that often results in preventive pretrial detention (Gottlieb, 1984).

Whether bail is granted is not exclusively determined by whether a crime is violent (Gaynes, 1982; Verrilli, 1982). More than a few defendants who are charged with nonviolent crimes are denied bail. Magistrates consider the **totality of circumstances** in setting bail on a case-by-case basis. A former bank president was denied bail in a case alleging fraudulent manipulation and theft of depositors' funds. Although the former bank president had substantial community ties and property interests to protect, he also had a recently acquired passport and travel visas to several foreign countries, where he also maintained property and business interests. In addition, $50 million in bank funds were missing, according to a federal audit. The magistrate considered the bank president a poor risk for bail. There was a strong likelihood that the bank president would flee the jurisdiction and live on the embezzled $50 million in some remote location.

Bail provisions of the U.S. Constitution have been challenged by the American Civil Liberties Union and other civil rights organizations. Their efforts, as well as the efforts of a variety of special interest groups, have prompted a number of bail reforms over the years. Some of the reasons given for such bail reforms have included the facts that (1) bail is inherently discriminatory against the poor or indigent defendant, (2) those who are unable to post a bail bond and must remain in jail cannot adequately prepare a defense or correspond effectively with their attorneys, (3) there is considerable variation from one jurisdiction to the next and from one case to the next within the same jurisdiction for establishing a bail bond for similar offenses, (4) withholding bail or prescribing prohibitively high bail offends our sense of the presumption of innocence until guilt is

NOBEL PRIZE AND CHILD SEXUAL ABUSE

The Case of Dr. Daniel Gajdusek

It allegedly happened in Frederick, Maryland. Dr. Daniel Gajdusek, chief of the Laboratory of Central Nervous System Studies, won the Nobel Prize for physiology or medicine in 1976 for his work on infectious diseases. Twenty years later at age seventy-two, Gajdusek was investigated and arrested by the FBI, which alleged that he had sexually molested a fifteen-year-old boy who had lived with him during the years 1987–1991. At the time of Gajdusek's arrest, four children were living with him in his home.

FBI spokesman Larry Foust said that Gajdusek was being charged with child abuse and unnatural perverted sex practices. He was being held in lieu of $1 million bail. Gajdusek told reporters outside a sheriff's office that he is not a pedophile. "No. Not in the way that you are using the term, so I say no." The boy he is accused of abusing was brought to the United States from Micronesia.

Source: Adapted from Associated Press, "Nobel Prize Winner Charged with Child Abuse in Maryland." *Minot* (N.D.) *Daily News,* April 6, 1996:A2.

proven in court, and (5) those who pose no risk to the community may suffer loss of job or other benefits from detention as the result of bail (Gibbs, 1975; Goldkamp, 1984). It would seem, therefore, that to deny a defendant bail would be contrary to the presumption of innocence that is an integral part of due process (Reed, 1983). Nevertheless, the right to bail is not absolute.

Race, gender, and socioeconomic status have been among the variables examined to determine their differential impact on bail decision making (Holmes et al., 1996). These variables are extralegal and should have absolutely no bearing on whether a defendant is granted bail. However, minorities seem to be at a definite disadvantage in the criminal justice system regarding bail decision making. Racial or gender differences seem to make a difference to judges when they are making pretrial release or bail decisions about particular defendants (Holmes et al., 1996). For instance, female defendants are granted more lenient pretrial release terms than men in many jurisdictions (Steury and Frank, 1990).

Katz and Spohn (1995:161–163) investigated whether these data might show a pattern of discrimination in bail decision making according to race or gender. A sample of 8,414 defendants was divided according to race and gender. Because of missing information, the sample consisted of records for 6,625 black defendants and 1,005 white defendants. A small percent of the sample were females. These researchers asked whether race or gender made any difference in the bail decision or the amount of bail. When offense and prior record are taken into account, race made no difference on the bail decision. However, gender did make a difference. For different types of offenses, female defendants faced significantly lower bail than their male counterparts. Regarding pretrial release decision making, however, white defendants were more likely to be released before trial than black defendants. Further, females tended to be granted pretrial release more than males. These findings are inconclusive, but they suggest that although race and gender may help to explain bail and pretrial release decisions, these variables may not be as influential as other investigators previously thought. Other researchers have found similar inconsistencies in bail decision making and race and gender variables (Albonetti, 1989).

THE BAIL REFORM ACT OF 1984. The bail reform movement assumes that bail is inherently discriminatory (Florida Governor's Task Force, 1981). The **Bail Reform Act**, passed in 1966, revised bail practices to assure that all people, regardless of their financial status, are not needlessly detained pending their appearance to answer charges. More recently, the **Bail Reform Act of 1984** vests magistrates and judicial officers with greater autonomy in setting bail and releasing arrestees on their own recognizance. At present, bail is available only to those entitled to it (Hirsch and Sheely, 1993), usually those who do not pose a threat to themselves or others and do not pose escape risks. There is nothing inherently unconstitutional about keeping arrestees jailed prior to their trials, however, under various forms of pretrial detention (*United States v. Salerno,* 1987). Some experts believe that pretrial detention of suspects is sometimes abused and that lawmakers should keep its use within reasonable limits (Miller and Guggenheim, 1990). One reason for this belief is that it is often difficult to forecast accurately who will be dangerous or good candidates for bail (O'Neill, 1983).

Several states have passed **sexual predator laws** that are targeted at violent sex offenders. Washington state, for instance, passed a sexual predator act in 1990 aimed at those likely to engage in future acts of sexual violence. However, the act was soundly criticized because of its failure to cite realistic predictive criteria that would identify *which* sex offenders would commit future dangerous sexual acts following some type of sex therapy or treatment (Brody and Green, 1994). Although such laws have drawn criticism from various civil rights groups, the U.S. Supreme Court upheld the constitutionality of such laws in 1998.

Interestingly, Nebraska passed a sexual predator law concerning a sex offender's right to bail in 1978, twenty years before the U.S. Supreme Court upheld the constitutionality of the Washington state sexual predator act. Nebraska amended its constitution to require the denial of bail to defendants charged with forcible sex offenses when the proof is evident and the presumption of guilt is great (Portman, 1982). Other jurisdictions, such as Texas and California, have enacted similar provisions (Collins, 1981; Pisula, 1980).

Other Forms of Pretrial Release

BAIL EXPERIMENTS. The 1984 Bail Reform Act was innovative in its provisions for judicial officers to release defendants subject to certain conditions, such as complying with a curfew; reporting on a regular basis to a designated law enforcement agency; abiding by specific restrictions on one's personal associations, place of abode, and travel; maintaining

IS THE STAND-UP COMIC ALSO A RAPIST?

The Case of Vinson Champ

It happened in Wisconsin, and in Nebraska, and in Iowa, and in Illinois, and in California. On several college campuses, female students and teachers were sexually assaulted by a man wearing a ski mask. Besides the ski mask, the rapist quizzed each of his victims about their sexual experiences and then asked them to pray for him. In California, police arrested Vinson Champ, a thirty-five-year-old stand-up comedian, after he was spotted running from an attempted rape scene on the campus of Pasadena City College.

Because of the different locations where the rapes occurred, police originally theorized that the attacker might be a traveling professor or perhaps an athlete. However, when California police arrested Champ, his travel and comedy club schedule coincided perfectly with the times and dates of the previous rapes.

Champ was released on bail from a Pasadena, California, jail. Shortly thereafter, he boarded a plane and headed for the Caribbean. However, an all-points bulletin was issued, and he was arrested at the Newark International Airport before he could leave the country. Several women have identified Champ as their attacker, and semen specimens at all of the rape scenes matched. A check of Champ's background disclosed that he had previous arrests for prostitution and for physically attacking his seventeen-year-old former girlfriend in 1996. One possible hindrance to prosecuting Champ is whether all victims will come forward to identify themselves and cooperate with the police. In June 1997, Champ was awaiting extradition to Nebraska, where he faced rape charges.

Source: Adapted from Patrick Rogers, "No Laughing Matter: Looking for the Link in a Series of Campus Rapes, Police Arrest a Traveling Stand-Up Comic." *People,* May 26, 1997:79.

or commencing an educational program; and maintaining employment or actively seeking employment if currently unemployed (Broderick et al., 1993; Vera Institute of Justice, 1995).

Before the Bail Reform Act of 1984 was passed, experiments were conducted to determine the effectiveness of ROR. A national bail study was conducted in twenty jurisdictions in the United States (Thomas, 1976, 1977) between 1962 and 1971. There was a significant drop in both felony and misdemeanor defendants who were detained in jails during those years and an accompanying increase in the numbers of defendants who were released on their own recognizance (ROR). More judges seemed to be relying on ROR for the pretrial release of defendants, which meant more limited use of cash bonds, a primary criticism of bail opponents.

Between January 1981 and March 1982, the **Philadelphia Experiment** was conducted concerning bail guidelines in the Philadelphia Municipal Court (Goldkamp and

A STOMACH FULL OF HASH

The Case of Ernest Henton

It happened in West Haven, Connecticut. Ernest Henton, forty-nine, had just returned from Jamaica with a stomach ache that wouldn't go away. When he went to the doctor for relief, X-rays revealed that Henton had swallowed 230 bags of hashish. With some laxatives, a rectal scope, and four days in the hospital, Henton passed more than two hundred tiny, marble-sized packets of cellophane-wrapped hashish, worth about $5,000. Doctors turned over about 1.3 pounds of hashish to police. When finally released from the hospital, Henton was charged with possession of a controlled substance and possession with intent to sell. He was held on $200,000 bond.

Do you think that the bond set in Henton's case was unreasonable, given the fact that the hashish he possessed was valued at only $5,000? What bond would you have imposed on Henton in these circumstances? What do you think?

Source: Adapted from the Associated Press, "Man Returns from Vacation with Hashish Packets in His Stomach." *Minot* (N.D.) *Daily News,* May 24, 1997:A2.

Gottfredson, 1984). Twenty-two judges were selected for the experiment. One objective was to create visible guidelines for judges to follow in using ROR in lieu of bail in pretrial release decisions. When bail was established, median bail figures for judges not following prescribed guidelines was $2,000, whereas the median bail figure was $1,500 for those judges adhering to the guidelines provided.

Although the findings were inconsistent regarding the use of ROR, the researchers said that the experiment yielded significant improvements in the equity of bail decisions for defendants generally. The study also encouraged greater use of supervised or conditional release programs, as outlined within the Bail Reform Act of 1984. As the Philadelphia Experiment suggested, this alternative would provide some degree of relief for jail overcrowding, at the very least.

Subsequently, the New York City Department of Correction discharged 611 jail inmates in November 1983 (Gerwitz, 1987), of which 75 percent were released on bail and 25 percent were released on their own recognizance. Only four ROR defendants were charged with felonies, but about 75 percent of the bail defendants were similarly charged. Forty percent of the released defendants failed to appear for at least one pretrial hearing. ROR defendants were far more likely than bail-release defendants to fail to appear in court later. Over one-third of the ROR defendants were rearrested prior to trial. **Failure to appear** means that people scheduled for trial who were temporarily released on bail or ROR do not show up in court on their scheduled trial dates. Other investigators concluded similarly that obligating defendants to post bail does not necessarily guarantee their subsequent court appearances, but it does result in fewer failures to appear, compared with those released on ROR (Pretrial Resources Service Center, 1994). Other researchers have reported similar findings (Bak, 1994; Block and Twist, 1995).

Bounty Hunters

BOUNTY HUNTERS AND JUMPING BAIL. It is advantageous for bonding companies if the defendant can post property assets as collateral for the bonding fee. Then, if a defendant leaves the jurisdiction before trial and jumps bond, the bonding company forfeits the bond it posted with the court, but it is entitled to seize the defendant's tangible assets or property to cover the cost of the forfeited bond. Defendants may bypass bonding companies altogether by pledging their own real property assets to the court as bond in lieu of confinement. Courts are permitted to accept other types of assets, such as bank deposits, securities, or valuable personal property. When defendants must post their own property as bail, they are more likely to appear in court later than those defendants who have bail posted for them by bonding companies (Pretrial Resources Service Center, 1994). The bail options available to defendants vary among jurisdictions (North Carolina Legislative Research Commission, 1987; Reynolds, 1994).

When bonding companies provide bond for defendants, they do so on the assumption that bailees will reappear later in court to face the criminal charges against them. Bonding companies avoid furnishing bail to those likely to jump bail and leave the jurisdiction to avoid a subsequent criminal prosecution. (**Jumping bail** means to leave the jurisdiction while on bail to avoid prosecution.) However, a certain number of defendants leave the jurisdiction and fail to appear later in court. When this happens, the bonding company forfeits its bond to the city or county court. The more bail jumpers a bonding company has, the less bonding funds it has available to use for other defendants. Sizable profits are lost, at least temporarily, whenever someone jumps bail. For this reason, many bonding companies post **bounties** or monetary incentives or employ **bounty hunters** to track down bail jumpers for a fee and bring them to court (Burton, 1984; Colorado Department of Regulatory Agencies, 1992). Unfortunately, we have been unable to devise foolproof mechanisms for predicting which defendants will jump bail. However, some prediction models work better than others (Cuvelier and Potts, 1993).

In recent years, there have been several incidents involving acts of irresponsibility by bail bondsmen and bounty hunters. Specifically, the wrong persons have been targeted as bail jumpers. As a result, several innocent victims have suffered serious injury or death as the result of bounty hunters' actions. Despite these inappropriate and indiscriminate actions by bounty hunters, bondsmen continue to enjoy a broad range of procedural safeguards in surety arrests under both federal and state statutes (Doane, 1986).

On Jumping Bail

The Case of Jeff Helgeson

Bail jumping is not new. Defendants jump bail all the time. Arrested in a jurisdiction where they have no roots, or if the bail set for an offense is low, many defendants simply leave the jurisdiction and go back to their homes in other states. For bonding companies who provide the bail for a defendant's early release, jumping bail is an unpleasant outcome. Bail companies have to reimburse courts for the bail amounts that have been provided if defendants fail to appear. On such occasions, bounty hunters may be employed to hunt down defendants and bring them bodily back to court, probably the only way a bonding company can get its money back.

In July 1995, Jeff Helgeson, forty-one, of Towner, North Dakota, was arrested for terrorizing. He was alleged to have forced his estranged wife from her home in Carrington, North Dakota, and attempted to beat her up and sexually assault her. He allegedly took her in her car to the Upham, North Dakota, area, where she escaped and notified police about Helgeson's actions. Helgeson was arrested shortly thereafter in Upham, where he had allegedly smashed his wife's car with a hammer. His offense was listed as terrorizing, a felony in North Dakota that carries a maximum penalty of five years and a $5,000 fine.

Shortly after Helgeson's arrest by police, he was released from jail after posting $7,500 bail. His trial was set for January 1996. When the trial date arrived, Helgeson was nowhere to be found. He had skipped town, and no one knew where Helgeson had gone.

It was not until January 27, 1998, that Helgeson surfaced in Fargo, North Dakota. He was arrested by North Dakota officers when he appeared in a federal courtroom in Fargo to face separate federal charges of buying a firearm by giving false information about his criminal history. His sentencing date in federal court was set for April 3, 1998. In the meantime, Helgeson was turned over to North Dakota authorities and held in a Bottineau, North Dakota, jail following his initial appearance on the bail-jumping charge. The trial for his bail-jumping charge was to be held on August 20, 1998. On August 25, 1998, he was scheduled to be tried on the state charges of terrorizing and simple assault. After North Dakota authorities had processed Helgeson, he was returned to federal authorities to await his April 3, 1998, trial for giving false information about his criminal history. He was denied bail on all charges, both federal and state.

Is everyone entitled to bail? What conditions would you prefer to use for qualifying a person for bail? Under what circumstances would you deny someone bail? Do you think Helgeson was entitled to bail in North Dakota the first time he was charged?

Source: Adapted from Jill Schramm, "Helgeson Pleads Not Guilty to Jumping Bail: Trials Set." *Minot (N.D.) Daily News,* March 5, 1998:B1.

Decriminalization, Alternative Dispute Resolution (ADR), and Diversion

Placement of a criminal case into the criminal justice system does not necessarily mean that the case will proceed through the entire system and be fully processed. Several factors determine whether specific cases will move further into the system or be removed from it. There is a great deal of pressure on prosecutors to resolve increasing numbers of cases expeditiously. Unfortunately, prosecutors' offices throughout the United States do not have sufficient staff or resources to prosecute all cases brought to their attention. Therefore, prosecutors must often prioritize cases and arrange them from the most to least serious. The most serious cases are likely to receive the full attention of prosecutors and move forward. However, a massive number of less serious criminal cases are relegated to lower priority for prosecution.

Several solutions have been devised or proposed to resolve these less serious cases without consuming valuable court time. For instance, a large number of cases involve possession of marijuana or recreational drug use. Some cases involve assault and battery or spouse abuse; individuals, married or otherwise, have physically injured one another, police have intervened, and one or both parties have been arrested. Although criminal laws have been violated, prosecutors do not always regard these types of offenses with the same degree of seriousness as armed robbery, rape, and murder.

In the case of illegal drug use, some people have advocated legalizing certain drugs, thus rendering their possession as a noncriminal act. Prosecutors do not think drug use is harmless, but they might inquire as to whether the criminal justice system is the best place to deal with illicit drug use and punish it. Should drug users be treated rather than punished? No one knows the answer to this question. Certainly, there are strong opinions favoring and opposing the legalization of certain drugs.

The following section explores several strategies devised by legislators and others to reduce the caseloads of prosecutors and accelerate the justice process by focusing on the most serious cases. Strategies for reducing the sheer numbers of criminal cases confronting overworked prosecutors' offices include decriminalization, alternative dispute resolution, and diversion.

Decriminalization

Decriminalization removes an act from the category of crime. Decriminalization might occur, for instance, in marijuana use. Some states, such as Oregon and Washington, have entertained legislation that would legalize marijuana. California decriminalized marijuana use for medical purposes in the mid-1990s. When crimes are decriminalized, they may be shifted to civil courts for noncriminal resolution. Thus, a fight at a football game between overly enthusiastic fans may be shifted from criminal court to some type of civil resolution.

Alternative Dispute Resolution

An increasingly used option to settle minor criminal cases is **alternative dispute resolution (ADR)**. ADR is community-based, informal dispute settlement between offenders

THE HASH-BASH

A Case for Decriminalization?

Ann Arbor, Michigan, was the site of a hash-bash, with thousands of people congregating to smoke pot at a weekend festival. The twenty-fifth annual event was marred by sixty-three arrests for possessing a controlled substance. Police said that at this regular event many persons interested in the legalization of marijuana get together each year, smoke pot, and advocate its unrestricted use in the United States.

In Michigan, possession of a controlled substance, a misdemeanor, is punishable by a $2,000 fine and a one-year jail sentence. The crowd of more than five thousand did not seem to care, however. John Sinclair, a long-time Ann Arbor marijuana activist, said, "Everything's cool. It's a beautiful day. Everyone's getting high." Banners proclaimed "Pot Is Fun" and "Hemp, Hemp, Hooray." Interestingly, the event is held annually on the campus of the University of Michigan, with additional thousands of onlookers, including police. Knowing in advance that there will be more than five thousand substance abusers in one place seemingly makes the enforcement of Michigan's drug laws easier. Police know in advance of the event, plan accordingly, and act whenever they observe illegal behavior in plain view.

Some spectators suggested that the aroma of marijuana was so strong in the air during the rally that someone who merely watched would get high from secondary smoke inhalation. Advocates of marijuana use claim that the medicinal benefits of marijuana far outweigh its criminal concomitants. Medicinal purposes include treatment for glaucoma and relief from arthritis pain. The event included prominent speakers, even physicians, who differentiated between marijuana and other drugs and alcohol. One rally participant boasted, "You can use it for a lot of different purposes. It came from the ground. God made it and we're going to smoke it."

The Washington State Legislature entertained a bill in the early 1990s aimed at the legalization of marijuana. The bill was narrowly defeated. Similar bills have been proposed in other states, including Michigan. The fact that not everyone was arrested in a crowd of more than five thousand people openly flouting the law says something about strength in numbers. It also suggests that in many jurisdictions, such as Michigan, the laws prohibiting marijuana use may not be treated with equal force as other drug laws.

Should marijuana be legalized? What standards should be set regarding the use of marijuana and under what circumstances? Who should decide? Would decriminalization of this drug lead to decriminalizing more serious abused substances, such as heroin or cocaine?

Source: Associated Press, "Thousands Rally for Marijuana Use." *Minot* (N.D.) *Daily News,* April 8, 1995:A2.

and their victims (Clarke et al., 1994). Most often targeted for participation in these programs are misdemeanants (van Dijk et al., 1996). Some overly excited fans at a football game may get into a fight; one person may assault another, causing physical injuries and broken teeth. Although criminal charges may be filed against the aggressor, such cases often consume considerable valuable court time. However, if offender and victim agree, ADR may be used to conclude these cases quickly and informally to the mutual satisfaction of all parties involved. Victim-offender mediation or ADR programs originated in the Midwestern United States. They are presently found in 100 U.S. jurisdictions, 54 in Norway, 40 in France, 26 in Canada, 25 in Germany, 18 in England, 20 in Finland, and 8 in Belgium (Umbreit, 1994:25). Umbreit (1994:25) notes that in most victim-offender programs, the process consists of four phases:

1. Case intake from referral sources
2. Preparation for mediation, during which the mediator meets separately with the offender and the victim
3. The mediation session, which consists of a discussion of what occurred and how people felt about it, followed by negotiation of a restitution agreement
4. Follow-up activities, such as monitoring restitution completion

Umbreit found in a cross-site study that 79 percent of the victims were satisfied with the results of the mediation, 87 percent of the offenders were satisfied, and 83 percent of all parties believed that the mediation process was fair for both the victims and the offenders. Examples of the volume of referrals in specific mediation agencies are 591 mediations in 1991 in Albuquerque, New Mexico; 903 mediations in Minneapolis, Minnesota, in 1991; 541 mediations in Oakland, California, in 1991; and 1,107 mediations in 1991 in Austin, Texas (Umbreit, 1994:28).

Another name for alternative dispute resolution is **restorative justice** (Bazemore, 1994). Restorative justice seeks to produce a civil remedy between victims and their victimizers. The intent is not simply to restore to victims that which was lost or the value of services or lost wages caused by injuries suffered. An additional objective is to heighten the accountability of the offender by requiring a bilateral agreement with the victim in an effort to reach a compromise that will be mutually satisfying. Although a criminal case has been transformed into a civil one, ADR involves the direct participation of the victim and offender, with the aim of mutual accommodation for both parties. The emphasis of ADR is upon restitution rather than punishment (DeMore, 1996). The costs associated with it are small compared with trials, and criminal **stigmatization** is avoided (Axon and Hann, 1995). Many criminal cases are being diverted from the criminal justice system through alternative dispute resolution (Merry and Milner, 1995). **Mediation** is increasingly used (Cook, 1996). ADR is recognized increasingly as a means by which differences between criminals and their victims can be resolved through civil means (Krapac, 1996).

MEDIATION IN ACTION. Morrill and McKee (1993:450) studied the Sunshine Mediation Center (SMC), the name for an urban mediation program founded in 1981 in a southwestern city. The SMC handled from 800 to 1,100 cases per year between 1985 and 1991. The problems and disputes the SMC handled included barking dog nuisances, landlord-tenant disputes, spouse and child abuse, broken financial obligations, and unpaid private and small commercial debts, as well as various misdemeanor cases. The basic premises of the SMC included:

1. Delivery of dispute settlement services
2. Personal growth
3. Community improvement

Mediation services provided by the SMC relieved congested criminal and civil courts. Volunteers were used as mediators. Often, they would resolve cases over the telephone between victims and offenders. Subsequently, a meeting was held between victims and offenders, and both parties worked out their differences and reached compromises or settlements. The SMC had a ninety percent success rate during the years investigated.

States vary in their use of ADR. For example, in North Carolina, there were nineteen mediation programs operating in 1991 (Clarke, Valente, and Mace, 1992). ADR is most frequently used to settle misdemeanor cases. To evaluate the effectiveness of mediation programs in North Carolina, an evaluation study compared several counties with programs with several counties without programs. A sample of 1,421 clusters of cases filed in 1990 that matched eligibility criteria were followed in the records of courts and mediation programs. Furthermore, interview data were collected from complainants and defendants. About fifty-nine percent of the referred cases were mediated, with almost all reaching mutually satisfactory mediations between offenders and victims. These resolutions of differences are often called just solutions (American Bar Association, 1994). ADR is another way of reallocating judicial business (Kaufman, 1990). ADR may or may not be operated by individual state courts (Keilitz, 1990).

ADVANTAGES AND DISADVANTAGES OF ADR. Alternative dispute resolution has the following advantages:

1. Offenders do not acquire a criminal record after a successful resolution of the dispute.
2. Victims have the satisfaction of seeing punishment imposed for the criminal act committed.
3. Court dockets are eased because of the diversion of disputes to ADR.
4. Prosecutor caseloads are alleviated.
5. The community benefits when community service orders are issued to perpetrators.
6. Accountability is heightened because victim compensation and restitution are required of offenders. (Palumbo, Musheno, and Hallett, 1994)

The disadvantages of ADR include:

1. Offenders who have committed crimes escape criminal convictions. Some persons regard this outcome as unjust and believe that a person who commits a crime should receive a criminal conviction as a result.

2. ADR is insufficient as a punishment and causes some persons to flout the law, knowing that they will not be harshly treated if caught. ADR is perceived as too lenient.

3. Reoffending may occur if perpetrators believe that they can get away with crimes, with only civil sanctions being imposed.

4. The criminal justice system image is tainted by excessive leniency from ADR programs.

5. The proportionate punishment is not the same as a criminal conviction and the record an offender would acquire as a result. (Clarke et al., 1994)

Impartial Arbiters and Their Qualifications

Impartial arbiters in ADR programs may be retired judges, attorneys, or interested citizens. ADR arbiters are appointed on the basis of their fairness and integrity (Reese and Solomon, 1996), and there are no special qualifications for arbiters. They do not have to have a precise and extensive knowledge of the law. Their actions are designed to be fair, and the resolutions they negotiate must be agreeable to both the offender and the victim. In the event that the arbiters cannot settle cases, then prosecutors can always reinstitute criminal charges against defendants and take these cases to court for resolution.

Victim Participation and Input

Victim involvement in offender sentencing and punishments has increased dramatically in recent years. Testimony from victims can add much emotional appeal to formal proceedings. Victim feedback through direct participation in such proceedings is not always negative. In more than a few cases, victims have spoken on behalf of perpetrators and made requests for leniency. However, in ADR victim participation ensures that all aspects of the offense and its results are brought to the attention of the arbiter. When prosecutors decide to divert cases to ADR, every effort is made to reconcile the dispute between victims and offenders. When victims have such input, often it is in the form of a **victim impact statement**, a written or oral summary of the damages or injuries suffered from the actions of the perpetrator. When the perpetrator and victim agree on the proposed punishment, under the supervision of an impartial arbiter, then **victim compensation** is discussed. It is usually a monetary award to be paid by the perpetrator to the victim for the loss of property or work time. Many jurisdictions have **victim compensation programs** to provide guidelines about how much perpetrators should pay for the suffering and losses they have caused to victims.

Victim–Offender Reconciliation

Victim–offender reconciliation is another version of ADR. Roy and Brown (1992) report that victim–offender reconciliation is a specific form of conflict resolution between the victim and the offender. Face-to-face encounter is the basic element in this process. Elkhart County, Indiana, has been the site of the **Victim–Offender Reconciliation Project (VORP)** since 1987. The primary aims of VORP are the following:

1. Make offenders accountable for their wrongs against victims
2. Reduce recidivism among participating offenders
3. Heighten responsibility of offenders through victim compensation and repayment for damages inflicted (Roy and Brown, 1992)

VORP was established in Kitchener, Ontario, in 1974 and was subsequently replicated as PACT or Prisoner and Community Together in northern Indiana near Elkhart. Subsequent replications in various jurisdictions have created different varieties of ADR, each variety spawning embellishments, additions, or program deletions deemed more or less important by the particular jurisdiction (Immarigeon, 1993:5–6). The Genessee County (Batavia), New York, Sheriff's Department established a VORP in 1983, followed by programs in Valparaiso, Indiana; Quincy, Massachusetts; and Minneapolis, Minnesota, in 1985. In Quincy, for instance, the program was named EARN-IT and was operated through the probation department (Umbreit, 1994). More than twenty-five different states have some version of VORP. ADR programs in other jurisdictions have been evaluated, and the results of these evaluations suggest that most victims and offenders are satisfied with the fairness of these proceedings. A high rate of restitution by offenders has been reported by many participating jurisdictions (Umbreit and Coates, 1993).

Pretrial Diversion

Pretrial diversion or simply **diversion** is the process by which criminal defendants are either diverted to a community-based agency for treatment or assigned to a counselor for social or psychiatric assistance (Fields, 1994). Pretrial diversion may involve education, job training, counseling, or some type of psychological or physical therapy (National Association of Pretrial Services Agencies, 1995). Diversion officially halts or suspends criminal proceedings against a defendant (Federal Judicial Center, 1994). The thrust of diversion is toward an informal administrative effort to determine (1) whether nonjudicial processing is warranted; (2) whether treatment is warranted; (3) if treatment is warranted, which one to use; and (4) whether charges against the defendant should be dropped or reinstated (McCarthy and McCarthy, 1997).

Most likely targeted for pretrial **diversion programs** are first-time petty offenders. If these programs are completed successfully, then the charges against these defendants are either downgraded or dismissed outright. The totality of circumstances of the offender's crime is ascertained by the prosecutor and the court, and a decision about diversion is made. Each case is evaluated and decided on its own merits. People charged with possessing marijuana may be diverted and required to attend counseling classes or sessions that feature drug abuse discussions. Diverted defendants usually pay monthly fees during the period of their diversion to defray a portion of the expenses for their supervision (Broderick et al., 1993).

In 1992, a diversion program was established in New Orleans, Louisiana (Mieczkowski, Mumm, and Connick, 1995). The New Orleans Diversionary Program is designed to monitor nonviolent offenders who have been previously arrested for drug use. The program conducts periodic drug tests among its clientele to see whether they have remained drug-free. Low offender recidivism was reported.

The History and Philosophy of Diversion

Diversion originated in the United States through the early juvenile courts in Chicago and New York in the late 1800s. Strong efforts were made by religious groups and reformers to keep children from imprisonment of any kind; at the time, children over eight years of age were considered eligible for adult court processing. Cook County, Illinois, implemented a diversion program for youthful offenders in 1899 (National Association of Pretrial Services Agencies, 1995).

The philosophy of diversion is community reintegration and rehabilitation. The objective is that offenders can avoid the stigma of incarceration and public notoriety. In most state courts where diversion is condoned, diversion does not entirely remove offenders from court processing, because the court usually must approve prosecutorial recommendations for diversion in each case. Because these approvals are often conducted in less publicized hearings, a divertee's crimes are less likely to be scrutinized publicly.

Functions of Diversion

The functions of diversion are as follows:

1. To permit divertees the opportunity of remaining in their communities, where they can receive needed assistance or treatment, depending on the nature of the crimes charged
2. To permit divertees the opportunity to make restitution to their victims when monetary damages were suffered and property destroyed
3. To permit divertees the opportunity of remaining free in their communities to support themselves and their families, and to avoid the stigma of incarceration
4. To help divertees avoid the stigma of a criminal conviction
5. To assist corrections officials in reducing prison and jail overcrowding by diverting less serious cases to nonincarcerative alternatives
6. To save the courts the time, trouble, and expense of formally processing less serious cases and streamlining case dispositions through informal case handling
7. To make it possible for divertees to participate in self-help, educational, or vocational programs
8. To preserve the dignity and integrity of divertees by helping them avoid further contact with the criminal justice system and assisting them to be more responsible adults capable of managing their own lives
9. To preserve the family unit and enhance family solidarity and continuity

Factors Influencing Pretrial Diversion

Excluded from diversion programs are recidivists with prior records of violent offending. Offenders who have drug or alcohol dependencies may be excluded from diversion programs, as are probation and parole violators. In view of these restrictive criteria, diversion is most often granted for low-risk, first-time property offenders. Although recidivism rates among property offenders are not particularly different from those of violent offenders and drug traffickers, property offenders pose less public risk and are less dangerous than these other types of criminals. Relevant criteria operating in most jurisdictions where diversion exists as an option include the following:

1. The age of the offender
2. The residency, employment, and familial status of the offender
3. The prior record of the offender
4. The seriousness of the offense
5. Aggravating or mitigating circumstances associated with the commission of the offense

   Residency, employment, and familial status are important considerations because they are indicators of a person's stability. More stable people are more likely to complete diversion programs successfully. Most diversion programs require at least some regular contact with probation agencies operated by state or local authorities. Unemployed and transient offenders are more likely to flee from the jurisdiction than those offenders who are gainfully employed and have families in the area.

Criticisms of Diversion

1. Diversion is the wrong punishment for criminals. Criminals ought to be convicted of crimes and sent to jail or prison. Diverting them to community programs is wrong.
2. Diversion assumes guilt without a trial. If prospective divertees accept diversion in lieu of a trial, this is regarded as their admission that they are guilty of the offenses alleged.
3. Diversion leads to net widening. When diversion programs exist in communities, there is a tendency for prosecutors to assign people to these programs who otherwise would not be prosecuted because of case backlogs and crowded court dockets.
4. Diversion excludes female offenders. At present, this criticism is no longer valid because many female offenders are diverted from criminal prosecutions.
5. Diversion ignores due process. When a case is diverted, the defendant is deprived of his or her right to a trial by jury, a mechanism whereby guilt must be established beyond a reasonable doubt. Diversion frustrates due process by avoiding a trial.
6. Diversion is too lenient with criminals. (Mackay and Moody, 1996)

Other Noncriminal or Criminal Sanctions

Community Service

Community service sentencing is one way of achieving offender accountability (Allen and Treger, 1990). Community service is different from restitution in that usually, though not always, offenders perform services for the state or community. The nature of community service to be performed is at the discretion of the sentencing judge or paroling authority (Crew, 1994). Judges may also impose **fines** as part of an offender's sentence for almost any crime, but in many jurisdictions fines are imposed only about a third of the time. Also, when fines are imposed, not all offenders pay them. The Victim and Witness Protection Act of 1982 made restitution to victims a mandatory part of an offender's sentence. Victim advocates strongly urge that restitution to victims be an integral feature of the sentencing process (U.S. General Accounting Office, 1991).

IS COMMUNITY SERVICE A PUNISHMENT? Community service is considered a punishment and is court imposed. Many types of projects are undertaken by offenders as community service. Usually, these projects are supervised by probation office staff, although supervisors may be recruited from the private sector (Majer, 1994). Some part of an offender's earnings is allocated to victims, as well as to the state or local public or private agencies that provide supervisory services (Meeker, Jesilow, and Aranda, 1992). Restitution to victims may be through periodic payments from offender earnings while on work release, probation, or parole. Sometimes, restitution takes nonmonetary forms, and offenders rebuild or restore property destroyed by their crimes.

IS COMMUNITY SERVICE EFFECTIVE? The release of many offenders into their communities for the purpose of performing community service raises a public risk issue for some people, although offenders selected for community service ordinarily are low risk and nonviolent (Parent, Auerbach, and Carlson, 1992). Other criticisms relate to the personal philosophies of judicial and correctional authorities, the offender eligibility and selection criteria used among jurisdictions, organizational arrangements, the nature of supervision over offenders performing community services, and how such services are evaluated. Most researchers regard community service and restitution as just and fitting punishments to accompany whatever incarcerative sentence is imposed by judges.

Restitution and Victim Compensation

Restitution is also a victim-initiated action (Parent, Auerbach, and Carlson, 1992). Restitution is the practice of requiring offenders to compensate crime victims for damages offenders may have inflicted (adapted from Davis and Lurigio, 1992:25). If the victim fails to notify the court of financial losses or medical expenses, the restitution order may be neglected. Currently, there are no reliable statistics concerning the proportion of convictions in which restitution orders are imposed, nor are there statistics showing the extent to which probationers and parolees must make restitution a part of their probation or parole programs (Venner, 1994). Several models of restitution have been described.

THE FINANCIAL/COMMUNITY SERVICE MODEL. The **financial/community service model** stresses the offender's financial accountability and community service to pay for damages inflicted on victims and to defray a portion of the expenses of court prosecutions. It is becoming more commonplace for probationers and divertees to be ordered to pay some restitution to victims *and* to perform some type of community service. Community service may involve clean-up activities in municipal parks, painting projects

ON HOUSE ARREST

The Case of Jubal Bear

It happened in New Town, North Dakota, an Indian reservation. On August 5, 1997, Jubal Bear, thirty-nine, was driving an automobile west of New Town. Jubal had been drinking. Subsequently, police would determine his blood alcohol level to be 0.24; at 0.10 or over, a person is presumed to be intoxicated.

As Bear was driving along a major highway two miles west of New Town at 10:40 P.M. one evening, his car crossed the center line and collided head-on with a car driven by Rosena Dye, fifty-eight. Dye was traveling east on the highway and had a baby strapped in an infant seat in the rear of her car. The crash killed Dye outright. The baby, though covered with glass and badly shaken, survived. Another car, driven by Brian Zelmer, had been following the Dye vehicle. When the accident occurred, Zelmer's car rammed the rear of the Dye vehicle. Zelmer was not seriously injured in the crash. Shortly after the crash, Bear's car caught on fire, but his nephew, Chad Bear, pulled him from the burning vehicle. Jubal Bear was charged with involuntary manslaughter.

Appearing before U.S. District Court Judge Patrick Conmy in Minot, Jubal Bear entered into a plea agreement with federal prosecutors. The plea agreement ordered Bear to three years of probation, including wearing an electronic monitoring device at a cost of $5 per day. Further, Bear was placed under house arrest or home confinement for sixteen months. An additional probation condition was that Bear would pay restitution in the amount of $9,000 to State Farm Insurance Company, $2,750 to Brian Zelmer, and more than $16,000 to the state Crime Victims' Reparations Fund. Bear was sentenced to home confinement because he had extensive medical problems following the accident. His left leg was shattered, and he sustained severe shoulder injuries.

Is home confinement appropriate for someone who has caused the death of another because of drunk driving? What guarantees are there that Bear will not become intoxicated again and seriously injure or kill others? What type of punishment would you impose if you were the judge in this case? Do you think house arrest and electronic monitoring are too lenient? What do you think?

Source: Adapted from Ken Crites, "New Town Man Sentenced to House Arrest." *Minot* (N.D.) *Daily News,* February 24, 1998:B1.

involving graffiti removal, cutting courthouse lawns, or any other constructive project that can benefit the community. These community service sentences are imposed by judges. Probation officers are largely responsible for overseeing the efforts of convicted offenders in fulfilling their community service obligations. These sentencing provisions are commonly called **community service orders**.

Community service orders involve redress for victims, less severe sanctions for offenders, offender rehabilitation, reduction of demands on the criminal justice system, and a reduction of the need for vengeance in society, or a combination of these factors. Community service orders are found in many countries and benefit the community directly (Sapers, 1990). Further, where convicted offenders are indigent or unemployed, community service is a way of paying their fines and court costs. Some of the chief benefits of community service are that (1) the community benefits because some form of restitution is paid; (2) offenders benefit because they are given an opportunity to rejoin their communities in law-abiding, responsible roles; and (3) the courts benefit because sentencing alternatives are provided (Bazemore and Maloney, 1994).

THE VICTIM/OFFENDER MEDIATION MODEL. The **victim/offender mediation model** focuses upon victim-offender reconciliation. Alternative dispute resolution is used as a mediating ground for resolving differences or disputes between victims and perpetrators (Patel and Soderlund, 1994).

THE VICTIM/REPARATIONS MODEL. The **victim/reparations model** stresses that offenders should directly compensate their victims for their offenses. Many states have provisions that provide **reparations** or financial payments to victims under the Victims of Crime Act (VOCA). VOCA is a federally financed program of reparations to those who suffer personal injury and to dependents of those killed as the result of certain criminal conduct. In many jurisdictions, a specially constituted board determines, independent of court adjudication, the existence of a crime, the damages caused, and other elements necessary for reparation (U.S. General Accounting Office, 1991; Venner, 1994).

REPAYING VICTIMS AND SOCIETY THROUGH RESTITUTION. President Ronald Reagan signed Public Law 98-473 on October 12, 1984, which established the Comprehensive Crime Control Act. Chapter 14 of this act is known as the **Victims of Crime Act of 1984** or the **Comprehensive Crime Control Act of 1984** (Parent, Auerbach, and Carlson, 1992). Currently, all states and the federal government have victim compensation programs. As a part of offender work-release requirements, part of their earned wages may be allocated to restitution and to a general victim compensation fund. In fact, in the federal system, the Federal Victim/Witness Protection Act of 1982 required federal judges to order restitution to the victim in all cases in which the victim suffered a financial loss, unless they state compelling reasons for a contrary ruling on the record (U.S. Department of Justice, 1990). Thus, fines, restitution, and some form of community service have become common features of federal sentencing (18 U.S.C. Sec. 3563(a)(2), 2001).

Summary

People who commit crimes are brought into the criminal justice system through arrest. Arrestees are booked and have an initial appearance before a magistrate or judicial official. Booking is a procedure for compiling personal information about arrestees. The initial appearance is a stage where charges are placed against defendants. Subsequently, defendants have a preliminary hearing or preliminary examination, when probable cause is determined. In about half of all jurisdictions, grand juries consider the charges against defendants and issue indictments, which are the result of establishing that probable cause exists. The issue determined by preliminary hearings and grand juries is the same: was a crime committed, and is there probable cause to believe that the person charged with the offense committed it?

Early in a defendant's processing, the defendant is considered for bail. Bail bonds are sureties to procure the release of those under arrest and to assure that they will appear in court later to face criminal charges filed against them. Not everyone is entitled to bail. Those who pose a danger to themselves or others or are likely to flee the jurisdiction if freed are typically denied bail. Bail is granted in a majority of criminal cases. Often, bail bond companies post bail for criminal suspects. Because of the sometimes arbitrary nature of bail decision making, most jurisdictions have undergone some amount of bail reform and changed the circumstances under which bail is granted. Sometimes no bail is required, and persons are released on their own recognizance (ROR). Bail reform acts have been passed by the U.S. Congress, as well as by different states. Numerous experiments have been conducted in various jurisdictions to determine the effects of granting or denying bail under certain experimental conditions. When certain defendants who are out on bail fail to appear in court and flee the jurisdiction, bounty hunters often track down these persons and return them to their original jurisdictions for trial. Bounty hunters are paid a portion of the bail amount for these services.

In the last several decades, the sheer numbers of criminal defendants have escalated in every jurisdiction. Court dockets are clogged, and prosecutors lack sufficient resources to perform their jobs effectively. It is not possible to prosecute every single case. In a growing number of jurisdictions, several options exist for diverting certain criminal defendants from the criminal justice system. One of these options is simply to decriminalize particular behaviors, such as possessing or smoking marijuana. By decriminalizing certain behaviors, some people are no longer considered criminals and can be overlooked by the criminal justice system.

Another option is alternative dispute resolution. For relatively minor crimes committed by first offenders, some of these cases are treated as civil wrongs and scheduled for alternative dispute resolution (ADR). ADR is a community-based, informal dispute settlement between offenders and their victims. Overseeing ADR are impartial third-party arbiters who may be retired judges, lawyers, or community leaders. These impartial arbiters oversee ADR proceedings and the subsequent enforcement of any agreement made between parties. The agreement must be consensual. There is substantial victim input. In some jurisdictions, victim-offender reconciliation projects (VORPs) have been conducted, which parallel the aims and functions of ADR. The aim of ADR, sometimes called restorative justice, is to compensate victims for their losses and heighten offender accountability. Not all ADR proceedings result in agreements. Under those conditions, cases are sent back into the criminal justice system and prosecuted. Also, if perpetrators fail to fulfill their part of the ADR agreement, criminal charges may be reinstated against them.

A third option is diversion or pretrial diversion. Diversion means to temporarily remove a case from the criminal justice process and subject divertees to various behavioral conditions for specific periods, such as six months or one year. Some of these conditions include paying monthly program maintenance fees, performing community service, and making restitution or providing compensation to victims. At the end of the diversion period, if there has been compliance with the diversion program conditions and the diversion is successful, the original charges against the defendant may be either dropped entirely or downgraded to less serious charges. Most divertees complete their diversion programs successfully. One outcome of diversion is that valuable court time is saved and more serious criminal cases can be prosecuted. Divertees almost always benefit, and often their criminal records are expunged. Not everyone favors diversion as a viable option to a criminal prosecution. Some believe that diversion imposes sanctions or punishments without benefit of trial and that it is based on a presumption of guilt. Under the U.S. system of justice, due process presumes that criminal defendants are innocent until they are proved guilty in court beyond a reasonable doubt. Yet others favor diversion because of its reintegrative prospects for first-time offenders and the fact that their accountability is heightened. Those opposing diversion argue that criminal offenders are not really punished and that diversion is too lenient a sanction. There is continuing controversy regarding the application of diversion.

KEY TERMS

Alternative dispute
    resolution (ADR)
Arrest
Arrestee
Bail
Bail bond
Bail bond companies
Bail bondsmen
Bail bondspersons
Bail Reform Act
Bail Reform Act
    of 1984
Booking
Bounties
Bounty hunters
Cash bail bond
Community service
Community service orders
Comprehensive Crime
    Control Act of 1984
Decriminalization

Diversion
Diversion programs
Excessive bail
Failure to appear
Felony
Financial/community
    service model
Fines
Impartial arbiters
Initial appearance
Jumping bail
Mediation
Misdemeanor
Philadelphia Experiment
Preliminary examination
Preliminary hearing
Pretrial diversion
Probable cause
Reasonable suspicion
Release on their own
    recognizance (ROR)

Reparations
Restitution
Restorative justice
Sexual predator laws
Stigmatization
Totality of circumstances
Victim
Victim compensation
Victim compensation
    programs
Victim impact statement
Victim/offender
    mediation model
Victim–offender reconcili-
    ation
Victim–Offender Recon-
    ciliation Project
    (VORP)
Victim/reparations model
Victims of Crime Act of
    1984

QUESTIONS FOR REVIEW

1. What are four types of victim–offender mediation? Describe each briefly.
2. Distinguish between diversion and alternative dispute resolution.

3. What is a bail bondsman? Is a bail bondsman also a bounty hunter? Distinguish between them.

4. What is a bail bond? How can arrestees obtain bail?

5. Is everyone entitled to bail? Under what circumstances might a person not be entitled to bail?

6. Describe the process of arrest, booking, and initial appearance.

7. What is a preliminary examination or hearing?

8. What does it mean to release someone on their own recognizance?

9. How are failure-to-appear rates affected by whether a person is granted bail or is released on his or her own recognizance?

10. What are the competing goals of bail?

11. What were some important provisions of the Bail Reform Act of 1984 in terms of how citizens were treated when arrested?

12. What are sexual predator laws? What is their significance regarding whether someone is granted bail?

13. What is meant by decriminalization?

SUGGESTED READINGS

Barra, Allen. (1998). *Inventing Wyatt Earp: His Life and Many Legends.* New York: Carroll and Graf.

Bonta, James, Suzanne Wallace-Capretta, and Jennifer Rooney. (1998). *Restorative Justice: An Evaluation of the Restorative Resolutions Project.* Toronto: Solicitor General of Canada.

Burton, Bob. (1984). *Bounty Hunter.* Boulder, CO: Paladin Press.

Chambliss, William J. (1999). *Power, Politics, and Crime.* Boulder, CO: Westview Press.

Cornelius, William J. (1997). *Swift and Sure: Bring Certainty and Finality to Criminal Punishments.* Irvington-on-Hudson, NY: Bridge Street Books.

Fish, Jefferson M. (ed.). (1998). *How to Legalize Drugs.* Northvale, NJ: Jason Aronson.

Merry, Sally Engle and Neal Milner (eds.). (1995). *The Possibility of Popular Justice: A Case Study of Community Mediation in the United States.* Ann Arbor: University of Michigan Press.

Myers, Bryan and Jack Arbuthnot. (1999). "The Effects of Victim Impact Evidence on the Verdicts and Sentencing Judgments of Mock Jurors." *Journal of Offender Rehabilitation* **29**:95–112.

Ostermeyer, Melinda and Susan L. Keilitz. (1997). *Monitoring and Evaluating Court-Based Dispute Resolution Programs: A Guide for Judges and Court Managers.* Williamsburg, VA: National Center for State Courts.

U.S. Office for Victims and Crime. (1999). *Promising Practices and Strategies for Victim Services in Corrections.* Rockville, MD: U.S. Office for Victims and Crime.

Uviller, H. Richard. (1999). *The Tilted Playing Field: Is Criminal Justice Fair?* New Haven, CT: Yale University Press.

PRETRIAL PROCEDURES: PLEA BARGAINING

CHAPTER **8**

IN NEW YORK CITY, a prosecutor was approached by a defense attorney representing a client charged with possession of cocaine with intent to distribute. The amount of cocaine involved was two ounces. According to New York law, this crime is punishable by imprisonment of up to ten years and a substantial fine. The defense counsel said to the prosecutor, "Look. My client has no prior record. She was only carrying the coke for her boyfriend. Personally, I don't think she should even be prosecuted. But if you prosecute, I wouldn't expect anything more than maybe probation, first offender, you know." The prosecutor said, "Well, that may be. But that's also a lot of cocaine. She does the crime, she's going to do the time. Tell you what. If she pleads [guilty] to simple possession, I'll recommend a two-year term, with one year suspended. But she'll have to do some community service and enroll in a counseling program for first offenders. Take it or leave it." The defense counsel said, "One year in jail is a little much. Why not three years' probation, maybe a thirty-day sentence, and community service?" The prosecutor said, "No way am I going to let her off with a thirty-day wrist-slap. She'll have to do at least nine months and two years in a community program, with some community service." The defense counsel said, "I'll take her the offer and see what she says." After two or three days, the defense counsel saw the prosecutor and said, "My client will plead if you make it six months and include the other stuff." The prosecutor hesitated, but finally he said, "OK. Have your client in my office tomorrow afternoon, and we'll sign the paperwork and take it before the judge."

IN GREENSBORO, NORTH CAROLINA, a 60-year-old man is being held for robbing a liquor store. During the robbery, he shot and seriously wounded a customer. He is charged with armed robbery and aggravated assault. In North Carolina, these crimes, considered separately, can mean at least forty years in prison. The man is indigent and

213

cannot afford an attorney. A novice attorney fresh out of law school is appointed from the public defender's office. The defense counsel confers with his client, who has a lengthy record of arrests and convictions for assault, burglary, vehicular theft, and a host of other offenses spanning twenty years. There is no question that North Carolina prosecutors can charge him as a habitual offender and go for a subsequent conviction and sentence involving life without parole. The prosecutor converses with the defense counsel in the prosecutor's office. The prosecutor says, "We have him cold on the robbery and assault charges. Plenty of eyewitnesses. We can also charge him as a habitual offender. He would probably die in prison. But if he pleads guilty to the assault and robbery charges, we won't prosecute on the habitual offender violation. I'll also recommend a twenty-year sentence. With good behavior, he can get out when he's 72 or so." The defense counsel says, "Let me speak with my client. But I think that is more than fair. I'll see what he says." Later, the defense counsel says, "My client says to take it. He'll plead guilty to those charges if you recommend only twenty years."

IN CARMEL, CALIFORNIA, a woman has just been arrested for attempting to cash a stolen $100 money order. The bank teller was suspicious when the woman didn't produce a valid ID. Subsequent verification determined that the money order is stolen. Local police arrest the woman and take her to jail. She is unable to post bond. A public defender visits her and says he's with the public defender's office and is assigned to assist her in her defense. The woman says that she is unemployed and was desperate at the time. She took the money order from a neighbor's purse. She's sorry for what she did, has never done anything like this before, and will never do it again. The defense counsel determines that she has no criminal record, was employed for many years, was laid off from her job a few years ago, and has worked off and on since. She recently divorced and fell on hard times. He arranges a meeting with the district attorney. At that meeting, he says, "My client is a victim of circumstances. In a confused moment, she took a money order and tried to cash it. She hadn't eaten for a while, was broke, and she acted without thinking. I don't think jail is the best thing for her. She is a good candidate for probation and counseling." The prosecutor, who has familiarized herself with the woman's file and background, agrees. The prosecutor says, "If your client will plead guilty to attempted fraud, I'll recommend probation. She must get some counseling. Also, I'll arrange to have her meet with some community corrections people so that she can have some employment assistance. She won't have to do any time, and after a year, she'll be out of the system. What do you think?" The defense counsel says, "She will like to hear that. I believe she'll take it."

These scenarios are played out under different circumstances every day throughout the United States. Prosecutors and defense counsel confer and discuss cases. Depending on the facts of the case, the prior criminal history of offenders, and whether there were victim deaths or serious injuries, prosecutors and defense counsel work out **plea bargains**, which are preconviction agreements to enter a guilty plea to one or more criminal charges in exchange for some form of leniency in sentencing. **Plea bargaining** occurs in almost every state, and its use accounts for more than ninety percent of all convictions.

Whether the crime alleged is possession of a controlled substance, armed robbery and aggravated assault, or fraud, plea bargaining is used to avoid protracted trials and spare valuable court time. As you can see from each scenario, some form of haggling occurs between prosecutors and defense counsels. Plea bargaining has often been referred to as horse trading because there are offers and counteroffers, back and forth, attempting to arrive at a mutually agreeable charge and sentence. Each side seeks a resolution of the case to its own advantage. The prosecutor wants to maximize the penalties against defendants, and the defense wants to minimize them. Seldom are maximum penalties imposed by judges. Thus, there is almost always some room within the minimum and maximum sentences to negotiate guilty pleas and acceptable penalties. Failing to negotiate mutually agreeable pleas and penalties will move the case along to the courtroom for formal resolution in a trial by jury.

Introduction

This chapter examines plea bargaining. Different types of plea bargaining can be distinguished according to who initiates the plea bargain, the number of charges involved against the defendant, and the implicit or explicit nature of penalties contemplated by either side. Subsequently, the advantages and disadvantages of plea bargaining are discussed in this chapter, especially the implications of plea bargaining for the state and the defendant.

This chapter also examines why plea bargaining has been banned in certain states. One reason for opposing plea bargaining is that defendants waive several important constitutional rights when they enter a voluntary guilty plea to criminal charges. We investigate this issue and consider what is waived against what is gained through the actual plea bargain agreement.

Because judges must approve all **plea bargain agreements** in all states and federal jurisdictions, the roles of judges in plea agreement hearings are described here. Judges are vested with the responsibility for determining whether there are factual bases for pleas entered and whether defendants have voluntarily and knowingly waived certain constitutional rights in this process. This chapter concludes with a retrospective examination of plea bargaining in the United States and projections for its future use.

Plea Bargaining: Negotiated Guilty Pleas

WHY SHOULD ANY DEFENDANT PLEA BARGAIN? Ideally, defendants who wish to enter guilty pleas to criminal charges know that they are guilty. There is substantial evidence against them. They have the right to compel the state to try them in a court of law because all criminals have a right to their day in court. However, if a defendant's guilt is not seriously contested, trials are perfunctory rituals with almost absolutely predictable results.

Unfortunately for criminal defendants, trial convictions usually result in more stringent application of sanctions. Judges tend to deal more harshly with convicted offenders who have insisted on trials despite substantial evidence of their guilt beyond a reasonable doubt. By contrast, pretrial agreements in which guilty pleas are entered often result in less severe sanctions or sentences. Early research on the differences in sentences imposed through plea bargaining or trial has highlighted a pattern of judicial sentencing behavior. In more than a few jurisdictions, judges have advised defendants of the sentences judges plan to impose. Judges further advise that if the plea bargain is rejected and the case proceeds to trial, convicted offenders are likely to incur a harsher sentence. Thus, those who contest their guilt are subjected to established practices whereby judges sentence them more harshly than those who plea guilty (Klein, 1971). The harsher sentence is imposed as a punishment for burdening the state with the responsibility of proving one's guilt beyond a reasonable doubt.

One example of a contemplated plea bargain offer by the prosecution was the high-profile California murder case of O. J. Simpson who was charged with murdering his ex-wife, Nicole Brown Simpson, and her friend Ronald Goldman in June 1994. Simpson's attorneys were advised by the Los Angeles District Attorney's Office that if Simpson pleaded guilty to these murders, then the prosecutors would not seek the death penalty against Simpson. Rather, Simpson would receive a sentence of life without the possibility of parole. Of course, we know that this offer was rejected and that Simpson was subsequently acquitted of the murder charges. Nevertheless, had Simpson been convicted in the jury trial, there is little doubt that the death penalty would have been imposed. In this case, the death penalty was the more severe of two possible sentences Simpson could receive if convicted. The plea bargain offered life without parole rather than death as the state's concession for leniency.

In less dramatic cases played out in courtrooms throughout the United States, prosecutors and defense counsel attempt to arrive at the most favorable sentences for state interests and for defendants' interests. Depending on whether the offenses alleged are felonies or misdemeanors, negotiations between prosecutors and defense counsel are geared to arrive at an appropriate term of years or months for defendants who wish to enter guilty pleas. The prosecution seeks to maximize these years or months, and the defense seeks to minimize them.

For instance, suppose a defendant is charged with burglary and conversion of stolen property. The burglary and conversion of stolen property statutes provide a $5,000 fine and up to five years in prison on each charge. A worst-case scenario would result in a jury trial and convictions on both charges, a $10,000 fine, and consecutive sentences of the maximum five years each, for a total of ten years. Seeking to avoid both the fine and a ten-year term of imprisonment, the defendant may enter into a plea bargain agreement and plead guilty to one of the charges, such as the burglary. The prosecutor would then drop the conversion of stolen property charge and recommend waiver of the $10,000 in fines. The prosecutor may suggest a two- or three-year prison term in exchange for a guilty plea to burglary. Although the defendant wishes to avoid prison entirely, he is faced with either accepting the two- or three-year sentence or taking his chances in court. There is a strong likelihood that he would be convicted of both offenses. Further, the judge would likely impose a harsher sentence, such as five or more years. Therefore, defendants have a powerful incentive to enter guilty pleas rather than face potentially harsher punishments in courts if they are subsequently convicted.

Fines attached to criminal statutes are imposed, but infrequently. One reason for not imposing fines is the state's inability to collect fines from convicted offenders, who are most frequently unemployed and indigent. Crime may be their only livelihood. When offenders are apprehended, convicted, and incarcerated, they have no way to earn money to pay off fines imposed earlier by judges. An offender's inability to pay fines cannot be used to lengthen a sentence. However, if certain defendants have assets, including real estate, automobiles, or expensive possessions, these items of value may be subject to seizure under asset forfeiture. An embezzler might have purchased property and other material possessions with money stolen from a business, and one way of restoring the business's money is to seize the offender's assets and liquidate them. The proceeds from such liquidations are given to the business from which the money was stolen.

In typical property offense cases, however, convicted offenders may be drug or alcohol dependent. Their drug or alcohol habits may cause them to steal to obtain money to purchase more drugs or alcohol. A gambling addiction may drive offenders to steal property and convert it to money to satisfy their gambling addiction. Thus, many offenders have no assets and are deeply in debt when arrested. Because there are no assets to seize, the government can impose fines of any amount with little or no expectation of ever recovering any of the fines imposed.

WHY SHOULD PROSECUTORS BARGAIN WITH CRIMINALS? Are prosecutors obligated to collaborate with defense counsel and work out negotiated guilty pleas for each defendant? No. The U.S. Supreme Court has declared that prosecutors are under no obligation to enter into plea bargain agreements with any criminal defendant (*United States v. Benchimol*, 1985). Plea bargain agreements are sought by both prosecutors and defense counsel. It is to a prosecutor's advantage to resolve criminal cases without formal trial proceedings. Trials involve considerable preparation and state expense, and juries do not always convict guilty defendants, regardless of how much evidence exists against them. Plea bargains avoid trials and the often difficult burden of proving defendants guilty beyond a reasonable doubt. Most successfully concluded plea agreements result in convictions. Prosecutors are driven to convict defendants by one means or another. By far the cheapest and easiest convictions for prosecutors are through plea bargain agreements.

The effectiveness of prosecutors is most often evaluated in terms of their record of successful prosecutions. Successful prosecutions are those resulting in convictions. The more convictions, the better a prosecutor's effectiveness. Fewer convictions mean less effectiveness. For prosecutors who have political aspirations, aspire to judgeships, or seek promotions within their own district attorney's offices, their conviction records are direct evidence of their effectiveness as prosecutors (McConville and Mirsky, 1995a). Their reputations are enhanced and their careers are furthered to the extent that they are effective at whatever they do. It is in the prosecutor's best interests to seek quick convictions through plea bargaining.

POLITICS AND PLEA BARGAINING. Thus, plea bargaining has subsequently emerged as a powerful political tool. It has become an increasingly visible and integral part of the criminal justice process. Politically, it has shifted a great deal of power to prosecutors, who have become the ultimate decision makers about a defendant's life chances (Bagley, 1970). Prosecutors now perform pivotal roles as they decide which cases should be prosecuted and which cases should be dropped.

Consider also that in most plea bargaining and the hearings that follow, judges ordinarily see only what prosecutors decide to reveal against criminal defendants. Judges may be unaware that other charges against specific defendants were not included in the plea agreement but simply ignored by the prosecutor to elicit a guilty plea. This ignorance is not the fault of judges. Usually, there are so many plea agreements submitted to judges for their approval that most judges lack the time to study each agreement in detail. Furthermore, many judges view plea bargaining as a fundamental feature of the criminal justice process, and they cooperate with prosecutors by approving plea agreements that are seen as a reasonable trade-off between crime control and due process (Worden, 1995). There are some important exceptions, however.

In an Alabama case, James Smith entered a guilty plea and was convicted of first-degree burglary and rape. Earlier, a grand jury had indicted Smith for burglary, rape, sodomy, and assault. In exchange for a thirty-year sentence, Smith entered a guilty plea to the burglary and rape charges, provided that the prosecutor dropped the sodomy charge. When the judge approved the plea agreement, he sentenced Smith to two concurrent thirty-year sentences. However, a procedural technicality raised later by Smith resulted in a higher court vacating his original thirty-year sentences. Subsequently, Smith went to trial on all four charges and was convicted by a jury. This time, the same judge sentenced Smith to life imprisonment on the burglary and sodomy convictions and 150 years on the rape conviction. The judge explained the different sentences because he had not been fully aware of the circumstances under which Smith had committed these terrible crimes. The trial disclosed all of these details. Smith appealed unsuccessfully to the U.S. Supreme Court, contending that the judge was deliberately being vindictive with the imposition of these enhanced sentences. Rejecting his appeal, the U.S. Supreme Court said that in cases that go to trial, greater and more detailed information is available to sentencing judges than the information contained in a plea bargain agreement. This additional information justified the court's harsher sentencing decision (*Alabama v. Smith*, 1989).

District attorneys and their assistants factor in a defendant's criminal history, age, gender, and numerous other factors to arrive at what they consider to be the **going rate** for particular offenses (Emmelman, 1996). Going rates are implicit sentence lengths and penalties associated with specific crimes. These going rates are influenced greatly by many factors, including the quality of the accused's defense counsel. Public defenders are at a disadvantage compared with private counsel, primarily because they often lack experience in negotiating plea bargains that are favorable to their clients. Further, because they do not receive much money for defending indigent clients, they are often involved in the defense only perfunctorily, simply going through the motions that will lead to a rapid conclusion of a case. Private counsel, however, are compensated well by a wealthier clientele. They also have a more intimate familiarity with the criminal justice system and the key actors who must be contacted in the right way to negotiate the best possible plea bargain for their clients (Bernstein et al., 1977).

Ultimately, however, the decision to charge any particular defendant with specific crimes lies with the district attorney's office. Whether prosecutors interact with private counsel or public defenders, they wield considerable power in deciding how rigorously certain cases should be pursued. Prosecutors have the greatest amount of power in cases with multiple offenses. If a gun was used during the commission of a robbery, for example, prosecutors can decide whether to include this charge in a subsequent indictment.

Usually, plea bargaining results in some reduction in the number of charges filed. If prosecutors can be persuaded by defense counsel to omit the fact that a weapon was used during the commission of a felony and charge simple robbery instead of armed robbery, the result is likely to be a guilty plea to the lesser charge. This is because use of weapons during felonies often involve mandatory incarcerative penalties. For example, Michigan has a provision for an automatic addition of two years of **flat time** added to a convicted offender's sentence if a weapon was used during the commission of a felony. It is to the defendant's advantage if the prosecutor decides not to file a weapons-related charge, and this fact becomes a bargaining chip for the prosecutor to elicit guilty pleas more easily from defendants who have committed weapons-related offenses.

Another factor that affects the prosecutor's decision making about which cases to pursue vigorously is case pressure. In jurisdictions where the volume of cases processed is high, prosecutors may elect to *nolle prosequi* or decline to prosecute marginal cases that might have been pursued for a guilty plea (Heumann, 1975). Prosecutorial options under these conditions might include reducing more charges against defendants, recommending lighter sentences, or demanding more severe sentences after a trial.

How Long Has Plea Bargaining Been Used in the United States? Historians have investigated the use of plea bargaining in the United States. Evidence suggests that plea bargaining occurred in the various areas during the period following the Declaration of Independence in 1776. A study of plea bargaining in New York during the period 1800–1865 shows a pattern of usage that escalated during the second half of the nineteenth century (McConville and Mirsky, 1995b). The use of plea bargaining accompanied the rise in importance of district attorney's offices, the presence of elected judges, the judicialization of magistrates, the reorganization of the police, the marginalization of juries, and the politicization of crime.

During the 1800s, plea bargaining was simply referred to as a **guilty plea**. No formal classification of guilty pleas existed. In the early part of the nineteenth century, jury trials were prescribed for almost all criminal offenses. State reliance on jury trials was strong. However, by the middle to late 1800s, the growth of attorneys' organizations and the increasing professionalization of police work modified greatly the art of criminal investigations. At the same time, court dockets became overcrowded, and the glut of jury trials worsened. Thus, guilty pleas with one or more prosecutorial concessions gained popularity as an alternative to formal courtroom trial procedure.

The professionalization of police meant that larger numbers of minor prosecutions were shifted to municipal and police courts, such as those in Boston during the period 1814–1850 (Ferdinand, 1992). Data analyzed from more than 30,000 cases in the Boston Police Court during the early to mid-1800s showed that between 1814 and 1850 the caseload for police courts doubled. During the same time interval, the municipal court docket load increased by more than a thousand percent. Plea bargaining in Boston became increasingly commonplace as a means of resolving most cases. At the same time, court officers became more professional, and formal courtroom procedures grew more intricate (Ferdinand, 1992). In just such a milieu, the modern criminal court was born. Today's criminal courts are high volume and multipurpose. The sheer numbers of cases crowding these court dockets made plea bargaining especially appealing, because valuable court time could be saved by out-of-court bargaining between prosecutors and defense attorneys.

The growth of formal legal education was apparent during this same period. More people were acquiring formal legal training from newly established law schools, and the numbers of lawyers invading criminal courts to represent growing numbers of clients meant more protracted litigation. A relief valve was plea bargaining. A more educated lawyer contingent made plea bargaining more attractive to criminals as well as to judges, because criminals could bargain their way to lesser penalties without formal trial proceedings. The trend toward more plea bargaining continued into the 1900s. Since the 1960s, plea bargaining has escalated in use to the extent that more than ninety percent of all criminal convictions are secured through plea negotiations. Because of the great savings in case-processing time, most courts today are able to function with only moderate delays. It is difficult to contemplate what our courts would be like today if plea bargaining were banned outright.

Is Plea Bargaining Unique to the United States? Many countries use some form of plea bargaining as a means of speeding up criminal case processing. Plea bargaining is used frequently in Australia (Douglas, 1988), Canada (Cohen and Doob, 1989; Ferguson, 1972), Germany (Ludemann, 1994), and the United Kingdom (Pickles, 1987). Citizen discontent with plea bargaining in these countries is about the same as it is in the United States. In Canada, for example, a survey of 1,049 citizens revealed that most disapproved of plea bargaining. One primary complaint was that plea bargaining appeared to result in insufficient penalties for criminals. However, these citizen-respondents also indicated that if judges were to take a more proactive role in the plea bargaining process to ensure fairness to victims and the punishment process generally, then they would be inclined to be supportive of it (Cohen and Doob, 1989). And in Germany, plea bargaining has been evaluated by prosecutors, judges, and defense counsels. Their opinions toward plea bargaining vary, depending on the various costs and benefits of plea bargaining versus trial (Ludemann, 1994).

How Much Plea Bargaining Is There Today? To understand both the need for and use of plea bargaining, we must first appreciate the magnitude of federal and state litigation and the rapid growth of criminal cases. In the federal system, for example, there were 44,144 criminal prosecutions in U.S. district courts in 1982 (Chaiken, 1996:2). This figure had risen to 64,000 in 1994, with approximately 49,000 convictions. Judges dismissed or threw out nearly 9,000 cases that same year for various reasons, including insufficiency of evidence. About 92 percent of all federal criminal convictions were obtained through plea bargaining and without an expensive and lengthy trial. At the same time, there were over 500,000 prosecutions in state courts in 1982. By 1994, there were 1.2 million prosecutions in state courts, resulting in 872,217 convictions (Langan and Brown, 1997a:1). Of these, 89 percent had entered guilty pleas, and the remaining 11 percent were convicted through trials.

The rate of plea bargaining remained fairly constant during the period 1970–2000. In the 1970s, at least ninety percent of all convictions were obtained through plea bargaining (Alschuler, 1976). Even with ninety percent of all guilty pleas in either state or federal courts resulting from plea bargaining, the trial court delays in the criminal justice system today are notorious. Some cases, such as the California murder trials of the Menendez brothers and O. J. Simpson, consume several months of court time before they are resolved. In the Menendez case, two brothers were accused of killing their parents. There was considerable incriminating evidence. Nevertheless, the brothers sought and got two juries to hear their cases, only to have both juries deadlocked at the conclusion of the first lengthy trial. A second trial, which resulted in guilty verdicts, took several months to conclude.

These cases are high profile and receive considerable media attention, but less celebrated cases also consume large amounts of court time. What about the length of time taken to prosecute low-profile cases? In 1995, for instance, federal courts conducted 7,421 criminal trials. Of these, 4,400 were concluded in one or two days, about 400 took ten days or more, and at least 110 of these trials took twenty days or longer. Most of these cases were low profile and received little media attention (Maguire and Pastore, 1997:493). Despite this inattention, these trials are sufficiently drawn out to underscore the necessity for plea bargaining. Without it, federal and state courts would probably come to a grinding halt. At the very least, case backlogs would be such that most scheduled criminal cases could not be heard for at least one year. These courts would be hard-pressed to comply with a defendant's right to a speedy trial.

DO ALL JURISDICTIONS USE PLEA BARGAINING? No. Most jurisdictions use it, but in some jurisdictions plea bargaining has been banned. The most visible jurisdiction prohibiting plea bargaining is Alaska (Carns and Kruse, 1991). The ban against plea bargaining was announced by the Alaska Judicial Council in 1975. Routine sentence agreements between prosecutors and defense attorneys were virtually eliminated after the ban and have not returned. At present, most defendants are sentenced by a judge at an open hearing, with participation by the prosecutor, defense, and presentence reporter. Thus, the responsibility for sentencing rests primarily with the judge (Carns and Kruse, 1991).

Some jurisdictions, such as Bronx County, New York, have sought to limit plea bargaining to specific phases of criminal processing. Whether a defendant has been indicted is significant here. A preindictment period is the time before criminal defendants are formally indicted for specific offenses; a postindictment period follows their indictment. Once indictments have been issued in Bronx County, plea bargaining has been discouraged under a new policy (Greenstein, 1994). At the same time, preindictment plea bargaining has been openly encouraged (Nelson, 1994).

In El Paso, Texas, a felony plea bargaining ban was implemented in 1975 (Holmes et al., 1992). Researchers investigated the effects of this ban on case processing and dispositions. While the conviction rate was generally unaffected, many more cases went to trial. As a result, there was a gradual decrease in the disposition rate. Thus, the plea bargaining ban in El Paso adversely affected the ability of district courts to move felony case dockets along efficiently.

Later in 1981, the Superior Court of Merrimack County, New Hampshire, banned plea bargaining in response to criticisms of the practice and the perceived decline in public confidence in the judicial system's ability to effectively administer criminal sanctions (Pellenberg-Fixen, 1983). Unexpectedly, the quality of indictments against criminal defendants in Merrimack County did not improve. Actual sentence lengths imposed for various criminal offenses have remained unaffected by the ban. Court backlogs were increasing when researchers conducted a two-year follow-up of the ban.

WHEN CAN PLEA BARGAINING OCCUR? In most jurisdictions, unless otherwise prohibited by either policy or legislative statements, plea bargaining can occur at virtually any stage of a criminal proceeding prior to a finding of guilt. Although most plea bargaining occurs before a trial is conducted, plea bargain negotiations may transpire throughout a trial.

In some cases, plea bargains have been struck while a case is in progress or while a jury is deliberating. In September 1997, for example, a television sportscaster, Marv Albert, was accused by a woman of sexual assault. The case went to trial in Virginia. During the trial, the alleged victim described to the jury how Albert attacked her. Later, the defense was able to impeach the woman's credibility with exculpatory evidence of their own. But the prosecution brought forth an additional witness who testified to similar treatment by Albert on another occasion and under different circumstances. Albert's attorney sought to introduce other evidence of an exculpatory nature, including testimony and records of the victim's past sexual behavior. But the judge ruled against the introduction of this evidence. Shortly thereafter, Albert's attorney announced that his client was going to plead guilty to a lesser included offense rather than sit through more disclosures by other witnesses. When the jurors were reconvened, the judge announced Albert's decision to plead guilty, and the jurors were dismissed.

Ironically, one of the jurors said that she did not think the state had presented a sufficiently strong case to convict Albert, even with the additional witness and her damaging testimony about Albert's alleged actions. No doubt Albert was thinking that if the jurors were persuaded by this later testimony (which they apparently were not), then he would be convicted and suffer a more severe sentence. In retrospect, Albert probably would have been acquitted of all charges.

Interrupting a criminal trial with a plea bargain has about the same effect as refusing to plea bargain in the pretrial and preindictment periods. Considerable expense has been incurred by the state in the defendant's prosecution, and judges are unhappy with such events. However, the prosecution bears some of the responsibility by entering into these late plea bargaining negotiations. Perhaps the prosecutor in the Albert trial believed that there was a good chance that Albert would be acquitted. Thus, the plea bargain was attractive because it would guarantee a conviction, even for a lesser included offense. In the Albert case, it seemed that neither side was willing to gamble on the jury outcome in view of the different types of evidence presented.

IS PLEA BARGAINING COERCIVE? There is no question that plea bargaining is coercive. Almost no offender wants to admit guilt to any wrongdoing. Therefore, when the prosecutor offers a defendant reduced charges to plead guilty or face prosecution on more serious charges, most defendants find this choice coercive. Even judges think plea bargaining is coercive (Worden, 1995). At the same time, however, judges concede that plea bargaining is a suitable trade-off between due process and crime control. Further, plea bargaining makes life much easier for these judges, prosecutors, defense counsel, and criminals (Fine, 1986).

The U.S. Supreme Court has ruled in several important cases that alleged coercion relating to plea bargaining. Three cases dealing with coercion in eliciting guilty pleas through plea bargaining are *McMann v. Richardson* (1970), *North Carolina v. Alford* (1970), and *Bordenkircher v. Hayes* (1978).

In the case of *McMann v. Richardson,* the defendant entered a guilty plea knowingly and voluntarily and pleaded guilty to murder. He was sentenced to thirty years in prison as the result of the plea bargain agreement. Later, he appealed, contending that his guilty plea had been coerced by the prosecutor. The U.S. Supreme Court heard his argument and ruled that no evidence existed to show that his guilty plea was coerced. Merely alleging coercion is insufficient to succeed on an appeal and have a conviction overturned.

In the case of *North Carolina v. Alford* (1970), Alford was indicted for first-degree murder and faced the death penalty if convicted. Alford maintained his innocence and that he had murdered no one. Subsequently, he was permitted to enter a *nolo contendere* plea to second-degree murder in exchange for a thirty-year sentence the judge imposed. *Nolo contendere* pleas are treated the same as guilty pleas, although they technically do not involve admissions of guilt by defendants. Rather, defendants enter such pleas and merely acknowledge the facts as set forth in indictments without actually admitting their guilt. Later, Alford contested the thirty-year sentence, arguing that he was coerced into pleading guilty to avoid the death penalty that may have resulted from a subsequent jury verdict. The U.S. Supreme Court was unsympathetic in a case when an accused, such as Alford, enters a plea voluntarily and knowingly, and understandingly consents to the imposition of a prison sentence even though he is unwilling to admit participation in the crime, even if his guilty plea contains a protestation of innocence, when, as here, he intelligently concludes that his interests require a guilty plea and the record strongly evidences his guilt. Put more simply, plea bargaining is not considered coercive when a defendant chooses a lengthy prison sentence to escape the possible imposition of the death penalty.

The leading case on this specific point is *Brady v. United States* (1970). Brady was a codefendant in a case involving kidnapping. The offense carried the maximum penalty of death. Brady initially pleaded not guilty to the kidnapping charge. However, Brady's codefendant decided to plead guilty to a lesser charge in exchange for his testimony against Brady in a later trial. Brady changed his mind and pleaded guilty to the kidnapping charge in exchange for a fifty-year sentence, which was subsequently commuted to thirty years. However, Brady brooded about the lengthy prison term and eventually filed an appeal, alleging that his guilty plea had been coerced. The U.S. Supreme Court heard Brady's appeal and upheld his conviction. It held that a plea of guilty is not invalid merely because it is entered to avoid the possibility of the death penalty. The U.S. Supreme Court further noted that although Brady's plea of guilty may well have been motivated in part by a desire to avoid a possible death penalty, it was convinced that his plea was voluntary and intelligently made and that his solemn admission of guilt was truthful.

A noncapital Kentucky case, *Bordenkircher v. Hayes* (1978), involved a career criminal, Paul Hayes. Hayes was arrested for check forgery in Fayette County, Kentucky. The possible punishment for check forgery was a prison sentence of two to ten years. Hayes had several prior felony convictions and thus was eligible to be prosecuted under Kentucky's habitual offender statute. Under this statute, Hayes faced a sentence of life imprisonment. The prosecutor offered Hayes a plea bargain, which included a guilty plea to a bad check charge in exchange for a three-year sentence in prison. Hayes rejected the plea bargain and proceeded to trial. Hayes was prosecuted on the forgery charge, as well as a habitual offender charge under the habitual offender statute. He was convicted and sentenced to life imprisonment. Later, he appealed to the U.S. Supreme Court and claimed that the prosecutor had attempted to coerce him into pleading guilty to one crime while threatening to prosecute him for another crime. The U.S. Supreme Court concluded that Hayes had not been coerced. If prosecutors have grounds for filing particular criminal charges, then their threats to file such charges if defendants do not plead guilty to lesser charges are not considered coercive. In sum, prosecutors may use additional charges against defendants as leverage to elicit guilty pleas to lesser charges whenever there is probable cause to believe that the additional crimes have been committed by the defendant. There must be a factual basis underlying any criminal charge.

If Promises Are Made by Prosecutors to Obtain Guilty Pleas from Defendants, Are Prosecutors Obligated to Fulfill These Promises?

Yes. If a prosecutor promises to recommend leniency or a specific sentence in a plea agreement, then the prosecutor is bound to observe that promise if it is used to elicit a guilty plea. A prosecutor cannot promise a specific form of leniency merely to elicit a guilty plea from a defendant. Prosecutors must follow through on their promises.

In the case of *Santobello v. New York* (1971), Santobello was charged with two felony counts and pleaded guilty to a lesser included offense following a prosecutor's promise *not* to make a sentence recommendation at the plea bargain hearing. However, the plea bargain hearing did not occur for several months. When the proceeding was conducted, a new prosecutor had replaced the earlier one. The new prosecutor, unaware of the earlier prosecutor's promise to Santobello, recommended the maximum sentence under the law, which was imposed by the judge. Santobello appealed, arguing that his guilty plea resulted from a promise by the former prosecutor not to recommend a particular sentence. Although the judge himself said that he was unaffected by the new prosecutor's statement to maximize Santobello's sentence, the U.S. Supreme Court saw things differently. Santobello's conviction and sentence were overturned because a promise had been made to Santobello as a means of inducing him to plead guilty. The U.S. Supreme Court held that the second prosecutor was honor-bound to observe the earlier prosecutor's promise. Santobello was allowed to withdraw his guilty plea. A prosecutor may not make promises to defendants to obtain guilty pleas from them unless the prosecutor fully intends to keep the promises.

This same idea works both ways. If a prosecutor offers a reduced sentence to a defendant in exchange for that defendant's testimony against another defendant, then the defendant must fulfill that promise to testify, or the plea bargain and sentence imposed are withdrawn. In the case of *Ricketts v. Adamson* (1987), Adamson was one of several codefendants charged with first-degree murder. Before his conviction, however, Adamson entered into a plea agreement with prosecutors to testify against his codefendants. In exchange for his testimony against other codefendants in separate trials later, Adamson was permitted to plead guilty to second-degree murder and receive a prison term instead of the death penalty. Adamson was convicted of second-degree murder. Later, when the trials of his codefendants were scheduled, Adamson refused to testify, breaking his earlier promise to prosecutors. The prosecutors appealed Adamson's conviction and sentence, and the Arizona Supreme Court overturned the conviction. New first-degree murder charges were filed against Adamson, and he was later convicted of this offense, which carried the maximum penalty. Adamson appealed to the U.S. Supreme Court, alleging that his right against double jeopardy had been violated with the new trial following his earlier conviction. The U.S. Supreme Court upheld his second conviction in that his breach of the original plea agreement removed the double jeopardy bar that otherwise would prevail, assuming that under state law second-degree murder is a lesser-included offense of first-degree murder. Therefore, even criminal defendants are obligated to keep their promises to make the plea agreement enforceable.

Types of Plea Bargaining

There are four types of plea bargaining: implicit plea bargaining, charge-reduction bargaining, judicial plea bargaining, and sentence recommendation bargaining. These types of plea bargaining are ordinarily distinguished according to which party initiates the bargaining. In three types of plea bargaining discussed next, either judges or prosecutors initiate plea negotiations with defense counsel and their clients. A fourth type of plea bargaining actually occurs through a mutual understanding among parties of what charges will result and what penalties will be expected in exchange for guilty pleas entered (Padgett, 1985).

Implicit Plea Bargaining

Implicit plea bargaining is an understanding between defense counsel and the prosecutor that a guilty plea will be entered to a specific offense that carries a conventional punishment. The expected and contemplated punishment is usually somewhat less than the maximum sentence that could be imposed. The key word in this definition is *understanding*. Much hinges on what sentences have been imposed for similar offenses in the past, depending on the jurisdiction. Those who have entered guilty pleas to burglary charges in the past have sustained penalties ranging from straight probation to four-year prison terms. There are also jurisdictional variations among cities and counties involving identical crimes, even within the same states (Myers and Reid, 1995).

In view of a defendant's prior record, age, mental state, and a host of other factors, defense attorneys are generally in a position to know the going rate for specific offenses. For first offenders, the going rate for burglary may be eighteen months in prison. Depending on the circumstances of the burglary (e.g., whether there were victim injuries, the amount of property loss or damage), a defendant may receive probation for a specified period, such as two or three years. In the case of chronic offenders who have multiple convictions for burglary and other crimes, courts are inclined to impose more severe sentences. Maximum sentences may be contemplated. Further, because the defendant is a habitual offender, there is an additional charge that could be filed by prosecutors. Most states have habitual offender statutes, meaning that a conviction on a habitual offender charge would lead to life imprisonment or life without parole.

Thus, when defense attorneys consult with their clients, they acquire an intimate familiarity with the defendant's prior record and other background factors. Defense counsel have a fairly good idea of what they can expect from the prosecutor's office regarding a plea bargain for their clients. A knowledge of the going rate for specific offenses enables them to advise their clients accordingly and to let them know what they can likely expect from the prosecutor and court.

The practice of implicit plea bargaining begins when a defense counsel advises his or her client that if the client enters a guilty plea to a specific charge, the result will probably be a particular sentence. The defendant is induced to plead guilty based on the defense attorney's expertise and familiarity with the legal system. Offers to enter guilty pleas in exchange for particular punishments are attractive to prosecutors, because they are relieved of having to prove the case against the defendant later in court. Because of the defense counsel's knowledge and the agreeability of prosecutors, most plea agreement negotiations are completed rather quickly.

Exceptions are high-profile cases or cases that are particularly offensive, such as child sexual abuse, mutilation or torture, or some type of perversion. However, court policy may dictate that no plea bargains will be struck with certain types of offenders. For instance, a large suburban county in the Midwest enacted a policy of no deals with dope pushers (Church, 1976). Those who dealt in illicit drugs knew that they could not plea bargain their way into lenient punishments. Thus, a strong law-and-order stance taken by the courts and prosecutors in this county was intended as a deterrent to drug dealing. However, even though prosecutors were not permitted to plea bargain drug cases, judges could still dispense with such cases quickly, often without trial. In these instances, judges dismissed more troublesome cases or made their own sentence recommendations to conclude cases. In short, one form of plea bargaining was replaced with another, as the responsibility for initiating bargains shifted from prosecutors to judges (McConville and Mirsky, 1995a).

As an example of implicit plea bargaining, suppose we have two criminals, Joe Jones and Phil Smith, both charged with burglary and larceny. Each has broken into homes and stolen jewelry and other valuables assessed at $2,000. Profiles of the two criminals are highlighted here:

	Joe Jones	*Phil Smith*
Age	25	24
Education	Ninth grade	Completed high school
Family stability	Stable	Stable
Marital status	Single, never married	Divorced, two children
Prior record	Three felony convictions for larceny, fraud	None
Employment	Unemployed	Employed as day laborer
Drug use	Yes	No
Alcohol use	Yes	Yes

This information is often derived from arrest reports and booking documents and is known to both the defense counsel and the prosecutor. Jones has a more serious record than Smith. The most important factor weighing against Jones is his prior record of three prior felony convictions for larceny and fraud. The most important factor weighing in favor of Smith is his lack of a criminal record. In other respects, compared with Smith, Jones has less education, has less chance for holding a steady job, and is involved with both drugs and alcohol. The going rate for Jones in the present case may be five to seven years in prison. The prosecutor may threaten to bring habitual offender charges against him, and these charges would be easily substantiated. In Smith's case, the going rate might be probation or a short jail sentence. The fact that Smith is a first offender, is employed, has two children from a prior marriage, and has a high school education makes him an ideal candidate for some form of probation or leniency.

One point made by this comparison is that the going rate varies according to an offender's prior record and general background. The same crime committed is punished differently because of the difference in criminal histories for two otherwise similar offenders. Another feature of implicit plea bargaining is that no specific agreement or bargain is reached between the defendant and the prosecutor. Guilty pleas are entered in the hope that leniency will be extended by both the prosecutor and the judge. In most situations, some form of leniency issues from judges in exchange for guilty pleas. However, there are no rules that obligate judges or prosecutors to extend leniency to anyone who enters a plea of guilty to any crime. Judges remind defendants of this very fact before the guilty plea is accepted (Pohlman, 1995).

Charge-Reduction Bargaining

Charge-reduction bargaining or **charge bargaining** is an offer from the prosecutor to minimize the number and seriousness of charges against defendants in exchange for their pleas of guilty to lesser charges. When crimes are perpetrated, often there are multiple offenses arising from the original crime. For instance, Joe Jones and Phil Smith steal a car, enter a convenience store and rob it at gunpoint with automatic weapons, wound two customers who attempt to intervene, shoot and kill the convenience store clerk who attempts to telephone police, elude police who chase them through four counties, cause extensive damage to multiple vehicles during the hot pursuit, engage in a shootout with police and wound several innocent bystanders, and severely wound a police officer before they are subdued and taken into custody. The list of charges against Jones and Smith include murder, attempted murder, armed robbery, menacing, eluding police, firing upon law enforcement officers, resisting arrest, hit-and-run, aggravated assault on the police and bystanders, vehicular theft, and possession of illegal automatic weapons.

Charge-reduction bargaining would involve the prosecutor, who would probably suggest a guilty plea to second-degree murder and armed robbery. The punishment sought would be life imprisonment. Without the plea bargain offer, the prosecutor would file all of these charges against these defendants. The death penalty would probably be sought as well. The result might well mean the imposition of the death penalty or consecutive life imprisonment terms. The offer to reduce the charges and the recommended punishment might sound attractive to Jones and Smith. After all, they avoid the death penalty and are parole eligible. But plea bargaining of this sort is not always one-sided (Worden, 1995). Negotiations include counteroffers from defense counsel. Thus, charge-reduction bargaining and several other forms of plea bargaining are considered episodic, occurring over time and involving multiple defense counsel—prosecutor encounters (Emmelman, 1996). Further affecting the use of charge-reduction bargaining is the bureaucratization of courts in different jurisdictions. The greater the sheer volume of cases in particular jurisdictions, the greater the use of charge-reduction bargaining as a technique to facilitate case processing and move more cases through the system more rapidly (Dixon, 1995).

In another case, this time involving two real defendants, two young men were under police surveillance and suspected of dealing drugs. They happened to be members of the 1990 University of Tennessee football team in Knoxville and were considered quite popular. Knoxville police, the Tennessee Bureau of Investigation, and the Knox County Sheriff's Department were involved in a coordinated effort to investigate them and determine the extent of their alleged drug dealing. An informant, another football player, agreed to plant a bug in the telephone of their apartment. Other listening devices were planted throughout the apartment at the order of a Knoxville criminal court. Subsequently, the young men were videotaped and telephonically recorded engaging in at least twenty-eight transactions. Each transaction involved class X felonies, which meant life-without-parole sentences on each count or charge, because the quantity of drugs (many kilos of cocaine, heroin, and marijuana) was substantial.

The young men were eventually arrested. The most prominent criminal defense attorneys were hired for them by the University of Tennessee football boosters' club and other private supporters. With this formidable defense and the local popularity of these football players, the prosecution knew that despite their clear-cut evidence of criminal conduct and seized drugs, there was a possibility that these men would either be acquitted or convicted of some downgraded charge. Thus, the prosecutor approached their attorneys with the following deal: have your clients plead guilty to simple possession of a controlled substance (cocaine), get six months' jail time (with time off during days and weekends to play football), and do an additional two years on probation with four hundred hours of community service. The plea agreement was concluded quickly, and the young men were sentenced to six-month jail terms. Each was permitted to leave during the day for football practice and required to report back to the jail during evening hours at 9 P.M. Weekends were spent playing football with the rest of the team.

Many citizens in Knoxville were irate at the excessive leniency the court doled out to these football players. It was believed that their status and popularity as football players overshadowed their otherwise criminal conduct, which under other circumstances would have qualified them for twenty-eight consecutive terms of life without parole. But the prosecutor defended his action by arguing that a jury may have thrown out the case against these defendants, despite the mountain of evidence that had been compiled, the incriminating drug deals videotaped and telephonically recorded, and the numerous statements of informants and undercover agents. The final irony of this case is that *both* players failed to comply even with the simplest of conditions associated with their jail terms. They failed to observe their 9:00 P.M. curfew on at least three occasions, and the judge invited them back to his courtroom, where four-year prison terms were imposed. The football players eventually were sent to the Tennessee State Penitentiary in Nashville.

Cases such as this have been cited to underscore the ethics of plea bargaining and the morality of prosecutorial discretion in reflecting public interest in honest law enforcement (Chilton, 1993). Cases with flagrant abuse of prosecutorial discretion, such as the football player scenario, do little to foster public perceptions of prosecutorial integrity. In fact, such prosecutorial indiscretions have functioned as platforms for plea bargaining and sentencing reforms in most states (Chilton, 1993; Weinreb, 1993). Some critics who consider plea bargaining to be a dismal failure contend that it is often unethical and actually counterproductive relative to the court's manifest goals of retribution, deterrence, incapacitation, and rehabilitation (Stitt and Chaires, 1993).

CHARGE-REDUCTION BARGAINING AND LABELING THEORY. Criminologists have investigated the nature and consequences of charge-reduction bargaining for different types of clients. It has been postulated that downgrading the seriousness of charges against certain defendants tends to be accompanied by greater public acceptance. Thus, charge-reduction bargaining is considered a socially acceptable punishment, especially for those of higher socioeconomic status (Bernstein et al., 1977). In the context of **labeling theory**, when potential felony charges are reduced to misdemeanors, for instance, this modification of criminal charges is far less likely to result in unfavorable labeling by others. It is logical that less serious charges are more socially acceptable and considered less deviant than more serious charges. Thus, being labeled as deviant is more forgivable if charges have been downgraded to misdemeanors from felonies. Convicted offenders are more likely to suffer only short-term impacts and adverse reactions from others. Therefore, charge-reduction bargaining often explains relations between allegations of deviance and societal reactions (Bernstein et al., 1977).

Judicial Plea Bargaining

Judicial plea bargaining occurs when judges make offers of sentences to defendants in open court in exchange for their guilty pleas. One of the most frequent uses of judicial plea bargaining involves petty offenses, such as public intoxication or disturbing the peace. Persons arrested for being drunk and disorderly appear before judges in the morning following their arrest. Very often, they are eager to leave the courtroom and get on about their business. The judge knows that the criminal punishment for their conduct is not especially severe.

In New Orleans, for instance, judges must face thousands of intoxicated arrestees every Mardi Gras. Bourbon Street and the French Quarter generate large numbers of targets inviting arrest by police for public intoxication. Although their crime is not especially serious, they may do themselves harm by being out on city streets in that condition. Thus, the drunk tanks of local jails fill rapidly and empty the following morning. Judges bring in twenty or more people charged with public intoxication and inform them as a group of the punishment contemplated. They are usually given fines and suspended sentences. Many courts accept credit cards in lieu of cash payments. The proceedings are concluded quickly, as justice is rapidly dispensed through judicial plea

POLICE DISHONESTY AND PLEA BARGAINING

The Case of Wesley Berg

His name is Wesley Berg. He used to be a member of the North Dakota Bureau of Criminal Investigation (BCI), the state counterpart to the FBI. Berg, thirty-eight, had been the former head of the South Sakakawea Narcotics Task Force. A part of his job involved handling buy money, funds available for state BCI agents working undercover for the purpose of capturing drug traffickers. It turned out that Berg was diverting large sums, more than $50,000, to his personal use, a misuse of public funds and a crime. He was reported by other BCI agents who became aware of his manipulation of these monies. The state attorney general, Heidi Heitkamp, fired Berg when she learned of the incident.

Subsequently, Berg entered into a plea bargain whereby he agreed to plead guilty to embezzlement of public funds in exchange for community service, restitution, and some jail time. According to the terms of the plea agreement, Berg would continue to work at a job with Benson-Quinn Co. Elevator in Underwood, North Dakota. Each evening, he must return to a community corrections center, located in Bismarck and operated by the Federal Bureau of Prisons. The community corrections center is similar to a halfway house and permits offenders to leave only for work or work-related business.

Additionally, Berg will be required to pay twenty-five percent of his income to the corrections center for his room and board. He is further required to pay $200 monthly in restitution payments, which will be adjusted once he leaves the center. The maximum penalty that could have been imposed for his crime was imprisonment for ten years and a $250,000 fine. Some critics viewed Berg's sentence as a mere wrist slap. However, federal prosecutors countered that Berg's sentence involves a substantial loss of liberty. Others viewed the sentence as very light because of Berg's former BCI membership.

Given the higher standard to which all law enforcement officers are held compared with the general public, do you think that Berg's sentence was fair punishment for his crime? Would you like to see the same punishment imposed on a minister who took $51,000 illegally from the collection box? Would you like to see the same punishment imposed on a bank executive who embezzled $51,000 from a local bank? What do you think?

Source: Adapted from the Associated Press, "Former BCI Agent Sentenced." *Minot* (N.D.) *Daily News,* June 21, 1997:B5.

bargaining. Anyone wishing to contest the matter can remain jailed and stand trial later, when the outcome is likely to be the same (McDonald, 1985).

Judicial plea bargaining is tantamount to a bench trial but without much of the formality of prosecutorial involvement. In many cases, defense attorneys are not involved. Historically, bench trials such as those described in New Orleans frequently involve a defendant's waiver of the right to a jury trial. However, defendants who waive this right are rewarded, and those who demand a jury trial are punished. Known as the **jury waiver system**, this method of concluding cases is far less restrictive of one's Sixth Amendment rights than plea bargaining per se (*University of Pennsylvania Law Review,* 1984).

The frequency with which judicial plea bargaining occurs has certain adverse consequences for defendants, however. Decisions to plead guilty are encouraged, and the circumstances under which judges offer specific sentences to defendants, even fines, are somewhat coercive and threatening. Many defendants do not take the time to consider their options and frivolously enter guilty pleas, even if there is the possibility that they are innocent. Being rushed into a guilty plea, therefore, compromises due process to an extent, especially regarding indigent defendants. In New York, for instance, data were obtained from 236 indigent defendants involved in 150 felony cases in 1984–1985 (McConville and Mirsky, 1995a). Assignment of counsel to these indigent defendants included showing defendants that they would receive more severe penalties if they failed to plead guilty. Then these defendants were given exactly fifteen seconds to accept or reject the pleas and sentences offered by these judges. Almost all defendants acceded to the judge's request for them to plead guilty to the recommended charge and accept the proposed sentences (McConville and Mirsky, 1995a).

One unfortunate consequence is that once a guilty plea has been entered, even to a minor charge, it cannot ordinarily be withdrawn later. If it is successfully withdrawn later, there is little to prevent prosecutors from using the initial plea of guilty to their advantage in the courtroom later if the case proceeds to trial (Bagley, 1970). Thus, defendants lose in several different ways, no matter what their decision might be.

Judicial plea bargaining also results whenever power is removed from prosecutors to strike deals or plea bargains with defendants. If charge-reduction or sentence recommendation bargaining is minimized or prohibited, then the responsibility for deciding punishments and negotiating with defendants shifts to judges (Church, 1976). When judges are given this additional responsibility, they become **concession givers**, roles previously performed by prosecutors. More than a few judges get bogged down in their docket loads when dealing with defense counsel who seek reassurances for their clients that probation or some minimal jail time will be imposed. Judges who are not prepared to grant probation in certain cases tend to develop docket problems (Church, 1976).

Sentence Recommendation Bargaining

The fourth type of plea bargaining is **sentence recommendation bargaining**. Sentence recommendation bargaining occurs when the prosecutor proposes a specific sentence in exchange for the defendant's guilty plea (Padgett, 1985). In one respect, sentence recommendation bargaining is an overt articulation of implicit plea bargaining. A prosecutor informs the defense counsel representing a client of the contemplated sentence in exchange for a guilty plea. In a take-it-or-leave-it fashion, the defense counsel relays the information to the client, who decides whether the proposed punishment is worth the guilty plea. It usually is.

Sentence recommendation bargaining is not entirely discretionary with the prosecutor. In fact, judges must approve all plea bargain agreements in all jurisdictions (Worden, 1995). Therefore, if the prosecutor proposes a punishment that is later rejected by the judge, this process is viewed as a waste of court time, and the prosecutor will be chastised accordingly. Thus, prosecutors must be knowledgeable about what the court will or will not accept. All actors (prosecutor, defense counsel, and judge) must have a general understanding of the going rate for any crime, given contextual factors and defendant backgrounds, including their criminal histories.

Sentence recommendation bargaining is often finely tuned, depending on a prosecutor's experience with the system and relationship with the judge. There is a clear relation between a judge's beliefs about the leniency and coerciveness of plea bargaining and the trade-off between crime control and due process, on the one hand, and, on the other hand, the judge's own willingness to cooperate with a prosecutor who attempts plea negotiations with defendants (Worden, 1995). In the mid-1990s, however, there were efforts underway in several jurisdictions to overhaul the architecture of plea bargaining to remove its extralegal properties. Various forms of sentencing classification have been proposed as guidelines in plea negotiations. Of course, this raises the informal nature of plea bargaining to a much more formal and predictable level. The clear intent of plea bargaining reformers is to structure the practice and eliminate the often protracted interplay between prosecutors and defense attorneys. In many respects, the reform envisioned would be similar to guidelines-based sentencing schemes such as those used in Minnesota and other state jurisdictions, as well as the federal court. Offense-specific charts would be consulted, where a defendant's crimes would be cross-tabulated with the defendant's criminal history. Where the points intersect would define a range of months or years that would determine the latitude of the plea bargainers. Jurisdictions such as Massachusetts have been experimenting with sentencing commissions vested with such powers over plea bargaining and certain sentencing issues (Kane, 1995).

One troubling feature of sentence recommendation bargaining and other plea bargaining forms is gender disparity. Gender disparity occurs when one gender receives preferential treatment or consideration in plea negotiations and sentencing. Gender disparity studies indicate that females with no prior records are more likely than similar males to receive charge reductions and less severe sentence recommendations from prosecutors (Farnworth and Teske, 1995). Farnworth and Teske tested the **typicality hypothesis**, which proposes that women are treated with chivalry in criminal processing, but only when their charges are consistent with stereotypes of female offenders. **Selective chivalry** suggests that decision makers extend chivalry disproportionately toward white females. Finally, **differential discretion** suggests that disparity is most likely in informal charge-reduction bargaining than in the final sentencing process and sentencing hearing (Farnworth and Teske, 1995). Records of 9,966 felony theft cases and 18,176 felony assault cases were investigated for the year 1988. Given the similarity of prior records, women were more likely than their male counterparts to receive charge reductions and probation.

We have also seen how indigents seem to receive unfair treatment during plea bargaining, especially when they are assigned public defenders who are usually courtroom novices (McConville and Mirsky, 1995b). Not only are they assigned less competent counsel but also they are rushed into accepting reduced sentences from prosecutors and judges in exchange for their guilty pleas. The coerciveness for indigents is that they almost always face the prospect of harsher penalties from a jury trial on more serious charges. Plea bargaining is the symbolic poster child for socioeconomic unfairness in the criminal justice system. "You get what you pay for" has special significance here.

Unfortunately, there is no easy way to eliminate socioeconomic status as a relevant extralegal variable in the complex plea bargaining equation. This is one reason plea bargaining was banned in Alaska in 1975 (Marenin, 1995). However, simply banning something does not mean its informal abandonment, as Marenin (1995) cautions. In fact, Marenin has said that plea bargaining did not disappear in Alaska following the ban and that it is now alive and well. Prosecutors and defense counsel have simply modified their strategies for circumventing the Alaska plea bargaining ban.

But because plea bargaining occurs at the front end of the criminal justice system and affects virtually every stage following it, the potential for disparities attributable to almost any variable must be carefully monitored (Meyers and Reid, 1995). Although the bureaucratic apparatus is in place to ensure strict compliance with sentences imposed through plea bargains, there is a glaring absence of controls to protect against the unwarranted intrusion of social status variables in any particular plea negotiation (Dixon, 1995).

The Pros and Cons of Plea Bargaining

Plea bargaining has its proponents and opponents. Following is an extensive list of reasons why plea bargaining is both popular and unpopular with the public and with justice experts.

Arguments for Plea Bargaining

REDUCING THE UNCERTAINTIES OF CRIMINAL TRIALS. There are several arguments favoring the use of plea bargaining in the United States. Plea bargaining reduces the uncertainties and risks inherent in a trial for willing participants (Church, 1976), which means that offenders who decide to plead guilty to one or more criminal charges know with some degree of certainty the nature and extent of their punishment, including about how much time they will serve, either on probation or in jail, and any other conditions contemplated by the prosecutor and approved by the judge. If the case were to go to trial and the defendant were convicted, it is more difficult to predict with certainty what the judge would impose. Case-processing time is more rapid through plea bargaining (Greenstein, 1994; McAllister, Atchinson, and Jacobs, 1991; Nelson, 1994; Vanagunas, 1987). Cases that are plea bargained are processed much faster than those that go to a lengthy trial.

FEWER TRIALS AND TRIAL DELAYS. Plea bargaining also means fewer trials and **trial delays** (Barnes, 1988; Budeiri, 1981; Sanborn, 1993a). Prosecutors do not have to prove critical elements in the state's cases against defendants (Klein, 1971). Trials obligate prosecutors to present arguments to the jury about the defendant's guilt beyond a reasonable doubt. Juries may not be easily convinced. Absence of a jury does not relieve prosecutors from proving a defendant's guilt, however. In any plea agreement, the prosecutor must lay out for the judge in writing what evidence would have been presented to show the defendants' guilt beyond a reasonable doubt if the case had gone to trial. This is called the **factual basis for the plea**. This evidence is often minimal, but it may be sufficient to convince most judges of the soundness of the prosecutor's case against the defendant. It should not be assumed literally that prosecutors do not have to prove anything against the accused in a plea bargain agreement. The prosecutor is obligated to furnish the judge who oversees the plea agreement with sufficient evidence that would have been introduced to show the defendant's guilt, if the case had gone to trial. Some plea bargain agreements have been rejected by judges because of insufficient evidence presented by prosecutors.

PLEA BARGAINING MEANS MORE CONVICTIONS. Plea bargaining results in larger numbers of convictions. Usually, the concessions arising from plea bargaining are sufficient to induce most defendants to plead guilty. Ninety percent or more of all convictions are obtained through plea bargaining. Without plea bargaining, trials would determine defendants' guilt or innocence. With juries deciding many cases, it is likely that there would be fewer convictions, even when the evidence against the accused is strong. There are fewer jail backlogs and less jail and prison overcrowding as the result of plea bargaining (Colorado Legislative Council, 1996) because probation and nonincarcerative alternative sentencing options (e.g., **home confinement**, **electronic monitoring**, **intensive supervised probation**) are seriously considered and often imposed as enticements to elicit guilty pleas.

Plea bargaining involves **negotiated guilty pleas**. Because these guilty pleas are negotiated, they are often better than trials in terms of the deals arranged for guilty defendants (Emmelman, 1996). Again, trials are often unpredictable in outcome. If a defendant is found guilty through a trial, then the punishment is often harsher than if the case had been concluded through plea bargaining. Plea bargaining avoids potential jury bias and the emotional influence of adverse evidence. More rational sentencing decisions through bargaining are achieved, and the factual circumstances of terrible crimes, such as murder or aggravated rape, are less emotionally charged (McConville and Mirsky, 1995a). Juries may be persuaded to find someone guilty of a serious crime because of sympathy the prosecutor generates for the victim and the victim's survivors. Emotional persuasion is often strong and overrides the sound, cold deliberations that are expected of jurors when both sides have presented their cases.

Offenders convicted through plea bargaining often avoid the taint of a formal criminal prosecution (Sanborn, 1993b). They do not spend much time in court, except to participate in the plea agreement hearing. Little fanfare accompanies such hearings, which are not attended by many people. As opposed to trials, plea agreement hearings are not usually announced to the public. Most plea agreement hearings, although open to the public, are held only with the judge, court reporter and other court officers, the prosecutor, defense counsel, and defendant. Thus, the specter of a lengthy courtroom drama is avoided. Judicial discretion is more limited because of the conditions and concessions outlined in plea agreements (Kennedy, 1988; Walker, 1993). Judges reserve the right to reject plea agreements if they feel that plea agreements are too lenient. However, judicial rejection of plea agreements is rare. Most plea agreements are rubber-stamped by most judges in most jurisdictions.

PLEA BARGAINING AND ANTICIPATED LENIENCY. Plea agreements may also soften the impact of sentencing guidelines in states that have them. Guideline schemes tend to be excessively rigid (Freed et al., 1992). Prosecutors may downgrade the seriousness of an offense or write the plea agreement in such a way as to subvert the intended impact of guidelines to systematize the sentencing process and create greater uniformity in sentencing. However, each case is developed and rests on its own merits. Each plea bargain agreement is slightly different from others, even in the same jurisdictions. Their uniqueness is about as varied as personalities.

REDUCING THE COSTS OF TRIALS. Regarding its cost-effectiveness, plea bargaining is far less expensive than jury trials (Pellenberg-Fixen, 1983; Gifford, 1983). In jury trials, witnesses must be subpoenaed. Experts must be obtained. Evidence must be examined in greater detail for use in court. The time of judges, court officers, and other key participants is expensive. Thus, from a pure economic standpoint, plea bargaining is a cheap way of getting a guilty plea. In the federal system, for instance, the U.S. sentencing guidelines have severely limited the use of plea bargaining with extremely lenient sentences to less than twenty percent (U.S. Sentencing Commission, 1991). In the indeterminate sentencing followed by the U.S. district courts before the guidelines, probation was granted to convicted offenders about sixty percent of the time. Under the **U.S. sentencing guidelines** that went into effect in October 1987, the use of probation as a sentence in federal courts decreased to about twelve percent. In fact, the U.S. sentencing guidelines table provides for probation in only the least serious misdemeanor or felony cases, and U.S. probation officers are obligated to file more complete reports under the federal sentencing guidelines. The additional mandatory information to be included negates any attempt by federal prosecutors to leave out details that would intensify the seriousness of an offense. Under previous indeterminate sentencing, prosecutors could leave out details, such as the use of a weapon during the commission of the crime, in an attempt to negotiate a more lenient sentence for a federal defendant in exchange for a guilty plea. The fact that federal judges previously used probation sixty percent of the time is strong evidence that presentence investigation reports were often modified to give judges the impression that they were sentencing less serious defendants.

Arguments against Plea Bargaining

THE SELF-INCRIMINATING NATURE OF PLEA BARGAINING. There is considerable opposition to the use of plea bargaining in negotiating guilty pleas. One argument is that defendants who plea bargain give up their constitutional right to a jury trial. Further, they give up the right to cross-examine their accusers. They also relinquish their right against **self-incrimination**. However, the greater leniency extended to defendants in exchange for giving up these rights is sufficient to justify their waivers of jury trials and insistence of observance of their constitutional rights to full due process. Many convicted offenders are thankful for plea bargaining because a jury trial would almost certainly have involved harsher punishment for them. As a consequence, there are fewer trials with plea bargaining, and thus fewer forums are convened where defendants can present the full body of exculpatory evidence showing their innocence (Holmes et al., 1992). More than a few experts are bothered by this fact. Their belief is that jury trials mean that all facts will be heard and that the fairest decision will be rendered by the jury hearing all the evidence.

THE LOSS OF JUDICIAL CONTROL. Plea bargaining may signify a loss of judicial control of courtrooms, giving lawyers free reign to divert jurors from the facts with theories that portray their clients as supposed victims of an unfair criminal justice system (Fletcher, 1995). Most defendants are more than willing to ride through this loss of judicial control with a relatively lenient plea agreement, however. If a defendant is convicted through a trial, the punishment is almost invariably harsher than whatever had been contemplated in a plea bargain. Once a defendant has entered a guilty plea and a sentence has been imposed by the judge, it is difficult to withdraw the guilty plea (Budeiri, 1981). Despite the predictability of plea bargaining, there is always an elusive element. This is **judicial privilege**, which means that judges may accept or reject one or more plea bargain agreement terms and substitute more or less punitive sentences. Thus, although clients have been reassured by their counsel and the prosecutor that entering a plea of guilty to a specific charge will probably result in one type of sentence, the judge may actually imose another type of sentence. Again, judges are not obligated to follow precisely every condition noted in plea agreements.

DEFENDANT IGNORANCE AND PLEA BARGAINING. Ignorance or mistakes often lead to guilty pleas. Therefore, the plea agreement process may lack sufficient guarantees to ensure proper application of the law and sentencing options (Bagley, 1970). Many defendants are ignorant of the law. Those who have some knowledge of the law may lack the foresight to appreciate and understand the seriousness of the guilty plea they enter. Criminal convictions are serious and often result in a loss of one's job. Or naive defendants may enter into plea agreements with prosecutors not knowing that they have the right to litigate fully any charges against them. Their own attorneys often fail to apprise them of their various legal options. Relevant defense evidence is not presented (Purdy and Lawrence, 1990). Opponents of plea bargaining single out this particular factor as most damaging to defendants. If the accused enters a guilty plea, crucial evidence that may have resulted in an acquittal had the case gone to trial is instead often overlooked or deliberately ignored. Thus, opponents of plea bargaining argue, the true extent of a case cannot be known unless it is subjected to a trial proceeding. But many defendants enter into plea agreements with hopes that some of the evidence against them will never be heard. They see plea bargaining as a way of slipping through the system with minimal damage. Plea bargains often offer more benefits to the accused than would be forthcoming at a trial, where circumstances could be much worse.

REJECTIONS OF GUILTY PLEAS AND JUDICIAL PAYBACK. Judges are more likely to be more severe with defendants who reject initial plea bargain agreements (Ferguson, 1972; Klein, 1971). Thus, one danger of plea bargaining is that if an offer to a defendant is made to plead guilty in exchange for what the prosecutor (and judge) believe is a reasonable punishment, refusal to accept that agreement and force the case to trial will sometimes disturb the judge. Upon conviction, the judge may exact some revenge by extending the defendant's sentence by one or more years (Carns and Kruse, 1991). Judicial intervention is minimized such that the issue of ineffective assistance of counsel cannot be adequately explored (Alschuler, 1976; Flanagan, 1976; Marcus, 1992). When plea agreements are negotiated, there is little or no opportunity to ascertain whether the defense counsel is representing the best interests of the client. Is defense counsel competent? With so many cases being plea bargained, and in fairly standard ways, there is no clear opportunity to evaluate defense competence.

The judge becomes an advocate intent on inducing a defendant to plead guilty when due process presumes a person to be innocent until proven guilty beyond a reasonable doubt (Ferguson, 1972). This particular factor is another sore point with plea bargaining opponents. They do not want judges to engage in a form of bribery by dangling attractive lenient sentences before defendants who would face much worse if they went to trial on the same charges. When plea bargaining is allowed, judges wield a great deal of power in the offers they make through judicial plea bargaining. There is a hint of coercion in plea bargaining, particularly implicit plea bargaining, when threats of greater punishments are implied if guilty pleas are not entered to less serious charges, that may cause some defendants to plead guilty to crimes they did not commit. Thus, some innocent people may accept criminal convictions to avoid harmful or fatal punishment. Usually, these cases occur when innocent defendants are swept into the criminal justice system through suspicious circumstances. Those who cannot account for their whereabouts when crimes have occurred or who appear to be involved may find themselves in the unenviable position of facing harsh punishments if convicted. Death rows throughout the United States have set free occasional convicts who were subsequently determined to be innocent through newly discovered evidence or confessions from the real perpetrators.

CIRCUMVENTING HABITUAL OFFENDER STATUTES. Plea bargaining may circumvent **habitual offender statutes** or **three-strikes-and-you're-out policies** if mandatory penalties are contemplated (Tonry, 1987). The danger of plea bargaining here is that chronic or persistent offenders with multiple felony convictions can avoid mandatory punishments an unlimited number of times through plea bargaining. However, the purpose of mandatory penalties is to remove chronic and persistent offenders from society by incarcerating them either for life or for substantial terms. Such punishments are thwarted through plea bargaining, however. Because of plea bargaining, therefore, there is an inconsistent application of mandatory penalties among jurisdictions (Vincent and

Hofer, 1994). Habitual offender statutes are frequently used as leverage for inducing guilty pleas from defendants. There is no apparent intent on the part of prosecutors to enforce such habitual offender statutes, however. Circumvention of sentencing guidelines is encouraged by plea bargaining (Vincent and Hofer, 1994). Sentencing guidelines are designed to establish fairness in sentencing. Whenever these guidelines are bypassed through plea bargaining, fairness is unevenly applied for those who do not plead guilty but rather go to trial.

SENTENCING REDUCTIONS FOR THOSE UNDESERVING OF SENTENCING REDUCTIONS. Sentences for many serious offenders are reduced when such sentences should not be reduced (Brooks, 1996; Neubauer, 1974). Sex offenders and child sexual abusers receive sentences that are often far too lenient, given the seriousness of their offending. Often, critical case information may be buried or overlooked in an attempt to get a plea bargain negotiated. Therefore, some very serious offenders may get lighter sentences, when in fact their punishments should be more severe. At the same time, such offenders may avoid helpful counseling and therapy that might otherwise occur through traditional trial convictions (Brooks, 1996). Some experts have claimed that plea bargaining reduces the sheer volume of criminal prosecutions (Neubauer, 1974). There is no reliable evidence, however, that the absolute number of prosecutions is abbreviated because of plea bargaining. Plea bargaining results from a prosecution. Therefore, a decision by a prosecutor to prosecute someone for a crime sets the stage for offers and counteroffers from defense counsel and prosecutors, as plea bargain agreements are negotiated.

CONCEALING HEINOUS ASPECTS OF CRIMES THROUGH PLEA BARGAINING. Prosecutors and others may be able to conceal more serious aspects of a crime from the sentencing judge by withholding certain information from a plea agreement (Campaign for an Effective Crime Policy, 1996). Some professionals object to this circumstance as ethically wrong (Stitt and Chaires, 1993). Justice somehow seems politicized by this process (McConville and Mirsky, 1995a). Defense lawyers who have cultivated amicable relations with prosecutors over the years are more seasoned and better prepared to negotiate desirable plea bargains for their clients. New lawyers performing public defender functions are at a disadvantage because they are often unaware of how the system works in a particular jurisdiction. Where who you know gets you a better deal in the plea agreement process, this is a fairly clear indication that plea bargaining has been politicized.

RUBBER-STAMPING PLEA AGREEMENTS. Judges tend to rubber-stamp plea bargain agreements without doing their jobs effectively. Judges are supposed to determine whether a factual basis exists for a defendant's plea of guilty. Judges must also determine whether guilty pleas are voluntary. Do defendants wish to relinquish critical constitutional rights, such as giving up the right to cross-examine accusers or give evidence on their own behalf? Because of the glut of court cases in many jurisdictions today, judges are often relieved to merely approve agreements when guilty pleas have been entered. They often are lax in performing their oversight functions (Worden, 1995). Plea agreements often result in more lenient treatment for offenders, who tend to acquire a cynical view of the criminal justice system. They may take subsequent chances by committing new crimes, expecting leniency in the future if it was extended in the past (Kane, 1995). They are not wrong in their appraisal of the criminal justice system, nor are they wrong in anticipating further leniency from prosecutors.

THE POTENTIAL FOR GENDER BIAS IN PLEA BARGAINING. It is claimed that women tend to benefit to a far greater degree from plea bargaining than men (Farnworth and Teske, 1995). Women tend to be granted probation more often than men with similar prior records, instant offenses, and other salient factors. Because of this less than even-handed application of justice, the goals of deterrence, incapacitation, and rehabilitation are either undermined or defeated (Stitt and Chaires, 1993). Another form of discrimination in the use of plea bargaining applies to the poor and those in a lower socioeconomic status (Holmes et al., 1993; McConville and Mirsky, 1995b). Courts are deluged with thousands of indigent defendants, often drawn into the criminal justice system through police sweeps in drug-infested sections of cities. Much street crime is perpetrated by those who are unemployed. Youthful offenders are drawn into the criminal justice system as well, especially minority youth (Conley, 1994). Less affluent defendants are less likely to avail themselves of jury trials, where private counsel are most effective.

DOES PLEA BARGAINING INVALIDATE THE JURY PROCESS? Some critics say that plea bargaining invalidates the jury system (McConville and Mirsky, 1995a). By bypassing a jury trial, defendants are dealt with more swiftly and without the benefits of jury trials. However, it is incumbent upon judges to advise defendants of their right to a trial by jury and ask whether they wish to voluntarily relinquish that right. In more than a few instances, it is disadvantageous to criminal defendants to air their cases before juries, in that the details and circumstances of their crimes may offend more sensitive jurors. This result, in turn, could lead to more serious criminal convictions with accompanying and commensurate sentencing consequences. Thus, for some offenders at least, jury trials are not desired and for good reason. Plea bargaining encourages more proactive policing and arrests of indigents (McConville and Mirsky, 1995a). According to this line of thinking, police officers are interested in making increasing numbers of arrests that will result in convictions. Street people, indigents, drug users, and youthful offenders who loiter or act suspiciously are often arrested and charged with assorted offenses. Police officers know that there is a strong likelihood that many of those arrested will be offered plea bargains that result in probation or charge reductions. Convictions lead to greater approval of the actions of law enforcement officers, and thus a self-reinforcing cycle is set in motion with predictable consequences.

HAMPERING EFFORTS TO REFORM SENTENCING. Sentencing reforms are hampered through plea bargaining (Kaune, 1993; Roberts, 1994; Vincent and Hofer, 1994). If ninety percent or more of all convictions are obtained through plea bargaining, it is more difficult for reformers to convince legislatures of the necessity for sentencing reform. Going rates and other traditional plea bargaining features have become institutionalized nationally. There is no dramatic need to reform a system that seems to be accepted by criminals, prosecutors, defense counsels, and judges (Gorr and Harwood, 1992). However, plea bargaining is blamed for some amount of sentencing disparity

How Serious Is Perjury?

The Case of Mark Fuhrman and the O. J. Simpson Criminal Trial

It seemed like such a little lie at the time. During the murder trial of O. J. Simpson—a television and sports personality—a detective, Mark Fuhrman, was a key witness against him. Simpson's former wife, Nicole Brown Simpson, and her friend Ronald Goldman had been found stabbed to death in front of her home in June 1994. Investigating police officers decided to contact her former husband, O. J. Simpson, because of Detective Fuhrman's knowledge that Simpson had previously been charged with spousal abuse. He was a key suspect.

Four detectives arrived at the Simpson estate in fashionable Brentwood, California, a few hours following the murders. Mark Fuhrman, the youngest detective among the four, scaled Simpson's gate and unlocked it for the other detectives. While each detective went to different locations on the estate to contact anyone who might be present, Fuhrman wandered around to the back of the estate to an apparently undisturbed walkway, grown over with brush and covered with cobwebs. Using a penlight, he allegedly spotted a black, bloodied glove. He retrieved the glove, which turned out to be a match for another bloody glove found at the crime scene. The inference made by Fuhrman and the other detectives was that whoever committed the murder dropped one glove at the crime scene and the other glove in the small walkway behind the Simpson estate. With this very incriminating information, the detectives believed they had their man. Simpson was subsequently arrested and charged with the murders of his former wife and Goldman.

During his testimony on the witness stand, Fuhrman gave incriminating testimony, claiming to have found the bloody glove and other blood evidence in inconspicious locations around Simpson's estate. Under cross-examination, F. Lee Bailey, one of Simpson's defense attorneys, asked Fuhrman about finding the glove. He also inquired of Fuhrman if Fuhrman was a racist and if he had ever used the word *nigger* to refer to an African American. Fuhrman vehemently denied ever using that word in the past ten years. No one thought much about that.

However, several months later, several witnesses were produced by Simpson's defense team to show that Fuhrman *had* used the racist term in depicting blacks. Furthermore, evidence was disclosed that indicated Fuhrman's feelings against blacks ran much deeper than he had previously indicated. Evidence suggested that Fuhrman had planted evidence at previous crime scenes or had set up black motorists for various forms of harassment.

The prosecution scoffed at the *minor* matter of Detective Mark Fuhrman making such racist statements. "What difference does that make?" asked one prosecutor. After all, Fuhrman was the one who found *other* blood evidence directly linking O. J. Simpson to a double homicide.

Under a well-known legal theory, if a witness is determined to have lied about one fact, it may be presumed that he may have lied about other facts given in earlier testimony. Thus, if it could be demonstrated that Detective Mark Fuhrman had lied about using the word *nigger* to describe African Americans, then that fact alone could be used to impeach his entire testimony, including the allegation that he discovered the matching bloody glove on the Simpson estate. Did he plant the glove? We will never know. But we *do* know that Fuhrman lied under oath about one issue, and that this means he may have fabricated other evidence given during his testimony.

A year following O. J. Simpson's acquittal of the murder charges, Mark Fuhrman pleaded no contest (*nolo contendere*) to the felony criminal charge of perjury that the California attorney general had filed against him. In effect, on October 2, 1996, Fuhrman confessed to lying under oath during the O. J. Simpson trial. In exchange for his plea, Fuhrman was sentenced to three years' probation. Legally, a plea of *nolo contendere* or no contest is treated as the equivalent of a guilty plea in criminal courts. Thus, Fuhrman was convicted of perjury. With this new evidence of his perjured testimony, legal theorists and journalists will be able to speculate for decades about whether Fuhrman's crucial testimony about the blood evidence found on the Simpson estate was also a product of Fuhrman's racist views and planted to incriminate Simpson.

What do you think? Can it be assumed that if Fuhrman lied about one thing, he may have lied about other crucial evidence? What if these racist views of Fuhrman were known at the time he gave his testimony against Simpson early in the trial proceedings? Was the sentence imposed on Fuhrman too light, given the gravity of the charges O. J. Simpson was facing and the seriousness of the trial?

Source: Adapted from Associated Press, "Fuhrman Pleads No Contest to Perjury Charge." *Minot (N.D.) Daily News,* October 3, 1996:A7.

(Jensen et al., 1991; Vincent and Hofer, 1994). One obvious disparity resulting from plea bargaining is the difference in sentencing severity between plea-bargained cases and convictions resulting from trials. Another type of disparity is more difficult to detect. Different attorneys continually network with various assistant state's attorneys or district attorneys to work out agreements for their diverse clientele. All plea bargains are individualized; therefore, there is an inherent inequality. Only judges monitor plea agreements, and little effort is made by these judges to ensure that sentencing uniformity occurs according to the salient factors that should influence sentencing decisions (e.g., prior record or criminal history, instant offense, victim injuries, and other aggravating or mitigating factors) (Van Kessel, 1992). Without any consistent monitoring mechanisms to govern plea bargaining in any particular jurisdiction, sentencing disparity must be assumed to occur. We do not know how much sentencing disparity results from plea bargaining.

RACIAL DISCRIMINATION AND PLEA BARGAINING. More people of color are discriminated against through plea bargaining, which means that much racial and ethnic discrimination occurs (American Bar Association, 1992; Conley, 1994; Kunkle and Washburn, 1979; Stitt and Chaires, 1993). Street crimes are given greater attention by police officers, and proactive policing, as discussed previously, targets street people most often. These people are frequently ethnic and racial minorities. Frequently indigent, they must accept defense counsel who often lack the experience and expertise of seasoned private attorneys retained by more affluent criminal clients (Arcuri, 1976; Conley, 1994). Efforts are currently being made to upgrade legal services for indigents (Uphoff, 1992), but such efforts are sporadic and unevenly applied across jurisdictions. Also, there is no one to monitor the actions of prosecutors (Aaronson, 1977; National Institute of Law Enforcement and Criminal Justice, 1979). Thus, a serious accountability problem exists (Aaronson, 1977; Chilton, 1993). Who should oversee the credibility and quality of case screening and prioritizing? Prosecutors in many jurisdictions have virtually unbridled authority to drop or pursue a case, adjust charges, and make recommendations. In short, prosecutors have too much decision-making power in charging decisions. Also, shifting greater decision-making power to prosecutors reduces justice system accountability as case decision making is shifted toward the front of the system. Rights activists are concerned that due process protections for the accused are jeopardized and that victim participation is minimized under widespread plea bargaining (McCoy, 1993; Pellenberg-Fixen, 1983; Welling, 1987).

THE BUREAUCRATIZATION OF NEGOTIATED GUILTY PLEAS. The perfunctory nature of plea bargaining has certain bureaucratic characteristics. If there is greater reliance on bureaucratization, then there is less individualized attention given to more important cases (Ferdinand, 1992). The existing administrative structures of some jurisdictions, such as Pennsylvania, are frequently relied on by prosecutors to ensure consistency in plea bargaining practices (Kunkle and Washburn, 1979). A positive consequence of bureaucratization in plea bargaining is that extralegal factors, such as race, social class, and gender, are less important in negotiating guilty pleas. In **coconspirator** cases, it is more difficult for innocent defendants to separate themselves from guilty defendants (Freed et al., 1992). If the guilty defendant enters into a plea agreement with prosecutors and agrees to testify against an innocent party named as a coconspirator, the innocent coconspirator is tainted. Thus, if the case comes to trial for the codefendant who does not plead guilty, such circumstances work to the disadvantage of the innocent party.

ARE LAWYERS VESTED WITH TOO MUCH AUTHORITY IN PLEA BARGAINING? Some critics say that plea bargaining gives too much authority to lawyers. There is little or no weight given to **fact-finders** or juries (Van Kessel, 1992). Essentially, this is a complaint that jurors are in a better position to determine guilt or innocence and evaluate evidence than a prosecutor–defense attorney plea agreement, where all pertinent facts about the crime may not be disclosed and weighed properly. Plea bargaining is so pervasive that many defense attorneys have become complacent about it. If defense counsel must

FAST FOOD FOR CONFESSIONS AND EASY CONVICTIONS?

A Case of Confessing for Meals

Does it happen only in Miami? Picture this: Police officers walk a criminal suspect into a nearby Burger King or McDonald's and treat the suspect to a Big Mac and Coke. Almost immediately, the suspect rattles off all he knows about the crime alleged and his involvement in it. In the process, other suspects are implicated, and police officers make additional arrests on the basis of reliable and incriminating evidence from accessories and coconspirators.

How does it happen? In Miami, for instance, Gerardo Plaza was arrested in 1995 on suspicion of robbery. The detectives took him to a local Burger King. They asked him what he wanted to eat, and he asked for a Whopper. They bought Plaza the Whopper combo meal, and between bites Plaza confessed to a liquor store robbery and murder. When Plaza finished his meal, he said to detectives, "Well, you got your Whopper's worth. I'm really hungry. Buy me a cheese steak," with the promise of more crimes to be confessed. Police took Plaza to another sandwich shop, where they accommodated his request. One homicide detective, Kent Hart, said, "As soon as he gets his sub, he is eating it. And he cops out to a couple of robberies in the city of Miami. We should open an account at Burger King. Every time we walk in, they ask, 'Are you taking confessions tonight?'"

At the request of prosecutors, police write down all meals they feed defendants. Sometimes they even take pictures to memorialize these confession events. David Waksman, a Dade County prosecutor and former New York City police officer, says, "The name of the game now is feed them and schmooze them." Waksman is grateful for all the confessions such feeding tactics have yielded. In one case, turkey was an inducement for getting a confession from a ranch hand suspected of killing a nine-year-old boy. Juan Carlos Chavez underwent more than fifty hours of questioning by police, all the while eating fast food. Eventually, he confessed to killing the boy, Jimmy Ryce. The lead investigator in the Ryce case, Detective Pat Diaz, said, "If I ate a turkey sandwich, he [Chavez] ate a turkey sandwich." Then he confessed.

Not everyone is happy with these confession scenarios, however. Defense attorney William Matthewman is especially incensed by the fact that police officers are able to entice criminals into confessing with offers of food. He says, "Offers of food, leniency, dismissal of charges and other similar types of inducements are what contribute to the very serious problem of false confessions. False confessions have previously put innocent people in jail, even on death row." However, Miami police say that thus far their methods have been supported with considerable circumstantial evidence that corroborates confessions given by their suspects. No one has ended up on death row in Florida as the result of their Burger King or McDonald's generosity.

defend indigents, these attorneys are not paid at rates equivalent to private counsel. Thus, the financial incentives do not exist to work hard for indigent clients. Particularly if indigents are involved, defense counsel are often quick to conclude a case with a plea bargain (Uphoff, 1992). If cases do go to trial, there are questions about the competence of the defense counsel required to represent indigents. Are they enthusiastic enough to present the best defense, or do they go through the motions of defending clients, taking the easiest path that will conclude the proceedings?

Why Is Plea Bargaining Banned in Some Jurisdictions?

Plea bargaining has been banned in various U.S. jurisdictions, most notably in Alaska. When Alaska announced that it was banning plea bargaining on a statewide basis in 1975, other jurisdictions were apprehensive (Marenin, 1995). Would such a ban mean a glut of trials involving petty offenders? Would the wheels of Alaskan justice come to a grinding halt as more cases were processed without informal plea agreements worked out in advance?

Although plea bargaining in Alaska was officially banned, it did not disappear. Marenin (1995) says that plea bargaining is alive and well in Alaska. What occurred, according to Marenin, is that plea bargaining gave prosecutors considerably greater charging powers. With greater power over charging decision making, prosecutors in Alaska were more careful to screen those cases destined for trials. One result was a reduction in the number of criminal prosecutions, as many cases that once were plea bargained were simply dropped.

A more significant consequence of the Alaska plea bargaining ban was to create greater charge bargaining. Prosecutors were vested with considerably more authority to decide which charges should be brought against defendants. Subsequent bans of plea bargaining by various jurisdictions, such as New Hampshire, have revealed a similar pattern, with a substantial increase in charge bargaining (Pellenberg-Fixen, 1983).

At the core of plea bargaining bans is the unfairness inherent in sentencing bargaining. Most plea agreements contemplate a particular punishment. Much of the punishment meted out through plea bargaining is more lenient than traditional punishments associated with trial convictions. Thus, the leniency of plea bargaining concerning sentences received by convicted offenders—often serious offenders—has been objectionable to more than a few citizens and lawmakers.

Reasons for Banning Plea Bargaining

1. Where plea bargaining has been banned, a greater amount of charge-reduction bargaining occurs (Carns and Kruse, 1991). This has shifted much of the decision-making power to prosecutors and away from judges. Some experts view this shift unfavorably.

2. Under a plea bargaining ban, there is a greater likelihood of incarceration (Carns and Kruse, 1991). Jail and prison overcrowding could be exacerbated by an absence of plea bargaining. On the one hand, those who favor strong get-tough anticrime measures will applaud the elimination of plea bargaining. On the other hand, jail and prison officials may not be pleased with the overcrowding that might result.

3. Under a plea bargaining ban, cases are more carefully screened by prosecutors (Carns and Kruse, 1991). Only the more serious cases for which strong evidence exists will move forward to criminal trials.

4. Selective bans against bargaining that target certain offenses (e.g., no deals with dope pushers) appear to work in selected jurisdictions. When offense-specific plea bargaining restrictions are implemented, prosecutors are prohibited from accepting reduced-charge guilty pleas from drug dealers (Church, 1976). This ban does not necessarily mean that convicted drug dealers will be treated harshly, however. Current sentencing policies in certain jurisdictions are intended to incarcerate more offenders who commit certain types of offenses, such as drug dealing, for longer periods of time (New York City Criminal Justice Agency, 1992).

5. Even if plea bargaining is banned, judges and others find ways to get around the ban (Church, 1976). It is virtually impossible to eliminate plea bargaining. Informal negotiations will always occur, no matter how stringent the controls or plea bargaining restrictions.

Judicial Instructions for Accepting Guilty Pleas and Rights Waivers

In most jurisdictions, judges are obligated to determine the factual bases for guilty pleas, encourage frank discussion of the facts of the case, and facilitate further consideration of sentencing alternatives. In federal district courts, for example, judges must observe all of the **Federal Rules of Criminal Procedure** relating to plea bargaining. Specifically, this is 18 U.S.C., Rule 11 (U.S. Code, 2001). Rule 11 outlines with considerable precision what judges must do in the process of approving plea agreements. Under Rule 11, federal judges must make sure that defendants who enter guilty pleas to criminal charges understand the following:

1. The nature of the charge(s) to which the plea is offered
2. The maximum possible penalty provided by law
3. The mandatory minimum penalty as provided by law
4. The effect of any special supervised release term and any special provisions for compensating victims
5. That a defendant who does not have an attorney has a right to one; if the defendant cannot afford an attorney, one will be appointed at state expense
6. That the defendant has the right to plead not guilty and to withdraw a guilty plea at any time
7. That the defendant has the right to a trial by jury and the right to the assistance of counsel at the trial
8. That the defendant has the right to confront and cross-examine prosecution witnesses
9. That the defendant has the right not to incriminate himself or herself
10. That if the plea of guilty or *nolo contendere* is accepted, there will be no further trial of any kind; therefore, the plea is a waiver of the right to a trial
11. That there is a factual basis for the plea
12. That the plea is voluntarily given and that it is not the result of force, threats, or coercion apart from a plea agreement
13. That the judge may accept or reject the plea agreement
14. That the plea is accurate
15. If the plea is the result of prior discussions between prosecutors and defendants or their attorney

Items 11, 12, 13, and 14 are of great significance to defendants. These items are to determine whether the guilty plea entered by a defendant is voluntary. There must be a factual basis for the plea, the judge may accept or reject the plea agreement, and the plea agreement is an accurate summarization of the facts. These provisions seemingly protect defendants from overzealous prosecutors who threaten long sentences and drawn-out prosecutions if guilty pleas are not entered and suggested sentences are not accepted. This is the ideal scenario. It does not always happen this way in the real world.

Federal judges have no special protocol for determining these and other facts about a defendant's guilty plea and the nature and terms of the plea agreement. The spirit of the law is that federal judges must ascertain these facts, in open court, by orally addressing the defendant. Each judge uses his or her own style for covering these important items. Thus, Rule 11 provides general guidelines for judges to follow. Past challenges from defendants about whether judges asked them about these items in precise ways have been unsuccessful; that is, federal judges are not compelled by Rule 11 to recite these questions precisely in the context of the rule.

If a federal judge is not satisfied with the evidence proffered by a U.S. attorney or assistant attorney, then the judge is not bound to accept the plea agreement. Judges can throw out charges against defendants if the evidence against them does not or would not support a subsequent conviction if the case proceeded to trial. A case in Tennessee provides a good example.

A man from Chattanooga, Tennessee, was charged with several felonies relating to copyright infringement governing the use of 16-mm films and their possession by private film collectors. He had collected feature films as a hobby, but the Motion Picture Association of America (MPAA) and the Film Security Office under the direction of President Jack Valenti instituted a series of legal actions against private collectors to prevent them from trafficking in these motion pictures. The government's theory, at the urging of the MPAA, was that no motion picture had ever been sold to private individuals; therefore, all motion picture 16-mm prints in the hands of film collectors must have been stolen or obtained in nefarious ways. Although there are several flaws in the government's theory about the critical elements of criminal copyright infringement, suffice it to say that the Chattanooga film collector was innocent of any criminal wrongdoing. He had purchased most of his 16-mm prints of these motion pictures from film rental companies or from film reclamation services. Thus, he had legal title to these pictures. At the time, film collecting was regarded by the MPAA as jeopardizing the profits of major motion picture film companies. In reality, the number of motion picture collectors was small, and the sum of their monetary profits from trafficking in motion pictures was trivial. Subsequently, these motion pictures have been made available in videotape format, and any private citizen may now own just about any motion picture sold in this format.

In Chattanooga, Tennessee, however, the defendant was a fairly high-volume trader of motion pictures at the time. Although he probably profited from motion picture film trades and sales, he never intended to defraud film companies of any revenue that they might obtain through film rentals or leases. In any event, the assistant U.S. attorney (AUSA) for the federal district court in Chattanooga brought several criminal copyright infringement charges against the film collector. The defendant was in his early fifties and had a heart condition. He was employed only on a part-time basis and supported himself from a portion of the revenue he realized from his film collecting.

The AUSA in Chattanooga approached the defendant with an offer—plead guilty to a **federal misdemeanor** and the AUSA would recommend a three-year probationary term. The defendant, who was assigned a court-appointed attorney, declined any offer to plead guilty to any criminal charge relating to his film-collecting hobby. However, a persuasive public defender pointed out to the defendant that a three-year probationary term was not bad compared with the thirty years and $200,000 fine associated with felony convictions on the criminal copyright infringement charges. Reluctantly, the defendant agreed to plead guilty.

On the day of the plea agreement hearing, however, the defendant stood before the federal district court judge and answered the different questions faithfully. When it came to the matter of whether the defendant wanted to plead guilty to this crime, a federal misdemeanor, the defendant balked. "I never committed any crime, judge," he said. With a frustrated expression on his face, the judge asked the defendant's attorney if he wanted to confer with his client before proceeding. The defense counsel had a lengthy discussion with his client, who later went back into court before the judge and entered the guilty plea. Here is where things get interesting.

The judge next asked the AUSA what evidence would have been submitted to show that the criminal elements existed and could have been proved beyond a reasonable doubt. The AUSA said that the evidence was summarized as a part of the plea agreement. The judge asked, "Is that all you have against this man?" The AUSA said, "Yes, your honor." At that point, the judge faced the defendant and said, "You are hereby freed, as I am dismissing all criminal charges against you." Then he turned to the AUSA and chastised him for bringing such a poorly prepared case before him. It was clear to the judge that the defendant had been cajoled into pleading guilty for fear of a harsher prosecution.

Unfortunately for many federal and state criminal defendants, not all judges are as judicious and meticulous in examining federal or state plea agreements and their contents. A majority of federal and state court judges rubber-stamp these plea agreements because the court is backlogged with many serious cases to be plea bargained. Many judges give plea agreements only a cursory glance and overview before holding plea agreement hearings. Thus, their actions relating to accepting plea agreements are often perfunctory.

CAN JUDGES PARTICIPATE IN PLEA NEGOTIATIONS BETWEEN PROSECUTORS AND DEFENSE COUNSEL?

No and Yes. At the federal level, district court judges are prohibited from participating in plea agreement negotiations between defense counsel and prosecutors. The policy about judicial participation in plea bargaining negotiations varies among the states. However, most states follow the federal government and prohibit judicial involvement in these negotiations. The primary reason is that involvement in these discussions places them in the position of configuring an agreement that they will most certainly approve later. This type of influence is considered unethical and inappropriate in most jurisdictions.

Only a few states, such as North Carolina, permit state court judges to participate in plea negotiations. Thus, defense counsel and prosecutors can confer with judges about what judges will accept or reject as plea agreement terms. Some opponents of judicial participation in plea bargain negotiations rightly note that the adversarial nature of the justice system is substantially removed through judicial intervention of any kind (Van Kessel, 1992; Worden, 1995).

SHOULD JUDGES BE EXCLUDED FROM PLEA BARGAINING NEGOTIATIONS BETWEEN PROSECUTORS AND DEFENSE COUNSEL?

Some researchers believe that judges should be an integral part of the plea bargaining process. Judges can give both parties a clearer idea of what the sentence will be, the specific parameters of plea negotiations, and various correctional options (Klein, 1971; Schlesinger and Malloy, 1981). Essentially, judges can tell prosecutors and defense attorneys, "This is the deal I will accept. Don't bring me anything more lenient than that."

Sometimes judicial concern focuses more on particular offenses, such as those involving drugs. Political sentiment and the judiciary in one jurisdiction, a county in the Midwest, established a policy of "no deals with drug pushers" (Church, 1976). In that Midwest jurisdiction, reduced-charge plea bargaining for drug cases was all but eliminated, but trial rates soared. Court dockets were incredibly crowded. Judges were hard-pressed to resolve their court cases quickly. Interestingly, judges became concession givers, a role abandoned in drug cases by the district attorney. Defense counsel shifted their attention to judges and negotiated with them instead of with prosecutors. If defense counsel could not obtain probation for their clients charged with various drug offenses, then they would insist on a full-fledged trial, a time-consuming proceeding. Judges were compelled to make concessions, usually by granting probation or short jail terms for a majority of charged drug offenders.

Some critics oppose judicial participation in plea negotiations because of the implication that the defendant is guilty (Ferguson, 1972). Traditionally and consistent with due process, judges are supposed to assume a stance of neutrality and consider all defendants innocent until their guilt is proven in court beyond a reasonable doubt. Suppose a judge agrees to approve a particular guilty plea from defendant X. Later, defendant X withdraws his guilty plea and goes to trial before the same judge. Can that judge continue to remain neutral and impartial in rulings on motions and other matters during defendant X's trial? It seems somewhat contradictory for a judge to be an advocate during plea bargaining who encourages the defendant to admit guilt, and then turn around in the trial and fairly judge a defendant who decides to reject the plea bargain agreement.

Sentencing Systems and Plea Bargaining

Plea bargaining has been modified in different jurisdictions, depending on the sentencing scheme adopted. One purpose of sentencing reform is to reduce sentencing disparities among judges that are attributable to extralegal factors, such as the defendant's race, age, ethnicity, gender, or socioeconomic status. Sentencing guidelines have been created in most jurisdictions to create sentencing uniformity, although no sentencing guideline scheme has completely eliminated the influence of extralegal factors in sentencing offenders.

SENTENCING GUIDELINES AND RESTRICTIONS ON PLEA BARGAINING. For federal courts, however, the U.S. sentencing guidelines have operated to limit the negotiating parameters of prosecutors and defense counsel. Prior to the establishment of U.S. sentencing guidelines, federal prosecutors could tailor their plea agreements in ways that would maximize a defendant's acceptance of the plea agreement terms and encourage more guilty pleas. If a firearm was used in the commission of a robbery, for instance, the prosecutor could leave that fact out of the plea agreement. This omission would enable prosecutors to downgrade more serious felonies to less serious ones and offer defendants more lenient (and acceptable) punishments. Probation was used about sixty percent of the time in most federally plea-bargained cases prior to the establishment of sentencing guidelines.

When the federal sentencing guidelines were established, new rules were instituted requiring U.S. probation officers to include all relevant legal variables in **presentence investigation reports (PSIs)**. Prosecutors were prohibited from omitting these relevant variables. Thus, if a federal defendant used a firearm during the commission of a felony (e.g., robbing a U.S. post office), this fact had to be reported and noted in subsequent plea agreements. Further, the use of probation under the new federal sentencing guidelines (October 1987) dramatically decreased to about twelve percent of all plea-bargained cases. Guidelines tables now exist that restrict the use of probation to only a limited number of minor federal offenses. If federal defendants are recidivists, then the chances for probation as a sentence are eliminated. Thus, federal prosecutors have lost an important plea bargaining chip in the game of negotiating plea agreements with those charged with federal crimes.

OTHER SYSTEMS AND PLEA BARGAINING. If a particular offense carries with it a mandatory term, then judges must impose a specific sentence as required by law. Their hands are effectively tied. However, under **indeterminate sentencing** or **determinate sentencing** schemes absent any guidelines or other restrictions, judges and prosecutors may operate more or less freely in configuring plea bargain agreements with various defendants. There is considerable jurisdictional variation in this regard. In many jurisdictions without definite guidelines in place for offender sentencing, judges' sentencing practices are often influenced more by their work circumstances, their close relationships with courtroom prosecutors, and an absence of competing recommendations from probation officers (Worden, 1995).

Summary

Plea bargaining accounts for more than ninety percent of all criminal convictions in the United States. Plea bargaining is a preconviction agreement in which prosecutorial leniency or concessions are exchanged for a plea of guilty from a criminal defendant. Four types of plea bargaining have been identified. One is implicit plea bargaining, when an understanding exists about the going rate as the punishment for particular offenses and considering the defendant's prior record of criminal behavior. Another type is judicial plea bargaining, when a judge proposes a guilty plea in exchange for some form of sentencing leniency. Charge-reduction bargaining is initiated by prosecutors who offer to downgrade the number and/or seriousness of offenses charged against defendants in exchange for their guilty plea to lesser charges. Sentence recommendation bargaining is a fourth type of plea bargaining in which prosecutors propose a specific sentence in exchange for a defendant's guilty plea.

Plea bargaining occurs in virtually every U.S. jurisdiction, and it is not unique to the United States. Plea bargaining can occur at any time during a criminal defendant's processing, even during jury deliberations following a trial. Plea bargaining is inherently coercive because some form of leniency is offered as a reward for a plea of guilty. Sentencing leniency is attractive to many criminal defendants because sentencing from judges following trials is often more severe than sentences contemplated during the plea bargaining process.

Plea bargaining proponents say that the use of plea bargaining frees courts to pursue more serious cases. Without plea bargaining, they argue, courts would quickly become glutted and overburdened. The costs of expensive jury trials are avoided, and judicial sentencing disparities are minimized. Those opposed to plea bargaining believe that defendants surrender valuable rights, such as the right against self-incrimination and the right to cross-examine one's accuser in court. Opponents also believe that everyone is entitled to either a bench or jury trial to determine their guilt. Plea bargaining deprives them of this process. Also it is believed that plea bargaining is coercive and that many defendants plead guilty to offenses they have not committed, simply to avoid harsher sanctions that might be imposed by a jury. Another argument against plea bargaining is that it is too lenient. Many offenders avoid harsher punishment, which they deserve. Although the various states have different laws regarding plea bargaining, including banning its use, it thrives everywhere throughout the United States in one form or another.

All plea-bargained guilty pleas must be supervised by a judge. The judge must address those entering guilty pleas in open court and determine the voluntariness of their pleas. Were any promises made to induce the guilty plea? Was any coercion used to elicit it? These judges must also satisfy themselves that there is a factual basis for the guilty plea. That is, if the case had gone to trial, what evidence would the prosecutor have introduced to show guilt beyond a reasonable doubt? Subsequently, all plea bargains must be approved by a judge. Some plea bargain agreements may be rejected, and charges may be dismissed against certain defendants. Judges also have the power to impose more stringent punishments than those contemplated by the plea agreement. Once defendants have entered guilty pleas to criminal charges, there is little likelihood that they will be allowed to withdraw their guilty pleas if they dislike the sentences judges subsequently impose. In most jurisdictions, judges are barred from participating in plea negotiations between the prosecution and defense.

KEY TERMS

Charge bargaining
Charge-reduction
  bargaining
Coconspirator
Concession givers
Determinate sentencing
Differential discretion
Electronic monitoring
Fact-finders
Factual basis for the plea
Federal misdemeanor
Federal Rules of Criminal
  Procedure
Flat time

Going rate
Guilty plea
Habitual offender statutes
Home confinement
Implicit plea bargaining
Indeterminate sentencing
Intensive supervised
  probation
Judicial plea bargaining
Judicial privilege
Jury waiver system
Labeling theory
Negotiated guilty pleas
Nolle prosequi

Plea bargain agreement
Plea bargaining
Plea bargains
Presentence investigation
  reports (PSIs)
Selective chivalry
Self-incrimination
Sentence recommendation
  bargaining
Three-strikes-and-you're-
  out policies
Trial delays
Typicality hypothesis
U.S. sentencing guidelines

QUESTIONS FOR REVIEW

1. What is plea bargaining? Why is it controversial?
2. Name four types of plea bargaining and differentiate between them. Which one do you prefer and why?
3. What is the nature of judicial participation in plea bargaining for individual states and the federal government?
4. Should plea bargaining be banned? Why or why not?
5. What is meant by the going rate?
6. Briefly outline the history of plea bargaining in the United States.
7. In some jurisdictions, such as Alaska, plea bargaining has been banned. Does plea bargaining still go on in Alaska, even though it has been banned?
8. What is the significance of Federal Rule of Criminal Procedure 11 as it relates to plea bargaining?
9. What specific rights are waived by defendants who enter into plea bargain agreements?
10. How does the type of sentencing scheme influence plea bargaining?

SUGGESTED READINGS

Boland, Mary L. (1997). *Crime Victim's Guide to Justice.* Naperville, IL: Sourcebooks.

Gerber, Rudolph J. (1998). "A Judicial View of Plea Bargaining." *Criminal Law Bulletin* **34**:16–31.

Mitchell, George A. and David Dodenhoff. (1998). *The Truth about Sentencing in Wisconsin: Plea Bargaining, Punishment, and the Public Interest.* Thiensville: Wisconsin Policy Research Institute.

Nasheri, Hedieh. (1998). *Betrayal of Due Process: A Comparative Assessment of Plea Bargaining in the United States and Canada.* Lanham, MD: University Press of America.

Pohlman, H. L. (1995). *Constitutional Debate in Action: Criminal Justice.* New York: HarperCollins.

Turpin-Petrosino, Carolyn. (1993). *Exploring the Effects of Plea Bargaining on Parole Decision Making in the State of New Jersey.* Ann Arbor, MI: University Microfilms International.

Vogel, Mary E. (1999). "The Social Origins of Plea Bargaining: Conflict and the Law in the Process of State Formation, 1830–1860." *Law and Society Review* **33**:161–246.

TRIAL PROCESS AND PROCEDURES

CHAPTER

A JURY TRIAL IS IN PROGRESS. The process of jury selection is continuing. A woman, Mary Smith, is accused of murdering her husband, Tony Smith, a factory worker. Mary claims self-defense, that Tony beat her frequently and that he had threatened her life on the night she shot him with his own handgun. Tony was asleep at the time, following a night of heavy drinking. Mary has two young children. Mary is unemployed but has worked as a waitress for several years. Tony's family disliked Mary, even before she married Tony. They claimed she was "trash," partly because she had been married twice before. Tony carried a $200,000 life insurance policy for himself, naming Mary as his sole bene-ficiary. Tony had a history of spousal abuse and had previously been arrested for abusing a wife from a former marriage. Mary has no record, although depositions from others suggest that she is hot-tempered and physically abusive. Neighbors say that Mary and Tony Smith fought frequently and that the children were "scared" and often ran next door to seek protection. It was seemingly very scientific. "Let's go with the unemployed mother of three," said the defense jury consultant. "She will be sympathetic with our client, who is also an unemployed mother." "Further, let's get rid of the two men, the welder and the machinist. They probably would identify with our client's dead husband, a former factory worker." The defense attorney advised the judge, "Prospective jurors number 3 and 6 are excused. Prospective juror number 8 is acceptable." At the other end of the table, another professional jury consultant whispers to the prosecutor, "Let's excuse the woman with the three children. She will be too sympathetic with the defendant. Let's also get rid of the two women, prospective jurors 1 and 12, who are housewives." The prosecutor rose and addressed the judge. "We wish to excuse prospective jurors 1, 8, and 12, your honor." The judge says, "Very well. Prospective jurors 1, 3, 6, 8, and 12 are hereby excused. Thank you for coming. We will now have the bailiff call the next five prospective jurors." The bailiff rises and says, "Will prospective jurors 36, 37, 38, 39, and 40 please take the vacated seats in the jury box?" Five persons rise from their seats in the courtroom and take the empty seats in the jury box. By now, after five hours of jury selection, the prosecution and defense have agreed on only seven jurors for the trial. They need to select five more jurors, plus alternates. And the jury selection process continues.

WHERE SHOULD THE LINE BE DRAWN? American courts are deluged with increasing amounts of crime and are expected to process offenders by offering them fair trials. However, this is becoming increasingly difficult in certain parts of the country, especially border areas, where there are greater numbers of illegal immigrants to be prosecuted every year. The federal courts where most of these cases are heard are increasingly glutted with immigration cases. Some federal prosecutors have said that they will no longer prosecute numerous but small-level drug busts made by federal agents at international bridges and checkpoints. The Customs Service and Border Patrol make numerous drug busts every year. Many of these are low-level, involving simple possession of small quantities of illegal substances, such as marijuana or cocaine. Nevertheless, these are crimes that must be prosecuted, according to federal law. In certain federal districts, however, illegal aliens, smugglers, and undocumented immigrants are attempting to enter the United States in increasing numbers. These cases have caused the caseloads and court dockets in certain districts to quadruple. In 1999, for instance, the San Antonio– based Western District Court in Texas filed nearly 3,800 felony cases, nearly four times as many as the Dallas-based Northern District Court. U.S. Attorney Bill Blagg said, "I'd rather not be No. 1." Blagg expected to have an additional five hundred felony cases per year once district attorneys in communities such as El Paso stop prosecuting small drug busts made by the Customs Service and Border Patrol. Logistically, it takes a sizable court staff to handle the increased caseload. During 1999, there was a budget freeze, and staff vacancies caused the number of felony case filings to drop to 3,700. But with several new hires during 2000, 4,000 felony case filings were expected. One problem with increased caseloads and crowded court dockets is that the number of legal mistakes increases. In some cases, dockets are so clogged that some offenders may escape punishment altogether because of violations of their right to a speedy trial. In one case, for instance, a marijuana smuggler halved his prison sentence after he complained that a possible error occurred on the part of the district court judge who, based in San Antonio, regularly handles cases in Del Rio. The judge had left the trial in the middle of it, placing the trial in the hands of a U.S. magistrate, who was not authorized to preside in such a serious case. An increase in the number of judges, clerks, and other courthouse staff along the border has been proposed, which Congress must approve. The escalating number of cases is such, however, that the new numbers of judges may still not be enough to handle the increased caseload. Should low-level drug offenders not be prosecuted, simply because there are strains on the criminal justice system that require longer time periods to prosecute them? Should we revise the legislation that entitles all defendants to a speedy trial? How should crowded court dockets be handled so that all offenders can be punished? What do you think? (*Source:* Adapted from Maro Robbins. "Border Justice at Risk." *San Antonio Express-News,* May 25, 2000:1A, 12A.)

Introduction

This chapter about the trial process describes different types of trial systems. Many trials involve juries of one's peers. Whenever jury trials are conducted, people from the community are selected for possible jury service and form the pool from which the jurors will be selected.

Several constitutional amendments pertain to jury trials and a defendant's right to a trial. The Sixth Amendment guarantees all persons the right to a trial by jury, and the Seventh Amendment provides that the right of trial by jury shall be preserved. Finally, the Fourteenth Amendment provides that no state shall make or enforce any law that deprives citizens of their right to due process or to enjoy all privileges and immunities as citizens.

The chapter begins by distinguishing between bench and jury trials. Next, the process of selecting jurors is described in detail, commencing with the creation of a list of prospective jurors and a **screening** process known as *voir dire*. Once jury members have been selected and the trial commences, judges are bound to observe rules of criminal procedure that govern the conduct of trial proceedings. Other rules, such as rules of evidence, govern the nature of evidence that may be introduced or excluded.

Trial proceedings are also accompanied by pretrial motions that are described and explained in this chapter. Both the prosecution and defense present opening statements. The government presents its case against the defendant, followed by the defense's case. Witnesses from both sides are called in these **adversarial proceedings**. These witnesses are cross-examined by the other side to determine their veracity and reliability. When the trial is concluded, the prosecution and defense present summations or closing arguments, and the jury deliberates. Juries either reach verdicts or judgments or fail to agree. The process of jury deliberation and voting is described. The federal government and the states have different criteria that govern jury deliberations and voting for a defendant's guilt or acquittal, and these different scenarios are described. The chapter concludes with an examination of the aftermath of jury deliberations and verdicts, as well as the judge's role in sentencing.

Bench Trials and Jury Trials Contrasted

Although the jury system first appeared in the United States in 1607 under a charter granted to the Virginia Company in Jamestown by King James I, jury trials existed as early as the eleventh century in England (Simon, 1980:5). A criminal trial is an adversarial proceeding within a particular jurisdiction, where a judicial examination and determination of issues can be made, and where a criminal defendant's guilt or innocence can be decided impartially by either a judge or jury (Black, 1990:52). There are nearly 600,000 criminal trials for felonies annually (Maguire and Pastore, 2000). The number of nonjury trials is many times that figure. About eighty percent of all jury trials are civil, and twenty percent are criminal.

In U.S. district courts, for example, there were 64,956 criminal cases concluded in 1997 (Maguire and Pastore, 2000:418). Federal district judges dismissed 7,411 of these cases (11.4 percent), and about 2 percent of the defendants were acquitted by either the judge or the jury. There were 56,570 defendants convicted, or about 87.1 percent. Of these, 93.3 percent (52,789) entered guilty pleas through plea bargaining or by pleading ***nolo contendere*** or "no contest." In federal criminal trials for the 4,756 defendants whose cases actually went to trial and were not plea bargained, federal juries found 3,260 of these defendants guilty, and judges found 521 defendants guilty. Thus, nearly 80 percent of those who went to trial were convicted.

In contrast, there were 997,970 felony convictions in state criminal courts in 1998 (Maguire and Pastore, 2000:453). The proportion of convictions attributable to plea bargaining were similar to the plea-bargained convictions in U.S. district courts, exceeding 90 percent. In both state and federal courts, therefore, trials are comparatively infrequent, inasmuch as plea bargaining is used most of the time to secure convictions. But in approximately 10 percent of all criminal cases, either bench trials or jury trials are conducted.

Bench Trials

A **bench trial**, also known as a **trial by the court** or **trial by the judge**, is conducted either for petty offenses when a jury is not permitted or when defendants waive their right to a jury trial. A judge presides, hears the evidence, and then decides the case, relying on rational principles of law.

Several popular television shows, such as *Judge Judy* and *Judge Joe Brown*, depict bench trials. In cases heard by these courts, litigants or parties to the lawsuits have waived their right to a jury trial and have permitted the judge to decide their cases. In criminal courts, defendants often waive their right to a jury trial and permit the judge to decide their cases based on the evidence introduced.

One reason for waiving one's right to a jury trial is that juries are sometimes more likely than judges to convict persons for felonies (Smith and Stevens, 1984). If the crimes alleged are especially heinous or involve emotionally charged issues, defendants often opt for a bench trial instead of a jury trial because juries might be more persuaded by emotional appeals and arguments from prosecutors than by the cold, hard facts of the case. In the early 1990s, for example, the Reverend Moon, known for his indoctrination of youth known as Moonies, was on trial for income tax evasion. Because of the sensationalism associated with his religion and the impact he had on thousands of teenage followers, his defense attorney requested a bench trial, where the judge would decide his guilt or innocence (Wettstein, 1992). Other cases involving child abuse in cults have also been decided by judges rather than juries, reflecting the defense counsel's belief that judges can be more impartial than juries when evaluating the factual evidence (Wettstein, 1992). Research has also revealed that judges are more likely to impose shorter sentences as the result of a bench trial as opposed to a jury trial, although other investigations do not support this view (Bodapati, Jones, and Marquart, 1995).

From a purely practical standpoint, bench trials are more efficient than jury trials. If the process of jury selection does not occur, judges can hear evidence and decide a case in less time, because jury deliberations are avoided. For instance, in New York City, the

Misdemeanor Trial Law was enacted and took effect in 1985. Its purpose was to reduce the incarcerative punishments for certain types of misdemeanors to six months or less, meaning that jury trials for defendants charged with these misdemeanor offenses could be avoided (Dynia et al., 1987; Dynia, 1990). Case backlogs were expedited and overall case processing time greatly decreased. Interestingly, sentencing patterns among judges were the same before and after the new law went into effect.

There are several criticisms of bench trials. When judges determine guilt or innocence, they may be influenced by extralegal factors, such as race, class, ethnicity, or gender (Stolzenberg, 1993; Williams, 1995). Judges are also influenced in their decision making by their own personal feelings about the types of charged offenses. For example, some judges impose more severe sentences on convicted offenders who commit specific types of heinous offenses, such as child sexual abuse, compared with sentences they might impose for rape, aggravated assault, and murder convictions (Champion, 1988).

When judges decide cases on their own, their susceptibility to corruption is increased. Some judges become open to bribery by influential defendants. In recent years, judges at the state and federal levels have been charged with corruption and accepting bribes to render favorable decisions. **Bribery** is the giving or offering of anything to someone in a position of trust to induce that person to act dishonestly (Driscoll, 1984). In 1987, the FBI investigated 105 Pennsylvania judges because of allegations of judicial misconduct. The results of these FBI investigations led the Pennsylvania Supreme Court to temporarily suspend fifteen of these judges for bribery. In another FBI investigation, Operation Greylord, a sting operation was conducted against several corrupt judges in 1978 in Cook County, Illinois. FBI agents tapped judges' telephones, recorded conversations, and initiated bogus bribery attempts to induce judges into acting dishonestly in deciding cases. Operation Greylord was successful over the next several years in obtaining convictions against more than sixty judges for various criminal misconduct charges, including bribery (Bensinger, 1988). Recommendations made by the American Bar Association following Operation Greylord included adopting new ethical requirements for judges and attorneys and the implementation of procedural safeguards to monitor judicial discretion.

Briefly summarized, the major advantages of bench trials are as follows:

1. Case processing is expedited.
2. Cases are usually decided on the merits of the case rather than on emotionally charged appeals in the case of heinous offenses.
3. The appearance of defendants may be undesirable to jurors, but judges can usually be dissuaded from considering such extralegal factors.
4. In complex cases, judges are often in a better position to evaluate the sufficiency of evidence against the accused and make fairer judgments.
5. Judges are less persuaded by media attention given to high-profile cases, whereas juries might be unduly influenced against defendants.
6. Bench trials are usually cheaper than jury trials because they take less time to complete and require less defense attorney time.

Some of the major disadvantages of bench trials are as follows:

1. Judges may impose more severe punishments on certain defendants, depending on the crimes they have committed.
2. Judges are more susceptible to corruption when left to their own decision making.
3. Defendants waive their right to a jury trial when the defendant's situation, appearance, and emotional appeal may work to the defendant's benefit.

Jury Trials

People charged with felonies are guaranteed the right to a jury trial in the United States. This guarantee also applies to the states. The landmark case of *Duncan v. Louisiana* (1968) specified an objective criterion that restricts the right to a jury trial only to those offenses other than petty crimes for which the possible punishment of imprisonment of more than six months can be imposed. Other cases such as *Baldwin v. New York* (1970) and *Blanton v. City of North Las Vegas, Nev.* (1989) have upheld this standard.

In the last few decades, the number of trials by jury has increased for both major crimes and lesser offenses or misdemeanors (Maguire and Pastore, 2000). However, the trend is that criminal convictions are obtained increasingly through plea bargaining (McDonald, 1985). In at least one major city, the number of jury trials conducted for all felony arrests has dropped to about two percent (Hans and Vidmar, 1986:6).

The Trial Process

Trial procedures vary greatly among jurisdictions, although the federal district court format is frequently followed by judges in state and local trial courts. Figure 9.1 shows a diagram of a typical trial from the indictment stage through the judge's instructions to jury members.

FIGURE 9.1 Diagram of a Typical Trial, from Indictment through Judges' Instructions to the Jury

Indictment ⟶ Defendant's plea ⟶ Prosecution opening statement ⟶ Defense opening statement ⟶ Witnesses presented ⟶ Defense closing arguments ⟶ Prosecution closing (observations of witnesses) arguments ⟶ Judge's instructions to jurors about procedures ⟶ Judge's instructions (presumption of innocence, determination of facts, admissibility of certain types of evidence, witness credibility, reasonable inferences, standard of proof) about verdicts ⟶ Final verdict ⟶ Defendent discharged if acquitted, or defendant sentenced if convicted

U.S. Supreme Court Cases about the Right to Jury Trials

Duncan v. Louisiana, 391 U.S. 145 (1968). States must provide jury trials for defendants charged with serious offenses. Duncan was convicted in a bench trial of simple battery in a Louisiana court. The crime was punishable as a misdemeanor, with two years' imprisonment and a fine of $300. In Duncan's case, he was sentenced to only sixty days and a fine of $150. He appealed, saying that he demanded a jury trial and none was provided for him. The U.S. Supreme Court agreed with Duncan, saying that a crime with a potential punishment of two years is a *serious crime,* despite the sentence of sixty days imposed. Thus, for serious crimes, under the Sixth Amendment, Duncan is entitled to a jury trial.

Baldwin v. New York, 399 U.S. 66 (1970). Baldwin was arrested and prosecuted for "jostling" (pickpocketing), a class A misdemeanor punishable by a maximum term of imprisonment of one year in New York. New York law prescribed at the time that this was a petty offense not entitling a defendant to a jury trial. Baldwin asked for and was denied a jury trial. The U.S. Supreme Court heard Baldwin's appeal and declared that petty offenses carrying a one-year incarcerative term are *serious* in that jury trials are required if requested. Specifically, the wording of Baldwin attaches great significance to the months of imprisonment constituting *serious* time. The U.S. Supreme Court said that a potential sentence in excess of six months' imprisonment is sufficiently severe by itself to take an offense out of the category of "petty" as respects a defendant's right to jury trial (at 1886, 1891). The U.S. Supreme Court overturned Baldwin's conviction and sent the case back to the lower court for a jury trial for Baldwin.

Blanton v. City of North Las Vegas, Nev., 489 U.S. 538 (1989). Melvin Blanton was charged with DUI (driving under the influence). Blanton requested but was denied a jury trial by the North Las Vegas, Nevada, Municipal Court. In Nevada, the maximum sentence for a DUI conviction was six months in jail, and the maximum fine was $1,000. Blanton's driver's license was suspended for ninety days, and he was ordered to pay court costs and perform forty-eight hours of community service while dressed in attire identifying him as convicted of a DUI offense. Blanton appealed, contending that he was entitled to a jury trial because the offense, he alleged, was "serious" and not "petty." The U.S. Supreme Court considered his appeal and upheld his DUI bench trial conviction, saying that the most relevant criteria for determining the seriousness of an offense is the severity of the maximum authorized penalty fixed by the legislature. Thus, any offense carrying a maximum prison term of six months or less, as does Nevada's DUI law, is presumed to be petty unless it can be shown that any additional statutory penalties are so severe that they might distinguish the offense as "serious." A further proclamation by the U.S. Supreme Court was that the $1,000 fine did not approach an earlier standard of $5,000 established by Congress in its 1982 definition of "petty" offense, Title 18, U.S.C. Section 1. Thus, the *Blanton* case clearly affirms the earlier holding in *Baldwin* that a defendant is entitled to a jury trial only if the possible incarceration is beyond six months.

Pretrial Motions

Before the start of court proceedings, attorneys for the government or the defense may make **pretrial motions**. Pretrial motions are **motions in limine**, and one purpose of such motions is to avoid potentially serious or embarrassing situations that may occur later during the trial, such as the attempt by either side to introduce evidence that may be considered prejudicial, inflammatory, or irrelevant. In a brutal murder case, for example, it may be considered inflammatory for the prosecution to introduce photographs of a dismembered body or a mutilated corpse. The jury may be emotionally persuaded to interpret the photographs as conclusive evidence that the defendant committed the crime. Such photographs might also enhance sentencing severity, if additional and over-whelming evidence exists of the defendant's guilt.

In some instances, a defense attorney will make a **motion to suppress** certain evidence from being introduced because it was illegally seized by police at the time the defendant was arrested (Bell, 1983). This **exclusionary rule** provides that evidence obtained in violation of the privileges guaranteed citizens by the United States Constitution must be excluded at the trial (Black, 1990:564). Generally, any evidence seized by law enforcement officers as the result of an illegal search would be considered inadmissible in court later. Such evidence would fall within the exclusionary rule and would be excluded as evidence against the accused. The leading case in the adoption of the exclusionary rule is *Mapp v. Ohio* (1961). This case involved an illegal search of Dollree Mapp's premises by police officers in Cleveland, Ohio, who were searching for a suspect in a bombing incident and believed he was hiding in Mapp's home. They entered her home without a warrant and proceeded to search it. They found nothing incriminating, but in their search they discovered crude pencil sketches in an old trunk in Mapp's basement. They considered these drawings obscene, and they charged Mapp with violating a Cleveland obscenity ordinance. She was subsequently convicted of possessing obscene materials.

Later, the U.S. Supreme Court overturned Mapp's conviction because of the illegal search, and they declared that the seizure of the "evidence" by police was unlawful and therefore inadmissible against Mapp. Without the evidence, there was no case against Mapp. The U.S. Supreme Court took that particular opportunity to chide the police officers who conducted the illegal search of Mapp's premises. They warned police officers that in future cases such misconduct would not be tolerated. Thus, the exclusionary rule was subsequently interpreted by police officers as "tying their hands" and limiting their investigative powers, although the real reason for the rule was to prevent police misconduct related to warrantless searches.

In another leading case, this one involving narcotics sales, a Chinese suspect, Wong Sun, was arrested by police, charged, and convicted of violating federal narcotics laws (*Wong Sun v. United States,* 1963). Earlier, federal agents had acted on a tip and, without a warrant, broke down the door of James Wah Toy's dwelling and arrested him. They searched his home for narcotics but found none. But later under questioning Toy told police that Johnny Yee was selling narcotics. Yee was arrested, and narcotics were taken from his home. Yee, in turn, implicated Wong Sun, who was also arrested. All of the subsequent action against Wong Sun stemmed from an original unlawful search of James

Wah Toy's premises and the illegally obtained statements from Toy when he was immediately arrested.

The U.S. Supreme Court overturned Wong Sun's conviction and declared that the statements implicating Wong Sun in narcotics sales were **fruits of the poisonous tree**. The fruits of the poisonous tree doctrine provides that evidence derived from an illegal search or an illegal interrogation is inadmissible against a defendant because it has been tainted (Green, 1990). If the tree is poison, then the fruit from the tree will also be poison. Similarly, if a search is illegal and evidence is seized, then the "fruits" of that search or the seized evidence will also be considered illegally seized. Such illegally seized evidence will be excluded later against the accused in court.

Often, a defense attorney will file **motions**, such as a **motion to dismiss**, which is a motion attacking the prosecutor's evidence as insufficient or to signify the absence of a key prosecution witness upon which a conviction depends. Such pretrial motions are ordinarily conducted outside the presence of the jury. The judge rules on these motions, and the trial proceeds. A summary of the more frequently used pretrial motions follows.

1. **Motion for dismissal of charges** (motion seeking to dismiss the case against an accused based on the failure of the prosecution to state a sufficient case to be prosecuted; alleges critical weaknesses in prosecution's case)

2. **Motion for discovery** (motion to obtain and examine certain documents and evidence collected by the prosecution and the list of the witnesses to be called)

3. **Motion for a bill of particulars** (motion to require the prosecutor to furnish a written statement of charges, outlining the crime(s) alleged, the time and place of crime, and other information)

4. **Motion for continuance** (motion to delay trial proceedings, usually in order to interview additional witnesses and collect additional evidence)

5. **Motion for severance** (if more than one defendant is charged in a conspiracy or crime in which several defendants are involved, attorneys for each client may wish to separate the cases so that each defendant can be tried independently to avoid any conflict of interest, whereby one defendant may incriminate other defendants)

6. **Motion for suppression of evidence** (motion to exclude incriminating evidence against the accused, such as any evidence illegally seized from the defendant's premises in violation of Fourth Amendment provisions against unreasonable searches and seizures; in the Denver, Colorado, federal trial of Timothy McVeigh and Terry Nichols, charged with bombing the Oklahoma City, Oklahoma, federal building in 1995, for example, several incriminating statements made by Nichols and a receipt for bomb materials with McVeigh's fingerprint on it were the subject of a motion to suppress by their defense attorney)

7. **Motion for determination of competency** (motion to question whether the defendant is competent or sufficiently sane to stand trial; an examination by a psychiatrist might be requested before the trial proceeds)

8. **Motion for a change of venue** (the trial of Timothy McVeigh for the bombing of the Murrah Federal Building in Oklahoma City in 1995 was moved from Oklahoma City to Denver, Colorado, where it was believed that a more impartial jury could be selected, which would be less prejudiced toward McVeigh than an Oklahoma jury)

9. **Motion for intention to provide alibi** (motion to demonstrate that the defendant did not commit the offense alleged because the defendant was elsewhere when the crime was committed)

10. **Motion for summary judgment** (motion requesting the judge to order a judgment for the defendant based on the insufficiency of evidence presented by the prosecution to sustain a conviction)

Opening Arguments

Unless both the prosecution and defense attorneys agree to waive their opening statements, the prosecutor makes an opening statement to the jury. Usually, this statement includes the state's theory about the case and why the defendant is guilty. Often, prosecutors tell the jury what they intend to prove and attempt to persuade them to consider the importance of certain kinds of evidence to be presented later. This outline or summary of the nature of the case is to advise the jury of the facts to be relied on and the issues involved (Black, 1990:1091).

The defense attorney is also permitted to make an opening statement. The defense is given considerable latitude by the court in addressing the jury. Basically, the defense's statement is intended to undermine the state's case against the defendant and to indicate that, in the final analysis, the accused should be acquitted of all charges.

The State Presents Its Case

The prosecution begins its case by calling **witnesses** and presenting evidence that a crime has been committed and that the defendant committed it. Each witness is **sworn in** by a court officer. Being sworn in means that a witness is obliged under the law to be truthful in all subsequent testimony given. This stage is termed **direct examination**. Direct examination is the question-answer exchange between the prosecutor and the prosecutor's witnesses or between the defense and the defense's witnesses.

The defense has the right to challenge any question asked a witness by the prosecution on direct examination. Usually, defense attorneys raise **objections** to certain questions, or they may object to an answer given by a witness. The presiding judge rules on such objections and either sustains or grants them or overrules or denies them. The same option is available to defense attorneys whenever evidence is introduced by the prosecution. Objections by either side may be raised at any time, and the judge sustains or overrules these objections. When the defense presents witnesses, prosecutors may also raise objections for the same purposes. Sometimes following an adverse ruling on an objection by the prosecution or defense, the prosecutor or defense counsel will say, "Exception." The judge will usually respond, "Exception noted." Although some older attorneys continue to use this term, this use of "exception" is outmoded in contemporary courtrooms because whenever a motion is denied or sustained, this ends further dialogue about the motion. More than anything else, the term is intended to annoy the judge because it is entirely unnecessary. In essence, it is an insulting remark and is intended by either side to chide the judge for whatever ruling is made about the particular motion.

The **Federal Rules of Evidence** contain explicit guidelines for judges and attorneys to follow regarding which types of evidence are admissible and which are inadmissible (Saltzburg and Redden, 1994). These are very elaborate and technical rules. If they are not followed by any of the major participants in the trial proceeding, such rule violations could be the basis for overturning a guilty verdict on appeal to a higher court. The prosecution is also entitled to appeal a not guilty verdict on similar grounds. If certain evidentiary rules were violated, the verdict in favor of the defendant could be reversed on appeal. This scenario actually occurred in the case of Stacey Koon and Laurence Powell, Los Angeles police officers who were convicted in a federal district court in the Rodney King beating. The federal judge was especially lenient in sentencing Koon and Powell, and the U.S. Attorney's Office appealed the lenient sentences to the Ninth Circuit Court of Appeals, which overruled the federal judge. Later, attorneys for Koon and Powell appealed the Ninth Circuit ruling to the U.S. Supreme Court, which rendered a mixed opinion in the matter. The point is that either side may appeal a judge's rulings or conduct to a higher court.

The Right of Cross-Examination

After the prosecution has questioned a witness, the defense has the right to ask that same witness questions. This is known as **cross-examination**. The right to cross-examine witnesses is not only a constitutional right but also illustrates the adversarial nature of the trial system. The defense attorney attempts to impeach the credibility of the prosecutor's witnesses or to undermine their veracity or truthfulness to the jury (Graham, 1985). Sometimes, defense attorneys can use prosecution witnesses to their own advantage and elicit statements from them that are favorable to the defendant.

REDIRECT EXAMINATION. Once testimony has been given by a witness from either side, that witness may be cross-examined by the opposition. Once such cross-examination has been completed, additional questioning of the witness may be done by the side that called the witness initially. This questioning is called **redirect examination**. The purpose of redirect examination is to clarify certain issues that may be confusing to juries or to cause the witness to elaborate on points the other side may have introduced that appear to be incriminating. In contrast with the direct examination, the lawyer conducting the cross-examination is allowed to proceed in a leading fashion. Typically, the lawyer during cross-examination uses short, clear statements that cannot reasonably be denied and that ultimately support the lawyer's version of events. Questions during cross-examination do not seek to disclose new information. Rather, this is an opportunity for the attorney to direct the testimony in support of the position of the questioning party.

For instance, a witness may testify on behalf of the defense in a case where the defendant, Mr. X, a noted sports figure, claimed to have cut his hand *after* a murder had been committed in Denver, Colorado, where the unknown assailant had been injured on the hand. Some blood at the crime scene does not appear to be the victim's blood. In fact, investigators suspect that the blood is from the perpetrator, probably from a cut sustained to his hand from a knife wound during the murder. However, the time interval is such that the defendant claims to have cut his hand on the day following the murder when the unknown assailant's injuries occurred. The defendant claims, for instance, that he boarded an airplane on the evening of the terrible murder. Investigators have fixed the time of death of the deceased at about 10 P.M. At 11:30 P.M., it is known that the defendant boarded an airplane and flew to New York. As a passenger on the airline, the defendant sat next to another passenger. The passenger and the defendant conversed. The following day, the defendant was notified of the murder and suspected of it. He flew back to Denver on another airline. He had a cut on his hand. The defendant claimed that when he learned of the death of the victim the following day, he smashed his hand down on a table in his hotel room while holding a glass. The glass shattered, and the pieces cut his fingers. While on the return flight to Denver, the defendant sat next to another passenger, and they conversed throughout the trip.

On the witness stand, the passenger who sat next to Mr. X on the first flight is called as a witness for the defendant. The witness is called to confirm that Mr. X did not have a cut hand or fingers later in the evening, after the murder had occurred. The witness is asked some questions by the defense counsel on direct examination.

DEFENSE: Did you sit next to Mr. X on Flight 161 to New York on the evening of February 26th?

WITNESS: Yes.

DEFENSE: Did you have a conversation with Mr. X during this flight?

WITNESS: Yes.

DEFENSE: Did you notice whether there were any cuts on Mr. X's hands while you were talking with him?

WITNESS: I didn't see any cuts on Mr. X's hands.

DEFENSE: Did you know Mr. X by reputation when you were sitting next to him?

WITNESS: Yes, I did.

DEFENSE: Did you make any special requests of Mr. X?

WITNESS: Yes, I asked him to autograph a pad of paper in my pocket.

DEFENSE: You asked Mr. X for his autograph?

WITNESS: Yes, I did.

DEFENSE: Did he sign something for you?

WITNESS: Yes, he signed the paper pad.

DEFENSE: Where exactly did he sign this pad, you know, did he sign it while holding it in his lap or did he write on some surface?

WITNESS: He wrote his autograph on the pull-out tray in front of my seat. He leaned over and signed my paper pad on my pull-out tray.

DEFENSE: The pull-out tray on *your* seat. OK. And therefore, this gave you a good opportunity to look closely at his hands?

WITNESS: Yes, it did.

DEFENSE: And you didn't see or notice any cuts on his hands or fingers?

WITNESS: No, I didn't.

DEFENSE: And the overhead lights were on when he gave you his autograph?

WITNESS: Yes, the lights were on.

DEFENSE: And you had a clear view of *both* of his hands?

WITNESS: Yes, he used one hand to hold the pad and the other to sign his name.

[The prosecutor takes over and cross-examines the witness.]

PROSECUTION: Sir, could Mr. X have been sitting in such a way so as to hide his hands from you?

WITNESS: I don't think so. We talked a lot that evening, and he was quite animated, using his hands.

PROSECUTION: But you cannot say for certain that there were *no* cuts on his hands when you were talking with him?

WITNESS: No, I can't say for certain.

PROSECUTION: And so if there *were* cuts, it is possible that you just didn't happen to see them that evening.

WITNESS: That's right. I didn't see any cuts when he gave me his autograph, but maybe I just didn't notice them.

[The defense *redirects*]

DEFENSE: Well, you say that you can't say for sure that there were no cuts on Mr. X's hands. Is that right?

WITNESS: Yes, that's right.

DEFENSE: But suppose there was a deep gash, or perhaps even several deep gashes on Mr. X's hands? If such gashes were there, they would probably be bloody. Perhaps you would notice, for instance, if Mr. X was wearing some sort of covering to protect such cuts if they were there?

WITNESS: I didn't see any bandages.

DEFENSE: But if there was a deep cut, and if it had been made a short time before Mr. X boarded the plane, then you would probably have noticed that, wouldn't you?

WITNESS: Sure, I probably would have noticed that. We were sitting side by side in adjacent seats. Lights were on overhead, and I could see both of his hands.

DEFENSE: And you saw no cuts?

WITNESS: No, I saw no cuts on his hands. I think I would have seen them if there had been cuts there.

DEFENSE: Was there any blood on the paper pad where he signed his autograph?

WITNESS: No. There was no blood on the paper pad. Just his autograph.

Now, suppose we have the second witness on the stand, the one who sat next to Mr. X on his return flight from New York back to Denver. The next witness, also called by the defense, is asked the following questions.

DEFENSE: Were you a passenger on Flight 215 from New York to Denver on the day of February twenty-seventh?

WITNESS: Yes, I was.

DEFENSE: And who did you sit next to while on the airplane, if anyone?

WITNESS: I sat next to Mr. X.

DEFENSE: Did you have a conversation with Mr. X while you flew from New York to Denver?

WITNESS: Yes, we talked with one another.

DEFENSE: Did you notice Mr. X's hands while you were talking to him?

WITNESS: Yes, I did.

DEFENSE: Was there anything unusual or extraordinary about them that you recall?

WITNESS: Yes, there was a big bandage on one of his fingers on his right hand. It looked like it was seeping with blood.

DEFENSE: You say the wound was seeping with blood?

WITNESS: That's the way it looked to me.

DEFENSE: Did Mr. X tell you how he received that wound?

WITNESS: Yes, he said he cut it on a glass in his hotel room.

DEFENSE: Did he say *when* he cut his hand?

WITNESS: Yes. He said he cut it that morning, after he received an upsetting telephone call.

[The prosecution cross-examines the second witness.]

PROSECUTION: When you saw this wound, you don't know precisely *when* the wound was made, do you?

WITNESS: Mr. X says it happened that morning, a few hours before the flight to Denver.

PROSECUTION: Yes, but you don't really know for sure *when* that cut was made, do you?

WITNESS: No, I don't.

PROSECUTION: It could have been the night before, couldn't it, maybe even around 10:00 P.M. at night?

WITNESS: I suppose so.

PROSECUTION: So you really don't know *when* the cut was made, and that it could perhaps have been made the night before, is that right?

WITNESS: That's right.

[The defense redirects.]

DEFENSE: Did you actually *see* the cut on Mr. X's hand or just the bandage covering it?

WITNESS: I saw the cut. He changed the bandage once, just before we landed.

DEFENSE: When you saw the cut, how did it look to you?

WITNESS: What do you mean?

DEFENSE: Did it look like an old cut or a new one?

WITNESS: It looked like a cut that was made fairly recently.

DEFENSE: If a cut like the one you saw had been made the night before you actually saw it, would it still be bleeding like that, as you have described?

WITNESS: I don't think so. It probably would have healed some. I don't know.

DEFENSE: And so you are saying that the cut looked entirely consistent with Mr. X's explanation that he had just cut his hand on some glass in his hotel room, is that it?

WITNESS: Yes, that's it.

As can be seen from this exchange, each side, the defense and prosecution, attempt to use these two witnesses in ways that work to their particular advantage. The prosecution wants the jury to think that the cut occurred when Mr. X, believed to be the murderer, used a knife to kill the victim. The defense wants to show that there were no hand or finger cuts when Mr. X left Denver late on the evening of the murder, but that a cut *was* there when Mr. X was seen by others the following day. If it can be established that Mr. X's hand cut occurred the day following the murder, then it could not have been made when the murder was committed. The prosecution wants the jury to believe that the cut occurred during the murder, not afterward. Both defense and prosecution are permitted to engage in redirect and recross-examinations of each witness until they feel that they have adequately made their respective points. They are shaping and forming versions of events that make a case for or against Mr. X. We might even consider redirect and recross-examinations as refinements of witness testimony, to know for sure what the witness saw or did not see. The jury listens and decides which version seems most believable.

RECROSS-EXAMINATION. Although some people consider **recross-examination** as prolonging an otherwise long trial, each side is entitled to recross-examine witnesses and recall witnesses to the stand for further questioning. This tactic is particularly important whenever new evidence is revealed from other witnesses. Judges may abbreviate extensive cross-examinations and recross-examinations if they believe that attorneys are merely covering previous information disclosed in earlier testimony.

IMPEACHING WITNESSES. Impeachment means to call into question the truthfulness or credibility of a witness. If either the prosecutor or the defense attorney can demonstrate that a particular witness may be lying or is otherwise unreliable, then that witness's testimony is called into question. Jury members may not believe such witnesses and the evidentiary information they provide for or against defendants. Of course, defendants themselves are subject to impeachment if they testify.

There are several ways defense attorneys can impeach a witness. Attorneys can obtain inconsistent testimony from the witness or can get the witness to admit confusion over certain facts recalled. Attorneys can also introduce evidence of the untruthfulness of the witness based on previous information acquired through investigative sources. Perhaps a witness previously has been fired from a company because of embezzlement. Embezzlement is one form of dishonesty, and jurors can make an inference that witnesses who were dishonest in their employment may not be telling the truth on the witness stand, even though they may be telling the truth in the present case. Of course, when the defense presents its witnesses, the prosecution has the same cross-examination rights and can make similar attempts to impeach the credibility of the witnesses called in the defendant's behalf.

Eyewitnesses and Expert Witnesses

In criminal law, expert testimony is often solicited (Penrod, Fulero, and Cutler, 1995). Experts can testify and identify blood samples, firearms, and ballistics reports; comment on a defendant's state of mind or sanity; and provide opinions about any number of other pieces of evidence that link the defendant to the crime. By the same token, defense attorneys can introduce expert testimony of their own to rebut or counter the testimony of the prosecutions' experts.

Expert witnesses are used by either side to interpret the meaningfulness of evidence presented by either the prosecution or defense (Ross, Read, and Toglia, 1994). Expert witnesses have extensive training and experience in matters of fact that may be introduced as evidence in a trial. Their opinions are given more weight than opinions of laypeople who do not have such training and experience. Complex issues or topics are clarified for jurors whenever expert testimony is presented (Penrod, Fulero, and Cutler, 1995).

Being an expert witness involves certain hazards or risks, however. Some expert witnesses have reported that they were harassed by defendants or their attorneys outside the courtroom. Some expert witnesses, particularly forensic psychiatrists who might testify as to a defendant's sanity or criminal motives, have reported actually being physically assaulted or threatened with harm (Read, Yuille, and Tollestrup, 1992). In a survey of 408 members of the American Academy of Psychiatry and the Law (representing 48 percent of the largest U.S. organization of forensic psychiatrists), 42 percent of the respondents reported harassment of some fashion from defendants, plaintiffs, victims, the press, and even from judges (D. Miller, 1985). A majority of cases involving harassment involved criminal cases or where the insanity defense was raised.

Eyewitnesses are also of significant value to both prosecutors and defense attorneys (Davies et al., 1995). They can provide opinions and interpretations of events they

SUSPECTED ZODIAC SLAYER CHARGED AND EXPERT WITNESSES TO TESTIFY

The Case of Heriberto Seda

A man police dubbed as the *Zodiac killer* was arrested and charged with murdering three people and attempting to murder another. For several years, New York City residents had been fearful of being the next victim of the Zodiac killer. Apparently, persons were killed at random, according to their astrological sign. If you're a Cancer, you're a target. If you're a Leo, you're a target. If you're a Gemini, you're a target. It made no difference, at least to the Zodiac killer.

Seda, twenty-six, was arrested after various notes and symbols he had written matched those possessed by police officers after the Zodiac killer mailed taunting messages to police. The notes berated the police methods used to apprehend the Zodiac killer, and they indicated that police could never catch him. Four men were shot in 1990—a Scorpio, a Gemini, a Taurus, and a Cancer. One was wounded, and the others died from sniper fire. The shootings always occurred on Thursdays and twenty-one days apart. A fifty-detective task force was created to catch the Zodiac killer. Police suspect that Seda is also responsible for four other Zodiac killer–related crimes in the boroughs of Queens, Brooklyn, and Manhattan. Seda was arrested following a police standoff, and he surrendered numerous weapons, some of which were linked with the murders. Seda also confessed to the crimes.

No doubt, expert witnesses will be very instrumental in the case against Seda. Some will testify about the markings on bullets fired from particular weapons. Other experts will testify about DNA samples taken from envelopes Seda sent to others, envelopes on which his saliva residue was found. DNA matches have been found between the Zodiac killer's saliva left on letters mailed to police and on letters known to have been mailed by Seda to some of his friends and family.

Source: Adapted from Associated Press, "Suspect Charged in Zodiac Slayings." *Minot* (N.D.) *Daily News,* June 22, 1996:A2.

actually experienced, and they can provide accounts of the defendant's involvement in the crime alleged. But some researchers have explored the impact of eyewitness testimony on jury verdicts and have suggested strongly that any such testimony should be corroborated with additional supportive evidence to be more fully reliable (J. Jackson, 1986).

A major problem faced by prosecutors is obtaining the cooperation of victims or witnesses to testify in court about pertinent information they might have about a particular case (Davis, 1983). The courtroom is a frightful experience for many people, and the thought of enduring questioning on the witness stand is not a desirable one. In an effort to allay fears of victim-witnesses, various victim-witness assistance programs have been initiated, particularly by prosecutors and courts in various jurisdictions (Finn and Lee, 1985).

Victim-witness assistance programs are services that are intended to explain court procedures to witnesses and to notify them of court dates (Finn and Lee, 1985). Additionally, such programs permit victim-witnesses to feel more comfortable with the criminal justice system generally. One particularly important function performed by such programs is to assist witnesses in providing better and clearer evidence in criminal prosecutions, with the result of more convictions (Finn and Lee, 1985).

Children As Eyewitnesses. One area that has received much attention in recent years is the reliability of the testimony of child witnesses, especially in cases alleging child sexual abuse (Dent and Flin, 1992; McGough, 1994). The scientific study of child witnesses by psychologists in the United States began during the early 1900s, and some researchers have concluded that children are the most dangerous witnesses of all (McGough, 1994). A child's memory of an especially traumatic event such as a rape or homicide is often distorted, and their recall or true impression of what actually occurred is often flawed in one respect or another (Dent and Flin, 1992; Mason, 1991).

A large number of child victims of sexual abuse are under age twelve, and nearly a third are under age six (McGough, 1994). By 1994, half of all states had adopted special hearsay exceptions when children are giving testimony about being abused, however. Of primary concern to the judge and other participants in the courtroom scene is the ability of children to distinguish between real and imagined events (Davies et al., 1995; Whitcomb et al., 1994).

In addition to the obvious trauma of being asked about emotionally disturbing events such as sexual molestation, the parents of sexually abused children are often reluctant to allow their children to testify in court. Some have suggested that children be permitted to testify in an isolated location away from the actual courtroom and that their testimony should be monitored through closed-circuit television (Whitcomb et al., 1994). Under the Sixth Amendment, however, defendants are entitled to a face-to-face confrontation with their accusers (Ceci and Bruck, 1995; Zaragoza et al., 1995). Thus, at least for the present, it would seem that the use of closed-circuit television in cases such as child sexual abuse will need to be assessed further by the U.S. Supreme Court before it is approved on a national scale.

At the conclusion of the state's case against the defendant, the defense attorney may make a motion for a **directed verdict of acquittal**. A directed verdict of acquittal requests the judge to dismiss the case against the defendant because the prosecution has not proved the defendant's guilt beyond a reasonable doubt. Thus, the defense believes that their client has not been proved guilty and should be freed. No evidence exists to indicate how often such a verdict is requested, but such a motion is probably made often in criminal cases. It does not cost the defense anything to make such a motion, and on occasion the motion may be granted. In most instances, if the case is being tried by a jury, the presiding judge is reluctant to grant such a motion. The jury is charged with the responsibility of determining the defendant's guilt or innocence. Judges may grant such a motion, however, if they believe that the state has failed to present a compelling case of the defendant's guilt. If the case is a high-profile one, such as the trial of O. J. Simpson, the judge is unlikely to grant such a motion. Such a motion was made in Simpson's trial in early 1996 following the prosecution's case, but presiding Judge Lance Ito denied it.

The Defense and Summation

The defense attorney presents all relevant evidence and calls all witnesses who have relevant testimony favorable to the defendant. The prosecutor may object to the introduction of certain witnesses or to any kind of evidence the defense intends to introduce. Defendants choose whether to testify in their own behalf. Their right not to testify is guaranteed under the Fifth Amendment of the U.S. Constitution, and no defendants may be compelled to give testimony against themselves. Evidence from defendants themselves may be self-incriminating, and the Fifth Amendment provides for the right against self-incrimination. Of course, if a defendant does not testify, the jury may believe that the defendant has something to hide. It is difficult to make juries understand that defendants are merely exercising their right not to testify under the Fifth Amendment and that no inferences should be made by jurors if defendants elect not to testify on their own behalf. It is the responsibility of the state—that is, the prosecution—to prove the case against the defendant beyond a reasonable doubt. The defendant is entitled to a presumption of innocence until guilt is established according to the "beyond a reasonable doubt" standard. The judge is charged with the responsibility of instructing the jury in this regard and acquainting them with the Fifth Amendment protections extended to defendants under the law.

Some people erroneously claim that if a jury finds a defendant not guilty and votes for acquittal, this decision does not necessarily mean that the defendant is innocent; that is, the status of being found "not guilty" is not the equivalent of the status of being acquitted of criminal charges. But this erroneous belief undermines the fundamental principles of the U.S. Constitution and the rights it conveys to all citizens, regardless of how guilty they may appear to the public or the media. Therefore, if we presume correctly that a defendant is innocent until proved guilty in a court of law, beyond a reasonable doubt, then an acquittal causes the presumption of innocence to remain unchanged. For instance, Fred Graham, a former attorney and expert commentator for *Court TV*, accepted a telephone call from an interested viewer following the O. J. Simpson trial. The caller posed the following question: "Mr. Graham, the fact that the jury found Simpson not guilty doesn't mean that Simpson is innocent, does it?" Graham answered, "That's right, it doesn't mean he is innocent." Graham was clearly wrong in his response to the anonymous caller. The presumption of innocence continues as part of our right to due process throughout a trial and its conclusion, unless a guilty verdict is declared by the jury. In the eyes of the law, therefore, O. J. Simpson continues to be viewed as innocent of the crimes previously alleged.

Interestingly, two quite different books appeared in 1996 following the verdict in the murder trial of sports figure O. J. Simpson. A work by Ron Huff, Arye Rattner, and Edward Sagarin, *Convicted but Innocent: Wrongful Conviction and Public Policy,* and another work, *Guilty: The Collapse of Criminal Justice* by Harold J. Rothwax, both address fundamentally different views of jury voting. Jury decisions may result in conviction of innocent persons, and jury decisions may result in acquittals of guilty persons. Rothwax, a former judge, suggests that current laws and procedures handicap the police and prosecutors from apprehending and convicting criminals and that they prevent the courts from resolving the primary question of whether the accused committed the crime. He explores various drastic changes in the laws so that the ends of justice might be served more effectively, through more frequent convictions and fewer reversals of convictions on technical grounds. The work by Huff and his colleagues examines various wrongful convictions, where innocent persons were convicted anyway, despite the fact that they were innocent. At present, we acknowledge that our legal system is flawed, and it probably will always be flawed.

Movies have portrayed various interesting scenarios of a guilty offender who is convicted of murder but later has his conviction overturned because evidence is found implicating another offender of the murder. The other offender has murdered several people, and so it is believed that he is fully capable of murdering one more person. The fact is that the second murderer has entered into an agreement with the first murderer. The agreement is that the second murderer wants his parents killed, and the first murderer (who really is a murderer) agrees to kill the second murderer's parents if the first murderer is freed. Therefore, a plot unfolds where evidence is suddenly discovered that leads to freeing the first murderer. Although this convoluted plot seems peculiar, it is no sillier than imagining scenarios where guilty suspects are acquitted and innocent suspects are convicted. In many murder cases, only the real murderers know for sure. Although these two books offer criticism of the criminal justice system that allows such events to occur, there is no foolproof way of preventing their occurrence, no matter what reforms are implemented.

CAN PROSECUTORS CRITICIZE DEFENDANTS FOR NOT TESTIFYING IN THEIR OWN BEHALF? The prosecution is forbidden from mentioning a defendant's refusal to testify to the jury (*Griffin v. California*, 1965). For instance, if the prosecutor said, "Ladies and gentlemen of the jury, if this defendant were innocent, he would get up here on the stand and say so," this statement would be improper, and the judge would order the statement stricken from the record. In fact, such an utterance by the prosecutor may cause the judge to declare a mistrial. Both prosecutors and defense attorneys alike are bound by legal ethics to comply with court rules when presenting a case or representing a client in the courtroom. But occasionally, some attorneys engage in unethical conduct, either deliberately or inadvertently. Sometimes, such conduct will result in the judge declaring a mistrial, and the case will have to proceed from the beginning in front of a new jury.

Ordinarily, judges give the jury instructions when it is ready to deliberate and decide the case. These instructions include statements about the rights of the accused and whether any inferences, either positive or negative, may be drawn from an accused's right not to testify in her or his own behalf. The jury is instructed not to consider the fact that a defendant chose not to testify. One reason for this admonition is to remind the jury that it is the prosecutor's burden to show, beyond a reasonable doubt, that the accused is guilty of the crime(s) alleged. It is not the responsibility of the defendants to prove themselves *innocent* to the jury. Although these admonitions may seem self-evident, more than a few jurors have been influenced by a defendant's refusal to testify. We cannot possibly know what impact this refusal to testify will have on jury decision making.

Each side is permitted a **summation** at the conclusion of all evidence presented. Ordinarily, defense attorneys present the final oral argument on behalf of their client. This argument is followed by the closing argument of the prosecuting attorney. Sometimes, with court consent, prosecutors may present a portion of their closing argument, followed by the closing argument of the defense, followed by the remainder of the prosecutor's closing argument. In short, the prosecutor gets in the final remarks to the jury. There is a very good reason for this order of summation. Because the burden of proving guilt beyond a reasonable doubt is so difficult, prosecutors are given the last word. It is assumed that if these prosecutorial remarks are the last words heard by the jury, besides the instructions they receive from presiding judges, then their subsequent deliberations will be tainted initially by these prosecutorial remarks. During jury deliberations, however, a critical examination of all evidence introduced will lead the jury to one conclusion or the other. If the prosecutor has failed to carry the burden of proof in the case, the jury will vote to acquit the defendant.

Jury Deliberations

After the prosecution and defense have presented their final arguments, the judge instructs the jury on the procedures it must follow in reaching a verdict, and the jury retires to the jury room to consider the evidence and arrive at a verdict. The judges' instructions to the jury often include a recitation of the charges against the defendant, a listing of the elements of the crime that the prosecution must prove beyond a reasonable doubt, and a charge for jurors to carefully weigh and consider the evidence and testimony of witnesses.

Again, depending on whether the case is in federal district court or in a state jurisdiction, the jury must either be unanimous or comply with the particular state rules governing jury verdicts. Federal juries must be unanimous. If a jury of twelve fails to agree, a mistrial will be declared by the federal judge. If one jury member becomes ill, an eleven-member federal jury, with court approval, is acceptable, and it must render a unanimous verdict as well. In states such as Louisiana and Oregon, the particular state rules governing jury verdicts have approved 9–3 or 10–2 majority votes for verdicts of guilty to be rendered. In six-person juries, the jury must reach a unanimous decision, according to the U.S. Supreme Court (*Burch v. Louisiana*, 1979).

Jury deliberations and the decision-making process of arriving at particular verdicts have also been targeted for study by social scientists (Kerr, 1994; Kerr and MacCoun, 1985). The primary difficulty confronting those interested in studying jury deliberation processes is that such deliberations are conducted in secret. Some investigators have participated as actual jury members in their respective jurisdictions, and the insight gained through such experiences has been instrumental in preparing defense attorneys to present convincing cases to juries on behalf of their clients (Greene, 1986).

Jury deliberations have often been the subject of feature films and novels. The 1957 drama *Twelve Angry Men*, starring Henry Fonda, epitomized the emotion and anger of jurors in a murder case. In that film, Fonda was the lone juror voting "not guilty" against the other eleven "guilty" votes. The remainder of the film describes the jury's attempt to convince Fonda that he was wrong. As it turned out, Fonda convinced the other jurors that *they* were wrong, and the defendant was acquitted. A 1996 novel by author-lawyer John Grisham, *The Runaway Jury,* depicts in detail jury deliberations, with an incredible amount of interplay among jurors and the ease with which jurors' opinions are changed by particularly dominant jury members.

Jury deliberations such as those in *Twelve Angry Men* are not uncommon (Simon, 1980). Jurors who differ in their estimation of the value of particular evidence attempt to persuade the other jurors to side with them. At the outset, jurors may take an informal ballot or vote to see where they stand for conviction or acquittal. More often than not, this initial ballot significantly influences the final verdict by presenting to all jury members the disposition or determination of the majority of jurors favoring guilt or acquittal (Kalven and Ziesel, 1966).

Hastie, Penrod, and Pennington (1993:119–120) have found that group pressure is responsible for changing minority factions in a jury to align themselves with the majority opinion. And in jurisdictions where the majority-rule option is in effect, such as Oregon and Louisiana, agreement among jurors is achieved more rapidly than in those states where unanimity of opinion is required. Figure 9.2 shows the jury deliberation task.

When deliberations commence, juries may or may not establish a deliberation agenda. Ordinarily, they discuss the relevance and importance of particular pieces of evidence and witness testimony. If there is an initial vote and the jury is in disagreement as to the verdict, deliberations continue until a verdict is reached. If the jury simply cannot agree on a verdict, or if the required majority cannot be obtained in those jurisdictions providing for a majority vote for conviction, the judge is likely to declare a mistrial.

Must a Jury Agree on a Verdict?

JURY VOTING IN U.S. DISTRICT COURTS. In federal district courts, juries consist of twelve people. The judge may or may not permit the selection of **alternate jurors**. Alternate jurors are used in the event that a one or more of the regular jurors become ill during the proceedings. Also, during jury deliberations, if a juror cannot continue to serve, Title 18 U.S.C., Rule 23 (2001) provides, "If the court finds it necessary to excuse a juror for just

FIGURE **9.2** Jury Deliberations

Deliberation commences ⟶ Deliberation agenda determined ⟶ Evidence review and instructions ⟶ Juror verdict preferences determined ⟶ Verdict returned if unanimous voting occurs ⟶ Deliberations continue if verdict is not unanimous ⟶ Progress toward consensus ⟶ Instructions requested from judge ⟶ Further deliberations ⟶ Deadlock instruction received from judge ⟶ Jury agrees and renders verdict, or jury does not agree ⟶ Judge declares mistrial or hung jury cause after the jury has retired to consider its verdict, in the discretion of the court a valid verdict may be returned by the remaining 11 jurors" (Title 18, U.S.C., 2001). In federal courts, whether a twelve- or eleven-member jury hears a case, the decision reached for either guilt or acquittal must be unanimous. If one or more jurors disagree and persist in their disagreement with the other jurors, the judge declares a hung jury and a mistrial is declared. Mistrials are erroneous, invalid, or nugatory trials (Black, 1990:1002). The entire case will have to be heard again before a new jury. Mistrials also occur during the trial, especially if irregularities or errors jeopardize a defendant's fair trial rights. Sometimes, inadmissible evidence may be admitted erroneously. A witness may make an utterance that may cause substantial jury bias. Whenever such trial irregularities and others errors occur, the judge ordinarily grants a motion by either side for a mistrial (Hodge, 1986; Institute for Court Management, 1983).

Jury Voting in State Courts. At the local and state levels, however, the federal rule for jury agreement or unanimity does not always apply. Under existing U.S. Supreme Court guidelines, state juries may vary in size from six to twelve. Actually, the U.S. Supreme Court has established the minimum number of jury members at six in the case of *Williams v. Florida* (1970), but no such precedent has been established for upper limits of jury sizes. It is conceivable that a defendant may request a jury of more than twelve, such as twenty-five or fifty jurors. This unusual request would pose severe logistical problems for courtrooms, where it would be difficult to find sufficient seating for all these jurors. Furthermore, all these jurors would have considerable difficulty in reaching agreement about the guilt or innocence of criminal defendants.

Six-member juries must be unanimous in their verdict (*Burch v. Louisiana,* 1979). However, for twelve-person juries, a majority verdict may be acceptable unless unanimity is required under state or local laws. For instance, in the cases of *Apodaca v. Oregon* (1972) and *Johnson v. Louisiana* (1972), the respective defendants were convicted by a majority of jurors, but there was no unanimity of agreement. In most states, however, unanimous verdicts are required by statute.

An example of a legitimate nonunanimous verdict is *Johnson v. Louisiana* (1972), in which Frank Johnson was arrested, tried, and convicted of armed robbery in 1968. The twelve-person jury convicted him by a 9–3 vote (the absolute minimum majority required under Louisiana law). In another case, *Apodaca v. Oregon* (1972), unanimity of jury voting was not required either. Robert Apodaca and several other defendants were convicted of assault with a deadly weapon by an 11–1 jury vote. In Oregon, the minimum vote required by a jury for conviction is 10–2. Their appeals were heard by the U.S. Supreme Court, which upheld their convictions and underscored the right of states to require only a majority vote in their jury trials. Also, in some states, such as Tennessee, the state legislature has copied the Federal Rules of Criminal Procedure and required their twelve-member juries to be unanimous in their voting. There are some exceptions to nonunanimous jury voting, however. In capital cases with a possible death penalty, the jury vote for conviction must always be unanimous.

Polling the Jurors. Judges frequently poll jurors once they have rendered their verdict. **Polling jurors** refers to asking each juror to state in open court whether the verdict is a true reflection of the juror's feelings and how he or she voted. For a particular juror to say to the judge that he or she did not agree with that vote is unusual. In jurisdictions where juries must be unanimous in their decision to convict or acquit defendants, such an event is especially important. In Louisiana or Oregon, where unanimous votes are not needed, polling individual jury members identifies the specific vote breakdown. However, in the event that one or more jurors disagree with the majority in a state or federal court where the jury vote must be unanimous, judges send the juries back to deliberate more extensively, until unanimity of voting is reached. If the jury deliberates for an unusually long period and cannot agree on a verdict, the judge declares a mistrial, and a new trial may be scheduled. Whether a new trial is scheduled is up to the prosecutor. Mistrials are sometimes based on unclear or insufficient evidence. If prosecutors believe that the issues to be resolved in particular criminal cases are so controversial that no jury is likely to agree in the future, then no further prosecution against the defendant will be conducted.

The Selling of Jury Deliberations. During the 1980s and 1990s, increasing interest was expressed in jury deliberations and factual accounts of what transpires in jury rooms (Kerr, 1994). Juries have become increasingly scrutinized bodies. Individual jury members have profited from their jury membership, and this phenomenon is not peculiar to the United States. Other countries, such as Australia and Great Britain, have found that jurors in particularly high-profile cases have focused on the profit motive as a primary reason for their jury involvement (Findlay and Duff, 1988).

In particularly sensational trials, jury members' opinions about jury deliberations are increasingly marketable products (Kleinig, 1989). Several jurors in the murder trial of O. J. Simpson were excused as jurors when the judge learned that they were planning to write books about their experience and actually negotiating with publishers for book contracts. One former juror had been keeping a journal of trial events, which was forbidden and regarded as juror misconduct. Another juror, a former airline attendant, was excused for a different reason. She had been approached by representatives of *Playboy* magazine and had agreed to pose nude for a large sum of money when the trial was completed. She was exploiting her role as a juror in the high-profile trial. Although posing nude for a men's magazine is not against the law, it raises serious questions about the juror's original motives for becoming a juror.

Whenever jurors in any trial consider the potential profits stemming from their roles as jurors, their veracity or truthfulness when the *voir dire* was originally conducted comes into question. If they have hidden agendas, such as writing a book about their experiences, no laws prohibit subsequent expressions of their opinions and views. However, it is juror misconduct to keep journals about their jury involvement and observations. If the prosecution or defense learns about such activities or behaviors, then these revelations become grounds to bar these jurors from further jury service.

In one New York City trial, for instance, a highly publicized event involving a racial attack occurred in the Howard Beach community. During the trial, several jurors contacted the media in an attempt to sell their story and give their account of jury deliberations. Some news reporters believed that such conduct by jurors was acceptable and within the boundaries of free speech. The court and prosecution took a different view by

JURIES ARE SOMETIMES WRONG FOR THE RIGHT REASONS

The Case of Kevin Lee Green

It happened in Santa Ana, California, in 1979. A pregnant woman was brutally raped and murdered. Her unborn baby died as the result of the attack as well. Police had their man, and justice would indeed be served! Arrested for these crimes was Kevin Lee Green, the *husband* of the murdered woman and father of the unborn baby. Green was tried quickly, convicted, and sentenced to life imprisonment in 1980.

Move in time to June 1996. Kevin Lee Green is suddenly brought back into court. The judge tells Green, "We made a mistake. You didn't kill your wife and unborn baby. Your conviction is hereby reversed and you are free to leave prison." What happened?

After sixteen years, DNA technology had advanced to the point of being able to identify, fairly precisely, the perpetrators of rape crimes, whenever their semen or blood has been left as evidence at the crime scene. A woman being raped might scratch her attacker. Forensics experts can recover skin scrapings from underneath the rape victim's fingernails, and from them the rapist's DNA can be recorded. Later, this DNA can be matched with other DNA from suspects, even many years after the actual crimes.

In Green's case, a technician recording DNA samples noted that Green's DNA did not match the rapist's DNA. In fact, a match *was* found, but it belonged to another person who was currently serving a term for another crime. When the other man, a convicted rapist, was confronted with this new evidence, he confessed to murdering Green's wife and unborn baby. Case solved!

Superior Court Judge Robert Fitzgerald apologized to Green in open court. "You're about to wake up after a seventeen-year nightmare," Fitzgerald said. "I want to congratulate you on the end result, and the court, on behalf of society, apologizes to you for your incarceration. I wish you have a good and happy remainder of your life."

In Green's case, circumstantial evidence led to his conviction for rape and murder in 1980. If DNA technology had existed then, perhaps Green would have been cleared of any wrongdoing, but the system made a mistake. A prosecutor developed a convincing case, beyond a reasonable doubt, in fact. The jury bought it and convicted Green. But a terrible mistake has been corrected. The question remains, how many other "Greens" are wrongfully incarcerated today?

What should the government do for Kevin Green to compensate him for his years in prison? What measures should be taken to ensure him employment at a job suiting his skills and education? Can the government ever repay a wrongfully convicted person sufficiently to undo what was done after seventeen years?

Source: Adapted from Associated Press, "Man Freed after 17 Years in Jail." *Minot* (N.D.) *Daily News*, June 22, 1996:A2.

condemning those jurors who sought to profit from their experiences as jurors, and the jurors were excused (Kleinig, 1989).

What if people seek to become jurors for the purpose of advancing some political view or social cause? Ideally, juries are made up of people who will render fair decisions and consider and weigh all factual information presented by both sides during the trial. Becoming sidetracked with collateral issues not directly relevant to the trial proceedings may impair jurors' ability to render fair judgments about what they have seen and heard.

The Verdict and Its Aftermath

After deliberating, the jury returns to the courtroom and delivers its **verdict** to either the judge or an officer of the court. The defendant rises and faces the jury, while either the jury foreman or the judge reads the verdict aloud. If the verdict is not guilty, the defendant is released. In some cases, acquitted defendants may be rearrested for other crimes, but ordinarily an acquittal effectively removes the defendant from the criminal justice system.

In the event that a guilty verdict is rendered by the jury, the defendant has the right to appeal the verdict. The defense attorney may again request the judge to issue a directed verdict of acquittal despite the jury's decision. The judge may, indeed, exercise this option. However, if the judge sets aside the jury verdict and declares the defendant acquitted, the prosecution may appeal that decision to a higher court.

If the judge does not grant the defense attorney's request, the defendant is sentenced. The appeals process may take many years. In all of the U.S. Supreme Court cases presented in this and previous chapters, the interval of time between the offense, the conviction, and the U.S. Supreme Court decision has been several years. Before a case goes before the U.S. Supreme Court, however, it must be reviewed by higher courts within the particular state jurisdiction where the original judgment was entered against the defendant. This appeals process consumes much time as well. Cases presented before the U.S. Supreme Court usually involve constitutional issues. Were a defendant's constitutional rights violated at any stage of the criminal proceeding? Were there procedural errors committed by different court participants, such as the judge, so that the original conviction might be set aside and a new trial ordered?

Summary

A trial proceeding provides defendants with the opportunity to confront and cross-examine their accusers and to offer exculpatory evidence favoring a verdict of not guilty. A trial is an adversarial proceeding in which the prosecution attempts to establish a defendant's guilt and the defense attempts to prove their client innocent of any offenses alleged.

Trial procedures vary from one jurisdiction to the next. Where a jury trial is conducted, the number of jurors ranges from six to twelve. At the federal level, a jury verdict must be unanimous. At the state and local levels, however, a unanimous verdict may or may not be required, depending upon the prevailing laws.

Juries are made up of people from the community or region that has jurisdiction over the crimes alleged. The selection of jury members involves questioning them concerning their possible biases or prejudices in the case before the court. Both prosecution and defense attorneys attempt to select jurors favorable to their particular interests. Jurors are excluded from jury duty for reasons of illness or other compelling circumstances, and both prosecution and defense attorneys may challenge any juror for cause. Jurors may also be excluded by means of peremptory challenges, as the prosecutor and defense attorney attempt to construct the most favorable jury for their particular position. These peremptory challenges may not be used for purposes of discrimination, however.

The science of jury selection is popular. Many attorneys turn to consulting firms that specialize in the selection of jury members. However, the results of studies investigating particular jury member characteristics and their decision-making inclinations have been inconsistent and disappointing. No one has been able to predict with certainty how particular jury members will vote in a given trial.

In any trial, both the prosecution and defense have specific roles and follow established protocol in presenting their evidence and witnesses. Each side is permitted to address the jury with an opening statement. Each side is also entitled to cross-examine witnesses and to object to the introduction and relevance of certain evidence. Witnesses can be reexamined in redirect and recross-examinations. The process continues until both sides are satisfied that the evidence before the jury has been adequately presented.

Jury deliberations are conducted following the presentation of witnesses and evidence from both the prosecution and defense, and a verdict is determined. If the jury cannot agree on a verdict as local, state, or federal law requires, the presiding judge declares a mistrial, which requires a new trial before a new jury. If a jury finds the defendant guilty of the crime alleged, the judge sentences the convicted offender, either at the conclusion of the trial or in a separate subsequent proceeding.

KEY TERMS

Adversarial proceedings
Alternate jurors
Bench trial
Bribery
Cross-examination
Direct examination
Directed verdict of
   acquittal
Exclusionary rule
Expert witnesses
Eyewitnesses
Federal Rules of
   Evidence

Fruits of the poisonous
   tree doctrine
Jury deliberations
Misdemeanor Trial
   Law
Motion for a bill of
   particulars
Motion for a change of
   venue
Motion for continuance
Motion for determination
   of competency
Motion for discovery

Motion for dismissal of
   charges
Motion for intention to
   provide alibi
Motion for severance
Motion for summary
   judgment
Motion for suppression of
   evidence
Motions
Motions *in limine*
Motion to dismiss
Motion to suppress

Nolo contendere	Screening	Trial by the judge
Objections	Summation	Verdict
Polling jurors	Sworn in	Victim-witness assistance
Pretrial motions	Trial	programs
Recross-examination	Trial by the court	Witnesses
Redirect examination		

QUESTIONS FOR REVIEW

1. What is a pretrial motion? What are some examples of pretrial motions?

2. Differentiate between a "bench trial" and a "jury trial." Is there any evidence to indicate that a defendant is better off having a bench trial as opposed to a jury trial?

3. What is a trial? What are some of the functions of a trial proceeding?

4. Does a criminal defendant charged with murder have to have a jury trial? Can the defendant waive his or her right to a jury trial? What constitutional amendment pertains to jury trials?

5. Identify three functions of juries. What U.S. Supreme Court decision pertained to setting lower limits for jury sizes? What was the limit established?

6. In a particular criminal case before a six-person jury, the jury brought back a verdict of guilty, but the vote was 5–1. Evaluate this verdict in view of what you have learned about jury size and unanimity of agreement among jurors.

7. On the basis of some of the research that has been conducted about jury size, is a twelve-member jury more representative of community interests than a six-person jury? What are some differences between these jury sizes other than the number of jurors?

8. What are five "maxims" believed by many attorneys and reported by Rita Simon about juror characteristics and accompanying juror attitudes?

9. What is meant by the "fruit of the poisonous tree"? What does it have to do with evidence? Explain briefly.

10. What is the exclusionary rule?

11. How reliable is the testimony of a child witness? Cite some research that has investigated the competency of child witnesses.

12. What is the purpose of a victim-witness assistance program?

13. Who usually gets the last word and closing argument in a criminal case before a jury?

SUGGESTED READINGS

Arrigo, Bruce A. (1996). *The Contours of Psychiatric Justice: A Postmodern Critique of Mental Illness, Criminal Insanity, and the Law.* New York: Garland.

Callahan, Cornelius P. (1997). *The Search for the Truth: An Introduction to the Jury Trial Process.* Chicago: Sextant Press.

Daley, Kathleen. (1994). *Gender, Crime and Punishment.* New Haven, CT: Yale University Press.

Epstein, Lee. (1995). *Contemplating Courts.* Washington, DC: CQ Press.

Fukurai, Hiroshi. (1997). "A Quota Jury: Affirmative Action in Jury Selection." *Journal of Criminal Justice* **25**:477–500.

George, Jody, Deirdre Golash, and Russell Wheeler. (1989). *Handbook on Jury Use in the Federal Courts.* Washington, DC: Federal Judicial Center.

Healey, Kerry Murphy. (1995). *Victim and Witness Intimidation: New Developments and Emerging Responses.* Washington, DC: U.S. National Institute of Justice.

Huff, C. Ronald, Arye Rattner, and Edward Sagarin. (1995). *Convicted but Innocent: Wrongful Conviction and Public Policy.* Thousand Oaks, CA: Sage.

Manzo, John F. (1996). "Taking Turns and Taking Sides: Opening Scenes from Two Jury Deliberations." *Social Psychology Quarterly* **59**:107–125.

Rothwax, Harold J. (1996). *Guilty: The Collapse of Criminal Justice.* New York: Random House.

SENTENCING AND APPEALS

THE KILLER OF SEVERAL UNIVERSITY OF FLORIDA COEDS sat at a table during the hearing to determine his sentence. Various people testified against him; several people testified in his behalf. Those against him were the families of the victims, who spoke out about the suffering they had been caused by this man's actions. One family member said that the convicted offender had cut off his daughter's head and placed it in a conspicuous place, on a bookshelf, where it would shock those who discovered it. Others spoke on behalf of the offender, saying that he had been a good boy and had done well in school. The death penalty would be wrong to apply in his case. A preacher who knew him as a child gave a compelling argument for why his life should be spared. Even the offender spoke on his own behalf. He apologized to the court and families for his misdeeds. His attorney spoke out in favor of a life sentence. The prosecutor demanded the death penalty for the heinous nature of the man's crimes. When all had testified, the jury deliberated and the judge sentenced the defendant to death.

THE KILLER OF A YOUNG GIRL sat impassively in the courtroom as different actors argued over his fate. He was vilified by his victim's family. Some people who knew him before he had committed this atrocity spoke out in favor of his being spared the death penalty. When the defendant spoke, he obliterated any hope for mercy by the court. He gave the finger to the television cameras. In a babbling discourse with many expletives, he said that his young victim had told him that she had been sexually abused by her own father, thus adding insult to the gravest of injuries. When the judge spoke, he sentenced the offender to death.

THE CONVICTED OFFENDER stood before the court as she heard the judge impose the maximum sentence—life without parole. She had been convicted of embezzlement. She had embezzled nearly $4 million over a two-year period as the secretary of a prominent businessman in the community. Facts uncovered at her trial revealed that she had embezzled before. On at least eight other occasions in different states, this woman had been convicted of fraudulent activities, largely embezzlement. She had made a living from crime and was known as a career offender. The judge imposed a sentence of life without parole, not because he wanted to but because he had to. It was the law.

THE MAN HAD BEEN CONVICTED OF BANK ROBBERY. He was a businessman, deeply in debt. He had experienced a sequence of devastating financial crises. He thought about suicide. His life was over, as far as he was concerned. He decided to rob a bank as a last resort because he needed some quick cash to survive. He had never robbed a bank before. He wore a fake mustache and gave the teller a note demanding money and claiming he had a bomb. The teller handed over some bills, and the man ran from the bank into the waiting arms of police. He was unarmed and did not possess a bomb. At his sentencing hearing, many of his friends and acquaintances spoke out in favor of leniency. No one spoke against him. The judge deliberated before pronouncing a sentence—four years' probation.

Introduction

This chapter is about **sentencing** offenders. Sentencing is the process of imposing punishment on convicted offenders for their conviction offenses. Punishments imposed for different kinds of crime can range from probation to **capital punishment**. However, sentencing is a complex process. It is far more than a judicial recitation about what the law is that was violated and an imposition of the maximum punishment proscribed. For especially serious offenses, there are several stages or events after a conviction.

Criminal courts are vested with a vast array of punishment powers. To apply these powers effectively, judges must be fully informed about the nature of the crime committed and how this crime affected not only the victim(s) but also others, including the offender. Most jurisdictions have a bureaucratic apparatus that enables judges to order investigations into the background of criminals, known widely as presentence investigations. They are summarized in presentence investigation reports and are usually prepared and submitted by probation officers who act at the judge's direction.

In sentencing hearings, the accused and the accusers can speak out, either for or against the accused. Victim testimony is solicited, as well as testimony from others with relevant factual information. Offenders submit summaries of their crimes, the defendant's sentencing memorandums, as part of the presentence investigation report. Judges consider the evidence presented in sentencing hearings and contained in presentence investigation reports and impose what they consider to be fair and impartial punishments.

Judges are guided in their decision making by rules governing the types of sentences that can be imposed. Jurisdictions vary in their sentencing systems, and judges are obligated to observe these rules. Following the imposition of sentences, convicted offenders may appeal them on various grounds. The most frequently appealed sentences are death sentences for capital crimes. All death penalty appeals are automatically appealable. This appeals process is especially lengthy, often taking many years before a death sentence is actually imposed. For noncapital cases, the appeals process is also lengthy. This chapter examines all these topics in detail and considers several important sentencing issues.

Functions and Goals of Sentencing

Sentencing offenders serves the following functions and aims: (1) punishment or "just deserts," (2) incapacitation and crime control, (3) rehabilitation, (4) reintegration, and (5) prevention and deterrence.

Punishment

Punishment is any sanction imposed following a criminal conviction. The primary function of sentencing is to punish offenders for their crimes. Each crime carries minimum and maximum penalties. When judges or juries find defendants guilty of committing one or more crimes, sentences are imposed that presumably punish offenders. Depending on the circumstances and the jurisdiction, judges can impose probation for a period of years or subject convicted offenders to incarceration in either a jail or prison. How harshly or leniently convicted offenders are treated should depend on the crime's seriousness. Ideally, the more serious the crime, the harsher the penalties. In reality, however, the system does not always work this way. Investigators can always find examples of some rapists and robbers, even murderers, who received probation instead of prison sentences, and some burglars and thieves receive lengthy sentences in jails or prisons.

Incapacitation and Crime Control

A second function of sentencing is **incapacitation**. A primary aim of sentencing is to incapacitate those convicted of crimes, particularly those who are persistent or chronic offenders. **Career criminals** who make their living from crime are frequently targeted by the criminal justice system to receive the harshest penalties. Special statutes have been written to make it possible to mete out stringent penalties for **chronic recidivists** or **chronic offenders**. Many state legislatures believe that while **persistent felony offenders** and chronic recidivists are confined in prison for prolonged periods through longer sentences, then they cannot commit new crimes against society. Thus, the system takes these offenders out of circulation for a period of years. If such offenders are allowed to remain in their communities through some form of probation, then probation departments maintain surveillance over these clients by monitoring their whereabouts. Home confinement and electronic monitoring systems are used, together with regular face-to-face visits with probation officers. These forms of managing convicted offenders in their communities do not prevent them from committing new crimes in any absolute sense but do exert some degree of crime control for many of these offenders.

Rehabilitation

One intended function of punishment is **rehabilitation**. A high degree of cynicism is prevalent in the criminal justice system, however, concerning just how well corrections in any form actually rehabilitates convicted offenders. Some experts believe that rehabilitation never occurs; others think that for many offenders, particularly those incarcerated in prisons, rehabilitative programs have enabled them to turn their lives around and become law-abiding citizens when they are eventually released back into society.

Most prisons include various vocational, technical, and educational programs for offenders who wish to take advantage of these rehabilitative services. Individual and group counseling and other forms of social and psychological assistance are provided for inmates. Some jails and prisons require inmates to participate in certain programs, whether or not they wish to participate. Literacy programs have been established in some jurisdictions, such as Virginia, which expects illiterate inmates who are serving long prison terms to learn to read and write as one condition for early release. Some authorities question whether voluntary or mandatory participation in any particular prison program is directly responsible for an inmate's rehabilitation over time.

Reintegration

A fourth function of sentencing is **reintegration**, or assisting criminals to fit into their communities and society. This aim is most closely associated with nonincarcerative sentences, including all forms of probation. When judges sentence offenders to probation, there are usually several conditions attached, such as mandatory participation in counseling programs, job placement services, restitution programs, and other activities intended to help offenders find employment and become self-sufficient without having to return to crime. Particularly for first offenders, community correctional programs can help them become reintegrated in society. They may remain with their families and receive their social support. Further, these offenders will not be exposed to the criminogenic influence of incarceration.

Prevention and Deterrence

Sentencing is also symbolic, both to convicted offenders and to those who are contemplating committing crimes. When judges impose sentences, there is a tacit expectation that others will consider the harshness of these sentences and refrain from crime because of their fear of punishment. Thus, sentencing is designed as a form of **crime prevention** or **deterrence**. One direct intention of the **get-tough movement** is to mete out harsher penalties for offenders to set examples and deter others from crime. Some people regard the death penalty as an effective deterrent for those who are contemplating capital offenses because no one wants to be executed. Theoretically, if the **death penalty** is the punishment for murder, then fewer murders will be committed. This view has been challenged by experts frequently, and most agree that the death penalty does not necessarily deter some people from killing others (Acker and Lanier, 1995; Long, 1995). Also, longer prison terms for those who deal in drugs do not prevent drug dealers from carrying out their illicit activities. Nevertheless, in an ideal world, sentencing is supposed to act as a deterrent and prevent others from committing crime. Largely because of this aim, the sentencing systems of all jurisdictions throughout the United States have been changed to maximize sentencing effectiveness. As discussed in the next section, sentencing reform has yielded several sentencing schemes to further the aim of crime deterrence and prevention. Unfortunately, all forms of sentencing have generated criticism from experts and the general public, with little agreement as to which sentencing scheme is best (Forst and Rhodes, 1982).

Forms of Sentencing

Federal and state judges tend to believe that the toughest part of their jobs is imposing punishments on convicted offenders. There are so many types of offenders with varied backgrounds and criminal histories that the act of sentencing them is one of the most stressful and complex decisions these judges make (National Council on Crime and Delinquency, 1974; Tauro, 1983). Assisting judges in their sentencing decision making are legislatively enacted sentencing schemes that provide a rational structure within which to make sentencing decisions. Currently, there are four types of sentencing schemes used by various jurisdictions throughout the United States: (1) indeterminate sentencing, (2) determinate sentencing, (3) presumptive or guidelines-based sentencing, and (4) mandatory sentencing.

Indeterminate Sentencing

In indeterminate sentencing, the judge imposes a sentence that includes a minimum term of years or months and a maximum term. After the minimum term is served, the offender's early release from prison is determined by a **parole board**. Whether the maximum term is served by any particular offender depends on that person's institutional behavior and other factors.

Indeterminate sentencing has its roots in early correctional history from the 1850s and 1860s. Influenced by penal reforms in Ireland, Scotland, and England, the United States was inclined to experiment with indeterminate sentencing as a means of providing incentives for inmates to behave well while confined. Provided that their institutional conduct was acceptable, once inmates had served the minimum portion of their sentences as imposed by judges, they would become eligible for parole or early release short of serving their full terms. Parole boards would decide whether to grant **early release** to these parole-eligible inmates. Their institutional conduct would be examined, together with the circumstances and seriousness of their conviction offenses, and the parole board would either grant or deny their parole. Those denied parole on one occasion could apply for it on subsequent occasions, usually at regular intervals such as annually or every two years. Most paroling authorities in the United States today continue to make such decisions.

However, indeterminate sentencing has been criticized for its potential for discrimination on the basis of race, gender, and socioeconomic status (Griset, 1995b; Kaune,

1993). Both judges and parole boards have been accused of abusing their sentencing and early-release discretionary authority by making decisions on factors other than legal ones. These **extralegal factors** are most often racially or ethnically based or related to gender or socioeconomic differences. Convicted black and other minority offenders more often receive longer sentences by judges or are denied early release by parole boards than white offenders who have a similar **criminal history**. Those with private counsel often are treated more leniently in sentencing than indigent convicted offenders who are represented by public defenders or **court-appointed counsel** (Marvell and Moody, 1996; Roberts, 1994; Stolzenberg, 1993). Because these factors should not be considered significant in such decision making, substantial efforts have been made by different interests to reform state and federal sentencing policies and practices (Austin et al., 1995; Griset, 1995b). In some instances, states and the federal government have abolished parole in favor of what they believe to be more equitable sentencing schemes (Marvell and Moody, 1996). One noticeable shift in many states has been from indeterminate sentencing to determinate sentencing (Goodstein and Hepburn, 1985).

Determinate Sentencing

Determinate sentencing is a sentence imposed by the judge that includes a fixed minimum term and a fixed maximum term. Early release from prison is determined by the accumulation of **good-time credit**, which is deducted from the maximum term. **Good time**, or good-time credit, is a fixed number of days inmates may accumulate based on the amount of time they serve. Some states enable offenders to accumulate up to thirty days for every thirty days they serve. Thus, an inmate who serves one year may accumulate one year of good-time credit. This credit is deducted from the maximum sentence originally imposed by the judge. It is conceivable, therefore, that inmates sentenced to ten years under a determinate sentencing system may only serve five years, with the accumulated good time deducted from their maximum ten-year sentences. Determinate sentencing is intended to produce greater certainty, proportionality, and rationality in punishment (Institute for Rational Public Policy, 1991).

Its proponents believe that determinate sentencing corrects the potential for discrimination according to extralegal factors by judges and parole boards (Roberts, 1994). With determinate sentencing, inmates can calculate their own approximate early-release dates, and there is greater release certainty than with indeterminate sentencing. But inmates may jeopardize their good-time credit by misbehaving while confined. They may receive write-ups from correctional officers for fighting or possessing illegal contraband or drugs. Violations of other institutional rules revoke or cancel good time.

Determinate sentencing has received mixed criticisms. Several states, such as Delaware, Colorado, Iowa, Minnesota, North Carolina, and Washington, have replaced indeterminate sentencing with determinate sentencing. Some of these states, including Minnesota and Washington, have opted for additional sentencing changes after experimenting with determinate sentencing for several years. Despite the promise of significant reform in curing the previous ills of discrimination in sentencing, determinate sentencing has not been as successful in this regard as originally projected (Key, 1991; Stolzenberg, 1993). More than a few states have opted for yet another variety of sentencing designed to curb judicial sentencing discretion and its potential for abuse. In the last few decades, guidelines-based or presumptive sentencing schemes have been proposed and implemented (Institute for Rational Public Policy, 1991; Stolzenberg, 1993).

Presumptive or Guidelines-Based Sentencing

Presumptive sentencing or **guidelines-based sentencing** is the establishment of fixed punishments for each criminal offense, graded according to offense severity and the offender's criminal history. Punishments for different offenses are ranged according to months. Punishment range midpoints are the presumptive number of months imposed according to a fixed table. Minnesota was one of the first states to implement **sentencing guidelines**. Subsequently, many other states established their own guidelines. The federal government established sentencing guidelines as well, following the extensive work of the **U.S. Sentencing Commission.** The U.S. Sentencing Commission originated as the result of the Comprehensive Crime Control Act of 1984 and promulgated punishment guidelines for all federal crimes. These guidelines were implemented in 1987. Federal parole was abolished in 1992 and replaced with supervised release.

An example of guidelines-based or presumptive sentencing is the U.S. sentencing guidelines, which are shown in Table 10.1. Across the top of the table are criminal history categories. These range from I, in which offenders have little or no criminal history, to VI, which reflects those who have the most extensive and serious criminal histories. Down the left-hand side of the table are offense levels ranging from 1 to 43. Every federal crime has an offense seriousness level. The more serious the crime, the higher the offense seriousness score. In the body of the table, where the criminal history and offense seriousness scores intersect, are ranges of months, the guidelines used by judges to sentence offenders. Judges must remain within these month ranges in most cases. The midpoint in each month range is considered the presumptive sentence judges must impose, unless certain factors dictate otherwise. For instance, if the month range is 40–50, the presumptive number of months is 45. If the range is 30–40 months, then 35 would be the presumptive number of months. Judges may move upward or downward within each range, depending on whether there are aggravating or mitigating circumstances. They may impose sentences outside any particular month range if they believe there are circumstances to justify such departures. They must provide in writing their rationale for such departures. Such was the case in *Koon v. United States* (1996).

A comprehensive study of various sentencing schemes completed in 1995 (Austin et al., 1995) examined the nature of sentencing reform and evaluated the various sentencing schemes now used. According to this report, by 1994, sixteen states and the federal government had adopted presumptive sentencing schemes. Another five states had adopted determinate sentencing systems. The most promising of all sentencing schemes was presumptive sentencing. Presumptive sentencing is considered most promising because of its potential for minimizing sentencing disparities according to extralegal factors, minimizing incarceration rates, and reducing prison overcrowding. Similar conclusions have been reached by those investigating different dispositional schemes for juvenile offenders (Ashford and LaCroy, 1993).

Table 10.1   U.S. Sentencing Guidelines in Months

Offense Level	Criminal History Category					
	I 0 or 1	II 2 or 3	III 4, 5, 6	IV 7, 8, 9	V 10, 11, 12	VI 13 or More
1	0–1	0–2	0–3	0–4	0–5	0–6
2	0–2	0–3	0–4	0–5	0–6	1–7
3	0–3	0–4	0–5	0–6	2–8	3–9
4	0–4	0–5	0–6	2–8	4–10	6–12
5	0–5	0–6	1–7	4–10	6–12	9–15
6	0–6	1–7	2–8	6–12	9–15	12–18
7	1–7	2–8	4–10	8–14	12–18	15–21
8	2–8	4–10	6–12	10–16	15–21	18–24
9	4–10	6–12	8–14	12–18	18–24	21–27
10	6–12	8–14	10–16	15–21	21–27	24–30
11	8–14	10–16	12–18	18–24	24–30	27–33
12	10–16	12–18	15–21	21–27	27–33	30–37
13	12–18	15–21	18–24	24–30	30–37	33–41
14	15–21	18–24	21–27	27–33	33–41	37–46
15	18–24	21–27	24–30	30–37	37–46	41–51
16	21–27	24–30	27–33	33–41	41–51	46–57
17	24–30	27–33	30–37	37–46	46–57	51–63
18	27–33	30–37	33–41	41–51	51–63	57–71
19	30–37	33–41	37–46	46–57	57–71	63–78
20	33–41	37–46	41–51	51–63	63–78	70–87
21	37–46	41–51	46–57	57–71	70–87	77–96
22	41–51	46–57	51–63	63–78	77–96	84–105
23	46–57	51–63	57–71	70–87	84–105	92–115
24	51–63	57–71	63–78	77–96	92–115	100–125
25	57–71	63–78	70–87	84–105	100–125	110–137
26	63–78	70–87	78–97	92–115	110–137	120–150
27	70–87	78–97	87–108	100–125	120–150	130–162
28	78–97	87–108	97–121	110–137	130–162	140–175
29	87–108	97–121	108–135	121–151	140–175	151–188
30	97–121	108–135	121–151	135–168	151–188	168–210
31	108–135	121–151	135–168	151–188	168–210	188–235
32	121–151	135–168	151–188	168–210	188–235	210–262
33	135–168	151–188	168–210	188–235	210–262	235–293
34	151–188	168–210	188–235	210–262	235–293	262–327
35	168–210	188–235	210–262	235–293	262–327	292–365
36	188–235	210–262	235–293	262–327	292–365	324–405
37	210–262	235–293	262–327	292–365	324–405	360–Life
38	235–293	262–327	292–365	324–405	360–Life	360–Life
39	262–327	292–365	324–405	360–Life	360–Life	360–Life
40	292–365	324–405	360–Life	360–Life	360–Life	360–Life
41	324–405	360–Life	360–Life	360–Life	360–Life	360–Life
42	360–Life	360–Life	360–Life	360–Life	360–Life	360–Life
43	Life	Life	Life	Life	Life	Life

Source: U.S. Sentencing Commission, *U.S. Sentencing Guidelines* (Washington, DC: U.S. Government Printing Office, 1987).

Many states have sentencing reform acts to change the ways convicted offenders are sentenced. Congress passed the **Sentencing Reform Act of 1984**, which led to the creation of the U.S. Sentencing Commission and a revision of the entire federal criminal code. In Washington, the state's Sentencing Reform Act of 1981 established determinate sentencing for felonies (Washington State Sentencing Guidelines Commission, 1996). But various deficiencies in determinate sentencing laws have caused state officials to modify their existing sentencing policy with a more structured one, a sentencing system that will obligate sentenced offenders to make frugal use of institutional resources in becoming rehabilitated. Thus, with new sentencing guidelines, the Washington State Sentencing Guidelines Commission expects to address the following issues: truth in sentencing, prosecution standards, sentencing standards and ranges, juvenile dispositions, and mentally ill offenders.

Perhaps the most immediate impact of newly implemented presumptive sentencing guidelines is the reduction of sentencing disparities, in which similar offenders receive widely divergent sentences. In Minnesota, for example, a 22 percent decline in **sentencing disparity** was observed in the year following the implementation of guidelines (Stolzenberg, 1993). A 60 percent reduction in sentencing inequality for the length-of-time-in-prison decision was also observed. But even presumptive sentencing guidelines can be circumvented by creative sentencing judges (Wallace and Wedlock, 1994). One way of curbing such abuses of discretion is through mandatory sentences, according to which judges must impose specific terms regardless of their own views and prejudices (Griswold, 1995).

Mandatory Sentencing

Mandatory sentencing is the obligatory imposition of a specified period of years or months for specific types of offenses. Judges are bound to impose a **mandatory sentence** for certain types of conviction offenses. For instance, Michigan has a mandatory penalty of two years for using a gun during the commission of a felony. The use-a-gun-and-go-to-prison law in Michigan is added to whatever sentence is imposed when offenders are convicted. Thus, a bank robber in Michigan might be sentenced to twenty years, with an additional two years as a mandatory sentence for using a firearm when robbing the bank. When all or part of the offender's twenty-year term is served, a mandatory additional two years must be served by the offender for the weapons offense. The intent of this mandatory law is to discourage criminals from using weapons when they commit crimes. Less use of weapons by criminals usually means fewer serious injuries or deaths resulting from their crimes. The deterrent effect of Michigan's law and similar laws in other states is currently unknown.

VIRGINIA EXILE. One of the more recent gun control measures enacted by a state is Virginia's **Virginia Exile**, which went into effect on July 1, 1999. It provides for a mandatory term of five years for anyone convicted of using a firearm during the commission of a felony. Although this idea is not new in view of Michigan's two-year tack-on for essentially the same type of offense, the length of mandatory flat time is unique among other mandatory laws governing the use of firearms during commissions of felonies. Virginia

JUDGES MAY STRAY FROM PRESUMPTIVE SENTENCING GUIDELINES

Koon v. United States, 518 U.S.81 (1996) Police officers Stacy C. Koon and Laurence M. Powell were convicted in federal court of violating the constitutional rights of motorist Rodney King under color of law during arrest and sentenced to thirty months' imprisonment. The U.S. district court trial judge used U.S. sentencing guidelines and justified a downward departure of eight offense levels from 27 to 19 to arrive at a 30–37 month sentence. The government appealed, contending that downward departure of eight offense levels from 27 was an abuse of judicial discretion and that the factors cited for the downward departure were not statutory. An original offense seriousness level of 27 would have meant imposing a sentence of 70–87 months. The Ninth Circuit Court of Appeals rejected all of the trial court's reasons for the downward departure, and Koon and Powell petitioned the Supreme Court, which upheld the Circuit Court of Appeals in part and reversed it in part. Specifically, it said that the primary question to be answered on appeal is whether the trial judge abused his discretion by the downward departure in sentencing. The reasons given by the trial judge for the downward departure from an offense level of 27 to 19 were that (1) the victim's misconduct provoked police use of force, (2) Koon and Powell had been subjected to successive state and federal criminal prosecutions, (3) Koon and Powell posed a low risk for recidivism, (4) Koon and Powell would probably lose their jobs and be precluded from employment in law enforcement, and (5) Koon and Powell would be unusually susceptible to abuse in prison. The Supreme Court concluded that a five-level downward departure based on the victim's misconduct that provoked officer use of force was justified, because victim misconduct is an encouraged (by the U.S. Sentencing Commission) basis for a guideline departure, but that the remaining three-level departure was an abuse of judicial discretion. Federal district judges may not consider a convicted offender's career loss as a downward departure factor. Further, trial judges may not consider an offender's low likelihood of recidivism, because this factor is already incorporated into the Criminal History Category in the sentencing guideline table. Considering this factor to justify a downward departure, therefore, would be tantamount to counting the factor twice. The Supreme Court upheld the trial judge's reliance on the offenders' susceptibility to prison abuse and the burdens of successive state and federal prosecutions, however. The case was remanded back to the district court, where a new sentence could be determined. Thus, a new offense level had to be chosen on the basis of the victim's own misconduct that provoked the officers, offender susceptibility to prison abuse, and the burden of successive state and federal prosecutions. The significance of this case for criminal justice is that the Supreme Court identifies specific factors to guide federal judges in imposing sentences on police officers convicted of misconduct and violating citizen rights under color of law. Victim response that provokes police use of force, an officer's susceptibility to abuse in prison, and the burden of successive state and federal prosecutions are acceptable factors for justifing downward departures in offense seriousness, but low recidivism potential and loss of employment opportunity in law enforcement are not legitimate factors.

Source: Powell v. United States, 518 U.S.81(1996).

Exile targets three crimes: (1) possession of a firearm by a convicted violent felon; (2) possession of a firearm on school property with the intent to use it, or displaying it in a threatening manner; and (3) possession of a firearm and drugs such as heroin and cocaine. The Virginia legislature has said that Virginia Exile gets straight to the point: a gun associated with drugs, felons, or school gets you five years in a Virginia prison. The offender will be going away—exiled—for a long time, with no suspended sentence, no probation, and probably no bail. Virginia Exile is modeled after Richmond's **Project Exile**, a highly effective federal, local, and state cooperative effort initiated by the U.S. Attorney's Office. Those who are arrested by city police and charged with illegal possession or use of firearms have been prosecuted under federal laws that generally have stiffer penalties. Thus, this is a tough new effort designed to reduce gun violence throughout the state.

The most important feature of mandatory sentencing is the obligation it places on judges to impose consistent sentences for a variety of convicted offenders, regardless of their gender, race or ethnicity, or socioeconomic status. Under these mandatory sentencing provisions, judges must impose specific sentences as authorized by their state legislatures. However, even mandatory sentencing policies may be circumvented. Prosecutors may choose to ignore those aspects of the crime that carry mandatory penalties. More plea bargains are obtained if certain facts about a crime are ignored. Armed robbery may be downgraded to simple robbery, for instance. The fact that a firearm was used in the offense is not mentioned. Even in the presentence investigation report prepared by probation officers, certain facts may be omitted. Thus, sentencing judges may never see the full set of circumstances involved in the crime committed. If crimes with mandatory penalties are not included in the prosecutor's information or charges, and if these facts are also omitted in the plea bargain agreement, the judge imposes a sentence consistent with presumptive guidelines or determinate sentencing.

Such a scenario occurs too frequently throughout the United States, according to some critics. Many law-and-order proponents advocate greater truth in sentencing. If someone uses a gun when committing a crime, then this fact ought to be made known to the court. Further, if the convicted offender is a recidivist with prior felony convictions, this information also ought to be made known to the court. All states have habitual offender statutes that apply to **habitual offenders** with lengthy criminal records. They are in jeopardy of being given a **life-without-parole sentence** as a mandatory sentence for their conviction as habitual offenders.

Habitual Offender Statutes and Truth in Sentencing

Habitual Offender Statutes

Chronic, persistent, and violent felony offenders pose the greatest risk to the public. These criminals commit new crimes frequently, and these crimes often result in serious victim injuries or deaths. There is also a broad class of chronic and persistent felony offenders who commit property crimes, such as larceny, vehicular theft, and burglary. All types of chronic recidivists have been targeted in recent decades for special and harsher treatment by the criminal justice system. Since the 1970s, virtually every jurisdiction throughout the United States has evolved habitual offender statutes (Hunzeker, 1985). In some jurisdictions, these laws are called **persistent offender statutes**. These laws prescribe life sentences for those who are convicted of three or more felonies.

The intent of habitual offender statutes is to incapacitate those who persist in committing crimes. If these high-rate offenders are removed from society, then some crime prevention or crime control occurs. The primary problem is that there are so many persistent and chronic felony offenders that there is not enough prison space to house them for extended terms (DeJong and Franzeen, 1993; Forer, 1994). Furthermore, some inmates convicted as habitual offenders have filed lawsuits challenging their lengthy prison sentences compared with the nonserious nature of their conviction offenses. These are usually habeas corpus actions that seek relief in the form of sentence reductions (Flango, 1994). Also, some experts do not consider these statutes as particularly beneficial as deterrents or methods of crime control (Tonry, 1993).

WHO ARE HABITUAL OFFENDERS? A key problem confronted by all jurisdictions with habitual offender statutes is defining who the habitual offenders are. Do habitual offenders include all types of offenders, or is the definition limited to those committing only the most serious and violent types of felonies? This problem seems universal in nature. England, for instance, has been vexed by the problem of habitual offender legislation and its inability to provide precise guidance about who qualifies as a habitual offender. Are habitual offenders only violent criminals who pose an immediate threat to society, or are they also the bumbling petty thieves and property offenders (Radzinowicz and Hood, 1980)?

Florida has attempted to refine the habitual offender definition by establishing a limited number of categories and a guideline matrix (Griswold, 1995). Thus, not every Florida felon with numerous convictions qualifies as a habitual offender. Further, Florida law provides for gradations in offense seriousness and in whether certain convicted offenders will be classified as habitual offenders.

A subsequent study of the application of Florida's habitual offender statute has generated an offender database of 25,806 people eligible for habitualization. Interestingly, only eighteen percent or 4,783 people from this database were actually prosecuted and convicted as habitual offenders (Florida Joint Legislative Management Committee, 1992).

This finding is consistent with the earlier work of Hunzeker (1985), who found that although every state has habitual offender statutes, relatively few inmates are serving sentences as habitual offenders. In fact, eight states have reported that two to three percent of the inmates were serving terms as habitual offenders. Nine states reported that less than one percent of their inmate populations were serving terms as habitual offenders.

The consensus is that all states have habitual offender statutes but *most* states do not enforce these habitual offender statutes with any consistency (Rodriguez and O'Connell, 1993). More often than not, prosecutors in most jurisdictions use habitual offender statutes as mechanisms of coercion to elicit guilty pleas from persistent offenders. Thus, prosecutors threaten to prosecute particular habitual criminals as habitual offenders unless they agree to plead guilty to other crimes. This sort of leverage is perfectly legal and is not considered coercive by the U.S. Supreme Court (*Bordenkircher v. Hayes*, 1978).

NARROWING THE HABITUAL OFFENDER DEFINITION: THREE STRIKES AND YOU'RE OUT! In recent years, the federal government and various states have enacted provisions to punish more serious felons with harsh punishments if they are convicted of three or more felonies. Such legislation is termed three strikes and you're out. Essentially, offenders convicted of three serious felonies are out, in that they are sentenced to life terms in prison (Long, 1995). The get-tough movement and general public seem supportive of legislation aimed at incapacitating persistent felony offenders (Kercher and Dull, 1981; Santa Clara County Office of the County Executive, 1995; U.S. House of Representatives, 1995a, 1995b).

California is one of several jurisdictions where three-strikes-and-you're-out legislation has been passed. Under this legislation, it is mandated that felons found guilty of a third serious crime must be locked up for twenty-five years to life. However, the long-term effect of such legislation on California's correctional population is grim. California does not have sufficient prison space to accommodate all of these offenders at present, despite the fact that it has one of the nation's most vigorous prison construction programs in progress (Bloom, Chesney-Lind, and Owen, 1994; Nicol, 1995).

A **cost–benefit analysis** of this new sentencing legislation has been conducted by the Rand Corporation under the direction of researcher Peter Greenwood and others (Greenwood et al., 1994). Greenwood investigated three-strikes legislation according to arrest rates, time served, prison populations, and length of criminal careers. He found that if the new law were fully implemented as written, serious felonies committed by adults would decrease by 22 to 34 percent. A third of all felonies eliminated (by incarceration) would be violent crimes such as murder and rape. The reduction in these types of crime would cost the California public about $4.5 to $6.5 billion annually, largely attributable to the costs of incarceration. Greenwood has speculated that California may not be able to afford this crime reduction as the law is presently written.

A FELONY IS A FELONY IS A FELONY. Some attempt has been made by California and other states to limit the types of offenses that qualify under the habitual offender statute and three-strikes legislation. Distinctions have been made between those who commit **violent felonies** (rape, murder, aggravated assault, armed robbery), **serious felonies** (robbery, drug dealing), and **felony property offending** (larceny/theft, vehicular theft, burglary). In theory, at least, the most serious persistent felons will be given twenty-five years to life, and less serious felons will receive shorter sentences. But few states, including California, have found the three-strikes legislation to be effective in reducing violent crime (Forer, 1994; Schiraldi, 1994; Shilton et al., 1994).

Furthermore, some critics have contended that three-strikes legislation has resulted in greater racial and ethnic discrimination by targeting proportionately larger numbers of blacks and other minorities for long mandatory sentences (Davis, Estes, and Schiraldi, 1996). In California, for instance, blacks are arrested at a rate 4.7 times higher than that of whites, blacks are incarcerated at a rate 7.8 times higher than that of whites, and blacks are incarcerated as habitual offenders at a rate 13 times higher than that of whites. California is not an isolated case, however. Disparities in mandatory sentencing laws according to race, gender, socioeconomic status, and ethnicity have been found in other jurisdictions (Campaign for an Effective Crime Policy, 1993; Forer, 1994).

Use-a-Gun-and-Go-to-Prison Statutes

Not all mandatory penalties involve **life imprisonment** or life without parole. Some mandatory penalties are intended to downgrade the seriousness of violent crimes whenever they are committed. One way of discouraging some violent offenders from using firearms when committing their crimes is to provide mandatory sentences of incarceration whenever firearms are used (Fischer and Thaker, 1992; McDowall, Loftin, and Wiersema, 1992). Other types of mandatory penalties are associated with crimes such as repeat-offense driving-while-intoxicated cases (Baxter and Kleyn, 1992).

Michigan has enacted a mandatory penalty for using a firearm during the commission of a felony. This penalty is a **flat term**, two-year sentence that must be served following whatever other sentence is imposed. If someone is convicted of armed robbery, a sentence of ten to twenty years might be imposed for the armed robbery charge, and then a separate sentence of two years will be added to the original sentence. This second sentence must be served in its entirety. If the offender is parole-eligible after serving fifteen years of the ten- to twenty-year sentence, then the two-year sentence commences. No time off for good behavior will be extended to those serving these mandatory sentences. California enacted such a law more than a decade before Michigan did (Buddingh, 1982). At present, most states have such mandatory sentencing provisions for firearms use whenever felonies are committed (Marvell and Moody, 1991).

Some critics believe that many of these mandatory sentences are primarily symbolic, in that they show the public that the legislature and other politicians are concerned about public safety and citizen fear of crime (Tonry, 1993b). Frequently, mandatory penalties are circumvented by defense counsel, prosecutors, and judges through plea bargaining, where the violations incurring mandatory penalties are carefully omitted from any reports or written documents. Many presentence investigation reports are doctored by probation officers at the request of prosecutors, so that judges will be more willing to impose variable sentences under indeterminate or determinate sentencing. If judges don't know whether particular defendants used a firearm when a felony was committed, then they cannot be compelled to impose mandatory penalties, even in Michigan. However, more than a few jurisdictions have made it increasingly difficult for these mandatory sentencing provisions to be circumvented (Austin et al., 1995). The federal sentencing guidelines and changed roles of U.S. probation officers have greatly restricted the degree to which certain aspects of an offender's crime can be ignored (Champion, 1989; Parnas et al., 1992).

Truth in Sentencing

The federal Crime Bill of 1994 provided monies to states that changed their sentencing provisions in the direction of harsher sanctions. For instance, convicted offenders in 1994 in North Dakota typically served about 35 to 40 percent of their maximum sentences. Offenders sentenced to ten years, therefore, would usually serve about three and a half to four years and then be paroled. Because of the incentive of federal money, North Dakota changed its sentencing policy in 1995 so that all convicted offenders would have to serve at least 85 percent of their maximum sentences before becoming parole-eligible. This type of sentencing reform is known as **truth in sentencing** (Delaware Statistical Analysis Center, 1989). The get-tough movement and the general public have been alarmed over the fact that inmates in North Dakota and many other states have been serving only fractions of their maximum sentences.

Although **truth-in-sentencing laws** have been enacted and the public's feelings have been assuaged to a degree, corrections departments have had to find more space for those offenders who are spending longer terms in prison. The direct result of truth in sentencing has been enormous prison population growth. Prison overcrowding is now a characteristic of all U.S. prisons. A significant contributing factor has been the **Crime Bill of 1994**. President Bill Clinton promoted this bill to provide for greater numbers of police officers on city streets as a means of preventing crime. Another provision of this bill was to maximize offender sentences so that convicted offenders must serve between 80 and 90 percent of their maximum sentences before being granted early release or parole.

Originally, the intent of truth-in-sentencing provisions was to make sure that inmates would serve a large portion of their prison terms. This has occurred in those jurisdictions where it has been mandated by state legislatures, but other problems have been created. For instance, in 1994 North Dakota was one of six states without an overcrowding problem. Its state prison in Bismarck could house about 650 inmates. Shortly after enacting truth-in-sentencing laws, however, North Dakota Penitentiary quickly became overcrowded, and a new prison facility had to be built in Jamestown. In 1998, North Dakota officials were planning two additional **tiers** in the Jamestown prison facility, as dramatic increases in the inmate population were projected. Thus, North Dakota taxpayers now face unprecedented tax increases to defray some or all of the cost of new prison construction. Although the public may want greater truth in sentencing and longer prison terms for inmates, they may not want to pay the dollar cost of new prison construction to keep this policy in place. North Dakota is not alone in dealing with prison overcrowding, however.

240-Year Sentence: How Long Do Prisoners Live?

Eyad Ismoil, His 240-Year Sentence, $10 Million Restitution, and $250,000 Fine

Eyad Ismoil was convicted of the 1993 World Trade Center bombing in November 1997, together with Ramzid Yousef. The bombing killed six people and injured more than a thousand others. Six other conspirators have already been convicted of this act of terrorism against the United States and have been sentenced to life imprisonment.

Prosecutors at Ismoil's sentencing hearing contended that Ismoil helped load the bomb into a van the day before the attack and then drove the van and Yousef to the World Trade Center the morning of the bombing. When the fuse was lit, both men fled in another car. Ismoil escaped from the United States, only to be apprehended in Jordan in 1995.

United States District Judge Kevin Duffy imposed a sentence of 240 years on Ismoil. He also ordered him to pay $10 million in restitution to the victims' families, as well as a $250,000 fine. The federal judge said, "I want to make sure that you [Ismoil] never make a dime out of this." In past cases, convicted offenders have profited from book royalties that depict how the crime was committed and what their own role was. Almost every jurisdiction has a law on the books now about prisoners being unable to profit personally from any injuries or deaths they may have inflicted on others.

What sort of sentence should the federal district judge have imposed on Ismoil? Would the death penalty have been appropriate? Why or why not? Is a 240-year sentence realistic, in that no one has ever lived that long? What do you think?

Source: Adapted from the Associated Press, "Man Gets 240 Years for Bombing." *Minot* (N.D.) *Daily News,* April 4, 1998:A2.

Sentencing Disparities

Sentencing disparity takes several different forms. Disparities in sentencing may occur when different judges within any given jurisdiction impose vastly different sentences on offenders charged with similar crimes (Hanke, 1995). Judges may be inclined to be more lenient with female offenders than with their male counterparts (Daly and Bordt, 1995). Blacks and Hispanics may receive harsher sentences than whites when the same kinds of offenses are involved (Lopez, 1995). Older offenders may receive less harsh sentences from judges than younger offenders, even when the same crimes have been committed (Smykla and Selke, 1995).

Promoters of sentencing reforms have been quick to point out these sorts of deficiencies in our sentencing system. Many states are modifying their existing sentencing systems from an indeterminate to a determinate form. Such changes are almost always accompanied by reductions in sentencing disparities attributable to racial, ethnic, gender, or socioeconomic qualities.

RACE AND ETHNICITY. Different jurisdictions report variations in sentencing attributable to race. A study of 183 defendants in Leon and Gadsden County Circuit Courts in Tallahassee and Quincy, Florida, revealed, for example, that black appellants who were sentenced in excess of the recommended maximum sentence were more likely to have the trial court's recommendation affirmed on appeal (Williams, 1995). Thus, at least in these jurisdictions, appellate decision making is far from "routine" as otherwise reported by official sources.

An investigation of sentencing disparities among 685 white and black women in Alabama during the period 1929–1985 showed that whites who killed interracially were more likely to have light sentences (of 1 to 5 years) than blacks who killed interracially. Black women who killed interracially tended to receive moderate (6 to 10 years) to heavy sentences (11 to 20 years) (Hanke, 1995). In, a sample of 755 defendants prosecuted for burglary and robbery, being Hispanic made no difference on the type of adjudication received, the verdict, or sentence severity in Tucson. However, in El Paso, Hispanic defendants were more likely to receive less favorable pretrial release outcomes than white defendants, were more likely to be convicted in jury trials, and consistently received more severe sentences when they were found guilty at trial (LaFree, 1985). Interviews with district attorneys and other officials in both cities indicated that these disparities may be partially attributable to differing language difficulties in the two jurisdictions, different mechanisms for providing attorneys to indigent defendants, and differences between established Hispanic Americans, less well-established Mexican American citizens, and Mexican nationals (LaFree, 1985).

Despite the increasing attention given to sentencing disparities and the sentencing reforms established to correct such disparate sentences, considerable evidence indicates that racial and ethnic sentencing disparities are becoming more disproportionate rather than diminishing (Tonry, 1995). Blacks are overrepresented at virtually every processing stage in the criminal justice system, and they are increasingly included in incarcerated populations. Scholars report that such disproportionate representation of blacks is due to greater offending rates of blacks, and such reports are supported by the literature. However, at the root of such disproportionate representation of blacks and other minorities in the criminal justice system are poverty and unemployment. It has been recommended, for instance, that judges should exercise greater use of special circumstances when sentencing minority offenders. With more honest sentencing policies, less disproportionate sentencing that is attributable to race or ethnicity should occur (Tonry, 1995).

Sentencing disparities attributable to race differences are particularly noticeable in the South. It has been shown, for instance, that for 21,169 convicted felons in Georgia for the years 1973–1980, blacks tended to receive longer sentences than whites (Clayton, 1983). As a matter of fact, blacks received sentences that were on average 2.5 years longer than sentences for whites convicted of the same crimes. Similar disparities have been observed and are considered pervasive in capital cases (Sorenson and Wallace, 1995).

GENDER. Do women receive more lenient sentences than men? A study of 1,027 male and female offenders in Minneapolis, Minnesota, who were convicted of theft, forgery, or drug law violations between 1972 and 1976 revealed that sex status does have a significant effect on sentencing severity in that women receive more lenient sentences than men who have committed similar offenses (Kruttschnitt, 1984). Women not only received more lenient sentences but also received more lenient treatment related to pretrial release. A related study of 1,558 convicted males and 1,365 convicted females in Minneapolis between 1965 and 1980 found that women were more likely to receive pretrial release than men, as well as receive less severe sentences for similar offenses (Kruttschnitt and Green, 1984).

Other research has largely supported the Minnesota study. For example, Daly and Bordt (1995) conducted an extensive statistical review of sentencing disparity literature to determine whether "sex effects" favoring women over men exist in sentencing. More than half of the fifty studies surveyed indicated gender effects favoring women over men existed. Both older and more recent data sets reveal similar patterns in which female offenders have received more lenient sentences than male offenders (Kruttschnitt, 1984; Kruttschnitt and Green, 1984).

The relation between gender and the application of the death penalty in capital cases has also been investigated. Both surveys of citizens and actual patterns of capital punishment use in selected states reveals that women convicted of capital crimes are far less likely to receive the death penalty than men convicted of a capital crime under similar circumstances (Farnworth and Teske, 1995; Sandys and McGarrell, 1995). Further, citizens surveyed tended to favor more lenient treatment for women convicted of capital offenses (i.e., life-without-parole sentences as opposed to death sentences). Farnworth and Teske (1995) suggest that one explanation for gender differentiation is the chivalry hypothesis, which is that decision makers or judges treat female offenders with chivalry during sentencing, and further that judges are inclined to dispense selective chivalry toward white women compared with other women or minorities of either gender. Data from 9,866 felony theft cases and 18,176 felony assault cases from California courts in 1988 show that female offenders with no prior record were more likely to receive charge reductions than male offenders. Also, female offenders' chances for probation were greater than that of a similar aggregate of male offenders (Farnworth and Teske, 1995).

As more states adopt reforms including presumptive and determinate sentencing systems, fewer sentencing disparities will be observed from one jurisdiction to the next. Also, judges seem to favor greater uniformity in their sentencing practices within the same jurisdictions. The adoption of consistent sentencing standards will gradually eliminate patterns of gender, ethnic, or racial discrimination in sentencing in future years.

SOCIOECONOMIC STATUS. An offender's socioeconomic status plays a significant part in explaining sentencing disparities. Offenders whose resources are limited cannot afford private counsel, and less experienced public defenders are often appointed to defend them. Further, the sentencing guidelines in many states tend to overpenalize street crimes, which are most often committed by those with lower socioeconomic status.

Evidence of sentencing disparities attributable to socioeconomic status is considerable. Studies of sentencing patterns in southeastern states have shown an inverse relation between socioeconomic status and sentence length (D'Allessio and Stolzenberg, 1993). Of 2,760 convicted offenders, those of lower socioeconomic status drew longer sentences than those of higher socioeconomic status. The study concluded that this extra-legal factor was significant in explaining differential sentence lengths of offenders, controlling for criminal history and conviction offense (D'Allessio and Stolzenberg, 1993). Other research has supported the idea that those with lower socioeconomic status are disenfranchised by the criminal justice system. However, the influence of socio-economic status may adversely affect certain offenders of higher socioeconomic status. A survey of white-collar offenders sentenced in seven U.S. district courts showed that these offenders tended to receive imprisonment more often than comparable offenders of lower status; furthermore, the sentences imposed on white-collar offenders were longer (Weisburd, Waring, and Wheeler, 1990). The general consensus seems to be that lower socioeconomic status offenders tend to receive harsher and longer sentences than offenders of higher socioeconomic status, although there are always exceptions.

The Sentencing Hearing

When offenders are convicted, they are sentenced by a judge to a term of years, either on probation or in jail or prison. In most felony cases, before offenders are sentenced, they must have a **sentencing hearing**. A sentencing hearing is a proceeding in which evidence and testimony are presented both for and against the offender. The hearing furnishes the sentencing judge with additional information about the offender, the crime, and the victims. In the context of this additional information, judges can make an informed decision about the best sentence to impose. Oral testimony is given by anyone who has relevant information. Usually, testimony is given by the offender and those speaking on her or his behalf. Victims and their families also offer their opinions and tell how they were affected by the offender's actions. This oral testimony is considered by the judge in making the sentencing decision.

WEIGHING THE AGGRAVATING AND MITIGATING CIRCUMSTANCES. The sentencing hearing is also important because it permits the judge to consider **aggravating circumstances** and **mitigating circumstances**. Aggravating circumstances are those factors that tend to intensify the severity of the punishment: whether the crime involved death or serious bodily injury, whether the offender was out on bail or on probation at the time the crime was committed, whether the offender has a prior criminal record, whether there was more than one victim, whether the offender was the leader in the commission of the offense involving two or more offenders, whether the victim was treated with extreme cruelty by the offender, and whether a dangerous weapon was used by the offender in committing the crime.

Mitigating circumstances are those that tend to lessen the severity of punishment: whether the offender was cooperative with police and gave information about others who may have been involved in the crime, whether the offender did not cause serious bodily injury or death to a victim, whether the offender acted under duress or extreme provocation, whether there was any possible justification for the crime, whether the offender was

Coroner Steals from the Dead

The Case of Lycoming County Coroner George Gedon

Ever heard of a coroner who burglarized the homes of the deceased? In Lycoming County, Pennsylvania, authorities arrested Coroner George Gedon and charged him with taking cash and jewelry from corpses he examined. It seems that Gedon also served as a funeral director. In these two capacities, Gedon had unlimited access to a deceased person's home. Witnesses claim that they saw Gedon take some coins and other valuables from the body of one of their relatives during a preliminary examination of the corpse.

Williamsport, Pennsylvania, residents are more than a little concerned about Gedon's behavior. Quite a few family members of deceased loved ones have filed complaints against Gedon, alleging that money, jewelry, or other valuable possessions were not returned to them when they knew that these possessions were on the deceased's body at the time of death. Shortly following these accusations, the funeral directors' association in Pennsylvania revoked Gedon's license to do business as a funeral director. However, Gedon retained his coroner's position temporarily, until the court could determine his guilt or innocence.

If Gedon is guilty of these charges, what should be his punishment? What types of controls should be in place to guard against tampering with valuable possessions of the deceased?

Source: Adapted from Associated Press, "Coroner to Stand Trial of Charges of Stealing from the Dead." *Minot* (N.D.) *Daily News,* August 11, 1996:A2.

mentally incapacitated or was suffering from some mental illness, whether the offender made restitution to the victim, whether the offender had no previous criminal record, or whether the offender committed the crime to provide necessities for self or family.

Judges consider these aggravating and mitigating circumstances to determine whether the aggravating circumstances outweigh the mitigating ones. If this is the case, then judges can mete out harsher sentences. However, if the mitigating circumstances outweigh the aggravating ones, then judges can be more lenient with offenders in their sentencing decisions.

When the jury or judge finds the defendant guilty, a sentence is not imposed immediately. Sentencing hearings are usually scheduled four to six weeks after the trial. Within the context of due process, defendants are presumed innocent of any crime until they are proven guilty beyond a reasonable doubt in court. At that point, most judges wish to gather additional information about the convicted offender, the circumstances surrounding the commission of the crime, and the impact of the crime on the victim(s). Probation officers are most frequently assigned the task of researching the background of each convicted offender in an effort to furnish judges with a fairly complete package of information. This information is compiled in a presentence investigation report or PSI. A **probation officer** needs time to gather all relevant information, which explains the lapse of time between conviction and sentencing. Probation officers interview the offender's employer, relatives, friends, church and school officials, and victims. The offender's criminal history is described as well. All this information is summarized in the PSI report and submitted to the judge. Defendants are also given the opportunity to describe their involvement in the crime and to take responsibility for what they did.

The Presentence Investigation Report: Contents and Functions

A presentence investigation (PSI) report is a probation officer's written summary of information about the convicted offender's background, the nature of the crime's commission, and the implications of the crime for all relevant parties, including victims. A sample presentence investigation report form for North Dakota is shown in Figure 10.1.

The North Dakota PSI report is a fairly standardized document that is typical of PSI reports prepared in other state jurisdictions. An inspection of this report shows that considerable background information must be compiled. Notice that the following information is required: the names of the judge, prosecutor, and defense attorney (private or appointed); county; file number; date PSI was ordered, due, and completed; docket or file number of case and location of court; name, address, telephone number, marital status, and dependents of defendant; whether home is rented or owned; how long defendant has lived at the address provided; occupation and income; Social Security number; employer and gross monthly income; education; military service record, if any, and type of discharge; general physical condition; prior criminal record; instant offense, seriousness, and offense classification; date of offense and arresting agency; days in custody following arrest; codefendants, if any; victim and victim address; defendant's version of crime (offender's **sentencing memorandum**); investigating officer's version of crime, or **narrative**; other information, including defendant's reputation, attitude, leisure time activities, and associates; comments by probation officer about sentencing alternatives, treatment proposals, and community service; and mandatory attachments, including criminal information/complaint, law enforcement investigation report, and victim impact statement (if applicable).

Probation officers sometimes locate school officials and associates of the offender and interview them. Likewise, victims and their families are interviewed. Probation officers summarize this information and make their own recommendations to the judge. Judges consider the PSI report in making their sentencing decision (Lanier and Miller, 1995).

Note that the judge considers both the sentencing hearing testimony and the contents of the PSI report. None of this information, even the recommendation of a sentence by the probation officer, binds the judge in any way (Cromwell and Killinger, 1994; Walsh, 1992). The judge has already presided at the trial where all relevant evidence was introduced. Judges know the facts of the case, and they may contemplate a particular

PRE-SENTENCE INVESTIGATION REPORT 1
NORTH DAKOTA PAROLE AND PROBATION DEPARTMENT
SFN 16394 (7-88)

County	File No.(s)	Date PSI Ordered
Judge	States Attorney	Date PSI Due
Defense Attorney ☐ Appointed ☐ Retained		Date PSI Completed

Name (Court Records)	Date of Birth	Race	Sex
Name (Alias)	Place of Birth		

Offense

Address	Telephone No.

Lives With (Name)	Relationship
☐ OWNS ☐ RENTS ☐ House ☐ Apartment ☐ Room	How Long At This Address?

Marital Status	Gross Monthly Income—All Sources	Number of Dependents
Occupation	Social Security No.	NDSID No.

Employer	How Long Employed
Previous Employer	How Long Employed

Reason For Leaving

Education

Military Service (Branch & Dates)	Type of Discharge

Current Physical Condition

☐ Drug Use ☐ Mental/Emotional Problems ☐ Alcohol Use (Give details under comments)

PRIOR RECORD (USE REVERSE SIDE IF NEEDED FOR ADDITIONAL SPACE)

Date	Offense	Arresting Agency	Disposition

COMMENTS AND RECOMMENDATIONS (Community Service and/or Treatment Proposals, etc.):

MANDATORY ATTACHMENTS:
Criminal Information/Complaint
Law Enforcement Investigation Report
Victim's Impact Statement (If applicable)

Probation/Parole Officer _____ Date _____

FIGURE 10.1 North Dakota Presentence Investigation Report Form

SFN 16395 Page 2

PRIOR RECORD (USE REVERSE SIDE IF NEEDED FOR ADDITIONAL SPACE)			
Date	Offense	Arresting Agency	Disposition

Offense and Penalty Classification	Days in Custody

Date of Offense	Arresting Agency

Co-defendants and disposition

Victim	Address

DEFENDANT'S VERSION OF CRIME

INVESTIGATING OFFICER'S VERSION OF CRIME

OTHER INFORMATION (Reputation, Attitude, Leisure time activities, Associates, etc.)

COMMENTS AND SENTENCING ALTERNATIVES (Community Service and/or Treatment Propsals, etc.):

MANDATORY ATTACHMENTS:
Criminal Information/Complaint
Law Enforcement Investigation Report
Victim's Impact Statement (If applicable)

Probation/Parole Officer   Date sentence. But before the actual sentence is imposed, judges have one final opportunity to consider any additional relevant information.

For instance, defendants do not have to testify in their own criminal trials. The sentencing hearing, therefore, gives them a chance to speak, to apologize, and to accept responsibility for what they have done. **Acceptance of responsibility** for one's crimes is considered an important first step toward rehabilitation (Shockley, 1988; Shein, 1988). Sometimes judges are persuaded to be more lenient when convicted offenders admit the wrongfulness of their actions and express genuine regret for what happened. However, additional testimony from victims may persuade the judge to deal more harshly with offenders who have so adversely affected the lives of others (Beckley, Callahan, and Carter, 1981; Clear, Clear, and Burrell, 1989).

Functions of PSI Reports

The functions of PSI reports are to (1) provide information for offender sentencing, (2) aid probation officers in determining the most appropriate treatment or rehabilitative programs for offenders in need of assistance, (3) assist prisons and jails in their efforts to classify offenders effectively, and (4) furnish parole boards with important offender background data to assist them in deciding about early release (*Federal Probation*, 1974). Probation officers attempt to solicit the most accurate information about the offender and victims (Vance, 1970). The contents of PSI reports are disclosed not only to judges but also to prosecutors and defense counsel (Zastrow, 1971) to ensure that they are accurate (Bergman, 1986). Disclosure of the contents of PSI reports is usually mandated by legislative provisions for both the states and federal government (Dubois, 1981; Townsend, Palmer, and Newton, 1978). Two important components of PSI reports are the offender's sentencing memorandum and the victim impact statements (Schmolesky and Thorson, 1982; Lanier and Miller, 1995).

The Offender's Sentencing Memorandum

A **defendant's sentencing memorandum** is a document prepared by the convicted offender that describes the crime, why it was committed, and the attitudes and feelings of the offender concerning his or her involvement. The memorandum also provides an opportunity for the offender to accept responsibility for the crime.

In recent years, the phrase *acceptance of responsibility* has become an increasingly important part of the sentencing process. The U.S. Sentencing Commission provided that acceptance of responsibility would enable sentencing judges to possibly mitigate an offender's sentence. Various states have added acceptance of responsibility to their sentencing provisions. Thus, offenders who admit their crimes and apologize in open court during the sentencing hearing may incur some leniency from judges. It is insufficient to merely declare, "Your honor, I'm sorry for what I've done and I accept responsibility for my actions." Much depends on the circumstances and sincerity of the person making such an admission. Many convicted offenders learn to act contrite and make false statements about their acceptance of responsibility. Judicial discretion is accorded great weight here (Forst and Rhodes, 1982). If the judge is convinced that the offender has truly accepted responsibility for the crime, then the judge may decide to mitigate the harshness of the penalties imposed. Defense counsel are often key players in the sentencing process. They have one final opportunity to summarize the facts as they see them and to make a case for judicial leniency toward their client (Shein, 1988; Weintraub, 1987).

Victim Impact Statements and Victim Input

Another important part of the sentence mosaic is the victim impact statement (VIS). Victim impact statements are oral and/or written testimony concerning how the victims and their close relatives were affected by the offender's crime. The nature of victim impact is very important, because judges can learn much more than what was originally disclosed about the crime during the trial (Davis and Smith, 1994). Most jurisdictions in the United States permit victims and their relatives to provide written or oral evidence of how the offender's crime has affected them. VISs are also used in other countries, such as Canada (Roberts, 1992).

The inclusion of VISs in sentencing hearings is not new. Many states have provided for victim involvement in the sentencing process in past years (Luginbuhl and Burkhead, 1995). However, victim involvement in sentencing decisions has dramatically increased (Davis and Smith, 1994; Erez and Tontodonato, 1992). In 1987, the admissibility of VISs was prohibited by the U.S. Supreme Court in the case of *Booth v. Maryland*. However, by 1992, the U.S. Supreme Court changed its position to allow VISs in most criminal proceedings, including sentencing hearings (*Payne v. Tennessee*).

One reason for increased victim participation in sentencing decisions is that many citizens regard the criminal justice system as far too lenient toward offenders, particularly those who have committed violent felonies. Many factors besides victim impact enter into the judge's sentencing decision. Logistical constraints, such as chronic prison overcrowding, may mean that not all convicted felons who deserved to be imprisoned actually are imprisoned. California, for instance, places about seventy percent of its convicted felons on probation annually, a fact that disturbs critics of the criminal justice system as well as the general public.

In an effort to make judges more accountable and impose sentences more in line with the seriousness of the offense, victims and their families have attempted to provide information that will cause judges to deal with offenders more harshly. Investigators have studied VISs and whether judicial sentencing practices have been influenced, one way or another, in different jurisdictions. The results are mixed (Davis and Smith, 1994; Roberts, 1992). Little evidence shows a direct correlation between how victims have been affected by a crime and the severity of sentences imposed by judges (Davis and Smith, 1994). However, there is evidence that victim participation in sentencing has a cathartic effect. Victims and their families who participate in the sentencing hearing tend to be more satisfied with the sentences judges impose (Erez and Tontodonato, 1992). Victim participation may not directly influence judicial sentencing decisions, but victims or their relatives may feel as though their input was influential.

Experiments have been conducted with mock juries in death penalty proceedings. At North Carolina State University, for example, ninety-nine undergraduate students were asked to place themselves in the position of jurors in a hypothetical death penalty case.

CASE LAW ON VICTIM IMPACT STATEMENTS

Booth v. Maryland, 482 U.S. 496, 107 S.Ct. 2529 (1987). Booth was convicted of first-degree murder in a Baltimore, Maryland, court. During his sentencing hearing, a victim impact statement (VIS) was read so that his sentence might be enhanced or intensified. Following the sentence of death, Booth appealed, alleging that the VIS was a violation of his Eighth Amendment right against cruel and unusual punishment. The U.S. Supreme Court agreed and said that during sentencing phases of capital murder trials, the introduction of VISs is unconstitutional. Among its reasons cited for this opinion, the U.S. Supreme Court said that a VIS creates an unacceptable risk that a jury may impose the death penalty in an arbitrary and capricious manner. At the time, therefore, VISs were considered unacceptable and inadmissible during the sentencing phase of a trial. The U.S. Supreme Court's position about VISs changed in 1991 in the case of *Payne v. Tennessee.*

Payne v. Tennessee, 501 U.S. 808, 111 S.Ct. 2597 (1991). Payne was convicted of a double murder. At the sentencing hearing, Payne introduced various witnesses on his behalf to avoid the death penalty. During the same hearing, the victims' relatives introduced their victim impact statement, pressing the jury to impose the death penalty on Payne. The death penalty was imposed and Payne appealed, contesting the introduction of damaging evidence and opinions expressed in the victim impact statement. The U.S. Supreme Court upheld Payne's death sentence, holding that victim impact statements do not violate an offender's Eighth Amendment rights. The significance of this case is that it supports and condones the use of victim impact statements against convicted offenders during sentencing hearings. At present, VISs are considered admissible during the sentencing phase of a trial.

Other students acted as victims and gave testimony about a convicted offender who had murdered their relative. Later, the students were polled to determine whether the VISs were influential in deciding whether the death penalty would be applied. Significant numbers of students disclosed that the VISs were important in persuading them to vote for the death penalty, where the options were the death penalty or life without parole (Luginbuhl and Burkhead, 1995). Although this experiment involved students reacting to an imaginary scenario, it does indicate how actual jurors might react to similar testimony from real victims in capital trials. Other researchers have arrived at similar conclusions (Erez, 1990; Erez and Tontodonato, 1990; McLeod, 1986).

VISs may contain errors of fact. Sometimes victims and their families exaggerate the adverse effects of the offender's actions, particularly where property losses were involved

(Davis, Fisher, and Paykin, 1984; McLeod, 1986). Some studies have revealed that female offenders are more favorably treated by victims than male offenders whenever VISs are provided (Erez and Tontodonato, 1990).

VISs have additional uses in the processing and imprisonment of offenders. For example, parole boards may rely on VISs in determining whether a particular offender should be granted early release (Texas Crime Victim Clearinghouse, 1989). Written VISs are maintained in an offender's file and used by parole board members whenever an inmate's early-release eligibility occurs. Some victims may participate in parole hearings and give additional oral testimony about why the offender should be denied parole (Posner, 1984). However, not all victims present oral testimony against their victimizers. In some cases, victims speak in favor of an offender's early release during parole hearings. These cases, though exceptional, do occur with some frequency (Erez and Tontodonato, 1990; Hellerstein, 1989).

Imposing the Sentence

When sentences are imposed by judges, they are guided by information provided in PSI reports, the offender's sentencing memorandum, probation officer recommendations, victim impact statements, and their own view of the offender and the crime's seriousness. Depending on the sentencing scheme used in each jurisdiction, judges may be bound to sentence offenders in a consistent way; that is, all convicted bank robbers in a given jurisdiction are supposed to receive a specified sentence as punishment, with consideration given to any aggravating or mitigating circumstances. But judges are permitted latitude under almost every sentencing scheme (Griset, 1996b). This is judicial discretion.

Each judge relies on previous rulings in similar cases and attempts to be fair and impartial when meting out a specific sentence (Austin et al., 1995). Elderly offenders may receive special consideration because of their age. If an offender is mentally ill, intellectually retarded, or in some other way impaired, judges may take these impairments into account for virtually every type of offender. Judicial sentencing decisions may be challenged, but appellate courts are inclined to assume that the original sentence imposed was correct (Washington State Sentencing Guidelines Commission, 1996). It is difficult to overcome such a presumption on appeal.

Shock Probation and Split Sentencing

Where judges are permitted great latitude in their sentencing discretion, they are inclined to impose probation for many first offenders convicted of minor offenses or less serious felonies. Judges assign offenders sentenced to some form of probation to a probation department or community corrections agency, where their behavior will be supervised for a period of time (Diroll, 1989).

One type of sentence designed to scare convicted offenders, particularly those who have never served time in a prison or jail, is **shock probation**, **shock incarceration**, or

THE SEVENTY-SEVEN-YEAR-OLD BANK ROBBER

About Ray Boeger

It happened in Santa Ana, California. Ray Boeger, seventy-seven, was a business-man and former advertising executive who had built a successful electric car company. However, bad business deals and investments led to hard times for Boeger. Also, his wife developed kidney problems and ran up huge medical bills. Ray was in over his head and didn't know what to do.

One morning, Ray met some friends at a bar. They drank and discussed Ray's business. Ray said that downing a large quantity of beer and getting criticism from his associates triggered bad feelings. Although he can't remember doing much of it, Ray went home and got a Halloween disguise and an unloaded gun. He then went to the Huntington Beach branch of the World Savings & Loan, walked in with the weapon, and asked a teller if she could cash an $800 check. The teller asked if Boeger had a gun, and he said, "Yes," and then he showed it to her. She and two other tellers began loading up a bag with bills. Boeger left the bank, but a short time thereafter some dye packets included with the bills went off, spraying Boeger with telling dye. Several witnesses saw his car as it left the bank area and noted the plate number. Boeger was arrested a few hours later by police. They found the dye-stained money, a dye-stained Boeger, and about $1,100 in cash.

Boeger said that his ailing wife was disappointed in him, and he felt like a failure. Police acknowledge that Boeger is not the typical armed bank robber. He had no prior criminal record. Further, Boeger had served earlier on the Seal Beach Police Commission and the Orange County Boy Scout Council. Boeger told news reporters, "I guarantee you I won't do it again. Because I'm not going to drink anymore."

Is Boeger the type of person who might qualify for a diversion program? Should Boeger be prosecuted for bank robbery? What mitigating factors can you think of that might lessen Boeger's punishment? What do you think?

Source: Adapted from the Associated Press, "Blaming Crime on Booze, Bills." *Minot* (N.D.) *Daily News*, September 22, 1997:A5.

shock parole. Shock probation and shock parole refer to planned sentences whereby judges order offenders imprisoned for statutory incarceration periods related to their conviction offenses. However, after 30, 60, 90, or 120 days of incarceration, these offend-ers are taken out of jail or prison and resentenced to probation or parole (Vaughn, 1993; Vito, 1984). Ohio introduced shock probation for the first time in 1965 (Vito, 1984). Since then, shock probation has spread to almost every U.S. jurisdiction.

The intent of shock probation is literally to shock or frighten convicted offenders through the incarceration experience (Scott, Dinitz, and Shichor, 1978; Vito and Allen,

1980). No one wants to be imprisoned. For those who have never experienced either short- or long-term confinements, the effect of being behind bars for a month or more can be sufficiently traumatic to deter them from further criminal activity. Early evidence suggests that recidivism rates among shock probationers are relatively low compared with other probationers who have not been imprisoned for short periods (Parisi, 1981).

SPLIT SENTENCING. In several jurisdictions, judges may engage in **split sentencing**. Split sentencing, also known as **mixed sentencing**, **intermittent sentencing**, and **jail as a condition of probation**, are combination sentences imposed by judges, part incarceration and part probation. If an offender has committed more than one offense, then the judge may impose a separate sentence for each offense. The sentence for one offense may be a year in jail, whereas the sentence for the second offense may be probation. This mixed sentence means that the offender will spend some time in jail as well as on probation.

Intermittent sentences involve offenders who are sentenced to partial confinement. These offenders may be sentenced to a jail on weekends but during the week work at a job to support themselves and their families. In jail as a condition of probation, the judge orders the offender to serve a specified term of months in a jail before being placed on probation (Parisi, 1981; Vito, 1984). The intent of these split sentencing options is to dramatize the seriousness of the offender's crime. Serving some time in jail or prison will make the point that crime is bad and should be avoided; otherwise, imprisonment will result. This simplistic view underscores the fact that many shock probationers take this experience to heart and never reoffend (Boudouris and Turnbull, 1985; Massachusetts Legislative Research Council, 1987). The effectiveness of shock probation varies among jurisdictions. Generally, shock probationers tend to have lower rates of recidivism than other types of offenders (Boudouris and Turnbull, 1985; Diroll, 1989; Massachusetts Legislative Research Council, 1987).

The Death Penalty and Bifurcated Trials

The most serious sentence criminal courts can impose is the death penalty. The death penalty is reserved for those who have committed capital crimes, primarily murder. In recent years, the death penalty has been approved for federal offenders who have been convicted of large-scale drug dealing.

The death penalty is controversial. However, surveys during the 1990s reveal that about seventy-five percent of all U.S. citizens support its use as a suitable punishment for capital offenses. In 1997, Timothy McVeigh was convicted of bombing a federal building in Oklahoma City, Oklahoma, and was given the death penalty for his role in this crime, which killed 169 people. Another participant in this bombing was Terry Nichols. In a separate federal trial, Nichols was convicted as a conspirator in the bombing, and the federal prosecutor sought the death penalty in his case. However, the jury was unable to agree on which punishment should be imposed, and the federal court sentenced Nichols to life without parole instead of death.

Furman v. Georgia (1972) and *Gregg v. Georgia* (1976). The death penalty is used as the maximum punishment in about two-thirds of all states. In 1972, the constitutionality of the death penalty in Georgia was challenged. Disproportionately large numbers of blacks were being executed, compared with whites, often in cases involving rape or assault. In 1972, the U.S. Supreme Court declared in *Furman v. Georgia* that the death penalty as it was currently being applied in a discriminatory manner in Georgia was unconstitutional. All states temporarily suspended the death penalty until more information could be obtained from the U.S. Supreme Court about the procedural appropriateness of the death penalty and its application.

In 1976, the U.S. Supreme Court held in *Gregg v. Georgia* that the revised procedural application of the death penalty in Georgia was constitutional. States resumed the application of the death penalty shortly thereafter. Gary Gillmore, a Utah murderer, was executed by firing squad in 1979, the first person executed after the U.S. Supreme Court approved of Georgia's new method for imposing death penalties on those convicted of capital crimes, which called for a **bifurcated trial** in all capital cases.

A bifurcated trial is a two-stage proceeding. The first stage is the main trial, when a defendant's guilt or innocence is established. If the defendant is found guilty of the crime, the jury meets in a second stage to consider the punishment, particularly whether the death penalty should be imposed. Aggravating and mitigating factors are weighed by juries, and the judge recommends the death penalty when the aggravating factors outweigh the mitigating ones.

Bifurcated trials are common in those states with death penalty provisions. The nature of bifurcated trials is thought to overcome the criticism that the death penalty is applied in a discriminatory manner. The offender's race is not a factor in these two-stage proceedings, which permit juries to consider both aggravating and mitigating circumstances. We have already examined the common set of statutory aggravating and mitigating circumstances that juries consider.

Another feature of bifurcated trials is that death penalties can no longer be automatically applied. It used to be the case that for some felony murders, such as police officers killed during a crime, those convicted of such crimes would automatically be sentenced to death. The *Gregg* case was significant in causing these automatic death penalty statutes to be declared unconstitutional. The 1980 case of *Woodson v. North Carolina* held that automatic death penalties were unconstitutional anyway, even though the essence of this holding was conveyed in *Gregg* four years earlier. The main reason is that automatic death penalties do not permit juries to weigh aggravating and mitigating circumstances.

Appeals of Sentences

THE PURPOSES OF AN APPEAL. Once defendants have been convicted of crimes, they are entitled to at least one appeal to a higher court. The primary purpose of an appeal is to correct a wrong that may have been committed by police, the prosecution, or the court. Errors may have occurred that influenced the trial outcome, and appeals are intended to correct these mistakes and errors.

SERIAL MURDERER STASHES BODIES IN MOM'S HOME

The Case of Gregory Clepper, Crack Addict and Serial Killer

To look at Gregory Clepper, a twenty-eight-year-old who lived in a crowded neighborhood and worked at lots of odd jobs, you would never guess that behind that mild and polite social exterior lurked a serial killer. "I've known him all his life. He was always polite and mannerable." said Lois Crane, fifty-nine, his neighbor up the street. Another neighbor, Anita Hodges, twenty-three, said, "He was just a regular guy."

Clepper's neighbors knew that the had a drug problem. They knew that he used crack cocaine and other drugs. But they also knew that as far as they were concerned, Gregory's drug use never interfered with his functioning around them. He never hurt *anybody.*

Imagine the surprise among Clepper's neighbors when police came to arrest him for killing at least twelve women. Beginning in the summer of 1991, Clepper strangled or beat prostitutes when they objected to his refusal to pay them. One body was left in the city's recycling center. Clepper was caught after a friend turned him in for bragging about killing Patricia Scott, a thirty-year-old prostitute who had been raped, strangled, and left in a high school trash bin on April 24, 1996. Actually, Clepper had killed the woman in his mother's home the day before and had stashed her body in a closet. Later, a friend of Clepper's, Eric Henderson, helped him carry Scott's body to a car.

Even more surprising was the fact that Gregory's mother was an accomplice. After some police questioning, Gregory's mother, Gladys Clepper, forty-six, admitted that she had helped her son dispose of at least one body earlier. Clepper was arrested and charged with twelve murders; Clepper's mother was arrested and charged with two counts of concealing a homicide, and Gregory's friend Henderson was also arrested and charged with concealing a homicide. Gregory confessed to all of the killings. Prosecutors were debating whether to seek the death penalty.

Who is to blame for Gregory Clepper's murders? Should he receive the death penalty? Does committing twelve murders qualify someone for capital murder? Why or why not? What would you suggest as an appropriate punishment for Clepper?

Source: Associated Press, "Chicago Man Charged with 12 Murders." *Minot* (N.D.) *Daily News,* May 3, 1996:A4.

A secondary purpose of an **appeal** is to render judgment about one or more issues that will influence future cases. Thus, when an appellate court hears a case from a lower trial court, their decision becomes a precedent for subsequent similar cases. This is the doctrine of ***stare decisis***, meaning that once a higher court has ruled a particular way on

U.S. Supreme Court Reviews Numbers of Death Row Appeals

The Case of Wayne Ellis Felker

Habeas corpus relief is taken for granted by death row inmates. Habeas corpus relief seeks to challenge the *fact, nature,* and *length* of confinement. Convicted murderers who are given death sentences use habeas corpus as a means of delaying their death sentences. On the basis of habeas corpus appeals, a condemned inmate can prolong execution for ten or more years. Wayne Ellis Felker is on death row in Georgia for murdering a college student, Joy Ludlum, in Warner Robins, Georgia, in 1981.

The get-tough movement and the Crime Bill of 1994 are dissatisfied with the liberal posture courts have taken on death penalty appeals. Housing inmates on death row costs a considerable amount of money and taxpayer dollars, and the longer they remain on death row, the more it costs. Some opponents of capital punishment have argued that such costs could be cut by abolishing the death penalty and keeping these prisoners in less costly incarceration. The American Civil Liberties Union (ACLU) and other groups want to ban the death penalty and thus favor any appeals process that delays or sets aside death sentences.

Not everyone is anti–capital punishment, however. Proponents of capital punishment outnumber its opponents in the United States, at least according to national polls. Legislators have been responsive to such surveys. In fact, Congress passed and President Bill Clinton signed into law the Anti-Terrorism and Effective Death Penalty Act of 1996, which limits death row appeals.

Normally, state prisoners may use the federal appeals process to prolong litigation and raise an unlimited number of questions about the sentences of death imposed upon them by alleging that their state court prosecutions violated one or more of their basic constitutional rights. They have had this right since 1867 under habeas corpus. Under the 1996 act, however, inmate appeals are limited to one federal appeal to a three-judge panel in any given federal circuit. The law states that the decision of the three-judge panel is final and that if an inmate's request for appellate review is denied, then the death sentence will be imposed, unless dramatic new evidence is discovered.

The ACLU argues that the one-appeal limitation substantially suppresses the oversight powers of the U.S. Supreme Court itself, and thus there is conceivably a conflict-of-interest issue remaining to be resolved. The U.S. Supreme Court does not agree, however. The limited appeals procedure streamlines the process and greatly reduces the time lag between the imposition of death sentences and their implementation. Civil rights groups, such as the ACLU, oppose such a streamlined process, however, because they believe that some convicted offenders are, in fact, innocent and that eventually exculpatory evidence may

surface that will set aside or overturn death sentences. In 1996, five U.S. Supreme Court justices regarded the pace of appellate review in past years as too slow, and it would seem that they would favor legislation to speed up the execution process.

Should death row appeals be limited? Is such a reduction in the number of appeals constitutional? Should prisoners have an unlimited number of appeals to challenge their death sentences?

Source: Adapted from Associated Press, "Trying to Escape the Electric Chair." *Minot* (N.D.) *Daily News,* June 3, 1996:A3.

a particular issue, lower courts are bound to make rulings consistent with higher court holdings whenever similar cases are heard. However, trial court judges have some discretion in deciding whether certain subsequent cases resemble previous cases on which appellate courts have ruled. Thus, trial court judges may decide that although a subsequent case is similar in various respects to previous cases already decided by higher courts, there may be sufficient differences in the cases so that trial judges decide that the higher court rulings do not apply.

APPEALS OF SENTENCES. All death sentences are automatically appealed (Coyne and Entzeroth, 1994). The appellate process for any case, capital or otherwise, begins with an appeal filed with the most immediate appellate court above the trial court level. When offenders are convicted in federal district courts, for instance, their appeals are directed to one of the thirteen circuit courts of appeal. In California, for example, Stacy Koon and Laurence Powell were two police officers convicted in a federal district court of inflicting great bodily harm on a motorist, Rodney King, under color of their police authority. Under the U.S. sentencing guidelines, these former officers were supposed to be sentenced to several years of prison. However, the federal district judge downgraded the seriousness of their offense and sentenced them to time served. The U.S. Attorney's Office in Los Angeles filed an appeal with the Ninth Circuit Court of Appeals, contending that the reasons cited by the federal judge for downgrading their offense were not appropriate. The Ninth Circuit reversed the trial judge and reinstated the original sentence called for under the U.S. sentencing guidelines. Koon and Powell appealed, this time to the U.S. Supreme Court, the court of last resort above the circuit courts of appeal.

In capital cases originating in state courts, state remedies must be pursued on appeal before the federal system is accessed. For instance, a person convicted of murder in Tennessee and sentenced to death must direct an appeal first to the Court of Criminal Appeals. If there is an unfavorable ruling by that appellate court, then the offender can direct an appeal to the Tennessee Supreme Court. If the ruling by this court is unfavorable for the offender, then a direct appeal may be made to the U.S. Supreme Court for relief.

APPELLANTS AND APPELLEES. **Appellants** are those who initiate appeals. **Appellees** are those who prevailed in the trial court and argue against reversing the decision of the lower court. Those convicted of capital crimes and sentenced to death are appellants. In most instances, the state is the appellee. Cases are given names to fit the two parties. Thus, we have *Furman v. Georgia, Gregg v. Georgia, Woodson v. North Carolina,* or *Payne v. Tennessee.* In each of these cases, the appellant is mentioned first and the appellee second. There are many grounds on which to base appeals, and death penalty appeals can drag out these cases for ten or fifteen years before the appellants are eventually executed.

Bases for Appeals

Appeals may be directed to appellate courts on diverse grounds. Appellants may raise questions about how they were originally arrested and processed. They may challenge the admissibility of certain evidence used to convict them or claim incompetence or ineffective assistance of counsel (del Carmen, 1995; Smith, 1995). They may challenge the sentence imposed by the judge. Almost all these challenges about their processing as criminal defendants can be included within the scope of a habeas corpus petition.

HABEAS CORPUS PETITIONS. *Habeas corpus* means, literally, "produce the body." A **habeas corpus petition** challenges three things: (1) the fact of confinement, (2) the length of confinement, and/or (3) the nature of confinement. The fact of confinement involves every event that led to the present circumstances of the appellant (Pursley, 1995). If the appellant is on death row because of a capital offense conviction, then any aspect of the justice process leading to the offender's placement on death row is a potential habeas corpus target (Hanson and Daley, 1995; U.S. House of Representatives (1995c).

For example, the fact of confinement was challenged in the case of *Preiser v. Rodriguez,* 411 U.S. 475 (1973). Rodriguez was a state prisoner who was deprived of good-time credits by the New York Department of Correctional Services because of disciplinary proceedings. Rodriguez filed a habeas corpus petition. The lower court dismissed the petition, saying that it was not relevant for challenging the fact and duration of his confinement. However, the U.S. Supreme Court overturned the lower court decision, holding that when state prisoners challenge the very fact or duration of their physical confinement, and the relief sought is a determination that they are entitled to immediate release from that imprisonment, the sole federal remedy is a writ of habeas corpus.

Length of confinement has often been challenged by prisoners who feel that their sentences are too long and disproportionately harsh in relation to the crimes they committed. In the case of *Hutto v. Davis,* 454 U.S. 370 (1982), for instance, Roger Davis was a Virginia inmate who had been sentenced to forty years in prison and a $20,000 fine for marijuana possession with intent to distribute. Davis sought habeas corpus relief, contending that the forty-year sentence was disproportionate to the crime and thus cruel and unusual punishment. Ultimately, after considerable hearing and rehearing through the appellate process, the U.S. Supreme Court decided the matter by upholding Virginia's authority to mandate sentences for crimes as they see fit without labeling such sentences as cruel and unusual. In Davis's case, the forty-year sentence was legislatively

CONVICTED CHILD KILLER REFUSES TO APPEAL DEATH SENTENCE

The Case of Daren Lee Bolton

It happened in Tucson, Arizona, in June 1986. Zosha Lee Pickett, a two-year-old girl, was abducted from her home, raped, stabbed, and left to die in an abandoned taxi a few blocks away. Earlier, in October 1982, a seven-year-old girl, Cathy Fritz, was kidnapped while she was walking home from a friend's house and then sexually assaulted and murdered. No apparent evidence, other than some unknown person's fingerprints, was found at either crime scene. However, police investigating both murders believed that the same perpetrator was involved.

In the meantime, Daren Lee Bolton moved from Tucson to Champaign, Illinois. He was arrested numerous times on various assault charges there. In 1990, a new computerized fingerprinting system was installed in the Tucson Police Department. Police tested the new equipment by attempting to match the prints at the two prior murder scenes with any prints in the national computer file. A match was found, and Bolton, then twenty-nine, was identified as the man whose prints were at both murder scenes. He was located in Illinois and extradited back to Arizona, where in 1993 he was convicted of Zosha Lee Pickett's murder and sentenced to death.

In an unusual move, Bolton fired his attorneys and refused to appeal his death sentence. He declared that he would rather die than stay behind bars for life. On Tuesday, June 18, 1996, Bolton was executed in the Arizona State Penitentiary by lethal injection, thus getting his wish. He had been scheduled for a second murder trial to commence in September 1996.

Did Bolton deserve the death penalty for the murder he committed? Given that his fingerprints were also found at the other murder scene and he admitted to that crime, was the sentence of death too severe in his case? What punishment would you impose on Bolton for these crimes?

Source: Adapted from Associated Press, "Man Executed for Killing Toddler." *Minot* (N.D.) *Daily News,* June 20, 1996:A2.

mandated, and the U.S. Supreme Court believed that it would be improper to interfere with state legislative sanctions. Davis's sentence was therefore upheld.

The **conditions of confinement** in jails or prisons are frequent grounds for habeas corpus relief. Prisoners who are ordered confined in jails rather than prisons for long periods may object to the lack of facilities and amenities in jails that would ordinarily be available in prisons. If prisoners had the choice, they would almost always prefer a prison, where there is a broad array of facilities and services for long-term inmates. Most jails are designed for inmates serving short sentences of less than a year and do not attempt to furnish their inmates with weight rooms and saunas, a general store, or outdoor or indoor recreational facilities.

In the case of *Youngberg v. Romeo,* 457 U.S. 307, 102 S.Ct. 2452 (1982), Romeo was a mentally retarded individual with a history of violence. Subsequently, he was involuntarily committed to a state mental hospital, where he sustained numerous physical injuries at the hands of others. His mother filed a habeas corpus action on his behalf, alleging that her son is entitled to safe conditions of confinement, freedom from bodily restraints, and training or rehabilitation. The U.S. Supreme Court heard the case and declared that Romeo is entitled to conditions of reasonable care and safety, reasonably nonrestrictive confinement conditions, and such training as may be required by these interests. The judge gave an improper jury instruction in Romeo's subsequent civil proceeding when he advised the jury to consider the standard of cruel and unusual punishment as set forth in the Eighth Amendment.

Another case about conditions of confinement was *Hutto v. Finney,* 437 U.S. 678, 98 S.Ct. 2565 (1978). In 1970, the Arkansas prison system was declared unconstitutional on various grounds through a habeas corpus petition filed by inmates. The U.S. Supreme Court ruled that the conditions of confinement were cruel and unusual, violating the Eighth Amendment. Subsequently, a check by federal officials revealed that the reforms to be implemented had not been completed. The court issued additional orders for prison official compliance: (1) limiting the number of prisoners who could reasonably be confined in one cell, (2) discontinuing particular types of nonnutritious meals, (3) maximizing the days of **solitary confinement** or **isolation** as punishment to thirty, and (4) obligating the state to pay for attorneys' fees and expenses. Arkansas Commissioner of Corrections Hutto appealed, contending that the thirty-day confinement standard was too lenient and that the court had wrongfully assigned attorneys' fees to the state. The U.S. Supreme Court heard the case and upheld the lower court. The thirty-day punitive limitation on solitary confinement was upheld, as well as the assessment of attorneys' fees against the state.

Habeas corpus relief is also sought for myriad problems arising from the time offenders are arrested all the way through to their sentencing dispositions. For instance, in the case of *Frazier v. Cupp,* 394 U.S. 731 (1969), Frazier was convicted of murder in Oregon. Prior to his conviction, Frazier was indicted, together with his cousin Rawls, who entered a guilty plea to the same murder. Some question arose about whether Rawls would testify against Frazier and whether the prosecutor ought to rely on such testimony. The prosecutor made statements in his opening remarks to the jury about what they could expect to hear from Rawls. This and other statements by the prosecutor were regarded as prejudicial to Frazier, especially a prosecutorial reference to a confession made by Rawls that implicated Frazier. Also, when Frazier was being questioned by police, he made a passing reference to "I had better get a lawyer," but he continued to answer questions. His appeal to the U.S. Supreme Court through a writ of habeas corpus was that his Miranda rights had not been observed when police questioned him, that there was prosecutorial misconduct, and that his due process rights had been violated. The U.S. Supreme Court upheld his conviction and rejected his claims. The prosecutor's comments were harmless errors, and Frazier had been advised of his Miranda rights and simply failed to exercise them.

Sometimes, offender-petitioners allege that the sentencing judge acted inappropriately by making prejudicial remarks in front of the jury. In the case of *Arave v. Creech*, 507 U.S. 463 (1993), for instance, Creech was convicted of the murder of another inmate while both were confined in the Idaho Penitentiary. At his trial and sentencing, the judge sentenced him to death and based his decision, in part, on aggravating circumstances. He used the phrase, "utter disregard" and the "cold-blooded pitiless slayer." Creech appealed the sentence, contending that the phrase "utter disregard" was facially invalid. The U.S. Supreme Court upheld Creech's conviction, holding that the phrase "utter disregard" does not violate any constitutional provisions.

Sometimes, inmates file habeas corpus petitions because they believe prosecutors acted in bad faith or engaged in improper conduct, such as suppressing exculpatory evidence. In one case (*Arizona v. Washington*, 434 U.S. 497 [1978]), for instance, George Washington was convicted of murder, but an Arizona court granted Washington a new trial because the prosecution had withheld exculpatory evidence during discovery. At the beginning of the second trial, defense counsel made various remarks in his opening statement concerning hidden information from the first trial. The prosecutor moved for a mistrial, which was granted. Washington was subsequently convicted in a third trial. As an inmate, however, Washington later filed a habeas corpus petition, seeking to have his conviction overturned because of the trial judge's decision to declare a **mistrial** in the second trial. Washington contended that the judge's decision to declare a mistrial was erroneous and led to his being placed in double jeopardy by a third trial. The U.S. Supreme Court rejected Washington's arguments, holding that the mistrial was properly declared by the judge. Thus, no previous trial had been concluded with an acquittal so that Washington was again being tried for the same offense.

Another reason for seeking habeas corpus relief is ineffective assistance of counsel. If convicted offenders believe that they were not properly represented by counsel because they were convicted, they may allege that their counsel was ineffective. Most of these types of petitions are denied by the U.S. Supreme Court. In the case of *Darden v. Wainwright*, 477 U.S. 168 (1986), Willie Darden was a convicted murderer under sentence of death. He filed a habeas corpus petition challenging the exclusion of a juror from his earlier trial, alleged improper remarks made by the prosecutor during his summation to the jury, and ineffective assistance of counsel. One prospective juror had been excused by the judge when the juror declared a moral and religious opposition to the death penalty, which was one option in Darden's case. Prosecutorial remarks Darden regarded as improper were references made to Darden's furlough program at the time he committed murder and the referral to him as an animal. The third allegation involved a one-half hour preparation by Darden's attorney between the trial's guilt phase and the trial's penalty phase. Darden did not believe this time interval gave his attorney sufficient time to prepare an adequate mitigation statement. The U.S. Supreme Court rejected all of Darden's arguments, holding that jurors may be excused from death penalty cases if their religious views or moral feelings would render them unable to vote for a death penalty if warranted. Further, the emotional rhetoric from the prosecutor was insufficient to deprive Darden of a fair trial. Finally, evidence showed that the defense counsel spent considerable preparatory time for both the trial and the mitigation statement during the penalty phase.

Other reasons for habeas corpus actions include allegations that the judge gave the jury improper instructions (*Cabana v. Bullock,* 474 U.S. 376 [1986]), failure of the court to provide counsel to the offender or to determine whether a guilty plea was indeed voluntary (*Carter v. People of State of Illinois,* 329 U.S. 173, 67 S.Ct. 216 [1946]), failure of defense counsel to inform the offender of possible sentence enhancements because a firearm was used during the commission of a felony (*Custis v. United States,* 511 U.S. 485 [1994]), the search by police was conducted without a **warrant** where the circumstances required the issuance of one for a lawful search (*Gerstein v. Pugh,* 420 U.S. 103 [1975]), and that cyanide gas is a cruel and unusual punishment (*Gomez v. United States District Court,* 503 U.S. 653 [1992]).

Over the years, inmates have frequently abused the writ of habeas corpus by submitting numerous petitions with frivolous claims (Smith, 1995b; U.S. House of Representatives, 1995c). The U.S. Supreme Court has limited such filings in recent years. Currently, the use of habeas corpus has been severely limited so that inmates must set forth all arguable issues encompassed by habeas corpus and not use a separate habeas corpus action per issue (*Delo v. Stokes,* 495 U.S. 320 [1990]). For instance, Winford Stokes was convicted of capital murder and sentenced to death. Following several habeas corpus petitions in which Stokes raised several issues on appeal, he was granted a stay of execution, and Missouri prosecutors sought an appeal to the U.S. Supreme Court. The U.S. Supreme Court heard the state's appeal and reversed a U.S. district judge's grant of a stay of execution in Stokes's case. Stokes had raised four habeas corpus petitions earlier, and he could have raised the present issue as a part of one of his earlier petitions. Thus, the U.S. Supreme Court said that granting a stay of execution to Stokes when he filed his fourth petition was abuse of judicial discretion for the federal judge. Thus, the application from the state to vacate the stay of execution was granted.

Furthermore, state prisoners must first exhaust all state appellate remedies before seeking relief directly from the U.S. Supreme Court. In the case of *Duckworth v. Serrano,* 454 U.S. 1 [1981]), an Indiana prisoner, Serrano, sought to challenge his conviction through a habeas corpus petition. He alleged that he was denied effective assistance of counsel at his trial, and thus his due process rights had been violated. Serrano had not sought relief in state courts first, however. The U.S. Supreme Court took significant notice of the fact that Serrano commenced his petition with the Court of Appeals in the Seventh Circuit, a federal appellate body, rather than in an Indiana state court. The U.S. Supreme Court dismissed his habeas corpus petition because he had failed to exhaust all state remedies. The significance of this case is that any petitioner who has been convicted of a state crime must first exhaust all state remedies before attempting to file petitions in federal courts. This case is considered a landmark because it obligates prisoners to direct their habeas corpus petitions first to state courts before they pursue federal remedies. This decision is no doubt calculated to reduce crowded federal court dockets.

This matter was underscored in the case of *McCleskey v. Zant,* 499 U.S. 467 [1991]), which limits access to the federal courts because all habeas corpus claims must be raised in the initial petition. McCleskey was charged with and convicted of murder and armed robbery. A cell mate of McCleskey's, Evans, was called to testify against him. Evans said that McCleskey boasted about the killing and admitted it. McCleskey was convicted and sentenced to death. He appealed, claiming that the cell mate–induced conversations were made without the assistance of his counsel. The U.S. Supreme Court rejected his claim, stating that it could have been made in an earlier appeal proceeding. The fact that McCleskey was making it in a subsequent proceeding nullified the claim. Thus, for such claims to be considered, they must be made in a timely way and at the right time, shortly after they occur, not after several appeals have been unsuccessfully lodged with state and federal courts.

New technological developments concerning identification of suspects through DNA testing or **DNA fingerprinting** and other forensic achievements have caused more than a few inmates to be released from prison after they were determined to be innocent of the crimes for which they were originally convicted. To obtain their release from prison or get new trials, inmates must file habeas corpus petitions (del Carmen, 1995), but the courts have been reluctant to cause old cases to be reopened, except under the most compelling of circumstances (Hanson and Daley, 1995; Weddington and Janikowski, 1996). This is consistent with the general policy change by the U.S. Supreme Court in recent years to make it more difficult for inmates to pursue habeas corpus writs without limit (Smith, 1995b).

Both the number of habeas corpus petitions filed by prisoners and the proportion of prisoners filing habeas corpus actions are declining steadily (Flango, 1994b). Even in capital cases, habeas corpus appeals have declined (Brennan et al., 1994; Coyne and Entzeroth, 1994; Dworaczyk, 1994). This is because of the greater restrictions imposed on such appeals by the U.S. Supreme Court and Congress. This trend is also observed in various states, including California (California Judicial Council, 1994; Flango, 1994b; Kadish, 1994).

WRITS OF *CERTIORARI*. A writ of *certiorari* is issued by a higher court directing a lower court to prepare the record of a case and send it to the higher court for review. It is also a means of accessing the U.S. Supreme Court for a case to be heard (Estreicher and Sexton, 1986). Writs of *certiorari*, especially from those on **death row**, must contain compelling arguments for the U.S. Supreme Court to grant them. Most writs of *certiorari* from those sentenced to death are denied. Of those petitions that are heard by the U.S. Supreme Court, only a handful each year overturn a death penalty. Usually, the U.S. Supreme Court may order a new trial if a particularly strong argument is presented showing a flagrant constitutional rights violation. These occasions are rare, however (Berlage, 1984; Riordan, 1986; West, 1986).

The Lengthy Process of Appeals

Appeals of any kind, especially death penalty appeals, consume a great deal of time. The interval between sentencing and execution averages about ten to eleven years. In some instances, the appeals process has taken fifteen years (Maguire and Pastore, 1997). One reason for the lengthy appeals process is that prisoners have been allowed to file new petitions with either state or federal courts, under a variety of theories. Although habeas corpus is the most frequently used type of appeal, there is almost no limit to the issues that may be raised by inmates and their counsel that could result in their convictions and/or sentences being overturned.

If an offender's case is reviewed by the U.S. Supreme Court and it rules in their favor, often the case is reargued in a new trial. When second or third trials occur, the results are almost always the same as in the first trial. However, some evidence shows that sentencing judges may abuse their sentencing discretion and punish these offenders with harsher penalties than earlier prescribed (Riordan, 1986). But the U.S. Supreme Court has usually condoned harsher sentences by judges, especially if judges have provided a logical written rationale for the enhanced or harsher sentence. Increased sentences have survived constitutional challenges as violations of double jeopardy, equal protection, and due process without limiting a trial judge's wide sentencing discretion (Riordan, 1986).

INITIATING APPEALS. Appeals are launched by appellants, those who lose in the trial court. Most frequently, appellants are convicted offenders. They must first file a **notice of appeal**, a written statement of the appellant's intent to file an appeal with a higher court. Such notices are required within a fixed time following an offender's conviction.

A copy of the court record or complete transcript of proceedings is forwarded to the appellate court for review. Also, a **brief** is filed with the appellate court, outlining the principal arguments for the appeal. These arguments may pertain to particular judicial rulings that are believed to be incorrect. Appellants are required to list the issues that are the substance of the appeal. If the appellant believes that thirty mistakes were committed by the trial judge, if the prosecutor was believed to have made prejudicial remarks to the jury where such remarks are prohibited, or if the police did not advise the offender of his Miranda rights when he was arrested, all of these mistakes or errors should be listed in the brief or legal argument. These errors or mistakes are considered appealable issues. An offender's first appeal should contain all of these issues because courts are unlikely to consider further appeals concerning omitted issues.

Appellees, or those who succeed in the trial court (usually the prosecution), may file briefs as well, noting why they believe there were no procedural irregularities or errors committed by different actors in the system. Thus, the groundwork is provided for **argument** later before the appellate court.

Most states and the federal government have criminal appellate courts, where offenders direct their appeals. These appellate courts frequently consist of three-judge panels that hear the legal arguments and decide whether the trial court was in error. Rulings by appellate courts that overturn a lower trial court are rare, however. One reason is that appellate courts assume that whatever transpired during the offender's trial was correct and that the criminal conviction was valid. This is a difficult presumption for appellants to overcome. They must often present overwhelming evidence of prosecutorial misconduct or judicial indiscretion to convince an appellate court to reverse or set aside their conviction. And if a conviction is reversed, this decision does not absolve the offender of any criminal liability. A new trial may be ordered, or a sentencing decision may be modified to be consistent with a higher court ruling.

Presenting the case for the appellant is the defense attorney in most criminal cases, and the district attorney or state prosecutor (the U.S. attorney or assistant U.S. attorney in federal courts) gives the government's position in the matter to be argued. This dispute process is **oral argument**. Once the appellate court has heard the oral argument from both sides and has consulted the trial transcript, it renders an **opinion.** An opinion is a written decision about the issue(s) argued and a holding as to which side, the appellant or the appellee, prevails. If the appellate court holds in favor of the appellant, and if the appellant is a convicted offender, then the case is **reversed and remanded** back to the trial court with instructions for modifying the original decision. Whenever the ruling favors the government, the appellate court is said to **affirm** the holding or judgment against the appellant-offender. When the case against the offender is affirmed by an appellate court, the offender may direct an appeal to the next higher appellate court. In state courts, this higher appellate court is the state supreme court or court of last resort within the state judicial system. If the state supreme court affirms the conviction, the offender may direct an appeal to the U.S. Supreme Court.

In some opinions by appellate courts, not all of the appellate judges agree about the decision rendered. The minority view is sometimes summarized in a **dissenting opinion**. Legal historians value dissenting opinions because they believe that appellate court policy change can be predicted over time, especially if those rendering dissenting opinions are younger judges on appellate panels. However, these minority or dissenting opinions have no impact on the appeal outcome. The majority opinion is the governing opinion in the case and the more important one. Appellate judges who write the majority opinion also outline the legal rationale for their opinion. These opinions are more or less lengthy.

THE DISCRETIONARY POWERS OF APPELLATE COURTS. Appellate courts may or may not decide to hear appeals from lower courts. Their powers in this regard are discretionary. They may choose which cases to review as well as decide which cases not to review. Usually, only a small proportion of cases are reviewed by appellate courts at the state and federal levels annually. For instance, the U.S. Supreme Court receives thousands of appeals from convicted offenders annually. However, only a small fraction, less than a hundred cases, are heard each year with written opinions provided. Most appeals from convicted offenders are denied. The U.S. Supreme Court is also a discretionary body, and the cases they hear are carefully chosen. Furthermore, the Rule of Four applies, according to which at least four of the justices must agree to hear the case. And even if the U.S. Supreme Court consents to hear a case, the sheer volume of scheduled cases may be such that the case may not be heard. The U.S. Supreme Court's time is quite limited, and more than a few scheduled cases are not heard each year because the court has run out of time. These cases are not carried over to the next term of the court. Rather, appellants must refile their appeals with the court the following term.

APPEALS BY INDIGENTS. Indigent defendants who are sentenced to death are entitled to counsel on their first nondiscretionary appeals (Mello, 1989). However, some inmates on death row have filed numerous subsequent appeals, almost always at taxpayer expense, with public defenders appointed to assist them. However, as we have seen, the U.S. Supreme Court has limited the number of appeals indigents may file, as well as their right to publicly appointed counsel each and every time they launch a new appeal (Dieter, 1984; Mello, 1989; Nagel et al., 1990).

Summary

When defendants have been convicted of one or more crimes, they are sentenced. A sentence is the process of imposing a punishment prescribed by law for particular crimes. The punishment may involve incarceration for a period of time in a jail or prison. However, many offenders are sentenced to probation and other community-based punishments. The aims of sentencing include punishment or just deserts, incapacitation or crime control, rehabilitation, reintegration, and prevention or deterrence. Depending on the jurisdiction, each of these aims is emphasized to a greater or lesser degree.

There are several different types of sentencing. The most common is indeterminate sentencing, in which a judge imposes a sentence of a period of months or years, and subsequently the offender's early release from prison or jail is contingent on the decision of a parole board. During the last few decades, sentencing practices have changed. One change is from indeterminate to determinate sentencing. Determinate sentencing also involves an incarcerative term imposed by the judge, but instead of a parole board determining the offender's early release, the accumulated good-time credits are deducted from the maximum sentence. Good-time credits are statutory for the most part. These credits are accumulated at different rates, depending on the state or federal government. One common good-time credit allocation is thirty days off the original maximum sentence for every thirty days served in prison. Thus, after a convicted offender serves approximately half of a prison sentence under this scheme, the inmate would be freed. Determinate sentencing, therefore, avoids any possible bias or prejudice that might exist among parole board members.

Presumptive or guidelines-based sentencing involves fixed punishments for particular offenses, usually expressed as a range of months. The middle range is the presumptive sentence, and the offender's sentence may be increased or decreased within the range of months by the presence of aggravating or mitigating circumstances. Sentencing guidelines are used by the federal government and several states. A key motivation for adopting sentencing guidelines and using presumptive sentencing is that judicial disparities in sentencing are minimized or eliminated.

A fourth type of sentencing is mandatory sentencing. Certain sentences must be imposed by judges for particular crimes. A common type of mandatory sentence is a sentence enhancement of several years for using a firearm during the commission of a felony. Another offense requiring a mandatory sentence is being a habitual or repeat offender. All states have habitual offender statutes that require mandatory terms of life imprisonment when habitual offenders are convicted. Unfortunately, there is laxity in the enforcement of mandatory sentences for particular crimes. One major reason is the serious and chronic jail and prison overcrowding. Enforcing mandatory sentencing laws would exacerbate already overcrowded conditions in many prison systems. Therefore, habitual offender statutes are seldom enforced. However, prosecutors may use such statutes as leverage in compelling particular defendants with lengthy criminal records to plead guilty to lesser offenses. At present, there is friction between those endorsing truth-in-sentencing laws and those favoring greater sentencing leniency. Truth-in-sentencing laws provide that convicted offenders will serve either all or most of their imposed sentences. States that use parole as the major means of granting inmates early release typically free inmates after they have served 40 percent or more of their sentences. The federal government considers inmates for early release after they have served at least 85 percent of their sentences. Truth-in-sentencing policies are controversial.

All those convicted of serious offenses receive a sentencing hearing, a formal proceeding following conviction when the judge listens to arguments for or against leniency for the offender. Victims and their families testify and attempt to persuade judges to impose harsher sentences. Relatives and friends of the convicted offender attempt to persuade the judge to be lenient. Cited are various aggravating and mitigating factors. Aggravating factors intensify the seriousness of the offense: whether death or serious bodily injury resulted from the defendant's actions, whether the offender has a prior criminal record, whether there was more than one victim, whether the crime was especially heinous and cruel, and whether the offender was a leader of others when the crime was committed. Mitigating factors are those that lessen the seriousness of the offense. The absence of a criminal record and no bodily injury or death to victims are two important mitigating factors. Other mitigating factors include whether the offender has a mental illness or is mentally incapacitated, whether the offender has made restitution to the victim(s), and whether the offender committed the offense while under duress or because of necessity. All of this factual information is disclosed during the sentencing hearing.

Assisting judges in their sentencing decisions are presentence investigation reports or PSIs. PSIs are prepared by probation officers at the court's direction, and they include a substantial amount of factual information about the offender, his or her background, the crime and its commission, and other sociodemographic information. PSIs also contain victim impact statements, which are written records of how the crime has affected one or more victims.

Judges impose different sentences on convicted offenders, depending on the circumstances of each case. Sometimes judges impose shock probation on defendants. Shock probation involves a full jail or prison sentence imposed, but the offender is removed from jail or prison after serving up to 130 days. The offender is brought before the judge once again and resentenced to probation. The objective of shock probation is to shock the offender, usually a first offender, with a short amount of incarceration to deter them from further offending. Some offenders are subject to split sentencing, mixed sentencing, or jail as a condition of probation, which are creative sentences from judges including some time served behind bars.

When offenders have been convicted of capital murder and are subject to the death penalty as the maximum punishment, special two-stage or bifurcated trials are conducted. The defendant's guilt is determined in the first stage, and a subsequent stage determines the punishment, or whether the defendant will receive a life sentence or the death penalty. Aggravating and mitigating circumstances are weighed during the second phase of these bifurcated trials. All death sentences are automatically appealed. The appeals process is lengthy, and the average length of time between conviction and a sentence of death and actual imposition of the death penalty is about ten years. Various states and the federal government have passed legislation aimed at shortening the time between conviction and execution. The death penalty is particularly controversial, especially because in recent years several people have been freed from death row because DNA and other compelling evidence have shown that they are innocent and should not have been convicted initially.

KEY TERMS

Acceptance of
    responsibility
Affirm
Aggravating
    circumstances
Appeal
Appellants
Appellees
Argument
Bifurcated trial
Brief
Capital punishment
Career criminals
Chronic offenders
Chronic recidivists
Conditions of
    confinement
Cost–benefit analysis
Court-appointed counsel
Crime Bill of 1994
Crime prevention
Criminal history
Death penalty
Death row
Defendant's sentencing
    memorandum
Deterrence
Dissenting opinion
DNA fingerprinting
Early release
Extralegal factors

Felony property offending
Flat term
Get-tough movement
Good time
Good-time credit
Guidelines-based
    sentencing
Habeas corpus
Habeas corpus petition
Habitual offenders
Incapacitation
Intermittent sentencing
Isolation
Jail as a condition of
    probation
Life imprisonment
Life-without-parole
    sentence
Mandatory sentence
Mandatory sentencing
Mistrial
Mitigating circumstances
Mixed sentencing
Narrative
Notice of appeal
Opinion
Oral argument
Parole board
Persistent felony offenders
Persistent offender
    statutes

Precedent
Presumptive sentencing
Probation officer
Project Exile
Punishment
Rehabilitation
Reintegration
Reversed and remanded
Sentencing
Sentencing disparity
Sentencing guidelines
Sentencing hearing
Sentencing
    memorandum
Sentencing Reform Act
    of 1984
Serious felonies
Shock incarceration
Shock parole
Shock probation
Solitary confinement
Split sentencing
Stare decisis
Tiers
Truth in sentencing
Truth-in-sentencing laws
U.S. Sentencing
    Commission
Violent felonies
Virginia Exile
Warrant

QUESTIONS FOR REVIEW

1. What is a habeas corpus petition? What are three types of issues challenged by such petitions?

2. What is a writ of *certiorari*? Under what circumstances might this type of writ be used?

3. What are some trends regarding the use of habeas corpus petitions by jail and prison inmates? What factors seem to account for such trends?

4. What are four general functions or aims of sentencing?

5. How does indeterminate sentencing differ from determinate sentencing?

6. What constraints are imposed on judges by presumptive or guidelines-based and mandatory sentencing schemes?

7. What is a habitual offender statute? Do most states have such statutes? Are these statutes used frequently by these states? Why or why not? Explain.

8. Differentiate between shock probation and split sentencing. What are three types of split sentences?

9. What is a use-a-gun-and-go-to-prison statute?

10. What is a sentencing hearing? What are the major functions of such hearings?

11. What is a presentence investigation report? Who prepares it, and how is it used to determine an offender's punishment?

12. What is a bifurcated trial? Under what circumstances is it used? What are two significant cases relating to bifurcated trials?

13. What is meant by truth in sentencing? How is truth in sentencing achieved?

14. What are victim impact statements? Where are such statements found, and what purposes do they serve in the sentencing process?

15. Why is the appeals process for death sentences so lengthy?

SUGGESTED READINGS

Allard, Patricia and Marc Mauer. (1999). *Regaining the Vote: An Assessment of Activity Relating to Felon Disenfranchisement Laws.* Washington, DC: The Sentencing Project.

Bauer, Jere M. (1999). *Felony Sentencing and Probation.* Madison: Wisconsin Legislative Fiscal Bureau.

Edwards, Todd. (1999). *Sentencing Reform in Southern States: A Review of Truth in Sentencing and Three-Strikes Measures.* Atlanta, GA: Council of State Governments Southern Office.

Hofer, Paul J., Kevin R. Blackwell, and Barry R. Ruback. (1999). "The Effect of the Federal Sentencing Guidelines on Inter-Judge Disparity." *Journal of Criminal Law and Criminology* **90**:239–321.

Irwin, John, Vincent Schiraldi, and Jason Ziedenberg. (1999). *America's One Million Nonviolent Prisoners.* Washington, DC: Justice Policy Institute.

Levin, David J., Patrick A. Langan, and Jodi M. Brown. (2000). *State Court Sentencing of Convicted Felons, 1996.* Washington, DC: U.S. Bureau of Justice Statistics.

Mauer, Marc, Cathy Potler, and Richard Wolf. (1999). *Gender and Justice: Women, Drugs, and Sentencing Policy.* Washington, DC: The Sentencing Project.

Reynolds, Mike, Bill Jones, and Dan Evans. (1996). *Three Strikes and You're Out! . . . A Promise to Kimber: The Chronicle of America's Toughest Anti-Crime Law.* Fresno, CA: Quill Driver Books.

Washington Sentencing Guidelines Commission. (2000). *The Sentencing Reform Act at Century's End: An Assessment of Adult Felony Sentencing Practices in the State of Washington.* Olympia: Washington Sentencing Guidelines Commission.

JUVENILE COURTS, JUVENILE RIGHTS, AND PROCESSING

CHAPTER **11**

THE CASE OF BRANDY MARTIN, MOTHER. Brandy Martin, 20, was peacefully holding her 1-year-old child in her arms one evening. She was sitting on the living room couch. Suddenly, three rounds from a rifle were fired through her front room window, one of them striking Brandy in the back of the head. She was killed instantly. Witnesses said that a car had driven by the home, with a rifle protruding through the passenger window. When the shots were fired, the witnesses took cover. When it was all over, the witnesses said the car was gone. Police observed that the Martin home was the scene of previous incidents. In the past year, a dud grenade was tossed through the front window, and another drive-by shooting at the same residence led to a juvenile's arrest and conviction. Martin and her family are unrelated to any gang members in the area. Thus, although the drive-by shootings were carried out by gang members, no one could say why the attacks on the Martin residence occurred. At home with Martin at the time of her murder were her mother, 53, and a 3-year-old child who was playing on the floor near Martin. Lieutenant Ken Landwehr said that "cowards shot at the occupants of that house on purpose. But I don't think they knew who was inside. They just fired at the house at random." The "random" shots took out Brandy Martin in the process. Gang members laughingly refer to such victims of gang shootings as "mushrooms," stemming from a video arcade game, Centipede, in which mushrooms emerge and turn into more powerful opponents. One game objective, survival, is continued by killing mushrooms whenever they appear. Thus, gang members have adopted some of this video game terminology to refer to innocent victims of drive-by shootings. What should be the punishment for those convicted of drive-by shootings? What do you think the juvenile court should do to juveniles as young as 8 or 10 who commit murders with impunity in these drive-by shooting scenarios? How would you judge a case if your own brother or sister was killed at random by drive-by 12-year-old shooters? What justice should the survivors of "mushrooms" seek in the juvenile courts? (*Source*: Adapted from Associated Press, "Woman Killed in Drive-By Shooting." *Minot (N.D.) Daily News*, February 4, 1997:A2.)

IT HAPPENED IN CINCINNATI, OHIO. At 12:45 A.M. one night, Cincinnati Police Officer Kevin Crayon, 40, thought the boy looked suspicious behind the wheel of an automobile in front of a convenience store. Certainly, the boy looked too young to drive a car. This might have been a routine stop and issuing of a citation, but subsequent events turned tragic. Officer Crayon approached 12-year-old Courtney Mathis, who was sitting behind the wheel of an automobile parked in front of a convenience store. He asked the boy to show him his driver's license, and the boy refused. Then the boy put the car in reverse and began backing out of the parking lot. The officer saw several small children who were in the path of the fleeing automobile and attempted to reach in and grab the keys. Courtney panicked and started driving off erratically, with the officer clinging to the window, his arm locked in the steering wheel. While he was being dragged by the accelerating car, Officer Crayon pulled out his service revolver and fired one shot, striking Mathis in the chest. The officer was dragged at least 800 feet under the vehicle before his body parted from it. He was dead, crushed to death by the fleeing car. In the meantime, Mathis drove the car home. On his way home, he struck several other cars. When he got home, he told family members that he had been shot by police. The family member who owned the car had no knowledge that Courtney had commandeered his vehicle that evening. The family members called 911, and paramedics rushed Mathis to the Children's Hospital Medical Center, where he underwent emergency surgery. He died about four hours later. Keith Fangman, president of the local Fraternal Order of Police, said "The officer died because some young punk was driving a car. It's unbelievable." Flags flew at half staff at police headquarters the next day. Crayon, a father of three, had been with the Cincinnati Police Department for about 4 years. Police Chief Thomas Streicher Jr., said of Crayon's actions, "I'd like to think the officer was trying to save the children from serious injury or death. Unfortunately, as the result of his own actions trying to save someone's life, he sacrificed his own life." What precautions should parents undertake to make sure their children do not have access to automobiles, especially late at night? Should automobiles be equipped with safety equipment to prevent youths from driving them? Was Officer Crayon's use of deadly force that evening justified? What do you think? (*Source:* Adapted from John Nolan and the Associated Press, "Officer, Boy Die in Violent Confrontation." *Laredo Morning Times,* September 2, 2000:7A.)

THE CASE OF THE EATON, COLORADO, EIGHT-YEAR-OLD POT SMOKERS. It happened in Eaton, Colorado, in April 1997. Principal Oren Nero had never seen anything like it before. Five of his third-graders were caught during early morning recess smoking marijuana cigarettes rolled with their homework paper. "I have been principal for 30 years, and this is a first for me," said Nero about the incident. "Earlier this same year, we caught this same group smoking plain old cigarettes, and this was even a first for me," said Nero. Police Chief Rod Hawkins said, "We're kind of fumbling our way through this right now, trying to figure out how to handle this. All of these kids are under age 10, and thus their names will not be released to the general public. They will not face criminal charges because they are so young and state law bans prosecution of children that young." The students were suspended after one of the boys rolled a marijuana cigarette, lit it, and began to puff it. What do you think ought to be done to regulate such behavior on school playgrounds? What safeguards should be employed by schools to ensure that students do not come to school with marijuana or any other drug contraband? Should children under age 10 be held accountable for actions that would be crimes if adults committed them? What do you think? (*Source:* Adapted from the Associated Press, "Third-Graders Caught Smoking Pot." *Minot* (N.D.) *Daily News,* April 27, 1997:A2.)

The Juvenile Justice System

The **juvenile justice system** or **process** is supposed to handle cases like these. The juvenile justice system is a loosely integrated network of agencies, institutions, organizations, and personnel that process juvenile offenders. This network is made up of law enforcement agencies, prosecutors, and courts; corrections, probation, and parole services; and public and private community-based treatment programs that provide youths with diverse services.

The first part of this chapter defines delinquency and delinquent youths and differentiates them from status offenders. Juveniles are usually referred to juvenile courts because of offenses they commit. These **referrals** sometimes result in petitions filed against them. Filing a **petition** results in an **intake screening**, or an initial attempt to determine the seriousness of the youthful offender. Depending on the outcome of this screening process, certain youths considered more serious will face prosecution in juvenile courts.

Prosecutors and judges make crucial decisions that affect the lives of youths who are processed by the juvenile court. Juvenile court judges decide or adjudicate each case. A resolution of a juvenile court case results in a **disposition**, several types of which are described in this chapter. For the most serious juvenile offenders, criminal court may be one solution to providing enhanced punishments. Some juveniles are defined as adults for the purpose of criminal prosecutions. Juveniles who fit this description are subject to **waivers, transfers**, or **certifications** as adults so that criminal courts can have jurisdiction over them. The transfer process is examined in detail in this chapter.

In the mid-1960s, a series of U.S. Supreme Court decisions vested all juveniles with rights ordinarily enjoyed by adult offenders. With greater rights, however, juveniles have been obligated to accept greater responsibility for their offenses. Thus, a discussion of juvenile rights and how these rights are exercised is an integral part of this discussion. The get-tough movement has created considerable pressure on state legislatures to take juvenile offending more seriously, especially violent juvenile offending. The prevalent belief is that juvenile courts are too lenient and that more punitive options should be available, to juvenile as well as criminal court judges. By the mid-1990s one-third of the states had adopted blended sentencing statutes, and the trend is toward greater punitive sanctions against the most violent juveniles. These blended sentencing statutes, as well as their implications for juvenile treatment in both juvenile and criminal courts, are examined. The chapter concludes with an examination of selected trends in juvenile justice.

Delinquency, Juvenile Delinquents, and Status Offenders

Juvenile Delinquents

JUVENILES. **Juvenile court jurisdiction** depends on established legislative definitions of who **juveniles** are and the offenses they commit. States vary as to which juvenile offenders are within the purview of juvenile courts. The federal government has no **juvenile court**. Rather, federal cases involving juveniles infrequently are heard in federal district courts, but adjudicated juveniles are housed in state or local facilities if the sentences involve incarceration. Ordinarily, upper and lower age limits are prescribed. However, these age limits are far from uniform among jurisdictions. The common law or **English common law** standard sets the minimum age of juveniles at seven, although no state is obligated to recognize this definition. In fact, some states have no lower age limits that would otherwise function to limit juvenile court jurisdiction.

States with the lowest maximum age for juvenile court jurisdiction, fifteen, are Connecticut, New York, and North Carolina. States whose maximum age is sixteen for juvenile court jurisdiction are Georgia, Illinois, Louisiana, Massachusetts, Michigan, Missouri, South Carolina, and Texas. All other states and the federal government use age eighteen as the maximum age for criminal court jurisdiction (Butts, 1996a:64–87).

In most jurisdictions, youths under the age of seven are often placed in the care of community agencies, such as departments of human services or social welfare. These children frequently have little or no responsible parental supervision or control. In many cases, the parents themselves may have psychological problems or suffer from alcohol or drug dependencies. Youths from such families may be abused or neglected and may be in need of supervision and other forms of care or treatment. Under common law in those states where common law applies, children under the age of seven are presumed incapable of formulating criminal intent. If a six-year-old child kills someone, for instance, deliberately or accidentally, he or she will probably be treated rather than punished.

JUVENILE DELINQUENCY. **Juvenile delinquency** is the violation of a criminal law of the United States, which would have been a crime if committed by an adult, by a person prior to her or his eighteenth birthday (18 U.S.C., Sec. 5031, 1997). Generally, juvenile delinquency is the violation of any state or local law or ordinance by anyone who has not yet become an adult. Any act committed by a juvenile that would be a crime if an adult committed it is a delinquent act. A **juvenile delinquent** is anyone who has committed juvenile delinquency.

Status Offenders

Status offenders are those who commit offenses that would not be crimes if adults committed them. Typical status offenses are runaway behavior, truancy, and curfew violation. Adults may run away from home, be truant from their classes, and stay out late at night without violating the law. However, juveniles are required to observe these laws that pertain specifically to them.

THE FELONIOUS FIRST-GRADER

The Case of Chantel Woodard

Chantel Woodard kicked, hit, and spit at an administrator and a police officer during a seventy-five-minute melee. Eventually, Woodard was subdued, arrested, and led away in handcuffs. Police charged her with felony battery. Chantel Woodard is a six-year-old girl.

The incident started when a police officer brought a tape about crime prevention to the first-grade class. While the tape was being shown to the class at Largo Central Elementary School in Largo, Florida, some students moved their chairs closer to the television set for a better view. Eventually, most of the class had converged very close to the television. Officer Paula Crosby asked the children to move back from the television so that all students could see the film. When Chantel Woodard was asked to move her chair back, she threw a tantrum. The tantrum escalated and required two large adults to restrain her. She was arrested and taken to jail because authorities did not know what else to do with her. "The whole idea was to get the child some help," said Police Captain Joe Gillette. He did not think that the case would ever be prosecuted.

Should Chantel have been arrested and handcuffed? How would you discipline a child in the first grade? What do you think?

Source: Adapted from the Associated Press, "First-Grader Charged with Felony." *Minot* (N.D.) *Daily News*, April 25, 1997:A2.

RUNAWAYS. In 1995, 201,459 **runaways** were reported to police (Maguire and Pastore, 1996:404). This is less than one percent of all offenses charged that year. More than half of these runaways were fifteen to seventeen years old. Runaways leave their homes, without permission or their parents' knowledge, and remain away from home for prolonged periods, ranging from several days to several years. Many runaways are eventually picked up by police in different jurisdictions and returned to their homes. Others return of their own free will.

TRUANTS AND CURFEW VIOLATORS. **Truants** absent themselves from school without either school or parental permission. **Curfew violators** remain on city streets after specified evening hours when they are prohibited from loitering unless they are in the company of a parent or guardian. In 1995, 105,888 youths were charged with curfew violation in the United States (Maguire and Pastore, 1996:404).

JUVENILE AND CRIMINAL COURT INTEREST IN STATUS OFFENDERS. Juvenile courts are interested in status offenders who habitually appear before juvenile court judges. Repeated juvenile court appearances may be symptomatic of subsequent adult criminality

(Benda, 1987). The chronicity of juvenile offending seems to be influenced by the amount of contact youths have with juvenile courts (Minnesota Criminal Justice Statistical Analysis Center, 1989). Greater contact with juvenile courts is believed by some experts to **stigmatize** youths and cause them either to be labeled or to acquire **stigmas** as delinquents or deviants (Florida Governor's Juvenile Justice and Delinquency Prevention Advisory Committee, 1994). Therefore, they recommend diversion of certain types of juvenile offenders from the juvenile justice system to minimize stigmatization (Fuller and Norton, 1993).

One way of removing status offenders from juvenile courts and their stigmatizing effects is to deprive juvenile court judges of jurisdiction over status offenders (Blackmore, Brown, and Krisberg, 1988). Another way of minimizing status offender stigmatization is to remove them from custodial institutions, such as industrial schools. These methods are known as **divestiture of jurisdiction** and **deinstitutionalization of status offenders (DSO)**, or simply **deinstitutionalization**.

DIVESTING JUVENILE COURTS OF THEIR JURISDICTION OVER STATUS OFFENDERS. Under divestiture, juvenile courts cannot detain, petition, adjudicate, or place youths on probation or in institutions for committing *any* status offense. In lieu of juvenile court intervention, community agencies and social services care for and place status offenders.

DEINSTITUTIONALIZATION OF STATUS OFFENDERS (DSO). Institutionalizing status offenders in juvenile industrial schools (i.e., prisons for juveniles) is thought to harden them, thus increasing their likelihood of committing more serious offenses in the future (U.S. Senate Judiciary Committee, 1984). Therefore, starting in the late 1960s, some status offenders were removed from juvenile penal institutions such as industrial schools. In 1974, the U.S. Congress passed enabling legislation to accomplish this objective on a national basis.

The **Juvenile Justice and Delinquency Prevention Act of 1974 (JJDPA)** (modified in 1984) was established in response to a national concern about growing juvenile delinquency and youth crime. This act authorized the establishment of the **Office of Juvenile Justice and Delinquency Prevention (OJJDP)**, which has been helpful and influential in disseminating information about juvenile offending and prevention and as a general data source. The JJDPA provides for a state relations and assistance division.

THE STATE RELATIONS AND ASSISTANCE DIVISION. This division addresses directly the matter of removing juveniles, especially status offenders, from secure institutions (facilities similar to adult prisons), jails, and lockups. The Research and Program Development Division examines how juvenile courts process juvenile offenders.

CHANGES AND MODIFICATIONS IN THE JJDPA. Congress modified the act in 1977 by declaring that the juveniles should be separated by both sight and sound from adult offenders in detention and correctional facilities. Also in 1977, states were given five years to comply with the DSO mandate. Congress prohibited states in 1980 from detaining juveniles in jails and lockups and also directed that states should examine their secure confinement policies relating to minority juveniles and determine reasons and

Truancy Leads to Boot Camps for Youths

Nixon High School

You are a teenager. You decide to cut school and be truant. In Texas, at least, state law says that until you are age eighteen, you must attend school when school is in session. Until 2000, the punishment for being truant was a school suspension and perhaps some low grades in classes missed, but this has all changed.

At Nixon High School in Laredo, Texas, truant students are being brought before the juvenile court judge, Judge Danny Valdez, who does not mess around. He orders truants to attend a mandatory boot camp at a local middle school on Saturday mornings at 5:00 A.M. In October 2000, Valdez had twenty-five cases of truant students who had missed 218 days of school without reason. For ten of these cases, Valdez ordered them to show up for 5:00 A.M. exercises and discipline at the Lamar Middle School the following Saturday morning.

Actually, parents receive these court orders to bring their children to the school at that early hour. Valdez says that students who do not attend class create discipline problems when they do attend. Once at the school, these truant students will learn military discipline, accept orders, and respond quickly with "Yes, sir!" or "No, sir!" The boot camp is an option for youth to redirect their lives and look positively toward the future. Military Sergeants Carlos R. Gonzalez and Pascualita Valdez are in the disciplinary team that directs these truant students in military-like exercises. One student says, "I'm not bothered by the sergeants. They are rerouting the path I was on. My goal is to be a pilot in the Air Force. I can now start reaching for my goal. I believe I have the opportunity to succeed when I enlist."

The sergeants directing the boot camp on Saturday mornings say that their program is based on intensive exercise and military discipline during each eight-hour session. Additionally, students cannot speak to each other during the day without permission from the sergeants. Gonzalez recalled that before the establishment of the boot camp, students missed more than a thousand days of school. In 1999, the number dropped to two hundred days.

"On their first day of boot camp, you can see the change on their faces, how proud they are of themselves. Afterward, the students return home and want to do nothing but sleep," says Gonzalez. During the first hour, the sergeants have the students exercise and allow them ten minutes of rest. Two more hours of exercise follow, along with memorization of information the sergeants give the students. No talking is permitted during the half-hour lunch break. The only noise visitors hear is the sound of utensils and glasses. Another hour is spent in discussion about their responsibilities as students and how they should prepare for the future. Sundays are spent exercising and marching for four hours, cleaning up the Lamar campus for three hours, and enjoying free time for another hour.

(continued)

> ### TRUANCY LEADS TO BOOT CAMPS FOR YOUTHS
>
> #### Nixon High School *(continued)*
>
> Gonzalez says that whenever students do not attend boot camp, a judge will issue an arrest warrant and have the student taken to juvenile detention or the county jail, where a fine must be paid before release. During the 1999–2000 school year, 330 students attended the boot camp, including about 80 girls.
>
> Should boot camps be used to punish truants? What do you think of the methods used in Laredo, Texas, for disciplining truants? What alternative strategies would you recommend to induce children to attend school?
>
> *Source:* Adapted from the Associated Press. "Weekend at Camp Decreases Truancy." *Laredo Morning Times,* October 16, 2000:1A, 10A.

justification for the disproportionately high rate of minority confinement. In 1992, Congress directed that any participating state would have up to twenty-five percent of its formula grant money withheld, to the extent that the state was not in compliance with each of the JJDPA mandates (Bilchik, 1995).

The Jurisdiction of Juvenile Courts

THE AGE JURISDICTION OF JUVENILE COURTS. Upper age limits for juveniles have been established in all U.S. jurisdictions (either under 16, under 17, or under 18 years of age). However, there is no uniformity concerning lower age limits. Technically, juvenile courts have jurisdiction over three-year-old murderers. However, no juvenile court will adjudicate a three-year-old delinquent and place the child in an industrial school. The type of jurisdictional control over such children by juvenile courts is more oriented toward care and treatment. This treatment and care may include placement of children or infants in foster homes or under the supervision of community service or human welfare agencies who can meet their needs. Neglected, unmanageable, abused, or other **children in need of supervision (CHINS)** are placed in the custody of these agencies, at the discretion of juvenile judges. Generally, juvenile courts have broad discretionary powers over most people under eighteen.

THE TREATMENT AND PUNISHMENT FUNCTIONS OF JUVENILE COURTS. Not all juveniles who appear before juvenile court judges are delinquents. Many youths in juvenile court have not violated any criminal laws (Feld, 1993c). Rather, their status as juveniles means that they are within juvenile court control. Several circumstances make these youths susceptible to juvenile court jurisdiction. The quality of their adult supervision, if any, may be inadequate. They may run away from home, be truant from school, or loiter on certain city streets during evening hours. Runaways, truants, or **loiterers** are considered status offenders because their actions would not be criminal if committed by adults.

Physically, psychologically, or sexually abused children are within the jurisdictional control of juvenile courts. Many of these juvenile courts are instead called family courts. The majority of youthful offenders who appear before juvenile courts are juvenile delinquents, but in some jurisdictions, a delinquent act is whatever juvenile courts say it is. Thus, juvenile courts have broad discretionary powers over all types of juveniles. Much of this state authority originated under the early English doctrine of *parens patriae.*

Parens Patriae

Parens patriae, literally "the father of the country," originated with the King of England during the twelfth century. Applied to juvenile matters, *parens patriae* means that the king is in charge of, makes decisions about, or has responsibility for all matters involving juvenile conduct. Within the scope of early English common law, parental authority was primary in the early upbringing of children. However, as children advanced to age seven and beyond, they acquired some measure of responsibility for their own actions. Accountability to parents was shifted gradually to accountability to the state whenever those seven years of age or older violated the law. In the name of the king, chancellors in various districts adjudicated matters involving juveniles and the offenses they committed. Juveniles had no legal rights or standing in any court. They were the sole responsibility of the king or his agents. Their future often depended largely on decisions made by the **chancellors**. In effect, children were wards of the court, and the court was vested with the responsibility to safeguard their welfare.

Because children could become wards of the court and subject to their control, a key concern for many chancellors was the future welfare of these children, which led to numerous rehabilitative and treatment measures. Children were placed in foster homes or assigned to work tasks for local merchants. Parental influence in these child placement decisions was minimal.

Modern Applications of Parens Patriae

Parens patriae is today pervasive in all juvenile court jurisdictions (Ellsworth, Kinsella, and Massin, 1992), as exhibited by the wide range of dispositional options available to juvenile court judges and others in earlier stages of offender processing in the juvenile justice system. Most of these options are either nominal or conditional, meaning that the confinement of any juvenile for most offenses is regarded as a last resort.

The strong treatment or rehabilitative orientation inherent in *parens patriae* is not acceptable to some juvenile justice experts (Schwartz, 1992). Contemporary juvenile court jurisprudence stresses individual accountability for the juvenile's actions. Consistent with a growing trend in the criminal justice system toward just deserts and justice, there is a similar trend throughout the juvenile justice system (Champion and Mays, 1991). This get-tough movement is geared toward providing law violators with swifter, harsher, and more certain punishment than the previously dominant rehabilitative philosophy of American courts.

ON THE AGE OF ACCOUNTABILITY

Child Middleton

In Pensacola, Florida, they took him into custody for assaulting the school counselor. He showed little remorse as he was led away in handcuffs to the backseat of the police car. At the jail, he was booked, fingerprinted, photographed, and placed in a room by himself.

The school counselor, fifty-one-year-old Linda Green, said that a warrant for his arrest had been issued earlier that day on charges of battery of an elected official or educator. In Florida, such a charge is a felony and punishable by one or more years in prison.

The arrestee is a five-year-old girl we will refer to as Child Middleton. Child Middleton is described as an out-of-control youngster who has a lot of pent-up hostility and rage. She has been in trouble with her parents and school officials on previous occasions. She has bitten and scratched school officials numerous times and was undergoing counseling at the time she assaulted her counselor. Her father, Lee Ernest Middleton, said that the arrest of his five-year-old daughter was the most ludicrous thing he has ever experienced, but school officials are making sure that the child does not get a chance to assault them again.

How would you judge Child Middleton? Obviously, the child needs counseling and substantial intervention by others. What type of intervention would you deem appropriate to control her rage and violence? The age of seven is regarded as the age of responsibility under common law. Should we apply this standard to Child Middleton? Are criminal charges against her appropriate here? What do you think?

Source: Adapted from the Associated Press, "5-Year-Old Arrested after Attack." *Minot* (N.D.) *Daily News,* February 21, 1998:A2.

The *parens patriae* doctrine has been greatly influenced by the changing rights of juveniles. Since the mid-1960s, juveniles have acquired greater constitutional rights, commensurate with those enjoyed by adults in criminal courts. Some professionals believe that as juveniles are vested with greater numbers of constitutional rights, the juvenile court is trending toward greater **criminalization** (Feld, 1993a, 1993b, 1993c). Interestingly, as juveniles obtain a greater range of constitutional rights, they become more immune to the influence of *parens patriae*. Quite simply, juvenile judges are gradually losing much of their former almost absolute autonomy over juveniles and their life chances.

Variations in Criminal and Juvenile Court Processing

Some of the major differences between juvenile and criminal courts follow.

1. Juvenile courts are civil proceedings exclusively designed for juveniles, whereas criminal courts are proceedings designed to try adults charged with crimes. The civil-criminal distinction is important because a civil adjudication of a case does not result in a criminal record.
2. Informality characterizes juvenile court proceedings, whereas criminal proceedings are formal. Juvenile court judges frequently address juveniles directly and casually. Formal criminal or evidentiary procedures are not followed rigorously, and hearsay from various sources is considered, together with factual evidence.
3. In thirty-nine states, juveniles are not entitled to a trial by jury, unless the juvenile court judge approves. In jurisdictions that do not provide jury trials for juveniles in special circumstances, judicial approval of a jury trial for juveniles is required.
4. Juvenile court and criminal court proceedings are adversarial.
5. All criminal courts are courts of record, whereas transcripts of most juvenile proceedings are made only at the judge's request. However, some juvenile court judges may have the resources or interest to provide for such transcriptions, particularly if serious offenses are alleged (Schwartz, 1992).
6. The **standard of proof** to determine the defendant's guilt in criminal proceedings is beyond a reasonable doubt. This same standard is applicable in juvenile courts if violations of criminal laws are alleged and incarceration in a juvenile facility is a possible punishment. However, the less rigorous civil standard of preponderance of evidence is used when the juvenile's loss of liberty is not at issue.
7. Criminal courts have the full range of penalties, including death and life without parole. Juvenile courts have limited jurisdiction, and they can dispose juveniles only to terms that terminate when they reach adulthood.

Juvenile Court History

A Brief History of Juvenile Courts in the United States. Juvenile courts are primarily an American creation. The first juvenile court was established in Illinois in 1899 under the **Illinois Juvenile Court Act**, although numerous agencies and organizations had been established earlier in other jurisdictions, particularly during the latter half of the 1800s.

Reformatories. The first public **reformatory** for juveniles was the **New York House of Refuge**, established in New York City in 1825 by the Society for the Prevention of Pauperism (Cahalan, 1986:101). This house of refuge had several goals, including providing food, clothing, and lodging for all poor, abused, or orphaned youths. However, the **Society for the Prevention of Pauperism** was made up, in part, of many benefactors, philanthropists, and clergy, and these individuals sought to instill a commitment to hard work, strict discipline, and intensive study. These houses were established in various parts of New York and staffed largely by volunteers who knew little or nothing about individual counseling, group therapy techniques, or interventions that might assist youths in surviving city hazards. Because the organization of these houses was decentralized, there were few, if any, external controls that could regulate the quality of care provided.

CHILD SAVERS. While houses of refuge operated to provide services for misplaced youths, other random efforts led to the creation of child-saving programs. **Child savers** referred to no one in particular, because anyone who wished to be of assistance in helping children and intervening in their lives for constructive purposes could define themselves as child savers. No one knows what child saving meant, but many people were involved in providing food, shelter, and other care for needy children.

COMMUNITY-BASED PRIVATE AGENCIES. **Jane Addams** established and operated **Hull House** in Chicago in 1889. It was a settlement home used largely by children from immigrant families in the Chicago area. Many adults worked long hours, and many unsupervised youths wandered about their neighborhoods looking for something to do. Using money from charities and philanthropists, Addams supplied many children with creative activities to alleviate their boredom and monotony. Addams integrated these activities with moral, ethical, and religious teachings. In her own way, she was hoping to deter these youths from lives of crime with her constructive activities and teaching.

TRUANCY STATUTES. In Massachusetts, where the first compulsory school attendance statutes were established, the state legislature passed truancy laws in 1852. By 1918, all jurisdictions had truancy statutes. Juveniles who did not attend school could be taken into custody. Such youths could be placed in state homes if it could be demonstrated that they had little, if any, adult supervision at home.

THE LACK OF JUVENILE COURT UNIFORMITY. Much variation exists among juvenile court organizations and operations in the United States (Butts, 1996b), even within the same state. Some jurisdictions have courts that adjudicate juvenile offenders as well as decide child custody. Thus, although all jurisdictions now have juvenile courts, these courts are not always called juvenile courts.

SPECIALIZED JUVENILE COURTS. Most early juvenile court proceedings were different from criminal courts. These proceedings often involved a juvenile charged with some offense; a petitioner claiming the juvenile should be declared delinquent, dependent, or neglected; and a judge who would decide things. Juveniles had no rights and no attorneys and were not permitted to call witnesses or testify on their own behalf. Juvenile court judges made decisions about juveniles according to what the judges believed to be in the best interests of the children. Thus, much individualized justice was dispensed by juvenile court judges.

THE CLOSED AND ARBITRARY NATURE OF JUVENILE COURT PROCEEDINGS. Early juvenile court proceedings were closed to the general public to protect the identities of the youthful accused. Mere allegations, together with uncorroborated statements and pronouncements from probation officers and others, were sufficient for juvenile court judges to declare any juvenile either delinquent or not delinquent. Penalties imposed ranged from verbal reprimands and warnings to incarceration in a state reform school or industrial school.

THE BUREAUCRATIZATION AND CRIMINALIZATION OF JUVENILE COURTS. Generally, juvenile courts are viewed as **due process courts** rather than **traditional courts** (Feld, 1995). Due process juvenile courts involve more formal case dispositions, a greater rate of intake dismissals, and more importance attached to offense characteristics and seriousness. Traditional courts are characterized as less formal, with greater use made of secure confinement. Both defense and prosecuting attorneys play more important roles in due process juvenile courts than in traditional ones (Butts, 1996b).

PUBLIC DEFENDERS FOR JUVENILES. There is today greater procedural formality in the juvenile justice system relating to the appointment of public defenders for juvenile indigents. Formerly, defense counsel for juveniles often were the juvenile's probation officer or a social caseworker with a vested interest in the case. It is not entirely clear how these officers and workers were able to separate their law enforcement and defense functions to avoid allegations of conflicts of interest. Little public interest was exhibited in the quality of defense in juvenile cases.

In recent years, juvenile court proceedings have become increasingly formalized (Champion, 1992, 1996). Further, public access to these proceedings in most jurisdictions is increasing. Defense counsel, an adversarial scenario, a trial-like atmosphere where witnesses testify for and against juvenile defendants, and adherence to Rules of Procedure for Juvenile Courts are clear indicators of greater formalization, bureaucratization, and criminalization (Feld, 1987b, 1995).

The Juvenile Justice Process

Referrals and Petitions

REFERRALS. Many juvenile encounters with the juvenile justice system are prompted by referrals from police officers (Butts, 1996a). Referrals are notifications made to juvenile court authorities that a juvenile requires the court's attention. Referrals may be made by anyone, such as concerned parents, school principals, teachers, and neighbors, but more than ninety percent of all referrals to juvenile court are made by law enforcement officers (Butts, 1996a:5). Arrest and being taken into custody are the first of three major processing points that indicate different degrees of entry into the juvenile justice system for juveniles. The other entry points include probation disposition and court disposition. Each of these entry points involves the exercise of discretion from various actors in the juvenile justice system.

PETITIONS. A petition is a legal document filed by interested parties alleging that a juvenile is delinquent, a status offender, or in need of adult supervision. The petition requests that the juvenile court decide whether the allegations are true and determine an

ARE JUVENILE MURDERS DECREASING?

Eric Paulding, 16

It happened in Boston, Massachusetts, on December 10, 1997. Sixteen-year-old Eric Paulding was shot and killed outside his girlfriend's house during an apparent altercation between several young people. The significance of Paulding's death is that it was the first teen murder that occurred since the death of Cassius P. Love, another sixteen-year-old, who was shot to death with a rifle in an argument over a bicycle—on July 10, 1995.

For several years, Boston has been a model for other cities to follow regarding low youth violence. President Clinton allocated $495 million to various cities in 1994 as a part of the Crime Bill to deter youth violence, and in Boston it seemed to be working. Boston credits a combination of programs run by youth workers, clergy, and police officers. Full-time youth officers keep kids busy with organized basketball games, job training, and counseling. Simultaneously, police, probation officers, and prosecutors target persistent troublemakers, tracking them down and threatening to go after them with the full force of the law. In many cases, Boston probation officers and police have shown up at the doors of troubled youngsters to make sure that they are observing curfew and remaining law-abiding.

The victim, Paulding, was no stranger to police. He had been known to them because of various status offenses, such as skipping school or lack of parental control. Although Paulding's death is regrettable, it may not signify a trend in escalating youth violence. Boston has done a good job thus far of keeping the lid on youth violence, and the efforts of many concerned youth workers and specialists are likely to continue to yield low crime rates among juveniles.

Do you think that one youth's murder is the beginning of a trend in youth violence for a city such as Boston? What can police and city officials do to continue maintaining Boston's low level of youth violence? What do you think?

Source: Adapted from Jon Marcus, "First Juvenile Killed in Boston Since '95." *Atlanta Constitution*, December 14, 1997:A11.

appropriate penalty or disposition. When a petition is filed against a particular juvenile, the juvenile is subjected to an intake hearing or simply, intake.

Intake

Intake, a screening procedure conducted by a court officer or a probation officer, varies in formality among jurisdictions (Worling, 1995). Some jurisdictions conduct **intake hearings**, where comments and opinions are solicited from significant others such as the police, parents, neighbors, and victims. These proceedings are important, regardless of their degree of formality, because one or several courses of action are recommended.

An **intake officer** is either a court-appointed official who hears complaints against juveniles and attempts early resolutions of them or, more often, a juvenile probation officer who performs intake as a special assignment. In many small jurisdictions, juvenile probation officers may perform diverse functions, including intake screenings, enforcement of truancy statutes, and juvenile placements. Intake officers consider youths' attitudes, demeanor, age, offense seriousness, and a host of other factors. If the offenses alleged are serious, what evidence exists against the offender? Should the offender be referred to certain community social service agencies, receive psychological counseling, receive vocational counseling and guidance, acquire educational or technical training and skills, be issued a verbal reprimand, be placed on some type of diversionary status, or be returned to parental custody? An intake officer may interview parents and neighbors as part of information gathering. In most jurisdictions, intake normally results in one of five actions, depending, in part, on the discretion of intake officers, who may do any of the following:

1. Dismiss the case, with or without a verbal or written reprimand.
2. Remand youths to the custody of their parents.
3. Remand youths to the custody of their parents, with provisions for or referrals to counseling or special services.
4. Divert youths to an alternative dispute resolution program, if one exists in the jurisdiction.
5. Refer youths to the juvenile prosecutor for further action and possible filing of a delinquency petition.

Juvenile Court Prosecutors and Decision Making

Like their criminal court counterparts, juvenile court prosecutors have broad discretionary powers. They may dismiss cases. They may screen cases by diverting some of the most serious ones to criminal court through waiver, transfer, or certification. A **prosecutorial waiver** is used for this purpose. Some cases are diverted out of the juvenile justice system for informal processing (Feld, 1995). Prosecutors may also file petitions or act on the petitions filed by others. These documents assert that juveniles fall within the categories of dependent or neglected, status offender, or delinquent, and the reasons for such assertions are usually provided (McCarthy and McCarthy, 1997). Filing a petition formally places the juvenile before the juvenile court judge in many jurisdictions.

Adjudicatory Proceedings

Most of the physical trappings of criminal courts are present in juvenile courts, including the judge's bench, tables for the prosecution and defense, and a witness stand. Juvenile court judges have almost absolute discretion in how their courts are conducted. Juvenile defendants may or may not be granted a trial by jury, if one is requested. Few states permit jury trials for juveniles in juvenile courts, according to legislative mandates. After hearing the evidence presented by both sides in any juvenile proceeding, the judge decides or **adjudicates** the matter in an **adjudication hearing**. An **adjudication** is a judgment or action on the petition filed with the court by others. If the petition alleges delinquency on the part of certain juveniles, the judge determines whether the juveniles are delinquent or not delinquent. If the petition alleges that the juveniles are dependent, neglected, or otherwise in need of care by agencies or others, the judge decides the matter. If the adjudicatory proceeding fails to support the facts alleged in the petition filed with the court, the case is dismissed and the youth is freed. If the adjudicatory proceeding supports the allegations, then the judge must sentence the juvenile or order another disposition.

Dispositions

Twelve dispositions are available to juvenile court judges, if the facts alleged in petitions are upheld. These dispositions may be grouped into (1) nominal, (2) conditional, or (3) custodial options.

NOMINAL DISPOSITIONS. **Nominal dispositions** are the least punitive of the three major courses of action available to juvenile court judges. They are usually verbal warnings or reprimands. Release to the custody of parents or legal guardians completes the juvenile court action.

CONDITIONAL DISPOSITIONS. All **conditional dispositions** are probationary options. Youths are placed on probation and required to comply with certain conditions during the probationary period. Juveniles are usually required to complete a given act or acts as conditions of the sentence imposed. If juveniles have been adjudicated as delinquent and the delinquency involved damage to a victim's property or bodily harm, restitution to victims may be required to pay for the property or the medical bills. Juveniles may perform community service, such as cutting courthouse lawns, cleaning up city parks, and cleaning debris from city highways or public areas. Group or individual therapy may be required of certain juveniles who exhibit psychological or social maladjustment. Juveniles who are alcohol or drug dependent may be required to participate in various recovery programs.

CUSTODIAL DISPOSITIONS. **Custodial dispositions** are either **nonsecure custody** or **confinement** or **secure custody** or **confinement**. Nonsecure custody is placing a juvenile into a **foster home, group home**, or **camp, ranch**, or schools. These are temporary measures, often designed to make more permanent arrangements for juvenile placement later. Juveniles have freedom of movement, and they can generally participate in school and other activities. For juveniles, secure custody is often the last resort most juvenile court judges consider. There is a general reluctance among judges to incarcerate youths because of adverse labeling effects. Furthermore, there are increasing numbers of alternatives to incarceration within communities. Judges are increasingly apprised of these programs and are assigning more youths to them in lieu of industrial school placements.

THIRTEEN-YEAR-OLD MURDERERS FACE LIFE IMPRISONMENT FOR DEATH OF 3-YEAR-OLD

The Cases of Justin Kennedy and Vernon Leroy James Jr.

It happened on July 6, 1997, in Oklahoma City, Oklahoma. Two brothers were roughhousing in their backyard swimming pool. Justin Kennedy, thirteen, and his thirteen-year-old common-law stepbrother, Vernon Leroy James Jr., grabbed their three-year-old stepbrother, Deangelo Jordan James, and held him under the water. The three-year-old was clamped tightly between Justin's legs under the water. Justin joked to Vernon, "Do y'all known where he [Deangelo Jordan James] is?" As they laughed, Deangelo drowned. When Deangelo was eventually pulled from the water, he was not breathing. The brothers refused to perform CPR on him because they said water and frothy liquid were flowing from his mouth.

Investigating police learned later that Justin and Vernon had been throwing Deangelo into the pool again and again, knowing that he could not swim. On at least one of these occasions, Deangelo's head hit the edge of the concrete pool hard. A prosecutor, Susan Caswell, said, "It may have started out as roughhousing . . . I don't know what they were thinking at the end." Justin was arrested by police on July 30, and Vernon was being sought. Both boys faced murder charges.

In many states, such as Oklahoma, increasing violence among younger juveniles has been met with tougher laws, including transfer of certain juveniles to criminal courts, where they conceivably can receive tougher, longer sentences. For those sixteen years of age or older, the death penalty is a possibility if they are ultimately convicted.

Justin Kennedy and Vernon James could be sentenced to life imprisonment without possibility of parole if convicted as adults. The death penalty is not an option, given their ages.

What do you think the punishment should be for two youths who deliberately drown a defenseless three-year-old? Is life imprisonment too severe for such an offense? Should we lower the age at which the death penalty can be administered? How can youth violence be deterred? What do you think?

Sources: Adapted from the Associated Press, "Brothers Charged with Drowning 3-Year-Old, Could Get Life If Guilty." *Minot* (N.D.) *Daily News,* July 31, 1997:A2; Associated Press, "Teenagers Charged in Pool Death of Boy, 3." *Honolulu Advertiser,* July 31, 1997:A11.

Changing Juvenile Court Practices

MINIMIZING THE CONFIDENTIALITY OF JUVENILE COURT RECORDS AND PROCEEDINGS. In 1995, twenty-two states had provisions for open hearings in juvenile or family court proceedings. Only eleven states did not provide for the release of the names of those juveniles charged with serious offenses, and only six states did not permit court record releases to interested parties. In fact, all states currently make available juvenile court records to any party showing a legitimate interest. In such cases, information is ordinarily obtained through a court order. Fingerprinting and photographing of juveniles are conducted routinely in most states. Half the states require registration of all juvenile offenders when they enter new jurisdictions. Also, most states now have state repositories of juvenile records and other relevant information about juvenile offending. Seventeen states prohibit sealing or expunging juvenile court records after certain dates, such as age of majority or adulthood (Bilchik, 1996:37–38). Therefore, juveniles today are considerably more likely to have their offenses known to the public in one form or another.

The protections previously given to juveniles are rapidly disappearing. The greater formality of juvenile proceedings, as well as their openness to others, may restrict the discretion of juvenile court judges, although this limitation is not particularly undesirable. Juvenile court judge decision making has often been individualized, and individualized decision making is inherently discriminatory. With more open proceedings, less individualization is evident, thus making due process a greater priority for juvenile court judges. Theoretically, at least, more open proceedings are fairer proceedings. Table 11.1 summarizes current developments in confidentiality provisions for serious and violent juvenile offenders for 1997.

THE PROSECUTION DECISION IN **2000.** The juvenile justice system has been slow in its **case processing** of juvenile offenders. In fact, delays in filing charges against juveniles and the eventual adjudicatory hearing are chronic in many jurisdictions. Juveniles arrested may wait a year or longer in some jurisdictions before their cases are heard by juvenile court judges. Juvenile court prosecutors may delay filing charges against particular juveniles for a variety of reasons. The most obvious reasons for delays—court **case backlogs**, crowded court dockets, insufficient prosecutorial staff, too much paperwork—are not always valid reasons. In many instances, the actors themselves are at fault. In short, prosecutors and judges may simply be plodding along at a slow pace because of their own personal dispositions and work habits. In jurisdictions where prosecutors and judges have aggressively tackled their caseload problems and forced functionaries to work faster, juvenile caseload processing has been greatly accelerated. The time between a juvenile's arrest and disposition has been shortened because of individual decision making and not because of any organizational constraints or overwork (Butts and Halemba, 1996:73–91).

However, in thirty states in 1997, juvenile court prosecutors were at liberty to file charges against juvenile offenders whenever they decided. No binding legislative provisions force these actors to act promptly and bring a youth's case before the juvenile court. In the meantime, twenty states have established time limits that cannot be exceeded between the time of a juvenile's court referral and the filing of charges by prosecutors.

Defense Counsels As Advocates for Juveniles

ATTORNEYS FOR JUVENILES AS A MATTER OF RIGHT. Juveniles are entitled to attorneys at all stages of juvenile proceedings. Despite this safeguard, attorney representation for juveniles in juvenile courts in most jurisdictions is less than 75 percent. In several

TABLE 11.1 Summary of Provisions Limiting Confidentiality for Serious and Violent Juvenile Offenders, 1997

State	Open Hearing	Release of Name	Release of Court Record[a]	Statewide Repository[b]	Finger-printing	Photo-graphing	Offender Registration	Seal/Exchange Records Prohibited
Totals:	30	42	48	44	47	46	39	25
Alabama			X	X	X	X	X	
Alaska	X	X	X	X	X	X	X	X
Arizona	X	X	X	X	X	X	X	
Arkansas		X	X	X	X	X	X	
California	X	X	X	X	X	X	X	X
Colorado	X	X	X	X	X	X	X	X
Connecticut			X		X	X		
Delaware	X	X	X	X	X	X	X	X
District of Columbia			X		X	X		
Florida	X	X	X	X	X	X	X	X
Georgia	X	X	X	X	X	X		X
Hawaii	X	X	X	X	X	X	X	
Idaho	X	X	X	X	X	X	X	
Illinois		X	X	X	X	X	X	
Indiana		X	X	X	X	X	X	
Iowa	X	X	X	X	X	X	X	X
Kansas	X	X	X	X	X	X	X	X
Kentucky		X	X	X	X	X		X
Louisiana	X	X	X	X	X	X	X	X
Maine	X	X	X	X		X	X	X
Maryland	X	X	X	X	X	X		
Massachusetts	X	X	X	X	X	X	X	
Michigan	X	X	X	X	X	X	X	X
Minnesota	X	X	X	X	X	X	X	X
Mississippi		X	X		X	X	X	
Missouri	X	X	X	X	X	X		X
Montana	X	X	X	X	X	X	X	X

(continued)

TABLE 11.1 (continued)

State	Open Hearing	Release of Name	Release of Court Record[a]	Statewide Repository[b]	Finger-printing	Photo-graphing	Offender Registration	Seal/Exchange Records Prohibited
Nebraska		X	X	X	X	X	X	
Nevada	X	X	X	X	X	X	X	X
New Hampshire		X	X			X	X	
New Jersey		X	X	X	X	X	X	
New Mexico	X			X	X	X	X	
New York			X	X	X	X		
North Carolina			X		X	X	X	X
North Dakota		X	X	X	X	X		
Ohio				X	X	X	X	
Oklahoma	X	X	X	X	X	X	X	X
Oregon		X	X	X	X	X	X	X
Pennsylvania	X	X	X	X	X	X	X	
Rhode Island		X	X	X			X	
South Carolina	X	X	X	X	X	X	X	X
South Dakota		X	X	X	X	X	X	X
Tennessee		X	X	X	X	X	X	
Texas	X	X	X	X	X	X	X	X
Utah	X	X	X	X	X	X	X	X
Vermont					X	X		
Virginia	X	X	X	X	X	X	X	X
Washington	X	X	X	X	X	X	X	X
West Virginia		X	X		X			X
Wisconsin	X	X	X	X			X	
Wyoming		X	X	X	X	X	X	X

Legend: X indicates the provision(s) allowed by each state as of the end of the 1997 legislative session.

[a] In this category, X indicates a provision for juvenile court records to be specifically released to at least one of the following parties: the public, the victims(s), the school(s), the prosecutor, law enforcement, or social agency; however, all states allow records to be released to any party who can show a legitimate interest, typically by court order.

[b] In this category, X indicates a provision for fingerprints to be part of a separate juvenile or adult criminal history repository.

Source: Patricia Torbet and Linda Szymanski, *State Legislative Responses to Violent Juvenile Crime: 1996–1997 Update.* Washington, DC: U.S. Department of Justice, 1998: 10.

states, only 50 percent of all adjudicated juveniles are represented by counsel (Champion, 1992).

DEFENSE COUNSEL AND ENSURING DUE PROCESS RIGHTS FOR JUVENILES. The manifest function of defense attorneys in juvenile courts is to ensure that **due process** is fulfilled by all participants. Defense attorneys are the primary advocates of fairness for juveniles who are charged with crimes or other offenses. Minors, particularly the very young, are more susceptible to the persuasiveness of adults.

ARE ATTORNEYS BEING USED MORE FREQUENTLY BY JUVENILE DEFENDANTS? Yes. At least a survey of five states during the 1980–1989 period (California, Montana, Nebraska, North Dakota, and Pennsylvania) found that attorney use by juvenile offenders increased across these years (Champion, 1992). Attorney use varies by jurisdiction, however. In the late 1980s, about 90 percent of all California juvenile cases involved either private or publicly appointed defense counsel; in Nebraska and North Dakota, juveniles used attorneys in about 60 percent of the cases.

DO DEFENSE COUNSEL FOR JUVENILES MAKE A DIFFERENCE IN THEIR CASE DISPOSITIONS? Having an attorney to represent you generally makes a difference in the case disposition, but not all dispositions are favorable for juveniles. The presence of attorneys may heighten juvenile court formality. Earlier in the processing of juveniles, attorney presence may cause intake officers to take sterner measures with juveniles who ordinarily would be dismissed from the system. Some intake officers, for instance, are intimidated by attorneys. Intake officers who would be inclined to divert a particular case from the juvenile justice system because of their judgment that the youth will probably not reoffend may not select this diversion decision if an attorney is present to represent the juvenile's interests. The intake officer may feel that the prosecutor or juvenile court judge should decide the case. However, in an otherwise attorney-free environment, the intake officer would act differently.

DEFENSE COUNSEL AS GUARDIANS *AD LITEM*. Defense counsel perform additional responsibilities as they attempt to protect children from parents who abuse them (Rodatus, 1994). A **guardian *ad litem*** is a special guardian appointed by the court to represent a youth, ward, or unborn person when litigation is pending (Black, 1990:706). Most juvenile court jurisdictions have guardian *ad litem* programs in which interested individuals serve in this capacity. In some cases, defense counsel for youths perform the dual role of defense counsel and the guardian *ad litem*. Guardians *ad litem* are supposed to benefit those they represent, and such guardians provide legal protection from others. Defense counsel working as guardians *ad litem* may act to further the child's best interests, despite a child's contrary requests or demands.

JUVENILE OFFENDER PLEA BARGAINING AND THE ROLE OF DEFENSE COUNSEL. Many juveniles plea bargain with juvenile court prosecutors (Sanborn, 1993a). Plea bargaining is an invaluable tool to eliminate case backlogs in some of the larger juvenile courts. Most frequently sought by defense counsel are charge reductions against their clients by prosecutors. Defense counsel are interested in reducing the stigma of a serious, negative juvenile court profile of their youthful clients. Prosecutors benefit because plea agreements decrease case processing time.

Jury Trials for Juveniles

In 1997, the National Center for Juvenile Justice investigated state jurisdictions to determine their present status concerning jury trials and other formal procedures for juveniles. The categories created by this investigation were states providing no right to a jury trial for juvenile delinquents under any circumstances, states providing a right to a jury trial for juveniles delinquents under any circumstances, states not providing a jury trial for juvenile delinquents except under specified circumstances, states providing the right to a jury trial for juvenile delinquents under specified circumstances, and states with statutes allowing juvenile delinquents with a right to a jury trial to waive that right.

STATES NOT PROVIDING JURY TRIALS FOR JUVENILE DELINQUENTS UNDER ANY CIRCUMSTANCES. These states were Alabama, Arizona, Arkansas, California, District of Columbia, Georgia, Hawaii, Indiana, Kentucky, Louisiana, Maryland, Mississippi, Nevada, New Jersey, North Dakota, Ohio, Oregon, Pennsylvania, South Carolina, Tennessee, Utah, Vermont, and Washington.

STATES PROVIDING JURY TRIALS FOR JUVENILES UNDER ANY CIRCUMSTANCE. These states were Alaska, Massachusetts, Michigan, and West Virginia.

STATES NOT PROVIDING JURY TRIALS FOR JUVENILE DELINQUENTS, EXCEPT UNDER SPECIFIED CIRCUMSTANCES. In Colorado, all hearings, including adjudicatory hearings, are heard without a jury; a juvenile not entitled to a trial by jury when the petition alleges a delinquent act that is a class 2 or class 3 misdemeanor, a petty offense, a violation of a municipal or county ordinance, or a violation of a court order if, prior to the trial and with the approval of the court, the district attorney has waived in writing the right to seek a commitment to the department of human services or a sentence to the county jail. In the District of Columbia and New Mexico, probation revocation hearings are heard without a jury. In Montana, hearings on whether a juvenile should be transferred to adult criminal court are heard without a jury, and probation revocation proceedings are heard without a jury. In Florida, Lousisana, Maine, North Carolina, and Nebraska, adjudicatory hearings are heard without a jury. In Texas, detention hearings are heard without a jury, hearings to consider the transfer of a child for criminal proceedings and hearings to consider waiver of jurisdiction are held without a jury, disposition hearings are heard without a jury unless the child is in jeopardy of a determinate sentence, and hearings to modify a disposition are heard without a jury unless the child is in jeopardy of a sentence for a determinate term. In Wisconsin, there is no right to a jury trial in a waiver hearing. In Wyoming, probation revocation hearings are heard without a jury.

STATES WHERE A JUVENILE DELINQUENT HAS A RIGHT TO A JURY TRIAL UNDER SPECIFIED CIRCUMSTANCES. In Arkansas, if the amount of restitution ordered by the court exceeds $10,000, the juvenile has right to a jury trial on all issues of liability and damages. In Colorado, there is no right to a jury trial unless otherwise provided, but a juvenile may demand a jury trial unless the petition alleges a delinquent act that is a class 2 or class 3 misdemeanor, a petty offense, a violation of a municipal or county ordinance, or a violation of a court order if, prior to the trial and with the approval of the court, the district attorney has waived in writing the right to seek a commitment to the department of human services or a sentence to the county jail. Also, any juvenile alleged to be an aggravated juvenile offender (defined in statute) has the right to a jury trial. In Idaho, any juvenile age fourteen to eighteen alleged to have committed a violent offense as defined in statute or a controlled substance offense has the right to a jury trial. In Illinois, any habitual juvenile offender, as defined by statute, has the right to a jury trial. In Kansas, any juvenile alleged to have committed an act that would be a felony if an adult committed it has the right to a jury trial. In Minnesota, a child who is prosecuted as an extended-jurisdiction juvenile has the right to a jury trial on the issue of guilt. Montana allows any juvenile who contests the offenses alleged in the petition the right to a jury trial. New Mexico specifies that a juvenile can demand a jury trial if an adult could have a jury trial for alleged offenses. In Oklahoma, a child has the right to a jury trial in an adjudicatory hearing. Rhode Island allows a child the right to a jury trial when the court finds the child is subject to certification to adult court. In Texas, a child has the right to a jury trial at an adjudicatory hearing at a disposition hearing only if the child is in jeopardy of a determinate sentence, and at a hearing to modify the disposition only if the child is in jeopardy of a determinate sentence on the issues of the violation of the court's orders and the sentence. In Virginia, a juvenile who is indicted has the right to a jury trial; if a juvenile is found guilty of capital murder, the court fixes the sentence with the intervention of a jury; and if appeal is taken by a child on a finding that he or she is delinquent and the alleged delinquent act would be a felony if done by adult, the child is entitled to a jury. Wyoming states that a juvenile has the right to a jury trial at an adjudicatory hearing.

STATES PROVIDING RIGHT TO A JURY TRIAL FOR JUVENILE DELINQUENTS WHERE JUVENILE DELINQUENTS CAN WAIVE THEIR RIGHT TO A JURY TRIAL. In Colorado and Montana, unless a jury is demanded, it is deemed waived. Illinois states that a minor can demand, in open court and with advice of counsel, a trial by the court without a jury. In Massachusetts, a child can file written waiver and consent to be tried by the court without a jury; this waiver cannot be received unless the child is represented by counsel or has filed, through his parent or guardian, a written waiver of counsel. Oklahoma allows a child the right to waive a jury trial. Texas states that a trial shall be by jury unless a jury is waived. In Wyoming, the failure of the party to demand a jury no later than ten days after the party is advised of the right is a waiver of this right (Szymanski, 1997).

ON THE VIOLENT IMPACT FORUM

The Cases of Tariq Khamisa and Tony Hicks

It happened in San Diego on a Saturday in January 1995. Tariq Khamisa, twenty, was delivering pizza for a local business. Tony Hicks was a troubled fourteen-year-old. Hicks had been molested by an older male acquaintance when he was six. When he was nine, his mother sent him to live with his grandfather, Ples Felix, in San Diego. Ples says, "My daughter and I felt he [Tony] needed a consistent male role model." Ples was seemingly a good role model. He had a master's degree and was a project manager for a local firm. He believed in gentle but firm discipline, and he was fairly strict with his grandson.

Tariq's father was also a good role model for his only son. Azim Khamisa was an investment banker who had fled from Africa to avoid religious persecution. His son, Tariq, was born in the United States. "He was a gifted writer, a very talented photographer who loved to laugh," said Azim of Tariq.

Tariq Khamisa had just moved into an apartment with his girlfriend. On that fateful Saturday night, Tariq had volunteered for night deliveries at the pizza store. Earlier that day, Tony Hicks had run away from home, linking up with some friends at an apartment used as a gang hangout. Tony met up with three other teenage males and a female. While hanging out, they decided that they would rob a pizza delivery man to get some extra money. The girl telephoned the pizza store where Tariq worked and ordered a pizza to be delivered to a non-existent apartment. The gang members, including Tony, placed themselves where they could watch the delivery man's arrival.

When Tariq arrived with the pizza, he could not find the right apartment. He went from apartment to apartment, ringing doorbells, as the four teenagers watched from a short distance. Then they surrounded Tariq and demanded the pizza and his money. Tariq refused. When Tariq began to walk back to his car, the oldest boy ordered Tony, the youngest, to shoot Tariq. He did. Tariq died almost instantly. The boys robbed him and fled with the money and the pizza.

Police could not contact Azim, his father, until the next day. A cleaning woman found a detective's calling card wedged in Azim's screen door at his home. When Azim called the police station, he was informed of the grisly incident. Unknown informants advised police that at least four teenagers were involved in Tariq's murder and provided details that led to Tony's arrest, along with the other three boys. "I felt rage," said Azim. "It was a rage at our society. There's something really wrong with our kids."

Tony Hicks was charged with murder and confessed to police that he was the one who had shot Tariq. He pleaded guilty to the killing and received a sentence that would keep him in a California prison until at least age thirty-seven. When asked about Tony's sentence, Azim Khamisa said, "Trying fourteen-year-olds as adults is not the answer. We've got to get to the root causes of violence."

Ples Felix, Tony's grandfather, said, "He [Tony] is a very sad and regretful kid. He's very anxious to help other kids not make the same mistake." Ples believes that his grandson can someday become a valuable member of society once again. "If we support him and give him what he needs, it can happen," added Ples.

In November 1995, Ples Felix went to the home of Azim Khamisa at Azim's invitation. He went to ask forgiveness for his grandson. As the result of this meeting, the Tariq Khamisa Foundation was established. This foundation now works with San Diego schools and community groups to educate children and parents about gang violence. Both men created a tape, *Too Many Victims,* and went on a ten-school tour. The tour was a two-phase program that included parents and siblings of students who were victims of violence and takes the message of nonviolence into the community and churches.

Should fourteen-year-olds be transferred to adult courts? How would you judge Tony Felix for his role in the shooting of Tariq Khamisa? What do you think?

Source: Adapted from Michael Ryan, "I Realized That Change Had to Start with Me." *Parade Magazine,* March 2, 1997:18–19.

Transfers, Waivers, and Certifications

A **transfer** means changing the jurisdiction of certain juvenile offenders to another jurisdiction, usually from juvenile court jurisdiction to criminal court jurisdiction. A transfer is also known as a **waiver**, referring to a change of jurisdiction from juvenile court judges to criminal court judges. Prosecutors or juvenile court judges decide that in some cases juveniles should be waived or transferred to the jurisdiction of criminal courts.

In Utah, juveniles are waived or transferred to criminal courts through a process known as certification. A certification is a formal procedure by which the state declares the juvenile to be an adult for the purpose of prosecution in a criminal court (Sanborn, 1994a). The results of certifications are the same as for waivers or transfers. Thus, certifications, waivers, and transfers result in juvenile offenders being subject to the jurisdiction of criminal courts, where they can be prosecuted as though they were adult offenders. A thirteen-year-old suspected murderer, for instance, might be transferred to criminal court for a criminal prosecution on the murder charge.

THE RATIONALE FOR TRANSFERS, WAIVERS, OR CERTIFICATIONS. The basic rationale underlying the use of waivers is that the most serious juvenile offenders will be transferred to the jurisdiction of criminal courts, where the harshest punishments, including capital punishment, may be imposed as sanctions (Dawson, 1992). The reasons for the use of transfers, waivers, or certifications include the following.

1. To make harsher punishments possible
2. To provide just deserts and proportionately severe punishments to those juveniles who deserve such punishments on account of their violent actions

3. To foster fairness in administering punishments according to the accused's serious offenses
4. To hold serious or violent offenders more accountable for what they have done
5. To show other juveniles who contemplate committing serious offenses that the system works and that harsh punishments can be expected if serious offenses are committed
6. To provide a deterrent to decrease juvenile violence
7. To overcome the traditional leniency of juvenile courts and provide more realistic sanctions
8. To make youths realize the seriousness of their offenses and induce remorse and acceptance of responsibility

THE CHARACTERISTICS OF TRANSFERRED JUVENILES. In 1993, 11,800 youths were transferred to criminal court. Most juveniles transferred were male, with only 500 females (0.4 percent) waived (Bilchik, 1996:24). About 6,500 (55.5 percent) of all transferred juveniles were black or another minority, despite the fact that white juveniles were about 64.5 percent of all cases referred to juvenile court. Furthermore, those charged with person offenses and waived to criminal court made up only 42 percent of those transferred. About 46.6 percent of those charged with property or public order offenses were waived to criminal courts, and about 10 percent of those waived were charged with drug offenses (Bilchik, 1996:13). As discussed later in this chapter, transfers are more common in recent years, although the system has not necessarily been targeting the *most* serious offenders for waivers.

YOUNGEST AGES AT WHICH JUVENILES CAN BE TRANSFERRED TO CRIMINAL COURT. In 1987, fifteen states and all federal districts indicated no specified age for transferring juveniles to criminal courts for processing. One state, Vermont, specified ten as the minimum age at which a juvenile could be waived. Montana established twelve as the earliest age for a juvenile waiver. Fourteen states used fourteen as the youngest transfer age, seven states and the District of Columbia set the minimum transfer age at fifteen, and seven states used the minimum transfer age of sixteen. During the 1990s, however, more states moved their juvenile age ranges lower for transfers or waivers. Table 11.2 shows states that have modified or enacted changes in their transfer provisions for juveniles during the 1992–1995 period.

As shown in Table 11.2, under **judicial waiver** modifications, eleven states lowered the age limit at which juveniles can be transferred to criminal court. One example of a significant age modification is Missouri, where the minimum age for juvenile transfers was lowered from fourteen to twelve for any felony. In the case of Texas, the minimum transfer age was lowered from fifteen to ten. Virginia lowered the transfer age from fifteen to fourteen. Table 11.2 also shows other modifications made to get tough toward juvenile offenders. Ten states added crimes to the list of those that qualify youths for transfer to criminal courts. In six states, the age of criminal accountability was lowered, and twenty-four states authorized additional crimes to be included that would automatically direct that the criminal court would have jurisdiction rather than the juvenile court.

TABLE 11.2 States Modifying or Enacting Transfer Provisions, 1996–1997

Types of Transfer Provision	Action Taken (Number of States)	States Making Changes	Examples
Discretionary waiver	Added crimes (7 states)	DE, KY, LA, MT, NV, RI, WA	Kentucky: 1996 provision permits the juvenile court to transfer a juvenile to criminal court if 14 years old and charge with a felony with a firearm.
	Lowered age limit (4 states)	CO, DE, HI, VA	Hawaii: 1997 provision adds language that allows waiver of a minor at any age (previously 16) if charged with first- or second-degree murder (or attempts) and there is no evidence that the person is committable to an institution for the mentally defective or mentally ill.
	Added or modified prior record provisions (4 states)	FL, HI, IN, KY	Florida: 1997 legislation requires that if the juvenile is 14 at the time of a fourth felony, and certain conditions apply, the state's attorney must ask the court to transfer him or her and certify the child as an adult or must provide written reasons for not making such a request.
Presumptive waiver	Enacted provisions (2 states)	KS, UT	Kansas: 1996 legislation shifts the burden of proofs to the child to rebut the presumption that the child is an adult.
Direct file	Enacted or modified (8 states)	AR, AZ, CO, FL, GA, MA, MT, OK	Colorado: 1996 legislation adds vehicular homicide, vehicular assault, and felonious arson to direct file statute.

(continued)

TABLE 11.2 *(continued)*

Types of Transfer Provision	Action Taken (Number of States)	States Making Changes	Examples
Statutory exclusion	Enacted provision (2 states)	AZ, MA	Arizona: 1997 legislation establishes exclusion for 15- to 17-year-olds charged with certain violent felonies.
	Added crimes (12 states)	AL, AK, DE, GA, IL, IN, OK, OR, SC, SD, UT, WA	Georgia: 1997 legislation adds crime of battery if victim is a teacher or other school personnel to list of designated felonies.
	Lowered age limit (1 state)	DE	Delaware: 1996 legislation lowers from 16 to 15 the age for which the offense of possession of a firearm during the commission of a felony is automatically prosecuted in criminal court.
	Added lesser-included offense (1 state)	IN	Indiana: 1997 legislation lists exclusion offenses, including any offense that may be joined with the listed offenses.

Source: Patricia Torbet and Linda Szymanski, *State Legislative Responses to Violent Juvenile Crime: 1996–1997 Update* (Washington, DC: U.S. Department of Justice, 1998), p. 5.

Types of Waivers

The four types of waiver actions are prosecutorial waivers, judicial or discretionary waivers, demand waivers, and legislative or automatic waivers.

PROSECUTORIAL WAIVERS. Prosecutorial waivers are also known as **direct file** or concurrent jurisdiction. Under direct file, the prosecutor has the sole authority to decide whether a particular juvenile case will be heard in criminal court or juvenile court. In Florida, one of the states where prosecutors have concurrent jurisdiction, prosecutors may file extremely serious charges (e.g., murder, rape, aggravated assault, robbery) against youths in criminal courts and present cases to grand juries for indictment action, or they may decide to file the same cases in the juvenile court.

JUDICIAL OR DISCRETIONARY WAIVERS. Most waivers from juvenile to criminal court annually come about as the result of direct judicial action. Judicial waivers give the juvenile court judge the authority to decide whether to waive jurisdiction and transfer the case to criminal court (Bilchik, 1996:3). Known also as **discretionary waivers**, judicial waivers typically involve a juvenile court judge's consideration of various criteria, including the juvenile's age, current offense, criminal history, and amenability to rehabilitation. This particular type of transfer is invoked following a motion by the prosecutor (Bilchik, 1996:3).

LEGISLATIVE OR AUTOMATIC WAIVERS. **Legislative waivers** or **automatic waivers** are statutorily prescribed actions that provide for a specified list of crimes to be excluded from the jurisdiction of juvenile courts if offending juveniles are within a specified age range and if the resulting action gives criminal courts immediate jurisdiction over these juveniles. By the mid-1980s, thirty-six states excluded certain types of offenses from juvenile court jurisdiction. These excluded offenses are either very minor or very serious, ranging from traffic or fishing violations to rape or murder (U.S. Department of Justice, 1988:79). Also, many state jurisdictions have made provisions for automatic transfers of juveniles to criminal court. Among those states with automatic transfer provisions are Washington, New York, and Illinois (Bilchik, 1996).

Automatic or legislative waivers are also known as **statutory exclusion** or **mandatory transfer**. Statutory exclusion generally refers to provisions that automatically exclude certain juvenile offenders from the juvenile court's original jurisdiction (Bilchik, 1996:3). An example of statutory exclusion is to simply lower the upper age of original juvenile court jurisdiction from eighteen to seventeen or sixteen. States with statutory exclusion make provisions for the statutory exclusion of offenders of particular ages who are alleged to have committed certain types of serious offenses. For instance, a state may prohibit juvenile courts from hearing any case involving a fifteen-year-old murderer. The age and offense are combined to create the statutory exclusion.

DEMAND WAIVERS. Under certain conditions and in selected jurisdictions, juveniles may submit motions for **demand waiver** actions. Demand waiver actions are requests or motions filed by juveniles and their attorneys to have their cases transferred from juvenile courts to criminal courts. If a juvenile's case is heard in a criminal court, the juvenile is entitled to the full range of rights available to adults charged with crimes.

OTHER WAIVER VARIATIONS. Thirteen states, including the District of Columbia, have established **presumptive waiver** provisions, which require that certain offenders should be waived unless they can prove that they are suited for juvenile rehabilitation (Bilchik, 1996:4). Essentially, juveniles are considered waived to criminal court unless they can prove that they are suitable candidates for rehabilitation. This rebuttable presumptive waiver, where the burden of proving rehabilitation potential rests with juveniles and their attorneys rather than the prosecutor, is used especially when juveniles have a history of frequent offending or have committed serious or violent offenses. Overcoming this presumption is difficult for any defense attorney if the juvenile client has committed an especially serious offense and has a prior record of violent offending.

ONCE AN ADULT, ALWAYS AN ADULT. The **once an adult, always an adult** provision is perhaps the most serious and long-lasting for affected juvenile offenders. Once juveniles at any age have been waived to the criminal court for processing or have been convicted and sentenced for one or more crimes by a criminal court, they are forever after considered adults for the purpose of criminal prosecutions.

Waiver and Reverse Waiver Hearings

All juveniles who are waived to criminal court for processing are entitled to a hearing on the waiver if they request one (Bilchik, 1996). A **waiver hearing** is a formal proceeding designed to determine whether the waiver action taken by the judge or prosecutor is the correct action and that the juvenile should be transferred to criminal court. Waiver hearings are normally conducted before the juvenile court judge. These hearings are to some extent evidentiary, because a case must be made for why criminal courts should have jurisdiction in any specific instance.

REVERSE WAIVER HEARINGS. For those jurisdictions with automatic or legislative waiver provisions, waiver actions may be contested through the use of **reverse waiver hearings**. Reverse waiver hearings are conducted before criminal court judges to determine whether to send the juvenile's case back to juvenile court. Reverse waiver hearings in those jurisdictions with automatic transfer provisions are also conducted in the presence of judges (Poulos and Orchowsky, 1994).

Implications of Waiver Hearings for Juveniles

THE CASE FOR HAVING ONE'S CASE DECIDED IN JUVENILE COURT. Among the benefits of having a case heard in juvenile court are the following:

1. Juvenile court proceedings are civil, not criminal; therefore, juveniles do not acquire criminal records.
2. Juveniles are less likely to receive sentences of incarceration.
3. Compared with criminal court judges, juvenile court judges have considerably more discretion in influencing a youth's life chances prior to or at the time of adjudication.

4. Juvenile courts are traditionally more lenient than criminal courts.
5. There is considerably more public sympathy extended to those who are processed in the juvenile justice system, despite the general public advocacy for a get-tough policy.
6. Compared with criminal courts, juvenile courts do not have as elaborate an information-exchange apparatus to determine whether certain juveniles have been adjudicated delinquent by juvenile courts in other jurisdictions.
7. Life imprisonment and the death penalty lie beyond the jurisdiction of juvenile court judges, who cannot impose these harsh sentences.

THE CASE AGAINST HAVING A CASE DECIDED IN JUVENILE COURT. Juvenile courts are not perfect, and they may be disadvantageous to many youthful offenders. Some of their major limitations are the following:

1. Juvenile court judges have the power to administer lengthy sentences of incarceration, not only for serious and dangerous offenders but also for status offenders.
2. In most states, juvenile courts are not required to provide juveniles with a trial by jury.
3. Because of their wide discretion in handling juveniles, judges may underpenalize a large number of those appearing before them on various charges.
4. Juveniles do not enjoy the same range of constitutional rights as adults in criminal courts.

Criminal Court Processing of Juvenile Offenders

THE CASE FOR AND AGAINST HAVING A CASE TRIED IN CRIMINAL COURT. When juveniles are transferred, waived, or certified to criminal court, then all rules and constitutional guarantees attach for them as well as for adults. For juveniles, being processed in criminal courts has both benefits and disadvantages. Positively, depending on the seriousness of the offenses alleged, a jury trial may be a matter of right. Adversely, periods of lengthy incarceration in minimum-, medium-, and maximum-security facilities with adults become a real possibility. Also negatively, criminal courts in a majority of state jurisdictions may impose the death penalty in capital cases. A sensitive subject with most citizens is whether juveniles should receive the death penalty if convicted of capital crimes. In recent years, the U.S. Supreme Court has addressed this issue specifically and ruled that in those states where the death penalty is imposed, the death penalty may be imposed as a punishment on any juvenile who was age sixteen or older at the time the capital offense was committed (*Stanford v. Kentucky*, 1989; *Wilkins v. Missouri*, 1989). Positively, the youthfulness of the accused works to the benefit of the defense. Jury sympathy is often evoked for a youth who has committed a horrible crime, because it can be shown that the juvenile's home life, sexual or physical abuse, and other factors are to blame for the defendant's present plight. Therefore, a jury often favors leniency for young offenders.

MENENDEZ REVISITED

The Case of Robert and Jeffrey Dingman

It happened in Rochester, New Hampshire, on the Maine state line. Eve and Vance Dingman were a typical middle-class family. Vance was an electrician, and Eve was a customer service representative at a nearby fabric plant. They lived in a small house in a middle-class neighborhood. Vance Dingman was a gun collector who had a number of rifles and pistols locked in a gun cabinet in the home. The Dingmans also had two sons—Robert, seventeen, and Jeffrey, fourteen—and a will leaving approximately $200,000 to their sons in the event of their deaths.

On Friday, February 9, 1996, Eve and Vance Dingman were shot to death in cold blood. When they failed to report for work at their respective jobs the following Monday, coworkers called their home to find out why they were absent. The sons advised their parents' coworkers that Eve and Vance had gone on a spur-of-the-moment vacation. Suspicious of this explanation, coworkers called the police, who showed up at the Dingman residence a short time later and asked the boys if they could look around. The boys gave their consent, and police eventually found the bodies. Vance was found wrapped in black plastic trash bags in the attic. Eve, also wrapped in black plastic trash bags, was found in the basement. The house was spotless, and it was not immediately known where the victims had been killed.

The younger son, Jeffrey, decided to cooperate with police. The tale he told was very disturbing. He said that earlier during the week of the murder the boys had been placed on a curfew and other restrictions. Robert, the elder brother, complained that his parents would not let him purchase a cell phone with the money he had earned working at two restaurants. More than a month before the actual murders, the boys plotted various scenarios involving the deaths of their parents. They mused about poisoning their parents. In another scenario, they envisioned staging a car crash and pushing their parents onto thin ice at a nearby lake. They even toyed with the idea of having a friend help them shoot their parents.

The ultimate decision was to simply shoot their parents with one or more weapons from Vance's gun cabinet. Jeffrey said that when his father came home that fateful Friday, Robert Dingman shot him in the chest. Vance Dingman said, "I can't believe my own son did this." Robert fired several more times. He shot his father again when Jeffrey observed Vance's arm move as they were trying to stuff him into a garbage bag.

The mother came home a few minutes later. She yelled about the stereo the boys had turned up to cover up the sound of their gunshots. Jeffrey then fired two or three quick shots at her. Jeffrey said that Robert also fired a few shots at her, saying "Die, bitch," as he shot her in the head.

The boys scrubbed down the walls and floors of the rooms where the shootings occurred. After the killings, the night was still young. Jeffrey had some Doritos and went to play basketball with a friend. Robert peeled off his rubber gloves and went to his girlfriend's house for a few hours. Subsequent police lab work positively identified blood stains on the walls and floors. Jeffrey's testimony was substantially incriminating.

What type of punishment would you impose for each of the boys? Should the older boy receive the death penalty? Do you believe the murders were premeditated?

Source: Adapted from the Associated Press, "Menendez Brothers East? Brothers Accused of Murdering Their Parents." *Minot* (N.D.) *Daily News,* May 17, 1997:B1.

Juvenile Rights and Standards of Proof

During the mid-1960s and for the next thirty years, there were significant achievements in juvenile rights. Although the *parens patriae* philosophy continues to be somewhat influential in juvenile proceedings, the U.S. Supreme Court has vested youths with certain constitutional rights. These rights do not encompass all rights extended to adults who are charged with crimes, but those rights conveyed to juveniles thus far have had far-reaching implications for how juveniles are processed. In the following section, several landmark cases involving juvenile rights are described.

Landmark Cases in Juvenile Rights

Regardless of the causes, several significant changes have been made in the juvenile justice system and juvenile defendant processing in recent decades. Each of the cases presented here represents attempts by juveniles to secure rights ordinarily extended to adults.

KENT V. UNITED STATES (1966). Morris A. Kent Jr., a fourteen-year-old in the District of Columbia, was apprehended in 1959 as the result of several housebreakings and attempted purse snatchings. He was placed on probation in the custody of his mother. In 1961, an intruder entered a woman's apartment, took her wallet, and raped her. Fingerprints at the crime scene were later identified as those of Morris Kent, who had been fingerprinted when he was apprehended for housebreaking in 1959. On September 5, 1961, Kent, sixteen, was taken into custody by police and interrogated for seven hours. He admitted the offense and volunteered information about other housebreakings, robberies, and rapes. Kent was summarily waived to criminal court by the juvenile court judge without a hearing on the waiver, which his attorney had demanded. Kent was later found guilty of six counts of housebreaking by a federal jury, although the jury found him not guilty by reason of insanity on the rape charge. Because of District of Columbia law, it was mandatory that Kent be transferred to a mental institution until such time as his sanity is restored. On each of the housebreaking counts, Kent's sentence was five to fifteen years, or a total of thirty to ninety years in prison. His mental institution commitment would be counted as time served against the thirty- to ninety-year sentence. The U.S. Supreme Court reversed Kent's conviction on appeal. The court held that Kent's rights to due process and to the effective assistance of counsel were violated when he was denied a formal hearing on the waiver and his attorneys' motions were ignored. Because of the *Kent* decision, waiver hearings are now considered critical stages that require an attorney's advice and presence.

IN RE GAULT **(1967).** *In re Gault* (1967) is perhaps the most significant of all juvenile rights cases. It is certainly the most ambitious in terms of the rights sought by Gault. The U.S. Supreme Court granted the following rights for all juveniles as the result of the *Gault* decision: (1) the right to a notice of charges, (2) the right to counsel, (3) the right to confront and cross-examine witnesses, and (4) the right to invoke the privilege against self-incrimination.

The facts are that fifteen-year-old Gerald Francis Gault and a friend, Ronald Lewis, were taken into custody by the Sheriff of Gila County, Arizona, in the morning of June 8, 1964. A verbal complaint had been filed by a neighbor of Gault, Mrs. Cook, alleging that Gault had called her and made lewd and indecent remarks. Gault was picked up and taken to Children's Detention Home while his mother and father were at work. They did not learn of their son's whereabouts until later that evening. Gault's parents proceeded to the home and were advised that a petition had been filed against Gault and that a hearing was scheduled in Juvenile Court the following day. No factual basis was provided for the petition, and Gault's parents were not provided with a copy of it in advance of the hearing. When the hearing was held, only Gault, his mother and older brother, Probation Officers Flagg and Henderson, and the juvenile court judge were present. The original complainant, Mrs. Cook, was not there. No one was sworn at the hearing, no transcript was made of it, and no memorandum of the substance of the proceedings was prepared. The testimony consisted largely of allegations by Officer Flagg about Gault's behavior and prior juvenile record. Gault was adjudicated delinquent by the judge and ordered to serve a six-year term in the Arizona State Industrial School (a juvenile prison). After exhausting their appeals in Arizona state courts, the Gaults appealed to the U.S. Supreme Court. Needless to say, the court was appalled that Gault's case had been handled in such a cavalier and unconstitutional manner. They reversed the Arizona Supreme Court, holding that Gault did, indeed, have the right to an attorney, the right to confront his accuser (Mrs. Cook) and to cross-examine her, the right against self-incrimination, and the right to have notice of the charges filed against him. Perhaps Justice Black summed up the current juvenile court situation in the United States when he said, "This holding strikes a well-nigh fatal blow to much that is *unique* [emphasis mine] about the juvenile courts in this Nation."

IN RE WINSHIP **(1970).** *Winship* was a less complex case than *Gault*, but it set an important precedent in juvenile courts with respect to the standard of proof used in establishing defendant guilt. The facts are that twelve-year-old Samuel Winship was charged with larceny in New York City. He purportedly entered a locker and stole $112 from a woman's pocketbook. Under Section 712 of the New York Family Court Act, a juvenile delinquent was defined as a person over age seven and less than sixteen who does any act that, if done by an adult, would constitute a crime. Although the juvenile court judge in the case acknowledged that the proof to be presented by the prosecution might be insufficient to establish the guilt of Winship beyond a reasonable doubt, he did adjudicate Winship delinquent and ordered him placed in a training school for eighteen months. The U.S. Supreme Court heard Winship's case and reversed the New York Family Court ruling on the basis that an eighteen-month loss of liberty was substantial enough to warrant a stronger standard of proof, such as beyond a reasonable doubt. Because this standard of proof was not used in Winship's case, he was unjustly adjudicated.

McKeiver v. Pennsylvania (1971). The *McKeiver* case was important because the U.S. Supreme Court held that juveniles are not entitled to a jury trial as a matter of right. (As of 1990, twelve states legislatively mandated jury trials for juveniles in juvenile courts if they requested such trials, depending upon the seriousness of the offense(s) alleged.) The facts are that in May 1968, Joseph McKeiver, age sixteen, was charged with robbery, larceny, and receiving stolen goods. While he was represented by counsel at his adjudicatory hearing and requested a trial by jury, the judge denied his request. McKeiver was adjudicated delinquent. On appeal to the U.S. Supreme Court, McKeiver's adjudication was upheld. The U.S. Supreme Court said that it is the juvenile court judge's decision whether to grant jury trials to juveniles.

Breed v. Jones (1975). This case raised the significant constitutional issue of double jeopardy. The U.S. Supreme Court concluded that after a juvenile has been adjudicated as delinquent on specific charges, those same charges may not be alleged against those juveniles subsequently in criminal courts through transfers or waivers. The facts of the case are that on February 8, 1971, in Los Angeles, seventeen-year-old Gary Steven Jones was armed with a deadly weapon and allegedly committed robbery. Jones was subsequently apprehended, and a petition was filed against him. He was adjudicated delinquent. The judge then transferred Jones through a judicial waiver to a criminal court, where he could be tried as an adult. In a later criminal trial, Jones was convicted of robbery and committed for an indeterminate period to the California Youth Authority. The California Supreme Court upheld the conviction. When Jones appealed the decision in 1971, the U.S. Supreme Court reversed the robbery conviction. Jones's conviction in criminal court was overturned on the basis that it was a violation of his right against double jeopardy. Jones had already been adjudicated on the same charge in juvenile court. Juveniles cannot be adjudicated on a given charge in juvenile court and then sent to criminal court to face conviction on the same charge.

Schall v. Martin (1984). In this case, the U.S. Supreme Court issued juveniles a minor setback regarding the state's right to hold them in preventive detention pending a subsequent adjudication. The court said that the preventive detention of juveniles by states is constitutional if judges perceive these youths to pose a danger to the community or an otherwise serious risk if released short of an adjudicatory hearing. This decision was significant, in part, because many experts advocated the separation of juveniles and adults in jails, the facilities most often used for preventive detention. Also, the preventive detention of adults was not ordinarily practiced at that time. (Since then, the preventive detention of adults who are deemed to pose societal risks has been upheld by the U.S. Supreme Court [*United States v. Salerno*, 1987].)

The facts are that fourteen-year-old Gregory Martin was arrested at 11:30 P.M. on December 13, 1977, in New York City. He was charged with first-degree robbery, second-degree assault, and criminal possession of a weapon. Martin lied to police at the time by giving a false name and address. Between the time of his arrest and December 29, when a fact-finding hearing was held, Martin was detained (a total of fifteen days). His confinement was based largely on the false information he had supplied to police and the seriousness of the charges pending against him. Subsequently, he was adjudicated a delinquent and placed on two years' probation. Later, his attorney filed an appeal, contesting his preventive detention as violative of the due process clause of the Fourteenth Amendment. The U.S. Supreme Court eventually heard the case and upheld the detention as constitutional. Table 11.3 summarizes some of the major rights available to juveniles and compares these rights with selected rights enjoyed by adults in criminal proceedings.

Blended Sentencing Statutes and the Get-Tough Movement

The most significant change in waiver patterns throughout the United States is that between 1992 and 1996, all but ten states had adopted or modified laws to make it easier to prosecute juveniles as adults in criminal courts (Bilchik, 1996:3). Some of the reasons suggested for this tougher stance toward juvenile offending are that juvenile rehabilitation has not been particularly effective at deterring juveniles from further offending and that the juvenile justice system is not punitive enough to impose the nature and types of punishments deserved by an increasingly violent juvenile offender population (Bilchik, 1996:3). The major ways of making juveniles more amenable to criminal court punishment are to lower the age at which they can be processed by criminal courts as adults, expand the number of crimes that qualify juvenile offenders as adults for criminal court action, and lower the age at which juveniles can be transferred to criminal courts for various offenses.

Blended Sentencing Statutes

Barry Feld (1995) observes that in recent years many states have legislatively redefined the juvenile court's purpose by diminishing the role of rehabilitation and heightening the importance of public safety, punishment, and accountability in the juvenile justice system. One of the most dramatic changes in the dispositional and sentencing options available to juvenile court judges is **blended sentencing**, the imposition of juvenile and/or adult correctional sanctions to serious and violent juvenile offenders who have been adjudicated in juvenile court or convicted in criminal court. Blended sentencing options are usually based on age or on a combination of age and offense (Bilchik, 1996:11).

TABLE 11.3 Comparison of Juvenile and Adult Rights Relating to Delinquency and Crime

Right	Adults	Juveniles
1. "Beyond a reasonable doubt" standard used in court	Yes	Yes
2. Right against double jeopardy	Yes	Yes
3. Right to assistance of counsel	Yes	Yes
4. Right to notice of charges	Yes	Yes
5. Right to a transcript of court proceedings	Yes	No
6. Right against self-incrimination	Yes	Yes
7. Right to trial by jury	Yes	No in most states
8. Right to defense counsel in court proceedings	Yes	No
9. Right to due process	Yes	No[a]
10. Right to bail	Yes	No, with exceptions
11. Right to cross-examine witnesses	Yes	Yes
12. Right of confrontation	Yes	Yes
13. Standards relating to searches and seizures:		
a. "Probable cause" and warrants required for searches and seizures	Yes, with exceptions	No
b. "Reasonable suspicion" required for searches and seizures without warrant	No	Yes
14. Right to a hearing prior to transfer to criminal court or to a reverse waiver hearing in states with automatic transfer provisions	N/A	Yes
15. Right to a speedy trial	Yes	No
16. Right to habeas corpus relief in correctional settings	Yes	No
17. Right to rehabilitation	No	No
18. Criminal evidentiary standards	Yes	Yes
19. Right to hearing for parole or probation revocation	Yes	No
20. Bifurcated trial, death penalty cases	Yes	Yes
21. Right to discovery	Yes	Limited
22. Fingerprinting, photographing at booking	Yes	No, with exceptions
23. Right to appeal	Yes	Limited

(continued)

TABLE 11.3 *(continued)*

Right	Adults	Juveniles
24. Waivers of rights:		
a. Adults	Knowingly, intelligently	
b. Juveniles	Totality of circumstances	
25. Right to a hearing for parole or probation revocation	Yes	No, with exceptions
26. "Equal protection" clause of Fourteenth Amendment applicable	Yes	No, with exceptions
27. Right to court-appointed attorney if indigent	Yes	No, with exceptions
28. Transcript required of criminal/delinquency trial proceedings	Yes	No, with exceptions
29. Pretrial detention permitted	Yes	Yes
30. Plea bargaining	Yes, with exceptions	No, with exceptions
31. Burden of proof borne by prosecution	Yes	No, with exceptions[b]
32. Public access to trials	Yes	Limited
33. Conviction/adjudication results in criminal record	Yes	No

Source: Compiled by the authors.

[a]Minimal, not full, due process safeguards assured.

[b]Burden of proof is borne by the prosecutor in twenty-three state juvenile courts; while the rest make no provision or mention of who bears the burden of proof.

There are five basic models of blended sentencing: (1) juvenile-exclusive blend, (2) juvenile-inclusive blend, (3) juvenile-contiguous blend, (4) criminal-exclusive blend, and (5) criminal-inclusive blend. These models are shown in Figure 11.1.

The **juvenile-exclusive blend** involves a disposition by the juvenile court judge to either the juvenile correctional system or the adult correctional system, but not both. Thus, a judge might order a juvenile adjudicated delinquent for aggravated assault to serve three years in a juvenile industrial school, or the judge may order the adjudicated delinquent to serve three years in a prison for adults. The judge cannot impose *both* types of punishment under this model, however. In 1996, only one state, New Mexico, provided such a sentencing option for its juvenile court judges.

FIGURE 11.1 Models of Blended Sentencing

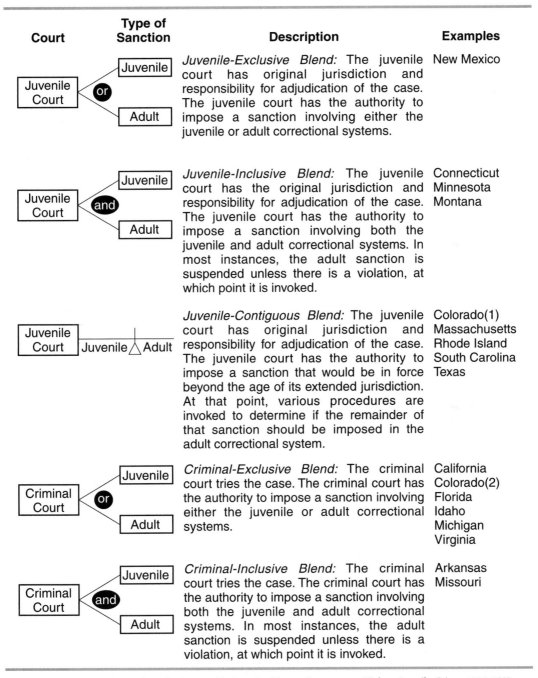

Court	Type of Sanction	Description	Examples
Juvenile Court (or)	Juvenile / Adult	*Juvenile-Exclusive Blend:* The juvenile court has original jurisdiction and responsibility for adjudication of the case. The juvenile court has the authority to impose a sanction involving either the juvenile or adult correctional systems.	New Mexico
Juvenile Court (and)	Juvenile / Adult	*Juvenile-Inclusive Blend:* The juvenile court has the original jurisdiction and responsibility for adjudication of the case. The juvenile court has the authority to impose a sanction involving both the juvenile and adult correctional systems. In most instances, the adult sanction is suspended unless there is a violation, at which point it is invoked.	Connecticut Minnesota Montana
Juvenile Court	Juvenile △ Adult	*Juvenile-Contiguous Blend:* The juvenile court has original jurisdiction and responsibility for adjudication of the case. The juvenile court has the authority to impose a sanction that would be in force beyond the age of its extended jurisdiction. At that point, various procedures are invoked to determine if the remainder of that sanction should be imposed in the adult correctional system.	Colorado(1) Massachusetts Rhode Island South Carolina Texas
Criminal Court (or)	Juvenile / Adult	*Criminal-Exclusive Blend:* The criminal court tries the case. The criminal court has the authority to impose a sanction involving either the juvenile or adult correctional systems.	California Colorado(2) Florida Idaho Michigan Virginia
Criminal Court (and)	Juvenile / Adult	*Criminal-Inclusive Blend:* The criminal court tries the case. The criminal court has the authority to impose a sanction involving both the juvenile and adult correctional systems. In most instances, the adult sanction is suspended unless there is a violation, at which point it is invoked.	Arkansas Missouri

Source: Patricia Torbet and Linda Szymanski, *State Legislature Responses to Violent Juvenile Crime; 1996–1997, Update* (Washington, DC: U.S. Department of Justice, 1998), p. 13.

The **juvenile-inclusive blend** involves a disposition by the juvenile court judge that is both a juvenile correctional sanction and an adult correctional sanction. Suppose the judge had adjudicated a fifteen-year-old juvenile delinquent on a charge of vehicular theft. The judge might impose a disposition of two years in a juvenile industrial school or reform school. Further, the judge might impose a sentence of three additional years in an adult penitentiary. However, the second sentence to the adult prison would typically be suspended unless the juvenile violated one or more conditions of the original disposition and any conditions accompanying the disposition. Usually, this suspension period would run until the youth reaches age eighteen or twenty-one. The offender who committed a new offense or violated one or more program conditions would immediately be placed in the adult prison to serve the second sentence originally imposed.

The **juvenile-contiguous blend** involves a disposition by a juvenile court judge that may extend beyond the jurisdictional age limit of the offender. When the age limit of the juvenile court jurisdiction is reached, various procedures may be invoked to transfer the case to the jurisdiction of adult corrections. States with this juvenile-contiguous blend include Colorado, Massachusetts, Rhode Island, South Carolina, and Texas. In Texas, for example, a fifteen-year-old youth who has been adjudicated delinquent on a murder charge can be given an incarcerative term of from one to thirty years. At the time of the disposition in juvenile court, the youth is sent to the Texas Youth Commission and incarcerated in one of its facilities (similar to reform or industrial schools). By the time the youth reaches age seventeen and a half, the juvenile court must hold a transfer hearing to determine whether the youth should be sent to the Texas Department of Corrections. At this hearing, the youth may present evidence in his or her favor to show why he or she has become rehabilitated and no longer should be confined. However, the prosecutor may present evidence of institutional misconduct to show that the youth should be incarcerated for more years in a Texas prison. This hearing functions as an incentive for the youth to behave well while confined in the juvenile facility.

The **criminal-exclusive blend** involves a decision by a criminal court judge to impose either a juvenile court sanction or a criminal court sanction, but not both. For example, a criminal court judge may hear the case of a fifteen-year-old youth who has been transferred to criminal court on a rape charge. The youth is convicted in a jury trial in criminal court. At this point, the judge has two options: sentence the offender to a prison term in an adult correctional facility or impose an incarcerative sentence for the youth to serve in a juvenile facility. The judge may believe that the fifteen-year-old would be better off in a juvenile industrial school rather than an adult prison. The judge may impose a sentence of adult incarceration but be inclined to place the youth in a facility where there are other youths in the offender's age range.

The **criminal-inclusive blend** involves a decision by the criminal court judge to impose both a juvenile penalty and a criminal sentence simultaneously. Again, as in the juvenile-inclusive blend model, the latter criminal sentence may be suspended, depending on the good conduct of the juvenile during the juvenile punishment phase. For example, suppose a twelve-year-old boy has been convicted of attempted murder. The boy participated in a drive-by shooting and is a gang member. The criminal court judge sentences the youth to a term of six years in a juvenile facility, such as an industrial school. At the same time, the judge imposes a sentence on the youth of twenty years to be spent in an adult correctional facility, following the six-year sentence in the juvenile facility. However, the adult portion of the sentence may be suspended, depending on whether the juvenile behaves or misbehaves during his six-year industrial school incarceration. There is an additional twist to this blend. If the juvenile violates one or more conditions of his confinement in the juvenile facility, the judge has the power to revoke that sentence and invoke the sentence of incarceration in an adult facility. With good behavior, the youth can be free of the system following the period of juvenile confinement; the adult portion of the sentence is suspended if the youth deserves such leniency. Arkansas has the revocation power and ability to place youths in adult correctional facilities (Bilchik, 1996:14).

Trends and Implications for Juvenile Offenders

A Summary of Juvenile Justice Trends

The trends discussed in this section pertain to the legal rights of juveniles; law enforcement; the prosecution of juveniles and juvenile courts; diversion, probation, and intermediate punishments; and juvenile corrections and aftercare.

1. The juvenile justice system will experience greater reforms in the area of juvenile rights commensurate with those enjoyed by adult offenders.
2. Juveniles will attain constitutional rights commensurate with adult offenders. Currently, there are no speedy-trial provisions for juvenile offenders.
3. Greater accountability and responsibility will be expected from juvenile offenders.
4. A deinstitutionalization of status offenses will occur. As we have seen, there is a general trend toward DSO as a means of diverting less serious offenders from the jurisdiction of juvenile courts.
5. Greater attention will be paid to preventing short-term detention of juveniles with adult offenders after arrest.
6. There will be greater use of transfers and waivers to adult criminal courts.
7. The juvenile court will become increasingly adversarial, in many respects paralleling the adult system.
8. Juvenile courts will become more formal.
9. The increased use of transfers of juveniles to criminal courts will continue, especially for serious offenses such as rape, robbery, and murder.
10. There will be a greater concern for juvenile rights.
11. More stringent standards will be applied for the admissibility of evidence in juvenile proceedings.
12. There will be greater use of plea bargaining.
13. There will be greater use of diversion.
14. Innovations in juvenile offender management will include electronic monitoring and/or home confinement.
15. There will be a greater emphasis on victim restitution and community service.

Summary

Paralleling the criminal justice system for adults is a juvenile justice system for youthful offenders. The juvenile justice system is a largely civil entity. The jurisdiction of juvenile courts is limited to youths who have not yet reached the age of their majority, which may be eighteen, nineteen, or twenty-one. The juvenile justice system distinguishes between juvenile delinquents, who have committed crimes, and status offenders, who have committed offenses that would not be crimes if adults committed them. Status offenses include runaway behavior, truancy, and violation of curfew. Also under the jurisdiction of juvenile courts are children in need of supervision (CHINS). Under common law, persons under age seven are presumed incapable of formulating criminal intent, and it is unusual for the juvenile justice system to hear cases involving especially youthful offenders under age ten.

In 1974, the Juvenile Justice and Delinquency Prevention Act was passed. It has been revised several times subsequently. This act provides in part for the removal of status offenders from secure facilities where juvenile delinquents are held. Secure facilities are prisonlike structures, although these institutions are not called prisons. One purpose for removing status offenders from secure institutions was to assist them in avoiding the adverse effects of labeling that result from incarceration. Most states today do not incarcerate status offenders.

Especially influential on the juvenile justice system is the fifteenth-century doctrine of *parens patriae*. This doctrine deemed the King of England as the father of his country in a figurative sense. He dispensed justice to people throughout England through his representatives, known as chancellors. The scope of their authority to decide matters of law encompassed juveniles as well as adults. Early U.S. juvenile courts were strongly influenced by *parens patriae*, and today many juvenile court judges relate to youths in paternalistic or maternalistic ways. Decisions are often made about youths on the basis of what is in their best interests. These decisions are highly individualized. Critics say that these individualized decisions, although well intended, are inherently discriminatory and deny youths due process. Therefore, substantial changes in the nature and functions of juvenile courts were made in the 1960s and 1970s, and due process received greater emphasis.

Major differences between juvenile and criminal courts include the following: juvenile courts are less formal; in most states, juveniles are denied the right to a jury trial; juvenile courts are not courts of record; the standard of proof when incarceration is not an option is the civil standard of preponderance of the evidence; and the range of punishments is much greater in criminal courts. In both types of courts, the proceedings are adversarial. In fact, many believe that juvenile courts are slowly being converted into criminal courts because of the additional rights juveniles have acquired.

Juveniles are brought to the attention of juvenile courts following alleged illegal conduct. They are arrested or taken into custody and are sent to intake, which is an informal proceeding conducted by a juvenile probation officer. More serious cases are sent to juvenile court prosecutors, usually through a petition, and eventually a portion of these cases is heard by the juvenile court judge. On the basis of the evidence, judges determine the truthfulness of the allegations against the juvenile, and the juvenile is adjudicated. An adjudication is a judicial decision. It may be dismissal of all charges against the juvenile, or it may be a determination that the juvenile is a delinquent, status offender, or child in need of supervision. Following an adjudication that found delinquency, the judge disposes the juvenile, which is the functional equivalent of an adult sentence. Juvenile court dispositions are nominal, conditional, or custodial. Nominal sanctions are verbal reprimands or warnings, conditional sanctions typically involve probation, and custodial sanctions involve incarceration in a secure or nonsecure juvenile facility.

More serious juvenile offenders are waived or transferred to criminal court for processing. Juveniles sent to criminal court for processing are believed to suffer harsher punishments, although there is considerable evidence to show that in most cases this result fails to occur. Nevertheless, almost every state has transfer, waiver, or certification provisions that permit youths to be treated as adults and sent to criminal courts to be prosecuted as though they were adult criminal offenders. More recent legislative changes relating to juvenile court processing have evolved blended sentencing statutes that empower juvenile or criminal court judges to impose either or both juvenile or criminal sanctions following a determination of guilt.

The juvenile court and juvenile justice system have been influenced significantly by several important U.S. Supreme Court decisions. Landmark cases include *Kent v. United States* (1966), which entitled youths to a hearing prior to being transferred to criminal court; *In re Gault* (1967), which gave youths the right to counsel, the right to confront and cross-examine witnesses against them and to give testimony in their own behalf, and the right against self-incrimination; *In re Winship* (1970), which changed the standard of proof in juvenile proceedings to beyond a reasonable doubt if incarceration for the juvenile was a serious option; *McKeiver v. Pennsylvania* (1971), which declared that juveniles are not automatically entitled to a jury trial in juvenile courts; *Breed v. Jones* (1975), which declared that juveniles cannot be adjudicated in juvenile court and convicted in criminal court on the same charge, which violates their right against double jeopardy; and *Schall v. Martin* (1984), which authorizes law enforcement to place youths in preventive detention.

At present, the juvenile court is undergoing various reforms, including lowering the age for treating juveniles as adults for the purpose of a criminal prosecution, creating greater standards of accountability for juvenile offenders, using more plea bargaining for juveniles, and emphasizing victim restitution and community service. The juvenile court is gradually changing from a traditional system to a due process system, with greater emphasis on defendants' legal rights. One reason for these changes is the rise in youth violence during the 1990s and the fact that youths are committing more violent offenses at younger ages. There is continuing debate concerning how best to deal with juveniles in court and which punishments are most appropriate for them.

KEY TERMS

Addams, Jane
Adjudicates
Adjudication
Adjudication hearing
Automatic waivers
Blended sentencing
Camp, ranch
Case backlogs
Case processing
Certification
Chancellors
Child savers
Children in need of
   supervision (CHINS)
Conditional dispositions
Criminal-exclusive blend
Criminal-inclusive blend
Criminalization
Curfew violators
Custodial dispositions
Deinstitutionalization
Deinstitutionalization
   of status offenses
   (DSO)
Demand waiver
Direct file
Discretionary waivers
Disposition
Divestiture of jurisdiction
Due process

Due process courts
English common law
Foster home
Group home
Guardian *ad litem*
Hull House
Illinois Juvenile Court Act
Intake
Intake hearing
Intake officer
Intake screening
Judicial waiver
Juvenile-contiguous blend
Juvenile court
Juvenile court jurisdiction
Juvenile delinquency
Juvenile delinquent
Juvenile-exclusive blend
Juvenile-inclusive blend
Juvenile Justice and
   Delinquency
   Prevention Act of
   1974, 1984 (JJDPA)
Juvenile justice system,
   process
Juveniles
Legislative waivers
Loiterers
Mandatory transfer
New York House of Refuge

Nominal dispositions
Nonsecure custody,
   confinement
Office of Juvenile Justice
   and Delinquency
   Prevention (OJJDP)
Once an adult, always
   an adult
Parens patriae
Petition
Presumptive waiver
Prosecutorial waiver
Referral
Reformatory
Reverse waiver hearings
Runaways
Secure custody,
   confinement
Society for the Prevention
   of Pauperism
Standard of proof
Status offenders
Statutory exclusion
Stigmas
Stigmatize
Traditional courts
Transfer
Truants
Waiver
Waiver hearing

QUESTIONS FOR REVIEW

1. Distinguish between a juvenile delinquent and a status offender. What has the federal government done to keep status offenders out of jails?

2. What is the jurisdiction of juvenile courts?

3. What is the doctrine of *parens patriae*? Why is it significant in the actions of juvenile courts today? In what ways does *parens patriae* influence judicial decision making?

4. What is a referral? Who can make referrals? What are their purposes?

5. Identify four types of waivers. Which types of waivers are made by judges? Which types of waivers are made by legislatures?

6. Can juveniles contest waivers? How can these waiver actions be reversed? Describe several methods to accomplish this task.

7. What is a blended sentencing statute? How does it relate to the get-tough movement?

8. Identify three major rights cases involving juveniles. What are the major rights conveyed in the cases you have identified?

9. Describe several important trends relating to juveniles and their processing in juvenile court.

10. What is meant by DSO? What was the enabling legislation leading to DSO on the federal level?

11. What are some general differences between criminal courts and juvenile courts?

12. Under what circumstances can juveniles have jury trials in juvenile courts?

SUGGESTED READINGS

Community Research Associates. (1998). *Female Juvenile Offenders: A Status of the States Report.* Washington, DC: U.S. Office of Juvenile Justice and Delinquency Prevention.

Dean, Bernard C. (1997). *Juvenile Justice and Disproportionality: Patterns of Minority Over-Representation in Washington's Juvenile Justice System.* Olympia: Sentencing Guidelines Commission in Washington.

Elrod, Preston and R. Scott Ryder. (1999). *Juvenile Justice: A Social, Historical, and Legal Perspective.* Gaithersburg, MD: Aspen.

Florida Inter-University Consortium for Child, Family, and Community Studies. (1999). *Young Chronic Offenders: Final Report.* Tallahassee: Juvenile Justice Accountability Board, Florida Department of Juvenile Justice.

Justice Research and Statistics Association. (1999). *Juvenile Justice Evaluation Needs in the States: Findings of the Formula Grants Program Evaluation Needs Assessment.* Washington, DC: Justice Research and Statistics Association.

Kassebaum, Gene, Nancy L. Marker, and Patricia Glancey. (1997). *A Plan for Prevention, Resolution, and Controls for the Problem of Youth on the Run.* Honolulu: Center for Youth Research, Social Science Research Institute, University of Hawaii at Manoa.

McDowell, Gary L. and Jinney S. Smith (eds.). (1999). *Juvenile Delinquency in the United States and the United Kingdom.* London: Macmillan; New York: St. Martins.

New York State Task Force on School Violence. (1999). *Safer Schools for the 21st Century.* Albany: New York State Office of the Lieutenant Governor.

Torbet, Patricia et al. (2000). *Juveniles Facing Criminal Sanctions: Three States That Changed the Rules.* Washington, DC: U.S. Office of Juvenile Justice Policy and Delinquency Prevention.

U.S. Department of Justice. (1999). *1997 National Youth Gang Survey.* Washington, DC: U.S. Department of Justice.

Watkins, John C. Jr. (1999). *Selected Cases on Juvenile Justice in the Twentieth Century.* Lewiston, NY: Edwin Mellen Press.

COURTS, MEDIA, AND THE LITIGATION EXPLOSION

CHAPTER **12**

REALITY CHECK: It never fails. During television broadcasts of courtroom drama, commentators and so-called experts provide up-to-the-minute extended drama to characterize court happenings. Before jurors can get to their homes from court each evening, the 6 P.M. news is broadcasting the latest court highlights for interested viewers. Unimportant gibberish, you say? Has no effect on jurors, you say? Has no effect on anyone, you say? Think again. In the well-publicized 1997 trial of sportscaster Marv Albert, Albert was charged with sexual assault and other crimes. As the prosecution was presenting its evidence against him, the victim testified, and others testified about Albert's alleged sexual appetite. Nightly commentary by talk show hosts and their legal experts gave a play-by-play recitation of the significance of these witnesses and their incriminating statements. Informed opinions from experts on sexual abuse were also given, and popular comedians parodied Albert. Jay Leno and David Letterman got considerable mileage from the Albert trial. Late-breaking developments came almost on a daily basis.

However, Albert's defense had not been presented yet. In the United States, trials are adversarial. Prosecutors make their case against defendants first, and they give it their most incriminating shot. When the prosecution finishes its case, the accused get their chance to tell their side of the story. Too many prosecutors are unethical and engage in unscrupulous conduct, all in the name of getting the conviction. But isn't a defendant presumed innocent of a crime until proven guilty beyond a reasonable doubt in a court of law? In Albert's case, besides the jury in the courtroom, the media were judging Albert, daily. "You know, Geraldo, it looks pretty bad for Albert." "Well, Mr. Grodin, I don't think Albert is going to be able to overcome those statements against him." "I think, Mr. Cochran and Company, Miss so-and-so looked pretty credible to me." Of course, all of these statements were premature. Why don't we wait and see what the defense is going to present?

Interestingly, in Albert's case, Albert and his attorneys were swayed by the court of public opinion and media coverage. Based on nightly summaries by the experts, Albert didn't stand a snowball's chance in hell of getting acquitted of these sexual assault charges. Just as the prosecution was winding down its case, yet another witness against Albert was said to be ready to come forth and say something deeply incriminating. Already humiliated and anticipating more of the same from another alleged former sexual partner, Albert told his attorneys to enter a guilty plea to a lesser-included offense, which the prosecution had offered earlier. The prosecution agreed, and the trial was ended. The judge advised the jurors that their services were no longer needed, and they were dismissed. Why? they asked. Because Albert had pleaded guilty. "But we were ready to acquit him," said several jurors. "The state hadn't presented a convincing case," they said in unison. Sorry, Marv, but you've committed yourself to a criminal conviction, and you can't take back the guilty plea.

Enter the experts once again. "Yes, now that you mention it, these witnesses against Albert weren't very convincing. We thought they were at the time, but we're only experts, not the jurors. We were only speculating and giving the testimony of witnesses different spins. It did make for some stimulating conversation, you've got to grant us that!" And the talk shows and comedians had another six months' worth of Albert material. The media had tried and convicted Albert, long before he had a chance to present his side of the story. And the media's case was so strong and consistent that even Albert himself and his highly paid attorneys caved in and accepted a plea bargain, thinking that they had no chance with the jury. If the nightly commentary on television sounds familiar in the Albert trial, it should. The O. J. Simpson murder trial and media coverage of it were a conspicuous forerunner of things to come for Marv Albert.

FICTITIOUS DIALOGUE between *Court TV* Host Mary Tuba and Court Expert Johnny Rockran.

TUBA: "Say, Johnny, you're an expert on jury selection. Do you think that Mr. Harris's [the defendant in a murder case] case was jeopardized when the black janitor testified that he saw Mr. Harris wearing what appeared to be a pair of black patent leather Jarmans at the Rolling Stones concert in Central Park two days before Mrs. Harris was murdered?"

ROCKRAN: "Well, you know, there was some black patent leather residue and scuff marks on Mrs. Harris's back doorstep. Mr. Fung, the criminalist, testified that the marks were consistent with black patent leather. And of course, we know that Harris himself denied ever having a pair of patent leather shoes. I think Harris is going to have a tough time explaining away how he got those shoes and wore them to the Rolling Stones concert. Yes, I think the janitor's remarks were damaging to Harris."

TUBA: "But you know, the fact that the janitor is black and Harris is black, do you think that fact had more credibility with the jury, which is predominantly black?"

ROCKRAN: "Well, yes, I think that if the janitor had been white, the jury might not have given it as much weight. But since the janitor was black, I mean, why would he want to give incriminating evidence against a black defendant if it were not true?"

TUBA: "Are you saying that white janitors might be more inclined to lie about the shoes worn by a black defendant?"

ROCKRAN: "Well, the race card cannot be discounted. Remember the O. J. Simpson trial!"

FICTITIOUS DIALOGUE on *CNN News* between Ted Boppel and former Attorney General Thornblow.

BOPPEL: "Mr. Thornblow, did you see Jana Bumpus get a little teary-eyed when the coroner testified about the 202 knife wounds in the back of her late husband, Jeffrey Bumpus?"

THORNBLOW: "Yes, Ted, there was a definite crack of emotion in that otherwise cold exterior. I think the jury was moved by it."

BOPPEL: "Well, Mr. Thornblow, we know Mrs. Bumpus says she had a blackout and doesn't remember attacking her husband with the kitchen butcher knife. She also claims that she doesn't remember picking up the knife, even though her prints were on it and she was covered in her husband's blood. She says she really loved her husband and wouldn't harm him in any way. But the $2 million insurance policy was a strong motivator, don't you think?"

THORNBLOW: "Well, Ted, we have to consider several theories. For one thing, it may be true that Mrs. Bumpus blacked out and didn't know what she had done. Then again, she could have simply stumbled into the room after an assailant had killed her husband, got caught up in panic and shock, tried to revive her dead husband, and in the process, she could have handled the knife and got a lot of blood on herself. Then she could have passed out and awakened later to call police. The money is certainly a consideration, but remember that Mrs. Bumpus has a high-paying job in an advertising agency."

BOPPEL: "OK, Mr. Thornblow, I'll grant you that a scene like that might have caused Mrs. Bumpus to go into shock. That might wash with the jury. And we might even forget about the $2 million life insurance policy. Mrs. Bumpus is such a fragile-looking thing. I mean, if I were a juror, I'd wonder if she had the strength to stab her husband 202 times. And then, that little show of emotion by her in the courtroom—I don't know what I'd think if I were a juror. It might cause me to think twice before deciding on a guilty verdict."

THORNBLOW: "Yeah, Ted. We can't forget about American justice and giving her every benefit of the doubt in the case."

Introduction

These scenarios and thousands of others are played out daily on television shows. In many cases, jurors themselves have an opportunity to watch these broadcasts and reruns late at night before returning to the courtroom the following morning. Defense attorneys, prosecutors, and judges also watch these shows. During the progress of the trial, subtle changes in the behaviors of court actors are detected, sometimes as reactions to such television commentary. According to the American system of justice, this media coverage of trials is supposedly irrelevant and should not be viewed by jurors. Jurors take an oath that they will remain impartial and objective. They are obliged to refrain from listening to, reading about, or watching anything related to the trial. In reality, many jurors keep in close touch with trial events and media coverage of them. And most people, including jurors, are affected by what they see and hear. We are in the midst of an era of media news frenzy, and in diverse ways almost everyone is influenced by the media and its news reports and characterizations.

Since the early 1900s, the courts have had an antagonistic relationship with the media. Increasing numbers of courtrooms are permitting limited or extensive television coverage. Such permissiveness is consistent with the public's right to know, public access to the courts, and freedom of speech. However, the media have almost always sought to dramatize court events in different ways to stimulate listeners, readers, and viewers. *Court TV* and *CNN News* shows have pioneered creative and innovative court reporting through the use of experts and panels of experts who debate, criticize, and overanalyze information bits from trial testimony and events. No court actor has escaped the intensive scrutiny of television cameras or the opinions, reactions, and interpretations of events through the eyes and ears of courtroom observers. Hourly reporting of who has testified, what the judge thought or seemed to think about the testimony, juror reactions, and other courtroom banter has riveted millions of television viewers. If the courtroom news has not been sufficiently dramatic, these shows often create their own news by giving less newsworthy events fictitious spins for audience consumption. Conjectures from guests and "what ifs" from news commentators or legal experts and analysts are often passed off as factual information, when in fact it may be simply their opinion.

Today, the public seems discontented with simple news reporting. Generally, judicial decisions are reported only when they seem newsworthy. When television producers or newspaper reporters determine that a judge has imposed a lenient sentence, a jury has failed to convict a guilty-appearing defendant, or an unusually large monetary award is made in a civil case by a jury, these outcomes are reported on the evening news or in daily newspapers. The selection of the news events to report is not particularly random. Rather, the news selection process is carefully calculated to yield the greatest public impact. The more sensational the news and its reporting, the greater the interest and viewership.

The police and prosecutors often have a symbiotic relationship with the media. In exchange for confidential information from the police or district attorney's offices, reporters slant their stories in ways favorable to police conclusions and prosecutorial theorizing about the crime, how it was committed, and who probably committed it. Seldom is equal time allocated to defendants so that they can give their version of events or their side of the story. The courts have increasingly relied on media technology to assist in processing cases. In many jurisdictions, initial appearances and arraignments are held by closed-circuit television. The defendant remains at the jail and enters a plea before the judge across town in the courthouse through closed-circuit television monitoring systems. Jurisdictions have adopted this alternative to minimize security problems and the costs of transporting defendants to and from their jails for short court appearances.

This chapter examines two important issues that shape our perceptions about the American court system. The first issue is the nature of the interplay between the courts and the media. This interplay has prompted much public discourse, especially as the direct result of several high-profile trials during the 1990s. The O. J. Simpson trial focused national attention on both court protocol and the personalities involved in the trial. All relevant actors were scrutinized, including the judge, the prosecution and defense counsel, jury members, and witnesses. All those watching the courtroom drama were active participants who critiqued the actions of the witnesses, attorneys, and the judge.

The second issue is our definition of justice as portrayed by the media. Has the legitimacy of the court system been undermined because our ideals of justice are inconsistent with courtroom reality delivered by the media into our homes through radio or television? Have the courts been effective and acted responsibly in their use of media technology? How has the media shaped our perceptions of the "litigation explosion"? We have witnessed seemingly outlandish jury judgments in civil cases extended to people who have filed lawsuits that appear frivolous. We have seen an array of courtroom tactics used successfully by plaintiff's attorneys against big businesses and corporate giants. The mentality of juries and the racial and ethnic composition of jurors have been analyzed extensively by the media, and we are inclined to view the average juror in a criminal or civil case in disparaging ways. Jurors are perceived as both pawns of the legal system and as self-styled vigilantes with their own political and social agendas. The buzzword of the 1990s was jury nullification, in which juries disregard the facts in favor of some alternative and contrary verdict that satisfies political ends rather than legal ones.

This chapter is organized as follows. First, a brief history is provided of the media and their uneasy association with the American justice system. Technological change has greatly modified the nature of courtroom intrusion by the media. Newspapers, radio, and television innovations have been significant in influencing what happens in courtrooms throughout the nation. Increasingly clear is the fact that the behaviors of courtroom actors have undergone a metamorphosis of sorts as courtrooms have been subjected to greater public scrutiny. The implications of these behavioral changes for the justice process are explored.

Several highly visible trials are described, together with the nature of media attention given to each. The media have been instrumental in promoting a defendant's guilt or innocence, depending on the specific case. Accordingly, jurors have been responsive to particular types of media coverage, such that it is questionable whether justice has been served in certain cases. Indeed, some jury verdicts have been reversed by the U.S. Supreme Court because of the undue influence of media trial coverage. Often, media coverage has been passed off and labeled as the **court of public opinion**. The media have magnified the popularity of this term over time, and many citizens accept media opinion as factually based and give considerable credence to it.

Next, pretrial publicity is described. Pretrial publicity is almost always prejudicial for the defense or prosecution. Sensationalized coverage of both spectacular and heinous crimes has created an emotionally charged milieu for many defendants. In certain cases, defense counsel have sought to change the site of a trial because of extensive adverse pretrial publicity. The trials of Timothy McVeigh and Terry Nichols were changed from Oklahoma City, Oklahoma, to Denver, Colorado, because it was believed that the amount of pretrial publicity indicated that they could not receive a fair trial in Oklahoma. Eventually, they were both convicted of bombing the Murrah Federal Building in

Oklahoma City and killing 167 people. This section also explores the factors that determine whether the prejudice generated by pretrial publicity is sufficient to jeopardize a defendant's right to a fair and impartial trial. Several ways to minimize the prejudicial effects of pretrial publicity are described.

Besides criminal trials, many civil trials have generated considerable publicity and media coverage. Often, these trials involve **tort actions**, in which monetary damages are sought instead of convictions. Tort actions may highlight negligence, wrongful death, or product liability. The **litigation explosion** is also depicted, with the burgeoning volume of civil cases in recent decades. The media have labeled our society as litigious, emphasizing quite appropriately the increasing interest of people in seeking monetary awards from their employers or from large corporations. The bases of these increasing numbers of lawsuits may be sexual harassment, product liability, or wrongful death. Judges dismiss many of these as **frivolous lawsuits.** Others are decided in civil courtrooms by juries. Again, the media are present and pervasive to assess and interpret what is going on and why. The chapter concludes with a discussion of tort reforms.

Trials and the Court of Public Opinion

The media have been instrumental in shaping our perceptions of justice. The media and the courts are often at odds because of their competing interests. The courts operate in a methodical fashion, following specific criminal or civil protocols that may at times frustrate the observer. A great deal of time is consumed over seemingly trivial details of events, although we are reminded by the experts on television talk shows that the most trivial details have profound importance in shaping trial outcomes. Verdicts are rendered only after juries have given careful review to factual details, expert witness testimony, and all relevant evidence. While the case proceeds at a snail's pace, the media have their story to tell. The most innocuous details of a case are given great weight. Thus, an otherwise boring media story is converted into an exciting one by creative media spins. The viability of a network television show is critically dependent on giving sensational coverage to the most mundane courtroom events.

There has been considerable debate about the role and influence of the media and the courts. The O. J. Simpson case brought all the arguments for and against media access to the courts into the public discourse. For instance, before the O. J. Simpson murder case, the presiding judge, Lance Ito, was initially reluctant to permit television cameras in his courtroom. Judge Ito believed that the presence of television cameras would undermine the justice process and cause viewers to misunderstand the proceedings. He also expected tabloidization of the judicial process. In retrospect, Judge Ito was right, although he permitted television cameras to cover most aspects of the trial anyway.

Judge Ito's reservations about the intrusion of television cameras and media representatives into his courtroom were grounded in scientific research. Several scholars and legal experts have provided compelling arguments both for and against television cameras in courtrooms (Thaler, 1994; Dershowitz, 1994; Spence, 1992; Libby, 1994). Although these arguments are inconclusive and inconsistent, the general sentiment is that television coverage of courtroom drama does influence what goes on in the courtroom. There is extensive debate about whether this influence jeopardizes a defendant's right to a fair trial, however. Media representatives emphasize that their interest in covering courtroom events is based on the public's right to be present inside courtrooms as public events. Thus, a judge's refusal to allow the media into courtrooms is perceived as a violation of the First Amendment. Technological change and the advent of television and closed-circuit broadcasting has done much to change the definition of public access to courtroom activities, however. To understand how the definition of public courtroom access has changed, we must first examine the early vestiges of courtroom coverage by the media.

History of Media and the Courts

Court reaction to media intrusion has gradually changed with changing media technology. Before the 1800s, trial outcomes or happenings were relayed by word of mouth. Information dissemination shifted from word of mouth to the printed page with the advent of newspapers. By the 1850s, trial events and court decisions were transmitted throughout the country by telegraph. Those eager to hear the results often gathered at the local telegraph office to wait for the trial results to be announced. The most widely acknowledged example of this process was the murder trial of Harry Thaw. He had killed millionaire Stanford White over the affections of a very young Evelyn Nesbit, also known as the "girl in the red velvet swing."

Soon, courtroom photographers and newsreel cameras were common in high-profile cases. The Tennessee trial of teacher John Scopes, known as the "monkey trial," was the first to be broadcast over the radio. Attorneys Clarence Darrow and William Jennings Bryan were well aware of the impact of the media presence and structured their trial tactics not only for the benefit of the jury but also for the benefit of the larger national audience. In fact, compared with today's standards, the media seemed to intrude on the court proceedings by making requests similar to those from a movie director to an actor rather than to court officers. For instance, media representatives have often made requests for the attorneys and judges to position themselves so that their cameras could get better picture angles.

The problems created by the media during the murder trial of Bartolomeo Vanzetti and Nicola Sacco in 1921 and during the trial of Richard Loeb and Nathan Leopold Jr. in 1924 prompted the American Bar Association to review the issue of news reporting and the courts. It took another "trial of the century" to force the courts to come to terms with the impact of the media on court proceedings.

The trial involved Bruno Hauptmann, a German immigrant. Hauptmann was accused of kidnaping and murdering the baby of Charles Lindbergh. The trial started with more than 700 representatives of the media, 120 of them cameramen. The trial was chaos. Witnesses were barraged by reporters and blinded by flashbulbs reminiscent of a Hollywood movie premiere. Hauptmann appealed his conviction, alleging that the extensive media coverage prevented him from receiving a fair trial. He lost

THE FIRST TRIAL OF THE TWENTIETH CENTURY

The Girl in the Red Velvet Swing

Stanford White was one of the brightest stars in New York society at the turn of the century. As an architect, he was a visionary. Many of the new millionaires of the industrial revolution flocked to White to have him design their mansions. His talent was recognized by officials of the city, and he was hired to design the New York Public Library and Madison Square Garden. White's appetite for design was matched only by his desire for young women. He had several apartments throughout Manhattan to which girls were often accompanied by White. At the turn of the century, the newest sensation in New York was sixteen-year-old Evelyn Nesbit. Nesbit had arrived in New York from Pittsburgh with her mother, a widowed seamstress. Evelyn was slim and beautiful and soon found work as an artist's model. Later, she landed a role in a Broadway musical and was an instant sensation. Soon, many admirers were waiting for her after the show, among them Stanford White.

In 1901, White convinced Nesbit to have lunch with him, the beginning of an affair that would last for five years. Nesbit was raped by White while she was intoxicated with champagne drunk at White's apartment during one of their meetings. She did not seem to be fazed by this development and continued the relationship. Nesbit eventually fell in love with White and made frequent visits to his apartment, where he encouraged her to swing on his red velvet swing—preferably naked.

Evelyn's mother knew that a long-term, financially secure future with White was not possible. White was married with children. Therefore, she encouraged her daughter to see other men, such as Harry Thaw, who stood to inherit $40 million from a Pittsburgh railroad fortune. Thaw courted Evelyn with antics like sending her roses individually wrapped in $50 bills. Thaw and White had more in common than an interest in Evelyn. Earlier, White had blackballed Thaw from many of New York's social clubs, which Thaw deeply resented. During the courtship of Nesbit and Thaw, she told Thaw how White had taken advantage of her by getting her drunk and raping her. Upon hearing this, Thaw became furious. A short time later during a trip to Europe, he tied her up and beat her with a whip until she was covered with welts. Six months later, she married him because she believed he was the only rich man who would propose to her.

On June 25, 1906, Stanford White sat on the rooftop Madison Square Garden theater enjoying a production, when Harry Thaw walked up and shot him three times, proclaiming, "I did it because he ruined my wife." At the trial, Nesbit testified about White's sexual behavior in an effort to "save a husband I didn't love from the chair." Thaw's mother went to considerable effort to demonstrate her son's insanity. She even testified that the entire Thaw family was crazy. The initial jury could not reach a verdict, and the second jury found Thaw not guilty by reason of insanity.

Why do the media seem to present us with a new "trial of the century" every decade? Do you feel if this offense happened today the nation would be transfixed on the case? Are these types of cases good measures of how the criminal justice system operates?

Source: Adapted from "Stanford White and Evelyn Nesbit." *People Weekly*, February 12, 45:79–80 (1999).

his appeal, but the trial prompted the American Bar Association (ABA) to review their position on camera access to court proceedings. They ultimately ruled in 1937 that photographing and broadcasting court proceedings should be prohibited. Most states adopted that position and forbade photographing and broadcasting trials and trial participants. In 1952, the ABA extended the media ban to include television coverage of court proceedings.

Texas was one of the states that ignored the ABA recommendation and allowed cameras into the courtroom at the discretion of the judge. In 1962, Texas provided the case that served as the basis for denying cameras into the courtroom. Billie Sol Estes, a friend of President Lyndon B. Johnson, was charged with swindling people out of large sums of cash. The trial judge decided to allow television cameras into the courtroom, but they were restricted to the back of the courtroom in a specially constructed booth. Like Hauptmann thirty years earlier, Estes argued that the media coverage deprived him of a fair trial. The Texas Court of Appeals declared that his due process rights had not been violated, and Estes appealed to the U.S. Supreme Court. In a 5–4 decision, the U.S. Supreme Court reversed Estes's conviction. The majority held that although no prejudice was actually shown, the circumstances of the case were suspect. Furthermore, Justice Clark believed that the presence of the cameras in the courtroom had a harmful effect on all those involved in the trial. In its decision, the U.S. Supreme Court did not address the issue of whether the First Amendment extended to the media to broadcast from the courtroom (*Texas v. Estes*, 1965).

After the Estes decision, states continued to experiment with media coverage. Judges were generally given the discretion to allow cameras. For the next twelve years, courts individually struggled with the decision to allow cameras. In 1977, the Florida Supreme Court approved a one-year pilot study that allowed the electronic media to cover all cases in Florida state courts without the consent of the participants. The crucial case that emerged during this year involved a fifteen-year-old boy who was charged with murdering an elderly neighbor while he and some friends burglarized the victim's house. The circumstances of the offense were not unusual. What attracted the media to the trial was the unusual defense of involuntary television intoxication. The defense alleged that Zamora (the boy) did not know what he was doing because of the massive amounts of crime and violence he had watched on television. The local media broadcast segments of the trial on the nightly news, and the worldwide audience was estimated at several million viewers. At the conclusion of the trial, Judge Paul Baker submitted a report including his observations about the effect of the media on the trial. He said that the equipment did not produce distracting noises or light flashes. In contrast, during the Estes trial, the cameras and lighting equipment created distractions. In the years between these cases, technology improved to the extent that media became less intrusive in the courtroom and seemed to have little impact on the courtroom actors.

Judge Baker spoke with jurors about their reactions to the presence of the media. The jurors believed that the cameras caused only slight distractions and the media did not hinder or distract the jurors from following the testimony, arguments of counsel, and judicial instructions. The judge also found no support for the assertion that judges would alter the way that they conduct business in the presence of the cameras.

Considering this information as well as evidence from other cases, in 1979 the Florida Supreme Court permanently allowed cameras in the courts with the approval of the presiding judge. The new provisions were put to the test with the Ted Bundy murder trial. Ted Bundy defended himself and appeared to enjoy playing to the cameras. However, the trial judge believed that the rules in place were effective and that the cameras did not hamper the court process. The court acknowledged that publicity could undermine a defendant's right to a fair trial. However, this risk did not require an absolute ban on news reporting and the broadcasting of trials. Essentially, the U.S. Supreme Court left the decision up to the individual states.

Current Status of Media Access to the Courts

As of 1994, only three states did not allow cameras into their courtrooms. Table 12.1 shows states that permit cameras in courtrooms. Most states have allowed cameras in their courtrooms either experimentally or permanently. States that have allowed cameras in the courtroom have developed guidelines for their usage. In most states, the consent of the presiding judge is required. Many states require a written application submitted in advance of the trial. Furthermore, in some states, if the defendant objects, cameras will not be permitted to record the trial proceedings.

Most states do not allow television coverage of cases involving juveniles, and coverage is limited for cases that include victims of sex crimes or trade secrets of business organizations. Fewer states limit coverage of jurors and the *voir dire* process. All states ban coverage of pretrial conferences and sidebars between the judge, prosecutor, and defense counsel in court. States have also developed guidelines that regulate media equipment and personnel. Courts specify which types of cameras are allowed and limit the movement and number of media personnel in the court.

TABLE 12.1 Current Status of the Use of Media in U.S. Courtrooms

States with Permanent Rules Permitting Cameras in Courtrooms at Trial and Appellate Levels, Both Civil and Criminal

Alabama,[c] Alaska, Arizona, California, Colorado, Connecticut, Florida, Georgia, Hawaii, Iowa, Kansas,[a] Kentucky, Maryland,[a,d] Michigan, Montana, Nevada, New Hampshire, New Mexico, New Jersey, North Carolina, Ohio,[b] Oklahoma,[b] Oregon,[a] Rhode Island, South Carolina, Tennessee,[b] Texas,[b] Vermont, Virginia, Washington, West Virginia, Wisconsin, Wyoming

States with Permanent Rules Permitting Cameras in Courtrooms for the Supreme Court

Idaho, North Dakota, Utah

States with Permanent Rules Permitting Cameras in Courtrooms for Appellate Courts Only

Illinois, Louisiana, Minnesota, Nebraska, New York

States with Permanent Rules Permitting Cameras in Courtrooms for Trial Courts Only

Maine[d]

Source: Compiled by the authors.

[a]Consent of some participants required.
[b]No coverage of defendants who raise objections.
[c]Approval required from individual courts.
[d]Civil courts only.

Pretrial Publicity

One of the primary concerns of those who study the courts-media relationship is the effect of **pretrial publicity**. Within this area are two different issues. The first is that extensive pretrial publicity makes it difficult, if not impossible, to locate jurors who have not heard of the case and developed some preconceived notions about the defendant's guilt or innocence. The second is that jurors, as the result of the pretrial publicity, recognize that their decision will be scrutinized by friends, family, neighbors, and the larger community. This pressure may ultimately influence them to vote on the basis of how their own lives will be affected rather than on the actual facts of the case. In the Estes decision, this issue seemed to concern the U.S. Supreme Court the most. And realistically, only the notorious trial will be broadcast because of the necessity of paid sponsorship. The conscious or unconscious effect of this factor on the juror's judgment cannot be evaluated, but experience indicates that it will probably have a direct bearing on

TELEVISION IN THE COURTROOM?

The Case of Judge Richard Catsch and the Timothy McVeigh Trial

Should high-profile trials be televised for the general public? Some judges say yes, and some say no. The trial of the Menedez brothers who killed their parents and the O. J. Simpson acquittal were televised. *Court TV* regularly invades courtrooms with its cameras to give viewers an up-to-the-minute glimpse of how justice is done in the United States. Obviously, the matter of whether television cameras should be allowed in courtrooms is not a constitutional issue because that issue has already been settled. The public *does* have the right of access to court proceedings. However, judges may decide who can be admitted to particular trials at particular times.

Depending on the defendant or the crime alleged, trials attract more or less interest from the general public. Sometimes, judges must consider whether television cameras in the courtroom will jeopardize a defendant's right to a fair trial. Both prosecutors and defense attorneys play to the in-court cameras when examining witnesses or making opening or closing arguments. Without such publicity, would these courtroom actors have acted differently, and would the outcomes of these trials differ from what actually occurred?

In mid-1996, a Denver federal judge, U.S. District Judge Richard Matsch, had to decide whether to allow televised coverage of the trial of Timothy McVeigh, a key suspect in the Oklahoma City bombing of the Alfred P. Murrah Federal Building, where more than 160 people were killed. An antiterrorism bill signed by President Bill Clinton in April 1996 required closed-circuit television coverage of federal trials that are moved more than 350 miles so that victims and survivors can follow the court proceedings. Televised coverage of the trial became an issue after the site of the trial was moved from Oklahoma City to Denver after McVeigh's attorneys alleged that he could not receive a fair trial in Oklahoma.

Favoring closed-circuit televised coverage of the trial were the prosecutors, who argued that the defendant's rights would not be jeopardized. Timothy McVeigh's attorneys opposed such televised coverage, arguing it would prejudice prospective jurors. The ultimate *judge* of whether cameras were allowed in the courtroom was Judge Richard Matsch himself, who was bound by no particular law either to ban or to permit television cameras in any federal trial over which he presides.

Should television cameras be allowed in any trial proceeding? In what ways would television coverage jeopardize a defendant's fair trial rights, if at all? What standards should be used to determine whether live television coverage should be permitted in any given courtroom?

Source: Adapted from Associated Press, "Judge Weighs Closed-Circuit Coverage." *Minot* (N.D.) *Daily News,* May 13, 1996:A6.

the juror's vote as to guilt or innocence. Where pretrial publicity of all kinds has created intense public feeling, aggravated by the telecasting or picturing of the trial, the televised jurors cannot help feeling the pressure of knowing that friends and neighbors have their eyes upon them. If the community is hostile to an accused, televised jurors, realizing they must return to neighbors who saw the trial themselves, may well be led "not to hold the balance nice, clear and true between the State and the accused" (*Estes v. Texas,* 1965:545).

Some people have argued that jurors' concerns over the impact of their decisions should not allow their identity to be concealed. In fact, juror anonymity should be allowed in only the rarest of cases, and jurors in high-profile cases should be regarded as citizen-soldiers in the quest for justice (Litt, 1992).

In the context of the day-to-day operations of the court, perhaps pretrial publicity should not be a concern. Daily, the courts process thousands of cases, usually in empty courtrooms. In fact, the larger problem facing the court is public apathy. When somebody wanders into a courtroom merely to watch the proceedings, the courtroom actors take notice. They assume that the observer must be a defendant; if this is not the case, they wonder why this person has nothing better to do than watch courtroom proceedings. Researchers have estimated that only seven percent of felony arrests are covered by the press (Frasca, 1988).

The concern over pretrial publicity occurs only when there is a high-profile case. The common assumption is that pretrial publicity almost always favors the prosecution and therefore limits the defendant's ability to receive a fair and impartial trial. Researchers have disclosed that most courtroom actors do not believe that pretrial publicity significantly affects juror behavior. Judges believe that the *voir dire* process is an effective method for removing jurors who have been prejudiced by the media. Prosecutors acknowledge that pretrial publicity usually works in their favor. Simon and Emermann (1971), for example, found that 65 percent of those exposed to pretrial publicity had pro-prosecution attitudes, compared with 45 percent of those not exposed to pretrial publicity. As prosecutors contend, whether defense attorneys can overcome this bias depends on the type of information prospective jurors are exposed to prior to the trial. Defense attorneys are most inclined to believe that pretrial publicity adversely affects their clients. However, journalists believe that pretrial publicity is an insignificant problem (Carroll et al., 1986). Surveys of the public reveal that pretrial publicity may affect juror attitudes about the case but that they believe that despite this information they could render objective and impartial judgments and base their decisions on the facts presented at trial (Constantini and King, 1980).

What Types of Information Do Potential Jurors Consider Prejudicial?

Researchers have identified two ways that jurors are affected by prejudicial information. The first is **case-specific pretrial publicity** (Greene, 1990), information about a specific case on which jurors must make a determination of guilt or innocence. An example of case-specific pretrial publicity might come from the Rodney King state and federal cases.

Most Americans were repeatedly exposed to the videotape showing police officers beating King as he lay on the ground. Jurors asked to serve in that case were probably exposed to that videotape numerous times prior to the trial. Their perceptions of the event were relevant only to this individual case.

The second type of pretrial publicity is **general pretrial publicity**, which includes information about crime, criminals, and the criminal justice system that is constantly in the media and shapes the perceptions of those asked to serve as jurors. For example, most of us have probably developed an opinion about the insanity defense based on several cases and stories about the insanity defense presented in the media. Jurors with these vague perceptions may have already formed an opinion about whether they might accept insanity as a valid defense before hearing any relevant evidence or testimony about a defendant's sanity in an actual trial. Many jurors may believe that a defendant found guilty but mentally ill will escape punishment or receive a light sentence.

Research has shown that jurors who are exposed to pretrial publicity revealing a confession or a prior lengthy criminal record of a particular defendant are more likely to believe the defendant is guilty. Furthermore, when information is released prior to the trial that the defendant has failed a lie detector test, jurors are more likely to infer guilt from this event.

Uncovering the effects of general pretrial publicity is more difficult. The best research comes from conducting experiments with mock juries. Greene and Loftus (1984) compared three groups of mock jurors. The first group read newspaper stories about a defendant who was mistakenly identified and convicted of rape. The second group was asked to read stories about how the testimony of an eyewitness led to the conviction of a mass murderer. The final group was exposed to no pretrial publicity and acted as the control group. All three groups were then asked to make a decision about guilt or innocence for cases involving alleged armed robbery and murder. The prosecution's case consisted primarily of the testimony of an eyewitness. The first group had a significantly higher acquittal rate than either of the other two groups. From this evidence, we might infer that the story about the miscarriage of justice influenced the jurors, made them more skeptical of law enforcement, and increased the probability of acquittal.

Research has also indicated that the entertainment media influence individuals' perceptions of criminality and the criminal justice system. Jurors may expect the courtroom to be an exciting and dramatic place if they have watched crime dramas such as *L.A. Law*, *Law and Order*, or *Perry Mason*. These shows do not accurately portray what happens in real courtrooms. Court proceedings are typically routine and bland, with no riveting revelations or courtroom confessions, and jurors are more likely to struggle to find ways to overcome boredom.

How to Minimize the Effects of Pretrial Publicity

Trial judges can minimize the effects of pretrial publicity by various methods. The most radical and least-used approach is to issue a **gag order**. This controversial approach raises serious First Amendment questions. Gag orders usually prohibit media from publishing or broadcasting any prejudicial information about a case. Sometimes gag orders are extended to include the attorneys in the case. When a gag order includes attorneys, they are under court order not to talk about the case, and they are prohibited from giving television interviews or appearing on talk shows while the trial is in progress.

Another possible remedy to minimize pretrial publicity is a **change of venue**, which shifts the trial from one location to another. The objective is that jurors selected from the new trial location have not been exposed to the same level of pretrial publicity as the potential jurors in the original jurisdiction. This remedy is rarely used because it is costly. All the people who have been called to testify have to travel to the new jurisdiction. Family and friends of the victim and the accused have to travel to the new jurisdiction as well, and this hardship increases their emotional and financial instability.

Granting continuances is another method judges use to lessen the effect of pretrial publicity. Most high-profile cases capture public and media attention for only a brief period until something new attracts media attention. Like our fleeting attention, memories also fade with time. Judges grant short trial delays in the hope of selecting jurors who have forgotten the media stories about a particular case. Minow and Cate (1991) found this method an effective remedy to pretrial publicity.

Another method used to minimize pretrial publicity is the use of **judicial instructions**. During the O. J. Simpson trial, Judge Ito gave the jury detailed judicial instructions about what they could and could not do. The question is whether jurors abide by the judge's wishes and follow these judicial instructions. In this area, much research points to the same conclusion. Judicial warnings do little or nothing to change juror behavior. In fact, judicial warnings seem to make matters worse. Kline and Jess (1966), Wolf and Montgomery (1977), and Kalven and Ziesel (1966) have all found that judicial warnings have no significant effect on jury attitudes and behaviors.

Many attorneys and judges believe that they can eliminate jurors who have been affected by pretrial publicity through **jury selection**. They assume that an intensive *voir dire* unmasks those prospective jurors who have been unduly influenced by the media. When publicity has reached most potential jurors, lawyers may have to permit some jurors to be seated who have been exposed to stories about the case but say they can disregard such media information and render an impartial verdict. Although their intentions may be honorable, research does not support their assertion. Jurors exposed to pretrial publicity who say that such publicity will not influence their ability to evaluate the facts are much more likely to convict defendants than those who have not been exposed to any pretrial publicity.

Legal scholars have suggested that juries can police themselves during jury deliberations. Once juries are in the jury room, other members of the jury can censure anyone who begins to depart from the judicial instructions and introduce information that was not presented during the trial. The evidence on the jury's self-policing ability has been inconsistent. Some evidence has shown that when a jury member with a particular bias joins with others who have similar biases, the group's determination is stronger and affects the decision more than the opinions of any individual juror. When reinforced, individual biases of the group are difficult for juries to overcome. Therefore, jury deliberations seem to strengthen rather than weaken juror biases.

Overall, these investigations of juror conduct indicate that eliminating biased jurors during *voir dire* is ineffective. The jury is unable to eliminate bias during deliberations,

Journalism versus the Courts: A Compromise

Journalists, judges, and legal experts have debated the limitations and merits of allowing cameras in the courts. At the heart of the matter is a conflict between the first and sixth amendments. Judges and lawyers argue that often the press limits a defendant's Sixth Amendment right to a fair trial. However, journalists argue that free press and free speech protections are equally as important under the First Amendment.

The press has argued that journalists should have more access to court proceedings. "The presumption of openness should be the first presumption," says Paul Masters, Freedom Forum First Amendment ombudsman. "When we increase the amount of secrecy, we increase the amount of suspicion and erode confidence in the system."

Legal scholars and lawyers believe that camera access to the courtroom may serve to erode public confidence in the legal system. Professor Peter Arenella of the UCLA Law School believes that erosion occurs when the public, acting as the thirteenth juror and seeing the testimony and other coverage, often reaches a different verdict from the jury. Ira Reiner, former Los Angeles district attorney and NBC commentator, believed that some coverage would shed light on courtroom weaknesses. Reiner has declared, "Live TV . . . revealed the single greatest weakness in the court system: inadequate judicial management of criminal trials."

Ten recommendations have been developed by judges, journalists, legal scholars, and lawyers.

1. Encourage and establish continuing interdisciplinary educational opportunities and dialogue for judges, journalists, and lawyers to foster an understanding of each other's roles through journalism schools, law schools, and the National Judicial College.

2. Assume accuracy in all court proceedings and records, and place the burden of proof for closure on the entity seeking secrecy. Privacy issues may overcome the presumption in appropriate cases.

3. Refrain from imposing gag orders on the news media or attorneys. The court should seek other remedies in lieu of gag orders except in extraordinary cases.

4. Establish and/or support bench-bar-media committees that meet regularly in every community to address issues of mutual concern.

5. Establish guidelines for press management in high-profile cases. Court officials should confer and consult with media representatives to avoid unanticipated problems and understand each other's legal constraints.

6. Adopt nonbinding professional standards for journalists, and encourage industry-administered certification.

7. Assume that cameras should be allowed in the courtroom, including the federal system, and that such access should be limited or excluded for only the strongest of reasons.
8. Encourage judges to explain, on the record, the reasons for their rulings.
9. Develop a national model to determine when it may be appropriate to compel reporters to testify or produce notes and tapes, with the understanding that the media cannot serve as an arm of law enforcement.
10. Encourage media organizations to develop an ombudsman system to hear recommendations from the courts and public wherever feasible.

Source: Adapted from Steve Geiman, "Journalism v. Courts." *The Quill.* July–August 1996:46–48.

and judicial instructions simply go unheeded. The most effective option available to judges is granting a continuance until the media fascination with the case has disappeared and people forget case details.

The Litigation Explosion

Like many children, Denise Richie was afraid of monsters and demons. However, Denise Richie's demons were real. For five years until she ran away from home, she was sexually abused by her father, and, as a result, she spiraled downward into depression, emotional distress, and several suicide attempts. Finally, when she was able to pull herself together, she brought criminal charges against her father, who was convicted and sent to jail for the sexual abuse. For Denise, the legal battle was not over. At the urging of her attorneys, she filed a lawsuit against her mother. Was the lawsuit against her mother because for a year she had turned a blind eye to the abuse of her daughter and two other family members? No, Denise had sued the Richie household because of an insurance policy covering negligence. Detractors argue that Denise did not sue to garnish wages from her father's paycheck but instead went for the "deep pockets" of the insurance company by arguing that her mother was negligent in her failure to respond to her suspicions regarding her husband's sexual abuse. A jury agreed and awarded $1 million against Mr. Richie in punitive damages and $1.4 million against Mrs. Richie in a negligence lawsuit ultimately paid by the insurance company. The Richie family seems to have overcome their differences because at the same time Denise was in court suing her mother, she was also in criminal court urging the judge to be lenient so that her father could keep his job and support her mother and younger brother.

Another example involves Texas attorney Joe Jamails. Jamails likes civil litigation. In his office, he proudly displays the $3 billion bank deposit slip that was his part of the $10.5 billion award to Pennzoil against Texaco. He often urges companies to settle their

One Perspective on Frivolous Lawsuits

One winter, an elevator in the Bronx cut off a man's head. He was getting off the elevator, and it started to go up fast with the door still open. He lost his balance and leaned toward the elevator, which cut off his head. The head rolled around in the car with the five other passengers, the body fell down the shaft, and for five minutes these people had to stand there looking at the head until they were rescued. The news account had all these people saying, What can we do to make sure this never happens again? Which state agency is responsible? Politicians demanded that the elevator company should check all its elevators to ensure that no more heads are cut off in the future. However, there are some things that are never going to happen again, and this is one of them. Why is it that when something like this happens, everybody wants to set up an Anti-Cut-Off-Your-Head Elevator Rights Committee? Do they really think that at the Otis Elevator Company a bunch of evil, shifty-eyed, fat guys sat around saying, "Yeah, sure these elevators could slice a guy's head off, and the head would go rolling around on the floor, but that's the risk we are willing to take"?

These are the times we live in. Every time a car blows up, a plane crashes, or somebody hits his head by slipping on a wet sidewalk, the first thing we think of is a lawsuit. The best lawsuit you can possibly have is when you're dead. You can get lots of money for being dead, especially if you became dead while doing something fun, like flying off a Jet-Ski or getting crushed by a rock concert stampede. Does the idea of an "accident" even exist anymore? Is there a single situation where something bad happens to somebody and people say, "Well, it was just an accident"? Is it always somebody's fault?

If you're using your Lawn Boy lawnmower and it flings a rock that beans a neighborhood kid and cuts his cheek, you end up in court nine months later, trying to decide: Is it the Lawn Boy user's fault that he didn't see the rock? Is it a requirement that before you use your Lawn Boy, you should check the tall grass searching for rocks? What if you did search for rocks, but somebody threw a fresh one in there right before you fired up the Lawn Boy? Maybe you had the blade set too low. Maybe Lawn Boy had a defective design, and the hard surface of the rock was supposed to stop the blade. Maybe the kid was standing too close to the mower. Maybe the owner of the Lawn Boy failed to warn the kid. Maybe he did warn the kid, but the kid ignored him

After a while, you have to scream at these people and say, "It was just an accident." What I'd really like to say to them is, please, don't move to West Texas, where everybody over the age of six has been cut, burned, beat up, hit with foul balls, injured by equipment, pummeled in schoolyard brawls, and lost family members in railroad accidents, wars, and car wrecks — and which has fewer "plaintiff's attorneys" per capita than any other place in America. Why? Because they still believe there's such a thing as being a "neighbor." And a neighbor says, "Don't worry about it, Joe. It was just an accident."

Source: Adapted from John Bloom, "Can Business Ever Make an Honest Mistake? Satire Criticizing Over-Regulation of Business and Litigiousness of Americans due to Failure to Acknowledge Accidents." *Business and Society Review,* Fall, 1995:41–45.

case rather than face him in court and suffer the same fate as Texaco. Tort cases have spread the wealth to other attorneys in the Houston area. In fact, five of the highest paid trial attorneys in the United States reside in the Beaumont suburb of Houston. In 1994, these attorneys collectively made a total of $188 million. They specialize in product liability cases, primarily breast implants and asbestos. There is no end in sight for such litigation and the enormous financial awards that follow. Jamails is estimated to be worth $600 million, and many other attorneys are looking forward to working out similar settlements with tobacco companies.

Within the last decade, there has been a concerted effort to limit tort litigation, fueled by allegations that the tort system is careening out of control. The arguments for reform revolve around two central themes. First, there has been a dramatic increase in the number of tort cases. Second, juries hand out excessive awards. A public opinion poll conducted for the Aetna Life and Casualty Insurance Company revealed that 59 percent of the American population believe that the number of lawsuits has been growing faster than the population; 68 percent of Americans polled believe that more people originate lawsuits than should and that many of these lawsuits are frivolous. More than half believe that the sizes of awards have risen faster than inflation, and 45 percent are convinced that the size of jury awards in personal injury cases has been excessive (Taylor, Kagay, and Leichenko, 1987).

Referendums to reform the tort system and the litigation explosion extend back in time for many decades. For instance, it was argued that the current trend in litigation would force the collapse of the court system, a sentiment that was echoed in the popular press. The *U.S. News & World Report* (1978) revealed in a survey that Americans from all walks of life are being buried under an avalanche of lawsuits. Doctors are being sued by patients, lawyers are being sued by clients, teachers are being sued by students, and merchants, manufacturers, and all levels of government, from Washington, D.C., to local sewer boards, are being sued by all sorts of persons. The "epidemic of hair-trigger suing," as one jurist calls it, has even infected the family. Children haul their parents into court, husbands and wives sue each other, brothers sue brothers, and friends sue friends.

Even Chief Justice Burger warned that one reason our courts have become overburdened is that Americans are increasingly turning to the courts for relief from a range of personal distresses and anxieties. Remedies for personal wrongs were once considered the responsibilities of institutions other than the courts, but now damages for personal wrongs are boldly asserted as legal entitlements. The courts have been expected to fill the void created by the decline of church, family, and neighborhood unity (Burger, 1982).

Torts

The emergence and development of **torts** and tort law in America can be attributed to three diverse but ultimately related phenomena: (1) the emergence of industrial capitalism, (2) changing legal doctrine and legislative intervention, and (3) a transformation of scholarly legal thought. In the following section, a brief description of each of these phenomena is provided.

Industrial Capitalism

Prior to industrial capitalism, interactions and transactions among strangers were governed by contract law. Those entering into a contract had the responsibility to uphold their obligations, or the contract would be declared null and void. This form of law was well suited for governing obligations between a small number of people. However, the emergence of industrial capitalism greatly reduced face-to-face interaction between producers and consumers. Consumers were inundated with an unprecedented array of products created by an ever-increasing number of manufacturers. Furthermore, because production became more efficient through mechanization, producers were able to sell larger numbers of products to consumers. Capitalism also increased stranger interaction because it increased urbanization. Richard Abel explains why this is problematic when he says that the frequency of interactions among strangers is significant because strangers, unlike acquaintances or intimates, have less incentive to exercise care not to injure one another inadvertently and find it more difficult to resolve differences that arises when such an injury occurs (Abel, 1990). Industrialization also has the dubious distinction of being directly related to increasing the number of personal injuries. As Friedman suggests, machines of the industrial revolution have had a marvelous capacity for smashing the human body (Friedman, 1985). Increasing the number of accidents is a natural result of increasing the number of people working with and around dangerous machinery. Because contract law was not developed to deal with these new forms of personal injury, an increasing number of injured people began to demand some alternative legal solution.

Changing Legal Doctrine and Legislative Intervention

Initial tort claims brought against organizations in the emerging industrial economy were usually unsuccessful because legal doctrines were generally more supportive of industry than of individuals. Also, the courts were hesitant to support claims that could cause irreparable harm to fledgling industries. Friedman says about this process that lawsuits and damages might injure the health of precarious enterprises. The machines were the basis for economic growth, national wealth, and the greater good of society (Friedman, 1985:468).

Doctrines that have guided American legal decisions had their origins in common law. According to Friedman, this occurred because England had experienced initial forms of the Industrial Revolution prior to America. The initial doctrines that guided legal decisions regarding tort law were the doctrine of contributory negligence, the fellow servant rule, and the doctrine of assumptive risk.

The **doctrine of contributory negligence** essentially held that the defendant was not negligent if the plaintiff was in any degree responsible for his or her own injury. This doctrine was first developed in England in 1809 and was transplanted into American law to deal with railroad cases. The courts believed that if a person crossing the tracks had any degree of negligence in relation to his or her injury, the railroad could not be held liable.

The **doctrine of assumptive risk** was equally problematic for plaintiffs. This doctrine generally held that a person could not recover any damages if he or she willingly placed himself or herself in danger. Superficially, this doctrine does not seem restrictive, but in reality it offered no satisfactory remedy for persons who knowingly worked in hazardous occupations.

Two new legal doctrines that first began to chip away at existing legal rules were last clear chance and *res ipsa loquitur* (Friedman, 1985). The **doctrine of last clear chance** was developed in England in the case of *Jarrett v. Madifari* (1942). This doctrine allowed some degree of negligence on the part of plaintiffs while holding defendants responsible for their actions if they had the slightest chance of avoiding the injury. In the Davies case, Mann failed to hobble his donkey, which wandered into the path of Davies's approaching wagon, which smashed into the donkey and killed it. It is clear that Mann contributed to the death of his own animal because he failed to control it, but the court ruled that Davies was also negligent because he had the "last clear chance" to avoid hitting the animal but failed to do so. The **doctrine of *res ipsa loquitur*** or "the thing speaks for itself" originated in *Byrne v. Boadle* (1863). This case is important because it shifted the burden of responsibility from the plaintiff to the defendant when negligence was alleged and damages were sought.

Developing simultaneously with the notion of assumptive risk was the **fellow servant rule**, which was the largest obstacle that faced injured plaintiffs. However, as the number of industrial accidents increased, so did the number of injured parties bringing suit against organizations rather than specific individuals. The courts began to realize that the plight of injured workers could not be ignored. This rule held that a servant or employee could not sue his master or employer for injuries caused by the negligence of another employee (Friedman, 1985:472). The doctrine essentially left no recourse for employees who were injured in the workplace. They had the option of bringing a lawsuit against the fellow employee who caused the injury, but this effort was often futile because the negligent employee was as impoverished as the employee bringing suit.

In the 1840s and throughout the 1860s, these doctrines were relatively unchallenged. However, by the 1890s, labor had obtained a collective voice, and there was diverse judicial opinion concerning personal injury cases. Furthermore, political and legislative intervention began to erode previously existing legal doctrines. One of the original legal rules that limited the fellow servant rule was the **vice principal doctrine**. As has been described by Friedman (1985), an employee could sue his employer in tort if the careless fellow servant who caused the injury was a supervisor or a boss, more like an employer than like a fellow servant.

Employer immunity for tort law has also been limited by federal and state legislatures. As early as the 1850s, statutes outlined safety regulations for railroads that forced trains to ring bells prior to passing through railroad crossings. Railroads were also responsible for any fires caused by their locomotives and had to compensate ranchers for any cattle killed by their trains.

The Influence of Legal Scholars

Around the middle of the eighteenth century, legal scholars began to rethink the role and purposes of law. Previously, law was believed to have naturalistic and religious origins, foundations that seemed less applicable to a world that was experiencing the radical social transformations of the Industrial Revolution. In general, post–Civil War intellectuals were interested in restoring the sense of order and unity that had characterized eighteenth-century thought, but they rejected efforts to derive order and unity from "mythologic" religious principles. A particular interest of the intellectuals in that period was the transformation of data into theories of universal applicability.

The two leading proponents of this legal reconceptualization were Nicholas St. John Green and Oliver Wendell Holmes Jr., who rejected the notion that law was static and bound by religious or naturalistic rules. Rather, they believed that law should be evolutionary. Holmes and Green were convinced that life was in constant flux and that laws and the legal system must adapt to address these social changes. Because contract law could not adequately address the changing social structure, Holmes and Green advocated the expansion of tort law.

More recent expansions of tort law, specifically enterprise liability, were profoundly influenced by twentieth-century legal scholars. In fact, Priest (1985) rejected the argument that tort expansion was significantly influenced by industrialization, urbanization, mechanization, and the expanding intervention of the federal government. Instead, Priest believes that the current form of tort law classified as enterprise liability was the handiwork of three legal scholars: Flemming James, Friedrich Kessler, and William Prosser. The literary and oratory confluence of James's notion of "risk distribution," Kessler's conviction that contract law was inadequate for monopolized capitalism, and Prosser's synthesis of contract and tort law gave rise to the current conception of enterprise liability. At present, many legal scholars, businesses, and interest groups believe that tort law has expanded too far and is in need of substantial legislative reform.

Arguments for Tort Reform

Advocates of **tort reform** argue for its necessity because (1) in the last few years the number of tort cases has increased dramatically, which can be attributed to the increased litigiousness of American society, and (2) juries are incompetent to handle tort cases because they are sympathetic to plaintiffs and consistently dole out large awards.

A Dramatic Increase in the Number of Tort Cases

Until the mid-1960s, most courts never kept records of the number and types of cases they decided. Consequently, gathering statistics for a longitudinal study of American litigiousness is extremely difficult. Within the last two decades, a handful of agencies have begun to compile statistics on litigation rates: the National Center for State Courts, the Administrative Office of the U.S. Courts, and the Rand Corporation's Institute for Civil Justice. Researchers at the Institute for Civil Justice have found that, overall, tort filings in state courts have increased between 2.3 percent and 3.9 percent annually. Federal courts experienced a similar annual increase of 4 percent. Galenter's analysis of tort filings in federal district courts between 1975 and 1984 shows a 46 percent increase during that nine-year period. This percentage may be misleading because the absolute percent increase of tort cases in this nine-year period was only 8.2 percent. During this same time interval, federal government suits against individuals for overpayments comprised 31.6 percent of the entire federal caseload (Galenter, 1986).

Statistics reveal as much as they conceal. The previous analyses suggest that tort litigation has slightly increased during the past twenty years. However, several interesting results are disclosed by controlling for the actual type of tort filing. For example, the rise in the litigation rate may be caused by an increased number of people injured by unsafe products. Perhaps large toxic torts, with a large number of claims processed in a short time, have exaggerated the litigation rate. Perhaps this increased rate is an anomaly of the federal system that should not be used as evidence of a litigation explosion because federal courts handle only five percent of all tort cases.

Juries Delivering Excessive Awards

When arguing about whether juries deliver excessive awards, both proponents and opponents of tort reform seem to have relevant statistics to support their positions. This does not mean that one group's statistics are wrong but rather that they may be the result of applying incorrect statistical techniques. When analyzing data that are extremely skewed (e.g., jury awards), the mean or arithmetic average is inappropriate because a few large cases can severely skew the results. The median, or the midpoint of the data, is more appropriate for analyzing jury awards and trends. Using data from San Francisco and Cook County, Illinois, the Institute for Civil Justice conducted a study of jury awards. Between 1960 and 1979, the median jury award for all tort cases was approximately $30,000. However, in 1979 the awards in Cook County decreased dramatically while in San Francisco the awards increased dramatically.

The awards declined in Cook County because of a shift to comparative negligence that may have increased attorneys' propensity to bring cases involving smaller damage amounts to trial. Conversely, the awards in San Francisco increased because a mandatory arbitration program eliminated most of the smaller cases from reaching the courts. When the median tort awards are disaggregated, the median award for auto claims ranges between $5,000 and $40,000. Meanwhile, in product liability cases, the juries award between $180,000 and $200,000 per case, an increase from the $70,000 to

$150,000 range since 1960. When arithmetic means are used as indicators of the average tort award, the picture is quite different. In 1960, for instance, the average award for all tort cases ranged from $50,000 to $75,000. By 1984 this number had increased to between $250,000 and $300,000. When the average award is disaggregated, the data reveal that malpractice awards average about $1.2 million. Average awards for San Francisco automobile accidents and personal injury awards were $150,000 and $250,000, respectively.

Proponents of tort reform have utilized mean awards to support their position that juries are delivering excessive awards and that legislative limits should be placed on the amount of these awards. In this regard, they have been relatively successful because, as of 1987, twenty states had passed legislation that limited maximum awards courts would approve. Furthermore, state legislatures have become convinced that tort law is out of control and in need of reform. By 1987, forty-one states had passed some form of tort-limiting legislation. These reforms have undoubtedly significantly altered the tort system, but scholars are beginning to ask whether these reforms are a benefit to citizens or to businesses.

Who Benefits from Tort Reform?

If reform measures were supportive of citizen's interests, their passage ought to increase insurance availability and decrease insurance premiums. In several instances, however, reform measures have had no appreciable impact on the availability or affordability of insurance. For example, Florida, Minnesota, Washington, Wisconsin, and Ontario have passed legislative reform measures. Despite these reforms, all locations have experienced increased insurance premiums, and in many locations insurance carriers are unavailable. In fact, allegations by manufacturers and the medical community that reform was necessary because their insurance rates were too high have no basis in fact. Abel (1990) has said that product, occupier, and general liability costs or insurance premiums plus damage payments have totaled less than 0.2 percent of sales; in the manufacturing sectors where these costs were highest (e.g., rubber and plastic manufacture), they constituted only 0.58 percent; even among hospitals, these costs were only 2.35 percent of gross income.

The research that focuses on the efficacy of jurors would contradict the notions of jurors portrayed by tort reformers. These reforms allege that juries are sympathetic to plaintiffs simply because they deliver large cash awards. However, research focusing on jury behavior finds the opposite true. Jurors are extremely careful and often frugal when deciding cash awards. Sometimes jurors make very precise calculations of medical expenses, repair bills, and other costs when determining awards to ensure that the plaintiffs got no more than they were entitled to receive. Such careful accounting, particularly in cases of tragic dimensions, contrasts sharply with the common view of juries as over-generous and free-spending.

Legislators are convinced that litigation has increased at a dramatic rate and that reform measures (e.g., alternative dispute resolution) might control this problem. Increased litigation rates would, indeed, be a problem if an increasing number of litigants were initiating frivolous cases while the injury rate remained the same. However,

A Medical Malpractice Lawyer's Perspective on Frivolous Lawsuits

Frivolous lawsuits are the bane of all doctors. In one case, an orthopedic surgeon was sued by a forty-two-year-old diabetic who had to have his toe amputated. Later, the surgeon was dumbfounded at being sued because he had seen the patient after surgery and he was walking around without any problems. Later, the surgeon learned that he was being sued because the patient alleged that after the toe was removed, he had been unable to perform sexually.

In another case, a young married couple sued their family physician because of his advice about birth control. The couple had used the birth control suggested by the doctor during their honeymoon, yet they found out seven weeks later that they were expecting their first child. The attorney was at a loss to understand why they believed the doctor should be held liable for the pregnancy, and he instructed them that condoms were not a foolproof form of birth control. The pregnant wife chimed in, "Far from it. The morning after the first time we had sex, I found the condom at the foot of the bed. The dumb doctor should have warned us that it could slip off, or at least he could have recommended a more reliable brand."

Do you think these types of cases are representative of the common lawsuit? Should we limit access to justice to prevent frivolous cases? What role do the media have in shaping our perceptions of the problem of frivolous cases?

Source: Evelyn W. Bradford. (1997). "Patients Try to Sue over Everything." *Medical Economics* 74:138–139.

the contrary seems to be true. Abel summarized research showing that among those who suffered major permanent partial disability as a result of medical malpractice, less than 17 percent filed claims and only 6.5 percent received any payment (Abel, 1990:785–788). Regarding workplace injury claims, only 37 percent of injured workers made workers' compensation claims. Rather than a litigious public, the majority of people who have legitimate injuries fail to make a claim. These results seem to indicate that tort reform measures are not intended to help the average citizen. In each of the examples cited, the reform measures have limited the recourse of injured individuals and benefited insurance companies, businesses, and other interest groups.

Summary

This chapter has examined some of the major issues that are facing the American court system. The first is the relationship between the courts and the media, which dates back to the 1800s. The media have always had a desire to report about cases that involve celebrities or are bizarre or unique in some respect. During the 1900s, there were many "trials of the century," including those of Bruno Hauptmann, Sacco and Vanzetti, John and Lorena Bobbit, and O. J. Simpson. In each of these cases, the media and the courts have battled to balance the power of the media with the objectives of justice. In most cases, the court has had to determine whether the defendant can have a fair trial in spite of pretrial publicity generated by the media.

Another issue facing the courts is the perception that juries are out of control and award excessive damage awards in civil cases. The evidence suggests that this is more myth than reality. Civil cases are more common today than several decades ago, although courts are not collapsing under their greater caseloads. Furthermore, large jury awards have often been reduced on appeal.

KEY TERMS

Case-specific pretrial
  publicity
Change of venue
Court of public opinion
Doctrine of assumptive
  risk
Doctrine of contributory
  negligence

Doctrine of last clear
  chance
Doctrine of *res ipsa
  loquitur*
Fellow servant doctrine
Frivolous lawsuits
Gag order
General pretrial publicity

Judicial instructions
Jury selection
Litigation explosion
Pretrial publicity
Tort actions
Tort reform
Torts
Vice principal doctrine

QUESTIONS FOR REVIEW

1. Select one of the "trials of the century" and describe the interaction between the court and the media.
2. How much pretrial publicity do you believe is necessary for a change of venue?
3. What are the pros and cons of allowing the media into courtrooms?
4. Discuss the opposing views of frivolous lawsuits and excessive jury awards. What perspective do you advocate?
5. What is meant by tort reform? Who benefits from tort reform?
6. What is meant by a change in venue?
7. Under what circumstances is pretrial publicity unfavorable to defendants?
8. What is the litigation explosion? Why do you believe that it has occurred?
9. What is a gag order? Why do judges impose gag orders on jurors and other participants in legal actions?
10. Do media representatives have a constitutional right to enter and record what is going on in U.S. courtrooms? What are your opinions on this issue?

SUGGESTED READINGS

Abel, Richard. (1990). "A Critique of Torts." *UCLA Law Review* **37**:785–831.

Galenter, Marc. (1983). "Reading the Landscape of Disputes: What We Know and Don't Know (and Think We Know) about the Allegedly Contentious and Litigious Society." *UCLA Law Review* **31**:4–71.

Giles, Robert and Robert W. Snyder (eds.). (1999). *Covering the Courts: Free Press, Fair Trials, and Journalistic Performance.* New Brunswick, NJ: Transaction.

Mason, Paul. (2000). "Lights, Camera, Justice? Cameras in the Courtroom: An Outline of the Issues." *Crime Prevention and Community Safety: An International Journal* **2**:23–34.

Strickland, Ruth Ann and Richter H. Moore, Jr. (1994). "Cameras in State Courtrooms: A Historical Perspective." *Judicature* **78**:128–135.

Surrette, Ray. (1999). "Media Choices: Systematic Effects of News Coverage." *Justice Quarterly* **16**:601–631.

GLOSSARY

ABA Model Code of Professional Responsibility
American Bar Association standards of behavior, which are voluntary and intended as self-regulating for lawyer conduct in the courtroom and between lawyers and clients.

Acceptance of responsibility A genuine admission or acknowledgment of wrongdoing. In federal presentence investigation reports, for example, convicted offenders may write an explanation and apology for the crime(s) they committed. A provision that may be considered in deciding whether leniency should be extended to offenders during the sentencing phase of their processing.

Accused Person alleged to have committed a crime; the defendant in any criminal action.

Acquittal Any judgment by the court, considering a jury verdict or a judicial determination of the factual basis for criminal charges, in which the defendant is declared not guilty of the offenses alleged.

Action, actions at law A court proceeding; either civil, to enforce a right, or criminal, to punish an offender. Court litigation in which opposing parties litigate an issue involving an alleged wrongdoing; may be for the protection of a right or for the prevention of a wrong.

Actus reus One component of a crime; any overt act that accompanies the intent to commit a crime (e.g., pulling out a pistol in front of a convenience store clerk while robbing the store is an *actus reus* or overt act); drawing plans of a bank floor layout while conspiring to rob the bank would be an overt act in furtherance of the criminal conspiracy.

Addams, Jane (circa 1860–1935) Founded Hull House in the 1890s in Chicago, a shelter for runaways and others who needed housing, food, and clothing.

Adjudicate To judge, decide a case, conclude a matter.

Adjudication Legal resolution of a dispute; when a juvenile is declared delinquent or a status offender, the matter has been resolved; when an offender has been convicted or acquitted, the matter at issue (guilt or innocence) has been concluded by either a judge or jury.

Adjudication hearing Formal proceeding involving a prosecuting attorney and a defense attorney during which evidence is presented and a juvenile's status or condition is determined by the juvenile court judge.

Administrative law The body of laws, rules, orders, and regulations created by an administrative agency.

Administrative Office of United States Courts Organization that hires federal probation officers to supervise federal offenders. Also supervises pretrial divertees; probation officers prepare presentence investigation reports about offenders at the request of a district judge.

Admissible An evidentiary term designating testimony or physical evidence that may be presented to the finders of fact (juries or judges) in criminal proceedings. Restrictions and conditions are usually articulated in federal and state rules of evidence.

Admission A confession; a concession as to the truthfulness of one or more facts, usually associated with a crime that has been committed. May also apply to tort actions.

Admit A plea of guilty, an acknowledgment of culpability, accuracy of the facts alleged in either an adult or juvenile proceeding.

Adversarial proceedings Opponent-driven court litigation, in which one side opposes the other; prosecution seeks to convict or find defendants guilty, while defense counsel seek to defend their clients and seek their acquittal.

Adversary system Legal system involving a contest between two opposing parties under a judge who is an impartial arbiter.

Affiant Person who makes an affidavit.

Affidavit A statement in writing given under oath before someone who is authorized to administer an oath.

Affirm To uphold the opinion or decision of a lower trial court; usually an action by an appellate court.

Affirmation In courts, an oath, declaration in place of an oath, for those whose religious beliefs prohibit oaths, to tell the truth and nothing but the truth when giving testimony.

Affirmative defenses Responses to a criminal charge where defendant bears the burden of proof (e.g., automatism, intoxication, coercion, duress, mistake). Goes beyond simple denial of facts and gives new facts in favor of the defendant, if facts in the original complaint are true.

Affirmative registration Action on the part of women to actively seek to be included on juries that were formerly comprised exclusively of men.

Age of majority Chronological date when a person reaches adulthood, usually either eighteen or twenty-one; when juveniles are no longer under the jurisdiction of the juvenile courts but rather the criminal courts; also age of consent.

Aggravating circumstances Events about crime that may intensify the severity of punishment, including bodily injury, death to the victim, or the brutality of the act.

Alford plea A *nolo contendere* plea whereby defendants plead "no contest" to the factual scenario as outlined in the charges; originated with the case of *North Carolina v. Alford* (1970), in which a defendant did not wish to admit guilt but entered a *nolo contendere* plea, admitting to certain facts as specified by the prosecution.

Alibi Defense to a criminal allegation that places an accused individual at some other place than the crime scene at the time the crime occurred.

Allegation Assertion or claim made by a party to a legal action.

Allege To aver, assert, claim; usually a prosecutor will allege certain facts in developing a case against a criminal defendant.

Allocution Right of convicted offenders to address the court personally prior to the imposition of sentences.

Alternate jurors These selected to replace any of the regular jurors who may become ill and cannot attend the full trial proceeding; these jurors have been vested with the same tasks as regular jurors who will hear and decide cases.

Alternative dispute resolution (ADR) Procedure whereby a criminal case is redefined as a civil one, the case is decided by an impartial arbiter, and both parties agree to amicable settlement. Usually reserved for minor offenses.

Amendment A modification, addition, deletion.

American Bar Association (ABA) National organization of U.S. lawyers headquartered in Chicago.

Amicus curiae. A friend of the court. People may initiate petitions on behalf of others, perhaps for someone who is in prison. Such *amicus* briefs are designed to present legal arguments or facts on behalf of someone else. A person allowed to appear in court or file a brief even though the person has no right to participate in the litigation otherwise.

Answer A written response in relation to a filed complaint prepared by a litigant or defendant.

Appeal, appeal proceedings Any request by the defense or prosecution directed to a higher court to contest a decision or judgment by a lower court.

Appearance Act of coming into a court and submitting to the authority of that court.

Appellant Person who initiates an appeal.

Appellate court A court hearing appeals emanating from lower courts. These courts typically do not try criminal cases.

Appellate jurisdiction Authority to rehear cases from lower courts and alter, uphold, or overturn lower court decisions.

Appellate review A comprehensive rehearing of a case in a court other than the one in which it was previously tried.

Appellee Party who prevailed in lower court, who argues on appeal against reversing the lower court's decision.

Argument Any rationale provided by the defense or prosecution to support their position in court; any oral persuasion attempted before a jury.

Arraignment Official proceeding in which a defendant is formally confronted by criminal charges and enters a plea; the trial date is established.

Arrest Taking people into custody and restraining them until they can be brought before court to answer the charges against them.

Arrestee Person who has been arrested by police for suspicion of committing a crime.

Assembly-line justice Term applied to overworked, inadequately staffed court that is unsympathetic and unfair to criminal defendants.

Assigned counsel system Program wherein indigent clients charged with crimes may have defense attorneys appointed for them; these defense attorneys may be private attorneys who agree to be rotated to perform such services for a low rate of reimbursement from the city, county, or state.

Assistant state's attorneys Prosecutors who serve under other prosecutors in local or state jurisdictions; government prosecutors.

Assistant U.S. attorneys (AUSAs) Government prosecutors who are subordinate to the U.S. attorney who heads the prosecutor's office for each federal district.

Attorney, lawyer, counsel Anyone trained in the law who has received a law degree from a recognized university and who is authorized to practice law in a given jurisdiction.

Attorney–client confidentiality and privilege Relation between a counsel and a client wherein any information exchanged between parties will not be disclosed to others, such as prosecutors; attorneys are protected from disclosing information about the clients they represent because of this privilege.

Attorney competence Standards for determining whether clients are fairly and intelligently represented by their lawyers when they are charged with crimes.

Attorney general Senior U.S. prosecutor in each federal district court. A cabinet member who heads the Justice Department.

Automatic waivers Jurisdictional laws that provide for automatic waivers of juveniles to criminal court for processing; legislatively prescribed directive to transfer juveniles of specified ages who have committed especially serious offenses to jurisdiction of criminal courts.

Automatism A set of actions taken during a state of unconsciousness.

Backdooring hearsay evidence Prosecutor comments about or mentions information that is otherwise inadmissible in court; remarks made in front of a jury for their emotional and persuasive effects, which are otherwise barred because of the inadmissibility of evidence.

Backlog Number of pending cases that exceeds the court's capacity and that cannot be acted on because the court is occupied in acting on other cases.

Bail Surety provided by defendants or others to guarantee their subsequent appearance in court to face criminal charges. Available to anyone entitled to it (not everyone is entitled to bail); is denied when suspects are considered dangerous or likely to flee.

Bail bond A written guarantee, often accompanied by money or other securities, that the person charged with an offense will remain within the court's jurisdiction to face trial at a time in the future.

Bail bond companies Any organization established for the purpose of posting bail for criminal suspects.

Bail bondsperson, bail bondsman Person who is in the business of posting bail for criminal suspects. Usually charges a percentage of whatever bail has been set.

Bail Reform Act Original act passed in 1966 to assure that bail practices would be revised to ensure that no person, regardless of financial status, will needlessly be detained to answer criminal charges.

Bail Reform Act of 1984 Revision of original 1966 Bail Reform Act to implement changes in bail practices to assure that all persons, regardless of their financial status, shall not needlessly be detained to answer criminal charges; gave judges and magistrates greater autonomy to decide conditions under which bail would be granted or denied. Does not mean that all persons are entitled to bail regardless of their alleged offense.

Bail revocation Judicial decision to deny previously granted bail for a defendant.

Bail system Practice of releasing defendants after they place a financial guarantee with the court to ensure their subsequent trial appearance. Usually, defendants may place the entire amount with the court or pay a premium to the bondsman.

Bailiff Court officer who maintains order in the court while it is in session. Bailiff oversees jury during a trial proceeding and sometimes has custody of prisoners while they are in the courtroom. Also known as messengers.

Bar Aggregate denoting all attorneys admitted to practice law in every jurisdiction.

Bench trial Tribunal where guilt or innocence of defendant is determined by the judge rather than a jury.

Bench warrant Document issued by judge and not requested by the police demanding that a specified person be brought before the court without undue or unnecessary delay.

Best evidence rule In the course of presenting evidence in court, this edict states that if factual information or tangible documents are offered as proof, the original information or documents are preferred; if such original information or documents are unavailable, then a reasonable facsimile is the next most preferred item (e.g., a photocopy of an unavailable automobile title would be the best evidence, in the event that the original automobile title was destroyed or missing).

Beyond a reasonable doubt Standard used in criminal courts to establish guilt of criminal defendant.

Bifurcated trial Tribunal in capital cases in which a jury is asked to make two decisions. The first decision is to determine the guilt or innocence of the defendant; if guilty, the jury meets to decide punishment, which may include the death penalty.

Bill of Rights First ten amendments to the U.S. Constitution, setting forth certain freedoms and guarantees to U.S. citizens.

Bind over Following a finding of probable cause that a crime has been committed and the defendant has committed it, a court action to cause the defendant to be tried on the charges later in a criminal court.

Blaming A step in the dispute process whereby the victim singles out someone as a potential target for legal action.

Blaming the victim The stereotypical practice of charging the socially and psychologically handicapped with the lack of motivation. An attitude or belief that the adverse conditions and negative characteristics of a group, often of minorities, are the group's own fault.

Blended sentencing Any type of sentencing procedure in which either a criminal or juvenile court judge can impose both juvenile and/or adult incarcerative penalties.

Blue-ribbon jury A jury considered by one side, prosecution or defense, to be ideal because of its perceived likelihood of rendering a verdict favorable to that side; jurors often are selected because of their higher educational level and intellectual skills.

Bona fide "In good faith." Without the attempt to defraud or deceive.

Bond Written document indicating that defendants or sureties assure the presence of these defendants at a criminal proceeding; if not, then the bond will be forfeited.

Booking Process of making a written report of arrest, including name and address of arrested persons, the alleged crimes, arresting officers, place and time of arrest, physical description of suspect, photographs (sometimes called "mug shots") and fingerprints.

Bounties, bounty hunters Monetary rewards offered for capture of persons who escape prosecution from a given jurisdiction. Often, such persons have posted a bond with a bonding company, and the bonding company hires a bounty hunter (person who earns a living by apprehending these persons) to track them down so that monies deposited with the courts by the bonding company can be recovered.

Brady materials Exculpatory materials must be disclosed through discovery to defense counsel by the prosecution when defendant is to be tried for a crime.

Brady violation Infraction of discovery rules when prosecutor fails to turn over exculpatory materials acquired during a criminal investigation to defense counsel. Violation occurs whenever three conditions are met: (1) the evidence at issue must be favorable to the accused, either because it is exculpatory or because it is impeaching; (2) the evidence must have been suppressed by the state, either willfully or inadvertently; and (3) prejudice must have ensued.

Bribery Crime of offering, giving, requesting, soliciting, or receiving something of value to influence a decision of a public official.

Brief A document filed by a party to a lawsuit to convince the court of the merits of that party's case.

Burden of proof The requirement to introduce evidence to prove an alleged fact or set of facts.

Bureaucracy Organizational model that vests individuals with authority and spheres of competence in a predetermined hierarchy with abstract rules and selection by test.

Camp, ranch Any of several types of similar correctional confinement facilities for adults or juveniles, usually located in rural areas.

Canons of Professional Ethics Part of ABA Model Code of Professional Responsibility formulated in 1908; nine canons pertain to representing clients in a competent way, improving the legal system, avoiding the appearance of impropriety, and observing client confidences.

Capacity Mental state of being legally responsible; having the mental acuity to know the difference between right and wrong and to realize and appreciate the nature and consequences of particular actions.

Capias "That you take." A general term for various court orders requiring that some named person be taken into custody.

Capital punishment Imposition of the death penalty for the most serious crimes; may be administered by electrocution, lethal injection, gas, hanging, or shooting.

Career criminals Those offenders who make their living through crime. Usually offenses occur over the lifetime of the offender.

Case Incident investigated by law enforcement officers. A single charging document under the jurisdiction of a court. A single defendant.

Case backlogs Crowded court dockets in either juvenile court or criminal court; a massive buildup of cases, where judges cannot hear all cases in a timely fashion.

Case law Legal opinions having the status of law as enunciated by the courts (e.g., U.S. Supreme Court decisions become case law and governing cases when identical or very similar cases are subsequently heard in lower courts).

Case processing The speed with which cases are heard in either criminal or juvenile court.

Case-specific pretrial publicity Direct familiarity with actual events that transpired in particular cases when persons are to serve as jurors; example is the Rodney King case, where millions of viewers watched the privately recorded videotape of the Rodney King beating by police on national television newscasts.

Cash bail bond Cash payment for situations in which charges are not serious and the scheduled bail is low. Defendants obtain release by paying in cash the full amount, which is recoverable after the required court appearances are made.

Centralization Limited distribution of power among a few top staff members of an organization.

Certification (juvenile) *See* Waiver.

Certiorari, **writ of** A writ issued by a higher court directing a lower court to prepare the record of a case and send it to the higher court for review; a means of accessing the U.S. Supreme Court in order for a case to be heard.

Challenge *See* Peremptory challenge.

Challenges for cause In jury selection, the method used by either the prosecution or defense attorneys to strike or remove prospective jurors from the available jury pool because of prejudices they might have, toward either the defendant or prosecution. Prospective jurors may also be excused from jury duty because of being law enforcement officers, relatives of law enforcement officers, court officers, or relatives of court officers. Any obvious bias for or against a defendant may result in the exclusion of the biased prospective juror.

Challenges of jurors Questions raised of jurors by the judge, prosecutor, and/or defense attorney relating to their qualifications as impartial finders of fact; a determination of juror bias one way or another, for or against the defendant.

Chambers Usually a judge's office in a courthouse.

Chancellors King's agents used to settle disputes between neighbors in his behalf, such as property boundary issues, trespass allegations, and child misconduct. The early equivalent of the chancellor with similar duties and responsibilities was the justice of the peace, dating back to about A.D. 1200.

Chancery court Tribunal of equity rooted in early English common law, where civil disputes are resolved. Also responsible for juvenile matters and adjudicating family matters such as divorce. Has jurisdiction over contract disputes, property boundary claims, and exchanges of goods disputes.

Change of venue A change in the place of trial, usually from one county or district to another. Changes of venue are often conducted to avoid prejudicial trial proceedings, where it is believed that a fair trial cannot be obtained in the specific jurisdiction where the crime was alleged to have been committed.

Charge A formal allegation filed against some defendant in which one or more crimes are alleged.

Charge reduction bargaining, charge bargaining Negotiation process between prosecutors and defense attorneys involving dismissal of one or more charges against defendants in exchange for a guilty plea to remaining charges, or in which prosecutor downgrades the charges in return for a plea of guilty.

Chief justice The presiding or principal judge of a court, possessing nominal authority over the other judges (e.g., the chief justice of the U.S. Supreme Court).

Child savers Groups who promoted rights of minors during the nineteenth century and helped create a separate juvenile court. Their motives have been questioned by modern writers, who see their efforts as a form of social control and class conflict.

Children in need of supervision (CHINS) Typically unruly or incorrigible children who cannot be supervised well by their parents. Also includes children from homes where parents are seldom present. State agencies exist to find housing for such children.

Chronic offenders Habitual offenders; repeat offenders; persistent offenders; youths who commit frequent delinquent acts.

Chronic recidivists Persons who continue to commit new crimes after being convicted of former offenses.

Circuit courts Originally, courts that were held by judges who followed a circular path, hearing cases periodically in various communities. Now refers to courts with several counties or districts within their jurisdiction.

Circumstantial evidence Material provided by a witness from which a jury must infer a fact.

Citation, citation to appear Any document issued by a law enforcement or court officer directing one to present oneself in court on a specific date and time.

Cite, citation Any legal reference in which a point of law is made. In law enforcement, a summons.

Civil action Any lawsuit brought to enforce private rights and to remedy violations thereof.

Civil law All state and federal law pertaining to noncriminal activities; also referred to as municipal law. Laws pertaining to private rights and remedies. A body of formal rules established by any society for its self-regulation.

Civil liability In tort law, the basis for a cause of action to recover damages.

Claiming The process in a dispute where a grievance is expressed and a cause of action is cited.

Class action, class action suit Any lawsuit on behalf of a segment of the population with specific characteristics, namely, that they are victims of whatever wrongs are alleged. The class of persons may persist over time and change, but the action is for all current and future members of the class.

Coconspirator Another party besides the defendant who is alleged to have committed the same crime in concert with the defendant.

Code A systematic collection of laws.

Code of ethics Regulations formulated by major professional societies that outline the specific problems and issues that are frequently encountered in the types of research carried out within a particular profession. Serves as a guide to ethical research practices.

Codefendants Two or more defendants charged with the same crime and tried in the same judicial proceeding.

Coercion Affirmative defense similar to duress, wherein defendants allege that they were made or forced to commit an illegal act.

Common law Authority based on court decrees and judgments that recognize, affirm, and enforce certain usages and customs of the people. Laws determined by judges in accordance with their rulings.

Community service An alternative sanction requiring offenders to work in the community at such tasks as cleaning public parks or working with handicapped children in lieu of an incarcerative sentence. Restitution involves paying back a victim through money received from one's work.

Community service orders Judicially imposed restitution for those convicted of committing crimes; some form of work must be performed to satisfy restitution requirements.

Complaint Written statement of essential facts constituting the offense alleged, made under oath before a magistrate or other qualified judicial officer.

Comprehensive Crime Control Act of 1984 Significant act that authorized establishment of the U.S. Sentencing Commission, instituted sentencing guidelines, provided for abolition of federal parole, and devised new guidelines and goals of federal corrections.

Concession givers Judges who make plea agreement offers to criminal defendants, wherein the defendants plead guilty to a criminal charge in exchange for judicial leniency in sentencing.

Conclusive evidence Any compelling evidence that is so strong that it cannot be disputed or discounted. Proof establishing guilt beyond a reasonable doubt.

Concurrent jurisdiction Situation in which offender may be held accountable in several different jurisdictions simultaneously. Courts in the same jurisdiction.

Concurring opinion A judge's written opinion agreeing with the result in the case but disagreeing with the reasoning of the majority opinion.

Conditional dispositions Decisions by a juvenile court judge authorizing payment of fines, community service, restitution, or some other penalty after an adjudication of delinquency has been made.

Conditions of confinement The nature of jail or prison incarceration; refers to heat and humidity, cleanliness of cell and surroundings, and general treatment; often is the basis for legal action filed as habeas corpus petitions.

Confidentiality Any privileged communication between a client and an attorney.

Confidentiality privilege Right between a defendant and his or her attorney where certain information cannot be disclosed to prosecutors or others because of the attorney–client relation; for juveniles, records have been maintained under secure circumstances with limited access, and only then accessed by those in authority with a clear law enforcement purpose.

Consent decree A formal agreement involving the child, parents, and the juvenile court in which the youth is placed under the court's supervision without an official finding of delinquency.

Constitutional law An area of study in law schools involving the U.S. Constitution and its amendments. An investigation and discussion of the principles articulated by the U.S. Supreme Court and its interpretations of the law in different legal contexts.

Constitutional rights Privileges guaranteed to all U.S. citizens by the U.S. Constitution and its amendments.

Contempt of court Disobeying orders from judges in their courtrooms. Failing to observe the proper decorum of legal proceedings. Crossing the line of proper conduct, either as a defense attorney or prosecutor (e.g., failing to give testimony when compelled to do so).

Contract system Providing counsel to indigent offenders by having an attorney under contract to the county handle some or all of these types of cases.

Conviction State of being judged guilty of a crime in a court, either by the judge or jury.

Corroboration Evidence that strengthens the evidence already given.

Cost–benefit analysis Method of analyzing the costs associated with particular policies and determining whether the benefits or value derived from those policies are justified on the basis of the results.

Court Public judiciary body that applies the law to controversies and oversees the administration of justice.

Court administrator Any individual who controls the operations of the court in a particular jurisdiction. May be in charge of scheduling, juries, judicial assignment.

Court-appointed counsel Attorneys who are appointed to represent indigent defendants.

Court calendar Docket; the schedule of events for any judicial official.

Court clerk Court officer who may file pleadings, motions, or judgments, issue process, and may keep general records of court proceedings.

Court of general jurisdiction Any court having the power to hear diverse types of cases, both civil and criminal.

Court of last resort The last court that may hear a case. In the United States, the Supreme Court is the court of last resort for many kinds of cases.

Court of limited jurisdiction *See* Trial court of limited jurisdiction.

Court of public opinion Informal reactions to legal cases by unofficial pollsters and media broadcasters who cover high-profile cases on television and in the newspapers; independent reactions to court events by persons who may have only a passing interest in cases.

Court of record Any legal proceedings where a written record is kept of court matters and dialogue.

Court order Any judicial proclamation or directive authorizing an officer to act on behalf of the court.

Court reporter Court official who keeps a written word-for-word and/or tape-recorded record of court proceedings. *See also* Transcript.

Courtroom work group The phrase denoting all parties in the adversary process who work together cooperatively to settle cases with the least amount of effort and conflict.

Courts of last resort Either state or federal supreme courts that function as the final stage for appeals from lower courts; the ultimate court of last resort is the U.S. Supreme Court.

Crime Act or omission prohibited by law, by one who is held accountable by that law. Consists of legality, *actus reus, mens rea,* consensus, harm, causation, and prescribed punishment.

Crime Bill of 1994 Legislation supported by President Bill Clinton designed to increase crime prevention measures and put more police officers on the streets; also established truth-in-sentencing laws to maximize the amount of time inmates must serve in relation to their maximum sentences.

Crime prevention Any overt activity conducted by individuals or groups to deter persons from committing crimes. May include "target hardening" by making businesses and residences more difficult to burglarize; neighborhood watch programs, in which neighborhood residents monitor streets during evening hours for suspicious persons or automobiles; and equipping homes and businesses with devices to detect crime.

Criminal courts Tribunals handling criminal cases. May also handle civil cases and are then called criminal courts only in reference to the criminal cases they handle.

Criminal-exclusive blend Form of sentencing by a criminal court judge where either juvenile or adult sentences of incarceration can be imposed, but not both.

Criminal history One's prior convictions, indictments, and arrests.

Criminal-inclusive blend Form of sentencing by a criminal court judge where both juvenile and adult sentences can be imposed simultaneously.

Criminal law Body of law that defines criminal offenses, prescribes punishments (substantive law), and delineates criminal procedure (procedural law).

Criminal trial An adversarial proceeding within a particular jurisdiction, in which a judicial determination of issues can be made, and in which a defendant's guilt or innocence can be decided impartially.

Criminalization Transformation of civil proceedings into criminal proceedings; the juvenile court has undergone a transformation toward greater criminalization as juveniles have acquired almost the same number of legal rights as adults.

Critical legal studies Movement involving an examination of the entire legal system; recognizes that law is subjective rather than objective.

Cross-examination Questioning of one side's witnesses by the other side's attorney, either the prosecution or defense.

Culpable, culpability State of mind of persons who have committed an act that makes them liable for prosecution for that act.

Curfew violators Any juveniles who are on the streets after certain hours, such as 7:00 P.M. or 10:00 P.M.; may include adults on probation or parole who must adhere to fixed times for being at their residences.

Custodial dispositions Outcomes by a juvenile judge following adjudication of a juvenile as delinquent. Includes nonsecure custody (in a foster home, community agency, farm, camp), secure custody (in a detention center, industrial, reform school).

Damages Monetary sums awazrded to prevailing litigants in civil actions.

De facto "In fact," as a matter of fact.

De jure "In law," as a matter of law.

De minimis Minimal.

De novo Anew, afresh, as if there had been no earlier decision.

Death penalty *See* Capital punishment.

Death row Arrangement of prison cells where inmates who have been sentenced to death are housed.

Decriminalization, decriminalize Legislative action whereby an act or omission, formerly criminal, is made noncriminal and without punitive sanctions.

Defendant Person against whom a criminal proceeding is pending.

Defendant dispositions Any one of several adjudication and dispositional options available to a judge at various times during a criminal proceeding, ranging from dismissal of the case to long-term imprisonment.

Defendant's sentencing memorandum Version of events leading to conviction offense in the words of the convicted offender. Memorandum may be submitted together with victim impact statement.

Defense A response by defendants in criminal law or civil cases. May consist of only a denial of the factual allegations of the prosecution (in a criminal case) or of the plaintiff (in a civil case). If defense offers new factual allegations in an effort to negate the charges, this is called an affirmative defense.

Defense attorney, counsel A lawyer who represents a client accused of a crime.

Defense of property Affirmative defense to justify illegal conduct, wherein defendants claim that they broke one or more laws to safeguard their property or possessions or the property or possessions of others.

Defense strategy Approach taken by defense counsel for defending a client; usually involves a particular defense to criminal charges.

Defenses to criminal conduct Includes claims based upon personal, special, and procedural considerations that defendants should not be held accountable for their actions, even though they may have acted in violation of criminal laws.

Deferred prosecution Temporary halting of a prosecution against a defendant while he or she is subjected to a program with particular requirements for a short period. *See also* Diversion.

Deinstitutionalization Providing programs in community-based settings instead of institutional ones.

Deinstitutionalization of status offenses (DSO) Movement to remove nondelinquent juveniles from secure facilities by eliminating status offenses from the delinquency category and removing juveniles from or precluding their confinement in juvenile correction facilities. Process of removing status offenses from jurisdiction of juvenile court.

Demand waiver Request by juveniles to have their cases transferred from juvenile courts to criminal courts.

Demonstrative evidence Material related to a crime that is apparent to the senses, in contrast to material presented by the testimony of others.

Deponent Person who gives testimony through a deposition. If someone cannot physically attend a trial and give testimony under oath, then a deposition is taken and read into the court record.

Depose To take a deposition from a witness, under oath, which may be admissible in court at a later date.

Derivative evidence Information obtained as the result of previously discovered evidence (e.g., residue from an automobile tire may suggest that a crime was committed in a part of the city where such residue is found, and police discover subsequent "derivative" evidence by investigating that area).

Determinate sentencing Sanctioning scheme in which the court sentences the offender to incarceration for a fixed period, which must be served in full and without parole intervention, less any good time earned in prison.

Deterrence, general or specific Actions that are designed to prevent crime before it occurs by threatening severe criminal penalties or sanctions. May include safety measures to discourage potential lawbreakers, such as elaborate security systems, electronic monitoring, and greater police officer visibility, and influencing by fear, where fear is of apprehension and punishment.

Differential discretion View that sentencing disparities are more likely to occur during informal charge-reduction bargaining than in the final sentencing process following the trial and the sentencing hearing.

Direct evidence Information and details offered by an eyewitness who testifies to what was seen or heard.

Direct examination Questioning by attorney of one's own (prosecution or defense) witness during a trial.

Direct file Prosecutorial waiver of jurisdiction to a criminal court; an action taken against a juvenile who has committed an especially serious offense, where that juvenile's case is transferred to criminal court for the purpose of a criminal prosecution.

Directed verdict of acquittal Order by a court declaring that the prosecution has failed to produce sufficient evidence to show the defendant guilty beyond a reasonable doubt.

Discovery Procedure in which the prosecution shares information with the defense attorney and defendant. Specific types of information are made available to the defendant before trial, including results of any tests conducted, psychiatric reports, and transcripts or tape-recorded statements made by the defendant. Also known as "Brady materials" after a specific court case.

Discretionary waivers Transfers of juveniles to criminal courts by judges, at their discretion or in their judgment; also known as judicial waivers.

Disposition Action by criminal or juvenile justice court or agency signifying that a portion of the justice process is completed and jurisdiction is relinquished or transferred to another agency or signifying that a decision has been reached on one aspect of a case and a different aspect comes under consideration, requiring a different kind of decision.

Disposition hearing Proceeding in juvenile court, conducted after an adjudicatory hearing and a finding of delinquency, status offender, or dependent or neglected, to determine the most appropriate punishment, placement, or treatment for the juvenile.

Disputants Opposing sides in a civil action or case.

Dispute resolution Civil action intended to resolve conflicts between two parties, usually a complainant and a defendant.

Dispute stage Public revelation of a dispute by filing of a legal action.

Dissenting opinion Any judicial opinion disavowing or attacking the decision of a collegial court.

District attorneys City, county, and state prosecutors who are charged with bringing offenders to justice and enforcing the laws of the state.

District court Trial courts at the state or federal level with general and original jurisdiction. Boundaries of their venue do not conform to standard political unit boundaries but generally include several states or counties.

Diversion Removing a case from the criminal justice system, while a defendant is required to comply with various conditions (e.g., attending a school for drunk drivers, undergoing counseling, performing community service). May result in expungement of record. Conditional removal of the prosecution of a case prior to its adjudication, usually as the result of an arrangement between the prosecutor and judge.

Diversion programs One of several programs preceding formal court adjudication of charges against defendants; defendants participate in therapeutic, educational, or other helping programs. *See also* diversion.

Divestiture of jurisdiction Juvenile court relinquishment of control over certain types of juveniles, such as status offenders.

DNA fingerprinting Deoxyribonucleic acid (DNA) is an essential component of all living matter and carries hereditary patterning. Suspects can be detected according to their unique DNA patterning, as each person has a different DNA pattern. Similar to fingerprint identification, in which no two people have identical fingerprints.

Docket A court record of the cases scheduled to appear before the court.

Doctrine of assumptive risk Theory that holds that plaintiffs who engage in dangerous enterprises must accept some or all of the responsibility when accidents happen to them.

Doctrine of contributory negligence Theory that holds that a plaintiff by his or her own actions has brought about injuries for which he or she seeks relief from a defendant.

Doctrine of last clear chance Theory that holds that when an accident occurs, the responsibility lies largely with the party who has the last clear chance to avoid the accident. An example is a person standing on a railroad track who is subsequently struck by the train; the person is more in the position of avoiding the train than the train is of avoiding the person, even if the train engineer sees the person on the tracks before striking him or her.

Doctrine of *res ipsa loquitur* "The thing speaks for itself"; blame in a legal action lies on the part of the defendant, because the instrument(s) bringing about the injury to a plaintiff were within the control of the defendant.

Document Any written paper, official or unofficial, having potential evidentiary importance.

Documentary evidence Any written evidence.

Double jeopardy Subjecting a person to prosecution more than once in the same jurisdiction for the same offense, usually without new or vital evidence. Prohibited by the Fifth Amendment.

Dual court system A system consisting of a separate judicial structure for each state, in addition to a national structure. Each case is tried in a court of the same jurisdiction as that of the law or laws broken.

Due process Basic constitutional right to a fair trial, presumption of innocence until guilt is proven beyond a reasonable doubt; and the opportunity to be heard, to be aware of a matter that is pending, to make an informed choice whether to acquiesce or contest, and to provide the reasons for such a choice before a judicial official. Actual due process rights include timely notice of a hearing or trial that informs the accused of charges, the opportunity to confront one's accusers and present evidence on one's own behalf before an impartial jury or judge, the presumption of innocence under which guilt must be proved by legally obtained evidence and the verdict must be supported by the evidence presented, the right of the accused to be warned of their constitutional rights at the earliest stage of the criminal process, protection against self-incrimination, assistance of counsel at every critical stage of the criminal process, and the guarantee that individuals will not be tried more than once for the same offense.

Due process courts Juvenile courts where the emphasis is on punishment and offender control rather than on individualized treatments and assistance.

Due process of law A right guaranteed by the Fifth, Sixth, and Fourteenth Amendments to the U.S. Constitution, generally understood to mean the due course of legal proceedings according to the rules and forms that have been established for the protection of private rights. *See also* Due process.

Duress Affirmative defense used by defendants to show lack of criminal intent, alleging force, psychological or physical, from others as the stimulus for otherwise criminal conduct.

Early release *See* Parole.

Electronic monitoring The use of electronic devices (usually anklets or wristlets) that emit electronic signals to monitor offenders, probationers, and parolees. The purpose of their use is to monitor an offender's presence in a given environment where the offender is required to remain or to verify the offender's whereabouts.

Element of the offense Any conduct, circumstance, condition, or state of mind that in combination with other conduct, circumstances, conditions, or states of mind constitutes an unlawful act.

En banc "In the bench." Refers to a session of the court, usually an appellate court, when all of the judges assigned to the court participate.

English common law *See* Common law.

Entrapment Activity by law enforcement officers that suggests, encourages, or assists others in the commission of crimes that would ordinarily not have occurred without officer intervention. Defense used by defendants to show that an otherwise criminal act would not have occurred without police intervention, assistance, and/or encouragement.

Equal protection Clause of Fourteenth Amendment of U.S. Constitution guaranteeing all citizens equal protection of the law, without regard to race, color, gender, class, origin, or religion.

Equity The concept that the relationships between men, women, and society should be just and fair and in accordance with contemporary morality.

Error in fact Any error made in a court of law, which may or may not affect a judicial decision or judgment.

Error in law Any error made by the court that may affect the case outcome (e.g., permitting the prosecution to show numerous bloody photographs of a crime scene to inflame the jury and enhance a defendant's likelihood of being convicted and harshly sentenced). *See also* Reversible errors, Harmless error.

Ethical code Canons of professional responsibility articulated by professional associations such as the American Bar Association.

Evidence All materials or means admissible in a court of law to produce in the minds of the court or jury a belief concerning the matter at issue.

Evidence, corroborating Any collateral evidence that enhances the value of other evidence.

Evidence-driven jury Body that decides to consider all evidence presented as relevant rather than selected evidence based on juror interest or preferences.

Evidentiary Pertaining to the rules of evidence or the evidence in a particular case.

Ex parte A hearing or examination in the presence of only one party in the case.

Ex post facto laws Regulations making criminal an act committed before they were passed or that retroactively increase the penalty for a crime. Such laws are unconstitutional.

Ex rel Latin term used in case citations to designate parties for whom others are acting.

Examination, direct and cross *See* Direct examination and Cross-examination.

Exception An objection to a ruling or comments made by the judge or attorneys.

Excessive bail Any bail amount that so grossly exceeds the proportionality of the seriousness of the offense as to be prohibited by the Eighth Amendment.

Exclusionary rule Provision that says that if evidence has been obtained in violation of the privileges guaranteed by the U.S. Constitution, such evidence may be excluded at the trial.

Exclusive jurisdiction Specific jurisdiction over particular kinds of cases. The U.S. Supreme Court has authority to hear matters involving the diplomats of other countries who otherwise enjoy great immunity from most other courts. Family court may have exclusive jurisdiction to hear child custody cases.

Exculpate, exculpatory Tending to exonerate a person of allegations of wrongdoing.

Exculpatory evidence Any information that exonerates a person of allegations of wrongdoing; any information that reflects favorably on the accused and shows that they are innocent of the crimes with which they are charged.

Expert testimony Any oral evidence presented in court by someone who is considered proficient and learned in a given field, if such evidence is relevant. Testimony provided by an expert witness.

Expert witnesses People who have expertise or special knowledge in a relevant field pertaining to the case at trial. Witness who is qualified under the Federal Rules of Evidence to offer an opinion about the authenticity or accuracy of reports and who has special knowledge that is relevant to the proceeding. Sometimes called "hired guns."

Expunge, expungement Deletion of one's arrest record from official sources. In most jurisdictions, juvenile delinquency records are expunged when one reaches the age of majority or adulthood.

Expungement orders Juvenile court orders to seal juvenile records.

Extenuating circumstances Conditions under which offenders might be excused from culpability in criminal conduct.

Extralegal factors Any element of a nonlegal nature. In determining whether law enforcement officers are influenced by particular factors when encountering juveniles on the streets, extralegal factors might include juvenile attitude, politeness, appearance, or dress. Legal factors might include age or specific prohibited acts observed by the officers.

Eyewitnesses People who testify in court as to what they saw when the crime was committed.

Facsimile A copy of an original object or document.

Fact A true statement. An actual event.

Fact-finders Juries who hear cases, criminal or otherwise.

Factual basis for the plea Evidence presented to the judge by the prosecutor that would have been used if a plea-bargained case had gone to trial; evidence of guilt beyond a reasonable doubt to substantiate a plea bargain agreement.

Factual question A question designed to elicit objective information from respondents regarding their background, environments, and habits.

Failure to appear When defendants fail to present themselves for trial or some other formal proceeding, such as arraignment or a preliminary hearing or examination.

Federal district court Basic trial court for federal government. Tries all criminal cases. Has extensive jurisdiction. District judges are appointed by the president of United States with the advice, counsel, and approval of the Senate.

Federal misdemeanor Any federal crime with a maximum punishment of less than one year in prison or jail.

Federal Rules of Criminal Procedure Contained in Title 18 of the U.S. Code, all protocols and regulations that must be followed during offender processing, from arrest to conviction.

Federal Rules of Evidence Official rules governing the introduction of certain types of evidence in U.S. district courts.

Fellow servant doctrine Theory holding employer responsible for actions of employees.

Felony Crime punishable by incarceration, usually in a state or federal prison, for periods of one year or longer.

Felony property offending Any crime punishable by more than one year in prison or jail that causes property loss or damage (e.g., burglary, larceny/theft, vehicular theft).

Feminist legal studies View that women use a different type of logic from men when interpreting the law, favoring less litigation and more mediation.

Filing The commencement of criminal proceedings by entering a charging document into a court's official record.

Financial/community service model Restitution model for juveniles that stresses the offender's financial accountability and community service to pay for damages.

Finding A holding or ruling by the court or judge.

Finding of fact Court's determination of the facts presented as evidence in a case, affirmed by one party and denied by the other.

Fine Financial penalties imposed at time of sentencing convicted offenders. Most criminal statutes contain provisions for the imposition of monetary penalties as sentencing options.

Flat term A specific, definite term for a conviction, not necessarily known in advance of sentencing.

Flat time Actual amount of time required to be served by a convicted offender while incarcerated.

Foster home An out-of-home placement of a youth in need of adult supervision; usually, a youth is placed in the home of another unrelated family for a short period of time until permanent placement can be made.

Frivolous lawsuits Legal actions commenced by one or more parties with little hope of a successful outcome; often groundless legal actions without sufficient bases.

Fruits of the poisonous tree A U.S. Supreme Court decision in *Wong Sun v. United States* (1963) holding that evidence that is spawned or directly derived from an illegal search or an illegal interrogation is generally inadmissible against a defendant because of its original taint.

Fundamental fairness Legal doctrine supporting the idea that as long as a state's conduct maintains the basic elements of fairness, the Constitution has not been violated.

Gag order Official declaration by the judge in a trial proceeding that all parties in the action, including the jurors, must refrain from discussing the case with the media.

General jurisdiction Power of a court to hear a wide range of cases, both civil and criminal.

General pretrial publicity Information about a legal case involving general details, including suspects, how the crime was committed, and names of victims and alleged perpetrators, as covered by the news media.

General sessions courts Tribunals in particular states that have limited jurisdiction to hear misdemeanor cases and some low-level felony cases.

General trial courts Any one of several types of courts, either civil or criminal, with diverse jurisdiction to conduct jury trials and decide cases.

Geographic jurisdiction The power to hear particular kinds of cases, depending on the legally defined boundaries of cities, counties, or states.

Get-tough movement General orientation toward criminals and juvenile delinquents that favors the maximum penalties and punishments for crime and delinquency; any action toward toughening or strengthening sentencing provisions or dispositions involving adults or juveniles.

Going rate Local view of the appropriate sentence or punishment for a particular offense, given the defendant's prior record and other factors; used in implicit plea bargaining.

Good time, good-time credit An amount of time deducted from the period of incarceration of a convicted offender, calculated as so many days per month on the basis of good behavior while incarcerated. Credits earned by prisoners for good behavior. Introduced in early 1800s by British penal authorities, including Alexander Maconochie and Sir Walter Crofton.

Grand jury Investigative body whose numbers vary among states. Duties include determining probable cause regarding commission of a crime and returning formal charges against suspects. *See also* true bill and no true bill.

Grievance, grievance procedure Formalized arrangements, usually involving a neutral hearing board, whereby institutionalized individuals have the opportunity to register complaints about the conditions of their confinement.

Group home Facilities for juveniles that provide limited supervision and support. Juveniles live in homelike environment with other juveniles and participate in therapeutic programs and counseling. Considered nonsecure custodial.

Guardian *ad litem* A court-appointed attorney who protects the interests of children in cases involving their welfare and who works with the children during the litigation period.

Guidelines-based sentencing *See* Sentencing guidelines.

Guilty plea A defendant's formal affirmation of guilt in court to charges contained in a complaint, information, or indictment claiming that he or she committed the offenses listed.

Habeas corpus Writ meaning "produce the body"; used by prisoners to challenge the nature and length of their confinement.

Habeas corpus petition Writ filed, usually by inmates, challenging the legitimacy of their confinement and the nature of their confinement. Document commands authorities to show cause why an inmate should be confined in either a prison or jail. Also includes challenges of the nature of confinement. A written order by the court to any person, including a law enforcement officer, directing that person to bring the named individual before the court so that it can determine if there is adequate cause for continued detention.

Habitual criminal statutes, laws Any laws that penalize offenders for two or more convictions; repeat-offender statutes are aimed at recidivists who continue to commit crime; often, life without parole is the punishment for habitual offenders.

Habitual offender statutes Regulations vary among states. Generally provide life imprisonment as a mandatory sentence for chronic offenders who have been convicted of three or more serious felonies within a specific time period.

Habitual offenders People who have been convicted of two or more felonies and may be sentenced under the habitual offender statute for an aggravated or longer prison term.

Harmful errors Mistakes made by judges that may be prejudicial to a defendant's case. May lead to reversals of convictions against defendants and to new trials.

Harmless error Any mistake or procedural error during a trial that is not deemed sufficient to harm the rights of parties in a legal action.

Harmless error doctrine The view that errors of a minor or trivial nature should not harm the rights of parties in a legal action. Cases are not reversed on the basis of harmless errors.

Hearing Any formal proceeding in which the court hears evidence from prosecutors and defense and resolves a dispute or issue.

Hearing, probable cause A proceeding in which arguments, evidence, or witnesses are presented and in which it is determined whether there is sufficient cause to hold the accused for trial or whether the case should be dismissed.

Hearsay evidence Information given by witnesses that is not firsthand but is based on an account given by another.

Hearsay rule Courtroom precedent that hearsay cannot be used in court. Rather than accepting testimony on hearsay, the trial process asks that those who were the original source of the hearsay information be brought into court to be questioned and cross-examined. Exceptions to the hearsay rule may occur when those with direct knowledge are either dead or otherwise unable to testify.

Hierarchical jurisdiction Distinction between courts at different levels, where one court is superior to another and has the power to hear appeals from lower-court decisions.

Holding The legal principle drawn from a judicial decision. Whatever a court, usually an appellate court, decides when cases are appealed from lower courts. When an appellate court "holds" a particular decision, it may be to uphold the original conviction, set it aside, overturn in part, or uphold in part.

Home confinement Housing of offenders in their own homes with or without electronic monitoring devices. Reduces prison overcrowding and prisoner costs. Sometimes an intermediate punishment involving the use of offender residences for mandatory incarceration during evening hours after a curfew and on weekends. Also called house arrest.

Hull House A shelter for homeless youth in Chicago, Illinois, operated by Jane Addams during the 1890s.

Hung jury Body that cannot agree on a verdict.

Illinois Juvenile Court Act Legislation establishing the first juvenile court in United States in 1899.

Impartial arbiters People such as judges, attorneys, or prominent citizens who are called on to be objective and neutral third parties in disputes between perpetrators and their victims under conditions of restorative justice or alternative dispute resolution.

Impeachment Proceeding for the removal of a political officer, such as a governor, president, or judge.

Implicit plea bargaining Occurs when defendant pleads guilty with the expectation of receiving a more lenient sentence. *See also* Plea bargaining.

In camera In a judge's chambers.

In delicto Fault, as to a crime or happening; a finding that one is at fault in causing an accident or committing a crime.

In flagrante delicto Caught in the act. The fact that the perpetrator of a crime was caught during the crime's commission is direct evidence of guilt.

In forma pauperis "In the manner of a pauper." Refers to the waiver of filing costs and other fees associated with judicial proceedings to allow indigent people to proceed with their case.

In loco parentis "In the place of the parents." Refers to someone other than a parent acting on behalf of a juvenile in any juvenile proceeding.

In re "In the matter of." Refers to cases filed for juveniles, who must have an adult act on their behalf when filing motions or appeals.

In toto Completely, entirely.

Inadmissible Evidentiary term used to describe something that cannot be used as evidence during a trial.

Incapacitation, isolation Philosophy of corrections espousing loss of freedom proportional to seriousness of offense. Belief that the function of punishment is to separate offenders from other society members and prevent them from committing additional criminal acts.

Inculpatory evidence Any information that places the defendant in an unfavorable light and increases the likelihood of his or her guilt.

Incumbents Political officers who are currently in power but seeking to be reelected or reappointed.

Indeterminate sentencing Punishment scheme in which a period is set by judges between the earliest date for a parole decision and the latest date for completion of the sentence. In holding that the time necessary for treatment cannot be set exactly, the indeterminate sentence is closely associated with rehabilitation.

Indigent defendants Poor people; anyone who cannot afford legal services or representation.

Ineffective assistance of counsel Standard for determining whether a client is defended in a competent way; guidelines for determining a counsel's effectiveness were articulated in the case of *Strickland v. Washington* (1984) and include (1) whether counsel's behavior undermined the adversarial process to the degree that the trial outcome is unreliable and (2) the counsel's conduct was unreasonable to the degree that the jury's verdict would have been different otherwise.

Information Written accusation made by a public prosecutor against a person for some criminal offense, without an indictment. Usually restricted to minor crimes or misdemeanors. Sometimes called criminal information.

Initial appearance Formal proceeding during which the judge advises the defendant of the charges, including a recitation of the defendant's rights and a bail decision.

Insanity Degree of mental illness that negates the legal capacity or responsibility of the affected person.

Insanity defense Strategy that seeks to exonerate accused people by showing that they were insane at the time they were believed to have committed a crime.

Insanity plea A plea entered as a defense to a crime. The defendant admits guilt but assigns responsibility for the criminal act to the condition of insanity presumably existing when the crime was committed.

Intake Review of a case by a court (juvenile or criminal) official. Screening of cases includes weeding out weak cases. In juvenile cases, intake involves the reception of a juvenile against whom complaints have been made. Decision to proceed or dismiss the case is made at this stage.

Intake hearings Proceedings, usually presided over by an intake officer, when determinations are made about whether certain juveniles should undergo further processing by the juvenile justice system; a screening mechanism for juvenile offenders.

Intake officer Process of screening juveniles who have been charged with offenses. Officer who conducts screening of juveniles. Dispositions include release to parents pending further juvenile court action, dismissal of charges against juvenile, detention, and treatment by some community agency.

Intake screening A critical phase when a determination is made by a juvenile probation officer or other official as to whether to release juveniles to their parents' custody, detain juveniles in formal detention facilities for a later court appearance, or release them to parents pending a later court appearance.

Intensive supervised probation Varies from standard probation by including more face-to-face visits between probation officers and probationers under community supervision.

Intent A state of mind, the *mens rea*, in which a person seeks to accomplish a given result, such as a crime, through a given course of action.

Inter alia "Among other things."

Interim judge Temporary judge who is appointed following the death, resignation, or retirement of another judge, usually to complete the original judge's term; after the interim judge serves, a new judge is appointed or elected according to the rules of judicial selection in the particular jurisdiction.

Interlocutory appeal An appeal during a trial proceeding in which the judgment of the trial court is suspended pending the success of an appeal.

Intermittent sentencing Imposed punishment according to which an offender must serve a portion of the sentence in jail, perhaps on weekends or specific evenings. Considered similar to probation with limited incarceration. *See also* Split sentencing.

Intoxication The state of being incapable of performing certain tasks legally, such as operating motor vehicles or boats. Can be induced through consumption of alcoholic beverages, inhaling toxic fumes from petroleum products, or consumption of drug substances. May also be a defense to criminal conduct, although the courts often rule that it is voluntary.

Ipso facto "By the mere fact." By the fact itself (e.g., "We can assume, *ipso facto,* that if the defendant was observed beating another person in a bar by ten witnesses, then he is probably guilty of the beating inflicted on the victim").

Isolation A sentencing philosophy seeking to remove the offender from other offenders when confined by placing prisoner in a cell with no communication with others. Also known as solitary confinement, which originated in Walnut Street Jail in Philadelphia in the late 1700s. Another use of this term is to segregate offenders from society through incarceration.

Jail as a condition of probation Sentence in which judge imposes limited jail time to be served before commencement of probation. *See also* split sentencing.

Jencks materials Discoverable materials available from either the prosecutor or defense counsel prior to trial; *see Jencks v. United States* (1957).

Judge A political officer who has been elected or appointed to preside over a court of law, whose position has been created by statute or by constitution and whose decisions in criminal and juvenile cases may be reviewed only by a judge of a higher court and may not be reviewed *de novo.*

Judgment Final determination of a case. A proclamation stating a person's guilt or innocence in relation to criminal offenses alleged. In tort law, a finding in favor of or against the plaintiff. The amount of monetary damages awarded in civil cases.

Judicial activism The U.S. Supreme Court's use of its power to accomplish social goals.

Judicial appointments Selections of judges by political figures, such as governors or presidents.

Judicial conduct commission Investigative body created in California in 1960, made up of other judges, attorneys, and prominent citizens; task was to investigate allegations of judicial misconduct, incompetence, and unfairness.

Judicial instructions Specific admonitions to jurors, prosecutors, and defense counsel to do or refrain from doing different things.

Judicial misconduct Departure of a judge from accepted modes of conduct becoming a judicial official; forms of misconduct are accepting bribes in exchange for money or services; making biased decisions favoring one side or the other during a trial; engaging in behaviors (e.g., drunkenness, driving while intoxicated, perjury) while serving on the bench.

Judicial plea bargaining Recommended sentence by a judge who offers a specific sentence and/or fine in exchange for a guilty plea. *See also* Plea bargaining.

Judicial powers Court jurisdiction to act in certain cases and decide punishments.

Judicial privilege Power of judges to change plea bargain agreements and substitute their own punishments; the power to override prosecutors and defense counsel concerning the agreed-upon terms of plea agreements.

Judicial process The sequence of procedures designed to resolve disputes or conclude a criminal case.

Judicial waiver Decision by a juvenile judge to waive a juvenile to the jurisdiction of criminal court.

Jumping bail Act by defendant of leaving jurisdiction where trial is to be held. Attempt by defendant to avoid prosecution on criminal charges.

Jurisdiction The power of a court to hear and determine a particular type of case. Also refers to territory within which a court may exercise authority, such as a city, county, or state.

Juror misconduct Any impropriety by a juror; acceptance of illegal gratuities in exchange for a favorable vote for or against the defendant; sleeping during the trial; reading newspaper accounts or listening to or watching newscasters voice their opinions about the case and then relating this information to other jurors in attempt to persuade them one way or another for or against the defendant.

Jury *See* Petit jury.

Jury deliberations Discussion among jury members concerning the weight and sufficiency of witness testimony and other evidence presented by both the prosecution and defense. An attempt to arrive at a verdict.

Jury misconduct Any impropriety exhibited by one or more jurors, such as sleeping during a trial, attempting to bias other jurors for or against a particular defendant by illegal means, or accepting bribes or gratuities from those interested in the case.

Jury nullification Jury refuses to accept the validity of evidence at trial and acquits or convicts for a lesser offense (e.g., although all of the elements for murder are proved, a jury may acquit defendants who killed their spouses allegedly as an act of mercy killing).

Jury panel A list of jurors summoned to serve on possible jury duty at a particular court. From the jury panel, the petit jury is selected.

Jury poll A poll conducted by a judicial officer or by the clerk of the court after a jury has stated its verdict but before that verdict has been entered into the record of the court, asking each juror individually whether the stated verdict is his or her own verdict.

Jury pool Aggregate of people from which a jury is selected; use of voter registration lists, driver's licenses, home ownership records, and other public documents are used to create such pools; also known as a venire or venireman list.

Jury selection The process by which a jury is impaneled for either a civil or criminal trial proceeding.

Jury sequestration The process of isolating a jury from the public during a trial; the objective is to minimize the influence of media publicity and exposure that might otherwise influence juror opinions about the guilt or innocence of the defendant.

Jury size Traditional twelve-member jury at the federal level and many state and local levels; may vary between six-member jury and twelve-member jury at state and local level.

Jury trial Proceeding in which guilt or innocence of the defendant is determined by a jury instead of by the judge.

Jury waiver system Defendants waive their constitutional right to a jury trial and enter into a plea bargain agreement with the prosecutor.

Juvenile-contiguous blend Form of blended sentencing by a juvenile court judge in which the judge can impose a disposition beyond the normal jurisdictional range for juvenile offenders (e.g., a judge may impose a thirty-year term on a fourteen-year-old offender, but the juvenile is entitled to a hearing on reaching the age of majority to determine whether the remainder of the sentence shall be served).

Juvenile court Formal adjudicatory hearing to determine whether a youth is a juvenile delinquent, a status offender, or in need of supervision.

Juvenile court jurisdiction Power of juvenile courts to hear cases involving people under the legal age of adulthood.

Juvenile delinquency The violation of criminal laws by juveniles. Any illegal behavior or activity committed by people who are within a particular age range and that subjects them to the jurisdiction of a juvenile court or its equivalent.

Juvenile delinquent Any minor who commits an offense that would be a crime if committed by an adult.

Juvenile-exclusive blend Blended sentencing form in which a juvenile court judge can impose either adult or juvenile incarceration as a disposition and sentence, but not both.

Juvenile-inclusive blend Form of blended sentencing in which a juvenile court judge can impose *both* adult and juvenile incarceration simultaneously.

Juveniles People who have not as yet achieved their eighteenth birthday or the age of majority.

Juvenile Justice and Delinquency Prevention Act of 1974 Act passed by Congress in 1974 and amended numerous times, including in 1984, encouraging states to deal differently with their juvenile offenders. Promotes community-based treatment programs and discourages incarceration of juveniles in detention centers, industrial schools, or reform schools.

Juvenile justice system, process The system through which juveniles are processed, sentenced, and corrected after arrests for juvenile delinquency.

Kales plan A 1914 version of the Missouri plan, in which a committee of experts creates a list of qualified people for judgeships and makes recommendations to the governor. *See also* Missouri plan.

Labeling theory Theory attributed to Edwin Lemert that people perceive themselves as deviant or criminal through labels applied to them by others; thus, the more people are involved in the criminal justice system, the more they acquire self-definitions consistent with the criminal label.

Landmark decision Holding handed down by the U.S. Supreme Court that becomes the law of the land and serves as a precedent for subsequent similar legal issues in lower courts.

Law The body of rules of specific conduct, prescribed by existing, legitimate authority, in a particular jurisdiction, and at a particular point in time.

Law in action Procedural law.

Law in books Substantive law.

Legal realism View that law and society are constantly evolving and that law should be the means to a social end rather than an end in itself.

Legislative waivers Provisions that compel juvenile court to remand certain youths to criminal courts because of specific offenses that have been committed or alleged.

Lex non scripta "The unwritten law" or common law. Law not written down in some codified form.

Lex talionis The law of retaliation or retribution. A form of revenge dating back to the Old Testament and used until the Middle Ages.

Libel A tort of defamation through published writing or pictures critical of others.

Lie detector An apparatus that records a person's blood pressure and other sensory responses and records reactions by means of a moving pencil and paper. Designed to determine whether someone is telling the truth during an interrogation. Also known as polygraphs. Results of tests are not admissible in court.

Life imprisonment Any sentence involving lengthy incarceration, presumably for the life expectancy of the convicted offender; however, life imprisonment in the United States averages about seven years.

Life-without-parole sentence Penalty imposed as maximum punishment in states that do not have the death penalty; provides for permanent incarceration of offenders in prisons, without parole eligibility; early release may be attained through accumulation of good-time credits.

Limited jurisdiction Court is restricted to handling certain types of cases such as probate matters or juvenile offenses. Also known as special jurisdiction.

Litigation Civil prosecution in which proceedings are maintained against wrongdoers, as opposed to criminal proceedings.

Litigation explosion Sudden increase in inmate suits against administrators and officers in prisons and jails during the late 1960s and continuing through the 1980s. Suits usually challenge nature and length of confinement or torts allegedly committed by administration, and they usually seek monetary or other forms of relief.

Loiterers People who stand around idly, hanging out. Often used as a provocation by police officers to stop and question citizens who appear suspicious or to describe vagrants, people who are in public places with no visible means of support.

Magistrate A judge who handles cases in pretrial stages. Usually presides over misdemeanor cases. An officer of the lower courts.

Magistrate courts Judicial benches of special jurisdiction, usually urban.

Mala fides Bad faith.

Mala in se **crimes** Illegal acts that are inherently wrong or intrinsically evil (e.g., murder, rape, or arson).

Mala prohibita **crimes** Illegal acts that have been codified or reduced to writing. Offenses defined by legislatures as crimes. Many state and federal criminal statutes are *mala prohibita*.

Malfeasance Misconduct by public officials. Engaging in acts that are prohibited while serving in public office.

Malicious prosecution Prosecutorial action against someone without probable cause or reasonable suspicion.

Mandamus *See* Writ of *mandamus*.

Mandatory sentencing, mandatory sentence Sentencing in which court is required to impose an incarcerative sentence of a specified length, without the option for probation, suspended sentence, or immediate parole eligibility.

Mandatory transfer Automatic waiver of certain juveniles to criminal court on the basis of (1) their age and (2) the seriousness of their offense (e.g., a seventeen-year-old in Illinois who allegedly committed homicide would be subject to mandatory transfer to criminal court for the purpose of a criminal prosecution).

Material witness Any witness who has relevant testimony about a crime.

Mediation Informal conflict resolution through the intervention of a trained negotiator who seeks a mutually agreeable resolution between disputing parties.

Mens rea Intent to commit a crime. Guilty mind.

Merit selection Reform plan in which judges are nominated by a committee and appointed by the governor for a given period. When the term expires, the voters are asked to signify their approval or disapproval of the judge for a succeeding term. If the judge is disapproved, the committee nominates a successor for the governor's appointment.

Miranda warning, rights Warning given to suspects by police officers to advise suspects of their legal rights to counsel, to refuse to answer questions, to avoid self-incrimination, and other privileges. Named after landmark case of *Miranda v. Arizona* (1966).

Misdemeanor Crime punishable by fines and/or imprisonment, usually in a city or county jail, for periods of less than one year.

Misdemeanor Trial Law Action by New York City passed in 1985 permitting low-level misdemeanor cases involving incarceration of six months or less to be disposed of by bench trials rather than jury trials; a time-saving strategy for more rapid criminal case processing.

Missouri plan Method of selecting judges in which merit system for appointments is used. Believed to reduce political influence in the selection of judges.

Mistake Affirmative defense that alleges that an act was not criminal because the person charged did not know the act was prohibited.

Mistake of fact Unconscious ignorance of a fact or the belief in the existence of something that does not exist.

Mistake of law An erroneous opinion of legal principles applied to a given set of facts. A judge may rule on a given court issue and the ruling may be wrong because the judge misunderstands the meaning of the law and how it should be applied.

Mistrial A trial that cannot stand and is invalid. Judges may call a mistrial for reasons such as errors on the part of prosecutors or defense counsel, the death of a juror or counsel, or a hung jury.

Mitigating circumstances Factors about a crime that may lessen the severity of the sentence imposed by the judge. Cooperating with police to apprehend others involved, youthfulness or old age of defendant, mental instability, and having no prior record are considered mitigating circumstances.

Mittimus An order by the court to an officer to bring someone named in the order directly to jail.

Mixed sentencing Two or more separate sentences imposed after offenders have been convicted of two or more crimes in the same adjudication proceeding. *See also* Split sentencing.

Modus operandi The characteristic method a person uses in the performance of repeated criminal acts.

Motion for a bill of particulars An action before the court asking that the details of the state's case against a defendant be made known to the defense. *See also* Discovery.

Motion for a change of venue Action requested by either the prosecutor or defense counsel to change the trial site to a different jurisdiction or geographical location, possibly because of extensive pretrial publicity and the belief that prospective jurors might be biased one way or another toward the defendant.

Motion for continuance An action before the court asking that the trial or hearing or proceeding be postponed to a later date.

Motion for determination of competency Action requested of the court by defense counsel to order a psychiatric examination of the defendant to determine whether the defendant is competent to stand trial for a crime.

Motion for discovery Action initiated by either prosecutor or defense counsel entitling either side to certain discoverable evidence, such as police reports and defendant interviews, and any other relevant evidentiary items that might be useful as the basis for case arguments at trial later.

Motion for dismissal of charges Action requested by defense counsel to have charges against defendant dismissed because of an insufficiency of evidence presented by the prosecutor.

Motion for intention to provide alibi A move by the defense to offer an alternative explanation of why the defendant did not commit the crime; motion seeks to show that defendant was elsewhere when crime was committed; motion is made in order to give prosecutor the opportunity to verify defendant's explanation for not being present when crime was committed.

Motion for severance Action requested by either the prosecutor or defense counsel to have separate trial proceedings for different people charged with the same offense who are accused of acting in concert to effect a crime.

Motion for summary judgment Request granted by judges who have read the plaintiff's version and defendant's version of events, and a decision is reached holding for the defendant.

Motion for suppression of evidence Action initiated by prosecutor or defense counsel asking the judge to bar the admission of certain evidence from the trial proceeding.

Motion to dismiss An action before the court requesting that the judge refuse to hear a suit. Usually granted when inmates who file petitions fail to state a claim upon which relief can be granted.

Motion to suppress An action before the court to cause testimony or tangible evidence from being introduced either for or against the accused.

Motions Oral or written requests to a judge asking the court to make a specific ruling, finding, decision, or order. May be presented at any appropriate point from an arrest until the end of a trial.

Motions *in limine* A pretrial motion, generally to obtain judicial approval to admit certain items into evidence that might otherwise be considered prejudicial or inflammatory.

Municipal courts Judicial benches of special jurisdiction whose jurisdiction follows the political boundaries of a municipality or city.

Naming Identifying a party in a legal action as the target of that action.

Narrative A portion of a presentence investigation report prepared by a probation officer or private agency that provides a description of the offense and offender. Culminates in and justifies a recommendation for a specific sentence to be imposed on the offender by judges.

Necessity A condition that compels someone to act because of perceived needs. An affirmative defense (e.g., when someone's automobile breaks down during a snowstorm and an unoccupied cabin is nearby, breaking into the cabin to save oneself from freezing to death is acting out of "necessity" and would be a defense to breaking and entering charges later).

Negligence Liability accruing to prison or correctional program administrators and probation or parole officers as the result of a failure to perform a duty owed clients or inmates or the improper or inadequate performance of that duty. May include negligent entrustment, negligent training, negligent assignment, negligent retention, or negligent supervision (e.g., providing probation or parole officers with revolvers and not providing them with firearms training).

Negotiated guilty pleas Admissions of guilt entered in exchange for some form of sentencing leniency during plea bargaining.

New trial Tribunal *de novo.* After a hung jury or a case is set aside or overturned by a higher court, a new trial is held to determine one's guilt or innocence.

New York House of Refuge Established in New York City in 1825 by the Society for the Prevention of Pauperism; school managed largely status offenders; compulsory education provided; a strict prisonlike regimen was considered detrimental to youthful clientele.

No bill *See* No true bill.

No true bill Grand jury decision that insufficient evidence exists to establish probable cause that a crime was committed and a specific person committed it.

Nolle prosequi An entry made by the prosecutor on the record in a case and announced in court to indicate that the specified charges will not be prosecuted. In effect, the charges are thereby dismissed.

Nolo contendere Plea of "no contest" to charges. Defendant does not dispute facts, although issue may be taken with the legality or constitutionality of the law allegedly violated. Treated as a guilty plea. Also known as "Alford plea" from leading case of *North Carolina v. Alford* (1970).

Nominal dispositions Juvenile court outcome in which juvenile is warned or verbally reprimanded but returned to the custody of parents.

Nonpartisan elections Voting process in which candidates who are not endorsed by political parties are presented to the voters for selection.

Nonsecure custody, confinement A facility that emphasizes the care and treatment of youths without the need to place constraints on them to ensure public protection.

Nonsuit A judgment in favor of a defendant because of the failure of the plaintiff to state a case upon which relief can be granted.

Notice An official document advising someone of a proceeding, which usually requires that person's attendance.

Notice of appeal Filing a formal document with the court to advise the court that the sentence is to be appealed to a higher court or appellate court.

Nullen crimen, nulla poena, sine lege "There is no crime, there is no punishment, without law."

Objections Actions by either the prosecutor or defense requesting that certain questions not be asked of witnesses or that certain evidence should or should not be admitted.

Office of Juvenile Justice and Delinquency Prevention (OJJDP) Established by Congress under the Juvenile Justice and Delinquency Prevention Act of 1974; designed to remove status offenders from jurisdiction of juvenile courts and dispose of their cases less formally.

Once an adult, always an adult Provision that once a juvenile has been transferred to criminal court to be prosecuted as an adult, regardless of the criminal court outcome, the juvenile can never be subject to the jurisdiction of juvenile courts in the future; in short, the juvenile, once transferred, will always be treated as an adult if future crimes are committed, even though the youth is still not of adult age.

Open court Any court where spectators may gather.

Opening statement Remarks made by prosecution and defense attorneys to jury at the commencement of trial proceedings. Usually these statements set forth what each side intends to show of the evidence to be presented.

Operation Greylord FBI undercover investigation of corruption among judges in Cook County (Chicago), Illinois, in 1978; results of investigation disclosed numerous instances of judicial corruption.

Opinion The official announcement of a court's decision and the reasons for that decision. In research methods, the verbal expression of an attitude.

Opinion of the court Opinion summarizing the views of the majority of judges participating in a judicial decision; a ruling or holding by a court official.

Oral argument Verbal presentation made to an appellate court by the prosecution or defense to persuade the court to affirm, reverse, or modify a lower court decision.

Order Any written declaration or proclamation by a judge authorizing officials to act.

Original jurisdiction First authority over a case or cause, as opposed to appellate jurisdiction.

Overrule To reverse or annul by subsequent action (e.g., judges may overrule objections from prosecutors and defense attorneys in court, nullifying these objections; lower court decisions may be overruled by higher courts when the case is appealed).

Parens patriae "Parent of the country." Refers to the doctrine that the state oversees the welfare of youth, originally established by the King of England and administered through chancellors.

Parole A conditional early release from prison subject to restrictions.

Parole board, paroling authority Body of persons either appointed by governors or others or elected, which determines whether those currently incarcerated in prisons should be granted parole or early release.

Parole evidence Oral testimony given in court.

Particularity Requirement that a search warrant must state precisely where the search is to take place and what items are to be seized.

Parties to offenses All people associated with the crime, either before or after it was committed, whether they actually committed the crime or assisted in some way in its planning; may include those who assist criminals in eluding capture.

Partisan elections Elections in which candidates endorsed by political parties are presented to the voters for selection.

Per curiam "By the court." Phrase used to distinguish an opinion rendered by the whole court as opposed to an opinion expressed by a single judge.

Per diem "By the day." The cost per day, here the daily cost of housing inmates.

Per se "By itself." In itself (e.g., the death penalty is not unconstitutional per se, but a particular method of administering the death penalty may be unconstitutional in some states).

Percentage bail A publicly managed bail service arrangement that allows defendants to deposit a percentage (about 10 percent) of the amount of bail with the court clerk.

Peremptory challenge Rejection of a juror by either prosecution or defense in which no reason needs to be provided for excusing juror from jury duty. Each side has a limited number of these challenges. The more serious the offense, the more peremptory challenges are given each side.

Perjury Lying under oath in court.

Persistent felony offenders Habitual offenders who commit felonies with a high recidivism rate.

Persistent offender statutes Any law prohibiting someone from being a habitual offender, or someone who has been convicted of several serious crimes.

Petit jury The trier of fact in a criminal case. The jury of one's peers called to hear the evidence and decide the defendant's guilt or innocence. Varies in size among states.

Petition A document filed in juvenile court alleging that a juvenile is a delinquent, a status offender, or a dependent and asking that the court assume jurisdiction over the juvenile or that the juvenile be transferred to a criminal court to be prosecuted as an adult.

Petition not sustained Finding by juvenile court at an adjudicatory hearing that there is insufficient evidence to sustain an allegation that a juvenile is a delinquent, status offender, or dependent.

Petitioner Person who brings a petition before the court.

Petty offenses Minor infractions or crimes, misdemeanors. Usually punishable by fines or short terms of imprisonment.

Philadelphia Experiment Study conducted involving setting bail guidelines in Philadelphia during 1981–1982 and the use of release on one's own recognizance (ROR); experiment led to greater equity in bail decision making for people of different socioeconomic status.

Pickpocketing The theft of money or valuables directly from the garments of the victim.

Plea Answer to charges by defendant. Pleas vary among jurisdictions. Not guilty, guilty, *nolo contendere,* not guilty by reason of insanity, and guilty but mentally ill are possible pleas.

Plea agreement hearing Meeting presided over by a trial judge to determine the accuracy of a guilty plea and the acceptability of the general conditions of a plea bargain agreement between prosecution and defense attorneys.

Plea bargain agreement Formal agreement between prosecutor and defense counsel wherein defendant enters a guilty plea to one or more criminal charges in exchange for some form of sentencing leniency.

Plea bargaining A preconviction deal-making process between the state and the accused in which the defendant exchanges a plea of guilty or *nolo contendere* for a reduction in charges, a promise of sentencing leniency, or some other concession from full, maximum implementation of the conviction and sentencing authority of the court. Includes implicit plea bargaining, charge-reduction bargaining, sentence recommendation bargaining, and judicial plea bargaining.

Plea bargains Formal agreements between prosecutors and defense concerning the defendant's offer of a guilty plea in exchange for some form of sentencing leniency.

Plea, guilty A defendant's formal answer in court to the charges in a complaint, information, or indictment; defendant states that the charges are true and that he or she has committed the offense(s) as charged.

Plea, initial The first plea offered in response to a given charge entered in a court record by or for a defendant.

Plea negotiation *See* Plea bargaining.

Plea *nolo contendere* *See Nolo contendere.*

Plea, not guilty A defendant's formal answer in court to the charges in a complaint or information or indictment, in which the defendant states that he or she has not committed the offense(s) as charged.

Plead To respond to a criminal charge.

Polling jurors A direct method of asking each juror to state whether he or she has voted in a particular way.

Polygraph test *See* Lie detector.

Postconviction relief Term applied to various mechanisms whereby offenders may challenge their convictions after other appeal attempts have been exhausted.

Postconviction remedies Various means convicted people have of seeking redress for their incarceration or conviction.

Pound's model Plan of court organization with three tiers: supreme court, major trial court, and minor trial court.

Power of attorney Authority given to another to act in one's place.

Precedent Principle that the way a case was decided previously should serve as a guide for how a similar case currently under consideration ought to be decided.

Preconflict stage Perception by individuals or groups that they are involved in a conflict situation in which a legal resolution is sought.

Prejudicial error Wrongful procedure that affects the rights of parties substantially and thus may result in the reversal of a case.

Preliminary examination *See* Preliminary hearing.

Preliminary hearing, preliminary examination Hearing by a magistrate or other judicial officer to determine if a person charged with a crime should be held for trial. Proceeding to establish probable cause. Does not determine guilt or innocence.

Preplea conference A discussion in which all parties participate openly to determine ways of bringing about an agreement on a sentence in return for a plea of guilty.

Preponderance of evidence Civil standard whereby the weight of the exculpatory or inculpatory information is in favor of or against the defendant; the greater the weight of information favoring the defendant, the greater the likelihood of a finding in favor of the defendant.

Presentence investigation report, presentence report (PSI) Report filed by probation or parole officer appointed by court containing background information, socioeconomic data, and demographic data about the defendant. Facts in the case are included. Used by the judge to influence sentence imposed and by the parole board considering an inmate for early release.

Presentment An accusation, initiated by the grand jury on its own authority, from the members' own knowledge or observation, which functions as an instruction for the preparation of an indictment.

Presiding judge The title of the judicial officer formally designated for some period as the chief judicial officer of the court.

Presumption of innocence Premise that a defendant is innocent unless proven guilty beyond a reasonable doubt. Fundamental to the adversary system.

Presumption of validity In constitutional law, the premise that a statute is valid until it is demonstrated otherwise.

Presumptive sentencing, presumptive sentences Statutory sentencing method that specifies normal sentences of particular lengths with limited judicial leeway to shorten or lengthen the term of the sentence.

Presumptive waiver Type of judicial waiver in which the burden of proof shifts from the state to the juvenile to contest whether the youth is transferred to criminal court.

Pretrial conference A meeting between opposing parties in a lawsuit or criminal trial for purposes of stipulating things that are agreed on and thus narrowing the trial to the things that are in dispute, disclosing the required information about witnesses and evidence, making motions, and generally organizing the presentation of motions, witnesses, and evidence.

Pretrial diversion *See* Diversion.

Pretrial motions *See* Motions *in limine.*

Pretrial publicity Any media attention given to a case before it is tried in court.

Prima facie **case** A case for which there is as much evidence as would warrant the conviction of defendants if properly proved in court. A case that meets the evidentiary requirements for a grand jury indictment.

Pro bono Literally "for the good," in legal terms, legal services provided at no cost to the defendant (e.g., indigent clients receive assistance from defense attorneys on a *pro bono* basis).

Pro forma According to form or a matter of policy or procedure; following specific rules.

Pro se Acting as one's own defense attorney in criminal proceedings. Representing oneself.

Probable cause Reasonable suspicion or belief that a crime has been committed and that a particular person committed it.

Probation officer Professional who supervises probationers.

Procedural law Rules that specify how statutes should be applied against those who violate the law. Procedures whereby the substantive laws may be implemented.

Process A summons requiring the appearance of someone in court.

Process of law Procedural law.

Project Exile Local, state, and federal cooperative effort providing for a five-year mandatory extension of one's sentence for using a firearm during the commission of a felony. Deemed a deterrent to the use of firearms in serious crimes, particularly those involving convicted violent felons, people who possess firearms on school property, and those who use both drugs and firearms.

Proof beyond a reasonable doubt Standard of proof to convict in a criminal case.

Property bond Setting bail in the form of land, houses, stocks, or other tangible property. In the event the defendant absconds prior to trial, the bond becomes the property of the court.

Prosecuting attorney *See* Prosecutor.

Prosecution Carrying forth of criminal proceedings against a person, culminating in a trial or other final disposition such as a plea of guilty in lieu of trial.

Prosecution agency, prosecutorial agency Any local, state, or federal body charged with carrying forth actions against a criminal. State legal representatives, such as district attorneys, or U.S. attorneys and their assistants, who seek to convict those charged with crimes.

Prosecutor Court official who commences civil and criminal proceedings against defendants. Represents state or government interest, prosecuting defendants on behalf of state or government.

Prosecutorial bluffing Attempt by prosecution to bluff the defendant into believing the case is much stronger than it really is. Used to elicit a guilty plea from the defendant to avoid a lengthy trial in which proof of the defendant's guilt may be difficult to establish.

Prosecutorial discretion The decision-making power of prosecutors based on the wide range of choices available to them in handling criminal defendants, scheduling cases for trial, and accepting bargained pleas. The most important form of prosecutorial discretion lies in the power to charge or not to charge a person with an offense.

Prosecutorial information A criminal charge against someone filed by the prosecutor.

Prosecutorial misconduct Any deliberate action that violates ethical codes or standards governing the role of prosecutors; usually the action is intended to injure defendants and illegally or unethically strengthen the case of prosecutors.

Prosecutorial waiver Authority of prosecutors in juvenile cases to have those cases transferred to the jurisdiction of criminal court.

Proximate cause The factor that is closest to actually causing an event, such as the death of a victim.

Public defender agency Any local, state, or federal organization, public or private, established to provide a defense to indigent clients or those who otherwise cannot afford to pay for their own defense against criminal charges. Because everyone is entitled to counsel, whether or not counsel can be afforded, such services exist to meet the needs of those without funds to hire private counsel.

Public defender system Means by which attorneys are appointed by the court to represent indigent defendants.

Punishment Any sanction imposed for committing a crime; usually a sentence imposed for being convicted of either a felony or misdemeanor.

Quash To vacate a sentence or annul a motion.

Real evidence Physical evidence such as a weapon, records, fingerprints, or stolen property.

Reasonable doubt Standard used by jurors to decide if the prosecution has provided sufficient evidence for conviction. Jurors vote for acquittal if they have reasonable doubt that the accused committed the crime.

Reasonable suspicion Warranted suspicion (short of probable cause) that a person may be engaged in criminal conduct.

Rebutting testimony, evidence Any questioning or presentation of evidence designed to offset, outweigh, or overwhelm evidence presented by the other side or to question the veracity or truthfulness of witnesses.

Recall election Special election called to remove a politician or judge from office.

Recognizance Personal responsibility to return to court on a given date and at a given time.

Recross-examination Opposing counsel further examines an opposing witness who has already testified.

Recusal Act of judges excusing themselves from proceedings, especially if they have an apparent conflict of interest in the case being tried.

Redirect examination Questioning of a witness following the adversary's questioning under cross-examination.

Referral Any citation of a juvenile to juvenile court by a law enforcement officer, interested citizen, family member, or school official; usually based on law violations, delinquency, or unruly conduct.

Reformatory Detention facility designed to change criminal behavior or reform it.

Refreshing one's memory, reminding During testimony, witnesses may have their memories refreshed by rereading some document or looking at pictures to enable them to recall with greater clarity something that happened some time ago.

Rehabilitation, rehabilitative ideal Correcting criminal behavior through educational and other means, usually associated with prisons.

Reintegration Punishment philosophy that promotes programs that lead offenders back into their communities. Reintegrative programs include furloughs, work release, and halfway houses.

Release on own recognizance (ROR) Arrangement in which a defendant is set free temporarily to await a later trial without having to post a bail bond; persons released on ROR are usually well known or have strong ties to the community and have not been charged with serious crimes.

Remand To send back (e.g., the U.S. Supreme Court may remand a case back to the lower trial court where the case was originally tried).

Remedy Any declared solution to a dispute between parties (e.g., if someone is found guilty of slashing another's automobile tires, the remedy may be to cause the convicted offender to compensate the victim with money for the full value of the destroyed tires).

Reparations Damages paid to victims for injuries incurred as a result of the actions of a perpetrator.

Res judicata "Things judged." Refers to matters already decided in court, not subject to relitigation.

Respondeat superior Doctrine under which liability is imposed on an employer for the acts of his employees that are committed in the course and scope of their employment.

Respondent A person asked to respond in a lawsuit or writ.

Responsible Legally accountable for one's actions and obligations.

Restitution Stipulation by court that offenders must compensate victims for their financial losses resulting from the crime. Compensation to victim for psychological, physical, or financial loss. May be imposed as a part of an incarcerative sentence.

Restorative justice Mediation between victims and offenders in which offenders accept responsibility for their actions and agree to reimburse victims for their losses; may involve community service and other penalties agreeable to both parties in a form of arbitration with a neutral third party acting as arbiter.

Reverse waiver hearings Any proceedings initiated by a juvenile defendant to have a case reassigned to the juvenile court instead of being tried in criminal court.

Reversed and remanded Decision by appellate court to set aside or overturn the verdict of a lower trial court with instructions to the trial court to rehear the case with suggested modifications.

Reversible errors Mistakes committed by judges during a trial that may result in reversal of convictions against defendants.

Review The procedure by which a higher court examines one or more issues emanating from a lower court on an appeal by the prosecution or defense.

Right of allocution Right of defendant to speak before sentence is pronounced.

Right to counsel Right to be represented by an attorney at critical stages of the criminal justice system. Indigent defendants have the right to counsel provided by state.

Rights of defendant Constitutional guarantees to all persons charged with crimes; includes representation by counsel at various critical stages, such as being charged with crimes, preliminary hearings, arraignments, trial, and appeals.

ROR *See* Release on own recognizance.

Rule of Four A U.S. Supreme Court rule whereby the court grants *certiorari* only on the agreement of at least four justices.

Rule of law Describes willingness of people to accept and order their behavior according to rules and procedures that are prescribed by political and social institutions.

Rules of Civil Procedure Rules governing civil cases where compensatory damages are sought. Rules governing courts of equity.

Rules of Criminal Procedure Rules legislatively established by which a criminal case is conducted. Law enforcement officers, prosecutors, and judges use rules of criminal procedure in discretionary actions against suspects and defendants.

Runaways Youths who leave their homes for several days or longer without permission or supervision.

Scientific jury selection Applying the scientific method to select jurors who, it is believed, will render favorable decisions for or against defendants.

Screening Process of jury selection by attempting to remove biased jurors and select only the most competent and objective ones.

Screening cases Procedure used by prosecutor to define which cases have prosecutive merit and which do not. Some screening bureaus are made up of police and lawyers with trial experience.

Seal To close from public inspection any record of an arrest, judgment, or adjudication, either criminal or juvenile.

Secure custody, confinement Incarceration of juvenile offender in facility that restricts movement in community. Similar to adult penal facility involving total incarceration.

Selective chivalry View that judges tend to favor white females in their sentencing decisions compared with females of other races or ethnicities or males.

Self-defense Affirmative defense in which defendants explain otherwise criminal conduct by showing necessity to defend themselves against aggressive victims.

Self-incrimination The act of exposing oneself to prosecution by answering questions that may demonstrate involvement in illegal behavior. Coerced self-incrimination is not allowed under the Fifth Amendment. In any criminal proceeding, the prosecution must prove the charges by means of evidence other than the testimony of the accused.

Self-representation *See Pro se.*

Sentence Penalty imposed on a convicted person for a crime. May include incarceration, fine, both, or some other alternative. *See also* Mandatory sentencing, Presumptive sentencing, Indeterminate sentencing, Determinate sentencing.

Sentence bargaining Any negotiation between prosecutors and defense attorneys for the prosecutor's recommendation of a reduced sentence in exchange for a guilty plea to a lesser charge from a defendant.

Sentence disparity *See* Sentencing disparity.

Sentence hearing *See* Sentencing hearing.

Sentence recommendation bargaining Negotiation in which the prosecutor proposes a sentence in exchange for a guilty plea. *See also* Plea bargaining.

Sentencing Process of imposing a punishment on a convicted person following a criminal conviction.

Sentencing disparity Inconsistency in sentencing of convicted offenders, in which those committing similar crimes under similar circumstances are given widely disparate sentences by the same judge. Usually based on gender, race, ethnic, or socioeconomic factors.

Sentencing guidelines Instruments developed by the federal government and various states to assist judges in assessing fair and consistent lengths of incarceration for various crimes and past criminal histories. Referred to as presumptive sentencing in some jurisdictions.

Sentencing hearing Optional hearing held in many jurisdictions in which defendants and victims can hear contents of presentence investigation reports prepared by probation officers. Defendants and/or victims may respond to the report orally, in writing, or both. A hearing precedes the sentence imposed by the judge.

Sentencing memorandum Court decision that furnishes a ruling or finding and orders it to be implemented relative to convicted offenders. Does not necessarily include reasons or rationale for sentence imposed.

Sentencing Reform Act of 1984 Act that provided federal judges and others with considerable discretionary powers to provide alternative sentencing and other provisions in their sentencing of various offenders.

Sequester, sequestration The insulation of jurors from the outside world so that their decision making cannot be influenced or affected by extralegal factors.

Sequestered jury A jury that is isolated from the public during the course of a trial and throughout the deliberation process.

Serious felonies Any crime punishable by more than a year in prison or jail that causes substantial property loss or fraud; may include some crimes against persons, such as robbery.

Service of process The act of serving a summons to notify someone to be in court at a particular time.

Severance Separation of related cases so that they can be tried separately in different courts.

Sexual predator laws Somewhat ambiguous laws enacted in various states to identify and control previously convicted sex offenders; may include listing such persons in public announcements or bulletins or some other form of community notification.

Shadow juries People who resemble actual jurors and are used by both prosecutors and defense counsel to test their ideas prior to trials; shadow juries emulate actual jurors in criminal cases in terms of their background characteristics and attitudes.

Shock incarceration *See* Shock probation.

Shock parole *See* Shock probation.

Shock probation Sentencing offenders to prison or jail for a brief period, primarily to give them a taste or "shock" of prison or jail life, and then releasing them into the custody of a probation or parole officer through a resentencing project.

Sides Opposing parties in an adversarial relation, usually in the courtroom; prosecutors and defense counsel are considered "sides" in the adversarial system of U.S. justice.

Social change Process whereby ideas and/or practices are modified either actively or passively or naturally.

Social control Informal and formal methods of getting members of society to conform to norms, folkways, and mores.

Society for the Prevention of Pauperism Philanthropic society that established the first public reformatory in New York in 1825, the New York House of Refuge.

Sociological jurisprudence View that holds that part of law should be devoted to making or shaping public policy and social rules.

Solitary confinement *See* Isolation.

Speedy trial Defined by federal law and applicable to federal district courts, where a defendant must be tried within 100 days of an arrest. Every state has speedy-trial provisions that are within reasonable ranges of the federal standard. Originally designed to comply with the Sixth Amendment of the U.S. Constitution. The longest state speedy-trial provision is in New Mexico, which is 180 days.

Speedy Trial Act of 1974 (amended 1979, 1984) Compliance with Sixth Amendment provision for a citizen to be brought to trial without undue delay thirty to seventy days from date of formal specification of charges, usually in arraignment proceeding.

Spirit of the law Efforts by police officers to exhibit leniency when law violations are observed. Usually first offenders may receive leniency because of extenuating circumstances.

Split sentencing Procedure whereby a judge imposes a sentence of incarceration for a fixed period, followed by a probationary period of a fixed duration. Similar to shock probation.

Spontaneous declaration An excited utterance, such as confessing to a crime during emotional stress at the crime scene.

Standard of proof Norms used by courts to determine validity of claims or allegations of wrongdoing against offenders; civil standards of proof are "clear and convincing evidence" and "preponderance of evidence," while the criminal standard is "beyond a reasonable doubt."

Standing A doctrine mandating that courts may not recognize a party to a suit unless that person has a personal stake or direct interest in the outcome of the suit.

Stare decisis Legal precedent. Principle whereby lower courts issue rulings consistent with those of higher courts, when the same types of cases and facts are at issue. The principle of leaving undisturbed a settled point of law or particular precedent.

State bar associations Professional organizations of lawyers bound to observe the laws of the various states where they reside; state affiliate organizations in relation to the national American Bar Association.

State's attorneys Government prosecutors.

Status offenders Juveniles who have committed an offense that would not be considered a crime if committed by an adult (e.g., a curfew violation would not be a criminal action if committed by an adult, but such an act is a status offense if engaged in by a juvenile).

Status offense Any act committed by a juvenile that would not be a crime if committed by an adult.

Statute of limitations Period of time after which a crime that has been committed cannot be prosecuted. No statute of limitations exists for capital crimes.

Statutes Laws passed by legislatures. Statutory definitions of criminal offenses are embodied in penal codes.

Statutory exclusion Provisions that automatically exclude certain juveniles and offenses from the jurisdiction of the juvenile courts (e.g., murder, aggravated rape, armed robbery).

Statutory law Authority based on enactments of state legislatures. Laws passed by legislatures.

Stigmas The result of the process of being labeled as a delinquent or unruly child by others.

Stigmatization Social process whereby offenders acquire undesirable characteristics as the result of imprisonment or court appearances. Undesirable criminal or delinquent labels are assigned to those who are processed through the criminal and juvenile justice systems.

Stigmatize The process of labeling someone as a delinquent or a criminal on the basis of their exhibited behavior.

Strike for cause *See* Challenge for cause.

Subject matter jurisdiction Term applied when certain judges have exclusive jurisdiction over particular crimes.

Subornation of perjury The crime of procuring someone to lie under oath.

Subpoena Document issued by a judge ordering a named person to appear in court at a particular time to either answer to charges or testify in a case.

Substantive criminal law Legislated rule that governs behaviors that are required or prohibited. Usually enacted by legislatures. Such law also specifies punishments accompanying such law violations.

Substantive due process Refers to the practice of having substantive law conform to the principles of fairness set forth in the U.S. Constitution.

Substantive law Body of law that creates, discovers, and defines the rights and obligations of each person in society. Prescribes behavior, whereas procedural law prescribes how harmful behavior is handled.

Summary judgment Any granted motion following the presentation of a case against a defendant in a civil court. Any argument countering the plaintiff's presented evidence. Usually the result of failing to state a claim on which relief can be granted.

Summary justice Trial held by court of limited jurisdiction, without benefit of a jury trial.

Summation Closing remarks and persuasive arguments made by the prosecutor and defense counsel at the end of a trial before the jury.

Summons Same form as a warrant, except it commands a defendant to appear before the magistrate at a particular time and place.

Superior courts The courts of record or trial courts.

Suppression hearing Session held before a judge who presides at a defendant's trial. Purpose of the session is to determine which evidentiary documents and/or statements will be permitted later at trial. Motions are heard from both the defense and prosecution to keep out or put in particular evidence, and the judge decides which evidence can and cannot be introduced at trial.

Supra "Above." In U.S. Supreme Court written opinions, references are made to earlier statements (e.g., in the case of *Doe, supra,* the matter was concluded in a particular way).

Supreme Court The federal court of last resort as specified by the U.S. Constitution. Any court of last resort in most kinds of cases at the state level.

Surety bond A sum of money or property that is posted or guaranteed by a party to ensure the future court appearance of another person. *See also* Bail bond.

Surrebuttal Introducing witnesses during a criminal trial to disprove damaging testimony by other witnesses.

Sustain To uphold (e.g., the conviction was sustained by a higher appellate court).

Sustained petitions Adjudication resulting in a finding that the facts alleged in a petition are true; a finding that the juvenile committed the offenses alleged, which resulted in an adjudication and disposition.

Sworn in The process whereby persons who offer testimony in court swear to tell the truth and nothing but the truth, usually by oath upon the Bible.

Texas model Also known as the "traditional" model of state court organization. Two "supreme" courts, one for civil appeals, one for criminal appeals. Has five tiers of district, county, and municipal courts.

Three strikes and you're out Legislation designed to prevent offenders from becoming recidivists; provides that those who commit three or more serious felonies are in jeopardy of being incarcerated for life terms.

Three-strikes-and-you're-out policies A crime prevention and control strategy that proposes to incarcerate those offenders who commit and are convicted of three or more serious or violent offenses; the usual penalty is life imprisonment or the life without parole option. The intent is to incarcerate high-rate offenders to reduce crime in society. *See also* Habitual offender statutes.

Tiers Different floor levels in prisons and jails where inmates are housed; usually, different tiers house different types of offenders according to their conviction offenses and offense seriousness.

Tort actions Any legal proceeding in which a plaintiff is seeking damages from a defendant for a civil wrong.

Tort reform Any action taken by an individual or group to revise existing rules governing tort actions in courts, including limiting monetary awards for prevailing in lawsuits.

Torts Private or civil wrongs or injuries, other than breach of contract, for which the court will provide a remedy in the form of an action for damages. A violation of a duty imposed by law. Existence of a legal duty to plaintiff, breach of that duty, and damage as a result of that breach.

Totality of circumstances Exception to exclusionary rule, whereby officers may make warrantless searches of property and seizures of illegal contraband on the basis of the entire set of suspicious circumstances; sometimes applied to bail decision making, where the entire set of circumstances is considered for people thought to be eligible for bail.

Traditional courts Juvenile proceedings characterized by individualized treatments and prescriptions for assistance; the opposite of due process courts.

Transcript A written record of a trial or hearing.

Transfer Proceeding to determine whether juveniles should be certified as adults for purposes of being subjected to jurisdiction of adult criminal courts, where more severe penalties may be imposed. Also known as certification or waiver.

Transfers Proceedings in which the jurisdiction over juvenile offenders shifts from the juvenile court to criminal court.

Trial An adversarial proceeding within a particular jurisdiction, in which a judicial examination and determination of issues can be made, and in which a criminal defendant's guilt or innocence can be decided impartially by either a judge or jury. *See also* Bench trial, Jury trial.

Trial by the court *See* Bench trial.

Trial by the judge *See* Bench trial.

Trial court of general jurisdiction Criminal court that has jurisdiction over all offenses, including felonies, and may in some states also hear appeals from lower courts.

Trial court of limited jurisdiction Criminal court in which trial jurisdiction either includes no felonies or is limited to some category of felony. Such courts have jurisdiction over misdemeanor cases, probable cause hearings in felony cases, and sometimes felony trials that may result in penalties below a specific limit.

Trial *de novo* A new judicial hearing or proceeding. A new adversarial proceeding occurring as though there had never been a first trial or proceeding, usually granted to defendants if egregious wrongs or misconduct occurred to nullify former adjudicatory proceedings.

Trial delays Any one of several legitimate reasons that may contribute to delaying or prolonging the occasion that a trial commences; may be due to crowded court dockets, requests from the defense or prosecution for more time in case preparation, or the health of different courtroom actors, such as the prosecutor, defense counsel, or defendant.

Trial judge *See* Judge.

Trial jury *See* Petit jury.

Trial sufficiency Presence of sufficient legal elements to ensure successful prosecution of a case. When the prosecutor's decision to prosecute a case is customarily based on trial sufficiency, only cases that seem certain to result in conviction at trial are accepted for prosecution. Use of plea bargaining is minimal. Good police work and court capacity are required.

Tribunal A court. A place where judges sit. A judicial weighing of information leading to a decision about a case.

Truants Any juveniles who are absent from their schools without a valid excuse.

True bill Grand jury decision that sufficient evidence exists that a crime has been committed and that a specific suspect committed it. A charge of an alleged crime. An indictment.

Truth in sentencing Policy of imposing a sentence, most of which must be served in prison or jail; maximizing a prisoner's incarceration under the law.

Truth-in-sentencing laws Any legislation intended to maximize sentences and time served for committing a crime; the intent is to compel offenders to serve at least eighty or ninety percent of their maximum sentences before they become eligible for parole or early release.

Typicality hypothesis View that women are given greater consideration than men during sentencing, but only when their criminal charges are consistent with stereotypes of female offenders.

Ultra vires Beyond the scope of one's prescribed authority.

U.S. attorneys Officials responsible for the prosecution of crimes that violate the laws of the United States. Appointed by the president and assigned to a U.S. district court jurisdiction.

U.S. Attorney's Office Chief prosecuting body affiliated with each U.S. district court in the federal court system.

U.S. Circuit Courts of Appeal Appellate courts from which U.S. district court decisions are appealed; cases appealed from the U.S. Circuit Courts of Appeal are appealed directly to the U.S. Supreme Court; there are thirteen circuit courts of appeal.

United States Code, United States Code Annotated Comprehensive compendium of federal laws and statutes, including landmark cases and discussions of law applications. Annotated version contains paragraphs of contemporary cases summarizing court decisions and applying specific statutes.

U.S. Courts of Appeals The federal circuit courts of appellate jurisdiction. As of 1996, there were thirteen circuit courts of appeal zoned throughout the United States and its territories.

U.S. District Courts The basic trial courts for federal civil and criminal actions.

U.S. magistrates Judges who fulfill the pretrial judicial obligations of the federal courts. Formerly, U.S. commissioners.

U.S. Sentencing Commission Body of people originating from Sentencing Reform Act of 1984 that promulgated sentencing guidelines for all federal crimes.

U.S. Sentencing Guidelines Rules implemented by federal courts in November 1987, obligating federal judges to impose presumptive sentences on all convicted offenders. Guidelines are based on offense seriousness and offender characteristics. Judges may depart from guidelines only by justifying their departures in writing.

U.S. Supreme Court The actual court of last resort; final and highest court, which decides particular issues, usually issues with constitutional significance.

Vacate To annul, set aside, or rescind.

Vacated sentence Any sentence that has been declared nullified by the action of a court.

Venire, venireman list, veniremen List of prospective jurors made up from registered voters, vehicle driver's licenses, or tax assessor's records. People must reside within the particular jurisdiction where the jury trial is held. People who are potential jurors in a given jurisdiction.

Venue Area over which a judge exercises authority to act in an official capacity. Place where a trial is held.

Venue, change of Relocation of a trial from one site to another, usually because pretrial publicity has made it possible that a jury might be biased and that a fair trial will be difficult to obtain.

Verdict Decision by judge or jury concerning the guilt or innocence of a defendant.

Verdict-driven jury Body that decides guilt or innocence first without adequately considering the relevant evidence in the case; jurors are polled initially to see to what extent they agree or disagree among themselves; if most or all jurors vote the same way, then they conclude their deliberations without further consideration of the evidence.

Verdict, guilty In criminal proceedings, the decision made by a jury in a jury trial, or by a judicial officer in a bench trial, that defendants are guilty of the offense(s) for which they have been tried.

Verdict, not guilty In criminal proceedings, the decision made by the jury in a jury trial, or by the judge in a bench trial, that defendants are not guilty of the offense(s) for which they have been tried.

Verstehen Understanding. The notion that social scientists can understand human behavior through empathy.

Vicarious liability Doctrine under which liability is imposed on an employer for the acts of employees that are committed in the course and scope of their employment.

Vice principal doctrine Theory holding that someone may be sued by another if he or she is a supervisor or boss, and not necessarily the owner of an organization.

Victim Person who has either suffered death or serious physical or mental suffering or loss of property resulting from actual or attempted criminal actions committed by others.

Victim compensation Any financial restitution payable to victims by either the state or convicted offenders.

Victim compensation programs Any plans for assisting crime victims in making social, emotional, and economic adjustments.

Victim impact statement Information or version of events filed voluntarily by the victim of a crime, appended to the presentence investigation report as a supplement for judicial consideration in sentencing the offender. Describes injuries to victims resulting from convicted offender's actions.

Victim–offender mediation model Meeting between criminal and person suffering loss or injury from the criminal during which a third-party arbiter, such as a judge, attorney, or other neutral party decides what is best for all parties. All parties must agree to the decision of the third-party arbiter. Used for both juvenile and adult offenders.

Victim–offender reconciliation Any agreement between the victim and the perpetrator concerning a satisfactory arrangement for compensation of injuries or financial losses sustained.

Victim–Offender Reconciliation Project (VORP) Form of alternative dispute resolution whereby a civil resolution is made by mutual consent between the victim and an offender; objectives are to provide restitution to victims, hold offender accountable for crime committed, and reduce recidivism.

Victim-reparations model Restitution model for juveniles in which juveniles compensate their victims directly for their offenses.

Victims of Crime Act of 1984 Also known as the Comprehensive Crime Control Act of 1984; includes sanctions against offenders such as victim compensation, community service, and restitution.

Victim-witness assistance programs Plans available to prospective witnesses to explain court procedures and inform them of court dates and to assist witnesses in providing better testimony in court.

Violent felonies Any crime punishable by more than one year in a prison or jail that causes serious bodily injury or death (e.g., rape, aggravated assault, murder).

Virginia Exile Program that targets three types of crimes: (1) possession of a firearm by a convicted felon, (2) possession of a firearm on school property with the intent to use it or displaying it in a threatening manner, and (3) possession of a firearm and drugs such as cocaine or heroin.

Virginia plan Scheme deriving from England's royal court system, projecting superior and inferior courts; also called "Randolph plan."

Voir dire "To speak the truth." Interrogation process in which prospective jurors are questioned by either the judge or the prosecution or defense attorneys to determine their biases and prejudices.

Voluntariness Willingness of a defendant to enter a plea or make an agreement in a plea bargain proceeding. Judges must determine the voluntariness of the plea to determine that it was not coerced.

Waiver, waiver of jurisdiction Made by motion, the transfer of jurisdiction of a juvenile to a criminal court, where the juvenile is subject to adult criminal penalties. Includes judicial, prosecutorial, and legislative waivers. Also known as certification or transfer.

Waiver hearing Motion by a prosecutor to transfer a juvenile charged with various offenses to a criminal or adult court for prosecution, making it possible to sustain adult criminal penalties.

Warrant A written order directing a suspect's arrest and delivered by an official with the authority to issue the warrant. Commands suspect to be arrested and brought before the nearest magistrate.

Warrant, arrest Document issued by a judge that directs a law enforcement officer to arrest a person who has been accused of an offense.

Warrant, bench Document issued by a judge directing that a person who has failed to obey an order or notice to appear be brought before the court without undue delay.

Warrant, search Any document issued by a judicial official, based on probable cause, directing law enforcement officers to conduct an inspection of an individual, automobile, or building with the intent of locating particular contraband or incriminating evidence as set forth in the document.

With prejudice To dismiss charges, and those same charges cannot be brought again later against the same defendant.

Without prejudice To dismiss charges, and those same charges can be brought again later against the same defendant.

Without undue delay or unnecessary delay Standard used to determine whether the suspect has been brought in a timely manner before a magistrate or other judicial authority after arrest. Definition of undue delay varies among jurisdictions. Circumstances of arrest, availability of judge, and time of arrest are factors that determine reasonableness of delay.

Witnesses People who have relevant information about the commission of a crime; any person who has seen or heard inculpatory or exculpatory evidence that may incriminate or exonerate a defendant.

Writ A document issued by a judicial officer ordering or forbidding the performance of a specific act.

Writ of *certiorari* An order of a superior court requesting that the record of an inferior court (or administrative body) be brought forward for review or inspection. Literally, "to be more fully informed."

Writ of error A writ issued by an appellate court for the purpose of correcting an error revealed in the record of a lower court proceeding.

Writ of habeas corpus *See* Habeas corpus.

Writ of *mandamus* An order of a superior court commanding that a lower court, administrative body, or executive body perform a specific function. Commonly used to restore rights and privileges lost to a defendant through illegal means.

Writ of prohibition An appellate court order that prevents a lower court from exercising its jurisdiction in a particular case.

REFERENCES

Aaronson, David E. (1977). *The New Justice: Alternatives to Conventional Criminal Adjudication.* Washington, DC: U.S. Government Printing Office.

Abel, Richard. (1990). "A Critique of Torts." *UCLA Law Review* **37:**785–831.

Abrams, Stan. (1995). "False Memory Syndrome vs. Total Repression." *Journal of Psychiatry and Law* **23:**283–293.

Acker, James R. and Charles S. Lanier. (1994). "In Fairness and Mercy: Statutory Mitigating Factors in Capital Punishment Cases." *Criminal Law Bulletin* **30:**299–345.

Acker, James R. and Charles S. Lanier. (1995). "Matters of Life or Death: The Sentencing Provisions in Capital Punishment Statutes." *Criminal Law Bulletin* **31:**19–60.

Adler, Stephen J. (1994). *The Jury: Trial and Error in the American Courtroom.* New York: Times Books.

Adler, Stephen J. (1995). *The Jury: Disorder in the Court.* New York: Doubleday.

Albonetti, Celesta A. (1989). "Criminal Justice Decision Making As a Stratification Process: The Role of Race and Stratification Resources in Pretrial Release." *Journal of Quantitative Criminology* **5:**57–82.

Albrecht, Peter Alexis and Otto Backes (eds.). (1989). *Crime Prevention and Intervention: Legal and Ethical Problems.* New York: Walter de Gruyter.

Alfini, James J. (1981). "Mississippi Judicial Selection: Election, Appointment, and Bar Anointment." In *Courts and Judges,* James A. Cramer (ed.). Beverly Hills, CA: Sage.

Allen, G. Frederick and H. Treger. (1990). "Community Service Orders in Federal Probation: Perceptions of Probationers and Host Agencies." *Federal Probation* **54:**8–14.

Alschuler, Albert W. (1976). "The Trial Judge's Role in Plea Bargaining." *Columbia Law Review* **76:**1059–1154.

American Bar Association. (1972a). *Recommendations As Amended.* Chicago: American Bar Association Section of Criminal Law.

American Bar Association. (1972b). *Standards Relating to the Function of the Trial Judge.* Chicago: American Bar Association Advisory Committee on the Judge's Function.

American Bar Association. (1975). *Standards Relating to Trial Courts.* Chicago: American Bar Association Standards of Judicial Administration Commission.

American Bar Association. (1978). *Trial by Jury* (2nd ed.). Washington, DC: American Bar Association Standing Committee on Association Standards for Criminal Justice.

American Bar Association. (1992). *Achieving Justice in a Diverse America.* Washington, DC: American Bar Association Task Force on Minorities and the Justice System.

American Bar Association. (1994). *Just Solutions: A Program Guide to Innovative Justice System Improvements.* Chicago: American Judicature Society and the American Bar Association.

American Correctional Association. (1993). *Classification: A Tool for Managing Today's Offenders.* Laurel, MD: American Correctional Association.

American Judicature Society. (1971). *The National Picture: Merit Judicial Selection and Tenure.* Chicago: American Judicature Society.

American Judicature Society. (1973). "State Court Progress at a Glance." *Judicature* **56:**427–430.

American Judicature Society. (1979). *Merit Selection 1979, Merit Selection of Judges: How Is It Working?* Chicago: American Judicature Society.

American Judicature Society. (1983). *Report to the Committee on Qualification Guidelines for Judicial Candidates.* Chicago: American Judicature Society.

Arcuri, Alan F. (1976). "Lawyers, Judges, and Plea Bargaining: Some New Data on Inmates' Views." *International Journal of Criminology and Penology* **4:**177–191.

Asch, Solomon E. (1966). "Effect of Group Pressure upon the Modification and Distortion of Judgments." *Group Dynamics* **14:**189–199.

Ashford, Jose B. and Craig Winston LaCroy. (1993). "Juvenile Parole Policy in the United States: Determinate versus Indeterminate Models." *Justice Quarterly* **10:**179–195.

Ashworth, Andrew J. (1993). "Sentencing Reform Structures." In *Crime and Justice: A Review of Research,* Vol. 16, Michael Tonry (ed.). Chicago: University of Chicago Press.

Associated Press. (1998). "Judge Who Drank after Trial Quits." *Minot* (N.D.) *Daily News,* April 8, 1998:A2.

Association of the Bar of the City of New York. (1979). *Final Report and Recommendations.* New York: Association of the Bar of the City of New York, Special Committee on Criminal Justice.

Austin, James et al. (1995). *National Assessment of Structured Sentencing.* Washington, DC: U.S. Bureau of Justice Statistics.

Axon, Lee and Robert G. Hann. (1995). *Court Dispute Resolution Processes: The Application of Alternative Dispute Resolution in the Courts.* Ottawa: Department of Justice, Research, Statistics and Evaluation Directorate.

Bagley, Harold. (1970). "Improvident Guilty Pleas and Related Statement Inadmissible Evidence at Later Trial." *Criminal Law Bulletin* **6:**3–25.

Bak, Thomas. (1994). *Defendants Who Avoid Detention: A Good Risk?* Washington, DC: Statistics Division, Administrative Office of the United States Courts.

Barbara, Michael A. (1970). "Noblesse Oblige—Duty of Prosecution to Disclose Evidence in a Criminal Case." *Washburn Law Journal* **10:**54–58.

Barnes, Allan R. (1988). *Disparities between Felony Charges at Time of Arrest and Those at Time of Prosecution.* Anchorage: Alaska Statistical Analysis Unit.

Baron, Stephanie B. (1981). "Pretrial Sentence Bargaining: A Cure for Crowded Court Dockets?" *Emory Law Journal* **30:**853–892.

Barrette, Joseph A. (1983). "Plea Bargains and New York's Newly Created Right of Prosecutors." *Syracuse Law Review* **34:**575–617.

Baum, Lawrence. (1983). "The Electoral Fates of Incumbent Judges in the Ohio Court of Common Pleas." *Judicature* **66:**420–430.

Baxter, Brent L. and Jeanne E. Kleyn. (1992). *Washington State's Second Offender Laws for Driving While Intoxicated: Results of Six Years of Evaluation.* Seattle: Alcohol and Drug Abuse Institute, University of Washington.

Bazemore, Gordon. (1994). "Developing a Victim Orientation for Community Corrections: A Restorative Justice Paradigm and a Balanced Mission." *APPA Perspectives* **18**:19–24.

Bazemore, Gordon and Dennis Maloney. (1994). "Rehabilitative Community Service: Toward Restorative Service Sanctions in a Balanced Justice System." *Federal Probation* **58**:24–34.

Beck, Robert Keith. (1972). "Discovery in New York: The Effect of the New Criminal Procedure." *Syracuse Law Review* **23**:89–112.

Becker, Jordan D. (1985). "Removing Temptation: Per Se Reversal for Judicial Indication of Belief in the Defendant's Guilt." *Fordham Law Review* **53**:1333–1356.

Beckley, Loren A., Christine Callahan, and Robert M. Carter. (1981). *Presentence Investigation Report Program.* Sacramento, CA: American Justice Institute.

Beckman, David L. (1986). "Sixth Amendment— Effective Assistance of Counsel: A Defense Attorney's Right to Refuse Cooperation in Defendant's Perjured Testimony." *Journal of Criminal Law and Criminology* **77**:692–712.

Beechen, Paul D. (1974). "Can Judicial Elections Express the People's Choice?" *Judicature* **57**:242–256.

Bell, Bernard P. (1983). "Closure of Pretrial Suppression Hearings: Resolving the Fair Trial/Free Press Conflict." *Fordham Law Review* **51**:1297–1316.

Belsky, Martin H. (1984). "On Becoming and Being a Prosecutor." *Northwestern University Law Review* **78**:1485–1521.

Benda, Brent B. (1987). "Comparison of Rates of Recidivism among Status Offenders and Delinquents." *Adolescence* **22**:445–458.

Bensinger, Gad J. (1988). "Operation Greylord and Its Aftermath." *International Journal of Comparative and Applied Criminal Justice* **12**:111–118.

Bergman, Jeffrey H. (1986). "Insuring the Accuracy of the Presentence Investigation Report in the Wisconsin Correctional System." *Wisconsin Law Review* **44**:613–631.

Berkson, Larry and Susan B. Carbon. (1980). *The United States Circuit Judge Nominating Commission: Its Members, Procedures, and Candidates.* Chicago: American Judicature Society.

Berkson, Larry and Steven Hays. (1977). "Applying Organization and Management Theory to the Selection of Lower Court Personnel." *Criminal Justice Review* **2**:81–91.

Berkson, Larry and Donna Vandenberg. (1980). *National Roster of Women Judges, 1980.* Chicago: American Judicature Society, National Association of Women's Judges.

Berlage, Derick P. (1984). "Pleas of the Condemned: Should Certiorari Petitions from Death Row Receive Enhanced Access to the Supreme Court?" *New York University Law Review* **59**:1120–1148.

Bermant, G. and J. Shapard. (1981).The Voir Dire Examination, Juror Challenges and Adversary Advocacy. *Perspectives in Law and Psychology: Vol 2, The Trial Process.* New York: McGraw-Hill.

Bernstein, Ilene N. et al. (1977). "Charge Reduction: An Intermediary Stage in the Process of Labeling Criminal Defendants." *Social Forces* **56**:362–384.

Bilchik, Shay. (1995). *Unlocking the Doors for Status Offenders: The State of the States.* Washington, DC: Office of Juvenile Justice and Delinquency Prevention.

Bilchik, Shay. (1996). *State Responses to Serious and Violent Juvenile Crime.* Pittsburgh: National Center for Juvenile Justice.

Black, Henry Campbell. (1990). *Black's Law Dictionary.* St. Paul, MN: West.

Blackmore, John, Marci Brown, and Barry Krisberg. (1988). *Juvenile Justice Reform: The Bellwether States.* Ann Arbor: University of Michigan.

Blankenship, Michael B., Jerry B. Sparger, and W. Richard Janikowski. (1994). "Accountability v. Independence: Myths of Judicial Selection." *Criminal Justice Policy Review* **6:**69–79.

Block, Michael K. and Steven J. Twist. (1995). *Evidence of a Failed System: A Study of the Performance of Pretrial Release Agencies in California.* Washington, DC: American Legislative Exchange Council.

Bloom, Barbara, Meda Chesney-Lind, and Barbara Owen. (1994). *Women in California Prisons: Hidden Victims of the War on Drugs.* San Francisco: Center on Juvenile and Criminal Justice.

Boaz, Julia E. (1985). "Summary Processes and the Rule of Law: Expediting Death Penalty Cases in the Federal Courts." *Yale Law Journal* **95:**349–370.

Bodapati, Madhava, Mark Jones, and James Marquart. (1995). "The Sentencing Practices of Judges and Juries: A Comparative Analysis Using Texas Drug Offenders." *Journal of Crime and Justice* **18:**181–203.

Borman, Paul and Barbara Smith. (1992). *Survey on the Impact of the U.S. Sentencing Guidelines on the Federal Criminal Justice System.* Washington, DC: American Bar Association, Criminal Justice Section.

Boudouris, James and Bruce W. Turnbull. (1985). "Shock Probation in Iowa." *Journal of Offender Counseling, Services and Rehabilitation* **9:**53–67.

Bowman, Matthew W. D. (1986). "The Right to Counsel during Custodial Interrogation: Equivocal References to an Attorney—Determining What Statements or Conduct Should Constitute an Accused's Invocation of the Right to Counsel." *Vanderbilt Law Review* **39:**1159–1164.

Bradley, Craig M. (1987). "Criminal Procedure in the Rehnquist Court: Has the Rehnquistion Begun?" *Indiana Law Review* **62:**273–294.

Bradley, Craig M. (1988). "Supreme Court Review." *Journal of Criminal Law and Criminology* **79:**573–1063.

Brady, James R. (1983). "Fair and Impartial Railroad: The Jury, the Media, and Political Trials." *Journal of Criminal Justice* **11:**241–263.

Braithwaite, William Thomas. (1971). *Who Judges the Judges? A Study of Procedures for Removal and Retirement.* Chicago: American Bar Foundation.

Brannigan, Augustine, J. C. Levy, and James C. Wilkins. (1985). *The Preparation of Witnesses and Pretrial Construction of Testimony.* Calgary: Research Unit for Socio-Legal Studies.

Brannon, Marilyn E. et al. (1990). "Toward the Nonpathological Assessment of Behavioral and Conduct Disordered Adolescents." *Journal of Addictions and Offender Counseling* **11:**20–30.

Bratton, Howard C. (1970). "Standards for the Administration of Criminal Justice." *American Criminal Law Quarterly* **8:**146–155.

Breckenridge, S. P. (1906). "Legislative Control of Women's Work." *Journal of Political Economy* **15:**115–120.

Brennan, William J. et al. (1994). "Symposium on Capital Punishment." *Notre Dame Journal of Law, Ethics, and Public Policy* **8:**1–419.

Broderick, Vincent L. et al. (1993). "Pretrial Release and Detention and Pretrial Services." *Federal Probation* **57:**4–79.

Brody, Arthur L. and Richard Green. (1994). "Washington State's Unscientific Approach to the Problem of Repeat Sex Offenders." *Bulletin of the American Academy of Psychiatry and the Law* **22:**343–356.

Brody, David C. (1995). "Sparf and Dougherty Revisited: Why the Court Should Instruct the Jury of Its Nullification Right." *American Criminal Law Review* **33:**89–122.

Brooks, Alexander D. (1996). "Megan's Law: Constitutionality and Policy." *Criminal Justice Ethics* **15:**56–66.

Brooks, Daniel. (1985). "Penalizing Judges Who Appeal Disciplinary Sanctions: The Unconstitutionality of 'Upping the Ante.'" *Judicature* **69:**95–102.

Browning, James R., Collins J. Seitz, and Charles Clark. (1986). *Illustrative Rules Governing Complaints of Judicial Misconduct and Disability.* Washington, DC: Federal Judicial Center.

Buddingh, Jan D. (1982). "California's 'Use a Gun—Go to Prison' Laws and Their Relationship to the Determinate Sentencing Scheme." *Criminal Justice Journal* **5:**297–324.

Budeiri, Priscilla. (1981). "Collateral Consequences of Guilty Pleas in the Federal Criminal Justice System." *Harvard Civil Rights–Civil Liberties Law Review* **16:**157–203.

Bulkey, Josephine A. (1985). *Evidentiary and Procedural Trends in State Legislation and Other Emerging Legal Issues in Child Sexual Abuse Cases.* Washington, DC: National Legal Resource Center for Child Advocacy and Protection, American Bar Association.

Bureau of Justice Statistics. (1988). *Criminal Defense of the Poor.* Washington, DC: U.S. Department of Justice, Bureau of Justice Statistics.

Bureau of Justice Statistics. (1997). *Felony Sentences in State Courts, 1994.* Washington, DC: Bureau of Justice Statistics, Office of Justice Programs, U.S. Department of Justice.

Burger, Warren. (1982). "Isn't There a Better Way?" *American Bar Association Journal* **68:**274–275.

Burton, Bob. (1984). *Bounty Hunter.* Boulder, CO: Paladin Press.

Butts, Jeffrey A. (1996a). *Offenders in Juvenile Court, 1994.* Washington, DC: Office of Juvenile Justice and Delinquency Prevention.

Butts, Jeffrey A. (1996b). "Speedy Trial in Juvenile Court." *American Journal of Criminal Law* **23:**515–561.

Butts, Jeffrey A. and Paul DeMuro. (1989). *Risk Assessment of Adjudicated Delinquents.* Ann Arbor: Center for the Study of Youth Policy, University of Michigan.

Butts, Jeffrey A. and Jeffrey Gable. (1992). *Juvenile Detention in Cook County and the Feasibility of Alternatives.* Pittsburgh: National Center for Juvenile Justice.

Butts, Jeffrey A. and Gregory J. Halemba. (1996). *Waiting for Justice: Moving Young Offenders through the Juvenile Court Process.* Pittsburgh: National Center for Juvenile Justice.

Butts, Jeffrey A. and Eileen Poe. (1993). *Offenders in Juvenile Court, 1990.* Washington, DC: Office of Juvenile Justice and Delinquency Prevention.

Butts, Jeffrey A. et al. (1996). *Juvenile Court Statistics, 1993: Statistics Report.* Washington, DC: Office of Juvenile Justice and Delinquency Prevention.

Byrne, James M. (1989). "The Effectiveness of the New Intensive Supervision Program." *Research in Corrections* **2:**1–75.

Cahalan, Margaret W. (1986). *Historical Corrections Statistics in the United States, 1850–1984.* Washington, DC: U.S. Department of Justice.

California Assembly. (1981). *Interim Hearing on the Future of Probation in Crime Control.* Sacramento: Assembly Publications Office.

California Judicial Council. (1993). *Effects of Proposition 115 on California Trial Court Caseloads.* San Francisco: California Judicial Council, Administrative Office of the Courts.

California Judicial Council. (1994). *Analysis of the Supreme Court's Workload.* San Francisco: California Judicial Council, Administrative Office of the Courts.

Camp, Camille Graham and George M. Camp. (1997). *The Corrections Yearbook ,1997.* South Salem, NY: Criminal Justice Institute.

Campaign for an Effective Crime Policy. (1993). *Evaluating Mandatory Minimum Sentences.* Washington, DC: Campaign for an Effective Crime Policy.

Campaign for an Effective Crime Policy. (1996). *The Impact of "Three Strikes and You're Out" Laws: What Have We Learned?* Washington, DC: Public Policy Reports Series.

Canada Law Reform Commission. (1979). *Studies on the Jury.* Ottawa: Canada Law Reform Commission.

Canon, Bradley C. (1972). "The Impact of Formal Selection Processes on the Characteristics of Judges Reconsidered." *Law and Society Review* **6:**579–593.

Cardinale, Philip J. and Steven Feldman. (1978). "The Federal Courts and the Right to Nondiscriminatory Administration of the Criminal Law: A Critical View." *Syracuse Law Review* **29:**659–696.

Carns, Teresa White and John Kruse. (1991). *Alaska's Plea Bargaining Ban Re-Evaluated: Executive Summary.* Anchorage: Alaska Judicial Council.

Carr, James G. (ed.). (1995). *Criminal Law Review, 1995.* Deerfield, IL: Clark Boardman Callaghan.

Carroll, John L. (1986). "The Defense Lawyer's Role in the Sentencing Process: You've Got to Accentuate the Positive and Eliminate the Negative." *Mercer Law Review* **37:**981–1004.

Carroll, J. et al. (1986). "Free Press and Fair Trial: The Role of Behavioral Research." *Law and Human Behavior* **10:** 187–202.

Ceci, Stephen J. and Maggie Bruck. (1995). *Jeopardy in the Courtroom: A Scientific Analysis of Children's Testimony.* Washington, DC: American Psychological Association.

Cecil, Joe S. and Thomas E. Willging. (1993). *Court-Appointed Experts: Defining the Role of Experts Appointed under Federal Rule of Evidence 706.* Washington, DC: U.S. Federal Judicial Center.

Celebrezze, Frank D. (1987). "Prosecutorial Misconduct: Quelling the Tide of Improper Comment to the Jury." *Prosecutor* **21:**51–56.

Chaiken, Jan M. (1996). *Federal Criminal Case Processing, 1982–1993.* Washington, DC: U.S. Department of Justice.

Champagne, Anthony. (1988). "Judicial Reform in Texas." *Judicature* **72:**146–159.

Champion, Dean J. (1988). "Private Counsels and Public Defenders: A Look at Weak Cases, Prior Records, and Leniency in Plea Bargaining." *Journal of Criminal Justice* **17:**253–263.

Champion, Dean J. (ed.). (1989). *The U.S. Sentencing Guidelines: Implications for Criminal Justice.* New York: Praeger.

Champion, Dean J. (1992). *The Use of Attorneys in Juvenile Courts in Five States: A Trend Analysis, 1980–1989.* Pittsburgh: National Center for Juvenile Justice.

Champion, Dean J. (1996). *Probation, Parole and Community Corrections* (2nd ed.). Upper Saddle River, NJ: Prentice Hall.

Champion, Dean J. (1997). *Criminal Justice in the United States.* Belmont, CA: Wadsworth.

Champion, Dean J. (1999). *Probation, Parole, and Community Corrections* (3rd ed.). Upper Saddle River, NJ: Prentice Hall.

Champion, Dean J. and G. Larry Mays. (1991). *Juvenile Transfer Hearings: Some Trends and Implications for Juvenile Justice.* New York: Praeger.

Chilton, Bradley S. (1993). "Reforming Plea Bargaining to Facilitate Ethical Discourse." *Criminal Justice Policy Review* **5:**322–334.

Church, Thomas. (1976). "Plea Bargains, Concessions and the Courts: Analysis of a Quasi-Experiment." *Law and Society Review* **10:**377–401.

Cirincione, Carmen. (1996). "Revisiting the Insanity Defense: Contested or Consensus?" *Bulletin of the American Academy of Psychiatry and the Law* **24:**165–176.

Citizens Crime Commission of Connecticut. (1984). *Court Delay: Report.* Hartford: Citizens Crime Commission of Connecticut.

Clarke, David C. (1994). *An Evaluation of the Department's Policy on Criminal Aliens: Four Year Post-Release Follow-Up of Criminal Aliens Released in 1988.* Albany: New York State Department of Correctional Services.

Clarke, Stevens H. (1987). *Felony Sentencing in North Carolina, 1976–1986: Effects of Presumptive Sentencing Legislation.* Chapel Hill: Institute of Government, University of North Carolina.

Clarke, Stevens H., Ernest Valente Jr., and Robyn R. Mace. (1992). *Mediation of Interpersonal Disputes: An Evaluation of North Carolina's Programs.* Chapel Hill: Institute of Government, University of North Carolina at Chapel Hill, Mediation Network of North Carolina.

Clarke, Stevens H. et al. (1994). *National Symposium on Court-Connected Dispute Resolution Research: A Report on Current Research Findings.* Washington, DC: State Justice Institute.

Clayton, Obie Jr. (1983). "Reconsideration of the Effects of Race in Criminal Sentencing." *Criminal Justice Review* **8**:15–20.

Clear, Todd R., Val B. Clear, and William D. Burrell. (1989). *Offender Assessment and Evaluation: The Presentence Investigation.* Cincinnati, OH: Anderson.

Cohen, Stanley A. and Anthony N. Doob. (1989). "Public Attitudes to Plea Bargaining." *Criminal Law Quarterly* **32**:85–109.

Cohn, Alvin W. and Michael M. Ferriter. (1990). "The Presentence Investigation: An Old Saw with New Teeth." *Federal Probation* **54**:15–25.

Cohn, Bob. (1991). "There Goes the Judge: Why Bush's Appeals-Court Nominee Was Rejected." *Newsweek,* April 22, 1991:31.

Collins, Marvin. (1981). "The Right to Bail in Texas." *Houston Law Review* **18**:495–517.

Colorado Department of Regulatory Agencies. (1992). *1992 Sunset Review of Colorado Regulation of Professional Bail Bondsmen.* Denver: Colorado Department of Regulatory Agencies.

Colorado Legislative Council. (1996). *An Overview of the Colorado Adult Criminal Justice System.* Denver: Colorado Legislative Council.

Comisky, Marvin, Philip C. Patterson, and William E. Taylor III. (1987). *The Judiciary: Selection, Compensation, Ethics, and Discipline.* New York: Quorum Books.

Conley, Darlene J. (1994). "Adding Color to a Black and White Picture: Using Qualitative Data to Explain Racial Disproportionality in the Juvenile Justice System." *Journal of Research in Crime and Delinquency* **31**:135–148.

Conrad, Clay S. (1998). *Jury Nullification: The Evolution of a Doctrine.* Durham, NC: Carolina Academic Press.

Constantini, G. and J. King. (1980). "The Partial Juror: Correlates and Causes of Prejudgment." *Law and Society Review* **15**:9–40.

Cook, D. (1978) "Interpersonal and Attitudinal Outcomes in Cooperating Interracial Groups." *Journal of Research and Development in Education* **12**:97

Cook, Stephen S. (1996). "Mediation as an Alternative to Probation Revocation Proceedings." *Federal Probation* **59**:48–52.

Cooper, Philip J. (1988). *Hard Judicial Choices: Federal District Court Judges and State and Local Officials.* New York: Oxford University Press.

Coppom, John T. (1979). *Felony Sentencing Patterns of Three Criminal Court Judges: A Regression Model.* Ann Arbor, MI: University Microfilms International.

Corrado, Michael Louis (ed.). (1994). *Justification and Excuse in the Criminal Law: A Collection of Essays.* New York: Garland.

Correctional Association of New York. (1993). *Court Case Processing in New York: Problems and Solutions.* New York: Correctional Association of New York.

Council of State Governments. (1978). *State Court Systems.* Lexington, KY: Council of State Governments.

Courtless, Thomas F. (1989). "The Rehabilitative Ideal Meets an Aroused Public: The Patuxent Experiment Revisited." *Journal of Psychiatry and Law* **27:**607–626.

Coyne, Randall and Lyn Entzeroth. (1994). *Capital Punishment and the Judicial Process.* Durham, NC: Carolina Academic Press.

Craig, Michael D. (1983). "Improving Jury Deliberations: A Reconsideration of Lesser Included Offense Instructions." *University of Michigan Journal of Law Reform* **16:**561–584.

Crew, Robert E. Jr. (1994). "Managing Victim Restitution in Florida." *Justice System Journal* **17:**241–245.

Criminal Law Reporter. (1969). *The Criminal Law Revolution, 1960–1969.* Washington, DC: Bureau of National Affairs.

Cromwell, Paul F. and George G. Killinger. (1994). *Community-Based Corrections: Probation, Parole, and Intermediate Sanctions.* Minneapolis: West Publishing.

Cuvelier, Steven Jay and Dennis W. Potts. (1993). *Bail Classification Profile Project, Harris County, Texas: Final Report.* Alexandria, VA: State Justice Institute.

D'Alessio, Stewart J. and Lisa Stolzenberg. (1993). "Socioeconomic Status and the Sentencing of the Traditional Offender." *Journal of Criminal Justice* **21:**61–77.

D'Alessio, Stewart J. and Lisa Stolzenberg. (1995). "The Impact of Sentencing Guidelines on Jail Incarceration in Minnesota." *Criminology* **33:**283–302.

Daly, Kathleen. (1989). "Gender and Varieties of White-Collar Crime." *Criminology* **27:**769–794.

Daly, Kathleen and Rebecca L. Bordt. (1995). "Sex Effects and Sentencing: An Analysis of the Statistical Literature." *Justice Quarterly* **12:**141–175.

Davies, Graham M. et al. (1995). "Seminar: A New Look at Eyewitness Testimony: Papers Presented at the BAFS Joint Seminar on 12 October 1994." *Medicine Science and the Law* **35:**95–149.

Davis, Christopher, Richard Estes, and Vincent Schiraldi. (1996). *"Three Strikes": The New Apartheid.* San Francisco: Center on Juvenile and Criminal Justice.

Davis, David. (1990). "The Frivolous Appeal Reconsidered." *Criminal Law Bulletin* **26:**305–316.

Davis, Robert C. (1983). "Victim/Witness Noncooperation: A Second Look at a Persistent Phenomenon." *Journal of Criminal Justice* **11:**287–299.

Davis, Robert C., Pamela Fisher, and Alice Paykin. (1984). "Victim Impact Statements: The Experiences of State Probation Agencies." *Journal of Probation and Parole* **16:**18–20.

Davis, Robert C. and Arthur J. Lurigio. (1992). "Compliance with Court-Ordered Restitution: Who Pays?" *APPA Perspectives* **16:**25–31.

Davis, Robert C. and Barbara E. Smith. (1994). "The Effects of Victim Impact Statements on Sentencing Decisions: A Test in an Urban Setting." *Justice Quarterly* **11:**453–512.

Dawson, Robert O. (1992). "An Empirical Study of *Kent* Style Juvenile Transfers to Criminal Court." *St. Mary's Law Journal* **23:**975–1054.

Death Penalty Information Center. (1992). *Killing Justice: Government Misconduct and the Death Penalty.* Washington, DC: Death Penalty Information Center.

Deitz, S. R., M. Littman, and B. J. Bentley. (1984). "Attribution of Responsibility for Rape: The Influence of Observer Empathy, Victim Resistance, and Victim Attractiveness." *Sex Roles* **10:**14–29.

DeJong, William and Stan Franzeen. (1993). "On the Role of Intermediate Sanctions in Correctional Reform: The Views of Criminal Justice Professionals." *Journal of Crime and Justice* **16:**47–73.

Del Carmen, Rolando V. (1995). *Criminal Procedure: Law and Practice* (3rd ed.). Belmont, CA: Wadsworth.

Delaware Statistical Analysis Center. (1989). *Impact of Truth in Sentencing on Jail and Prison Populations.* Dover: Delaware Statistical Analysis Center.

DeMore, Rosemary. (1996). " 'I'm Not a Criminal': Working with Low-Risk Supervisees." *Federal Probation* **59:**34–40.

Dent, Helen and Rhona Flin (eds.). (1992). *Children As Witnesses.* Chichester, UK: Wiley.

Dershowitz, Alan. (1994). "Court TV: Are We Being Fed a Steady Diet of Tabloid Television? Yes: Its Commercialism Hides Its Potential." *American Bar Association Journal.* **80:** 46

Dieter, Richard C. (1984). *The Future of the Death Penalty in the United States: A Texas-Sized Crisis.* Washington, DC: Death Penalty Information Center.

DiGennario, Judith. (1983). "Sex-Specific Characteristics As Defenses to Criminal Behavior." *Criminal Justice Journal* **6:**187–203.

Dillehay, R. C. and M. T. Nietzel. (1985). "Juror Experience and Jury Verdicts." *Law and Human Behavior* **9:**179–191

Diog, Alan (ed.). (1995). "Selected Papers from ECPR Workshop on Forms & Dimensions of Public Corruption." *Crime, Law, and Social Change* **22:**303–414.

Diroll, David. (1989). *The Use of Community Corrections and the Impact of Prison and Jail Crowding on Sentencing.* Columbus, OH: Governor's Office of Criminal Justice Services.

Dixon, Jo. (1995). "The Organizational Context of Criminal Sentencing." *American Journal of Sociology* **100:**1157–1198.

Doane, Mary Lee. (1986). "Liability of Bail Bondsmen Under Section 1983." *Washington and Lee Law Review* **42:**215–245.

Dobbs, Dan B. (1971). "Contempt of Court: A Survey." *Cornell Law Review* **56:**183–284.

Doble Research Associates. (1995). *Crime and Corrections: The Views of the People of Oregon.* Englewood Cliffs, NJ: Doble Research Associates.

Dombrink, John, James W. Meeker, and Julie Paik. (1988). "Fighting for Fees: Drug Trafficking and the Forfeiture of Attorney's Fees." *Journal of Drug Issues* **18:**421–436.

Donzinger, Steven R. (ed.). (1996). *The Real War on Crime: The Report of the National Criminal Justice Commission.* New York: Harper.

Douglas, Roger. (1988). "Tolerated Contests? Pics and Sentence in the Victorian Magistrate's Courts." *Journal of Criminal Justice* **16:**269–290.

Driscoll, Lois Regent. (1984). "Illegality of Bribery: Its Roots, Essence, and Universality." *Capital University Law Review* **14:**1–42.

Dubois, Philip L. (1981). "Disclosure of Presentence Reports in the United States District Courts." *Federal Probation* **45:**3–9.

Dubois, Philip L. (1990). "Voter Responses to Court Reform: Merit Judicial Selection on the Ballot." *Judicature* **73:**238–247.

Dvoskin, Joe. (1978). "Legal Alternatives for Battered Women Who Kill Their Abusers." *Bulletin of the American Academy of Psychiatry and the Law* **6:**335–354.

Dworaczyk, Kellie. (1994). *After the Death Sentence: Appeals, Clemency and Representation.* Austin, TX: House Research Organization.

Dynia, Paul A. (1990). *Misdemeanor Trial Law: Is It Working?* New York: New York City Criminal Justice Agency.

Dynia, Paul A. et al. (1987). *Misdemeanor Trial Law Study: Final Report.* New York: New York City Criminal Justice Agency.

Echikson, Thomas. (1986). "Sixth Amendment: Waiver after Request for Counsel." *Journal of Criminal Law and Criminology* **77:**775–795.

Edelhertyz, Herbert and Thomas D. Overcast. (1990). *A Study of Organized Crime Business-Type Activities and Their Implications for Law Enforcement.* Kirkland, WA: Northwest Policy Studies Center.

Elliston, Frederick A. (1985). "Deadly Force and Capital Punishment: A Comparative Appraisal." *In Police Ethics: Hard Choices in Law Enforcement,* William C. Heffernan and Timothy Stoup (eds.). New York: John Jay Press.

Elliston, Frederick A. and Norman Bowie (eds.). (1982). *Ethics, Public Policy and Criminal Justice.* Cambridge, MA: Oelgeschlager, Gunn & Hain.

Ellsworth, Thomas, Michelle T. Kinsella, and Kimberlee Massin. (1992). "Prosecuting Juveniles: *Parens Patriae* and Due Process in the 1990s." *Justice Professional* **7:**53–67.

Emmelman, Debra S. (1996). "Trial by Plea Bargain: Case Settlement As a Product of Recursive Decision Making." *Law and Society Review* **30:**335–360.

Erez, Edna. (1990). "Victim Participation in Sentencing: Rhetoric and Reality." *Journal of Crime and Justice* **18:**19–31.

Erez, Edna and Pamela Tontodonato. (1990). "The Effect of Victim Participation in Sentencing on Sentence Outcome." *Criminology* **28:**451–474.

Erez, Edna and Pamela Tontodonato. (1992). "Victim Participation in Sentencing and Satisfaction with Justice." *Justice Quarterly* **9:**393–417.

Erez, Edna et al. (1994). "Victim Participation in Sentencing." *International Review of Victimology* **3:**17–166.

Erickson, William H., William D. Neighbors, and B. J. George. (1987). "Pronouncements of the United States Supreme Court Relating to Criminal Law, 1985–1986 Term." *Prosecutor* **20:**1–68.

Estreicher, Samuel and John Sexton. (1986). "Improving the Process: Case Selection by the Supreme Court." *Judicature* **70:**41–47.

Etzioni, Amitai. (1974). "Creating an Imbalance." *Trial* **10:**28.

Evans, Walter and Frank Gilbert. (1975). "The Sentencing Process: Better Methods Are Available." *Federal Probation* **39:**35–39.

Farnworth, Margaret and Raymond H. C. Teske Jr. (1995). "Gender Differences in Felony Court Processing: Three Hypotheses of Disparity." *Women and Criminal Justice* **6:**23–44.

Fay, Peter T. (1979). "Voir Dire: Some Impressions." *Florida Bar Journal* **53:**144–149.

Feazell, David M., Herbert C. Quay, and Edward J. Murray. (1991). "The Validity and Utility of Lanyon's Psychological Screening Inventory in a Youth Services Agency Sample." *Criminal Justice and Behavior* **18:**166–179.

Federal Judicial Center. (1981). *The Effects of Sentencing Councils on Sentencing Disparity.* Washington, DC: Federal Judicial Center.

Federal Judicial Center. (1994). *Planning for the Future: The Results of a 1992 Federal Judicial Center Survey of United States Judges.* Washington, DC: U.S. Government Printing Office.

Federal Probation. (1974). "The Selective Presentence Investigation Report." *Federal Probation* **38:**47–54.

Feeley, Malcolm M. (1982). "Plea Bargaining and the Structure of the Criminal Process." *Justice System Journal* **7:**338–360.

Feeley, Malcolm M. (1983). *Court Reform on Trial: Why Simple Solutions Fail.* New York: Basic Books.

Feld, Barry C. (1987a). "The Juvenile Court Meets the Principle of the Offense: Changing Juvenile Justice Sentencing Practices." Unpublished paper presented at the American Society of Criminology meetings, Montreal, November.

Feld, Barry C. (1987b). "The Juvenile Court Meets the Principle of the Offense: Legislative Changes in Juvenile Waiver Statutes." *Journal of Criminal Law and Criminology* **78:**471–533.

Feld, Barry C. (1987c). "*In re Gault* Revisited: The Right to Counsel in the Juvenile Court." Unpublished paper presented at the American Society of Criminology meetings, Montreal, November.

Feld, Barry C. (1988a). "The Juvenile Court Meets the Principle of Offense: Punishment, Treatment, and the Difference It Makes." *Boston University Law Review* **68:**821–915.

Feld, Barry C. (1988b). "*In re Gault* Revisited: A Cross-State Comparison of the Right to Counsel in Juvenile Court." *Crime and Delinquency* **34:**393–424.

Feld, Barry C. (1988c). "The Right to Counsel in Juvenile Court: An Empirical Study of When Lawyers Appear and the Differences They Make." Unpublished paper presented at the American Society of Criminology meetings, Chicago, November.

Feld, Barry C. (1989a). "Bad Law Makes Hard Cases: Reflections on Teen-Aged Axe-Murderers." *Law and Inequality: A Journal of Theory and Practice* **8:**1–101.

Feld, Barry C. (1989b). "The Right to Counsel in Juvenile Court: An Empirical Study of When Lawyers Appear and the Difference They Can Make." *Journal of Criminal Law and Criminology* **79:**1185–1346.

Feld, Barry C. (1993a). "Criminalizing the American Juvenile Court." In *Crime and Justice: A Review of Research,* Vol. 17, Michael Tonry (ed.). Chicago: University of Chicago Press.

Feld, Barry C. (1993b). *Justice for Children: The Right to Counsel and the Juvenile Courts.* Boston: Northeastern University Press.

Feld, Barry C. (1993c). "Juvenile (In)justice and the Criminal Court Alternative." *Crime and Delinquency* **39:**403–424.

Feld, Barry C. (1995). "Violent Youth and Public Policy: A Case Study of Juvenile Justice Law Reform." *Minnesota Law Review* **79:**965–1128.

Feldman, Michael. (1973). "A Hearing on Judicial Misconduct." *NLADA Briefcase* **31:**451–459.

Felker, Charles J. (1990). "A Proposal for Considering Intoxication at Sentencing Hearings." *Federal Probation* **54:**3–14.

Felstiner, William, Richard Abel, and Austin Sarat. (1980). "The Emergence of Disputes: Naming, Blaming, and Claiming." *Law and Society Review* **15:**631–634.

Ferdinand, Theodore. (1992). *Boston's Lower Criminal Courts, 1814–1850.* Newark: University of Delaware Press.

Ferguson, Gerald A. (1972). "The Role of the Judge in Plea Bargaining." *Criminal Law Quarterly* **15:**26–51.

Fields, Lea L. (1994). "Pretrial Diversion: A Solution to California's Drunk-Driving Problem." *Federal Probation* **58:**20–30.

Findlay, Mark and Peter Duff (eds.). (1988). *The Jury under Attack.* Sydney, Australia: Butterworths.

Fine, Ralph Adam. (1986). *Escape of the Guilty.* New York: Dodd, Mead.

Finn, Peter and B. Lee. (1985). "Collaboration with Victim-Witness Assistance Programs: Payoffs and Concerns for Prosecutors." *Prosecutor* **18:**27–36.

Fischer, Daryl R. and Andy Thaker. (1992). *Mandatory Sentencing Study.* Phoenix: Arizona Department of Corrections.

Fischer, Gloria J. (1991). Cognitive Predictors of Not-Guilty Verdicts in a Simulated Acquaintance Rape Trial." *Psychological Reports* **86:**1199–1206.

Fischer, Gloria J. (1997). "Gender Effects on Individual Verdicts and on Mock Jury Verdicts in a Simu-lated Acquaintance Rape Trial." *Sex Roles: A Journal of Research* **36**:491–502.

Flanagan, Tara A. (1986). "The Grand Jury Subpoena: Is It the Prosecutor's 'Ultimate Weapon'?" *Pepperdine Law Review* **13**:791–821.

Flanagan, William J. (1976). "New Federal Rule of Criminal Procedure 11(e): Dangers in Restricting the Judicial Role in Sentencing Agreements." *American Criminal Law Review* **14**:305–318.

Flango, Victor E. (1979). "What Difference Does Method of Judicial Selection Make? Selection Proce-dures in State Courts of Last Resort." *Justice System Journal* **5**:25–44.

Flango, Victor E. (1994a). "Federal Court Review of State Court Convictions in Noncapital Cases." *Justice System Journal* **17**:153–170.

Flango, Victor E. (1994b). *Habeas Corpus in State and Federal Courts.* Williamsburg, VA: National Center for State Courts.

Flango, Victor E. and Craig R. Ducat. (1979). "What Difference Does Method of Judicial Selection Make? Selection Procedures in State Courts of Last Resort." *Justice System Journal* **5**:25–44.

Fletcher, George P. (1995). *With Justice for Some: Victims' Rights in Criminal Trials.* New York: Addison-Wesley.

Florida Governor's Juvenile Justice and Deliquency Prevention Advisory Committee. (1994). *Non-delinquents Placed in Florida's Secure Juvenile Detention Facilities, 1991.* Tallahassee: Florida Gover-nor's Juvenile Justice and Deliquency Prevention Advisory Committee.

Florida Governor's Task Force. (1981). *Balancing Equity, Safety, and Justice through Pretrial Reform.* Tallahassee: Florida Governor's Task Force on Criminal Justice System Reform.

Florida Joint Legislative Management Committee. (1992). *An Empirical Examination of the Appli-cation of Florida's Habitual Offender Statute.* Tallahassee: Florida Joint Legislative Management Committee Economic and Demographic Research Division.

Florida Senate Committee on Corrections, Probation, and Parole. (1993). *Sentencing Guidelines and the Management of the Prison Population: An Executive Summary of Events and Policy Choices.* Tallahassee: Florida Senate Committee on Corrections, Probation, and Parole.

Forer, Lois G. (1994). *A Rage to Punish: The Unintended Consequences of Mandatory Sentencing.* New York: W.W. Norton.

Forst, Brian and William M. Rhodes. (1982). "Structuring the Exercise of Sentencing Discretion in the Federal Courts." *Federal Probation* **46**:3–13.

Fowler, W. Gary. (1984). "Judicial Selection under Reagan and Carter: A Comparison of Their Initial Recommendation Procedures." *Judicature* **67**:265–283.

Frank, Jerome. (1913). "Justice According to Law." *Columbia Law Review* **13**:696–733.

Frasca, G. (1988). "Estimating the Occurrence of Trials Prejudiced by Press Coverage." *Judicature* **72**:162–169.

Fredrich, Dolores. (1978). "Six-Person Nonunanimous Verdicts: Further Cutbacks on the Right to a Jury Trial." *Hofstra Law Review* **7**:185–213.

Freed, Daniel et al. (1992). "Symposium: Punishment." *Yale Law Journal* **101**:1681–2077.

Freedman, Warren. (1989). *Summary Judgment and Other Preclusive Devices.* Westport, CT: Quorum.

Friedman, Lawrence. (1984). *American Law: An Introduction.* New York: W.W. Norton.

Friedman, Lawrence. (1985). *History of American Law* (2nd ed.). New York: Simon and Schuster.

Friedman, Lawrence M. and Robert V. Percival. (1981). *The Roots of Justice: Crime and Punishment in Alameda County, California, 1870–1910.* Chapel Hill: University of North Carolina Press.

Fuller, John R. and William M. Norton. (1993). "Juvenile Diversion: The Impact of Program Philosophy on Net Widening." *Journal of Crime and Justice* **16**:29–45.

Galenter, Marc. (1986). "The Day after the Litigation Explosion." *Maryland Law Review* **46**:3–39.

Garofalo, James and Anita R. Neuberger. (1987). *Reducing Avoidable Felony Case Attrition through Enhanced Police-Prosecutor Coordination.* Albany: Hindelang Criminal Justice Research Center, State University of New York at Albany.

Gaynes, Elizabeth. (1982). *Typology of State Laws Which Permit the Consideration of Danger in the Pretrial Release Decision.* Washington, DC: Pretrial Services Resource Center.

Gazell, James A. (1972). "Developmental Syndromes in Judicial Management." *Brooklyn Law Review* **38**:587–621.

Gazell, James A. (1975). *State Trial Courts As Bureaucracies: A Study in Judicial Management.* New York: Dunellen Publishing.

Genego, William J. (1986). "Risky Business: The Hazards of Being a Criminal Defense Lawyer." *Criminal Justice* **1**:39–44.

Georgetown Law Journal. (1982). "Twelfth Annual Review of Criminal Procedure: United States Supreme Court and Courts of Appeal, 1981–1982." *Georgetown Law Journal* **71**:253–828.

Georgetown Law Journal. (1987). "Sixteenth Annual Review of Criminal Procedure: United States Supreme Court and Courts of Appeal, 1985–1986." *Georgetown Law Journal* **75**:713–1340.

Gershman, Bennett L. (1985). "The Burger Court and Prosecutorial Misconduct." *Criminal Law Bulletin* **21**:217–226.

Gershman, Bennett L. (1986). "Why Prosecutors Misbehave." *Criminal Law Bulletin* **22**:131–143.

Gershman, Bennett L. (1995). "Prosecutorial Misconduct in Presenting Evidence: 'Backdooring' Hearsay." *Criminal Law Bulletin* **31**:99–112.

Gerwitz, Marian. (1987). *Court-Ordered Releases—November 1983.* New York: New York City Criminal Justice Agency.

Gibbs, John J. (1975). "Jailing and Stress." In *Men in Crisis: Human Breakdowns in Prison,* H. Toch (ed.). Chicago: Aldine.

Gifford, Donald G. (1983). "Meaningful Reform of Plea Bargaining: The Control of Prosecutorial Discretion." *University of Illinois Law Review* **1**:37–98.

Glick, Henry R. and Craig F. Emmert. (1987). "Selection Systems and Judicial Characteristics: The Recruitment of State Supreme Court Judges." *Judicature* **70**:228–235.

Goldkamp, John S. (1984). "Bail: Discrimination and Control." *Criminal Justice Abstracts* **16**:103–127.

Goldkamp, John S. and Michael R. Gottfredson. (1984). *Judicial Guidelines for Bail: The Philadelphia Experiment.* Washington, DC: U.S. Government Printing Office.

Goldman, Sheldon. (1983). "Reagan's Judicial Appointments at Mid-Term: Shaping the Bench in His Own Image." *Judicature* **66**:334–347.

Goldman, Sheldon. (1985). "Reorganizing the Judiciary: The First-Term Appointments." *Judicature* **68**:313–329.

Goldman, Sheldon. (1987). "Reagan's Second Term Judicial Appointments: The Battle at Midway." *Judicature* **70**:324–339.

Goodstein, Lynne and John Hepburn. (1985). *Determinate Sentencing and Imprisonment: A Failure of Reform.* Cincinnati, OH: Anderson Publishing.

Gorman, Warren F. (1983). "Are There Impartial Expert Psychiatric Witnesses?" *Bulletin of the American Academy of Psychiatry and the Law* **11**:379–382.

Gorr, Michael and Sterling Harwood (eds.). (1992). *Controversies in Criminal Law: Philosophical Essays on Responsibility and Procedure.* Boulder, CO: Westview Press.

Gottlieb, Barbara. (1984). *Public Danger As a Factor in Pretrial Release: Summaries of State Danger Laws.* Washington, DC: Toborg.

Gottschall, Jon. (1983). "Carter's Judicial Appointments: The Influence of Affirmative Action and Merit Selection on Voting on the U.S. Courts of Appeals." *Judicature* **67**:165–173.

Gottschall, Jon. (1986). "Reagan's Appointments to the U.S. Courts of Appeals: The Continuation of a Judicial Revolution." *Judicature* **70**:48–54.

Graham, Michael H. (1985). *Witness Intimidation: The Law's Response.* Westport, CT: Quorum.

Grano, Joseph D. et al. (1989). "Symposium: The Future of Criminal Justice under the Constitution." *Criminal Law Bulletin* **25**:5–112.

Green, Bruce A. (1988). "The Ethical Prosecutor and the Adversary System." *Criminal Law Bulletin* **24**:126–145.

Green, Bruce A. (1990). "The Good Faith Exception to the Fruit of the Poisonous Tree Doctrine." *Criminal Law Review* **26**:509–533.

Greene, Edith. (1986). "Is the Juvenile Justice System Lenient?" *Criminal Justice Abstracts* **28**:104–118.

Greene, J. (1990). "Media Effects on Jurors." *Law and Human Behavior* **14**:439–450.

Greene, M. and C. Loftus. (1984). What's News in the News? The Influence of Well-Publicized News Events on Psychological Research and Courtroom Trials." *Basic and Applied Social Psychology* **5**:123–135.

Greenhill, Joe R. and John W. Odam Jr. (1971). "Judicial Reform of Our Texas Courts: A Re-Examination of Three Important Aspects." *Baylor Law Review* **23**:204–226.

Greenstein, Steven C. (1994). *The Impact of Restrictions on Post-Indictment Plea Bargaining in Bronx County: The Processing of Indictments Already Pending.* Albany: New York State Division of Criminal Justice.

Greenwood, Peter W. et al. (1994). *Three Strikes and You're Out: Estimated Benefits and Costs of California's New Mandatory Sentencing Law.* Santa Monica, CA: Rand.

Griset, Pamala L. (1995a). "Determinate Sentencing and Agenda Building: A Case Study of the Failure of Reform." *Journal of Criminal Justice* **23**:349–362.

Griset, Pamala L. (1995b). "Early-Release Policies in Florida and New York: Comparing Determinate and Indeterminate Sentencing Systems." *Criminal Justice Policy Review* **7**:155–184.

Griset, Pamala L. (1995c). "The Politics and Economics of Increased Correctional Discretion over Time Served: A New York Case Study." *Justice Quarterly* **12**:307–323.

Griset, Pamala L. (1996a). "Determinate Sentencing and Administrative Discretion over Time Served in Prison: A Case Study in Florida." *Crime and Delinquency* **42**:127–143.

Griset, Pamala L. (1996b). "Discretion, Disparity, and Discrimination in Sentencing: Where Have All the Critics Gone?" *Judges' Journal* **35**:2–9.

Griswold, David B. (1995). "Florida at the Crossroads: Integrating Sentencing with Corrections?" *Criminal Justice Policy Review* **7**:301–308.

Grodin, Joseph R. (1987). "Judicial Elections: The California Experience." *Judicature* **70**:365–371.

Gullick, Robert. (1970). "Right to Jury Trial: Indiana's Misapplication of Due Process Standards in Delinquency Hearings." *Indiana Law Journal* **45**:578–594.

Hall, Kermit L. (1984). "Progressive Reform and the Decline of Democratic Accountability: The Popular Election of State Supreme Court Judges, 1850–1920." *American Bar Foundation Research Journal* **2**:345–369.

Halpern, Susan M. (1984). "Federal Rule 81(c) and Jury Demand in a Removed Action: A Procedural Trap for the Unwary." *Albany Law Review* **47**:661–696.

Hammer, Thomas J. et al. (1986). "Offense Definition in Wisconsin's Impaired Driving Statutes." *Marquette Law Review* **69**:159–329.

Hanke, Penelope J. (1995). "Sentencing Disparities by Race of Offender and Victim: Women Homicide Offenders in Alabama, 1929–1985." *Sociological Spectrum* **15**:277–297.

Hans, Valerie P. and Neil Vidmar. (1986). *Judging the Jury.* New York: Plenum.

Hanson, Roger A. and Henry W. K. Daley. (1995). *Federal Habeas Corpus Review: Challenging State Court Criminal Convictions.* Washington, DC: U.S. Bureau of Justice Statistics.

Hanson, Roger A. et al. (1992). *Indigent Defenders Get the Job Done and Done Well.* Williamsburg, VA: National Center for State Courts.

Harmsworth, Esmond. (1996). "Bail and Detention: An Assessment and Critique of the Federal and Massachusetts Systems." *New England Journal on Criminal and Civil Confinement* **22**:213–290.

Harris, Joan S. (1990). *The Public Costs of Driving under the Influence Processing: A Study in the California Municipal Courts.* Oakland, CA: Office of Court Services, Alameda County.

Hastie, Reid, Steven Penrod, and Nancy Pennington. (1993). "Jury Deliberations" in Reid Hastie (ed.). *Inside the Juror: The Psychology of Juror Decision Making.* Cambridge: Cambridge University Press.

Hawaii Office of the Auditor. (1992). *Sunset Evaluation Report: Bail Bond Agents.* Honolulu: Hawaii Office of the Auditor.

Haynes, Peter. (1977). *Judicial Planning.* Washington, DC: American University Law Institute.

Heffernan, William C., John Kleinig, and Shirley R. Schnitzer. (1992). "Penalty Enhancement for Hate Crimes." *Criminal Justice Ethics* **11**:3–63.

Hellerstein, Dina R. (1989). "The Victim Impact Statement: Reform or Reprisal?" *American Criminal Law Review* **27**:391–430.

Hennessey, Edward F. (1976). "Disparity in Sentencing." *New England Journal on Prison Law* **3**:5–14.

Hertz, Randy and Robert Weisberg. (1981). "In Mitigation of the Penalty of Death: *Lockett v. Ohio* and the Capital Defendant's Right to Consideration of Mitigating Circumstances." *California Law Review* **69**:317–376.

Heumann, Milton. (1975). "A Note on Plea Bargaining and Case Pressure." *Law and Society Review* **9**:515–528.

Hewitt, William E. (1995). *Court Interpretation: Model Guides for Policy and Practice in the State Courts.* Williamsburg, VA: National Center for State Courts.

Heymann, Philip B. et al. (1980). "Symposium: White-Collar Crime." *American Criminal Law Review* **17**:271–408.

Hirsch, Alan and Diane Sheely. (1993). *The Bail Reform Act of 1984.* Washington, DC: Federal Judicial Center.

Hodge, John L. (1986). "Deadlocked Jury Mistrials, Lesser Included Offenses, and Double Jeopardy: A Proposal to Strengthen the Manifest Necessity Requirement." *Criminal Justice Journal* **9**:9–44.

Hoebel, E. Adamson. (1954). *The Law of Primitive Man: A Study in Comparative Legal Dynamic.* Cambridge, MA: Harvard University Press.

Hoff, Philip H. (1969). "Modern Courts for Vermont." *Judicature* **52**:316–320.

Holderman, James F. (1980). "Pre-Indictment Prosecutorial Conduct in the Federal System." *Journal of Criminal Law and Criminology* **71**:1–31.

Holmes, Malcolm D. et al. (1992). "Plea Bargaining Policy and State District Court Caseloads: An Interrupted Time Series Analysis." *Law and Society Review* **26**:139–159.

Holmes, Malcolm D. et al. (1993). "Judges' Ethnicity and Minority Sentencing: Evidence Concerning Hispanics." *Social Science Quarterly* **74:**496–506.

Holmes, Malcolm D. et al. (1996). "Ethnicity, Legal Resources, and Felony Dispositions in Two Southwestern Jurisdictions." *Justice Quarterly* **13:**11–30.

Holmes, Oliver Wendell. (1897). *Courts and the Law.* New York: Knopf.

Holmes, Robert E. (1992). *Sentencing in California: Where Are We Today? Where Are We Going?* Sacramento: California Research Bureau.

Holten, Gary N. and Melvyn E. Jones. (1982). *The System of Criminal Justice.* Boston: Little, Brown.

Holten, Gary N. and Lawson L. Lamar. (1991). *The Criminal Courts: Structures, Personnel, and Processes.* New York: McGraw-Hill.

Huff, C. Ronald, Arye Rattner, and Edward Sagarin. (1996). *Convicted but Innocent: Wrongful Conviction and Public Policy.* Thousand Oaks, CA: Sage.

Hughes, Graham. (1985). "Legal Aspects of Predicting Dangerousness." In *Critical Issues in American Psychiatry and the Law,* Richard Rosner (ed.). New York: Plenum.

Hunzeker, Donna. (1985). "Habitual Offender Statutes." *Corrections Compendium* **10:**1–15.

Hunzeker, Donna. (1992). *Bringing Corrections Policy into the 1990s.* Denver: National Conference of State Legislatures.

Hutton, Mary C. (1987). "Child Sexual Abuse Cases: Reestablishing the Balance within the Adversary System." *University of Michigan Journal of Law Reform* **20:**491–541.

Illinois Supreme Court. (1993). *Final Report.* Chicago: Illinois Supreme Court Special Commission on the Administration of Justice.

Immarigeon, Russ. (1993). "Victim-Offender Reconciliation in a Penal Setting." *Corrections Compendium* **18:**5–7.

Institute for Court Management. (1983). *Evaluation of Telephone Conferencing in Civil and Criminal Court Cases.* Denver: Prepared for the National Institute of Justice and the National Science Foundation; American Bar Association Action Commission to Reduce Court Costs and Delay.

Institute for Rational Public Policy. (1991). *Arizona Criminal Code and Corrections Study: Final Report to the Legislative Council.* Phoenix: Institute for Rational Public Policy.

Institute of Judicial Administration. (1977). *Standards Relating to Pretrial Court Proceedings.* Cambridge, MA: Ballinger.

Iowa Equality in the Courts Task Force. (1993). *Final Report of the Equality in the Courts Task Force.* Des Moines: The Supreme Court of Iowa.

Jackson, J. D. (1986). "The Insufficiency of Identification Evidence Based on Personal Impression." *Criminal Law Review* **16:**203–214.

Jackson, Michael. (1986). "The Right to Counsel in Prison Disciplinary Proceedings." *University of British Columbia Law Review* **20:**221–283.

Jacobs, Nancy F., Ellen Chayet, and Charles Meara. (1986). *Bang the Gavel Slowly: Felony Case Processing in New York City's Supreme Court.* New York: Criminal Justice Center, John Jay College of Criminal Justice.

James, Howard. (1968). *Crisis in the Courts.* New York: David McKay.

Jensen, Magdeline et al. (1991). "The Sentencing Reform Act of 1984 and Sentencing Guidelines." *Federal Probation* **55:**4–57.

Johnson, Herbert. (1988). *History of Criminal Justice.* Cincinnati, OH: Anderson Publishing.

Johnston, Robert G. (1974). "The Grand Jury–Prosecutorial Abuse of the Indictment Process." *Journal of Criminal Law and Criminology* **65:**157–169.

Jonakait, Randolph N. (1987). "The Ethical Prosecutor's Misconduct." *Criminal Law Bulletin* **23:**550–567.

Kadish, Sanford H. et al. (1994). "Supreme Court Review." *Journal of Criminal Law and Criminology* **84:**679–1175.

Kales, A. H. (1914). *Unpopular Government in the United States.* Chicago: University of Chicago Press.

Kalven, Harry Jr. and Hans Ziesel. (1966). *The American Jury.* Chicago: University of Chicago.

Kamm, Frances M. (1987). "The Insanity Defense, Innocent Threats, and Limited Alternatives." *Criminal Justice Ethics* **6:**61–76.

Kane, Robert J. (1995). "A Sentencing Model for the 21st Century." *Federal Probation* **59:**10–15.

Katz, Charles M. and Cassia Spohn. (1995). "The Effect of Race and Gender on Bail Outcomes: A Test of an Interactive Model." *American Journal of Criminal Justice* **19:**161–184.

Katz, John W. (1969). "Pretrial Discovery in Criminal Cases: The Concept of Mutuality and the Need for Reform." *Criminal Law Bulletin* **5:**441–462.

Kauder, Neil and Robert LaFountain. (1996). *Findings from the National Trial Court Network. Caseload Highlights: Examining the Work of the State Courts.* Williamsburg, VA: National Center for State Courts.

Kaufman, Irving R. (1990). "Reform for a System in Crisis: Alternative Dispute Resolution in the Federal Courts." *Fordham Law Review* **49:**1–38.

Kaune, Michael Merlin. (1993). *The Impact of Sentencing Reform on Sentencing Practices in Four States.* Ann Arbor, MI: University Microfilms International.

Keil, K. Douglas et al. (1994). "Election, Selection, and Retention." *Judicature* **77:**290–321.

Keilitz, Susan. (1990). "A Court Manager's Guide to the Alternative Dispute Resolution Database." *State Court Journal* **14:**24–31.

Kennedy, Duncan. (1982). "Legal Education As Training for Hierarchy." In *The Politics of Law: A Progressive Critique,* David Kairy (ed.). New York: Pantheon.

Kennedy, Thomas D. (1988). "Determinate Sentencing: Real or Symbolic Effects?" *Journal of Crime and Justice* **11:**1–42.

Kercher, Glen A. and Thomas R. Dull. (1981). *Texas Crime Poll, 1981.* Huntsville, TX: Sam Houston State University, Criminal Justice Center.

Kerr, Norbert L. (1994). "The Effects of Pretrial Publicity on Jurors." *Judicature* **78:**120–127.

Kerr, Norbert L. and Robert J. MacCoun. (1985). "The Effects of Jury Size and Polling Method on the Process and Product of Jury Deliberation." *Journal of Personality and Social Psychology* **48:**349–363.

Key, Clarence Jr. (1991). *The Desirability and Feasibility of Changing Iowa's Sentencing Practices: Comparison Study of Five States and Their Sentencing Structures.* Des Moines: Division of Criminal and Juvenile Justice Planning, Iowa Department of Corrections.

Kilpatrick, James J. (1986). "Commentary. *Miranda v. Arizona:* Twenty Years Have Not Improved It." *Criminal Justice Ethics* **5:**59–60.

Klein, Andrew R. (1991). "Restitution and Community Work Service: Promising Core Ingredients for Effective Intensive Supervision Programming in Juvenile Probation and Parole." In *Intensive Interventions with High-Risk Youths: Promising Approaches,* Troy L. Armstrong (ed.). Monsey, NY: Criminal Justice Press.

Klein, Daniel. (1971). "Judicial Participation in Guilty Pleas: A Search for Standards." *University of Pittsburgh Law Review* **33:**151–160.

Klein, Fannie J. and Ruth Wilztum. (1973). *Judicial Administration 1972–1973.* New York: Institute of Judicial Administration.

Klein, Irving J. (1986). *Constitutional Law for Criminal Justice Professionals* (2nd ed.). Miami, FL: Coral Gables Publishing.

Klein, Richard. (1986). "The Emperor Gideon Has No Clothes: The Empty Promise of the Constitutional Right to Effective Assistance of Counsel." *Hastings Constitutional Law Quarterly* 13:625–693.

Klein, Richard and Robert Spangenberg. (1993). *The Indigent Defense Crisis.* Washington, DC: Section of Criminal Justice, American Bar Association.

Kleinig, John. (1986). "The Conscientious Advocate and Client Perjury." *Criminal Justice Ethics* 5:3–15.

Kleinig, John. (ed.). (1989). "Ethics in Context: The Selling of Jury Deliberations." *Criminal Justice Ethics* 8:26–34.

Kline, G. and R. Jess. (1966). "Prejudicial Publicity: Its Effect on Law School Mock Juries." *Journalism Quarterly* 43: 113–116.

Kling, Susan. (1986). "A Mandatory Right to Counsel for the Material Witness." *University of Michigan Journal of Law Reform* 19:473–497.

Knab, Karen M. (ed.). (1977). *Courts of Limited Jurisdiction: A National Survey.* Washington, DC: U.S. National Institute of Law Enforcement and Criminal Justice.

Koenig, Linda and Doris Taylor Godinez. (1982). "The Need for Greater Double Jeopardy and Due Process Safeguards in RICO Criminal and Civil Actions." *California Law Review* 70:724–785.

Krapac, D. (1996). "The Position of the Victim in Criminal Justice." *European Journal of Crime, Criminal Law, and Criminal Justice* 3:230–240.

Kruttschnitt, Candace. (1984). "Sex and Criminial Court Dispositions." *Journal of Research in Crime and Delinquency* 21:213–232.

Kruttschnitt, Candace and Donald E. Green. (1984). "The Sex-Sanctioning Issue: Is It History?" *American Sociological Review* 49:541–551.

Kunen, James S. (1983). *How Can You Defend Those People? The Making of a Criminal Lawyer.* New York: Random House.

Kunkle, John H. and H. Gordon Washburn. (1979). *Plea Negotiation in Pennsylvania: An Exploratory Report.* Harrisburg: Pennsylvania Crime and Delinquency Commission.

Lafferty, Elaine. (1994) "Now, a Jury of His Peers." *Time,* November 14, 83.

LaFree, Gary D. (1985). "Official Reactions to Hispanic Defendants in the Southwest." *Journal of Research in Crime and Delinquency* 22:213–237.

Langan, Patrick A. and Jodi M. Brown. (1997a). *Felony Sentences in State Courts, 1994.* Washington, DC: U.S. Department of Justice.

Langan, Patrick A. and Jodi M. Brown. (1997b). *Felony Sentences in the United States, 1994.* Washington, DC: U.S. Department of Justice.

Lanier, Mark M. and Cloud H. Miller III. (1995). "Attitudes and Practices of Federal Probation Officers toward Pre-Plea/Trial Investigative Report Policy." *Crime and Delinquency* 41:364–377.

Lawrence, Richard A. (1990). "Diverting Offenders from Prison to Restitution Centers." *Journal of Crime and Justice* 13:27–41.

League of Women Voters of New York State. (1979). *The Judicial System in New York State.* New York: League of Women Voters of New York State.

Leo, Richard A. (1996). "The Impact of Miranda Revisited." *Journal of Criminal Law and Criminology* 86:621–692.

Levin, Martin H. (1988). "The Jury in a Criminal Case: Obstacles to Impartiality." *Criminal Law Bulletin* 24:492–520.

Libby, G. (1994). "Court TV: Are We Being Fed a Steady Diet of Tabloid Television? No: Tacky or Not, It Helps Bring the Law to Life." *American Bar Association Journal* **80:**47.

Lipetz, Marcia J. (1983). *Routine Justice: Processing Cases in Women's Court.* New Brunswick, NJ: Transaction.

LIS, Inc. (1995). *Status Report on Parole, 1995: The Results of an NIC Survey.* Longmont, CO: U.S. National Institute of Corrections.

Lithner, Klas. (1967). "The Prosecutor's Role." *Annales Internationales de Criminologie* **6:**437–457.

Litt, Marc O. (1992). " 'Citizen Soldiers' of Anonymous Justice." *Columbia Journal of Law and Social Problems* **25:**371–421.

Llewellyn, Karl. (1931). "Some Realism about Realism: Responding to Dean Pound." *Harvard Law Review* **44:**1222–1235.

Long, Robert Emmet (ed.). (1995). *Criminal Sentencing.* New York: H. W. Wilson.

Lopez, Antoinette Sedillo (ed.). (1995). *Latinos in the United States: History, Law and Perspective.* New York: Garland.

Lord, Vivian B., Denis O. Gray, and Samuel B. Pond III. (1981). "The Police Stress Inventory: Does It Measure Stress?" *Journal of Criminal Justice* **19:**139–150.

Louisiana Task Force on Women in the Courts. (1992). *Final Report.* Baton Rouge: Louisiana Task Force on Women in the Courts.

Lovrich, Nicholas P. Jr., John C. Pierce, and Charles H. Sheldon. (1989). "Citizen Knowledge and Voting in Judicial Elections." *Judicature* **73:**28–33.

Lovrich, Nicholas P. Jr. and Charles H. Sheldon. (1984). "Voters in Judicial Elections: An Attentive Public or an Uninformed Electorate?" *Justice System Journal* **9:**23–39.

Lovrich, Nicholas P. Jr. and Charles H. Sheldon. (1994). "Is Voting for State Judges a Flight of Fancy or a Reflection of Policy and Value Preferences?" *Justice System Journal* **16:**57–71.

Ludemann, Christian. (1994). "Land without Plea Bargaining? How the Germans Do It." *Euro-Criminology* **7:**119–140.

Luginbuhl, James and Michael Burkhead. (1995). "Victim Impact Evidence in a Capital Trial: Encouraging Votes for Death." *American Journal of Criminal Justice* **20:**1–16.

Lundstrom, Bruce D. (1986). "Sixth Amendment—Right to Counsel: Limited Post-Indictment Use of Jailhouse Informants Is Permissible." *Journal of Criminology and Criminal Law* **77:**743–774.

MacCarthy, Terence F. and Kathy Morris Mejia. (1984). "The Perjurious Client Question: Putting Defense Lawyers between a Rock and Hard Place." *Journal of Criminal Law and Criminology* **75:**1197–1221.

Mackay, Robert E. and Susan R. Moody. (1996). "Diversion of Neighborhood Disputes in Community Mediation." *Howard Journal of Criminal Justice* **35:**299–313.

Madrigal-Dean, Veronica. (1989). *An Examination of Differences in Clinical Recommendations of Criminal Sexual Offenders, 1982–1987.* Ann Arbor, MI: University Microfilms International.

Maguire, Kathleen and Ann L. Pastore. (1996). *Sourcebook of Criminal Justice Statistics, 1995.* Albany, NY: Hindelang Criminal Justice Research Center.

Maguire, Kathleen and Ann L. Pastore. (1997). *Sourcebook of Criminal Justice Statistics, 1996.* Albany, NY: Hindelang Criminal Justice Research Center.

Maguire, Kathleen and Ann L. Pastore. (1999). *Sourcebook of Criminal Justice Statistics, 1998.* Albany, NY: Hindelang Criminal Justice Research Center.

Maguire, Kathleen and Ann L. Pastore. (2000). *Sourcebook of Criminal Justice Statistics, 1996.* Albany, NY: Hindelang Criminal Justice Research Center.

Majer, Richard D. (1994). "Community Service: A Good Idea That Works." *Federal Probation* **58:**20–23.

Mande, Mary and Joan Crouch. (1987). *Getting Tough on Crime in Colorado.* Denver: Colorado Division of Criminal Justice.

Marcus, Martin. (1992). "Above the Fray or into the Breach: The Judge's Role in New York's Adversarial System of Criminal Justice." *Brooklyn Law Review* **57:**1193–1219.

Marenin, Otwin. (1995). "The State of Plea Bargaining in Alaska." *Journal of Crime and Justice* **18:**167–197.

Markowitz, Jeffrey A. (ed.). (1984). "Eighteenth Annual Symposium: Alternative Dispute Resolution." *Villanova Law Review* **29:**1219–1539.

Marvell, Thomas B. (1995). "Sentencing Guidelines and Prison Population Growth." *Journal of Criminal Law and Criminology* **85:**696–709.

Marvell, Thomas B. and Carlisle E. Moody. (1991). *Ultimate Impacts of Sentencing Reforms and Speedy Trial Laws.* Williamsburg, VA: Justice Research.

Marvell, Thomas B. and Carlisle E. Moody. (1996). "Determinate Sentencing and Abolishing Parole: The Long-Term Impacts on Prisons and Crimes." *Criminology* **34:**107–128.

Mason, Mary Ann. (1991). "A Judicial Dilemma: Expert Witness Testimony in Child Sex Abuse Cases." *Journal of Psychiatry and Law* **19:**185–219.

Massachusetts Legislative Research Council. (1987). *Report Relative to Alternative Sentencing.* Boston: Massachusetts Legislative Research Council.

McAllister, William, James Atchinson, and Nancy Jacobs. (1991). "A Simulation Model of Pretrial Felony Case Processing: A Queuing System Analysis." *Journal of Quantitative Criminology* **7:**291–314.

McBarnet, Doreen. (1983). "Victim in the Witness Box: Confronting Victimology's Stereotype." *Contemporary Crises* **7:**293–303.

McCart, Samuel W. (1964). *Trial by Jury: A Complete Guide to the Jury System.* New York: Chilton Books.

McCarthy, Belinda R. and Bernard J. McCarthy. (1997). *Community-Based Corrections.* Monterey, CA: Brooks/Cole.

McConville, Mike and Chester Mirsky. (1995a). "Guilty Plea Courts: A Social Disciplinary Model of Criminal Justice." *Social Problems* **42:**216–234.

McConville, Mike and Chester Mirsky. (1995b). "The Rise of Guilty Pleas: New York, 1800–1865." *Journal of Law and Society* **22:**443–474.

McCoy, Candace. (1993). *Politics and Plea Bargaining: Victims' Rights in California.* Philadelphia: University of Pennsylvania Press.

McCoy, Candace and Illya Lichtenberg. (1999). "Providing Effective *Habeas* Counsel for Indigents in Capital Cases." *Justice System Journal* **21:**81–87.

McDonald, Douglass C. (1983). "Will Fixed Sentencing Fix the Courts?" *New York Affairs* **8:**49–64.

McDonald, William F. (1985). *Plea Bargaining: Critical Issues and Common Practices.* Washington, DC: U.S. National Institute of Justice by the Institute of Criminal Law and Procedure, Georgetown University.

McDowall, David W., Colin Loftin, and Brian Wiersema. (1992). "A Comparative Study of the Preventive Effects of Mandatory Sentencing Laws for Gun Crimes." *Journal of Criminal Law and Criminology* **83:**378–398.

McFatter, Robert M. (1986). "Sentencing Disparity: Perforce or Perchance?" *Journal of Applied Psychology* **16:**150–164.

McGough, Lucy S. (1994). *Fragile Voices in the American Legal System*. New Haven, CT: Yale University Press.

McLeod, Maureen. (1986). "Victim Participation at Sentencing." *Criminal Law Bulletin* **22:**501–517.

McManus, Edgar J. (1993). *Law and Liberty in Early England: Criminal Justice and Due Process, 1620–1692.* Amherst: University of Massachusetts Press.

Meeker, James W., Paul Jesilow, and Joseph Aranda. (1992). "Bias in Sentencing: A Preliminary Analysis of Community Service Sentences." *Behavioral Sciences and the Law* **10:**197–206.

Meese, Edwin. (1987). "Promoting Truth in the Courtroom." *Vanderbilt Law Review* **40:**271–281.

Mello, Michael A. (1989). "Is There a Federal Constitutional Right to Counsel in Capital Post-Conviction Proceedings?" *Journal of Criminal Law and Criminology* **79:**1065–1104.

Menkel-Meadow, Carrie. (1986). "The Comparative Sociology of Women Lawyers." *Osgood Law Journal* **24:**897–918.

Merry, Sally Engle and Neal Milner (eds.). (1995). *The Possibility of Popular Justice: A Case Study of Community Mediation in the United States.* Ann Arbor: University of Michigan Press.

Mershon, Jerry L. (1991). *Juvenile Justice: The Adjudicatory and Dispositional Process.* Reno, NV: National Council of Juvenile and Family Court Judges.

Meyers, Laura B. and Sue Titus Reid. (1995). "The Importance of County Context in the Measurement of Sentence Disparity: The Search for Routinization." *Journal of Criminal Justice* **23:**223–241.

Michigan Law Review. (1971). "Involving Summary Criminal Contempt Procedures Use or Abuse? *United States v. Dellinger* and the 'Chicago Seven' Contempts." *Michigan Law Review* **69:**1549–1575.

Michigan Yearbook of International Legal Studies. (1983). *Transnational Aspects of Criminal Procedure.* New York: Clark Boardman.

Mieczkowski, Thomas, Rosemary Mumm, and Harry F. Connick. (1995). "The Use of Hair Analysis in a Pretrial Diversion Program in New Orleans." *International Journal of Offender Therapy and Comparative Criminology* **39:**222–241.

Miethe, Terance D. and Charles A. Moore. (1987). *Evaluation of Minnesota's Felony Sentencing Guidelines.* St. Paul, MN: Unpublished paper.

Miller, Benjamin. (1991). "Assessing the Functions of Judicial Conduct Organizations." *Judicature* **75:**16–19.

Miller, D. (1985). "The Harassment of Forensic Psychiatrists Outside of Court." *Bulletin of the American Academy of Psychiatry and the Law* **13:**337–344.

Miller, J. L., Marilyn Roberts, and Charlotte A. Carter. (1981). *Sentencing Reform: A Review and Annotated Bibliography.* Williamsburg, VA: National Center for State Courts.

Miller, Marc and Martin Guggenheim. (1990). "Pretrial Detention and Punishment." *Minnesota Law Review* **75:**335–426.

Miller, Robert D. et al. (1995). "Public Evaluations of Unrepresented Defendants." *Bulletin of the American Academy of Psychiatry and Law* **23:**93–103.

Minnesota Criminal Justice Analysis Center. (1989).*Violent and Chronic Juvenile Crime.* St. Paul: Minnesota Criminal Justice Analysis Center.

Minnesota Supreme Court Advisory Task Force on the Juvenile Justice System. (1994). *Final Report.* St. Paul: Minnesota Supreme Court Advisory Task Force on the Juvenile Justice System.

Minow, F. and H. Cate. (1991). "Who Is an Impartial Juror in an Age of Mass Media?" *American University Law Review* **40:** 631–664.

Missouri Task Force on Gender and Justice. (1993). *Report of the Missouri Task Force on Gender and Justice.* Jefferson City: The Missouri Bar.

Moenssens, Andre A. et al. (1993). "Symposium on Scientific Evidence." *Journal of Criminal Law and Criminology* **84:**1–238.

Moore, Lloyd E. (1988). *The Jury: Tools of the King, Palladium of Liberty.* Cincinnati, OH: Anderson Publishing.

Morgan, Thomas D. (1983). *Legal Ethics.* Chicago: Harcourt Brace Jovanovich.

Morrill, Calvin and Cindy McKee. (1993). "Institutional Isomorphism and Informal Social Control: Evidence from a Community Mediation Center." *Social Problems* **40:**445–463.

Morse, Stephen J. (1976). "The Twilight of Welfare Criminology: A Reply to Judge Bazelon." *Southern California Law Review* **49:**1247–1268.

Moskowitz, Herbert (ed.). (1992). "Problems with DWI Arrests: Convictions and Sentencing." *Alcohol, Drugs, and Driving* **8:**1–76.

Muehlenhard, C. L. and S. W. Cook. (1988). "Men's Self-Reports of Unwanted Sexual Activity." *Journal of Sex Research* **24:**58–72.

Muraskin, Roslyn et al. (1990). *Issues in Justice: Exploring Policy Issues.* Bristol, IN: Wyndham Hall.

Murchison, Kenneth M. (1994). *Federal Criminal Law Doctrines: The Forgotten Influence of National Prohibition.* Durham, NC: Duke University Press.

Nader, Laura. (1979). "Disputing within the Force of the Law." *Yale Law Journal* **88:**998–1043.

Nader, Laura and Harry F. Todd (eds.) (1978). "Introduction" In *The Disputing Process: Law in Ten Societies,* Laura Nader and Harry F. Todd (eds.). New York: Columbia University Press.

Nagel, Ilene H. et al. (1990). "Supreme Court Review." *Journal of Criminal Law and Criminology* **80:**883–1280.

Nagel, Stuart S. (1986a). *Causation, Prediction, and Legal Analysis.* New York: Quorum Books.

Nagel, Stuart S. (1986b). *Law, Policy, and Optimizing Analysis.* New York: Quorum Books.

National Advisory Commission on Criminal Justice Standards and Goals. (1973). *Courts.* Washington, DC: U.S. Government Printing Office.

National Association of Pretrial Services Agencies. (1995). *Performance Standards and Goals for Pretrial Release and Diversion.* Frankfort, KY: National Association of Pretrial Services Agencies.

National Center for State Courts. (1976). *State Judicial Training Profile.* Denver: National Center for State Courts.

National Center for State Courts. (1990). *Bail Policy for Criminal Defendants before, during and after Trial in Pennsylvania .* Andover, MA: National Center for State Courts, Northeastern Regional Office.

National Center for State Courts. (1995). *State Court Caseload Statistics, 1993: Court Statistics Project.* Williamsburg, VA: National Center for State Courts.

National Council on Crime and Delinquency. (1974). *Guides for Sentencing.* Hackensack, NJ: National Council on Crime and Delinquency, Council of Judges.

National Institute of Law Enforcement and Criminal Justice. (1979). *Courts of Limited Jurisdiction: More Than Limited Importance.* Washington, DC: U.S. Government Printing Office.

Nelson, James F. (1994). *The Impact of Restrictions on Post-Indictment Plea Bargaining in Bronx County: A Comparative Analysis of Historical Practice and Initial Impact.* Albany: New York State Division of Criminal Justice.

Neubauer, David W. (1974). "After the Arrest: The Charging Decision in Prairie City." *Law and Society Review* **8:**495–517.

New York City Criminal Justice Agency. (1992). *An Evaluation of the Impact of New York State's Felony Drug Statute.* New York: New York City Criminal Justice Agency.

Nicholson, Marlene Arnold and Bradley Scott Weiss. (1986). "Funding Judicial Campaigns in the Circuit Court of Cook County." *Judicature* **70:**17–25.

Nicol, Chuck. (1995). *Accommodating Prison Population Growth.* Sacramento: State of California Legislative Analyst's Office.

Nissman, David M. and Ed Hagen. (1982). *The Prosecution Function.* Lexington, MA: Lexington Books.

North Carolina Courts Commission. (1971). *Report.* Raleigh: North Carolina Courts Commission.

North Carolina Legislative Research Commission. (1987). *Bail Bondsmen, Bail Bond Forfeiture, and Pretrial Release.* Raleigh: North Carolina Legislative Research Commission.

North Dakota Century Code. (2000). *North Dakota Century Code.* Bismark: North Dakota State Legislature.

Northern Kentucky Law Review. (1982). "Selecting Judges in the States: A Brief History and Analysis." *Northern Kentucky Law Review* **9:**459–473.

Northwestern Law Review. (1971). "Sentencing and the Exclusionary Rule: Deterrence and Judicial Integrity." *Northwestern Law Review* **66:**698–713.

Norton, Jerry E. (1970). "Discovery in the Criminal Process." *Journal of Criminal Law and Criminology* **61:**11–38.

Olsen, Frances. (1982). "The Sex of Law." In *The Politics of Law: A Progressive Critique,* David Kairy (ed.). New York: Pantheon.

O'Neill, Terrence B. (1983). "Due Process and the Pretrial Detention Provisions of the Federal Criminal Code Reform Bill of 1981." *Albany Law Review* **47:**645–679.

O'Rouke, W. (1972). *The Harrisburg 7 and the New Catholic Left.* New York: Thomas Y. Crowell.

Ostermeyer, Melinda and Susan L. Keilitz. (1997). *Monitoring and Evaluating Court-Based Dispute Resolution Programs: A Guide for Judges and Court Managers.* Williamsburg, VA: National Center for State Courts.

Padgett, John F. (1985). "The Emergent Organization of Plea Bargaining." *American Journal of Sociology* **90:**753–800.

Palumbo, Dennis J., Michael Musheno, and Michael Hallett. (1994). "The Political Construction of Alternative Dispute Resolution and Alternatives to Incarceration." *Evaluation and Program Planning* **17:**197–203.

Panton, James H. (1974). "Personality Differences between Male and Female Prison Inmates." *Criminal Justice and Behavior* **1:**332–339.

Parent, Dale G., Barbara Auerbach, and Kenneth E. Carlson. (1992). *Compensating Crime Victims: A Summary of Policies and Practices.* Washington, DC: U.S. National Institute of Justice.

Parisi, Nicolette. (1981). "A Taste of the Bars?" *Journal of Criminal Law and Criminology* **72:** 1109–1123.

Parker, L. Craig. (1980). "Social Scientists and Jury Selection." In *Legal Psychology, Eyewitness Testimony, Jury Behavior* Craig L. Parker (ed.). Springfield, IL: Charles Thomas.

Parman, Steven D. (1983). "Twisting the Purposes of Discovery: Expert Witnesses and the Deposition Dilemma." *Vanderbilt Law Review* **36:**1615–1645.

Parnas, Raymond I. et al. (1992). "Symposium: Making Sense of the Federal Sentencing Guidelines." *UC Davis Law Review* **25:**563–771.

Patel, Jody and Curt Soderlund. (1994). "Getting a Piece of the Pie: Revenue Sharing with Crime Victims Compensation Programs." *APPA Perspectives* **18:**22–27.

Pellenberg-Fixen, Amy R. (1983). "Plea Bargaining: The New Hampshire Ban." *New England Journal on Criminal and Civil Confinement* **9:**387–405.

Penrod, Steven D., Solomon M. Fulero, and Brian L. Cutler. (1995). "Expert Psychological Testimony on Eyewitness Reliability before and after Daubert: The State of the Law and Science." *Behavioral Sciences and the Law* **13**:229–259.

Pettegrew, Hillary L. (1986). "Sixth and Eighth Amendments: Erosion of the Defendant's Right to an Impartial Jury and a Fundamentally Fair Trial." *Journal of Criminal Law and Criminology* **77**:796–820.

Pickles, James. (1987). *Straight from the Bench.* London: Dent.

Pinello, Daniel R. (1995). *The Impact of Judicial Selection Method on State Supreme Court Policy: Innovation, Reaction, and Atrophy.* Westport, CT: Greenwood Press.

Pisula, Kathy M. (1980). "Forcible Rape and the Right to Bail." *San Diego Law Review* **17**:1061–1091.

Pohlman, H. L. (1995). *Constitutional Debate in Action: Criminal Justice.* New York: HarperCollins.

Pollack, Harriet and Alexander B. Smith. (1983). "White-Collar v. Street Crime Sentencing Disparity: How Judges See the Problem." *Judicature* **67**:174–182.

Pollock-Byrne, J. M. (1989). *Ethics in Crime and Justice: Dilemmas and Decisions.* Pacific Grove, CA: Brooks/Cole.

Portman, Sheldon. (1982). "*Murphy v. Hunt:* The Right to Counsel and Equal Protection in Nebraska." *Pretrial Services Annual Journal* **5**:56–65.

Posner, Amy K. (1984). "Victim Impact Statements and Restitution: Making the Punishment Fit the Victim." *Brooklyn Law Review* **50**:301–338.

Poulos, Tammy Meredith and Stan Orchowsky. (1994). "Serious Juvenile Offenders: Predicting the Probability of Transfer to Criminal Court." *Crime and Delinquency* **40**:3–17.

Pound, Roscoe. (1912). "The Scope and Purpose of Sociological Jurisprudence." *Journal of Political Economy* **25**:489–500.

Powell, Lee. (1980). *Court Reform in Seven States.* Williamsburg, VA: National Center for State Courts.

President's Commission on Law Enforcement. (1967). *President's Commission on Law Enforcement and the Administration of Justice.* Washington, DC: U.S. Government Printing Office.

Pretrial Resources Service Center. (1994). *Commercial Surety Bail: Assessing Its Role in the Pretrial Release and Detention Decision.* Washington, DC: Pretrial Services Resource Center.

Priest, George. (1985). "The Invention of Enterprise Liability: A Critical History of the Intellectual Foundations of Modern Tort Law." *Journal of Legal Studies* **14**:461–527.

Provine, Doris Marie. (1986). *Judging Credentials: Nonlawyer Judges and the Politics of Professionalism.* Chicago: University of Chicago Press.

Purdy, Donald A. Jr. and Jeffrey Lawrence. (1990). "Plea Agreements under the Federal Sentencing Guidelines." *Criminal Law Bulletin* **26**:483–508.

Puritz, Patricia et al. (1995). *A Call for Justice: An Assessment of Access to Counsel and Quality of Representation in Delinquency Proceedings.* Washington, DC: Juvenile Justice Center, American Bar Association.

Pursley, Robert D. (1995). "The Federal *Habeas Corpus* Process: Unraveling the Issues." *Criminal Justice Policy Review* **7**:115–141.

Queensland. (1993). *The Bail Act.* Queensland, Australia: Government Publications Office, Working Paper No. 41.

Quinney, Richard. (1974). *Criminal Justice in America.* Boston: Little, Brown.

Radzinowicz, Leon and Roger Hood. (1980). "Incapacitating the Habitual Offender: The English Experience." *Michigan Law Review* **78**:1305–1389.

Ray, Patrick Joseph. (1984). *Neutral versus Adversarial Models of Expert Mental Health Testimony in Criminal Responsibility.* Ann Arbor, MI: University Microfilms International.

Read, J. Don, John C. Yuille, and Patricia Tollestrup. (1992). "Recollections of a Robbery: Effects of Arousal and Alcohol upon Recall and Person Identification." *Law and Human Behavior* **16:**425–446.

Reed, Patricia A. (1983). "Pretrial Bail: A Deprivation of Liberty or Property with Due Process of Law." *Washington and Lee Law Review* **40:**1575–1599.

Reese, James T. and Roger M. Solomon. (1996). *Organizational Issues in Law Enforcement.* Quantico, VA: Federal Bureau of Investigation.

Reitan, Eric. (1993). "Why the Deterrence Argument for Capital Punishment Fails." *Criminal Justice Ethics* **12:**26–33.

Reskin, B. F. and C. A. Visher. (1986). "The Impacts of Evidence and Extralegal Factors in Jurors' Decisions." *Law and Society Review* **9:**423–437

Reynolds, Morgan O. (1994). *Using the Private Sector to Deter Crime.* Dallas, TX: National Center for Policy Analysis.

Riordan, Henry Jeremiah. (1986). "*Wasman v. United States*: Vindictiveness in the Resentencing Process." *New England Journal on Criminal and Civil Confinement* **12:**151–175.

Roberts, Albert R. (ed.). (1994). *Critical Issues in Crime and Justice.* Thousand Oaks, CA: Sage.

Roberts, Tim. (1992). *Assessment of the Victim Impact Statement Program in British Columbia.* Ottawa: Canada Department of Justice.

Robinson, Paul H. et al. (1993). "Supreme Court Review." *Journal of Criminal Law and Criminology* **83:**693–1054.

Rodatus, Robert V. (1994). "Legal, Ethical and Professional Concerns When Representing Children in Abuse Cases in Juvenile Court." *Juvenile and Family Court Journal* **45:**39–50.

Rodriguez, Labarca Jorge and John P. O'Connell. (1993). *Mandatory Sentencing in Delaware, 1981–1991.* Dover: Delaware Statistical Analysis Center.

Rogers, Patrick, Sharon Cotliar, and Steve Erwin. (2000). "Judgment Day." *People,* November 6, 2000:87–91.

Romine, June and Daniel L. Skoler. (1971). "Local Government Financing and Law Enforcement." *American County* **16:**17–20.

Ross, David Frank, J. Don Read, and Michael P. Toglia. (1994). *Adult Eyewitness Testimony: Current Trends and Developments.* Cambridge: Cambridge University Press.

Rothwax, Harold J. (1996). *Guilty: The Collapse of Criminal Justice.* New York: Random House.

Rotman, Edgardo. (1990). *Beyond Punishment: A New View of the Rehabilitation of Criminal Offenders.* Westport, CT: Greenwood.

Rottman, David, Carol Flango, and Sehdine Lockley. (1995). *State Court Organization, 1993.* Washington, DC: Bureau of Justice Statistics.

Rowland, C. K., Donald Songer, and Robert A. Carp. (1988). "Presidential Effects on Criminal Justice Policy in the Lower Federal Courts: The Reagan Judges." *Law and Society* **22:**191–200.

Roy, Sudipto and Michael Brown. (1992). "Victim-Offender Reconciliation Project for Adults and Juveniles: A Comparative Study in Elkhart County, Indiana." Unpublished paper presented at the annual meeting of the American Society of Criminology, San Francisco, November.

Sachs, Albie and Joan H. Wilson. (1978). "Sexism and the Legal Profession: A Study of Male Beliefs and Legal Bias in Britain and the United States." *Women's Rights Law Reporter* **5:**53–70.

Saltzburg, Stephen A. and Kenneth R. Redden. (1994). *Federal Rules of Evidence Manual.* Charlottesville, VA: Michie.

Sams, Julia P. (1986). "The Availability of the 'Cultural Defense' as an Excuse for Criminal Behavior." *Georgia Journal of International and Comparative Law* **16**:335–354.

San Francisco Jail Overcrowding Committee. (1985). *Report to the Mayor from the Jail Overcrowding Commit.* San Francisco: Mayor's Criminal Justice Council.

Sanborn, Joseph B. Jr. (1993a). "Philosophical, Legal, and Systemic Aspects of Juvenile Court Plea Bargaining." *Crime and Delinquency* **39**:509–527.

Sanborn, Joseph B. Jr. (1993b). "The Right to a Public Jury Trial: A Need for Today's Juvenile Court." *Judicature* **76**:230–238.

Sanborn, Joseph B. Jr. (1994a). "Certification to Criminal Court: The Important Policy Questions of How, When and Why?" *Crime and Delinquency* **40**:262–281.

Sanborn, Joseph B. Jr. (1994b). "Remnants of *Parens Patriae* in the Adjudicatory Hearing: Is a Fair Trial Possible in Juvenile Court?" *Crime and Delinquency* **40**:599–615.

Sanborn, Joseph B. Jr. (1995). "How Parents Can Affect the Processing of Delinquents in the Juvenile Court." *Criminal Justice Policy Review* **7**:1–266.

Sandys, Marla and Edmund F. McGarrell. (1994). "Attitudes toward Capital Punishment among Indiana Legislators: Diminished Support in Light of Alternative Sentencing Options." *Justice Quarterly* **11**:641–677.

Santa Clara County Office of the County Executive. (1995). *Up-Date "Three Strikes, You're Out": Workload in Process within the Justice System in Santa Clara County, California.* Santa Clara County, CA: Santa Clara County Office of the County Executive Center for Urban Analysis.

Sapers, Howard. (1990). "The Fine Options Program in Alberta." Unpublished paper presented at the annual meeting of the American Society of Criminology, Baltimore, November.

Scheb, John M. II. (1988). "State Appellate Judges' Attitudes toward Judicial Merit Selection and Retention: Results of a National Survey." *Judicature* **62**:170–174.

Schiraldi, Vincent. (1994). *Racial Disparities in the Charging of Los Angeles County's Third "Strike" Cases.* San Francisco: Center on Juvenile and Criminal Justice.

Schlesinger, Steven R. and Elizabeth A. Malloy. (1981). "Plea Bargaining and the Judiciary: An Argument for Reform." *Drake Law Review* **30**:581–598.

Schmalleger, Frank (ed.). (1990). *Ethics in Criminal Justice: A Justice Professional Reader.* Bristol, IN: Wyndham Hall.

Schmolesky, John M. and Timothy K. Thorson. (1982). "The Importance of the Presentence Investigation Report after Sentencing." *Criminal Law Bulletin* **18**:406–441.

Schulhofer, Stephen J. (1979). *Prosecutorial Discretion and Federal Sentencing Reform.* Washington, DC: Federal Judicial Center.

Schulhofer, Stephen J. (1986). "The Future of the Adversary System." *Justice Quarterly* **3**:83–93.

Schwartz, Ira M. (ed.). (1992). *Juvenile Justice and Public Policy.* New York: Lexington Books.

Scott, Joseph E., Simon Dinitz, and David Shichor. (1978). "Pioneering Innovations in Corrections: Shock Probation and Shock Parole." *Offender Rehabilitation New York* **3**:113–122.

Shein, M. G. (1988). *Sentencing Defense Manual: Advocacy/Practice/Procedure.* New York: Clark Boardman.

Sheldon, Charles H. (1971). "The Degree of Satisfaction with State Judicial Selection Systems: Lawyers vs. Judges." *Judicature* **54**:331–334.

Sheldon, Charles H. and Nicholas P. Lovrich Jr. (1983). "Knowledge and Judicial Voting: The Oregon and Washington Experience." *Judicature* **67**:235–245.

Sheriff, Ellen. (1981). "Defense Witness Immunity: Constitutional Demands and Statutory Change." *Journal of Criminal Law and Criminology* **73**:1026–1054.

Sherwood, Fabre Liese. (1987). "An Evaluation of Federal Pretrial Services: Impact on Pretrial Decisions and Outcomes." *Evaluation Review* **11**:3–31.

Shilton, Mary K. et al. (1994). "Mandatory Minimum Sentencing." *IARCA Journal on Community Corrections* **6**:4–35.

Shockley, Carol. (1988). "The Federal Presentence Investigation Report: Postsentence Disclosure under the Freedom of Information Act." *Administrative Law Review* **40**:79–119.

Simon, H. and J. Emermann. (1971). "The Jury Finds Not Guilty: Another Look at Media Influence on the Jury." *Journalism Quarterly* **48**: 343–344.

Simon, Rita J. (1980). *The Jury: Its Role in American Society*. Lexington, MA: Lexington Books.

Smith, Brent L. and Edward H. Stevens. (1984). "Sentence Disparity and the Judge-Jury Sentencing Debate: An Analysis of Robbery Sentences in Six Southern States." *Criminal Justice Review* **9**:1–7.

Smith, Christopher E. (1987). "Who Are the U.S. Magistrates?" *Judicature* **71**:143–150.

Smith, Christopher E. (1992). "From U.S. Magistrates to U.S. Magistrate Judges: Developments Affecting the Federal District Courts' Lower Tier of Judicial Officers." *Judicature* **75**:210–215.

Smith, Christopher E. (1995a). "Federal *Habeas Corpus* Reform: The State's Perspective." *Justice System Journal* **18**:1–11.

Smith, Christopher E. (1995b). "Judicial Policy Making and *Habeas Corpus* Reform." *Criminal Justice Policy Review* **7**:91–114.

Smith, Michael et al. (1996). *Crime and Politics for the 1990s: Creating Demand for New Policies*. Washington, DC: Campaign for an Effective Crime Policy.

Smith, Steven K. and Carol J. DeFrances. (1996). *Indigent Defense*. Washington, DC: U.S. Department of Justice.

Smykla, John Ortiz and William L. Selke. (1995). *Intermediate Sanctions: Sentencing in the 1990s*. Cincinnati, OH: Anderson.

Solomon, Rayman L. (1984). "The Politics of Appointment and the Federal Court's Role in Regulating America: U.S. Courts of Appeals Judgeships from T.R. to F.D.R." *American Bar Foundation Journal* **2**:285–343.

Sorensen, Jonathan R., and Donald H. Wallace. (1995). "Arbitrariness and Discrimination in Missouri Capital Cases: An Assessment Using the Barnett Scale." *Journal of Crime and Justice* **18**:21–57.

Spaeth, Edmund B. et al. (1988). "Symposium: Limitations on the Effectiveness of Criminal Defense Counsel: Legitimate Means or 'Chilling Wedges?' " *University of Pennsylvania Law Review* **136**:1779–1973.

Spangenberg, Robert L. (1990). *Overview of the Fulton County, Georgia Indigent Defense System*. West Newton, MA: Georgia Indigent Defense Council.

Spence, Jerry. (1992). "Justice: The New Commodity." *American Bar Association Journal* **78**:46.

Spohn, Cassia. (1992). "An Analysis of the 'Jury Trial Penalty' and Its Effect on Black and White Offenders." *Justice Professional* **7**:93–112.

Stalmaster, Irvin. (1931). *What Price Jury Trials?* New York: Penguin.

Steelman, David C., and Samuel D. Conti. (1987). *Representation of Indigent Criminal Defendants in the Courts of Hamilton County, Ohio*. North Andover, MA: National Center for State Courts.

Stern, Ronald A. (1980). "Government Appeals of Sentences: A Constitutional Response to Arbitrary and Unreasonable Sentences." *American Criminal Law Review* **18**:51–89.

Steury, Ellen Hochstedler and Nancy Frank. (1990). "Gender Bias and Pretrial Release: More Pieces of the Puzzle." *Journal of Crime and Justice* **18**:417–432.

Stitt, B. Grant and Robert H. Chaires. (1993). "Plea Bargaining: Ethical Issues and Emerging Perspectives." *Justice Professional* **7:**69–91.

Stolzenberg, Lisa. (1993). *Unwarranted Disparity and Determinate Sentencing: A Longitudinal Study of Presumptive Sentencing Guidelines in Minnesota.* Ann Arbor, MI: University Microfilms International.

Subin, Harry I., Chester L. Mirsky, and Ian S. Weinstein. (1993). *The Criminal Process: Prosecution and Defense Functions.* St. Paul, MN: West Publishing.

Suggs, David and Bruce Sales. (1981). "Juror Self-Disclosure in the *Voir Dire*: A Social Science Analysis." *Indiana Law Journal* **56:**245–271.

Suny, Ellen Yankee. (1987). "Subpoenas to Criminal Defense Lawyers: A Proposal for Limits." *Oregon Law Review* **65:**215–308.

Sviridoff, Mitchell. (1980). "What's New in Dispute Resolution." *New York Law Journal* **13:**8–26.

Swain, F. W. (1985). *Of God and His Conscience: Judicial Selection in Louisiana.* Baton Rouge: Louisiana State Legislature.

Szymanski, Linda A. (1997). *Juvenile's Right to a Jury Trial in a Delinquency Hearing (1996 Update).* Pittsburgh: National Center for Juvenile Justice.

Talarico, Susette M. and Martha A. Myers. (1987). "Split Sentencing in Georgia: A Test of Two Empirical Assumptions." *Justice Quarterly* **4:**611–629.

Tauro, Joseph G. (1968). "The Few and the Many." *Judicature* **51:**215–218.

Tauro, Joseph L. (1983). "Sentencing: A View from the Bench." *New England Journal on Criminal and Civil Confinement* **9:**323–330.

Taylor, Humphrey, Michael Kagay, and Stuart Leichenko. (1987). *Public Attitudes toward the Civil Justice System and Tort Law Reform.* New York: Louis Harris and Associates for Aetna Life and Casualty Insurance Company.

Texas Crime Victim Clearinghouse. (1989). *Crime Victim Impact: The Report of the Crime Victim Clearinghouse.* Austin: Texas Crime Victim Clearinghouse.

Thaler, Paul. (1994). *The Watchful Eye: American Justice in the Age of the Television Trial.* Westport, CT: Praeger.

Thomas, Wayne. (1976). *Bail Reform in America.* Berkeley: University of California Press.

Thomas, Wayne. (1977). *National Evaluation Program: Pretrial Release Programs.* Washington, DC: Law Enforcement Assistance Administration.

Tomasi, Timothy B. and Jess A. Velona. (1987). "All the President's Men: A Study of Ronald Reagan's Appointments to the U.S. Courts of Appeals." *Columbia Law Review* **87:**766–793.

Tonry, Michael. (1987). *Sentencing Reform Impacts.* Washington, DC: U.S. National Institute of Justice.

Tonry, Michael. (1988). "Structuring Sentencing." *In Crime and Justice: A Review of Research,* Norval Morris and Michael Tonry (eds.). Chicago: University of Chicago Press.

Tonry, Michael. (1993a). "Mandatory Penalties." In *Crime and Justice: A Review of Research,* Vol. 16, Michael Tonry (ed.). Chicago: University of Chicago Press.

Tonry, Michael. (1993b). "Sentencing Commissions and Their Guidelines." *In Crime and Justice: A Review of Research,* Vol. 17, Michael Tonry (ed.). Chicago: University of Chicago Press.

Tonry, Michael. (1995). *Malign Neglect: Race, Crime and Punishment in America.* New York: Oxford University Press.

Torbet, Patricia et al. (1996). *State Responses to Serious and Violent Juvenile Crime.* Washington, DC: U.S. Office of Juvenile Justice and Delinquency Prevention.

Torbet, Patricia and Linda Szymanski. (1998). *State Legislative Responses to Violent Juvenile Crime: 1996–1997 Update.* Washington, DC: U.S. Department of Justice.

Townsend, David A., John W. Palmer, and Jennifer B. Newton. (1978). *Technical Issue Paper on Presentence Investigation Reports.* Westerville, OH: Center for Law Enforcement and Correctional Justice.

Trotto, Salvatore and James J. Golbin. (1987). *Investigation Review Process Selection Criteria for Identification of Jail Bound Felony Case.* Yaphank, NY: Suffolk County Department of Probation.

Turner, Susan and Joan Petersilia. (1996). "Work Release in Washington: Effects on Recidivism and Corrections Costs." *The Prison Journal* **76:**138–164.

Umbreit, Mark S. (1994) "Victim Empowerment through Mediation." *APPA Perspectives* **18:**25–28.

Umbreit, Mark S. and Robert B. Coates. (1993). "Cross-Site Analysis of Victim-Offender Mediation in Four States." *Crime and Delinquency* **39:**565–585.

Unger, Roberto. (1986). *The Critical Studies Movement.* Cambridge, MA: Harvard University Press.

U.S. Advisory Commission on Intergovernmental Relations. (1971). *For a More Perfect Union—Court Reform.* Washington, DC: U.S. Government Printing Office.

U.S. Congress Committee on the Judiciary. (1993). *Innocence and the Death Penalty: Assessing the Danger of Mistaken Executions.* Washington, DC: U.S. Congress Committee on the Judiciary Subcommittee on Civil and Constitutional Rights.

U.S. Department of Justice. (1988). *Report to the Nation on Crime and Justice.* Washington, DC: U.S. Department of Justice, Bureau of Justice Statistics.

U.S. Department of Justice. (1990). *Report to Congress.* Washington, DC: U.S. Department of Justice Office for Victims of Crime.

U.S. General Accounting Office. (1991). *Victims of Crime Act Grants: Better Reporting Needed for Compensation and Assistance Programs.* Washington, DC: U.S. General Accounting Office.

U.S. General Accounting Office. (1991). *Federal Criminal Justice: Cost of Providing Court-Appointed Attorneys Is Rising, but Causes Are Unclear.* Washington, DC: U.S. Government Printing Office.

U.S. House Committee on the Judiciary. (1984). *Sentencing Revision Act of 1984: Report.* Washington, DC: U.S. Government Printing Office.

U.S. House of Representatives. (1995a). *Correcting Revolving Door Justice: New Approaches to Recidivism.* Washington, DC: U.S. Government Printing Office.

U.S. House of Representatives. (1995b). *Federal Minimum Mandatory Sentencing.* Washington, DC: U.S. House of Representatives Committee on the Judiciary.

U.S. House of Representatives. (1995c). *Habeas Corpus.* Washington, DC: U.S. Government Printing Office.

U.S. National Commission on Reform of Federal Criminal Laws. (1971). *Final Report: A Proposed New Federal Criminal Code.* Washington, DC: U.S. Government Printing Office.

U.S. News & World Report. (1978). "Why Is Everybody Suing Everybody?" *U.S. News & World Report,* December 4, 50.

U.S. Senate Judiciary Committee. (1984). *Deinstitutionalization of Juvenile Non-Offenders: Hearing.* Washington, DC: U.S. Government Printing Office.

U.S. Sentencing Commission. (1991). *The Federal Sentencing Guidelines: A Report on the Operation of the Guidelines System and Short-Term Impacts.* Washington, DC: U.S. Sentencing Commission.

University of Pennsylvania Law Review. (1986). "Constitutional Alternatives to Plea Bargaining: A New Waive." *University of Pennsylvania Law Review* **132:**327–353.

Uphoff, Rodney J. (1992). "The Criminal Defense Lawyer: Zealous Advocate, Double Agent, or Beleaguered Dealer?" *Criminal Law Bulletin* **28:**419–456.

Uppal, Jay C. (1974). "Approaches to the Selection of Judges." *State Government* **47**:46–49.

Vago, Steven. (1997). *Law and Society,* 5th ed. Upper Saddle River, NJ: Prentice Hall.

Vanagunas, Stanley. (1987). "Crime Control: An Old Problem in Search of Fresh Solutions." In *Police and Law Enforcement,* Daniel B. Kennedy and Robert J. Homant (eds.). New York: AMS.

Vance, William M. (1970). *Presentence Investigations in Felony Cases.* Columbus: Ohio Committee on Crime and Delinquency.

Vandenberg, Donna. (1983). "Voluntary Merit Selection: Its History and Current Status." *Judicature* **66**:265–273.

Van Dijk, Jan J. M. (1994). "Understanding Crime Rates: On the Interactions between Rational Choices of Victims and Offenders." *British Journal of Criminology* **34**:105–121.

Van Dijk, Jan J. M. et al. (1996). "Crime and Justice in the City." *European Journal on Criminal Policy and Research* **4**:5–107.

Van Kessel, Gordon. (1992). "Adversary Justice in the American Criminal Trial." *Notre Dame Law Review* **67**:403–552.

Vaughn, Michael S. (1993). "Listening to the Experts: A National Study of Correctional Administrators' Responses to Prison Overcrowding." *Criminal Justice Review* **18**:12–25.

Venner, Melissa. (1994). "Harris County's Victim Offender Restitution Program." *APPA Perspectives* **18**:53.

Vera Institute of Justice. (1995). *Bail Bond Supervision in Three Counties: Report on Intensive Pretrial Supervision in Nassau, Bronx, and Essex Counties.* New York: Vera Institute of Justice.

Verrilli, Donald B. (1982). "The Eighth Amendment and the Right to Bail: Historical Perspectives." *Columbia Law Review* **82**:328–362.

Villamoare, Edwin and Virginia V. Neto. (1987). *Victim Appearances at Sentencing Hearings under the California Victims' Bill of Rights.* Washington, DC: U.S. National Institute of Justice.

Villanova Law Review. (1982). "Judicial Selection in Pennsylvania: A Proposal." *Villanova Law Review* **27**:1163–1178.

Vincent, Barbara S. and Paul J. Hofer. (1994). "The Consequences of Mandatory Minimum Prison Terms: A Summary of Recent Findings." Washington, DC: U.S. Government Printing Office.

Virginia Department of Criminal Justice Services. (1986). *Felony Justice in Virginia.* Richmond: Virginia Department of Criminal Justice Services.

Vito, Gennaro F. (1984). "Developments in Shock Probation: A Review of Research Findings." *Federal Probation* **48**:22–27.

Vito, Gennaro F. and Harry E. Allen. (1980). "Shock Probation in Ohio: Use of Base Expectancy Rates As an Evaluation Method." *Criminal Justice and Behavior* **7**:331–340.

Volcansek, Mary L. (1983). "Money or a Name? A Sectional Analysis of Judicial Elections." *Justice System Journal* **8**:46–58.

Volcansek, Mary L. (1990). "British Antecedents for U.S. Impeachment Practices: Continuity and Change." *Justice System Journal* **14**:40–62.

Volcansek, Mary L. (1993). *Judicial Impeachment: None Called for Justice.* Champaign: University of Illinois Press.

Volcansek, Mary L., Maria Eisabetta DeFranciscis, and Jacqueline Lucienne Lafron. (1996). *Judicial Misconduct: A Cross-National Comparison.* Gainesville: University Press of Florida.

Walker, Samuel. (1993). *Taming the System: The Content of Discretion in Criminal Justice, 1950–1990.* New York: Oxford University Press.

Wallace, Harvey and Shanda Wedlock. (1994). "Federal Sentencing Guidelines and Gender Issues: Parental Responsibilities, Pregnancy and Domestic Violence." *San Diego Justice Journal* **2:**395–427.

Walsh, Anthony. (1992). *Correctional Assessment, Casework, and Counseling.* Laurel, MD: American Correctional Association.

Walsh, Joseph T. (1968). "The Attorney and the Dispositional Process." *Saint Louis University Law Journal* **12:**644–659.

Wanamaker, John L. (1978). "Computers and Scientific Jury Selection: A Calculated Risk." *Journal of Urban Law* **55:**345–370.

Washington State Sentencing Guidelines Commission. (1996). *Sentencing Policy in Washington: An Assessment.* Olympia: Washington State Sentencing Guidelines Commission.

Weddington, Mary Margaret and W. Richard Janikowski. (1996). "The Rehnquist Court: The Counter-Revolution That Wasn't." *Criminal Justice Review* **21:**231–250.

Weidholz, Jean M. (1989). *Transition from Prison to the Community: A Prerelease Program.* Ann Arbor, MI: University Microfilms International.

Weinreb, Lloyd L. (ed.). (1993). *Leading Constitutional Cases on Criminal Justice.* Westbury, NY: Foundation Press.

Weintraub, Benson B. (1987). "The Role of Defense Counsel at Sentencing." *Federal Probation* **51:**25–29.

Weisburd, David, Elin Waring, and Stanton Wheeler. (1990). "Class, Status, and the Punishment of White-Collar Criminals." *Law and Social Inquiry* **15:**223–243.

Welling, Sarah N. (1987). "Victim Participation in Plea Bargains." *Washington University Law Quarterly* **65:**301–356.

Wells, Robert C. (1990). "Considering Victim Impact: The Role of Probation." *Federal Probation* **54:**26–29.

Wely, Theodore. (1904). *Hygene of Occupation.* New York: Jena.

West, John M. (1986). "Expert Services and the Indigent Criminal Defendant: The Constitutional Mandate of *Ake v. Oklahoma.*" *Michigan Law Review* **84:**1326–1362.

Wettstein, Robert M. (ed.). (1992). "Cults and the Law." *Behavioral Sciences and the Law* **10:**1–140.

Whitcomb, Debra et al. (1994). *The Child Victim As a Witness.* Washington, DC: U.S. Office of Juvenile Justice and Delinquency Prevention.

White, Welsh S. (1980). "Death-Qualified Juries: The Prosecution's Proneness Argument Reexamined." *University of Pittsburgh Law Review* **41:**353–406.

Wilkins, Leslie T. et al. (1976). *Sentencing Guidelines: Structuring Judicial Discretion.* Albany, NY: Criminal Justice Research Center.

Wilkins, William W. Jr. (1988). "Plea Negotiations, Acceptance of Responsibility, Role of the Offender, and Departures: Policy Decisions in the Promulgation of Federal Sentencing." *Wake Forest Law Review* **23:**181–202.

Williams, Jimmy J. (1995). "Race of Appellant, Sentencing Guidelines, and Decision Making in Criminal Appeals: A Research Note." *Journal of Criminal Justice* **23:**83–91.

Winston, Norma A. and William E. Winston. (1980). "The Use of Sociological Techniques in the Jury Selection Process." *National Journal of Criminal Defense* **6:**79–97.

Wolf, A. J. (1988). *Cross-Examination on Trial.* St. Paul, MN: Butterworth.

Wolf, Daniel. (1986). " 'I Cannot Tell a Lie:' The Standard for a New Trial in False Testimony Cases." *Michigan Law Review* **83:**1925–1949.

Wolf, J. and P. Montgomery. (1977). "Effects of Inadmissible Evidence and Level of Judicial Admonishment to Disregard on the Judgement of Mock Jurors." *Journal of Applied Social Psychology* 7:205–219.

Wootewn, Harold B. and Mary K. Shilton. (1993). "Restructuring Probation: What Prosecutors, Defense Attorneys, and Judges Can Do." *Criminal Justice* 7:12–15.

Worden, Alissa Pollitz. (1990). "Policymaking by Prosecutors: The Uses of Discretion in Regulating Plea Bargaining." *Judicature* 73:335–340.

Worden, Alissa Pollitz. (1991). "Privatizing Due Process: Issues in the Comparison on Assigned Counsel, Public Defender, and Contracted Indigent Defense Systems." *Justice System Journal* 143:390–418.

Worden, Alissa Pollitz. (1995). "The Judge's Role in Plea Bargaining: An Analysis of Judges' Agreement with Prosecutors' Sentencing Recommendations." *Justice Quarterly* 12:257–278.

Worling, James R. (1995). "Adolescent Sex Offenders against Females: Differences Based on the Age of Their Victims." *International Journal of Offender Therapy and Comparative Criminology* 39:276–293.

Wright, J. Skelly et al. (1974). "The Grand Jury–Prosecutorial Abuse of the Indictment Process." *Journal of Criminal Law and Criminology* 65:157–169.

Wright, Jack and Peter W. Lewis. (1978). *Modern Criminal Justice.* New York: McGraw-Hill.

Yarrow, C. (1992). "Jury Renders Mixed Verdict in Attica Case." *New York Times,* February 5, B4.

Zaragoza, Maria S. et al. (1995). *Memory and Testimony in the Child Witness.* Thousand Oaks, CA: Sage.

Zastrow, William G. (1971). "Disclosure of the Presentence Investigation Report." *Federal Probation* 35:20–22.

Zimmerman, Joseph F. (1981). *The Government and Politics of New York State.* New York: New York University Press.

Zumwalt, William James. (1973). "The Anarchy of Sentencing in the Federal Courts." *Judicature* 57:96–104.

CASE INDEX

INDEX